Work and Family

An International Research Perspective

SERIES IN APPLIED PSYCHOLOGY

Edwin A. Fleishman, George Mason University,
Jeanette N. Cleveland, Pennsylvania State University
Series Editors

Manuel London
Job Feedback: Giving, Seeking, and Using Feedback for Performance Improvement, Second Edition

Manuel London
How People Evaluate Others in Organizations

Manuel London
Leadership Development: Paths to Self-Insight and Professional Growth

Robert F. Morrison and Jerome Adams
Contemporary Career Development Issues

Michael D. Mumford, Garnett Stokes, and William A. Owens
Patterns of Life History: The Ecology of Human Individuality

Kevin R. Murphy
Validity Generalization: A Critical Review

Kevin R. Murphy and Frank E. Saal
Psychology in Organizations: Integrating Science and Practice

Susan E. Murphy and Ronald E. Riggio
The Future of Leadership Development

Steven A. Y. Poelmans
Work and Family: An International Research Perspective

Erich P. Prien, Jeffery S. Schippmann and Kristin O. Prien
Individual Assessment: As Practiced in Industry and Consulting

Ned Rosen
Teamwork and the Bottom Line: Groups Make a Difference

Heinz Schuler, James L. Farr, and Mike Smith
Personnel Selection and Assessment: Individual and Organizational Perspectives

John W. Senders and Neville P. Moray
Human Error: Cause, Prediction, and Reduction

Frank J. Smith
Organizational Surveys: The Diagnosis and Betterment of Organizations Through Their Members

George C. Thornton III and Rose Mueller-Hanson
Developing Organizational Simulations: A Guide for Practitioners and Students

Yoav Vardi and Ely Weitz
Misbehavior in Organizations: Theory, Research and Management

---

For more information on LEA titles, please contact Lawrence Erlbaum Associates, Publishers, at www.erlbaum.com.

Work and Family

An International Research Perspective

Edited by

Steven A. Y. Poelmans

IESE Business School, Barcelona, Spain

 LAWRENCE ERLBAUM ASSOCIATES, PUBLISHERS

2005 Mahwah, New Jersey   London

Senior Acquisitions Editor:	Anne Duffy
Assistant Editor:	Kristin Duch
Cover Design:	Kathryn Houghtaling Lacey
Textbook Production Manager:	Paul Smolenski
Full-Service Compositor:	TechBooks
Text and Cover Printer:	Sheridan Books, Inc.

This book was typeset in 10/12 pt. Bookman ITC Roman, Bold, and Italic. The heads were typeset in Futura, Futura Bold, and Futura Bold Italic

Lawrence Erlbaum Associates, Inc., Publishers
10 Industrial Avenue
Mahwah, New Jersey 07430
www.erlbaum.com

Library of Congress Cataloging-in-Publication Data

Work and family : an international research perspective / edited by Steven A. Y. Poelmans.
   p. cm.—(Series in applied psychology)
  Includes bibliographical references and index.
  ISBN 0-8058-4881-9 (case : alk. paper)—ISBN 0-8058-4882-7 (pbk. : alk. paper)
   1. Work and family. I. Poelmans, Steven A. Y., 1968– II. Series.

  HD4904.25.W6625 2005
  306.3′6—dc22   2004029676

Contents

Series Foreword

Jeanette N. Cleveland
The Pennsylvania State University

Edwin A. Fleishman
George Mason University

Series Editors

There is a compelling need for innovative approaches to the solution of many pressing problems involving human relationships in today's society. Such approaches are more likely to be successful when they are based on sound research and applications. This Series in Applied Psychology offers publications that emphasize state-of-the-art research and its application to important issues of human behavior in a variety of social settings. The objective is to bridge both academic and applied interests.

We are pleased to welcome this book, "Work and Family: An International Research Perspective" edited by Steven Poelmans, into our Series in Applied Psychology. The book joins the volume edited by Ellen Kossek and Susan Lambert in our Series, entitled "Work and Life Integration: Organizational, Cultural, and Individual Perpectives." The publication of both of these books at this time reflects the growing diversity of research and practice in this area. Changes in family structures are transforming the workplace while changes in parental work patterns are transforming family life. There has been a dramatic increase in the rates of paid employment globally among mothers with children. Further, the research on work and family during the past 30 years has been fueled by the growing proportion of employees who are dual-earner partners or single parents.

Research on work and family issues draws from numerous disciplines including human development, psychology, sociology, labor relations, economics, women's studies, and management. In the volume
edited by Poelmans, these issues are addressed from a more global,
international perspective. Few texts come to mind that have such a
wide range of countries represented addressing work and family research and practice issues. Authors of individual chapters represent
20 different countries. Further, the chapters discuss this topic from
multiple levels of analyses including micro- or individual level, the
meso- or organizational level, and the macro- or socio- cultural level.
Poelmans has skillfully brought together a diverse set of chapters in
order to portray the complexities of implementing work-life policies
and programs in today's international business environment.

Beginning with the first chapter, Poelmans provides a comparative overview of the work and family research drawing from U.S. and
international literatures. The theme of simultaneously tapping U.S.
and international literatures is carried throughout the book as chapters address key work and family constructs in such locations as the
Netherlands, Sub-Saharan Africa, Israel, Spain, and China. Another
strength of the book is the strong theoretical contribution across the
chapters. For example, in chapter 2, Kossek et al. tap the acculturative stress and conservation of resources frameworks to understand
the unique cultural and work–family stresses facing U.S. mid-western
Latino migrant workers.

Two general approaches have been used to examine work and family issues. A *work or management* perspective focuses on employee
perceptions of work and family and its relationship to work attitudes,
performance and profit. The *family* perspective often collects spousal
and children's perceptions of the effects of work on non-work stakeholders. The present book represents an example of the former approach yet the family perspective on work and family is presented in
chapter 15 by Jennifer Bowes.

This book provides important multi-cultural and country perspectives on work–life programs. This enhances the degree to which we can
generalize research findings and practical solutions, and better defines the situational factors that interact with these findings. The book
highlights the importance of research and practice on work–life initiatives and their human resource interfaces. The book will appeal to academic researchers in management, organizational behavior, human
resources management, as well as in industrial and organizational
psychology. Importantly, it can serve as a central text or supplemen-
tary one in a course on international management as well as work and
family. It also will be a useful resource for human resource practitioners especially those employed in organizations with global partners.

F oreword

Canaries in the Mine: Reflections on Women in Management and Work and Family Research

Virginia E. Schein
Gettysburg College

It was August 1978, and I was preparing to speak at the International Congress of Applied Psychology in Munich. Seated at the podium, I looked out over a large crowd of people, many of whom were wearing headphones to listen to my English presentation in French or German. As I stood up to speak, an infant, held by his father in the back of the room, let out a loud wail. All heads turned to the infant and then swung back to the podium as I declared, in three languages, "That's my son."

Had that event taken place today, it would have been viewed as a work–family moment—"Mom giving a talk, Dad sitting in the back for support, and their 4-week-old child in tow to complete the family picture." But 25-years ago terms such as the *work–family interface* were not part of the mainstream academic lexicon. In the 1970s, the issue was the limited number of women in management positions. Research focusing on how to increase the number of women in management was just emerging. In 1978, my Congress presentation on the psychological barriers to women in management was a pioneering event. Only years later would the presence of my infant son be seen as an integral aspect of these pioneering efforts.

Although women have always worked, either in the home or in low-level positions, the entrance of women into managerial positions in significant numbers brings work and family issues to center stage.

As women make significant strides into management, the spotlight shifts from issues of entry and equality of access to the consideration of the work–family conflicts and to the difficulties posed for women in managerial positions.

To some extent, women's advancement into management serves a function similar to that of the canaries once used by miners to alert them to poisonous gases. If the canaries died, then the air was not healthy to breathe. Women's entry into positions heretofore held predominantly by men surfaces the difficulties of successfully performing both managerial and family roles. The conflicts between work and family demands are felt most strongly at these work levels. The presence of women in managerial positions often reveals a corporate atmosphere that is poisonous to those seeking to function successfully in both managerial and family roles. New research questions arise out of the efforts to clean up this air. Once women's entry into management is established, work and family research and concomitant applications based on new understandings are an absolute necessity if women are to be full and equal participants in the leadership of organizations.

THE UNITED STATES EXPERIENCE

In the United States, women have made significant progress in entering and advancing in management. Today, women comprise 45.9% of all managerial workers (U.S. Department of Labor, 2003). Over the past 20 years, this proportion has risen almost continuously from 32.4% in 1983 (U.S. Department of Labor, 1984). The steady progression of women into managerial roles has been accompanied by numerous and wide-ranging changes at the individual, social group, and organizational levels.

As the number of women managers increases, so too do the pressures to recognize and deal with the family responsibilities that these new entrants into management carry with them. Research focusing on work and family has both shed light on the conflicts and encouraged organizational changes to minimize or reduce such conflicts. Today, in the United States, there are a variety of benefits and programs designed to accommodate the family obligations of an increasing number of full-time managerial employees. These changes include maternity and parental leaves, child-care programs and benefits, flexible working hours, telecommuting, and so forth.

Although these changes are beneficial, at the executive level it is the demands and requirements of the work itself that conflict with family obligations. Most executive positions, having been occupied predominately by males since the beginning of industrialized society, have been designed under the assumption of a gender-based division of labor. Indeed, in the late 1940s and early 1950s, Talcott Parsons, a leading sociologist, considered this separation of work and family as essential to the smooth running of the enterprise (Kanter, 1977). Over the years, these job demands and requirements have become acceptable and assumed necessary behaviors. The original assumption upon which the design was based was not questioned.

As canaries in the mine, the presence of significant numbers of women in management calls for the re-examination of the way managerial work is done (Schein, 1993). Efforts to enhance women's status in management must focus on changing the design and structure of the work itself in order to facilitate the interface between work and family. To do this, basic assumptions need to be questioned. What is needed is to examine the time frames, priorities, scheduling expectations, and valued behaviors from the perspective of: "What is convenient to the corporation?" and "What is job-related?" What demands, activities, and expectations are convenient only in the old order of a gender-based division of labor, and what activities and expectations are valid and essential to the productivity of the enterprise?

For example, last-minute meetings, urgent requests, and unscheduled high priority business trips appear to be a fact of corporate life. These can be hurdles in the race to the top that can trip up the woman manager with family responsibilities. Perhaps these crisis situations are corporate convenient—assumed and unexamined when there is a wife at home to take care of the children and to adjust the family to the corporate demands.

Similarly, the relationship between how time is spent and performance evaluation needs to be examined. Performance is often judged on the basis of how late you work or how early you arrive at the office on Saturday. Neither the necessity of such long hours nor their relationship to actual performance is typically questioned in the old order of a gender-based division of labor. However, such work schedules can have serious consequences for a woman with work and family responsibilities.

When basic assumptions about work requirements are examined and distinctions between "what is corporate convenient?" and "what is job related?" are made, a new and different set of valued performance behaviors and expectations emerges. For example, if family obligations on the part of all managerial employees are the norm, advance planning becomes the rule and true corporate emergencies the exception. The manager accustomed to last minute firefighting and receiving praise for acting swiftly in an emergency might be chastised for not planning ahead and foreseeing and preventing so-called crisis situations. Expectations regarding the hours of work become different as well. Workdays that extend into the night and Saturdays at the office might be viewed as time spent only by the poor performer or inefficient worker.

If a work and family interface is the norm, the responsibly for any negative impact of vital job-related activities on required family obligations would be shared by the corporation and the manager. For example, Amoco reimburses employees for dependent care when they travel overnight on business and no family member is available to care for the child or elderly parent. Similarly, Chevron Texaco and Dorsey & Whitney pay for child care costs if an employee's business travel creates a need for additional child care during evenings or on weekends (Lawlor, 1998).

In the United States, the increasing number of women advancing into positions of power and influence is fostering a re-examination of the nature of managerial work. As canaries in the mine, women in management are bringing to light assumptions about the way managerial work is done that are no longer viable in today's society and are challenging the value of behaviors and expectations that are merely corporate convenient. The research and concomitant organizational changes stemming from this re-examination facilitate a managerial work environment conducive to the advancement of women. A focus on the work and family interface enhances the ability of women and men to function successfully in both managerial and family roles.

A GLOBAL LOOK

Globally, the status of women in management continues to improve. Although there are wide variations among countries in terms of the percentage of women who occupy management positions, there is no doubt that women are progressing in management around the world.

Wirth (2001) examined women's managerial status in 41 countries for which internationally comparable 1998–1999 data were available. The study was based on data collected by the International Labor Organization (ILO), using its 1988 International Standard Classification of Occupations. Major Group 1 includes legislators, senior officials, and managers.

Wirth (2001) found that in nearly half of the 41 countries, women typically hold between 20 and 30% of legislative, senior official, and managerial positions. These countries include Austria, Germany,

Greece, Israel, Peru, and Singapore. In 16 of the 41 countries, women hold between 31 and 39% of such jobs. These countries include New Zealand, Poland, Portugal, and the United Kingdom. In a few countries, such as the Republic of Korea and Sri Lanka, women hold less than 10% of legislative, senior official, and managerial positions. In Wirth's study, internationally comparable data from Africa were not available. According to the United Nations (2000), women's participation in management and administrative positions averages 15% across 26 African countries.

Using the same Major Group 1 classification, Wirth also reports that women worldwide are gradually increasing their share of management positions. Over about a 5-year period (approximately 1993–1998) 13 out of the 24 countries for which data were available showed increases in the share of managerial positions held by women. Significant increases occurred in El Salvador, from 26 to 35%; in Ireland, from 19 to 27%; in New Zealand, from 31 to 37%; and in Slovakia, from 23 to 30%.

Studies based on ILO national classifications and national surveys also reveal the significant strides women are making in some countries. For example, in Canada, the proportion of women managers rose from 13% in 1970, to 25% in 1980, and to 40% in 1990. In 1998, women in Australia comprised 27.3% of managers, compared to 17.2% in 1990 (Wirth, 2001). In Hungary, women increased their share of enterprise and organization managers from 16 to 25% between 1980 and 1990. In Thailand, the proportion of women managers grew from 8% in 1974 to 19% in 1990 (Wirth, 1998).

Even with large proportional increases, many countries still have a very small number of women in management positions. In Japan, 8.9% of managerial workers are women (French, 2003). Similarly, the percentage of women managers in Bahrain, Bangladesh, Niger, Pakistan, and Tunisia, as examples, is below 10% (Wirth, 2001).

Overall, all indications are that women are moving into management globally, albeit at different country rates. This progress portends a heightening of interest in work and family issues. Within their own countries, women's presence in traditionally male jobs will continue to surface work and family conflicts previously unexamined in a gender-based division of labor perspective.

There are already indications that the assumptions about the nature of managerial work are being questioned, similar to the challenges to corporate convenient in the United States. In 1997, at the invitation of the ILO, participants from 20 countries met to discuss factors impeding women's progress in management. As reported by Wirth (1998), a key issue that emerged from both the meeting and ILO research was that breaking the glass ceiling implies a significant transformation of the workplace itself, such as management approaches and work organization and structure. According to Wirth (1998), a major question is whether or not a standard 60-hour or longer workweek for managers is detrimental to business, health, families, and gender equality. Hence, as canaries in the mine, the increase in women managers globally seems to be revealing the unhealthy aspects of a previously assumed corporate convenient culture of long hours.

Women's entry into management around the globe brings work and family issues to center stage worldwide. Within and across national borders, the examination of work and family issues becomes critical to ensuring women's continued success in management. The challenge is to address the work and family interface from an international perspective. This edited volume meets that challenge. The editor, Steven Poelmans, has assembled an outstanding group of contributors who, in total, provide us with a foundation for building an international work and family research agenda.

Work and family research with a broad international base and cross-cultural comparisons is rare. Greenhaus and Parasuraman (1999), in their review of recent research in the work and family area, observe that most of the reviewed research was conducted on American samples. They conclude their review with a recommendation that "investigations of cross-cultural and cross-national influences play a prominent role in the future research agenda on the work–family interface" (p. 411). Poelmans' volume makes this recommendation a reality. He and his contributors have internationalized the work and family research agenda.

This volume employs a wide variety of comparisons and also emphasizes integration within and across studies. Some research studies examine work and family issues among different ethnicities or organizational cultures. Others use differing government policies or organizations in varying states of change as their basis for comparison. Several studies use a multination framework, allowing for international comparisons and integration within each of these investigations. Concluding overviews furnish integration across work and family research studies. In its totality, this volume provides a broad and deep international and cross-cultural research perspective.

The use of a wide and multicultural lens allows new ways of thinking about work and family issues to come into view. My experiences at the Munich Congress in 1978 showed me the significant role that cross-cultural interchange can play, one that highlights the value of the cross-cultural learning provided by this edited volume. Following my presentation on women in management, initial questions about methodology and applications were easily answered. However, I was totally unprepared to respond to questions from two French applied psychologists. They challenged my definition of success and queried me about other avenues for success. As someone enmeshed in the culture of the United States, these questions were startling. In the 1970s in the United States, most research and applied efforts focused on enhancing women's access to the corporate routes to success traditionally followed by men. All eyes were on the prize, the same one the men had successfully captured. Questioning the value and meaning of the prize or considering alternative paths to its acquisition was not part of society's discussion.

Today in the United States, topics such as "what price success?" "having it all," and the "meaning of success" are forming the debate and dialogue about the role of work in our lives, as both women and men struggle with work and family interface issues. What the United States culture was blind to at the time, other cultures saw clearly. An international focus early on might have brought these issues to the surface much sooner.

The work of Poelmans and his colleagues takes these cultural blinders off. It is exciting to consider what new ways of thinking will emerge as a result of the contributions of this volume. For example, across and within cultures, what assumptions about work and family will be challenged and how will these challenges be similar and different cross culturally? What challenges will be made to people and organizations and their way of working that will ripple similarly across cultures as women advance into management? If the transition of some countries is smoother than others, does that reveal a preexisting set of work and family assumptions conducive to women's entry? To what extent will lessons learned in one culture open the eyes of those in other cultures? What assumptions might be challenged by the rich interplay of research across cultures?

The advancement of women in management globally may well hinge on resolving the issues surrounding the work and family interface. Work structures based on the traditional gender-based division of labor operate to impede women's progress. Work demands and requirements must be evaluated on the basis of their relationship to organizational effectiveness rather than on their convenience to those locked within an outdated view of the world of work. As observed by Dr. Frene Ginwala, speaker of the South African National Assembly, "the institutions that discriminate are man-shaped and must be made people-shaped. Only then will women be able to function as equals within these institutions" (see Adler, 1999, p. 260).

A global perspective on the integration of work and family is a key element in bringing about the changes necessary for women to have full and equal participation in management. The international research perspective of the theoretical, empirical, and practitioner-oriented contributions in this volume provides us with this much-needed global viewpoint. In comparing and contrasting work and family research across borders around the globe the air is rich with possibilities. By applying the lens of culture, what will we see? What blinders will we be called upon to remove? What new approaches for enhancing the status of women in management internationally will emerge? What will we learn about managing the work–family interface individually and in the firm that will improve the quality of life of women and men in the workforces globally? The canaries may fly high in the clean air of change and possibilities.

REFERENCES

Adler, N. J. (1999). Global leaders: Women of influence. In G. N. Powell (Ed.), *Handbook of gender and work* (pp. 239–261). Thousand Oaks, CA: Sage.

French, H. W. (2003, July 25). Japan's neglected resource: female workers. *The New York Times*, A, p. 3.

Greenhaus, J. H., & Parasuraman, S. (1999). Research on work, family, and gender: Current status and future directions. In G. N. Powell (Ed.), *Handbook of work and gender* (pp. 391–412). Thousand Oaks, CA: Sage.

Kanter, R. M. (1977). *Work and family in the United States: A critical review and agenda for research and policy.* New York: Sage.

Lawlor, J. (1998, July 12). Minding the children while on the road. *The New York Times*, 3, p. 10.

Schein, V. E. (1993). The work/family interface: Challenging "corporate convenient." *Women in Management Review, 8,* 22–27.

United Nations. (2000). *The world's women 2000: Trends and statistics.* New York: United Nations.

U.S. Department of Labor, Bureau of Labor Statistics (1984, January). *Employment and earnings, 31,* Table 22.

U.S. Department of Labor, Bureau of Labor Statistics (2003, June). *Employment and earnings, 50,* Table 11.

Wirth, L. (1998). Women in management: closer to breaking through the glass ceiling? *International Labor Review, 137,* 93–102.

Wirth, L. (2001). *Breaking the glass ceiling: Women in management.* Geneva: International Labor Office.

Editorial Introduction

When in April 2002, I was approached by Dr. Jan Cleveland, editor of the Applied Psychology Series of Lawrence Erlbaum Associates, to put together an edited volume on international work–family research I was deeply honored. Dr. Cleveland proposed this idea to me after a symposium on cross-cultural research at the 2002 conference of the Society of Industrial and Organizational Psychology in Toronto. In this symposium I could count on the valuable contributions of Dr. Mina Westman of Tel Aviv University (Israel); Dr. Laura den Dulk, then at Erasmus University, now at Utrecht University (the Netherlands); Dr. Susan Lewis of Manchester Metropolitan University (UK); Dr. Aminah Ahmad of Putra University (Malaysia); and Dr. Nini Yang of San Francisco State University (USA). Dr. Virginia Schein of Gettysburg College (USA) was so kind to support our symposium by chairing the session. This symposium was a first step in encouraging the academic work–family community to initiate collaborative international research, in order to test the models mostly developed in the United States or to develop new models that could capture the complexity and diversity of work–family experiences around the globe.

At that time, I was coordinating a European research group (Kairos), which gathered for the first time at the founding conference of the European Academy of Management (EURAM) in Barcelona. The Kairos group recognized the necessity of taking into account the influence of diverse cultural and legislative contexts for the study of work–life policies and culture and developed an elaborate proposal for doing a longitudinal study in eight European multinationals. Although we were unsuccessful in obtaining European funding and realizing the study, our Dutch colleagues Dr. Sabine Geurts and Josje Dikkers of Radboud University Nijmegen, Dr. Laura den Dulk of Utrecht University, and Dr. Bram Peper of Erasmus University (all from the Netherlands) pursued this study in their own country. Their findings are reported in Chapter 6 of this book. Other participants of the Kairos group contributed to this book. Dr. Ulla Kinnunen and Dr. Saija Mauno of the University of Jyvaeskylae (Finland) wrote a review chapter for the book and Susan Lewis of the Manchester Metropolitan University (UK) co-authored the epilogue. The first Kairos meeting at EURAM developed into a separate conference track on work and family in the following annual conferences in Stockholm (2002), Milan (2003), and St. Andrews (2004). Every year, we receive submissions from a wide range of countries. It was at the Stockholm conference that I had the privilege of meeting Rhona Rapoport who is still very active in promoting this important issue through her action research in companies. In the epilogue of the book, Dr. Rapoport draws on her long work experience to give a vision of the field in a context of globalization, together with two thought leaders in the field, Dr. Lotte Bailyn of MIT (USA) and Dr. Susan Lewis (UK), and Dr. Lewis' colleague at the Manchester Metropolitan University, Richenda Gambles.

Most contributions in the 2002 SIOP symposium in Toronto were from individual countries from four continents, with the exception of Dr. Yang's comparative study of Americans and Chinese and Dr. den Dulk's comparison of four European countries (Sweden, the Netherlands, Italy, and the UK). Two years later and a few weeks before submitting the final manuscript of this book, at the 2004 SIOP conference in Chicago, we could proudly present three major collaborative international research (CIR) projects in progress. Once again, Dr. Virginia Schein chaired the symposium. Each one of the CIR projects focuses on the work–family interface: the Collaborative International Study of Managerial Stress (CISMS II), headed by Dr. Paul Spector of the University of South Florida and Dr. Cary Cooper of Lancaster University; Project 3535 headed by Dr. Zeynep Aycan of the Koç University; and a project led by Margaret Shaffer and Anne Marie Francesco of the Hong Kong Baptist University and Janice Joplin of the University of Texas at El Paso. Together, these three projects cover more than 30 countries around the world. The objectives and research methodology of these studies were presented in a special issue of the *International Journal of Cross-Cultural Psychology* (Winter, 2003). In this book, you will find some empirical results of the CISMS I project and of the Hong-Kong group.

Two years after the 2002 SIOP conference, I still wonder why Dr. Jan Cleveland approached me. Maybe she noticed my passion for the topic, which had led me to study the work–family interface in my doctoral dissertation and early career, generously supported by my employer, IESE Business School. Maybe she approached me because of my clumsy, but well-intended attempt to offer an integrating framework at the end of this symposium, calling full enthusiasm for more multilevel, cross-cultural research. Whatever her reason, I will be eternally grateful for that day and for the confidence she and Anne

Duffy of Lawrence Erlbaum Associates have given me. While editing a book is certainly a major challenge, it is also a privilege, because it allowed me to invite and get personally acquainted with some of the finest researchers in the field, a selection of seasoned pioneers, high-potential entrants, and widely quoted experts.

It would have been impossible to put together this volume alone. Therefore I would like to express my gratitude to everyone who helped me to make this book possible. First of all, I would like to thank all colleagues who reviewed a chapter of the book. They deserve a special applause because their contributions are very generous considering that I could only offer a special acknowledgment in this book in exchange for their effort. Each reviewer carefully read a chapter and made suggestions for improvement. Their contributions have been essential for improving the quality of the book.

REVIEWERS:

Zeynep Aycan, Koç University, Istanbul, Turkey
Lotte Bailyn, Massachusetts Institute of Technology, Boston, United States
Rabi Bhagat, University of Memphis, Memphis, United States
Jennifer Bowes, Macquarie University, Sidney, Australia
Prishnee Datta, Catholic University Leuven, Belgium
Chantal Epio, The Lagos Business School, Victoria Island, Lagos, Nigeria, Africa
Michele Gelfand, University of Maryland, Maryland, United States
Leslie B. Hammer, Portland State University, Portland, United States
Fiona Jones, University of Leeds, Leeds, United Kingdom
Karen Korabic, University of Guelph, Canada
Donna Lero, University of Guelph, Canada
Sadia Nadeem, Cass Business School, London, United Kingdom
Michael O'Driscoll, University of Waikato, Hamilton, New Zealand
Rhona Rapoport, Institute of Family & Environmental Research, London, United Kingdom
Steven Rogelberg, University of North Carolina, Charlotte, United States
Teresa Rothausen, University of St. Thomas, Minneapolis, United States
Cynthia Thompson, Zicklin School of Business, New York, United States

Second, I would like to thank my editorial assistant, Barbara Beham, who took on the daily management of the book and made sure we didn't lose sight of any single aspect. Her dedication and eye for detail made it possible to keep an overview of this complex responsibility. Many thanks also to Khatera Sahibzada, who reviewed the English of all chapters in this book, a special challenge when you edit a book with so many international authors writing in their second, third, or fourth languages. Last and certainly not least, I would like to thank my employer IESE Business School, and more specifically my dear colleagues Dr. Nuria Chinchilla and Dr. Pablo Cardona, who have proven to be much more than my supervisors, colleagues, and tutors. They supported me throughout my formation and early career development as true friends and mentors. The support of IESE Business School has made it possible to accept this assignment as a book editor and has meanwhile resulted in the foundation of an own research centre at IESE Business School, the International Centre of Work and Family (http://www.iese.edu/en/RCC/ICWF/Home/Home.asp).

The foreword and epilogue have been written by some of the pioneers and life-long defenders of the integration of women in management, gender equality and work–personal life integration: Virginia Schein, Rhona Rapoport, Lotte Bailyn, Richenda Gambles, and Susan Lewis. This work unfolds chapter by chapter into a book that provides many perspectives and research methodologies. My biggest challenge was to compose a well-equilibrated volume, offering a truly international perspective, addressing different levels of analysis and a wide choice of topics pertinent to the field, while safeguarding its coherence. The book holds contributions of 54 authors of more than 20 different countries spread over the five continents, and addresses three different levels of analysis, the micro- or individual level, the meso- or organizational level, and the macro- or socio-cultural level. The book consists of 16 chapters, organized in five sections, looking at the (1) individual level in an international perspective (Chapter 1–3); (2) the organizational level in an international perspective (Chapter 4–8) and the cross-cultural perspective (Chapter 9–12); (4) case studies; and (5) conclusions and recommendations for future research (Chapter 13–16).

The aspects of the work–family interface studied by scholars around the world are as diverse as their cultural background, so I had to make sure to include some review and overview chapters in order not to scatter the attention of the reader too much. The result is a volume that combines four review chapters, two theoretical contributions, seven empirical studies, four quantitative and three qualitative studies, and four concluding overview chapters in order to appeal to a broad audience of work–family researchers and practitioners around the globe. I also invited all authors to reflect on a case study and give their input to the accompanying teaching note. As a result, the readers of the book are also offered some materials to teach on the topic using two case studies, one situated at the individual–couple level of analysis, and one at the organizational–country level of analysis. These cases are suited to use in classes on organizational behaviour, career management, human resource management, change management, or family counselling.

On behalf of the whole team of the International Centre of Work and Family at the IESE Business School and Lawrence Erlbaum Associates, I wish you a pleasant journey through this book. But more than anything, I hope that it will provide you with the inspiration to initiate innovative research projects that will develop this field further into the many directions it needs. I especially hope, as I will reiterate in Chapter 16, that incoming Ph.D. students and recent graduates will find the courage to undertake longitudinal, qualitative, and cross-cultural studies that are so desperately needed to move the field forward. I encourage their thesis supervisors and leaders of research centers around the world to support them despite the increasing pressures to publish in a short term. If we want to bring this field forward we need to dig deeper than we have done until now. The journey has only just begun.

—Steven Poelmans

Work and Family

An International Research Perspective

I

Individual—International Perspective

1

An Overview of International Research on the Work–Family Interface

Steven Poelmans
IESE Business School/University of Navarra
Barcelona, Spain

Michael O'Driscoll
University of Waikato, Hamilton, New Zealand

Barbara Beham
IESE Business School/University of Navarra
Barcelona, Spain

INTRODUCTION

In this chapter we review the international literature on the antecedents, consequences, and moderators of work–family conflict. Our purpose especially is to overview studies published outside North America and to acknowledge the importance of different geo-political, socioeconomic, and cultural contexts for the experience of work and family. In an era of increasing globalization, international and expatriate assignments, and virtual and diverse teams, organizations and managers are increasingly confronted with different work and family values and, as a consequence, with varying interfaces between work and family. We need to critically assess the generalizability of models developed in the United States and Canada, because it cannot be assumed that the context, work ethos, and family values of these countries are universally relevant. Because cross-cultural research has only recently started to emerge (Poelmans, 2003), most of the studies we will review are simply set in a different context. Still, by systematically reviewing this less well known literature, we hope to trace inspiring trends of what could be promising avenues for future research.

In developing this chapter, we have not attempted to review all of the research conducted outside North America. As a starting point, we used a number of criteria to select manuscripts. First, to ensure the academic quality and reliability of the findings, we focused on manuscripts published in peer-reviewed journals. That means we excluded nonrefereed research papers, dissertations, book chapters, and conference presentations. Second, we limited our search to relatively recent research conducted since 1985. Third, although we will make reference to studies conducted in the United States and Canada as points of reference, our major focus is on research conducted outside North America. Fourth, we searched databases such as PsychInfo and Proquest, using as keywords "work–family conflict" and "work–family enhancement." Although scholars in diverse disciplines, ranging from family studies to political science, may have written manuscripts on the broad issue of work and family, we aim to primarily focus on the disciplines of psychology, management, and sociology, where the term work–family conflict is quite established. This also means that we focus on the micro-level of analysis, i.e., perceptions of individuals of themselves and their context, and exclude studies on organizational work–family policies in a broader sociopolitical context. Note that we talk about both conflict and enhancement to address the suggestions of scholars such as Edwards and Rothbard (2000), Parasuraman and Greenhaus (2000), and Frone (2003) that a broader set of work–family interactions should be considered. Unfortunately, as readers will observe in the next paragraphs, we found very few references to positive spillovers in the literature.

This chapter is divided into five major parts. First, to give an overall framework for the chapter, we briefly review the literature on work–family theories and models. We give special attention to theories that try to explain differences between people of different countries and cultural contexts. Second, we focus on the antecedents of work–family conflict. Although many studies use cross-sectional, correlational designs that do not distinguish between causes and consequences, we can use logical reasoning to determine that variables such as work stressors and family involvement are antecedents rather than consequences of work–family conflict. Third, we review some of the major consequences of work–family conflict, both for well-being, productivity, and the strength of the relationship with the firm. Fourth, we review moderators that have been reported to reduce the strength of the associations between work–family conflict and its antecedents and consequences. Finally, we identify some key issues and directions in this field of research.

THEORETICAL MODELS

Conflict between work and family is a widely researched topic in contemporary organizational behavior research. The origin of this research domain can be situated in the late 1970s with the seminal works of Rapoport & Rapoport (1969), Renshaw (1976), Kanter (1977), Pleck (1977), and Handy (1978). However, one could argue that this domain has its roots in research examining the mutual impact of employment and family life (Marshall, 1992a, 1992b). A major theme in this literature is that both work and family claim time and energy. Work is an important source of income, financial security, and status, whereas the family functions as a nucleus, where two partners find intimacy and support and raise children. Hence, work and family are not independent (Kanter, 1977) and consequently conflicts will inevitably arise.

Since the pioneering work of Pleck (1977), there is a general consensus that work and family influence each other in a positive and negative way: time, tasks, attitudes, stress, emotions, and behavior spill over between work and family (Greenhaus & Beutell, 1985). A distinction was made between the work–family interface (work influencing family) and the family–work interface (family influencing work; Frone, Russell, & Cooper, 1992; Greenhaus, 1988; Greenhaus & Beutell, 1985; Gutek, Searle, & Klepa, 1991). It was found that the interface is asymmetric: work tends to influence family more than vice versa (Frone, Russell, & Cooper, 1992b; Gutek, Searle, & Klepa, 1991; Hall & Richter, 1988; Wiley, 1987). Several scholars concluded that these two types of conflict are conceptually and empirically distinct constructs (Duxbury, Higgins, & Lee, 1994; Frone, Russell, & Cooper, 1992a; O'Driscoll, Ilgen, & Hildreth, 1992; Wiley, 1987).

The field has been dominated by role theory, which was derived from the seminal Michigan study of organizational stress (Kahn, Wolfe, Quinn, Snoek, & Rosenthal, 1964). According to role theory, conflicting expectations associated with different roles have detrimental effects for well-being. This rationale basically fits the logic of a stressor–strain model (Cohen & Wills, 1985; Karasek & Theorell, 1990), with work–family conflict as a stressor. Many published studies test a theoretical model that links antecedents, moderators, and consequences (Bedeian, Burke, & Moffet, 1988; Frone, Russell, & Cooper,

1992; Gutek, Searle, & Klepa, 1991; Judge, Boudreau, & Bretz, 1994; Kelly & Voydanoff, 1985). Frone, Yardley, and Markel (1997) offer a general, integrative framework of the work–family interface. Structural equations analysis supported their model, which integrates social support, time commitment, and overload (both at work and in the family) as antecedents, work–family conflict, and family–work conflict as core variables, and distress, dissatisfaction, and performance as outcomes. In this chapter, we will use this model as a framework to distinguish between antecedents and consequences of work–family conflict.

Another influential theory is spillover theory (Piotrkowski, 1979; Staines, 1980; Zedeck & Mosier, 1990), based on Pleck's (1977) early notion of asymmetrically permeable boundaries between the life domains of work and family. These studies invited scholars to consider other types of interfaces between work and family, such as compensation (Champoux, 1978), independency, and instrumentality (Evans & Bartolomé, 1981). Lambert (1990) and more recently Edwards and Rothbard (2000) reviewed all different linkages, specifying the sign and causal relationships and how these are influenced by personal intent.

More recently, a series of articles suggested alternative theories, such as Hobfoll's (1989) conservation of resources theory (COR; Grandey & Cropanzano, 1999; Poelmans, Spector, Cooper, Allen, O'Driscoll, & Sanchez, 2003; Rosenbaum & Cohen, 1999), Higgins, Bond, Klein, & Strauman's (1986) self-discrepancy theory (Polasky & Holahan, 1998), Tajfel & Turner's (1985) social identity theory (Lobel, 1991a), and Homans' (1958, 1974) and Blau's (1964) social exchange theory (Lambert, 2000). Several authors also proposed new theories, such as Nippert–Eng (1996) segmentation–integration theory, Campbell Clark's border-crossing theory (2000), Barnett and Hyde's (2001) expansionist theory, and Poelmans' (2004) decision–process theory. Very few of these theories have offered explanations for cultural differences and seem to operate on the assumption that these theories are universally valid, which only empirical tests and time can show.

Only very recently have authors started to formulate propositions that explicitly address cultural differences in the experience of work–family conflict. Yang, Chen, Choi, and Zou (2000) were among the first to suggest that cultural values, and more specifically individualism–collectivism, could be used to explain cultural differences in the experience of work–family conflict. Yang focused more in-depth on this issue in chapter 11. In a recent special issue of the *International Journal of Cross-Cultural Management* a series of authors speculate on other macro-socioeconomic factors and cultural values that may be used in explaining differences among citizens in different parts of the world. Cultural values that are proposed to be relevant include individualism–collectivism (Poelmans et al., 2003; Korabik, Lero, Ayman, 2003; Joplin, Shaffer, Francesco, & Lau, 2003), gender role ideology (Korabik et al., 2003; Joplin et al., 2003), uncertainty avoidance and power distance (Peters & Den Dulk, 2003; Joplin et al., 2003), and monochronic–polychronic time orientation (Korabik et al., 2003). Together, these papers cover a wide spectrum of cultural values and propositions that link these cultural values with the experience of work–family conflict. In his multilevel "fit" model of work and family, Poelmans (2003) suggests that above and beyond causes at the individual, organizational, and cultural model, misfits between variables at different levels of analysis should not be overlooked in explaining work–family conflict. In chapter 14, Gelfand & Knight elaborate on these theoretical frameworks and make suggestions for future research.

ANTECEDENTS OF WORK–FAMILY CONFLICT

As pointed out above, theoretical models of the work–family interface differentiated two directions of work–family conflict: work-to-family interference (WFI) and family-to-work interference (FWI). Investigations in Western countries, particularly the United States, identified a higher prevalence of the former (WFI) than the latter (FWI), suggesting that family "boundaries" are more permeable than job boundaries (Carlson & Frone, 2003). In other words, individuals may perceive that they have more flexibility in terms of engaging in family commitments and responsibilities than they do for work commitments. Specifically, time on the job is frequently dictated by the person's employment contract or the organization, whereas family time is more discretionary. Hence, there is a greater likelihood that people will perceive negative spillover from the job to the family environment rather than the converse. Nevertheless, this does not imply that the impact of FWI on people's attitudes, behavior, and well-being will necessarily be greater than the effects of WFI (see our discussion of work–family conflict consequences later in this chapter).

Involvement in job and family extends beyond time. Carlson and Frone (2003) also discussed psychological involvement, which reflects "the investment of cognitive and emotional resources" (p. 516) in each domain, that is, "the degree to which individuals identify with a role domain and see it as important to their self-concept" (p. 521). A high degree of psychological involvement in a role (e.g., the job role, the family role) will result in the person being somewhat mentally preoccupied with their performance in that role and perhaps being more influenced by events that occur in that context. Conceptually, therefore, it would seem evident that psychological involvement would have significant implications for levels of work-to-family and family-to-work interference. As noted by Carlson and Frone (2003), however, research investigating the relationship of psychological involvement with work–family conflict has obtained very inconsistent results. Although some research has confirmed a positive relationship between involvement in one role and conflict between the two domains, other studies have obtained no significant association between these variables.

There may be multiple explanations for this inconsistency in findings, including use of different measures of both psychological involvement and work–family conflict. In addition, the assumption that involvement in one role (e.g., the job) necessarily precludes attention to another (e.g., family), or leads to interference between role commitments, is not inherently logical. It would be quite possible, for instance, for an individual to have high levels of psychological involvement in both job and family and to adopt coping strategies that prevent negative spillover between the two domains. To date, research has not explored these possibilities in any systematic fashion. In their U.S. study, Carlson and Frone (2003) found that both psychological involvement and behavioral (time) involvement in the job were significantly related to WIF, but the same did not apply for the relationship between family involvement and FIW. Clearly, more research is required to explore the dynamic interplay between psychological involvement and work–family spillover before definitive conclusions can be drawn about the role of psychological involvement in the work–family conflict process.

A comprehensive overview and discussion of work–family conflict and work–family "balance" was provided recently by Frone (2003), who summarized findings from the (overwhelmingly U.S.-based) research in this area. Frone noted that family boundaries may be more permeable than job boundaries and hence levels of work-to-family interference (WFI) are typically reported as being higher or more intense than those for family-to-work interference (FWI). Numerous empirical studies in the United States and other Western countries have confirmed this finding. These studies frequently examined two categories of antecedents to work–family conflict: (a) work-related and family-related conditions in which individuals function and (b) personal or dispositional factors relating to levels of conflict between work and family. Most of the research in this field has examined (a), characteristics of work and family environments which may have an impact on people's experience of WFI and FWI. Before turning to these studies, however, investigations of personal and dispositional factors will be summarized.

Of the personal variables, gender is the most obvious candidate as a predictor of work–family conflict. Some commentators (e.g., Pleck, 1977; Gutek et al., 1991) suggested that, because of their different roles and responsibilities, men and women may experience different levels of interrole conflict, with men exhibiting greater interference between work and family (WFI) and women reporting more interference from family to work (FWI). However, although some studies report significant gender differences, with females showing greater FWI and males more WFI, this pattern has not been uniformly replicated across studies, and many have found no gender differences at all in either WFI or FWI (Grzywacz & Marks, 2000). Few international studies have sought to compare males and females directly. In a French-Canadian sample of physical therapists and psychologists, Senecal, Vallerand, and Guay (2001) found no differences between males and females in their levels of work–family conflict. In one of the few cross-national studies that have been conducted to date, Yang et al. (2000) found that men in China reported higher levels of work–family conflict than their female counterparts, but the measure of work–family conflict used in this study was nondirectional, hence it is not possible to determine whether one direction of conflict was experienced more by men than women. However, in another Chinese study (among Hong Kong workers), Fu and Shaffer (2001) did obtain gender differences, with women displaying higher levels of FWI and men more WFI. This finding was explained in terms of gender role expectations in Chinese families, with women being expected to take the major responsibility for household and family chores, hence there is a greater likelihood that they would experience interference from these family commitments with their work. In contrast, according to Fu and Shaffer (2001), the predominant expectation is that men will be the major breadwinners, and hence males may invest more time in their jobs, with a consequent negative spillover to family life (time-based conflict).

With a few exceptions, however, there appears to be little systematic international research on gender differences in both levels of work–family conflict or relationships among work–family conflict and other variables (such as job and family satisfaction or psychological strain). This is surprising, given the overall salience of the topic and the potential for significant gender issues to emerge. It is possible, of course, that some studies including both male and female participants may have obtained no differences and were simply not reported. Furthermore, the primary focus may have been on antecedents and consequences of work–family conflict rather than gender similarities and differences per se. Indeed, as we discuss shortly, a number of international studies sampled one gender only, typically women.

There have been a few recent investigations of other dispositional antecedents to work–family conflict, in particular personality factors. Some researchers (e.g., Bernas & Major, 2000; Grandey & Cropanzano, 1999; Grzywacz & Marks, 2000) illustrated that high levels of hardiness, extraversion, and self-esteem are linked with reduced work–family conflict (both directions), whereas neuroticism may be positively associated with work–family conflict (Grzywacz & Marks, 2000). Following an earlier study by Carlson (1999), Bruck and Allen (2003) examined relationships of negative affectivity, Type A behavior disposition, and "big five" personality variables with both work-to-family interference and family-to-work interference. In their research, after controlling for demographic variables and hours worked per week, negative affectivity was the single most predictive variable of both WIF and FIW. Other dispositional variables included in their hierarchical regressions displayed no consistent significant relationships with the two directions of conflict. A similar result was obtained when Bruck and Allen disaggregated time-based, strain-based, and behavior-based work–family conflict. Again, although its contribution was significant only in the case of strain-based conflict, negative affectivity showed the highest beta weights in the hierarchical regressions. As a set, the dispositional variables accounted for most variance in strain-based conflict and least in behavior-based conflict, confirming Carlson's (1999) supposition that different forms of work–family conflict may be predicted by different antecedents.

The above research by Carlson (1999) and Bruck and Allen (2003), as well as an earlier study by Frone, Russell, and Cooper (1993), which obtained similar findings, was conducted in the United States. An online literature search identified few international investigations of the relationship between personality factors and work–family conflict. A notable exception is a study reported recently by Stoeva, Chiu, and Greenhaus (2002), who examined the role of negative affectivity among a sample of executive civil servants in Hong Kong. Consistent with the U.S. findings, Stoeva et al. (2002) found that negative affectivity was significantly, but modestly, correlated with both WFI and FWI, although the contribution of this variable diminished once job stressors and family stressors were entered into the regression equations. They also observed a moderator effect for negative affectivity, which will be discussed later.

Although the existing evidence is suggestive of the potential impact of dispositional factors on people's experience of work–family conflict, clearly more systematic investigation is required before we can definitively conclude that variables such as negative affectivity play a major role in determining levels of WFI and FWI, and in the relationship between these and other variables. Frone (2003) observed that personality characteristics may exacerbate (e.g., negative affectivity, neuroticism) or ameliorate (e.g., resilience) both WFI and FWI. International investigations that consider the interactions between dispositional and cultural variables (e.g., cultural values) would be particularly valuable. We are aware of no international studies to date that have systematically examined these interactions. As with gender, an understanding of the role of dispositional factors would be enhanced by explicitly incorporating personality variables into research on work–family conflict in diverse cultural contexts. By the same token, cross-cultural research on the interplay between personality and work–family conflict variables would also be informative.

In contrast to the relative paucity of research on personal and dispositional antecedents, there has been a plethora of studies, both in the United States and internationally, on situational predictors of work–family conflict. Evidence from the United States studies consistently demonstrated that work demands, work-related stressors, and strain are predictive of work-to-family interference, whereas family responsibilities and stressors (such as conflict within the family) appear to contribute more directly to family-to-work interference (Frone, 2003). In addition, social support (in both domains) has been associated with reduced work–family conflict. Work-related social support (e.g., from one's supervisor or work colleagues) is more associated with reduced WFI, and family support (e.g., from partner or spouse) correlates more closely with reduced FWI. Hence, social support would seem to be a primary determinant of (reduced) levels of work–family conflict. Frone (2003) concluded that research has illustrated that the two directions of interrole conflict are separate albeit interrelated, that antecedents of WFI reside primarily in the job domain, whereas antecedents of FWI lie mainly in the family domain, that "both dimensions of work–family conflict are affected by similar types of role characteristics, such as behavioral involvement, psychological involvement, stressors, and resources" (p. 152).

In a large U.S. study, Grzywacz and Marks (2000) also found that social support at work and from one's spouse were negatively related to levels of work–family conflict. Low levels of support at work were strongly correlated with negative spillover from work to family (WFI), especially for women. Another interesting gender difference was that spouse-affectual support appeared to have more influence on reduced WFI for men than for women. Spouse support was also closely related to reduced negative spillover from family to work (FWI) for both men and women. Grzywacz and Marks (2000) suggested that building supportive relationships at work and also at home may be more effective antidotes to the negative effects of work–family conflict than other strategies such as flextime and increasing control–decision latitude.

Several international studies also examined the antecedents of work–family conflict in different countries. Internationally, one of the most prominent research programs over the past 10 years or so was developed by Samuel Aryee and his colleagues in Hong Kong (Aryee, Fields, & Luk, 1999). Their studies largely confirmed findings that emerged from research in the United States. For example, Aryee, Fields, and Luk (1999) examined within-job and within-family role conflicts, along with job involvement and family involvement, as predictors of WFI and FWI. This study was conducted to partially replicate a model and findings presented by Frone, Russell, and Cooper (1992a) in the United States. Aryee et al.'s (1999) results were similar to those obtained by Frone and his colleagues, in that WFI and FWI were reciprocally related: within-job conflict predicted WFI and within-family conflict predicted FWI. However, in contrast to Frone et al.'s (1992a) results, Aryee and his colleagues (1999) did not obtain significant paths from job and family involvement to the two forms of work–family conflict. They attributed these differences to the overall importance of family life in Chinese culture (compared with the United States culture) and "the lack of significant relationship between family involvement and family–work conflict .... may occur because the centrality of the family in Hong Kong leads to perceptions that investment of time in the family does not interfere with work responsibilities" (p. 508). No explanation was provided for the finding that increased job involvement was not significantly associated with work-to-family interference, except that the authors noted that among Chinese employees, commitment to the work role may be a means to an end (that is, family security) rather than an end in itself.

In another study published in the same year, Aryee, Luk et al. (1999) studied the potential impact of work overload and parental overload on interrole conflict among Hong Kong employees in dual-earner families. As with their previous research, Aryee, Luk et al. (1999) found a reciprocal relationship between the two directions of work–family conflict. They also observed that WFI was significantly higher than FWI, and that males reported higher levels of WFI whereas females experienced more FWI. A key issue in this study, however, was the impact of role stressors on both WFI and FWI. Work overload was the primary contributor to both forms of interference, but parental overload also contributed to increased FWI (but not WFI). Aryee, Luk et al. (1999) also explored the potential impact of social support from the spouse, both as an antecedent of (reduced) work–family conflict and as a potential moderator of the relationship of work and family overload with WFI and FWI. (Moderator effects will be discussed later in this chapter.) They found that spousal support was negatively related with work-to-family interference, but not with family-to-work interference, suggesting that provision of a supportive home environment by spouses/partners may have a positive impact on spillover between family and work life, but cannot ameliorate the negative effects of work interfering with family life.

Another Hong Kong study, conducted by Fu and Shaffer (2001), looked at the three dimensions or forms of interrole conflict specified by Greenhaus and Beutell (1985), time-based conflict, behavior-based conflict, and strain-based conflict. Family-specific factors (such as hours spent on household work, parental demands, and whether or not the person's spouse was also in paid employment) were found to significantly predict time-based family-to-work interference (FIW), but not strain-based or behavior-based FIW. On the other hand, job-role demands stressors (especially role conflict, role overload, and hours spent at work) contributed to all three forms of work-to-family interference (WIF), although again the contribution of these predictors to time-based WIF was greater than it was to the other forms of WIF. These findings are consistent with those obtained in U.S. studies.

Additional findings from Hong Kong were published recently by Lo (2003), who interviewed married female professionals to ascertain their perceptions of factors that contributed to work–family conflict. Although this study did not specifically distinguish between the two directions of interrole conflict, respondents were asked to identify factors from both domains. The most frequently mentioned causes of conflict were: lack of support from the respondent's husband, feelings of exhaustion and burnout (from work and family demands), lack of time for family activities, and the amount of homework required of children. The last of these factors may be particularly relevant to Hong Kong, where the expectations of children's performance at school are very high and considerable amounts of out-of-school homework are required. Given that in Hong Kong, women are typically regarded as having most responsibility for household tasks and child-rearing (Aryee, Luk et al., 1999), the added burden of supervising children's school homework may be considerable.

Parallel to the above research conducted in Hong Kong, Kim and Ling (2001) investigated three forms of work–family conflict among female entrepreneurs in Singapore. The three forms of conflict included were: job–spouse conflict, job–parent conflict, and job–homemaker conflict. Of these, interference between job and homemaker roles was

found to the most intense form of conflict. Job stressors (a conglomer-
ate of work pressures, within-role ambiguity, and conflicting demands
allied with the entrepreneurial role, along with business-related problems) were more closely linked with the three forms of conflict than
were family stressors. However, age of children correlated positively
with job–parent conflict, which is somewhat contrary to previous research, which has found a negative correlation between children's age
and work–family conflict. Kim and Ling noted that the majority of
women in their sample had adolescent children and that this may be
a difficult age for parents and place high demands on their coping
ability. Finally, as in other studies, level of support from the (male)
spouse was negatively related to job–spouse conflict.

Research implemented in Western countries, other than the United
States, reflects similar trends to those observed in the above Asian investigations. For instance, Burke and Greenglass (1999) examined the
impact of restructuring (particularly downsizing) of Canadian hospital organizations, along with demographic variables, on both WFI and
FWI experienced by nurses. The prediction, which was confirmed, was
that the stress associated with restructuring would lead to increased
WFI, whereas demographic variables (such as age and whether or not
the respondent had children) would be closely associated with FWI
but unrelated to WFI. In this study, social support from spouse contributed to FWI, but not to WFI.

Elloy and Smith (2003) reported findings from a comparison of
dual-career and single-career lawyers and accountants in Australia.
As noted by these authors, the increasing prevalence of dual-earner
and dual-career couples requires organizations to consider the possibly differing needs of individuals functioning in these relationships,
compared with their counterparts who function in a single-career family. Their research did not differentiate between WIF and FIW, but used
the measure of overall interrole conflict constructed by Kopelman,
Greenhaus, and Connolly (1985). Although dual- and single-career
individuals differed on some variables, such as the amount of stress
reported, work overload, work role ambiguity, and role conflict, they
did not differ substantially on levels of overall work–family conflict.
Elloy and Smith (2003) suggested that organizations need to take account of the differential impact of role demands and stressors on
employees whose work–family contexts may differ.

Jansen, Kant, Kristensen, and Nijhuis (2003) conducted a longitudinal study of the antecedents and consequences of work–family
conflict in the Netherlands. They observed that the reported prevalence of work–family conflict was considerably lower (males 11% and
females 9%) in their sample of over 12,000 Dutch workers than had

been reported in the United States (Frone et al., 1992a) and Finland (Kinnunen & Mauno, 1998). Nevertheless, similar antecedents to work–family conflict were found to those reported in the United States and other countries, with work demands, job insecurity, and interpersonal conflict with peers and supervisors being major contributors to interrole conflict for men, and physical work demands, overtime, commuting time, and having dependent children contributing to interrole conflict for women. One limitation of this study, however, is that it utilized a single-item measure that did not differentiate between work-to-family and family-to-work interference.

Some of the above research has illustrated the positive benefits of social support from one's partner or spouse, especially for women. As noted previously, Kim and Ling (2001) found that social support from the spouse was associated with reduced work–family conflict in a sample of Singaporean female entrepreneurs. A Japanese study by Matsui, Ohsawa, and Onglatco (1995) also examined husband support among employed women (although in this case the respondents were office employees rather than entrepreneurs). Matsui et al. (1995) examined both directions of work–family conflict, and observed that (consistent with U.S. findings) reported levels of WIF were greater than those for FIW. A major finding of their study was that parental demands were closely associated with FIW, but not significantly related to WIF. Unfortunately, however, they did not include work-related demands in their research design; hence, it was not possible to determine if the converse applied for work demands. Support from the respondent's husband was associated with reduced family-to-work interference (FWI), but bore no relationship to work-to-family interference (WFI). Husband support also exhibited a moderator effect on the relationship between parental demands and FWI, which will be discussed later in this chapter. Similar findings were reported by Noor (2002a), who identified the number of work hours and work-role overload as significant predictors of an undifferentiated measure of work–family conflict among Malaysian employed married women. Furthermore, lack of spouse social support also contributed significantly to conflict between job and family. Lack of autonomy, however, was not a significant correlate of work–family conflict in this study.

A somewhat different approach to the issue of work–family interface was proposed by Senecal, Vallerand, and Guay (2001), whose research was mentioned earlier. Senecal et al. (2001) discussed work–family conflict from a motivational perspective. Their model suggests that being motivated to engage in family activities and work play a key role in determining levels of family commitment. A person who lacks what they refer to as "self-determination" (an intrinsic motivational force) will experience alienation from their family, which in turn induces feelings of work–family conflict. Their research on French-Canadian professionals supported the notion that motivational factors contribute to feelings of alienation from family and that family alienation leads to heightened work–family conflict. Although this process was replicated among both males and females in their study, who reported similar levels of work–family conflict, unfortunately the measure of conflict utilized did not distinguish work-to-family from family-to-work interference.

There has been relatively little attempt to directly compare U.S. findings concerning work–family conflict with those from other countries. This is perhaps surprising, given the substantial differences among countries in terms of cultural values, individualism–collectivism, and the centrality of family life. Although it is recognized that globalization of markets and international economic factors (among other factors) have increased the salience of work–family issues in all societies (Yang et al., 2000), research in the field has been conducted predominantly in Western countries. Yang et al. (2000) noted that "work and family issues are intricately related to cultural beliefs, values, and norms" (p. 113); hence, it is important to consider the determinants and outcomes of work–family conflict in different cultural contexts. Yang and colleagues compared sources of work–family conflict in the United States with those in China. Unfortunately, the measure of work–family conflict did not differentiate the different directions of conflict, but instead was a global index of conflict between the two domains. Nevertheless, they found that Chinese and U.S. respondents reported comparable levels of work–family conflict. Although patterns of relationships in the two countries displayed some similarity, in China both work and family demands contributed significantly to perceptions of work–family conflict, whereas in the United States only family demands predicted work–family conflict. Furthermore, in China, the coefficients for work and family demands were not significantly different, and the impact of work demands on work–family conflict was stronger in China than in the United States. The authors note that further research on the relative impact of demands from the two domains is warranted, along with additional cross-national and cross-cultural research on the antecedents of work–family conflict.

To summarize this discussion of the antecedents of work–family conflict: although there has been a multitude of studies conducted in the United States, research in other Western countries and non-Western countries has been less prolific. Nevertheless, similar patterns of results have emerged from both U.S. and non-U.S. studies, in terms of factors predicting levels of work-to-family interference and family-to-work interference. Findings are also consistent in demonstrating that work-to-family interference and family-to-work interference are separate, but frequently intercorrelated, dimensions, and that the demands and stressors occurring in each domain (e.g., the job) tend to have a greater impact on interference from that domain toward the other (e.g. family). Furthermore, social support, especially from one's partner or spouse, would appear to be a major contributor to reduced work–family conflict, especially family-to-work interference. At this point, however, there have been too few cross-cultural investigations to draw firm conclusions about similarities and differences among the experiences of people in different cultural contexts, but the research cited above by Yang et al. (2000) was a promising start. Clearly, there is a need for more systematic investigation of cultural norms and values and other cultural differences to determine whether antecedents of work–family conflict are culture-specific or cut across cultural boundaries. There also needs to be exploration of a greater range of potential contributors, including the role played by individual coping strategies and organizational policies or interventions intended to alleviate the negative impact of work–family conflict.

CONSEQUENCES

The negative effects of work–family conflict have been extensively documented and can be categorized in four main groups: (a) health (mental and physical), (b) satisfaction, (c) performance, and (d) commitment both in the work domain (e.g., burnout, work productivity, job satisfaction, and turnover intentions) and family–general life domain (e.g., anxiety, performance in parental role, marital satisfaction, and divorce intentions), respectively. In addition, authors such as Frone and his colleagues suggested domain-specific paths of antecedents and consequences for work-to-family conflict (affecting family outcomes) and family-to-work conflict (impacting work; Frone et al., 1992a), and feedback mechanisms between work and family life (Frone, Yardley, & Markel, 1997). Allen, Herst, Bruck, & Sutton (2000) conducted a valuable meta-analysis of the consequences of work–family conflict in the United States.

Health Outcomes

The most studied dependent variable is undoubtedly strain or mental health experienced by the person, in Frone, Russell, and Yardley's model (1997) referred to as work and family distress. A person occupying multiple roles has been associated with role strain, psychological distress, and somatic complaints (Cooke & Rousseau, 1984; Frone, Russell, & Cooper, 1991, 1992a; Menaghan & Parcel, 1990). Burke (1988) tested a model in which work–family conflict leads to psychosomatic symptoms and negative feeling states. Interference between job and family life has also been related to depression, irritation, and anxiety in married female managers (Greenglass, 1985). O'Driscoll et al. (1992) found a positive association between work/nonwork conflict and general psychological strain. Frone (2000) found work–family conflict to be related to having mood, anxiety, and substance dependence disorder. Boles, Johnston, and Hair (1997) linked work–family conflict with emotional exhaustion and job dissatisfaction in salespersons, and they found that these two consequences were in turn related to the propensity to leave one's job.

These detrimental effects were also found in non-U.S. respondents. Richardsen, Burke, and Mikkelsen (1999) found that work–family conflict was associated with emotional exhaustion and psychosomatic complaints in Norwegian female managers. Grant-Vallone and Ensher (1998) studied expatriates and reported that work interference with personal life resulted in reduced vitality and depression. Matsui et al. (1995) found that both WFI and FWI were significantly related to vocational, psychological, interpersonal, and physical strain in Japanese married women working full-time (in mostly clerical jobs). In a sample of 310 Malaysian employed women studied by Noor (2002b), work–family conflict was a significant predictor of psychological distress.

Geurts, Rutte, & Peeters (1999) tested a comprehensive model of work–home interference (WHI) among medical residents in an academic hospital in the Netherlands. The results showed that WHI was positively associated with psychosomatic health complaints and sleep deprivation (i.e., general health indicators), and with emotional exhaustion and depersonalization (i.e., work-related health indicators). Jansen et al. (2003) found that work–family conflict has important mental health implications, such as the development of an elevated need for recovery from work and prolonged fatigue. Using the General Health Questionnaire (assessing, for example, mental health, coping with difficulties in life, and enjoyment of daily activities), Rosenbaum and Cohen (1999) conducted a study assessing the effect of WFC on the level of distress of Isreali mothers of young children who had full-time outside employment. It was found that women who had at least one resource (resourcefulness self-control skill or spousal support) were less distressed than women who did not have either of these resources.

The impact of work–family conflict on well-being has also been demonstrated in a few qualitative and longitudinal studies. Frone, Russell, and Cooper's (1997) study of employed parents is one of the few longitudinal studies of the effects of work–family conflict. They found that FWI was related to elevated levels of depression and poor physical health and to the incidence of hypertension. In contrast, WFI was related to elevated levels of heavy alcohol consumption. The results of the study of Grzywacz & Bass (2003) suggest that higher levels of both work-to-family and family-to-work conflict are associated with poor mental health (depression, anxiety disorder). Another frequently studied work-related psychological consequence is burnout (Burke, 1988; Kinnunen & Mauno, 1998; Montgomery, Peeters, Schaufeli, & Den Ouden, 2003; Netemayer, Boles, & McMurrian, 1996). Allen et al. (2000) reported a weighted mean correlation of 0.42 between burnout and work–family conflict.

Satisfaction Outcomes

Kossek & Ozeki's (1998) meta-analysis shows that regardless of the type of measure used, a consistent negative relationship exists among all forms of work–family conflict and job and life satisfaction. Work–family interference has been associated with a decrease in life satisfaction in North American samples (Bedeian et al., 1988; Judge et al., 1994; Parasuraman, Greenhaus, & Granrose, 1992), and in a Malaysian sample of female researchers (Ahmad, 1996), but not in a Hong-Kong sample (Aryee, Luk et al., 1999). Family–work interference has been associated with job dissatisfaction (Duxbury & Higgins, 1991; Judge et al., 1994; Kopelman et al., 1985). Ahmad (1996), Ayree, Luk et al. (1999), Chiu (1998), and Ngo & Lui (1999) confirmed in Malaysian and Hong Kong samples the finding of Adams, King, and King (1996) that work–family conflict is also associated with job dissatisfaction. Bruck, Allen, and Spector (2002) examined the relation between work–family conflict and job satisfaction using both global and composite measures of job satisfaction. Their results indicated that WFI related significantly to both types of job satisfaction, but the relation was significantly stronger to composite job satisfaction than to global job satisfaction.

Ayree et al. (1999) found that neither WFI nor FWI were associated with family dissatisfaction. This can be explained by a combination of Chinese Confucianism and Hong Kong metropolitan modernism, resulting in what Ayree et al. call "utilitarianistic familism." According to this philosophy, the family is the central unit of society taking precedence over individual members, but work is prevalent to cope with a high cost of living and is considered as instrumental for family purposes. Therefore, conflicts between work and family are not associated with family dissatisfaction, because engagement in work is viewed as instrumental to family well-being. Interestingly, Ahmad (1996) also found a lack of relationship between work–family conflict and family dissatisfaction in Malaysia suggesting that the instrumentality model may apply across (at least some) Asian cultures.

Ayree (1992) more closely examined three specific types of work–family conflict (job–spouse conflict, job–homemaker conflict, and job–parent conflict) in a sample of married Singaporean professional women. He found that job–homemaker conflict had little or no influence on three measures of satisfaction (marital, job, and life satisfaction), whereas job–spouse conflict had a significant impact on all three types of satisfaction. This high impact of job–spouse conflict on job, marital, and life satisfaction was also confirmed by a study among Singapore women entrepreneurs (Kim & Ling, 2001). Surprisingly, Aryee (1992) found a relationship between job–parent conflict and job satisfaction and marital satisfaction, but not with life satisfaction. We could have expected though that a conflict between the job and the role as a parent would result in life dissatisfaction. The author does not offer an explanation for this intriguing finding and points out that "there is nothing distinctive about the experience of work–family conflict among married professional women in Singapore, an Asian country" (Ryan, McFarland, Baron, & Page, 1999) and that his findings "highlight the generality of the phenomenon of work–family conflict as a characteristic of modern industrial societies" (Aryee, 1992).

An important type of satisfaction in family domain is marital satisfaction. Several studies have provided support for the impact of work–family conflict on marital well-being (Campbell & Snow, 1992; Coverman, 1989). Greenglass, Pantony, and Burke (1988) found a clear association between role conflict and marital dissatisfaction, in both men and women. According to Kingston and Nock (1987), the time that couples spend together is determined by the number of hours they work, whereas sociocultural and life cycle variables have little influence. This is important because the researchers also found a clear relationship between hours together and marital satisfaction. Burley (1995) stated that social support from the partner and an equal distribution of domestic tasks between partners plays an important mediating role in the relationship between work–family conflict and marital satisfaction in men and women. Barling (1990) found that job satisfaction was related to marital satisfaction and work stress to marital dysfunction. Matthews, Congers, and Wickrama (1996) demonstrated that work–family conflict affects marital quality and stability via increased levels of distress and marital hostility and decreased marital warmth and supportiveness.

Research outside the United States has confirmed marital satisfaction as a consequence to be taken into account when studying work–family conflict. In a survey of mostly female Singaporean workers, Skilmore Sariati Ahmad (2003) found that work–family conflict serves as a link between work-related stress and marital dissatisfaction. Chiu (1998) also found work–family conflict to negatively affect marital and life satisfaction and job satisfaction. Mauno and Kinnunen (1999) gave a more detailed picture of this relationship in a sample of Finnish dual-earner partners, pointing out that work–family conflict is indirectly associated with marital satisfaction, through the mediation of job exhaustion and psychosomatic health. However, they did not find crossover effects, contrary to their expectations.

Another work-related satisfaction measure is career satisfaction. Results here are controversial. Whereas Peluchette (1993) found that multiple stresses in the work and family domain were associated with more subjective career dissatisfaction, Ayree and Luk (1996a) did not find any significant relationship with career satisfaction in their research on Hong Kong dual-earners. They explained this with the fact that many Chinese dual-earners count on paid domestic workers, thereby insulating especially the women from the stresses of combining work and family roles. The reason may be simply that their measure (adopted from Kopelman, Greenhaus, & Connolly, 1985) only captured work-to-family interference (WFI), whereas the significant impact on career satisfaction is expected to come from the interference of family with work (FWI).

Performance Outcomes

Frone, Yardley, and Markel (1997) showed that WFI is associated with family performance and FWI with job performance, respectively. Ayree (1992) examined the relationship of three types of work–family interference with work quality and found that only job–parent conflict was related with lower work quality, but not job–homemaker and job–spouse conflict.

The influence of work–family conflict on job performance is not so clear cut. Netemeyer et al. (1996) found a negative relationship only between family–work conflict and self-rated performance, whereas Frone, Yardley, and Markel (1997) reported a negative relationship between conflict originating from both domains and a performance measure that corresponds basically to an evaluation of the overall in-role behavior. Allen and her colleagues (2000) reported in their meta-analysis a mean weighted correlation of −0.12 between job performance and work–family conflict.

Career progression typically signals the success and performance levels of employees. Linehan and Walsh (2000) found that work–family conflict prevented many female European international managers from progressing to senior management. Ngo & Lui (1999) confirmed those findings in a sample of 772 managers in Hong Kong. Work–family interference, but not family interference with work, had a significant negative impact on job satisfaction, subjective career achievement, and perceived work pressure. A case study of East Asian Airlines (EAA) conducted by Ng, Fosh, and Naylor (2002) reported a sharp decrease in the number of women, especially women with families, in EAA's higher grades. This finding, coupled with the finding that men with dependent children had relatively greater experience of work–family conflict, suggests that this sharp decrease may be due to women with family responsibilities quitting EAA employment. Alternatively, this decrease may be due to women lowering their career ambitions and not seeking promotion to higher grades in anticipation of intolerable work–family conflict if they ardently pursue an their organizational career.

A range of studies has demonstrated that work has an indirect but clear impact on family performance. Work stressors such as long working hours cause strain in the employee, which can spill over into home life, where it is source of many problems: physical (e.g., fatigue, headache, tension) or mental (e.g., absentmindedness, worries, irritation). Thus, the impact is indirect and goes via the employee, who feels strained and consequently performs less well in a partner or parent role (Atkinson, Liem, & Liem, 1986; Dew, Bromet, & Shulberg, 1987). In Chapter 15, Bowes discusses the impact of work on family from a family research perspective. Here we only briefly highlight some of the consequences not mentioned earlier.

Important are consequences for children's performance in school. Goldberg, Greenberger, and Nagel (1996) studied the influence of the number of working hours and work involvement of the mother on the development and school performance of the child. A higher number of working hours per week was related with weaker teachers' evaluations of school performance, work habits, and performance related personality traits, but better school performance in girls, and weaker school performance, work habits and self-control in boys. A higher work motivation in the mother was associated with more support of the mother for the performance of the child and a stronger motivation in girls. Crouter, Bumpus, Maguire, and McHale (1999) found that the effects of work pressure on adolescent well-being were mediated by parental role overload and parent–adolescent conflict. We found no references in studies outside the United States to the impact of work–family interference on children's well-being. This is clearly an avenue for future research.

Commitment Outcomes

Organizational commitment, and particularly affective commitment, is another attitudinal outcome that has been associated with negative interaction between work and family life. The results are highly comparable to those concerning job satisfaction. Conflict between both domains was found to be negatively associated with organizational commitment by Allen et al. (2000) and Netemayer et al. (1996).

Withdrawal behaviors represent the opposite of commitment to one's work. It has been suggested that WFI and FWI have distinct paths leading to withdrawal behavior, with WFI leading to withdrawal from the family and FWI to withdrawal from work (MacEwen & Barling, 1994). Relationships with work–family conflict were found for both temporary withdrawal behavior, such as lateness and absenteeism (Hammer, Bauer, & Grandey, 2003; MacEwen & Barling, 1994; Goff, Mount, & Jamison, 1990), and permanent withdrawal behavior, such as turnover intentions (Allen et al., 2000; Ayree, 1992; Grandey & Cropanzano, 1999; Netemeyer et al., 1996) and actual turnover (Greenhaus, Collins, Singh, & Parasuraman, 1997). Whereas Thomas and Ganster (1995) did not find a relationship between work–family conflict and absenteeism, Goff et al. (1990) and Hammer et al. (2003) did. The latter authors also found significant crossover effects for both types of work–family conflict on withdrawal behaviors, meaning that conflict in one spouse causes withdrawal behavior in the other spouse. Whereas Ayree (1992) found that two specific types of work–family conflict (job–parent and job–spouse conflict) were related with turnover intentions in Singaporean married women, Shaffer, Harrison, Gilley, and Luk (2001) found that work–family conflict was associated with assignment withdrawal cognitions in expatriates in a diverse set of countries, especially among those with greater affective commitment. In other words, "when an expatriate has devoted a great deal of personal or psychological resources to his or her organization, it exacerbates the risk of WFC leading to plans for premature departure" (p. 112). Gignac, Kelloway, and Gottlieb (1996) found in a Canadian study that FWI was associated with withdrawal from employment (both permanent and temporary).

Other Outcomes

Work–family conflict not only has a negative effect on job and life satisfaction, but also is also related to less emotional and instrumental support from the family. Buelens and Poelmans (1996) found in a sample of Belgian professionals and managers that social support from the spouse is more associated with family satisfaction and support from the supervisor with job satisfaction. This means that the negative impact of work–family conflict is double and self-reinforcing. Not only does it have a direct impact on satisfaction, but also it increases the levels of stress by undermining social support from the family—hence work–family conflict also decreases the most important buffer against stress and social support. We will now explore these buffering or moderating effects more systematically.

MODERATORS OF WORK–FAMILY CONFLICT

Research in the field of work–family conflict has examined moderator effects in two distinct ways. First, some variables (e.g., gender) have been studied as possible moderators of the relationship between work or family demands/pressures and levels of interrole conflict. The moderator effect tested in these studies is that the impact of demands and pressures on work–family conflict variables will vary for different people (e.g., males versus females). The second potential moderation effect is on the relationship between work–family conflict variables (WFI and FWI) and certain "outcomes" (such as psychological strain, and job and family satisfaction), with the prediction being that this relationship will again vary for different people (e.g., males versus females). Diagrammatically, these two possible moderating effects are depicted in Fig. 1.1.

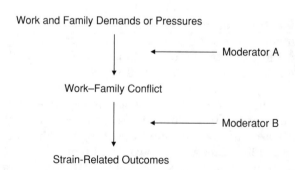

FIG. 1.1. Potential moderator effects relating to work–family conflict.

Compared with research on antecedents and consequences of work–family conflict, the volume of research on moderator effects is relatively small, and research using non-U.S. samples is very sparse indeed. Nevertheless, two potential moderator variables have received some attention: gender and social support. Moderating effects of gender have been the focus of several research projects. The so-called "gender role" hypothesis (Gutek et al., 1991) is that levels of work-to-family interference (WFI) will be greater for men than for women, whereas family-to-work interference (FWI) will be greater among women than men. Furthermore, it is expected that family-related characteristics (such as the number and ages of children) will have more impact on FWI for women than for men, whereas work-related characteristics (e.g., job demands) will impinge more upon men's levels of WFI. These anticipated differences are sometimes explained in terms of asymmetrical boundaries between work and family for men and women (Pleck, 1977), which suggests that family factors will spill over into the job context more for women than for men, whereas the converse will be true for job-related factors.

Recent research in the United States by Grzywacz and Marks (2000) illustrates the logic underlying the proposed moderating effect of gender. Using data from the National Survey of Midlife Development, these authors found that males and females did not differ in their reported levels of work-to-family and family-to-work negative spillover (interference). They then examined the interaction effects of gender, a range of family factors, work characteristics, and individual (demographic) characteristics on work–family conflict. Their findings demonstrated that low levels of social support at work were more strongly related to WFI for women than for men. In contrast, support from the person's partner or spouse was more related to WFI for men than women; among women in their sample, there was no relationship between spouse support and negative spillover from work to family.

These findings illustrate two important issues. First, it is important to consider the direction of interference (WFI versus FWI) when examining possible gender moderation effects. In the Grzywacz and Marks (2000) study, no systematic gender moderation effects were observed for family-to-work interference, which is inconsistent with the traditional gender role hypothesis (predicting that family and work characteristics would be more strongly associated with FWI among women than men), but some moderation effects were found for WFI. Second, the mechanisms underlying work–family conflict may vary among individuals. For example, in their study, social support (from the partner/spouse) appeared to serve different functions for men and women, in terms of its impact on levels of work–family conflict. Further exploration of these differential patterns is clearly warranted.

Grzywacz and Marks (2000), along with other commentators (e.g., Frone, 2003), suggested that research on gender differences in work–family conflict is by no means conclusive. As noted earlier, some studies found gender differences (Duxbury, Higgins, & Lee, 1994), whereas others have not (Eagle, Miles, & Icenogle, 1997). More importantly in the context of possible moderator effects, no consistent picture has emerged from U.S.-based research on how gender moderates either antecedents–conflict or conflict–consequences relationships.

In contrast, studies of the moderating effects of social support have generated substantially more uniform results. Three sources of support have been considered: support from the family (often the partner/spouse), support from work colleagues and supervisors, and overall organizational support. A few examples of international research on moderating effects of these forms of support will be discussed here. In Hong Kong, Aryee, Luk et al. (1999) examined the potential buffering effect of social support from the spouse among a sample of Hong Kong Chinese males and females. As noted earlier in this chapter, these investigators observed that social support was directly associated with reduced work-to-family interference (WFI), but showed no significant relationship with family-to-work interference (FWI). However, they also found that support from the spouse buffered the direct relationship between parental overload and FWI. In other words, when individuals reported greater support from their spouse, the correlation between overload and interference was reduced. This finding is consistent with those obtained in a sample of Japanese female workers by Matsui et al. (1995), who also found that spousal support (in this case, support from their husband) served as a buffer between parental overload and family-to-work interference. Aryee et al. (1999), however, found no moderating effect of spouse support in terms of the relationship between work demands and work–family conflict, and Matsui et al. (1995) did not explore the contribution of work demands to work–family conflict variables.

Whereas Aryee, Luk et al. (1999) focused on the moderating effects of support on the relationship between work–family conflict and "outcomes," which is represented as moderator B in Figure 1.1, in another Hong Kong sample, Fu and Shaffer (2001) examined the role of social support in the relationship between domain-specific demands and interrole conflict. In addition to measuring spouse/partner support, these investigators asked respondents the extent to which they received support from their supervisor and coworkers. However, in contrast to the findings reported by Aryee, Luk et al. (1999), Fu and

Shaffer (2001) found no significant moderating effect of spouse support on FIW, nor was colleague support a buffer of relationships between work role stressors and WFI. Supervisor support, on the other hand, did alleviate the negative effects of conflict within the work role on work-to-family interference.

A study in the Netherlands by Jansen et al. (2003) also identified social support as a significant moderator of the relationship between demands and work–family conflict. Although their study did not distinguish between the two directions of interference, they observed that support from both coworkers and supervisors buffered the impact of high work demands on non-directional work–family conflict, especially for men. In addition, decision latitude in relation to job task completion was another moderator variable for men, but not for women.

Noor's (2002a) study of Malaysian female employees found that support from the partner or spouse can moderate some relationships but not others. For instance, in this study, spouse support moderated the impact of longer work hours on work–family conflict, but not the effects of other work stressors, such as work overload and lack of autonomy. Noor (2002a) suggested that these work-related stressors may fall outside of the spouse's ability to help. An implication of this finding is that to obtain a substantial moderator (buffering) effect for social support, there needs to be a match between the stressor and the source of support (Fenlason & Beehr, 1994).

The literature on work–family balance suggests that, in addition to support from specific individuals (such as partner/spouse or supervisors), more general support from the organization may also be an important contributor to employee well-being. To date, however, although there has been international research on the direct relationship between this kind of support and employee outcomes (see, for example, Richardsen et al., 1999 study of Norwegian professional and managerial women), there have been relatively few empirical investigations of the moderating effects of organizational support. Following the work of Allen (2001), who developed and validated a measure of perceived organizational family-supportiveness, a recent study in New Zealand (O'Driscoll et al., 2003) found that a key variable in the process is the individual's perception of the organization as being supportive of work–family balance, and that organizational policies and practices per se bore little relationship to levels of work–family conflict or well-being. This perception would appear to be enhanced when the individual has supportive supervisors and managers.

Some international studies have examined other possible moderators of either antecedent–conflict or conflict–outcomes relationships.

For example, Aryee, Luk and their colleagues (1999) assessed whether use of various coping strategies to ameliorate the effects of work–family conflict on well-being. Specifically, they explored whether problem-focused coping and emotion-focused coping would function as buffering variables in this relationship. Their findings indicated, however, that problem-focused coping was ineffective in reducing the impact of either WFI or FWI on job satisfaction, family satisfaction, and overall life satisfaction. They suggested that this lack of buffering may be due to individuals feeling they had little control over the stressors that created work–family conflict, and that this feeling of low control might induce a sense of helplessness that cannot be alleviated by direct action. On the other hand, emotion-focused coping did display one significant moderating effect, on the negative relationship between FWI and job satisfaction. Aryee, Luk et al. (1999) suggested that FWI may negatively influence job performance and consequently the receipt of rewards associated with job performance. If so, then emotion-focused coping "may help to reduce one's expectations regarding the receipt of job rewards, which minimizes the extent of job dissatisfaction" (p. 274).

A dispositional variable that has emerged in U.S. research as a potential moderator of stressor–strain relationships is negative affectivity. It was suggested (Moyle, 1995; Jex & Spector, 1996) that negative affectivity (NA) moderates these relationships because individuals who score highly on NA are more vulnerable and less resilient to environmental stressors and may not utilize effective strategies for dealing with them. As mentioned earlier in this chapter, Stoeva, Chiu, & Greenhaus (2002) investigated the effects of negative affectivity among Hong Kong senior civil servants. Their study demonstrated not only direct associations between NA and job/family stressors, but also a moderating effect of negative affectivity on the relationship between family stressors and family-to-work interference (FWI). However, there was no significant moderating effect of NA on the parallel relationship between work stressors and work-to-family interference (WFI). Stoeva and colleagues (2002) suggested that this differential moderation may be due to job stressors being more difficult than family stressors for individuals to contend with and that people may receive less support from the work domain.

Finally, Matsui et al. (1995) found that role definition can serve an important moderating function in respect to work–family conflict. Specifically, they found that Japanese women who were able to redefine their family role, for example, by changing their own and others' expectations and delegating domestic chores were less likely to experience psychological strain as a result of interference between their family and work roles (FWI). Work-role redefinition, however, did not serve a parallel moderating function in terms of mitigating the impact of work-to-family interference (WFI). Given that the overwhelming majority of their sample were clerical workers, it is possible that redefining work roles was not available to them as a mechanism for reducing the effects of work–family conflict, whereas redefinition of family roles may have been more readily accomplished.

RECOMMENDATIONS FOR FUTURE RESEARCH

Although the studies mentioned above certainly have contributed to a more scientifically-based understanding of the antecedents and consequences of work–family conflict and family-supportive policies, we still have a long road to travel to develop a comprehensive map of the processes underlying work–family conflict and its linkages with other variables. A striking characteristic of this field of research is a lack of direct empirical testing or comparison of different theories. Often work–family researchers have not based their predictions on strong conceptual frameworks (Hobfoll, 1989). The field has been dominated by role theory (Kahn et al., 1964), which is undoubtedly the most cited theory by work–family researchers, together with spillover and segmentation theory (Piotrkowski, 1979; Zedeck & Mosier, 1990). Although these theories offer a rationale for the consequences of work–family conflict, they are limited in explaining actual behavior, interaction between actors, or decision making or prioritizing in case of work–family conflict (Poelmans, 2004). As mentioned, more recently a whole range of alternative theories have been suggested, but they remain untested.

From a methodological perspective, one salient criticism of extant research is the almost total reliance on quantitative, cross-sectional research designs, although work–family conflict is a dynamic, complex phenomenon, evolving over time and involving interactions among various actors. Few empirical studies, however, have closely examined the process by which work–family conflict develops and *how* it impacts other variables (for some exceptions, see Frone, Russell, & Cooper, 1997; Jones & Fletcher, 1996; Repetti, 1989; Williams & Alliger, 1994). There is clearly a need for more longitudinal research and studies that explore work–family conflict processes and outcomes. Additional qualitative research examining people's understanding and conceptualization of work–family relations and the impact of conflict between these two domains would also be valuable.

A further limitation of empirical research in this field is that few studies have focused on couples' joint experiences. In the context of a relationship between two people, work–family conflict is a dynamic process between two individuals who are mutually interdependent. To illustrate this, Hammer, Allen, and Grigsby (1997) found important crossover effects of work–family conflict among couples and concluded that future research on work–family conflict should focus on the couple as the unit of analysis. Other researchers have also echoed this call for more couple-oriented research on crossover effects (e.g., Greenhaus et al., 1989; Gupta & Jenkins, 1985; Jones & Fletcher, 1993; Parasuraman et al., 1992; Westman & Etzion, 1995). In addition, researchers need to take into account other variables that can moderate or reinforce work–family conflicts, such as mutual understanding, intellectual and professional equivalence, mutual support, emotional dependence of one partner, or rivalry. Interesting in this regard are the studies of Buunk & Peeters (1994) and Repetti (1989). Buunk & Peeters (1994) looked at the interplay between stress at work and social support, using an event-contingent recording approach. Repetti (1989) used surveys on three consecutive days to study the dynamic interaction among work demands, social withdrawal, and expression of anger of one spouse in function of social support of the other spouse.

A specific group that warrants specific attention are managers and managerial couples, because we can expect that the work–family nexus may be more acute in families in which one or both members have managerial responsibilities. Female managers in particular may be expected to experience high levels of stress and work–family conflict (Beatty, 1996). Still, studies of work–family conflict in this specific group are scarce (Judge et al., 1994; Lyness & Thompson, 1997; Spector et al., 2004; Spector et al., this volume, chapter 3). The same applies to entrepreneurs (Parasuraman, Purohit, & Godschalk, 1996), couples that are simultaneously business and marriage partners (Foley & Powell, 1997), and independent professionals such as doctors (Swanson, Power, & Simpson, 1998). One final group that can be expected to experience elevated levels of work–family conflict are single mothers or fathers with children, who are an increasingly important group in the population. Also, more studies are needed of specific professional groups that because of irregular or demanding work schedules (such as night shifts) can be expected to experience high levels of work–family conflict, for example, nurses (Bacharach, Bamberger, & Conley, 1991) and air-traffic controllers (Repetti, 1989).

Only a few researchers have made an effort to test models and relationships at a cross-cultural level (Poelmans, 2003). Most studies we found were developed in Anglo-Saxon countries (especially the United States, the United Kingdom, and Canada), which have relatively comparable populations. Attempts to test models of work–family conflict *across* cultures are only starting to emerge (e.g., Ayree, Fields, & Luk, 1999; Yang et al., 2000). The studies reported in the special issue of the *International Journal of Cross Cultural Management* (Poelmans, 2003) are a first step in that direction. An important suggestion for future research is the development of a two-directional culturally sensitive measure of work–family interference. Moreover, data are missing from countries where work–family conflict is especially relevant because of some culture-specific aspect. For instance, we would expect to find this in cultures where the family as an institution is very strong (such as Eastern and Latin countries) or cultures where female labor participation is on the rise and where we can expect high levels of conflict resulting from the transition from traditional to dual-earner families.

An important factor is the impact of the job content and presence of job stressors on work–family conflict. At the same time, it is clear that the family as a system and stressors in the family may have a very different impact on a person. Contrary to many models of work–family conflict that model the antecedents, processes, and consequences of work–family conflict and family–work conflict in a symmetrical way, real cases show that the permeability (in terms of receptivity or resistance) and internal logic of work and family can be substantially different for the two directions of interference. This calls for a very different treatment of work-to-family interference and family-to-work interference. While studying cross-cultural differences in the experience of work–family interference, researchers are recommended to analyze in detail the different antecedents and consequences of the two directions of conflict (WFI and FWI) in different cultures.

Something that particularly struck us is the distinction that some authors make between work and family stress. One could argue that people act according to stereotypes associated with roles and expectations (cf. role theory), and that the sources of stress can be situated at work (work stressors) and in the family (family stressors). However, we invite scholars to be cautious in believing that a respondent can distinguish between the resultant work and family strain. A person accumulates strain from sources at work, in the family, and in other domains, which combine to produce a general level of strain. When the individual is asked to explain the general experience of strain in terms of work and family, we depend on the individual's interpretation (appraisal/attribution) of his or her strain. As we know from cognitive theories, such as attribution theory, that these appraisals are subject to biases and can be misleading. Because most studies rely on self-report measures, we should be cautious with making these distinctions or forcing a respondent to make these distinctions. A more realistic approach is probably to recognize that several sources of stress and support interact and counteract to result in an overall level of strain.

An antecedent that has been associated with work–family conflict is involvement, more specifically, daily involvement in family roles (Williams & Alliger, 1994) and job involvement (Adams et al., 1996; Frone, Russell, & Cooper, 1992a; Greenhaus & Beutell, 1985; Higgins, Duxbury, & Irving, 1992). This points to the importance of considering interindividual differences while evaluating the development of work–family conflict and consequently the differential impact of work–family policies. Future studies should take into account not only the more obvious sociodemographic differences among individuals (e.g., gender, number and age of children), but also the interindividual differences in personality, values, motivations, and involvement. Most WFC measures do not go beyond a superficial measure of work pressure, family pressure, and the resulting work–family conflict. Underlying motivations, values, or choices are generally ignored. However, work–family conflicts will undoubtedly have different consequences for the satisfaction or health of the person if the person consciously chooses to *allow* spillover because she or he clearly gives priority to her/his work or family. In other words, an appreciation of the effects of work and family pressures depends on the underlying motivational structure of the person and his/her needs and priorities. Work–family conflict may be basically an intermotivational conflict or an ethical conflict. For instance, Lobel (1992) suggested that work–family conflicts stem from conflicting values of work and family roles. She suggested that work and family should integrate instrumental and affective values. There have been calls for greater consideration of underlying motivations, values, or choices while studying the relationship between work–family conflict and possible consequences (Edwards & Rothbard, 2000). Given that values differ significantly across cultures, once again we need to call for more cross-cultural studies looking at the moderating effects of culture-specific values.

Another variable that seems to be missing in most studies on work–family conflict is control or decision latitude. In terms of the demand-control-support theory (Karasek & Theorell, 1990), the fact of combining a family and a career may be a deliberate choice. Second, these conflicts may be well within control of the person, as he or she has the opportunity to work less or leave earlier from work. As a consequence, work–family conflicts are within the decision latitude of the person and may as such have fewer consequences in terms of stress or health. A very different case is a person who is forced to work in an unfavorable job, experiences high pressure to work extra hours, and is afraid to leave his or her job, because of financial demands or because of family responsibilities. Here, work–family conflicts are not within the control of the person. Surprisingly, this variable is rarely taken into account when measuring work–family conflict.

A variable that has been generally addressed is social support. Here we want to signal that one should define social support very broadly. In countries characterized by collectivistic values, one should take into account grandparents and other family members, neighbors, and members of the extended family, who in some cases take on major part of domestic tasks and the care and education of the children. By limiting social support to obvious sources such as spouse and supervisor, one could miss out an important group that make a difference between a conflict-free or conflicting work–family interface, especially in an international context.

As noted earlier in this chapter, another striking limitation of the accumulated research findings is that they are generally limited to Anglo-Saxon (mostly North American) contexts. Taking into account the heterogeneity of legislative contexts in countries outside Canada and the United States, and the argument that institutional pressures play an important role in the adoption of work–family policies (Goodstein, 1994; Ingram & Simons, 1995), it is critical to consider the generalizability of North American findings to other sociocultural contexts. Different cultures are characterized by different work and family values, practices and habits, which highlight the need for more cross-cultural studies of work–family policies and programs.

To conclude, although there has been considerable investigation of the antecedents and consequences of work–family conflict, more systematic cross-cultural research is required to determine the generalizability of theoretical models and frameworks and the relevance of various family-supportive policies and practices that organizations might implement. In addition, rather than focusing solely on the individual as the unit of analysis, more research on the experiences of couples would contribute to our understanding of the process by which work–family conflict is developed and is managed in the context of a relationship. Finally, we recommend that research designs be extended to incorporate longitudinal designs and the collection of qualitative data that might enhance our understanding of the meaning and process underlying the work–family nexus.

ACKNOWLEDGMENTS

We thank the Faculty of Arts and Social Sciences of The University of Waikato, New Zealand for the academic research visitor grant that allowed the authors to collaborate on this manuscript in the summer of 2003.

REFERENCES

Adams, G. A., King, L. A., & King, D. W. (1996). Relationships between job and family involvement, family social support, and work–family conflict with job and life satisfaction. *Journal of Applied Psychology, 81*, 411–420.

Ahmad, A. (1996). Work–family conflict among married professional women in Malaysia. *Journal of Social Psychology, 136*, 663–665.

Allen, T. (2001). Family-supportive work environments: The role of organizational perceptions. *Journal of Vocational Behavior, 58*, 414–435.

Allen, T. D., Herst, D. E. L., Bruck, C. S., & Sutton, M. (2000). Consequences associated with work-to-family conflict: A review and agenda for future research. *Journal of Occupational Health Psychology, 5*, 278–308.

Aryee, S. (1992). Antecedents and outcomes of work–family conflict among married professional women: Evidence from Singapore. *Human Relations, 45*, 813–837.

Aryee, S. (1993). Dual-earner couples in Singapore: An examination of work and nonwork sources of their experienced burnout. *Human Relations, 43*, 1441–1468.

Aryee, S., & Luk, V. (1996a). Work and nonwork influences on the career satisfaction of dual earner couples. *Journal of Vocational Behavior, 49*, 38–52.

Aryee, S., & Luk, V. (1996b). Balancing two major parts of adult life experience: Work and family identity among dual-earner couples. *Human Relations, 49*, 465–487.

Aryee, S., Fields, D., & Luk, V. (1999). A cross-cultural test of a model of the work–family interface. *Journal of Management, 25*, 491–511.

Aryee, S., Luk, V., Leung, A., & Lo, S. (1999). Role stressors, interrole conflict, and well-being: The moderating effect of spousal support and coping behaviors among employed parents in Hong Kong. *Journal of Vocational Behavior, 54*, 259–278.

Ayree, S., Luk, V., & Stone, R. (1998). Family-responsive variables and retention-relevant outcomes among employed parents. *Human Relations, 51*, 73–87.

Atkinson, T., Liem, R., & Liem, J. (1986). The social costs of unemployment: implications for social support. *Journal of Health and Social Behavior, 27*, 317–331.

Bacharach, S. B., Bamberger, P., & Conley, S. (1991). Work-home conflict among nurses and engineers: Mediating the impact of role stress on burnout and satisfaction at work. *Journal of Organizational Behavior,* *12,* 39–53.

Barling, J. (1990). *Employment, stress and family functioning.* Chichester, England: Wiley.

Barnett, R. C., & Hyde, J. S. (2001). Women, men, work, and family. An expansionist theory. *American Psychologist, 56,* 781–796.

Beatty, C. A. (1996). The stress of managerial and professional women: Is the Price Too High? *Journal of Organizational Behavior, 17,* 233–251.

Beena, C., & Poduval, P. R. (1992). Gender differences in work stress of executives. *Psychological Studies, 37,* 109–113.

Bedeian, A. G., Burke, B. G., & Moffett, R. G. (1988). Outcomes of work–family conflict among married male and female professionals. *Journal of Management, 14,* 475–491.

Bernas, K. H., & Major, D. A. (2000). Contributors to stress resistance: Testing a model of women's work–family conflict. *Psychology of Women Quarterly, 24,* 170–178.

Blau, P. (1964). *Exchange and power in social life.* New York: Wiley.

Boles, J. S., Johnston, M. W., & Hair, J. F., Jr. (1997). Role stress, work–family conflict and emotional exhaustion: Interrelationships and effects on some work-related consequences. *Journal of Personnel Selling & Sales Management, 17,* 17–28.

Bond, M. H., & Smith, P. B. (1996). Cross-cultural social and organizational psychology. *Annual Review of Psychology, 47,* 205–235.

Bruck, C. S., Allen, T. D., & Spector, P. E. (2002). The relation between work–family conflict and job satisfaction: A finer-grained analysis. *Journal of Vocational Behavior, 60,* 336–353.

Bruck, C. S., & Allen, T. D. (2003). The relationship between big five personality traits, negative affectivity, type A behavior, and work–family conflict. *Journal of Vocational Behavior, 63,* 457–472.

Bruck, C. S., & Allen, T. D. (2003). The relationship between big five personality traits, negative affectivity, type A behavior, and work–family conflict. *Journal of Vocational Behavior, 63*(3), 457–472.

Buelens, M., & Poelmans, S. (1996). The work–family interface. Typology based on physical and mental spill-over of stress. Paper presented at the Conference of the International Stress Management Association, Sydney, Australia.

Bures, A. L., Henderson, D., Mayfield, J., Mayfield, M., & Worley, J. (1995–1996). The effects of spousal support and gender on worker's stress and job satisfaction: A cross national investigation of dual career couples. *Journal of Applied Business Research, 12,* 52–58.

Burke, R. J. (1988). Some antecedents and consequences of work–family conflict. *Journal of Social Behavior and Personality, 3,* 287–302.

Burke, R. J., & Greenglass, E. R. (1999). Work–family conflict, spouse support and nursing staff well-being during organizational restructuring. *Journal of Occupational Health Psychology, 4,* 327–336.

Burley, K. A. (1995). Family variables as mediators of the relationship between work–family conflict and marital adjustment among dual career men and women. *The Journal of Social Psychology, 135,* 483–497.

Buunk, B. P., & Peeters, M. C. W. (1994). Stress at work, social support and companionship: Towards an event-contingent recording approach. *Work & Stress, 8*, 177–190.

Caligiuri, P. M., Hyland, M. M., Joshi, A., & Bross, A. (1998). Testing a theoretical model for examining the relationship between family adjustment and expatriates's work adjustment. *Journal of Applied Psychology, 83*, 598–614.

Campbell, J. L., & Snow, B. M. (1992). Gender role conflict and family environment as predictors of men's marital satisfaction. *Journal of Family Psychology, 6*, 84–87.

Campbell Clark, S. (2000). Work/family border theory: A new theory of work/family balance. *Human Relations, 53*, 747–770.

Carlson, D. S., Kacmar, K. M., & Williams, L. J. (1998). The development and validation of a multidimensional measure of work–family conflict. *Academy of Management Proceedings, 1998*, San Diego.

Carlson, D. (1999). Personality and role variables as predictors of three forms of work/family conflict. *Journal of Vocational Behavior, 55*, 236–253.

Carlson, D. S., & Frone, M. R. (2003). Relation of behavioral and psychological involvement to a new four-factor conceptualization of work–family interference. *Journal of Business and Psychology, 17*, 515–535.

Champoux, J. E. (1978). Perceptions of work and nonwork: A re-examination of the compensatory and spillover models. *Sociology of Work and Occupations, 5*, 402–422.

Chiu, R. K. (1998). Relationships among role conflicts, role satisfaction, and life satisfaction: Evidence from Hong Kong. *Social Behavior and Personality, 26*, 409–414.

Clark, C. S. (2002). Employees' sense of community, sense of control, and work–family conflict in native American organizations. *Journal of Vocational Behavior, 61*, 92–108.

Cohen, S., & Wills, T. A. (1985). Stress, social support, and the buffering hypothesis. *Psychological Bulletin, 98*, 310–357.

Cooke, R. A., & Rousseau, D. M. (1984). Stress and strain from family roles and work-role expectations. *Journal of Applied Psychology, 69*, 252–260.

Coverman, S. (1989). Role overload, role conflict and stress: Addressing consequences of multiple role demands. *Social Forces, 67*, 965–982.

Crouter, A. C., Bumpus, M. F., Maguire, M. C., & McHale, S. M. (1999). Linking parents' work pressure and adolescents' well-being. Insights into dynamics in dual-earner families. *Development Psychology, 35*, 1453–1461.

Dew, M., Bromet, E., & Shulberg, H. (1987). A comparative analysis of two community stressor's long term mental health effects. *American Journal of Community Psychology, 15*, 167–184.

Duxbury, L. E., & Higgins, C. A. (1991). Gender differences in work–family conflict. *Journal of Applied Psychology, 76*, 60–74.

Duxbury, L. E., Higgins, C. A., & Lee, C. (1994). Work–family conflict: A comparison of gender, family type and perceived control. *Journal of Family Issues, 15*, 449–466.

Eagle, B. W., Miles, E. W., & Icenogle, M. L. (1997). Interrole conflicts and the permeability of the work and family domains: Are there gender differences? *Journal of Vocational Behaviour, 50,* 168–184.

Earley, P. C., & Erez, M. (Eds.) (1997). *New perspectives on international industrial/organizational psychology.* San Francisco: The New Lexington Press.

Edwards, J. R., & Rothbard, N. P. (2000). Mechanisms linking work and family: Clarifying the relationship between work and family constructs. *Academy of Management Review, 25,* 178–199.

Elloy, D. F., & Smith, C. R. (2003). Patterns of stress, work–family conflict, role conflict, role ambiguity and overload among dual-career and single-career couples: An Australian study. *Cross-Cultural Management, 10,* 55–66.

Elloy, D. F., & Mackie, B. (2002). Overload and work–family conflict among Australian dual-earner families: Moderating effects of support. *Psychological Reports, 91,* 907–913.

Escobedo, A. (1999). Doing cross-national work on parental leave. In P. Moss & F. Deven (Eds.), *Parental leave: Progress or pitfall?* Vol. 35, pp. 173–192. The Hague/Brussels: NIDI/CBGS Publications.

Evans, P., & Bartolomé, F. (1981). *Must success cost so much? Avoiding the human toll of corporate life.* New York: Basic Books.

Evans, P., & Bartolomé, F. (1986). The dynamics of work–family relationships in managerial lives. *International Review of Applied Psychology, 35 (Special Issue),* 371–395.

Fallon, B. J. (1997). The balance between paid work and home responsibilities: Personal problem or corporate concern? *Australian Psychologist, 32,* 1–9.

Fenlason, K., & Beehr, T. (1994). Social support and occupational stress: Effects of talking to others. *Journal of Organizational Behavior, 15,* 157–175.

Foley, S., & Powell, G. N. (1997). Reconceptualizing work–family conflict for business/marriage partners: A theoretical model. *Journal of Small Business Management, October,* 36–47.

Frone, M. R., Russell, M., & Cooper, M. L. (1991). Relationship of work and family stressors to psychological distress: The independent moderating influence of social support, mastery, active coping, and self-focused attention. *Journal of Social Behavior and Personality, 6,* 227–250.

Frone, M. R., Russell, M., & Cooper, M. L. (1992a). Antecedents and outcomes of work–family conflict: Testing a model of work–family interface. *Journal of Applied Psychology, 1,* 65–78.

Frone, M. R., Russell, M., & Cooper, M. (1992b). Prevalence of work–family conflict: Are work and family boundaries asymmetrically permeable? *Journal of Organizational Behavior, 13,* 723–729.

Frone, M. R., Russell, M., & Cooper, M. (1993). Relationship of work–family conflict, gender, and alcohol expectancies to alcohol use/abuse. *Journal of Organizational Behavior, 14,* 545–558.

Frone, M. R., Russell, M., & Cooper, M. L. (1997). Relation of work–family conflict to health outcomes: A four year longitudinal study of employed parents. *Journal of Occupational and Organizational Psychology, 70,* 325–335.

Frone, M. R., Yardley, J. K., & Markel, K. S. (1997). Developing and testing an integrative model of the work–family interface. *Journal of Vocational Behavior, 50,* 145–167.

Frone, M. R. (2000). Work–family conflict and employee psychiatric disorders: The National Comorbidity Survey. *Journal of Applied Psychology, 85,* 888–895.

Frone, M. R. (2003). Work–family balance. In J. C. Quick & L. E. Tetrick (Eds.), *Handbook of occupational health psychology* (pp. 143–162). Washington, DC: American Psychological Association.

Fu, C. K., & Shaffer, M. A. (2001). The tug of work and family: Direct and indirect domain-specific determinants of work–family conflict. *Personnel Review, 30,* 502–522.

Gignac, A. M., Kelloway, E. K., & Gottlieb, B. H. (1996). The impact of caregiving on employment: A mediational model of work–family conflict. *Canadian Journal on Aging, 15,* 525–542.

Goff, S. J., Mount, M. K., & Jamison, R. L. (1990). Employer supported child care, work–family conflict and absenteeism: a field study. *Personnel Psychology, 43,* 793–809.

Goldberg, W. A., Greenberger, E., & Nagel, S. K. (1996). Employment and achievement: Mother's work involvement in relation to children's achievement behaviors and mother's parenting behaviors. *Child Development, 67,* 1512–1527.

Goodstein, J. D. (1994). Institutional pressures and strategic responsiveness: employer involvement in work–family issues. *Academy of Management Journal, 37,* 350–382.

Grandey, A. A., & Cropanzano, R. (1999). The conservation of resources model applied to work–family conflict and strain. *Journal of Vocational Behavior, 54,* 350–370.

Grant-Vallone, E. J., & Ensher, E. A. (1998). *The effect of work and personal life conflict and organizational support.* Paper presented at the Academy of Management Conference, San Diego, CA.

Greenglass, E. R. (1985). Psychological implications of sex bias in the workplace. *Academic Psychology Bulletin, 7,* 227–240.

Greenglass, E. R., Pantony, K. L., & Burke, R. J. (1988). A gender-role perspective on role-conflict, work stress and social support. *Journal of Social Behavior and Personality, 3,* 317–328.

Greenhaus, J. H. (1988). The intersection of work and family roles: Individual, interpersonal, and organizational issues. *Journal of Social Behavior and Personality, 3,* 23–44.

Greenhaus, J., & Beutell, N. (1985). Sources of conflict between work and family roles. *Academy of Management Review, 10,* 76–88.

Greenhaus, J. H., Collins, K. M., Singh, R., & Parasuraman, S. (1997). Work and family influences on departure from public accounting. *Journal of Vocational Behavior, 50,* 249–270.

Greenhaus, J. H., Parasuraman, S., Granrose, C. S., Rabinowitz, S., & Beutell, N. J. (1989). Sources of work–family conflict among two-career couples. *Journal of Vocational Behavior, 34,* 133–153.

Grzywacz, J. G., & Marks, N. F. (2000). Reconceptualizing the work–family interface: An ecological perspective on the correlates of positive and negative spillover between work and family. *Journal of Occupational Health Psychology, 5,* 111–126.

Grzywacz, J. G., & Bass, B. L. (2003). Work, family and mental health: Testing different models of work–family fit. *Journal of Marriage and Family, 65,* 248–262.

Geurts, S., Rutte, C., & Peeters, M. (1999). Antecedents and consequences of work–home interference among medical residents. *Social Science & Medicine, 48,* 1135–1148.

Gupta, N., & Jenkins, G. D. (1985). Dual-career couples: Stress, stressors, strain, and strategies. In T. A. Beehr & R. S. Bhagat (Eds.), *Human stress and cognition in organizations: An integrated perspective* (pp. 141–175). New York: Wiley-Interscience.

Gutek, B., Searle, S., & Klepa, L. (1991). Rational versus gender role explanations for work–family conflict. *Journal of Applied Psychology, 76,* 560–568.

Hall, D. T., & Richter, J. (1988). Balancing work life and family life: What can organizations do to help? *Academy of Management Executive, 2,* 213–223.

Hammer, L. B., Allen, E., & Grigsby, T. D. (1997). Work–family conflict in dual-earner couples: Within-individual and crossover effects of work and family. *Journal of Vocational Behavior, 50,* 185–203.

Hammer, L. B., Bauer, T. N., & Grandey, A. A. (2003). Work–family conflict and work-related withdrawal behaviors. *Journal of Business and Psychology, 17,* 419–437.

Handy, C. (1978). The family: Help or hindrance? In Cooper, C. L. & Payne, R. *Stress at work* (pp. 107–123). Chichester: John Wiley and Sons.

Heiligers, P. J. M., & Hingstman, L. (2000). Career preferences and the work–family balance in medicine: Gender differences among medical specialists. *Social Science and Medicine, 50,* 1235–1246.

Higgins, E. T., Bond, R. N., Klein, R., & Strauman, T. (1986). Self-discrepancies and emotional vulnerability: How magnitude, accessibility, and type of discrepancy influence affect. *Journal of Personality and Social Psychology, 51,* 5–15.

Higgins, C. A., Duxbury, L. E., & Irving, R. H. (1992). Work–family conflict in the dual-career family. *Organizational Behavior and Human Decision Processes, 51,* 51–75.

Hill, E. J. (2000). *A global perspective on work/life issues: Work/life surveys in Europe and Latin America.* Paper presented at the 15th Annual conference of the Society for Industrial and Organizational Psychology, New Orleans, LA.

Hobfoll, S. E. (1989). Conservation of resources: A new attempt at conceptualizing stress. *American Psychologist, 44,* 513–524.

Homans, G. C. (1958). Social behaviour and exchange. *American Journal of Sociology, 63,* 597–606.

Homans, G. C. (1974). *Social behaviour: Its elementary forms* (Rev. ed.). New York: Harcourt Brace Jovanovich.

Honda-Howard, M., & Homma, M. (2001). Job satisfaction of Japanese career women and its influence on turnover. *Asian Journal of Social Psychology, 4,* 23–38.

Ingram, P., & Simons, T. (1995). Institutional and resource dependence determinants of responsiveness to work–family issues. *Academy of Management Journal, 38,* 1466–1482.

Jacobs, J. A., & Gornick, J. C. (2002). Hours of paid work in dual-earner couples: The United States in cross-national perspective. *Sociological Focus, 35,* 169–187.

Jansen, N. W. H., Kant, I., Kristensen, T. S., & Nijhuis, F. J. N. (2003). Antecedents and consequences of work–family conflict: A prospective cohort study. *Journal of Occupational and Environmental Medicine, 45,* 479–491.

Jex, S., & Spector, P. (1996). The impact of negative affectivity on stressor-strain relations: A replication and extension. *Work & Stress, 10,* 36–45.

Jones, F., & Fletcher, B. (1993). An empirical study of occupational stress transmission in working couples. *Human Relations, 46,* 881–901.

Jones, F., & Fletcher, B. C. (1996). Taking work home: A study of daily fluctuations in work stressors, effects on moods and impacts on marital partners. *Journal of Occupational and Organisational Psychology, 69,* 89–106.

Joplin, J. R. W., Shaffer, M. A., Francesco, A. M., & Lau, T. (2003). The macro environment and work–family conflict: Development of a cross-cultural comparative framework. *International Journal of Cross-Cultural Management, 3,* 305–328.

Judge, T. A., Boudreau, J. W., & Bretz, R. D., Jr. (1994). Job and life attitudes of male executives. *Journal of Applied Psychology, 79,* 767–782.

Kahn, R. L., Wolfe, D. M., Quinn, R. P., Snoek, J. D., & Rosenthal, R. A. (1964). *Organizational stress: Studies in role conflict and ambiguity.* New York: Wiley.

Kanter, R. (1977). *Work and family in the United States: A critical review and agenda for research and policy.* New York: Sage.

Karasek, R. A., & Theorell, T. (1990). *Healthy work. Stress, productivity, and the reconstruction of working life.* Basic Books: New York.

Kelly, R., & Voydanoff, P. (1985). Work–family role strain among employed parents. *Family Relations, 34,* 367–374.

Kim, J. L. S., & Ling, C. S. (2001). Work–family conflict of women entrepreneurs in Singapore. *Women in Management Review, 15,* 2001.

Kingston, P. W., & Nock, S. L. (1987). Time together among dual-earner couples. *American Sociology Review, 52,* 391–400.

Kinnunen, U., Koivunen, T., & Mauno, S. (1995). Work–family interface among dual-earner couples. *Psykologia, 32*(2), 105–115.

Kinnunen, U., Loikkanen, E., & Mauno, S. (1995). Interaction between work and family in women's and men's lives. *Psykologia, 30*(5), 381–389.

Kinnunen, U., & Mauno, S. (1998). Antecedents and outcomes of work–family conflict among employed women and men in Finland. *Human Relations, 51*, 157–177.

Kinnunen, U., & Mauno, S. (2001). Dual-earner families in Finland: Differences between and within families in relations to work and family experiences. *Community, Work & Family, 4*, 87–107.

Kopelman, R., Greenhaus, J., & Connolly, T. (1985). A model of work, family and interrole conflict: A construct validation study. *Organizational Behavior and Human Performance, 32*, 198–215.

Korabik, K., Lero, D. S., & Ayman, R. (2003). A multi-level approach to cross cultural work–family research. *International Journal of Cross Cultural Management, 3*, 289–303.

Kossek, E. E., & Ozeki, C. (1998). Work–family conflict, policies, and the job–life satisfaction relationship: A review and directions for organizational behavior—Human resources research. *Journal of Applied Psychology, 83*, 139–149.

Kossek, E. E., & Ozeki, C. (1999). Bridging the work–family policy and productivity gap: A literature review. *Community Work and Family, 2*(1), 7–32.

Lambert, S. J. (1990). Processes linking work and family: A critical review and research agenda. *Human Relations, 43*, 239–257.

Lambert, S. J. (2000). Added benefits: The link between work–life benefits and organizational citizenship behaviour. *The Academy of Management Journal, 43*, 801–815.

Lewis, S., & Cooper, C. L. (1987). Stress in dual-earner couples and stage in the life cycle. *Journal of Occupational Psychology, 60*, 289–303.

Lewis, S., & Cooper, C. L. (1999). Balancing the work/home interface: A European perspective. *Human Resource Management Review, 5*, 289–305.

Lewis, S., & Cooper, C. L. (1999). The work–family research agenda in changing contexts. *Journal of Occupational Health Psychology, 4*, 382–393.

Lewis, S., & Lewis, J. (Eds.) (1996). *The work–family challenge. Rethinking employment.* London: Sage.

Linehan, M., & Walsh, J. S. (2000). Work–family conflict and the senior female international manager. *British Journal of Management, 11*, S49–S58.

Ling, Y., & Powell, G. N. (2001). Work–family conflict in contemporary China. *International Journal of Cross-Cultural Management, 1*, 357–373.

Lo, S. (2003). Perceptions of work–family conflict among married female professionals in Hong Kong. *Personnel Review, 32*, 376–390.

Lobel, S. A. (1991a). Allocation of investment in work and family roles: Alternative theories and implications for research. *Academy of Management Review, 16*, 507–521.

Lobel, S. A. (1992). A value-laden approach to integrating work and family life. *Human Resource Management (Special Issue on Work and Family), 31*, 249–266.

Luk, M. D. (2002). An investigation of work–family conflict: A cross-cultural comparison. *Dissertation Abstracts International, 62*, 10-A, 3470.

Lyness, K. S., & Thompson, D. E. (1997). Above the glass ceiling? A comparison of matched samples of female and male executives. *Journal of Applied Psychology, 82*, 359–375.

MacEwen, K. E., & Barling, J. (1994). Daily consequences of work interferences with family and family interference with work. *Work & Stress, 8*, 244–254.

Mari, M., Infante, E., & Rivero, M. (2002). Internal pressure from work and/or family sphere as antecedents of work–family conflict. *Revista de Psicologia Social, 17*, 103–112.

Marshall, C. M. (1992a). The influence of employment on family interaction, well-being, and happiness. In S. J. Bahr (Ed.), *Family research: A sixty-year review, 1930–1990*. New York: Lexington.

Marshall, C. M. (1992b). Family influences on work. In S. J. Bahr (Ed.), *Family research: A sixty-year review, 1930–1990*. New York: Lexington.

Martinez-Perez, M. D., & Segovia, A. O. (2002). Psychometrical analysis of the Spanish version of the Inventory of Family Support for Workers. *Psicothema, 14*, 310–316.

Martinez-Perez, M. D., & Osca, A. (2002). Psychometrical study of the Spanish version of the "Work Family Conflict Scale" of Kopelman, Greenhaus and Connoly (1983). *Revista de Psicologia Social, 16*, 43–58.

Matsui, T., Ohsawa, T., & Onglatco, M. (1995). Work–family conflict and the stress-buffering effects of husband support and coping behavior among Japanese married working women. *Journal of Vocational Behavior, 47*, 178–192.

Matsui, T., Tsuzuki, Y., & Onglatco, M. L. (1999). Some motivational bases for work and home orientation among Japanese college women: A rewards/costs analysis. *Journal of Vocational Behavior, 54*, 114, 126.

Matthews, L. S., Conger, R. D., & Wickrama, K. A. S. (1996). Work–family conflict and marital quality: Mediating processes. *Social Psychology Quarterly, 59*, 62–79.

Mauno, S., & Kinnunen, U. (1999). The effects of job stressors on marital satisfaction in Finnish dual-earner couples. *Journal of Organizational Behavior, 20*, 879–895.

Menaghan, E. G., & Parcel, T. L. (1990). Parental employment and family life: Research in the 1980s. *Journal of Marriage and Family, 42*, 1079–1089.

Mirrashidi, T. (1999). Integrating work and family: Stress social support, and well being among ethnically diverse working women. *Dissertation Abstracts International, 60*, 5-B: 2355.

Montgomery, A. J., Peeters, M. C. W., Schaufeli, W. B., & Den Ouden, M. (2003). Work–home interference among newpaper managers: Its relationship with burnout and engagement. *Anxiety, Stress & Coping: An International Journal, 16*, 195–211.

Moss, P. (1991). Work, family and the care of children: Issues of equality and responsibility. *Children and Society, 4*, 145–166.

Moyle, P. (1995). The role of negative affectivity in the stress process: Tests of alternative models. *Journal of Organizational Behavior, 16*, 647–668.

Netemeyer, R. G., Boles, J. S., & McMurrian, R. (1996). Development and validation of work–family conflict and family–work conflict scales. *Journal of Applied Psychology, 81*, 400–410.

Nippert-Eng, C. E. (1996). *Home and work: Negotiating boundaries through everyday life* (pp. xvii, 325). Chicago, London: University of Chicago Press.

Ng, C. W., Fosh, P., & Naylor, D. (2002). Work–family conflict for employees in an East Asian airline: Impact on career and relationship to gender. *Economic and Industrial Democracy, 23*, 67–106.

Ngo, Hang-Yue, & Lau, Chung-Ming (1994). Work–family conflict of men and women executives in Hong Kong. *Proceedings of the Second International Federation of Scholarly Associations of Management*, 198–199, Dallas, TX.

Ngo, Hang-Yue, & Lui, Siu-Yun (1999). Gender differences in outcomes of work–family conflict: The case of Hong-Kong managers. *Sociological Focus, 32*, 303–316.

Noor, N. M. (2002a). The moderating effect of spouse support of the relationship between work variables and women's work–family conflict. *Psychologia, 45*, 12–23.

Noor, N. M. (2002b). Work–family conflict, locus of control, and women's wellbeing: Tests of alternative pathways. *Journal of Social Psychology, 142*, 645–662.

Nordenmark, M. (2002). Multiple social roles—A resource or a burden: Is it possible for men and women to combine paid work with family life in a satisfactory way? *Gender, Work & Organization, 9*, 125–145.

O'Driscoll, M. P., Ilgen, D. R., & Hildreth, K. (1992). Time devoted to job and off-job activities, interrole conflict, and affective experiences. *Journal of Applied Psychology, 77*, 272–279.

O'Driscoll, M. P., Poelmans, S., Spector, P. E., Kalliath, T., Allen, T. D., Cooper, C. L., & Sanchez, J. I. (2003). Family-responsive interventions, perceived organizational and supervisor support, work–family conflict and psychological strain. *International Journal of Stress Management, 10*, 326–344.

Parasuraman, S., Greenhaus, J. H., & Granrose, C. S. (1992). Role stressors, social support, and well-being among two-career couples. *Journal of Organizational Behavior, 13*, 339–356.

Parasuraman, S., & Greenhaus, J. H. (2000). Toward reducing some critical gaps in work–family research. *Human Resource Management Review, 12*, 299–313.

Parasuraman, S., Purohit, Y. S., & Godschalk, V. M. (1996). Work and family variables, entrepreneurial career success, and psychological well-being. *Journal of Vocational Behavior, 48*, 275–300.

Peluchette, J. V. E. (1993). Subjective career success: The influence of individual difference, family and organizational variables. *Journal of Vocational Behavior, 43*, 198–208.

Peters, P., & Den Dulk, L. (2003). Cross-cultural differences in managers' support for home-based telework: A theoretical elaboration. *International Journal of Cross-Cultural Management, 3*, 3.

Piotrkowski, C. S. (1979). *Work and family system.* New York: The Free Press.

Pleck, J. H. (1977). The work–family role system. *Social Problems, 24*, 417–427.

Polasky, L. J., & Holahan, C. K. (1998). Maternal self-discrepancies, interrole conflict, and negative affect among married professional women with children. *Journal of Family Psychology, 12*, 388–401.

Poelmans, S. A. Y., Spector, P. E., Cooper, C. L., Allen, T. D., O'Driscoll, M., & Sanchez, J. I. (2003). A cross-national comparative study of work/family demands and resources. *International Journal of Cross-Cultural Management, 3*, 275–288.

Poelmans, S. (2003). Editorial. The multi-level "fit" model of work and family. *International Journal of Cross-Cultural Management, 3*, 267–274.

Poelmans, S. (2004). The decision process theory of work and family. In E. E. Kossek and S. Lambert (Eds.), *Managing work–life integration in organizations: Future directions for research and practice.* Mahwah, NJ: Lawrence Erlbaum Associates.

Rapoport, R., & Rapoport, R. N. (1969). The dual-career family: A variant pattern and social change. *Human Relations, 22*, 3–30.

Renshaw (1976). An exploration of the dynamics of the overlapping worlds of work and family. *Family Process, 15*, 143–157.

Repetti, R. L. (1987). Linkages between work and family roles. In S. Oskamp (Ed.), *Applied social psychology annual: Vol. 7. Family processes and problems* (pp. 98–127). Beverly Hills, CA: Sage.

Repetti, R. L. (1989). Effects of daily workload on subsequent behavior during marital interaction: The roles of social withdrawal and spouse support. *Journal of Personality and Social Psychology, 57*, 651–659.

Richardsen, A. M., Burke, R. J., & Mikkelsen, A. (1999). Job pressures, organizational support, and health among Norwegian women managers. *International Journal of Stress Management, 6*, 167–177.

Rosenbaum, M., & Cohen, E. (1999). Equalitarian marriages, spousal support, resourcefulness, and psychological distress among Israeli working women. *Journal of Vocational Behavior, 54*, 102–113.

Ryan, A., McFarland, L., Baron, H., & Page, R. (1999). An international look at selection practices: Nation and culture as explanations for variability in practice. *Personnel Psychology, 52*, 359–392.

Sahoo, F. M., & Bidyadhar, S. (1994). Critical factors of work–family linkage: An application of lens model to generate indigenous dimensions. *Psychology and Developing Societies, 6*, 169–185.

Senecal, C., & Vallerand, R. J. (1999). Construction and validation of the Family Activities Motivation Scale. *European Review of Applied Psychology, 49*, 261–274.

Senecal, C., Vallerand, R. J., & Guay, F. (2001). Antecedents and outcomes of work–family conflict: Towards motivational model. *Personality and Social Psychology Bulletin, 27,* 176–186.

Shaffer, M. A., Harrison, D. A., Gilley, K. M., & Luk, D. M. (2001). Struggling for balance amid turbulence on international assignments: Work–family conflict, support and commitment. *Journal of Management, 27,* 99–121.

Siew Kim, J. L., & Seow Ling, C. (2001). Work–family conflict of women entrepreneurs in Singapore. *Women in Management Review, 16,* 204–222.

Skilmore Sariati Ahmad, M. (2003). Work–family conflict: A survey of Singaporean workers. *Singapore Management Review, 25,* 35–53.

Smyrnios, K. X., Romano, C. A., & Tanewski, G. A. (1998). *Antecedents of work–family conflict and emotional well-being: A model for family business.* National Mutual Family Business Research Unit, Monash University.

Spector, P. E. et al. (2004). A cross-national comparative study of work–family stressors, working hours, and well-being: China and Latin America versus the Anglo World. *Personnel Psychology, 57,* 119–142.

Staines, G. L. (1980). Spillover versus compensation: A review of the literature on the relationship between work and nonwork. *Human Relations, 33,* 111–129.

Standen, P., Daniels, K., & Lamond, D. (1999). The home as a workplace: Work–family interaction and psychological well-being in telework. *Journal of Occupational Health Psychology, 4,* 368–381.

Stoeva, A. Z., Chiu, R. K., & Greenhaus, J. H. (2002). Negative affectivity, role stress, and work–family conflict. *Journal of Vocational Behavior, 60,* 1–16.

Swanson, J. L. (1992). Vocational behaviour, 1989-1991: Life span career development and reciprocal interaction between work and nonwork. *Journal of Vocational Behavior, 41,* 101–161.

Swanson, V., Power, K. G., & Simpson, R. J. (1998). Occupational stress and family life: A comparison of male and female doctors. *Journal of Occupational and Organizational Psychology, 71,* 237–260.

Tajfel, H., & Turner, H. (1985). The social identity theory of intergroup behaviour. In S. Worchel & W. Austin (Eds.), *Psychology of intergroup realtions* (2nd ed., pp. 7–24). Chicago: Nelson-Hall.

Thomas, L. T., & Ganster, D. C. (1995). Impact of family-supportive work variables on work–family conflict and strain: a control perspective. *Journal of Applied Psychology, 80,* 6–15.

Thompson, C. A., Beauvais, L. L., & Lyness, K. S. (1999). When work–family benefits are not enough: The influence of work–family culture on benefit utilization, organizational attachment, and work–family conflict. *Journal of Vocational Behavior, 54,* 392–415.

Takeuchi, R., Yun, S., & Tesluk, P. E. (2002). An examination of cross-over and spillover effects of spousal and expatriate cross-cultural adjustment on expatriate outcomes. *Journal of Applied Psychology, 87,* 655–666.

Vanfossen, B. E. (1981). Sex differences in the mental health effects of spouses support and equity. *Journal of Health and Social Behavior, 22,* 130–143.

Watanabe, S., Takahashi, K., & Minami, T. (1998). The emerging role of diversity and work–family values in a global context. In P. C. Earley & M. Earley (Eds.), *New Perspectives on international industrial/organizational psychology* (pp. 319–332). San Francisco: New Lexington Press.

Westman, M. (2001). Stress and strain crossover. *Human Relations, 54*, 717–751.

Westman, M., & Etzion, D. (1995). Crossover of stress, strain and resources from one spouse to another. *Journal of Organizational Behavior, 16*, 169–181.

Westman, M., & Piotrkowski, C. S. (1999). Introduction to the Special Issue: Work–family research in occupational health psychology. *Journal of Occupational Health Psychology, 4*, 301–306.

Wiersma, U. J. (1990). Gender differences in job attribute preferences: Work–home role conflict and job level as mediating variables. *Journal of Occupational Psychology, 63*, 231–243.

Wiersma, U. J. (1994). A taxonomy of behavioral strategies for coping with work–home role conflict. *Human Relations, 47*, 211–221.

Wiersma, U. J., & v.d. Berg, P. (1991). Work–home conflict, family climate, and domestic responsibilities among men and women. *Journal of Applied Psychology, 21*, 1207–1217.

Wiley, D. L. (1987). The relationship between work/nonwork role conflict and job-related outcomes: Some unanticipated findings. *Journal of Management, 13*, 467–472.

Williams, K., & Alliger, G. M. (1994). Role stressors, mood spillover, and perceptions of work–family conflict in employed parents. *Academy of Management Journal, 37*, 837–868.

Yang, N. (1998). An international perspective on socio-economic changes and their effects on life stress and career success of working women. *SAM Advanced Management Journal, Summer, 15–19*, 38.

Yang, N., Chen, C. C., Choi, J., & Zou, Y. (2000). Sources of work–family conflict: A Sino-U.S. comparison of the effects of work and family demands. *Academy of Management Journal, 43*, 113–123.

Zedeck, S. (Ed.). (1992). *Work, families, and organizations.* Jossey-Bass: San Francisco.

Zedeck, S., & Mosier, K. L. (1990). Work in the family and employing organization. *American Psychologist, 45*, 240–251.

2

U.S. Latino Migrant Farm Workers: Managing Acculturative Stress and Conserving Work–Family Resources

Ellen Ernst Kossek, Darrell Meece,
Marguerite E. Barratt,* and Beth Emily Prince
Michigan State University

ABSTRACT

Drawing on theorizing on acculturative stress (Berry, in press; Berry & Sam, 1997; Bhagat & London, 1999) and conservation of resource views of stress (Hobfoll, 1989) as organizing frameworks, this chapter presents original qualitative date from 79 interviews conducted with low income Latino migrant farm working mothers from five camps in Michigan in the United States. We discuss the migrant's work and family experiences in terms of the demands, opportunities, and constraints they face. We conclude with suggestions for future research on buffers of the stress-strain relationship and resilience for low skill migrant workers.

---

*Dr. Barratt is now at the U.S. National Science Foundation.

INTRODUCTION

Rosa, is a 41-year-old mother of five children: a three-month-old male infant, four-year-old boy and girl twins, and two sons ages eleven and twelve. Her husband Juan is 42 years old. They both have been working as migrant workers for the last 21 years, and have been coming to a midwestern U.S. camp in lower western Michigan with their family for the past three years, traveling from Florida in search of work. Both Rosa and Juan work picking and packing squash. Soon the squash season will be over and they will start sorting other vegetables. Their combined weekly earnings for last week were $175.00. Although this may not seem like a lot, Rosa says, "It is early in the season and the grower is expecting more work later in the season." Rosa does not know exactly how much she makes per hour, but comments that "Some people say that "he" (the grower) take taxes out of our pay checks." Rosa and Juan work very hard, and despite these conditions, Rosa is quite positive and thankful for the opportunity to work. Rosa and Juan's school-age children attend the Migrant Summer School and their preschool children attend Migrant Head Start. Even though Rosa is a new mother, she must work in the fields with her husband. The family cannot afford for her to stay home (in the temporary housing provided by the grower) to care for the new baby. Rosa is happy with her children's at the Migrant Head Start, but she is concerned because her baby is so small and has not started eating solid food yet. She is glad that her children have a place to go and learn and be taken care of while she and her husband work. It is really too hot for the children out in the field. Rosa completed the 5th grade in Mexico. After that she started working in the fields.

Large-scale migration of workers with their families is a global phenomenon that has grown dramatically over recent decades. Yet this topic has received relatively little attention in the mainstream work–family literature. Over 150 million people live temporarily outside their country of origin, and of these the International Labor Organization reports that nearly 100 million are migrant workers (Robinson, 2001). The United Nations Convention defines seasonal migrant workers as those who are employed in a state in which they are not nationals and where they are dependent on seasonal conditions (Hune, 1985). Robinson (2001) notes that ironically, many of the stresses that lead migrant workers and their families to see a new homeland in the first place, such as discrimination and poor access to education, health care, and employment, remain as barriers, despite border-crossing.

Recent migrants to developed countries such as the United States often represent two distinct occupational groups: (a) highly skilled and educated professionals and (b) workers with low skills and education. The later group, despite these constraints, still contributes far more to the economy than they receive in social services (Bhagat & London, 1999). Drawing from theorizing on acculturative stress (Berry, in press; Bhagat & London, 1999) and managing stress through conservation of resources (Hobfoll, 1989) as organizing frameworks, the goal of this chapter is to present an original case study of the unique cultural and work and family stresses facing the U.S. midwestern Latino migrant farm worker. Rosa and Juan, who are from the low-skilled immigrant group, typified the families we studied. We begin by providing brief background on U.S. midwestern Latino migrant workers. The comprehensive social and cultural issues examined may be relevant to other countries that depend on low-skill immigrants in their labor markets and to researchers conducting international and cross-cultural research on the work and family interface. For example, every year, a phenomenon similar to U.S. migrant stream occurs in Europe as Eastern-European workers migrate throughout Europe to harvest crops.

Michigan migrant farm workers are a key segment. The collective of U.S. Latino migrant farm workers is the largest re-occurring cyclical migrant population in the world and a major U.S. latino migrant worker segment (Martin, 1999). Most (88%) are of Latino origin and come from Florida, Texas, California, and Mexico. Yet they are ethnically diverse with origins in Cuba, Mexico, Puerto Rico, Central America, and South America. The migrant work force that comes to the United States from Mexico is equivalent to the size of one-eighth of the entire Mexican workforce (Cuellar, 2002). Although migrant jobs are highly undesirable and under paid, their loss could result in a U.S. farm worker shortage and hurt the world food supply and the Mexican economy (Martin & Martin, 1994).

The migrant farm worker represents the core of the fruit, vegetable, and horticulture industry today (National Center for Farmworker Health, Inc., 2002). These jobs include the picking a wide range of fruits and vegetables; their processing, grading, and packaging; and other horticultural labor, such as tree trimming and Christmas tree harvesting. The U.S. Department of Agriculture defines migrant farm workers as those who earn over 50% of their wages harvesting or working in agricultural labor and who spend the night away from home in order to seek agricultural work. Comprising 42% of the U.S. farm labor force (U.S. Department of Labor), migrants harvest more than 85% of the fruits and vegetables yielded by hand in the United States (National Center for Farmworker Health, Inc., 2002). They are also extremely economically disadvantaged (Rosenbaum, 2001b). For example, the U.S. poverty guidelines for officially living in poverty for a family of seven, the size of Rosa's family, is at or below $27,340 per year, over four times Rosa's earnings noted in the opening vignette (U.S. Federal Register, 2002).

U.S. migrant farm working families typically follow one of three main crop corridors. The eastern corridor originates in Florida and extends up the east coast and tends to have Haitian, African American, or Puerto Rican workers. The western corridor, comprising Mexican Americans, originates in southern California or Mexico and extends up the west coast. The Midwestern corridor is also primarily Mexican–American and originates in Texas or Florida, extending to the Great Lakes and plains states (U.S. Dept. of Labor, 2000; Barger & Reza, 1994).

This chapter focuses on migrant working mothers in Michigan from the third corridor. According to Michigan Agricultural Statistics, nearly 45,000 migrants farmed 45 Michigan crops in 2000 (Lansing State Journal, 2003), making Michigan the fourth largest migrant employer state in the United States (Michigan Commission on Spanish Speaking Affairs, 1997). Unlike other streams where there is greater movement following different crops, most Michigan migrants typically stay in one location and sit out various crops. In Michigan, migrant work can begin in February with the pruning of cherry trees, followed by the planting of early season crops such as asparagus, apples, and sugar beets, and ending with the farming of Christmas trees in December.

THEORETICAL FRAMEWORK

Acculturation research arose from study of how immigrants change as a result of resetting in a new culture. Berry and Sam (1997) define acculturative stress as "a stress reaction in response to life events that are rooted in the experience of acculturation, which is the process of cultural and psychological change as the result of cross-cultural contact." Building on this theory, later work by Bhagat and London (1999, p. 353) viewed acculturative stress as resulting from uncertainties associated with changing to the new culture and included the process of adopting to the dominant values or culture of the host country. Although Bhagat and London's model (1999) focused on professionals, their theory of acculturative stress can be used to understand the stress-related demands, opportunities, and constraints faced by migrants and their families. Demand stresses relate to perceived or real conflict with the cultural values of the mainstream society of the culture. Opportunity stresses relate to the ability of immigrants to achieve at a higher level than possible in home country. Constraint stresses are those that constrain individuals from integrating in the mainstream. These three factors influence cognitive appraisal of how well one and one's family are able to manage stress and assimilation.

Berry (in press) argues it is likely that the migrant may adopt acculturation strategies that are cognitively seen as minimizing resource losses. One of the most common strategies adopted by migrants is marginalization in which the family holds on to its old heritage in ways that preserve the family resources, but may at the same time be dysfunctional in taking advantage of opportunities in the new culture, thereby limiting full assimilation. The belief that individuals act based on their cognitive appraisal of the optimal way to conserve resources is aligned with Hobfoll's (1989) conservation of resources theory of stress. This theory holds that when an individual perceives or experiences environmental circumstances that threaten or cause depletion of resources, he or she psychologically responds in ways that minimize loss of resources. For example, resources might include self-esteem, and employment (Hobfoll, 1989). Migrating to a new land, acculturating oneself and family, and handling new work and family role integration demands can threaten or actually deplete resources and increase stress.

Hobfoll (1989) and Bhagat and London's (1999) theories are aligned and can be easily integrated. For example, opportunities often relate to resources, such as child care, and employment. Constraints and demands typically involve factors that can threaten or actually deplete resources, such as poor working conditions, language barriers, or high family mobility. We integrate these theoretical concepts to organize our case study along the themes of (a) resources and opportunities, (b) demands and potential for resource losses, and (c) constraints.

METHOD

Sample

This dataset was collected in 2001–2002 from users of Migrant Head Start Centers located at five different migrant work camps in the central and southern parts of Michigan. Face-to-face interviews lasting one to two hours were conducted with 79 low-income migrant working mothers. All interviews were conducted in Spanish by a Latino interviewer. All mothers had at least one infant. The study was part of a larger research project entitled The Michigan Child Care Partnership (Barratt, Meece, & Kossek, 2000). It was funded by the Gerber

Foundation to assess child and infant care for low-income working mothers.

Measures

The data used to develop the themes in this chapter are mainly qualitative. They were drawn from an interview protocol designed to assess work experiences, social and cultural integration, child care, individual well-being, educational background, health care, transportation, and work and family stressors. We also collected some quantitative data on demographics and some exploratory Likert scales were used to measure work–family conflict and job quality (reported elsewhere because of space restrictions and the fact that the purpose of this chapter was to develop substantive qualitative themes; Meece, Barratt, Kossek, & Hawkins, 2003).

Analysis

This case study following an inductive, grounded theory development process (Glaser and Strauss, 1967) as opposed to a priori hypotheses. In the results section, we give descriptive statistics and then we analyze our data by the main themes noted above, which we drew from Hobfoll (1989) and Bhagat & London (1999).

RESULTS

Descriptive Statistics

Eighty-two percent of the sample reported Mexican ethnicity, whereas 18% reported Hispanic. Approximately two thirds were legal immigrants. Nearly all (97.5%) were married. The age range of the mothers was from 16–48 years. Most were young—nearly 70% were between the ages of 19 to 29 years old. All had children. Two thirds (53) had one or two children. One fifth (18) had three children. One fifth had four or more children. Nearly all (93%) of the infants were cared for at Migrant Head Start with the rest (7%) in relative care. Most (96%) were poorly educated with only a grade school education of sixth grade or less. Only one had completed high school and two had no formal education. Self-reported household income ranged from $70.00 per week up to $600.00 per week. The mean was $284.93 with a standard deviation of $123.01. Two thirds (70%) earned less than $300 a week. Most households had two or more employed members. Eighty percent of our sample had worked in their jobs at least four years.

Over a third had their schedule change every week, and over a third were called into work at the last minute or had to work after 6 p.m. Ten percent sometimes brought their infants with them to the field.

Opportunities and Resources

To assimilate into the new culture and also earn a living, child care is a critical resource. When Migrants come into a migrant camp, local childcare often is not accessible, nor is it affordable. An exception is when there is a Migrant Head Start Center located at or near the camp. A unique aspect of our sample is that nearly all relied on Migrant Head Start for infant and toddler care. This enabled us to examine the lives of migrant workers under conditions in which there was public support for child care. This chapter focuses on migrants who did not have to search for childcare in order to work and who had access to quality care and additional resources to aid acculturation.

Serving over 30,000 migrant children annually and operating in 33 states, Migrant Head Start is sponsored by the U.S. government to provide child care for low income families (U.S. Department of Health and Human Services, 2001). This federal program is run by local contractors to provide free childcare and comprehensive developmental services for children from 2 weeks to 5 years of age. It can operate from 6 weeks to 10 months a year, depending on harvest schedule. Many sites are open 12 hours a day, 6 to 7 days a week. In Michigan, and 10 additional states, it is run by Telamon Corporation, a private nonprofit organization whose purpose is to provide human transitional services to improve the lives of migrant and other low-income workers (www.telemon.org).

Migrant Head Start not only provides high quality child care, but also provides other services for the whole family. These services include English literacy training; employment assistance; an AIDS/HIV education program; parent training in education, health, dental, and mental health; immunizations; help for children with disabilities; meals; transportation; and social services (www.telamon.org). Migrant Head Start childcare can be seen as an acculturation resource providing a first step toward setting up roots in a community. This linkage is illustrated by the following observation made by our interviewer about a 22-year-old married farm laborer with an infant and toddler:

> ...is so happy over the fact that in this state there is free childcare for ... (the family's) children and that wasn't the case in Florida. The family is considering settling down around here, if they can stand the cold winter months.

Although Migrant Head Start is publicly funded, the fact that it is located at or near the migrant camps led many workers to see it as part of employer support for quality childcare. We found that the more that migrant workers perceived that their employers or supervisors were supportive of childcare, such as providing childcare information, for example, the higher the care quality was rated and the lower the turnover intentions.

Child care is also important for ensuring labor force participation and economic opportunity. Following Hobfoll (1989), the lack of access to Migrant Head Start could result in perceived or actual resource loss. An illustration of this linkage comes from the situation of a young 23-year-old mother with an 8-month-old baby. With a high school diploma, she was the most highly educated individual in our sample. Yet she was unemployed and separated from her husband. Although she lives with her mother, father, grandparents, and uncle who could ostensibly provide care, our interviewer commented she was waiting for a Head Start opening:

> The mom seems very upbeat even though she hasn't been able to work because of childcare. I don't work because there isn't an opening at the Head Start school. She sits at home with her baby while her parents and brother go to work in the field harvesting or weeding celery.

The potential loss of family resources resulting from a shift of other members toward caregiving may be another factor. When Head Start is not available, if another family member provides care, then some of the potential wages earned for the family are threatened.

Not only are there potential economic losses if the resource of child care is not available, but also there are family health risks. If there is no room at Head Start, family members may decide to take children with them into the fields. This exposes these children to chemical pesticides, extreme heat, dangerous equipment, and hazardous conditions. A married 18-year-old mother with two children (13 months and 3 years) works in the fields picking blueberries. Soon the season will be over and she will begin picking apples. She has completed ninth grade and comments about her life as a migrant worker and when she gets to spend time with her children:

> Usually after school, they spend one hour by her in the field. I realize that I married very young and it has been hard but I want to get out of this kind of life. I want my children to attend one school and not have to leave in the middle of the school year.

Despite these hardships, this work experience also provides opportunities and resources. Working allows the mother to enhance multiple life role accumulation, by adding a work role to her repertoire (Lerner, 1994). Our interviewer commented on the mother's raised expectations:

> This young mother has a lot going for her. She's educating herself with the help of the Catholic Church (nuns) that visit her home four times a week. She wants to graduate so badly. She wants to get more education to be able to help her family with a better job.

Demands and Perceived or Actual Resource Losses

Resource losses include job demands and exposure to health risks that threaten livelihood, employer mistreatment because of immigrant status, and family demands resulting from separation and loss of family time.

Migrant farm-working jobs are physically and emotionally demanding with hazardous working conditions from exposure to chemicals to risks of injury from accidents. Two thirds of our sample agreed that they had daily health concerns about their safety on the jobs. Health losses from unsafe work are a critical job demand that hurts family well-being and future economic livelihood. Migrant work is dangerous and creates health concerns for workers and families (Slesinger, 1992). The Environmental Protection Agency estimates that 300,000 farm workers suffer acute pesticide poisoning each year. Many of these workers do not seek treatment or are misdiagnosed because symptoms can mimic a viral infection (National Center for Farmworker Health, Inc., 2002). Migrants' lack of education and economic desperation can also contribute to health concerns. One study of 460 hired farm workers in Washington State found that 89% did not know the name of a single pesticide to which they had been exposed, and 76% of workers had not received any information on appropriate protective measures (National Center for Farmworker Health, Inc., 2002).

According to Nixon (1996), pesticide exposure represents the greatest health threat to the children in agriculture. He notes children are more susceptible to pesticides because they absorb more per pound of body weight and because of their developing nervous system and organs. Exposure to fertilizers and pesticides on a daily basis had the workers from our sample concerned. This 26-year-old married mother of two children was finished picking blueberries and beginning the apple picking season. She has been a migrant worker for the last 5 years and has a seventh grade education:

> Yes, we could fall off the ladders and hurt ourselves. Our clothes are dirty because of the dust that remains on the leaves of the plants. We breathe that dust daily.

Dermatitis and respiratory problems are a common occurrence (National Center for Farmworker Health, Inc., 2002). Additional occupational health hazards of farm work include tuberculosis, diabetes, cancer, and HIV. All these conditions, which require frequent medical treatment, are difficult to treat because of the mobility of the population. Yet many migrant workers are fearful of losing their jobs and therefore do not ask for the needed medical attention.

Another example comes from a mother of two children who does not work because she just had a baby and her husband has been ill. She is concerned about the financial implications her husband's illness can have on their family:

> My husband was so sick, he had a fever, but was afraid to take time off because the farmer gets very angry when they miss work. His younger brother got hurt by a machine and had the tip of his finger cut off. They expect him to go back to work soon.

Unfortunately, migrants are dependent on their incomes and have no choice but to stay, despite the health risks. We also spoke with a married, 37-year-old migrant mother of three, who picks and packs squash and has a ninth grade education. Her family has been coming to this same farm for the last 7 years. She is concerned about her family's economic problems because of her husband's injury:

> My family is struggling. My husband had an accident while pruning apple trees. The branch from the apple tree didn't hold the ladder and he fell to the ground and broke his ankle. He had some type of surgery but his ankle and whole left foot were all swollen.

Job demands also create demands for family. Families spend little time together because the work hours threaten *family time*, which can be experienced as a cultural loss associated with migrant work. Often asked to work 50 to 60 hours per week, these migrant mothers rarely see their children. A 29-year-old married mother of mother of five children ages 1, 2, 6, 7, and 14 years old was concerned about the lack of family time. Her highest level of education completed is sixth grade. She had been working for 4 years as a migrant worker and will return to Florida in the fall. This season she is picking and packaging tomatoes. Our interviewer comments:

> This family doesn't say much because they need the jobs and have to feed their children... They have started harvesting the tomatoes. The women work together with the men picking the tomatoes. At 5:00 p.m.,

the men can go home and then the women are asked to work in the shed to sort and pack the tomatoes. Some of the women that I've interviewed have told me that soon they'll be starting to work from 6:00 a.m. until 9:30–10:00 p.m. They say that they are so tired at night that they don't even get to see their children.

Thus, at times the women are asked to work longer hours than men because of their skill in packing produce. They must go back to work at night after the picking shift is over to start packing. This structuring of the timing of work in which various family members may work longer and differing shifts may result in a loss of family time, an important family resource. We conducted some coding of family hours of the time that the mother and father are spending together. We found that the average amount of time spent together was only *1 hour* a week. This is in contrast to our findings from our other research on low-income mothers. For that sample, the average time parents spent together was 37 hours a week (Meece et al., 2003). Although migrant families may appear on paper to have the same or even higher number of adults living in the household, what appears to be happening is that after working in the fields, migrant mothers may come home only to work a separate shift of domestic chores alone.

A recent report from the Institute of Agricultural and Natural Resources indicates that family obligations are of great importance to Latino farm working people (Zanner & Stevens, 2001). The family is honored by both a strong work ethic and strong family obligations in the dual prevailing beliefs that although family should take precedence over work, work is also seen as an obligation to meet family responsibilities (Zanner & Stevens, 2001).

Consequently, some migrant workers travel north for a better wage and work to support family even if this sometimes means leaving some older children and family members behind. This hardship of family separation is a common occurrence in the migrant life. Our interviewer noted the emotional challenge this created for a 35-year-old farm laborer with a sixth grade education who works as a laborer doing various jobs such as weeding, pruning, and packing fruit. The migrant mother has three children from 11 months to 4 years here and several other older children she left behind:

> The family works very hard to take care of their family. They are separated from some of their children that are still in Mexico. Their main concern right now is arranging some kind of a plan to complete their immigration papers. Their wish is for their children to be able to come and live with them soon. Then they will all be together as a family once more.

Besides fragmenting families, another family demand that creates cultural stress stems from long term separation from one's permanent home. Our interviewer interviewed a young mother with a baby 4 months old, whose job was weeding young plants. The interviewer commented:

> The mother is very young but she seems to know the needs of her baby. She said that she and her husband work hard to be able to earn money for their family. She gives so much of herself to her baby. I thought that she seemed to miss her home down south but understood that they had to venture up north to work for better wages.

Constraints and Daily Life Hassles

Migrant farm working families have to cope with many daily life hassles, which pose serious structural constraints to cultural assimilation and the family's ability to manage stress and improve long-term overall social and economic well-being. Notwithstanding the health and employer concerns noted in the demands section above, the biggest constraint faced was *extreme poverty*, as our entire sample's household incomes were far below U.S. federal poverty guidelines. Seventy percent made less than $300 a week. Migrant workers tend to be poorer than the typical poor in the host country and Latino immigrants have higher poverty rates than overall U.S. Latino population. U.S. Census Bureau (1999) statistics show that whereas 28% of Latino families lived at or below the U.S. poverty level, the rate jumps to one third (34%) for Mexican immigrants, for example. National data show that one half of all farm working families earn less than $10,000 per year (National Center for Farmworker Health, Inc., 2002). This income is well below the 2002 U.S. poverty guidelines for a family of four of $18,100 (U.S. Federal Register, 2002). Under good working conditions, instead of an hourly minimum wage or lower, employees over age 16 can be paid for how much they pick ranging from .55 cents to $1.25 for a bushel of apples in southern Michigan (Lansing State Journal, 2003). Although these wage rates have increased in the past decade, when adjusted for inflation, wages have actually decreased by 5% in that time (National Center for Farmworker Health, Inc., 2002), and a minimum weekly level of work hours is not guaranteed. Given this limited income, it is not surprising that two thirds of our sample agreed or strongly agreed that with the statement, "If I stopped working, my family could not cover expenses."

Besides being poorer, migrant families tend to be *atypical from other low income families* in the U.S. host country in a number of other ways. Consistent with their high value on family grounded in their Latino heritage, migrant working mothers are also more likely to be married. Although ironically marriage is usually a vehicle for rising from poverty in the United States, the incomes of migrant families do not seem to significantly benefit from the marriage effect. (For an overview of U.S. low income working families, see Heyman, 2000.) All of the migrant families we studied lived in poverty yet were married, despite the fact that the majority of poor U.S. families are headed by single parents (Heyman, 2000). Migrant workers tend to be more dependent on their employer for social and community linkages than other low-income families. Their employment situation is the truly larger context in which their family is embedded as their childcare and housing are all in camps often located at or near the employer.

High mobility and transience are unique constraints emanating from migrant families' dual cultural ties. They serve as barriers to accumulating human and social capital and to assimilating into either dominant or minority host country cultures, constraints also faced by other migrant families around the globe.

Constant mobility creates a less stable work and family environment and has limited migrant workers' socioeconomic circumstances. Research by Roeder and Millard (2000) suggested that the cyclical mobility of migrant workers exacerbates their poverty, which makes migrants more susceptible to psychological problems, causes greater difficulty integrating into the community and establishing social ties, and creates educational challenges. These issues create difficulty into assimilating into either Anglo or Latino communities.

Mobility has a large constraint on human capital accumulation, especially its negative effects on immigrants' *education and skill levels*, which are well below the national average. According to the U.S. Census Bureau in March 2000, only 15.9% of persons 25 years and older did not graduate from high school. Latino farm workers have less education than their nonfarm working Latino counter parts. Although educational attainment varies by ethnicity, (Hispanics, Cubans, and other Hispanics), the breakdown of educational levels for this population is remarkably different from our sample. Of the Hispanics 25 years and older, 57% of the population in the United States have at least a high school education. The Mexican population is at 51%, Puerto Rican 65.3%, Cuban 73%, and Central and South American is at 64.3%. (U.S. Census Bureau, 2000). This lack of education also increases the division between year-round Latino families and the migrating Latino families and Anglos. Because migrant farm workers have less education on average, they are less able to compete for jobs outside the agricultural arena not only because of low skills, but also because of language barriers. It was surprising to us that not only

Anglos, but also nonmigrant Latinos were rarely mentioned by our interviewees.

Children's education is often neglected or inconsistent because of family economic pressures and the mobile life. The children usually start the school year in the farming location and then travel back to their home base to continue their school year for the winter months. Often these children are then taken out of school in early spring to make the journey back northward so the family can start to work on the early crops. This struggle for economic family stability forces the migrant lifestyles to revolve around working, moving on to find other work, and perhaps then migrating south at the end of the season. In our Latino sample, 5% have moved four or more times within the last year, 47.6% have moved two to three times within the year, and 40% have moved once. Consequently, children find themselves enrolled in different schools each year; in fact children of migrant farm working families may attend 14 to 15 schools by the time they reach high school (McCloskey, 2000). As a result, up to half of migrant children are behind their grade level, and one third of the children are retained by second grade (Morse, 1988). Many children need 3 years of education just to advance one grade level of skills (Kuperschmidt & Martin, 1997).

Many schools and communities lack understanding of the mobile migrant culture and the social supports required for effective acculturation. The constant interruption of their school year creates the inability of the school to meet their needs, although California has a policy that makes it easy for school records to follow these transient children (www.mnaonlineorg/pplmi.htm).

Regular transportation to Head Start during the fall and spring bridge seasons is another constraint. A mother who picks blueberries and apples is married with two children ages 11 months and 3 years old. She is 19 years old and has a sixth grade education and complains:

> I can't work. There isn't any transportation for my kids to get to the Head Start School. We don't own a car. It's hard for my son, he really liked school. Most of the bus drivers went back to their original jobs with the public schools. According to a Telamon contract, he said, that this happens almost every year. The funding (for transportation) starts to dwindle, even thought the parents will stay to work through the month of October.

Chronic social and school mobility also places migrant children at higher psychological and economic risk (Kuperschmidt & Martin, 1997). One study found two thirds of the children of migrant farm workers had one or more psychiatric disorders with anxiety being the most prevalent (Kuperschmidt & Martin, 2003). Because of their economic circumstances, children also may face additional stress because working can be expected of them. Boys begin to be treated as adults at age 15 or 16 when they can earn as much in the fields as their fathers. Girls are treated as adults when they are capable of having children and managing a household. Because there is no tradition of mandatory education in their culture, children are allowed to drop out of school to work and help support the family (Velazquez, 1996).

Low educational attainment keeps families in poverty. As noted, most (96%) of our sample only had no more than a grade school education. This lack of education creates additional language and social barriers to these families ability to adapt to a different culture. In order to assimilate, migrant workers need to adopt the language, values, and behaviors of the dominant U.S. culture and abandon the home culture and language. Yet many migrant workers have not been able to readily adopt the culture and have had difficulty adapting to the Anglo culture. They have a strong traditional background of beliefs and practices and ethnic identity (Zanner & Stevens, 2001), which is reinforced by physical isolation. The lack of English-speaking families in the camps fosters isolation and marginalization. Approximately, one in four (24%) Latinos over the age of 5 live in linguistically isolated houses compared with only 1.6% of non-Latinos, and over one third of Latino adults report not speaking English "very well" (Zambrana & Dorrington, 1998).

Because of low wages, migrant farm workers face significant difficulties finding *housing* and paying over 30% of their monthly income for housing or using substandard "free" employer housing. One national survey reports that less than one third of migrant workers nationally have adequate housing (McCloskey, 2000). Of the units that were substandard and crowded in a national farm worker housing survey (www.ruralhome.org), 74% had children. The average number of rooms in a single family dwelling for a migrant family is between 1 and 2.6, and the dimensions of the rooms are approximately 10 by 12 feet or 12 by 15 feet. Indoor running water is only available in 64.8% of the camps, and laundry facilities are generally not available (U.S. National Advisory Council on Migrant Health, 1995).

One campsite worker was a 17-year-old married mother of an 8-month-old. She picks squash in the fields where she wears long sleeves and gloves to protect herself from the plants and sharp knives she uses to cut the squash off of the plant. She has had no schooling. The interviewer comments on the living conditions:

Their living quarters are in very poor condition. She keeps her child on top of the bed most of the times because the floor (rug) is so dirty. They are preventing the baby from crawling. The furniture was so old and I mean rickety old, I think that I can find better furniture along side people's front yards when they discard them.

These deplorable living conditions can exacerbate existing health risks issues for this already struggling population.

A final set of constraints we examined was migrants' general *lack of social power in relation to government and their employers.* Paradoxically, while Migrant Head Start was valued and was the main point of governmental and community contact, our sample accessed other forms of public assistance at much lower rates than other families living in poverty (Boswell, 1996). Only 13% of migrant farm workers used Medicaid, and only 10% used WIC (Women, Infants, and Children) and food stamps (National Center for Farmworker Health, Inc., 2002).

Many were afraid or unable to access government services because they do not want to draw attention to themselves or do not meet the minimum 6-month residency requirements many states have put in place to qualify for welfare. Estimates show that 50% of the seasonal agricultural work force is undocumented; that number rises to 70% during the harvest time (Aleinikoff, 1999). The high mobility of migrant workers also makes applications for health services very difficult for this population. By the time the information is processed, the crop is harvested and the family is moving on.

This could be one explanation why this population has remained invisible to the public and to policy makers. The lack of information about the magnitude of the number of workers is a problem with regard to policy implementation. Yet overall, 80% of migrant farm workers are U.S. citizens or in the country legally (Fix & Pascal, 1994). They often pay taxes and reflect an important part of the national and global economy.

Another constraint is migrants' lack of power in dealing with their employers. Migrant workers are dependant on crop performance, and they must share the economic risk with their employer. The welfare of the migrant farm worker depends on the value of the crop, which can sometimes be wiped out by bad weather. Their income is based on the quality and quantity of produce. We also found evidence of threats and mistreatment by some supervisors who use their higher power in the U.S. culture to take advantage of the workers. Below are our interviewer's observations based on her interview with a mother of five children who had been picking and packing tomatoes for 4 years. The family will return to Florida in the fall:

> Several of these families have been threatened by their employer, that if they don't do the work the way that he wants it, he would deport them by calling the immigration department. Some of the families don't understand English but the few who understand have told the rest that he had threatened them. (The employer) has also gotten very angry when someone has been injured because he has to pay for the hospital for his injuries. This family doesn't say much because they need the jobs and have to feed their children.

The migrant workers are forced to take what money they can or face losing their job to another who will. In summary, migrant workers are constrained by the fact they are more dependent on their employer for survival than are other poor workers. They are less likely to be able to find another job and they may not utilize welfare or other established government programs aimed at helping the working poor.

Government regulators report many farmers find ways to short workers on their wages. A frequent practice is to shave a couple of hours off each workday as a way to lower the daily wage. It appears that little can be done about the treatment of the workers. Often it is never reported for fear of recourse.

A married 24-year-old mother of two children ages 3 months and 3 years was concerned about the family income because she had just had a baby. Her husband had been sick and had missed work. He used to pick and pack tomatoes. There is no sick pay or compensation for this family:

> The farmer is not paying them by the same pay scale each day. If he feels that a lot of the tomatoes have spoiled, he won't pay them as much. The tomatoes have to be good for the market, otherwise their pay scale goes down.

Although poor treatment by employers is common, there are exceptions. Many migrant workers relocate back to the same farm every year, especially when they have good employer relations. Social support for family from supervisors was less prevalent, as two thirds of our sample felt they could not share work and family concerns with their supervisors. Across the five camps, there was a marked split in our sample about employer support for children at work, perhaps reflecting cultural tensions on whether to bring children to work when care was not available. Although 40% disagreed or strongly disagreed with the statement, "My employer does not mind if my children came to work," 55% agreed or strongly agreed that their employer did mind. There seemed to be some cultural tensions over preferences on how to manage care.

Summary of Results: Implications for Cognitive Appraisal

Overall, the demands and constraints faced by our sample far outweighed their resources. The more an individual had a difficult job that was of low quality or had a constantly changing schedule, the higher their depression and intention to turnover. Yet these factors seemed to be kept psychologically separate and unrelated to their attitudes toward childcare. In fact, the more positive the individual felt about childcare, the better they felt about their job and family performance and the less negative they were about the demands and constraints we have noted, regardless of job demands.

Migrant Head Start and its quality childcare were bright spots in their lives and seemed to provide positive buffering social psychological effects that go beyond the mere instrumental provision of care services. What was surprising was that our sample generally felt very positive overall about juggling work and family and about the U.S. culture despite its hardships. Even with extreme poverty and other serious life constraints, less than half (42.6%) reported that they were worried about issues such as family and income. Even in the face of difficult working conditions, 90% did not find health a problem for holding a job. The workers in our sample had horrible jobs, yet a strong work ethic. They often got dirty on the job. Most did not know their work hours until that day, and they did not have any "sick leave" for themselves or their children. They did not have health care, yet they did manage. This is really amazing and more research is needed on the social and cultural work and family identities of migrant workers, especially women. More research is needed on how low-income working families living in extreme poverty develop resilience. The traditional work and family literature is silent on this theme. We believe the positive resource effects of Migrant Head Start did buffer families. We also note several other resources and acculturation mechanisms that seemed to buffer families from stress.

Clearly, the high value placed on family and maintaining two-parent households was beneficial. Consider our interviewer's comments on how a 24-year-old young married mother with an infant was doing. The mother has a first grade education and works packing pickles:

> The family is so supportive of each other. Their family's strength comes from the support that they all seem to have for each other. They like

this country and its people very much. They said that most Americans are very nice people toward their child as well as toward them.

The family ethic of our sample was strong and had positive affect: 86% percent believed their family thinks they fulfill family responsibilities. It was noteworthy that 83% of our migrant mothers saw their identities as equally attached to both work and family, which means they highly value both work and family roles. Even though the role quality of most of our migrant mothers' jobs was what the U.S. culture would deem as poor, the additional role accumulation seemed to have positive benefits for the mothers' well-being. Two roles, even of poor quality, seemed to be better than just one.

Although both a constraint and a resource, one strategy often using by migrants to manage acculturative stress is to maintain a strong sense of ethnic identity. The acculturation process can be (a) one way, integration, in which the minority group assimilates into the host culture, (b) two way in which the minority group becomes bicultural (Manaster, Chan, & Safady, 1992), or a third path of marginalization in which the minority group does not fully fit into either culture, in this case the host Anglo or Latino cultures (van de Vijver, Helms-Lorenz, & Feitzer, 1999). Young Latino children are likely to have a bicultural identity rather than reject their home ethnic origin (Zanner & Stevens, 2001). As each generation begins to learn English, they do not give up their use of Spanish in the home. Although this impedes assimilation, it also helps them develop pride in their cultural identity. Their strong identity and use of marginalization acculturation strategies allows them to feel good about themselves.

Although isolating them from the rest of the mainstream U.S. culture, the rural migrant camps that serve as temporary homes for our sample, paradoxically also may buffer them from recognizing how seriously less well off they are from the American dream and other cultural assimilation tensions. They socially construct their family situation as better off than what they left in Mexico. They reevaluate the family resources they have in the new cultural context. Yet they remain a marginalized minority from other nonmigrant Latino groups and may be viewed as a minority within a minority group.

DISCUSSION

This chapter begins to unpack and embrace the complexity of the work and family worlds of the U.S. midwestern Latino migrant worker. Little theorizing or qualitative empirical work in the work–family integration field has drawn on migrant farm workers, who are in shifting employment and social systems and face multiple concurrent demands and constraints on work and family well-being.

The issue of mobility and, in particular, cyclical mobility in work and its negative implications for the development of social and human capital is rarely integrated into work–family theorizing. An exception is research on mobility that has been conducted on international expatriates and executives or family relocation (cf Eby, DeMatteo, & Russell, 1997). Cyclical mobility creates temporary social systems and forces families to have to manage constant and additional transitions and additional risk factors emanating from frequent moves and the lack of social stability. Our study also has relevance for low-skill jobs in other cyclical industries such as construction, hotel, or restaurant.

Although migrant's annual migration allows for the family to survive economically, it is made with great sacrifice, stress, and suffering, and the high mobility makes it difficult for subsequent generations to rise from poverty and acculturate into the U.S. majority or Latino minority cultures. This mobility creates a physical isolation that supports a marginalization acculturation strategy as a means to manage stress, yet also feeds into language and cultural constraints that inhibit and stall future social prospects. Thus, migrant workers are a minority within a minority. More research is needed to develop measures that tap into the resources, demands, and constraints we have identified and to assess possible stress buffers and identify resilience factors. If quality employer childcare, strong family bonds, dual work and family attachment, and bicultural identity do provide the buffering effects we have noted, then more studies are needed to document these resources and follow children and families longitudinally. Study is needed on how to help migrant workers ameliorate demands from jobs on self and family, help them effectively conserve meager family resources, and develop mainstream acculturation strategies that promote greater stability and social advancement.

Hovey (2001) reports five primary stressors for migrant workers: (a) migrant journey and physical environment stressors, (b) social and cultural stressors, (c) language and communication stressors, (d) social support and isolation stressors, and (e) work environment and conditions stressors. This research can be reviewed with the conservation of resources frameworks in which social support serves as a moderator of cognitive appraisal of well-being. Stressors can be understood as demands or constraints on the net accumulation of family resources.

Our study also reinforces the fact that the face of the low-income global work force is changing. In the United States in particular, we must increase research to enable greater understanding of work–family issues for Latino families, who are now the largest U.S. minority. Study is needed on how to develop interventions that promote breadwinning and caregiving. Research on how to improve the integration of impoverished minorities within larger cultural majority and minority ethnic groups is rarely considered in traditional work and family theorizing.

The chapter highlights the need for more research to countervail migrant stereotypes that support discrimination and the inability to fully tap social services and manage employer relations. For example, despite prevailing stereotypes, we found that most migrant families did not necessarily return to Mexico. Many migrant workers see leaving agriculture and the migrant lifestyle as the main ways to move out of poverty. Increasingly, migrant workers may live in the United States all year, although they may still have family in Mexico and visit. Another misconception is that migrant farmers keep moving all season—instead most of these families stay in one place for the whole season and work in different crops as the season progresses.

Our migrant families were atypical poor and had characteristics challenging many existing assumptions in the current research on families living in poverty. Many poor mothers are single, and we presume (and research shows us) that having a partner makes life easier. However, these are struggling two-parent families. More research is needed on how to overcome the barriers of mobility and transience and to better link to educational and cultural systems as a way to accumulate social and human capital and improve the integration of these families.

A unique aspect of migrant workers' challenges, which can help foster innovative thinking in work and family theory and practice, is that their problems are not due to a lack of public policy programs. There are some excellent whole family programs such as Migrant Head Start. The problem is some migrants are illegal workers who do not want to draw attention to themselves or adopt dysfunctional acculturation strategies out of necessity to conserve family resources. They also do not have the support of growers or the government. They may encounter prejudice when they access services if they do not speak English well. Migrant Head Start works to link families with healthcare, child care, and parental education. It is a whole child and family program. More research is needed how this intervention might expand and improve its effectiveness in the United States and around the globe. Yet even with public supported high quality childcare, migrant families have a very difficult life. It takes more than free high quality childcare to make migrant families' lives work well. Some of the programs we studied operated 7 days a week or many hours a day. The lack of research on a personal level with the migrant population is evident as many of the reports we examined bemoaned the lack of quality data or statistics. Future work family research should triangulate qualitative and quantitative methods to enable better understanding of the work and family issues faced by unique populations, such as migrant families. The constraints migrants face such as extreme poverty, cyclical mobility, and low education; the multiplicative effects of resources such as quality free childcare; the measurement of job and family demands; and linkages to acculturation strategies need to be considered in models of work–family stress.

ACKNOWLEDGMENTS

We thank the Gerber Foundation, and the Institute for Children Youth and Families, and the Families and Communities Together Foundation both at Michigan State University for their support of this research. We also thank Steven Poelmans and Rabi S. Bhagat for helpful comments on a first draft of this chapter.

REFERENCES

Aleinikoff, T. (1999, December). The green card solution. *American Prospective, 11,* 32–37.

Barger, W. K., & Reza, E. M. (1994). *The farm labor movement in the Midwest.* Austin, Texas: University of Texas Press.

Barratt, M., Meece, D., & Kossek, E. (2000.) *Proposal to the Gerber Foundation.* East Lansing, MI: Michigan Child Care Research Partnership, Appendix.

Berry, J. W. (in press). Acculturation. In W. Friedlmeier (Ed.), *Culture and human development.* Amsterdam: Swets & Seitlinger.

Berry, J., & Sam, D. (1997). Acculturation and adaptation. In W. Berry, M. H. Segall, & C. Kagitcibasi (Eds.), *Handbook of cross-cultural psychology: Social behaviour and applications* (Vol. 3, ch. 8). Boston: Allyn & Bacon.

Bhagat, R. S., & London, M. (1999). Getting started and getting ahead: Career dynamics of immigrants. *Human Resource Management Review, 9,* 349–365.

Boswell, T. D. (1996). *Latino poverty in the United States* (Issue Paper). Miami, FL: Policy Center Cuban American National Council.

Cuellar, I. (2002, May). *Mexican-origin migration in the U.S. and mental health consequences,* (JSRI Occasional Paper #40). East Lansing, MI: The Julian Samora Research Institute, Michigan State University.

Eby, L. T., DeMatteo, J. S., & Russell, J. E. A. (1997). Employment assistance needs of accompanying spouses following relocation. *Journal of Vocational Behavior, 50,* 291–307.

Fix, M., & Pascal, J. S. (1994). *Immigration and immigrants: Setting the record straight.* Washington, DC: The Urban Institute.

Heyman, J. (2000). *The widening gap: Why America's working families are in jeopardy and what to do about it.* New York: Basic Books.

Hobfoll, S. E. (1989). Conservation of resources: A new attempt at conceptualizing stress. *American Psychologist, 44,* 513–524.

Hovey, J. D. (2001). *Mental health and substance abuse.* Program for the study of immigration and mental health, The University of Toledo.

Hune, S. (1985). Drafting an international convention on the protection and rights of all migrant workers and their families. *International Migration Review, Autumn,* 570–615.

Kuperschmidt, J. B., & Martin, S. L. (1997). Mental health problems of children of migrant and seasonal farm workers: A pilot study. *Journal of American Academy of Child and Adolescent Psychiatry, 36,* 224–232.

Kuperschmidt, J. B., & Martin, S. L. (June 20, 2003). Migrant farm workers finding success in MSU program. *Lansing State Journal, 1,* 4A.

Lerner, J. (1994). *Working women and their families.* Thousand Oaks, CA: Sage.

Manaster, G. J., Chan, J. C., & Safady, R. (1992). Mexican-American migrant students academic success: Sociological and psychological acculturation. *Adolesence, 27, 105,* 123–136.

Martin, P. (1999). Guest worker policies: An international survey. In A. Berstein & M. Weiner (Eds.), *Migration and refugee policies: An overview* (pp. 45–83). London: Pinter.

Martin, P. L., & Martin, D. A. (1994). *The endless quest: Helping america's farm workers.* Boulder, CO: Westview Press.

McCloskey, D. (October 2000). Working with children of migrant farm workers: Some practical interventions. *National Association of School Psychologists Communique.* Bethesda, MD: National Mental Health and Education Center.

Meece, D., Barratt, M., Kossek, E., & Hawkins, D. (2003, April). *Family, work, and infant care in limited income Latino migrant farm-working and Anglo non-migrant families.* Paper presented at the biannual meeting of the Society for Research in Child Development, Tampa, FL.

Michigan Commission on Spanish Speaking Affairs. (1997). *Michigan's Hispanic community: A profile.* Lansing, MI: Department of Civil Rights.

Morse, S. (1988, October). *Characteristics of migrant secondary students* (Outreach Meeting Report. ERIC No. ED 319 550).

National Center for Farmworker Health, Inc. (2002). *Overview of America's farmworkers: The agricultural economy.* [On-line]. Retrieved February 19, 2002, from http://www.ncfh.org/index.shtml.

Nixon, R. (1996). Caution: Children at work. *The Progressive, 60,* 30–32.

Robinson, M. (2001). The protection of human rights in migrant flows. *Migration World Magazine, 29,* 5.

Roeder, V. D., & Millard, A. V. (2000, August). *Gender and employment among Latino migrant farmworkers in Michigan*, (JSRI Working Paper #52). East Lansing, MI: The Julian Samora Research Institute, Michigan State University.

Rosenbaum, R. P. (2001b). *The direct economic impact of migrant farmworkers on southeastern Michigan*, (JSRI Working Paper #56). East Lansing, MI: The Julian Samora Research Institute, Michigan State University,

Slesinger, D. P. (1992). Health status and needs of migrant farm workers in the United States: A literature review. *Journal of Rural Health, 8*, 227–234.

United States Census Bureau. (1999). *Profile of foreign-born population in the United States: 1997*. (Current Populations Reports, 23–195).

United States Census Bureau. (2000). *The Hispanic population in the United States: 2001*. (Populations Characteristics, 5).

United States Department of Health and Human Services, Administration for Children and Families (2001). *Head Start Fact Sheet*, p. 4.

United States Department of Labor. (2000). [On-line]. Available: www.dol.gov.

United States National Advisory Council on Migrant Health. (1995). *Losing ground: The condition of farmworkers in America*. Bethesda, MD: U.S. Department of Health and Human Services, Health Resources and Services Administration.

U.S. Federal Register, February 14, 2002, Vol. 67, No. 31 pp. 6931–6933 or http://aspe.hhs.gov/poverty/02poverty.htm

van de Vijver, F. J., Helms-Lorenz, M., & Feitzer, M. 1999. *International Journal of Psychology, 34*(3), 149–162.

Velazquez, L. C. (1996). Voices from the fields: Community-based migrant education. *New Directions for Adult and Continuing Education, 70*, 27–35.

Zambrana, R., & Dorrington, C. (1998). Economic and social vulnerability of Latino children and families by subgroup: Implications for child welfare. *Child Welfare, 77*, 5–27.

Zanner, K., & Stevens, G. (October 2001). *A guide to better understanding of Latino family culture*. Lincoln, NE: Institute of Agricultural and Natural Resources, Cooperative Extension.

3

An International Comparative Study of Work–Family Stress and Occupational Strain

Paul E. Spector and
Tammy D. Allen
University of South Florida

Steven Poelmans
IESE, University of
Navarra, Spain

Cary L. Cooper
University of Manchester
Institute of Science and
Technology, UK

Peggy Bernin
National Institute for
Psychosocial Factors and
Health, Sweden

Peter Hart
University of Melbourne,
Australia

Luo Lu
Fu-Jen University, Taiwan

Karen Miller
University of
Witwatersrand,
South Africa

Lucio Renault de Moraes
Federal University of Minas
Gerais, Brazil

Gabrielle M. Ostrognay
University of Melbourne,
Australia

Horea Pitariu
Babes-Bolyai University,
Romania

Vladimir Salamatov
Ukrainian Academy of
Public Administration,
Ukraine

Jesus Salgado
University of Santiago,
Spain

Juan I. Sanchez
Florida International
University, U.S.

Oi Ling Siu
Lingnan University, Hong
Kong

Mare Teichmann
Tallinn Technical University,
Estonia

Töres Theorell
National Institute for
Psychosocial Factors and
Health, Sweden

Peter Vlerick
Ghent University, Belgium

Maria Widerszal-Bazyl
Central Institute for Labour
Protection, Poland

Shanfa Yu
Henan Institute of
Occupational Medicine,
China

INTRODUCTION

As businesses continue to globalize, organizational research from an international perspective has become increasingly important. The area of work and family is no exception. To develop general models of the work and family interface, we need a better understanding of work and family issues within different cultural contexts. Yet strikingly little work and family research has been conducted outside of the United States and other Western nations. In this chapter, data from the Collaborative International Study of Managerial Stress (CISMS), which includes a sample of managers from 18 diverse countries throughout the world, will be described. Descriptive data concerning the linkages between work–family pressure and several known correlates (work hours, number of children, job satisfaction, mental well-being, and physical well-being) will be presented. Differences in reported levels of each of these variables will also be described. First, we provide a brief review of the relevant existing literature.

THEORETICAL FRAMEWORK

According to the rational model of work–family conflict (WFC), conflict will increase in proportion to the amount of time expended in a role (Gutek, Searle, & Klepa, 1991; Pleck, 1985). Consistent with this view, research generally shows that as the number of work hours increases, the greater the likelihood that individuals will report experiencing WFC (e.g., Frone, Russell, & Cooper, 1993; Gutek et al., 1991; Holahan & Gilbert, 1979). These findings have held in studies conducted in nonwestern countries such as Singapore (Aryee, 1992) and Israel (Shamir, 1983). Interestingly, in the one comparative work and family stress study, Yang, Chen, Choi, and Zou (2000) investigated the relationship between work hours and work–family conflict using samples from China and from the United States. In support of their speculation that time at work is time away from family for individualists but not collectivists, working hours related significantly to work–family conflict for Americans, but not for Chinese. Thus, Yang et al. (2000) provided some initial evidence that the relationship between work–family conflict and work hours may not be universal across all cultural contexts.

Having children in the home increases one's obligations to the family role and heightens the opportunity for work and family conflicts to occur. The demands increase as the number of children increase. Indeed, research generally demonstrates that the greater the number of children in the home, the greater the level of work–family conflict reported (e.g., Beutell & Wittig-Berman, 1999; Carlson, 1999; Eagle, Miles, & Icenogle, 1997; Grandey & Cropanzano, 1999). These findings have also been reported with a sample of Finnish dual-career couples (Kinnunen & Mauno, 1998). However, it is interesting to note that Shamir (1983) did not find a higher level of conflict among hotel employees in Israel with dependent children than employees without children. Because the amount of support provided to working parents, such as child-care assistance and paid parental leave, varies substantially from country to country (see Waldfogel, 2001 for a review), it is likely that the relationship between number of children and work–family stress also differs across countries.

One of the most frequently studied variables in relation to work–family conflict has been job satisfaction (Bruck, Allen, & Spector, 2002). Several meta-analytic studies demonstrated a moderately strong relationship between work–family conflict and job satisfaction (Allen, Herst, Bruck, & Sutton, 2000; Kossek & Ozeki, 1998). Some of this research includes studies conducted in cultural contexts outside of the United States. For example, greater work–family conflict has been negatively associated with job satisfaction among hotel workers in Jerusalem (Shamir, 1983); Israeli male prison guards (Drory & Shamir, 1988); Canadian professional and managerial women (Beatty, 1996); married nurses, managers, and social workers from Hong Kong (Chiu, 1998); and professionals employed in Singapore (Aryee, 1992; Chan, Lai, Ko, & Boey, 2000). However, not all research outside the United States has been as consistent. Specifically, several studies conducted in Hong Kong found no relationship between work–family conflict and job satisfaction (Aryee & Luk, 1996; Aryee, Luk, Leung, & Lo, 1999).

One of the most critical reasons to be concerned with work–family conflict is that it has been associated with decreased mental and physical well-being. Allen et al. (2000) reported a mean correlation of .29 between work–family conflict and general psychological strain and a mean correlation of .29 between work–family conflict and somatic symptoms. Their review of the literature concerning psychological and physical well-being revealed only two studies conducted in nonwestern settings (Kinnunen & Mauno, 1998; Matsui, Ohsawa, & Onglatco, 1995). However, it should be noted that a relationship between WFC and burnout has also been reported based on samples from Singapore (Aryee, 1993) and Israel (Izraeli, 1988). Perhaps one of the most compelling studies of the detrimental impact of work–family conflict on well-being was recently provided by Frone (2000). Frone examined the relationship between WFC and employee psychiatric disorders using a large nationally representative U.S sample. Results showed that participants who reported family interfered with work (FIW) were 30 times more likely to report a mood disorder than those not experiencing FIW. Moreover, individuals who reported work interfered with family (WIF) were three times more likely to report a mood disorder than those not experiencing WIF. Because of the consistent results across a variety of studies, we expect that the relationship between WFC and well-being may be quite reliable across a variety of cultural contexts.

As mentioned previously and as demonstrated throughout our brief review, the research involving common correlates of work–family conflict includes very little work conducted outside of the United States and other Western cultures. Furthermore, little of this research has been comparative, contrasting results across countries. The CISMS study provided a unique opportunity to begin addressing questions concerning the universality of several established relationships in the work and family literature. Although most work–family studies have focused specifically on work–family conflict, our study investigated a related construct of work–family pressure. Rather than asking the extent to which work and family demands are in conflict, the pressure scales ask the extent to which work–family demands are a source of pressure or distress. In this chapter, we explore relations of work–family pressure with other variables across a diverse sample of countries. We included variables expected in Western countries to relate to pressure, either as potential antecedents (number of children, working hours) or consequences (job satisfaction, mental strain, and

physical strain). Our purpose was to see if results from Western countries could be generalized.

METHOD

Sample

The data reported here are a subset of the 31 country/territory Collaborative International Study of Managerial Stress (CISMS) founded
in 1996 by Cary L. Cooper and Paul E. Spector. More details on the
participants and method can be found in Spector, Cooper et al. (2001,
2002). For this chapter we chose data from 18 countries/territories
that met the following conditions: Sample size was at least 87, no
more than 89% of the sample was of the same gender, and all variables
were included. There were 3,397 participants across the 18 samples,
but 26 were dropped due to missing data on the country variable,
and 55 were dropped for having extreme values on work hours (see
description of work hours measure below), leaving 3,316 for analysis. Sample size, percent of males, and mean age for each sample is
shown in Table 3.1. Because of missing data on individual variables,

TABLE 3.1
Summary of Demographic Variables for Country Samples

Country	Sample Size	Percent Male	Mean Age
Australia	277–283	60	44
Belgium	172	70	35
Brazil	117	64	37
China (PRC)	194	70	41
Colombia	90–97	70	35
Estonia	150–151	57	39
Hong Kong	250	58	35
Mexico	102–103	83	41
Poland	239–240	60	45
Portugal	82–87	86	41
Romania	131	50	40
South Africa	120	72	37
Spain	148–158	83	38
Sweden	228–232	79	46
Taiwan	306–309	56	38
UK	200	56	44
Ukraine	196	49	39
US	116–117	56	44

Note. Sample sizes were variable due to missing data for some countries

sample sizes varied somewhat across analyses. Sample sizes per sample ranged from 87 (Portugal) to 309 (Taiwan). All participants in the analyses were managers, varying in level from first line supervisors to top management.

Measures

The data reported here came from a larger questionnaire of managerial stress. Included was the UK developed Occupational Stress Indicator-2 (OSI2; Cooper & Williams, 1996), questions concerning demographics and working hours, and additional scales not of interest here. The Work–Family Pressure Scale consisted of nine items from the OSI2 pressure subscale. Six response choices ranged from *very definitely is not a source* to *very definitely is a source* of pressure or stress. Each item dealt with issues that involved work and home, such as "taking my work home" and "demands my work makes on relationships with spouse/children." High scores represent high levels of work–family pressure. As noted above, the pressure scale is more of a measure of work–family distress or the extent to which work–family issues serve as stressors than it is a measure of work–family conflict per se. As shown in Table 3.2, the internal consistency reliabilities (coefficient alpha) ranged from .71 to .86 across samples.

Three scales assessed well-being at work: job satisfaction, mental well-being, and physical well-being. High scores indicate well-being and low scores indicate strain. The *job satisfaction* scale contained 12 items using 6-point scales ranging from *very much dissatisfaction* to *very much satisfaction*. A sample item is "The kind of work or tasks that you are required to perform." Internal consistencies ranged from .83 to .92 across samples (see Table 4.1). The *mental well-being* scale consisted of 12 items, each of which had 6 response choices that varied across items. For example, the item "concerning work and life in general, would you describe yourself as someone who is bothered by their troubles or a 'worrier'?" had choices ranging from *definitely yes* to *definitely no*. Internal consistencies (see Table 4.1) ranged from .75 to .87. The *physical well-being* scale had 6 items with 6 response choices ranging from *never* to *very frequently*. The items concerned physical symptoms, such as "feeling unaccountably tired or exhausted." Internal consistencies ranged from .70 to .84 across the 18 samples (see Table 4.1).

A single question asked gender (coded male = 1, female = 2) and number of children living in the home. A question also asked about hours worked in a typical week. Cases were considered outliers and

TABLE 3.2
Internal Consistency Reliabilities (Coefficient Alpha) for Multi-Item Measures

Country	Work–Family Pressure	Job Satisfaction	Mental Well-Being	Physical Well-Being
Australia	.85	.90	.87	.76
Belgium	.82	.85	.81	.76
Brazil	.71	.91	.78	.83
China (PRC)	.82	.91	.75	.74
Colombia	.77	.91	.78	.78
Estonia	.82	.84	.76	.70
Hong Kong	.84	.91	.84	.76
Mexico	.84	.92	.81	.83
Poland	.83	.89	.84	.77
Portugal	.78	.92	.83	.76
Romania	.74	.88	.78	.78
South Africa	.83	.91	.85	.82
Spain	.81	.92	.82	.76
Sweden	.78	.83	.83	.75
Taiwan	.81	.92	.80	.82
UK	.85	.89	.76	.84
Ukraine	.84	.86	.82	.82
US	.86	.90	.86	.84

excluded if they reported working fewer than 15 hours/week or more than 89 hours/week.

Procedure

The main CISMS questionnaire was designed by the project's organizers. Partners in countries where English was not the native language (except for Sweden where the English version was used) translated and then back-translated the questionnaire to ensure meaning equivalence. In the majority of cases, methods were used to assure reasonably representative samples from native companies (as opposed to foreign multinationals). In a few cases samples were limited to a small number of companies. Data were all sent to the organizers for analysis, which was done with SAS 8.02.

Results

One-way analyses of variance were conducted on the six major variables in the study (see Tables 3.3 and 3.4). In all cases, there were

TABLE 3.3
Mean Comparisons for Work–Family Pressure, Work Hours, and Number
of Children

Work–Family Pressure		Work Hours		Number of Children	
Country	Mean	Country	Mean	Country	Mean
Taiwan	35.6[a]	Colombia	52.7[a]	Mexico	2.6[a]
Hong Kong	34.6[a]	Spain	52.3[a]	Portugal	2.5[a]
Portugal	34.2[a-b]	Sweden	50.9[a-b]	Spain	2.1[b]
Poland	32.6[b-c]	US	50.0[b]	Colombia	2.0[b]
Brazil	32.5[b-c]	Hong Kong	49.6[b-c]	Sweden	1.4[c]
Spain	32.2[c-d]	Mexico	49.5[b-c]	Brazil	1.3[c-d]
Romania	32.2[c-d]	Portugal	49.1[b-c]	Taiwan	1.2[c-e]
Mexico	32.1[c-e]	Australia	49.0[b-c]	Poland	1.2[c-e]
Belgium	30.9[c-e]	South Africa	49.0[b-c]	Romania	1.2[c-e]
Estonia	30.8[c-e]	Taiwan	47.5[c-d]	China (PRC)	1.1[c-f]
Colombia	30.6[c-e]	Belgium	46.7[d-e]	Australia	1.1[d-f]
South Africa	30.4[d-e]	Poland	46.6[d-e]	Estonia	1.1[e-f]
Sweden	29.5[e]	UK	46.2[d-e]	UK	1.0[e-f]
China (PRC)	29.1[e]	Estonia	46.2[d-e]	South Africa	1.0[e-f]
US	26.9[f]	Romania	45.8[d-e]	Ukraine	1.0[f]
Ukraine	26.2[f-g]	Brazil	45.2[e-f]	Belgium	1.0[f]
UK	25.8[f-g]	China (PRC)	43.3[f]	US	0.6[g]
Australia	24.9[g]	Ukraine	40.0[g]	Hong Kong	0.5[g]

$F(17, 3139) = 32.8$, $R^2 = .15$ $F(17, 3398) = 22.5$, $R^2 = .10$ $F(17, 3253) = 42.5$, $R^2 = .18$

Note. Means within columns with the same superscript numbers are not significantly
different from one another.

significant differences among the countries/territories at $p < .0001$.
As can be seen in the table, Taiwan and Hong Kong reported the highest levels of work–family pressure, whereas the UK and Australia reported the lowest. Colombia and Spain reported working the most
hours, whereas China and Ukraine reported the fewest. Mexico and
Portugal had the most children, and United States and Hong Kong had
the fewest. As far as well-being, it can be seen that Mexico, Sweden,
United States, and Belgium were consistently near the top on all three
measures. The UK was lowest on all three with Hong Kong also being
consistently low.

Table 3.5 contains correlations of work–family pressure with work
hours, number of children, and the three measures of well-being.
Of note is that the correlation with work hours was significant only
for Australia, the UK and the United States. In all these cases, more
hours were associated with higher work–family pressure. Number of
children was related to work–family pressure for Australia and for
the United States and for Romania and Sweden, with more children

TABLE 3.4
Mean Comparisons for Job Satisfaction, Mental Well-Being and Physical Well-Being

Job Satisfaction		Mental Well-Being		Physical Well-Being	
Country	Mean	Country	Mean	Country	Mean
Mexico	53.5[a]	US	52.3[a]	Portugal	28.8[a]
Colombia	51.0[b]	Belgium	51.1[a-b]	Sweden	28.6[a]
Estonia	50.3[b-c]	Mexico	49.6[b-c]	Belgium	28.1[a-b]
Sweden	50.2[b-d]	China (PRC)	49.6[b-c]	US	27.6[a-c]
Belgium	49.9[b-d]	Portugal	49.3[b-c]	Colombia	27.2[b-c]
US	49.8[b-d]	Australia	49.3[b-c]	Spain	26.9[b-d]
Ukraine	48.9[b-e]	Sweden	49.2[b-c]	Romania	26.5[c-e]
Portugal	48.7[b-e]	Poland	48.0[c-d]	Mexico	26.5[c-e]
Poland	48.1[c-e]	South Africa	47.9[c-d]	Estonia	26.4[c-e]
Spain	47.9[d-e]	Taiwan	47.5[c-d]	Australia	25.6[d-f]
Brazil	47.3[e-f]	Romania	46.9[d-e]	Poland	25.5[d-f]
Taiwan	47.3[e-f]	Spain	46.5[d-e]	Ukraine	25.3[e-f]
Australia	46.7[e-g]	Brazil	46.5[e]	Taiwan	25.1[e-f]
South Africa	45.4[f-h]	Hong Kong	46.4[d-f]	Brazil	24.9[f]
Romania	45.2[f-h]	Colombia	46.3[d-f]	China (PRC)	24.6[f]
China (PRC)	44.7[g-h]	Estonia	46.3[d-f]	South Africa	24.3[f]
Hong Kong	43.3[h-i]	Ukraine	45.2[e-f]	Hong Kong	22.9[g]
UK	42.0[i]	UK	44.2[f]	UK	20.8[h]

$F(17, 3287) = 16.6$, $R^2 = .08$ $F(17, 3286) = 8.6$, $R^2 = .04$ $F(17, 3293) = 23.2$, $R^2 = .11$

Note. Means within columns with the same superscript numbers are not significantly different from one another.

associated with more pressure. However, in Hong Kong, the relation was significant but reversed, with more children associated with lower pressure. There were 6 of 18 significant correlations with job satisfaction. Most of the samples showed significant negative correlations of mental and physical well-being with pressure (14 and 15 significant correlations for mental and physical well-being, respectively).

Discussion

The goal of this study was to provide comparative data on work–family stress across a diverse group of countries in order to show if findings from Western countries similar to the United States would generalize. Results showed that in some cases results were fairly universal but in others they were not. Furthermore, there were significant mean differences for all of our variables compared across our 18 samples. Clearly, results are not the same everywhere.

TABLE 3.5
Correlations of Work–Family Pressure with Work Hours, Number of Children,
and Well-Being

Country	Work Hours	Number of Children	Job Satisfaction	Mental Well-Being	Physical Well-Being
Australia	.23*	.16*	−.06	−.47*	−.40*
Belgium	−.09	.11	.07	−.37*	−.23*
Brazil	−.05	−.12	−.11	−.18	−.27*
China (PRC)	−.06	−.00	−.03	−.22*	−.15*
Colombia	−.07	−.01	−.24*	−.21*	−.24*
Estonia	.04	−.10	−.12	−.21*	−.22*
Hong Kong	−.08	−.14*	−.14*	−.14*	−.17*
Mexico	.01	−.04	−.15	−.46*	−.37*
Poland	.07	.02	−.07	−.13	−.11
Portugal	.16	.01	.08	−.18	−.26*
Romania	.04	.19*	−.04	.03	−.19*
South Africa	.03	.06	.06	−.25*	−.10
Spain	−.08	.03	−.16*	−.17*	−.26*
Sweden	−.13	.17*	−.18*	−.23*	−.17*
Taiwan	.01	−.08	−.18*	−.25*	−.14*
UK	.27*	.10	−.05	−.20*	−.01
Ukraine	−.03	−.03	−.29*	−.42*	−.31*
US	.23*	.23*	−.07	−.24*	−.32*

$*p < .05.$

Our measure of work–family pressure differed considerably across countries. To some extent, the more Western countries, such as Australia, the UK and the United States had lower levels than Asian (Taiwan and Hong Kong) and East European (Poland and Romania) countries, but the pattern was not completely clear-cut, as one Asian country (PR China) was fifth lowest and was not significantly different from Sweden.

Weekly work hours were quite varied from 40 (Ukraine) to 52 (Columbia). Number of children residing with the participant also differed considerably from an average of .5 children in Hong Kong to 2.6 in Mexico. Despite its low level of children in the home, Hong Kong was second highest in work–family pressure. The pattern of means across samples was not completely consistent for job satisfaction and the two well-being measures. Job satisfaction tended to be relatively high for Latin countries (Mexico and Colombia) and low for Asians (PR China and Hong Kong), although this distinction is not completely consistent (e.g., Brazil and Taiwan were not significantly different from one another). The most consistent country was the UK, which was lowest on all three measures.

One should be cautious in the interpretation of the work–family pressure, job satisfaction, and well-being measures. One cannot be certain if the differences found reflect real discrepancies in these variables or merely reflect cultural response bias (Triandis, 1994; Van de Vijver & Leung, 1997). For example, an Asian tendency toward modesty might have reduced their scores on job satisfaction and well-being.

Our results were consistent with Yang et al. (2000) in showing that in the U.S. sample there was a significant correlation between work–family pressure and work hours, but there was no significant correlation in any of the three Chinese samples, and in fact in two of the cases (PR China and Hong Kong) the sign of the correlation was opposite to that of the U.S. sample. Furthermore, only Australia and the UK joined the United States in having a significant correlation, suggesting that working hours might be important only in Anglo countries. Yang et al. (2000) suggest that these differences may be due to culture values, specifically individualism-collectivism. Individualistic Westerners tend to view long work hours differently from collectivistic Asians and others. However, the lack of correlation occurred even in countries that tended to be individualistic, such as Belgium and Sweden, so there are apparently other culture/country differences beyond I-C that contribute to these results. Further research is needed to further explore why there are inconsistent results across countries. One factor to consider is how time is spent outside of work. For example, fewer working hours may not translate into less work–family pressure if the time spent outside of work is on low-schedule-control chores such as preparing meals, doing laundry, and other household tasks (Barnett & Gareis, 2002). Indeed, working more hours could free individuals from engaging in these types of nonwork tasks that also contribute to work–family pressure and conflict.

Number of children in the home also related to work–family pressure in the United States as expected, but again this was not a universal finding. A similar significant correlation was found in Australia and Sweden, but in Hong Kong the relation was opposite to the United States (more children was associated with lower pressure). This suggests that the impact of children in the home may well be different in most countries outside of the United States. The differences may be due to the great deal of variation in family support systems such as government sponsored childcare (Waldfogel, 2001) and kinship ties (Rothausen, 1999) that exist across countries. Another possibility is that for those in countries with high unemployment, such as East Europe, economic stressors may be far more important than number of children and may overshadow its potential impact.

We expected to find a correlation between work–family pressure and job satisfaction in the United States, but results were counter to our predictions. One possible explanation is that we did not assess work–family conflict, which has been linked consistently to job satisfaction. Work–family pressure might not be related to job satisfaction in the United States (or most of our other samples), as perhaps it relates more strongly to general family satisfaction or general well-being. In fact, in most of our samples, this work–family measure was significantly related to both mental and physical well-being, suggesting that this link may be almost universal.

One factor to consider in reviewing this research is that our measure of work–family pressure was developed within a Western context. Accordingly, it may not have fully captured the types of work–family pressures found in non-Western countries. The content validity of work and family measures developed by Western researchers when applied cross-nationally remains an issue for future research.

The results of this study illustrate the need for cross-national comparative research in the work–family area. Two established antecedents of work–family conflict, children in the home and work hours, related to work–family pressure as expected in our U.S. sample but not in most of our other samples from across the globe. On the other hand, mental and physical well-being related to work–family pressure in most cases, suggesting close to universality. Clearly, more comparative research is needed in the area to help us understand how the dynamics of work and family within a cultural and national context, contributes to stress and well-being.

REFERENCES

Allen, T. D., Herst, D. E. L., Bruck, C. S., & Sutton, M. (2000). Consequences associated with work-to-family conflict: A review and agenda for future research. *Journal of Occupational Health Psychology, 5,* 278–308.

Aryee, S. (1992). Antecedents and outcomes of work–family conflict among married professional women: Evidence from Singapore. *Human Relations, 45,* 813–837.

Aryee, S. (1993). Dual-earner couples in Singapore: An examination of work and nonwork sources of their experienced burnout. *Human Relations, 46,* 1441–1468.

Aryee, S., & Luk, V. (1996). Work and nonwork influences on the career satisfaction of dual-earner couples. *Journal of Vocational Behavior, 49,* 38–52.

Aryee, S., Luk, V., Leung, A., & Lo, S. (1999). Role stressors, interrole conflict, and well-being: The moderating influence of spousal support and coping behaviors among employed parents in Hong Kong. *Journal of Vocational Behavior, 54*, 259–278.

Barnett, R. C., & Gareis, K. C. (2002). Full-time and reduced hours work schedules and marital quality: A study of female physicians with young children. *Work and Occupations, 29*, 364–379.

Beatty, C. A. (1996). The stress of managerial and professional women: Is the price too high? *Journal of Organizational Behavior, 17*, 233–251.

Beutell, N. J., & Wittig-Berman, U. (1999). Predictors of work–family conflict and satisfaction with family, job, career, and life. *Psychological Reports, 85*, 893–903.

Bruck, C. S., Allen, T. D., & Spector, P. E. (2002). The relation between work–family conflict and job satisfaction: A finer-grained analysis. *Journal of Vocational Behavior, 60*, 336–353.

Carlson, D. S. (1999). Personality and role variables as predictors of three forms of work–family conflict. *Journal of Vocational Behavior, 55*, 236–253.

Chan, K. B., Lai, G., Ko, Y. C., & Boey, K. W. (2000). Work stress among six professional groups: The Singapore experience. *Social Science & Medicine, 50*, 1415–1432.

Chiu, R. K. (1998). Relationships among role conflicts, role satisfactions, and life satisfaction: Evidence from Hong Kong. *Social Behavior and Personality, 26*, 409–414.

Cooper, C. L., & Williams, S. (1996). *Occupational Stress Indicator Version 2.0*. Windsor, UK: NFER-Nelson.

Drory, A., & Shamir, B. (1988). Effects of organizational and life variables on job satisfaction and burnout. *Group & Organization Studies, 13*, 441–455.

Eagle, B. W., Miles, E. W., & Icenogle, M. L. (1997). Interrole conflicts and the permeability of work and family domains: Are there gender differences? *Journal of Vocational Behavior, 50*, 168–183.

Frone, M. R. (2000). Work–family conflict and employee psychiatric disorders: The national comorbidity survey. *Journal of Applied Psychology, 85*, 888–895.

Frone, M. R., Russell, M., & Cooper, M. L. (1993). Relationship of work–family conflict, gender, and alcohol expectancies to alcohol use/abuse. *Journal of Organizational Behavior, 14*, 545–558.

Grandey, A. A., & Cropanzano, R. (1999). The conservation of resources model applied to work–family conflict and strain. *Journal of Vocational Behavior, 54*, 350–370.

Gutek, B., Searle, S., & Klepa, L. (1991). Rational versus gender role explanations for work–family conflict. *Journal of Applied Psychology, 76*, 560–568.

Holahan, C. K., & Gilbert, L. A. (1979). Conflict between major life roles: Women and men in dual career couples. *Human Relations, 32*, 451–467.

Izraeli, D. N. (1988). Burning out in medicine: A comparison of husbands and wives in dual-career couples. *Journal of Social Behavior and Personality, 3,* 329–346.

Kinnunen, U., & Mauno, S. (1998). Antecedents and outcomes of work–family conflict among employed women and men in Finland. *Human Relations, 51,* 157–177.

Kossek, E. E., & Ozeki, C. (1998). Work–family conflict, policies, and the job-life satisfaction relationship: A review and directions for organizational behavior-human resources research. *Journal of Applied Psychology, 83,* 139–149.

Matsui, T., Ohsawa, T., & Onglatco, M. (1995). Work–family conflict and the stress-buffering effects of husband support and coping behavior among Japanese married working women. *Journal of Vocational Behavior, 47,* 178–192.

Pleck, J. H. (1985). *Working wives/working husbands.* Beverly Hills, CA: Sage.

Rothausen, T. J. (1999). 'Family' in organizational research: A review and comparison of definitions and measures. *Journal of Organizational Behavior, 20,* 817–836.

Shamir, B. (1983). Some antecedents of work–family conflict. *Journal of Vocational Behavior, 23,* 98–111.

Spector, P. E., Cooper, C. L., Sanchez, J. I., O'Driscoll, M., Sparks, K., Bernin, P., Büssing, A., Dewe, P., Hart, P., Lu, L., Miller, K., Renault de Moraes, L., Ostrognay, G. M., Pagon, M., Pitariu, H., Poelmans, S., Radhakrishnan, P., Russinova, V., Salamatov, V., Salgado, J., Shima, S., Siu, O. L., Stora, J. B., Teichmann, M., Theorell, T., Vlerick, P., Westman, M., Widerszal-Bazyl, M., Wong, P., & Yu, S. (2001). Do national levels of individualism and internal locus of control relate to well-being: An ecological level international study, *Journal of Organizational Behavior, 22,* 815–832 .

Spector, P. E., Cooper, C. L., Sanchez, J. I., O'Driscoll, M., Sparks, K., Bernin, P., Büssing, A., Dewe, P., Hart, P., Lu, L., Miller, K., Renault de Moraes, L., Ostrognay, G. M., Pagon, M., Pitariu, H., Poelmans, S., Radhakrishnan, P., Russinova, V., Salamatov, V., Salgado, J, Shima, S., Siu, O. L., Stora, J. B., Teichmann, M., Theorell, T., Vlerick, P., Westman, M., Widerszal-Bazyl, M., Wong, P., & Yu, S. (2002). A 24 nation/territory study of work locus of control in relation to well-being at work: How generalizable are western findings? *Academy of Management Journal, 45,* 453–466.

Triandis, H. C. (1994). *Culture and social behavior.* New York: McGraw-Hill.

Van de Vijver, F., & Leung, K. (1997). *Methods and data analysis for cross-cultural research.* Thousand Oaks, CA: Sage.

Waldfogel, J. (2001). International policies toward parental leave and child-care. *The Future of Children, 11*(1), 101.

Yang, N., Chen, C. C., Choi, J., & Zou, Y. (2000). Sources of work–family conflict: A Sino-U.S. comparison of the effects of work and family demands. *Academy of Management Journal, 41,* 113–123.

II

Organizational–International Perspective

4

Work–Family Culture in Organizations: Theoretical and Empirical Approaches

Ulla Kinnunen and Saija Mauno
University of Jyväskylä, Finland

Sabine Geurts and Josje Dikkers
Radboud University Nijmegen, The Netherlands

ABSTRACT

In this chapter, we shall discuss the role of work–family culture reconciling the demands of work and family in organizations. We have three primary aims: The first is theoretical: to theorize work–family culture from the perspective of organizational culture; the second is empirical: to present a review of the existing literature on work–family culture and provide directions for future research; and the third is practical: to make suggestions for creating family-friendly organizations.

INTRODUCTION

It is widely assumed that work–family policies (e.g., child care, reduced working hours, job sharing) can enhance the positive reconciliation of employment and family life. On the one hand, such policies enhance opportunities for women in working life and are seen as a practical response to the increasing proportion of women in the work force. On the other hand, men are placing increasing value on their family roles and showing greater willingness to modify their work in the interests of their families, particularly among the younger generation. Work–family policies, therefore, enhance opportunities for men to become more involved in family life.

However, although organizations may have formal work–family policies in place, employees may be reluctant to take advantage of them. It seems that these policies are generally perceived as enabling those with family commitments to work at the margins, seldom challenging the traditional patterns of work as the norm and ideal (Lewis, 2001). According to Lewis (1997, 2001), the traditional male model of work, one which constructs the ideal worker as one who works continuously and full-time and does not allow family to interfere with work, continues to prevail the norm. Because the male model of work is deeply embedded in most organizational cultures, we need to move beyond the formulation of policies to organizational culture, in seeking an answer to this basic problem of the lack of use of work–family initiatives (Blair-Loy & Wharton, 2002; Judiesch & Lyness, 1999; Lewis, 1997, 2001).

In addition to this theoretical aim—understanding work–family culture from the perspective of organizational culture—we have also an empirical aim, that is, to present a review of the findings of the empirical studies in the field. In this review, we focus on the following issues: Does the prevailing work–family culture truly contribute to the utilization of work–family arrangements, as has been suggested? What do we know about the outcomes of work–family cultures for employees and the organizations? Finally, we try to put the theory as well as the empirical findings into a practical context and give some suggestions on how family-friendly organizations might be created.

THEORETICAL FRAMEWORK: WORK–FAMILY CULTURE IN ORGANIZATIONS

General Perspectives on Organizational Culture Theories

Organizational culture is a very complex multilevel dynamic phenomenon and for this reason it is difficult to provide any universal definition for the concept (see Martin, 2002, for a review of different definitions). Consequently, it is not possible within the scope of this article to provide a comprehensive overview of organizational culture; rather our intention is to introduce some of the basic and commonly agreed characteristics of organizational culture.

Despite the fact that different organizational culture theories emphasize different constructs and processes (e.g., basic assumptions, practices, or values), some general agreement exists on the characteristics of organizational culture. For example, the overwhelming majority of scholars (see e.g., Isaac & Pitt, 2001; Lundberg, 2001; Martin, 2002; Sackmann, 2001) agree that organizational culture is a socially learned and transmitted group-level phenomenon, comprising many different visible or conscious, and invisible or subconscious, "deep" cognitive, behavioral and emotional aspects. These aspects are responsible for the rules governing organizational behavior and for the particular characteristics of an organization or a unit/group within that organization.

There is also some agreement on how organizational culture manifests itself in organizations. In our view, this can be seen to occur at two different levels, either as phenomena at the abstract (ideal) level or as phenomena at the concrete (material) level (see also Martin, 2002). At the more abstract level, are those phenomena that cannot easily be detected or known, values in particular, but this category also includes ideologies, beliefs, meanings, and discourses that the employees of a particular organization or work unit share. However, even though many scholars agree on these cultural manifestations, they disagree on the extent to which they are open to examination. For example, regarding values, Hofstede (2001) considers these to be invisible cultural phenomena that are so abstract and "deep" that examining them for organizational differences is extremely difficult. Other researchers perceive values as the most important cultural manifestation and one that can be examined both inside and between organizations, e.g., via surveys (e.g., Cameron & Quinn, 1999; Denison, 2001). At the more concrete or material level, in turn, are those issues that are easier to see, "feel," and research, for example, physical arrangements, dress codes, everyday practices in organizations, symbols, and rituals (e.g., Schein, 1985, 1990, 1999). According to Hofstede (2001), therefore, organizational culture within an organization manifests itself most visibly via organizational practices, encompassing such everyday actions as how things get done, how people in the organization are expected to behave, think, and feel as well as symbols and rituals (see also Sackmann, 2001).

As stated above, researchers seem to agree—at least to some degree—on the most typical characteristics of organizational culture. However, they do not agree on the epistemological or methodological issues relating to organizational culture. Consequently, organizational culture is usually approached from either an interpretative or functionalistic perspective (Davey & Symon, 2001; Martin, 2002;

Sackmann, 2001). Adopting the former approach means that organizational culture should be defined and studied as a unique construct, specific to a particular organization (or within an organization). On this definition, the interpretative, inductive research paradigm using qualitative research methods is regarded as the most appropriate in organizational culture research (see Czarniawska-Joerges, 1992; Sackmann, 2001; Schein, 1990, 1999).

The latter, functional perspective, in turn, aims at revealing the role of organizational culture in the various functions of an organization. This type of research is typically concerned with the relationships among organizational culture and productivity, organizational changes, or employees' well-being (e.g., Denison, 2001; Kotter & Heskett, 1992; Kristoff, 1996; O'Reilly, Chatman, & Caldwell, 1991). Hence, functional researchers are often interested in examining "cause-effect" links between culture and various outcomes, for which the deductive research paradigm using quantitative methods is adopted (e.g., Cameron & Quinn, 1999).

However, many researchers have recently emphasized the need for methodological triangulation in exploring organizational culture (Davey & Symon, 2001; Martin, 2002; Sackmann, 2001), suggesting, among other things, that both quantitative and qualitative research methods should be applied in a single study. Unfortunately, this kind of triangulation in studying organizational culture remains rare.

Organizational Culture Theories in the Context of the Work–Family Interface

Recently, some organizational culture theories—or at least some of their ideas—have been adopted in the context of the work–family interface. Of these, we shall briefly discuss the perceived organizational support (POS) theory, the border theory by Sue Campbell Clark and, finally, Susan Lewis' ideas about how to utilize Schein's theory in this context.

Perceived Supportiveness and Work–Family Culture. From the organizational viewpoint, one particularly important concept has been *supportiveness*, which generally refers to the extent that an environment is family-supportive. According to Thomas and Ganster (1995), a family-supportive work environment is composed of two major components: family-supportive policies and family-supportive supervisors. Both components exemplify organizational efforts to support employee needs to balance work and family responsibilities. The group of supportive persons in the organization has been broadened to include colleagues as well as managers and supervisors (e.g., Haas, Allard,

& Hwang, 2002; Dikkers, den Dulk, Geurts, & Peper, 2004; Secret, 2000).

More recently, a supportive work–family culture has been defined as the shared assumptions, beliefs, and values regarding the extent to which, for women and for men, an organization supports and values the integration of work and family lives (Thompson, Beauvais, & Lyness, 1999). According to Thompson et al. (1999), this definition is consistent with both Schein's (1985) and Denison's (1996) conceptualizations of organizational culture as "the deep structure of organizations, which is rooted in values, beliefs, and assumptions held by organizational members" (Denison, 1996, p. 264). Managerial support and sensitivity to employees' family responsibilities form one component of the operationalization of this definition.

No matter what supportive structures and practices an organization has in place, ultimately an organization's supportiveness in work–family issues rests upon employees' perceptions. According to the perceived organizational support (POS) theory, supportiveness is defined as employees' global beliefs concerning the extent to which the organization values their contributions and cares for their well-being (see Behson, 2002; Eisenberger, Huntington, Hutchison, & Sowa, 1986). Perceived organizational support describes employees' attitudinal responses to the organization as a whole, as distinct from the attitudinal response that an employee may form regarding his or her immediate supervisor. Recently, it has been suggested that perceived organizational support (POS) should also include the organization's supportiveness toward the demands of its employees' families (see Allen, 2001); and these employee perceptions are referred to as family-supportive organization perceptions (FSOP).

In line with organizational culture theories, it has been assumed that concrete and abstract manifestations of supportiveness are also learned through socialization processes; i.e., the members of organizations or teams become accustomed to perceiving and treating family life as either a resource or as a burden, which implies that the culture takes either a supportive or a non-supportive attitude to family life (Lewis, 1997; Thompson et al., 1999).

Border Theory and Work–Family Culture. Campbell Clark (2000) has introduced a theoretical framework linking the concepts of the work–family interface and corporate culture. She has developed the work–family border theory, which takes into account the cultural differences between working and family lives. Accordingly, differences exist in the purposes, acceptable behavior, task accomplishment, and communication appropriate at work and at home. Employees, in turn, are seen as "border-crossers," making continuous, daily transitions between their work and family lives (and cultures). For some individuals, the transition (border-crossing) may be slight, as where, for example, language and customs are highly similar in both domains. For others, the language and behavior expected in the work domain are very different from what is expected in the family domain, and thus a more extreme transition is required.

The work–family border theory attempts to explain how individuals manage the borders between work and family in order to balance these two domains. A main proposition of the model is that weak borders (i.e., permeable and flexible) will facilitate the work–family balance where the domains are similar, whereas the opposite (i.e., strong borders) is functional when the domains are very different. According to the theory, the "central participants" in a domain (i.e., those who have influence in that domain because of their competence, affiliation with central members within the domain, and their internalization of the domain's culture and values) have a good ability to control the border with the other domain and, consequently, to attain a good balance between work and family. The opposite is true for so-called "peripheral participants," that is, those who have less influence within the domain because they ignore domain values, have not achieved full competence and do not interact sufficiently with other (central) members within the domain (e.g., supervisors in the work domain, and spouses in the home domain).

According to the theory, organizations can alter domains and borders to enhance the work–family balance, for example, by adding flextime, flex-place, and leave policies or improving the supportiveness of the relationship between border-keepers, such as supervisors, and employees. However, when borders are changed, analogous changes have to be made to the domain's culture and values. For example, a more flexible workplace should be more like employees' homes in terms of values and purposes, but if organizations create flexible work policies to serve their own interests and not those of their employees and families, this leads to unrealized expectations and disillusionment. If it is impossible for an organization to change its culture, then the borders should be kept strong in both directions so that employees can maintain a good balance between work and home.

Schein's Theory and Work–Family Culture. One particular theory, i.e., Edgar Schein's (1985, 1990, 1999) organizational culture theory, has been most widely adopted as a theoretical framework in explaining cultural aspects of the work–family interface. Schein (1990, 1999) proposes that there are three fundamental levels at which culture manifests itself. The first, surface level includes *artifacts,* encompassing every-thing from the physical layout (both organization and personnel) to archival manifestations such as company records and annual reports. The second level includes the kinds of *values, strategies, and ideolo-gies* that are often explicated in organizations, forming both official goals for action and performance and "ideal worker" characteristics. At the most fundamental, "deep" level, are *underlying assumptions,* or paradigms, which are taken for granted, determining all percep-tions, thought processes, feelings, and behavior in an organization. Deeply held assumptions often start out historically as values, but gradually come to be taken for granted and then take on the charac-ter of assumptions (Schein, 1990).

Susan Lewis (1997) has shown how Schein's theory can be utilized in this context. In line with Schein's three operational levels of cul-ture, family-friendly policies can be seen as artifacts, that is, surface level indicators of organizational intentions. These are underpinned by values, such as valuing and wanting to retain highly trained women with family commitments, valuing long hours in the workplace, and valuing employees who do not allow family commitments to intrude in their working lives. Finally, organizational discourses can be re-garded as indicators of values and assumptions, that is, the way in which time, productivity, and commitment are socially constructed. These organizational discourses related to values and assumptions about entitlements and time are seen as major barriers to the effec-tiveness of family-friendly policies.

According to Lewis (2001), the male model of work, which may have seemed appropriate at a time when male breadwinners were the norm, is still deeply embedded in most organizational cultures. Lewis (1999, 2001) mentions at least four assumptions made in the traditional male model of work. First, and most fundamental, are gendered assumptions about the separation of work and home and about the division of labor (men at work, women at home), which result in the greater valuing of male workers or those without active family commitments.

Second, the prevailing traditional male model of work assumes full-time work as the norm, and those who prioritize their family at some stage in their life work cycle are thus constructed as deviant, less com-mitted and less valued employees than those whose family commit-ments remain invisible (Lewis, 1997). Lewis (2001) points out that such expectations of long working hours are largely a middle-class experience, characteristic of white-collar and professional work and have contributed to the relative undervaluing of part-time work across most occupations, which is usually defined as atypical or nonstandard work, with the implication that it deviates from a generally accepted and relatively fixed norm. In practice, part-time work is often perceived as second-class or marginal by organizations, and it remains predominantly female.

Third, one consequence of the emphasis on time spent visibly in the workplace in the traditional male model of work is that co-workers, and supervisors may construct those who make time for their family as less committed and productive than those working longer hours. This in turn can lead to feelings of inequity among those who do not currently have pressing family commitments and who do not view those who do, as being entitled to differential treatment.

Fourthly, employees' perceptions as to whether workplace practices, which set out to facilitate the reconciliation of family and employment are regarded as favors or as rights are important and affect the sense of personal entitlement. Thus, employees who work in organizations that have formal work–family policies in place, may view themselves as fortunate, even though they may feel that if they use benefits, it is at the cost of other rewards, for example, career advancement.

To conclude, organizational culture is both a multilevel and dynamic phenomenon: artifacts and values are visible and conscious, whereas basic assumptions remain less visible and less conscious, and the three levels constantly interact with each other. This interaction may be either reinforcing or contradictory. If levels contradict each other, an organization behaves or "feels" differently than its espoused values or artifacts would suggest. For example, an espoused value of an organization can be related to the concept of time: an organization may formally value its personnel's leisure and family time— even give it written format, as in HR strategies—but, simultaneously, long working hours are expected and are regarded as signs of high commitment (see Blair-Loy & Wharton, 2002; Lewis, 1997).

A Summary of Theoretical Viewpoints

Although some theoretical advance have been made in explaining or interpreting work–family issues in terms of organizational culture theories, the short review above also shows that in general organizational culture theories have not thus far been extensively utilized for this purpose. In fact, only one theory, that is, the psychodynamic theory of Edgar Schein, has inspired some empirical research. Susan Lewis (1997, 2001) utilized a qualitative case study approach and Thompson et al. (1999) a quantitative survey approach in examining work–family and associated workplace culture issues on the basis of

Schein's organizational culture theory. The work–family border theory by Campbell Clark (2000) seems to remain at the level of abstraction as it is difficult to test empirically (see Geurts & Demerouti, 2003, for a review).

In addition to culture on the organizational level, organizations operate within broad national and social contexts. The prevailing sociopolitical culture (e.g., liberal, conservative, sociodemocratic), that is, the role of the state in creating family-friendliness in the society, varies between countries, a fact that has to be remembered when discussing the findings of studies on work–family issues or performing cross-cultural studies (e.g., den Dulk, van Doorne-Huiskes, & Schippers, 1999; Treas & Widmer, 2000). The Value Survey Module (VSM) developed by Geert Hofstede (1994, 2001) for studying values related to work–family issues cross-nationally would provide an interesting framework in addition to new quantitative methods. Thus, although Hofstede regards value differences as hard to detect between organizations at the national level, he considers them worth studying cross-nationally. Comparing and understanding values and practices both among different countries and among different organizations within countries would yield important new information regarding the role of organizational culture in the work–family context.

REVIEW OF EXISTING EMPIRICAL STUDIES OF WORK–FAMILY CULTURE

Existing studies of work–family culture may be categorized into two groups: qualitative case studies and quantitative studies. The first category utilizes an inductive research paradigm, aiming primarily to understand (not to explain or predict) the role of organizational culture in the work–family context (e.g., Lewis, 1997, 2001; Lewis & Smithson, 2001). The latter category, in turn, has adopted a functional, deductive research paradigm, aiming to explain, predict, and generalize the role of organizational culture in the work–family interface (e.g., Allen, 2001; Thompson et al., 1999).

The emphasis in our literature review is on quantitative work–family culture studies (see Table 4.1). This is because our aim is functional, that is, to reveal the relationships between culture and various outcomes. Furthermore, following the tradition of multidimensional measurement of general organizational culture surveys (see e.g., Cameron & Quinn, 1999; Cooke & Lafferty, 1987; Denison, 2001), we concentrate only on those studies in which work–family culture has been defined and operationalized by a multidimensional measure, i.e., via separate—even though usually related—scales.

TABLE 4.1

A Summary of the Characteristics and Findings of Quantitative Studies Examining Work–Family Culture (Only Published Studies Have Been Taken Into Account)

Authors and Date of Study	Country and Sample	Measure of W–F Culture	Main Research Questions and Hypotheses	Main Findings
1. Thompson, C., Beauvais, L., & Lyness, K. (1999)	USA; $n = 276$ managers and profes- sionals in a variety of or- ganizations	21 items measuring perceptions of the overall extent to which the organization facilitates employees' efforts to balance work and family responsibilities, as well as three components of W–F culture: managerial support ($\alpha = .91$), career consequences ($\alpha = .74$), and organizational time demands ($\alpha = .80$) (invented for the study)	(1) Employees who are female, married or have children living at home or who perceive a more supportive work–family culture will be more likely to utilize work–family benefits than others. (2) Perceptions of a supportive work–family culture will be positively related to organizational attachment and negatively related to work–family conflict.	(1) Work-family benefit utilization was greater among women, married employees and those with children living at home than among other employees. Perceptions of a supportive work-family culture were related to employees' use of work-family benefits. (2) Both work-family benefit availability and a supportive work-family culture were positively related to affective organizational commitment and negatively related to work-family conflict and intentions to leave the organization.

Study	Sample	Measures	Hypotheses	Findings
2. Lyness, K. Thompson, C. Francesco, A.-M. & Judiesch, M. (1999)	USA; n = 86 pregnant women at work	9 items from Thompson et al.'s (1999) scale measuring managerial support ($\alpha = .74$), career consequences ($\alpha = .76$), and organizational time demands ($\alpha = .58$)	Pregnant women whose organizations provide family-responsive benefits and who perceive more supportive organizational work–family cultures will be more committed to their organizations, will plan to work later into their pregnancies, and will plan to return to work more quickly after childbirth than other pregnant women.	Family-responsive benefits were not related to women's organizational commitment, but those women with similar guaranteed jobs after maternity leave planned to work later into their pregnancies and return sooner than other women. Supportive work–family culture was positively related to organizational commitment and plans to return to work sooner, but not to timing of maternity leave.
3. Allen, T. (2001)	USA; n = 522 individuals from a variety of occupations and organizations	14 items measuring employees' perceptions on the extent that work environment is family-supportive (FSOP) ($\alpha = .91$) (invented for the study)	(1) FSOP will positively correlate with supervisor family support and family-friendly benefits offered in the organization and used by the employees.	(1) FSOP correlated especially with supervisor support but also, of the benefits offered and used, with flexible work arrangements.

(Continued)

TABLE 4.1
(Continued)

Authors and Date of Study	Country and Sample	Measure of W–F Culture	Main Research Questions and Hypotheses	Main Findings
			(2) FSOP will be negatively related to work–family conflict and turnover intentions, and positively related to job satisfaction and organizational commitment. (3) FSOP will mediate the relationships between family-friendly benefits available and supervisor support and work–family conflict, job satisfaction, organizational commitment, and turnover intentions.	(2) FSOP was negatively related to work–family conflict and turnover intentions and positively related to job satisfaction and organizational commitment. (3) FSOP fully mediated the relationship between family-friendly benefits available and the dependent variables of work–family conflict, affective organizational commitment and job satisfaction. FSOP fully mediated the relationship between supervisor support and work–family conflict and evidence for partial mediation was found concerning job satisfaction, organizational commitment, and turnover intentions.

4. Campbell Clark, S. (2001)	USA; $n = 179$ individuals from a variety of family situations and organizations	13 items measuring the extent of temporal flexibility ($\alpha = .84$), operational flexibility ($\alpha = .83$) and supportive supervision ($\alpha = .86$) (based on Bailyn's (1997) three cultural aspects)	(1) Temporal and operational flexibility and support from supervisors will be related to decreased role conflict, and increased work satisfaction and employee citizenship behavior. Operational flexibility and supportive supervision will be related to increased home satisfaction and better family functioning. (2) The relationship between work cultures and the dependent variables will be moderated by the presence of risk characteristics (dual-earner family, several dependents, long working hours).	(1) Operational flexibility (i.e., flexibility of the work itself) was associated with increased work satisfaction and better family functioning; supportive supervision was associated with increased employee citizenship; temporal flexibility (i.e., flexibility of working times) was not associated with any outcome. (2) Number of dependents moderated the relationship between supportive supervision and both home satisfaction and family functioning for employees with: three or more dependents, the more supportive the supervision, the less satisfaction with home

(Continued)

TABLE 4.1
(Continued)

Authors and Date of Study	Country and Sample	Measure of W–F Culture	Main Research Questions and Hypotheses	Main Findings
				life and the less functional the family. Dual-career moderated the relationship between supportive supervision and family functioning: the more supportive supervision, the more functional the family for those who are not in a dual-career situation.
5. Behson, S. (2002)	USA; $n = 147$ individuals from a variety of organizations and jobs	Family-supportive organization perceptions (FSOP) were measured using Allen's (2001) 14-item scale; work-family culture was measured using Thompson et al.'s (1999) 20-item scale	(1) Job satisfaction and organizational commitment will be better explained by perceived organizational support, perceived fair interpersonal treatment, and trust in management than by work-family culture and FSOP.	FSOP and work-family culture explained better outcomes related to work and family (work-family and family-work conflict) than general employee attitudes (job satisfaction, affective organizational commitment), which were better explained by

Study	Sample	Measures	Research Questions	Findings
			(2) Work–family conflict and family–work conflict will be better explained by work–family culture and FSOP than by perceived organizational support, fair treatment, and trust in management.	general organizational context (organizational support and trust in management).
6. Haas, L., Allard, K., & Hwang, P. (2002)	Sweden; $n = 317$ fathers in six companies (motor, tree, metal, chemical, finance, transport)	Company-level organizational culture included values of (1) masculine ethic ($\alpha = .77$), (2) caring ethic ($\alpha = .72$), (3) level of father friendliness, (4) support for women's equal employment opportunity, and (5) fathers' perceptions of support from top managers ($\alpha = .80$). Workgroup level organizational culture consisted of (1) supervisors' support for	(1) Does organizational culture—at the company level and work group level—affect men's use of parental leave? (2) What are the effects of men's individual and family attributes on taking parental leave?	(1) Men's use of parental leave was affected by company level organizational culture. More specifically, the composite culture index consisting of masculine and caring ethic was the most important factor explaining fathers' use of parental leave. In addition, at workgroup level, long hours culture (work group norms) explained whether or not fathers took leave. (2) A partner's reported willingness to share

(Continued)

TABLE 4.1
(Continued)

Authors and Date of Study	Country and Sample	Measure of W–F Culture	Main Research Questions and Hypotheses	Main Findings
				parenting explained a father's use of parental leave (after controlling for variables of culture).
7. Mauno, S., Kinnunen, U., & Piitulainen, S. (2004)	Finland; $n = 1,114$ individuals from 4 organizations in public (municipal social and health care department and municipal education department) and private (a paper mill and an IT organization) sectors	men's participation in childcare ($\alpha = .82$), (2) workgroup support ($\alpha = .88$), and (3) workgroup norms. 14 items from Thompson et al.'s (1999) scale measuring managerial support ($\alpha = .83$), career consequences ($\alpha = .81$) and organizational time demands ($\alpha = .74$)	(1) Does work–family culture vary according to such characteristics as organization, sector, and gender? A more positive work–family culture is hypothesized to prevail in the female-dominated public sector, compared to the male-dominated private sector organizations. (2) Is work–family culture linked to subjectively experienced phenomena such as	(1) Work–family culture was assessed more positively within the public sector than in the private sector; W-F culture was experienced least positively in the paper mill and most positively in the municipal education department. (2) Poorer perceptions of work–family culture were related to decreased work–family balance, decreased job satisfaction, and decreased positive job-related mood experiences.

8. Dikkers, J., den Dulk, L., Geurts, S., & Peper, B. (2004)	The Netherlands; $n = 1,171$ individuals from 2 organizations (financial consultancy firm and manufacturing company in electronic industry)	21 items partly based on Thompson et al.'s (1999) and Campbell Clark's (2001) scales measuring organizational support ($\alpha = .84$), supervisor support ($\alpha = .82$), colleague support ($\alpha = .78$), career consequences ($\alpha = .75$), and time demands ($\alpha = .77$)	(1) Does a supportive work-family culture contribute to the utilization of work-life arrangements? H1: Employees make more use of available work-life arrangements, the more supportive the work-life culture is perceived. (2a) Does a supportive work-life culture and	(1) Supportive culture was positively related to the use of flextime and working from home; however, users of child care arrangements and parental leave perceived more barriers in work-life culture (i.e., negative career consequences and high time demands) than others. (2a) Supportive culture contributed to work-life

work-family balance, job satisfaction, and job-related mood? It is expected that a supportive work-family culture will be associated with higher work-family balance, positive job-related mood, and increased job satisfaction.

(Continued)

TABLE 4.1
(Continued)

Authors and Date of Study	Country and Sample	Measure of W–F Culture	Main Research Questions and Hypotheses	Main Findings
			(2b) the utilization of work–life arrangements contribute to employees' work–life balance and well-being? H2: Employees experience a better work–life balance, the more supportive they perceive the work–life culture and the more they use work–life arrangements.	balance; on the contrary, the more barriers were perceived, the higher the work–life imbalance. In addition, supportive work–life culture was strongly related to organizational commitment. (2b) Using child care arrangements contributed to better work–life balance, but other arrangements examined either did not have any associations with well-being or the associations were negative.

Those studies defining and measuring work–family culture via one dimension—usually supportiveness—has already been shortly discussed in a previous section.

The work–family culture studies included in our analysis, shown in Table 4.1, were published mainly as articles in peer-reviewed journals. Two international databases (PsycINFO and Sociological Abstracts, 1990–2003) were searched using the keywords "work–family culture," "organizational culture and work–family," "culture and work–family," "work and family and organizational culture," and "work and family and culture." Altogether, we found eight studies that met our criteria; that is, the studies were quantitative and used a multidimensional measure of work–family culture. In this section, first we show how researchers have defined and operationalized work–family culture in these studies and, second, discuss their main findings.

Different Measures of Work–Family Culture

The search revealed four different multidimensional operationalizations of work–family culture (Table 4.1). The *first* of these was developed and published by Thompson et al. in 1999. They distinguished three dimensions in work–family culture: (a) *managerial support* (11 items, e.g., "In general, managers in this organization are quite accommodating of family-related needs") concerns the social support and sensitivity shown by managers to employees' family responsibilities; (b) *career consequences* (5 items, e.g., "In this organization employees who use flextime are less likely to advance their careers than those who do not use flextime," reverse scored) refers to the perception of negative career development opportunities as a consequence of utilizing work–family arrangements or spending time in family-related activities; and (c) *organizational time demands* (4 items, e.g., "Employees are often expected to take work home at night and/or on weekends," reverse scored) refer to expectations that employees prioritize work above family.

The foundations for these three scales are based on the assumptions that, first, supervisors play a key role in the effectiveness of work–family policies and programs, because they may either encourage or discourage employees' participation in these programs. Second, taking up work–family programs makes employees "less visible" at work, which may be taken as an indicator of diminished commitment to work, resulting in poor career development and promotion prospects (see Bailyn, 1993; Campbell Clark, 2001). Finally, working long hours often serves as an indicator of commitment, but forms an obstacle to the meeting of family requirements (Bailyn, 1993) and may reduce the sense of being entitled to work in ways compatible with family life (see Lewis, 1999).

The *second* measure, chronologically, was developed by Campbell Clark (2001). This measure is based on the three characteristics of family-friendly work cultures identified by Bailyn (1997): temporal flexibility (flexible work scheduling), operational flexibility (flexible work processes), and an understanding by management that family needs are important. Specifically, Campbell Clark (2001) measured both *temporal flexibility* (e.g., whether employees are able to arrive and depart from work when desired) and *operational flexibility* (e.g., the extent to which employees are in charge of their own activities at work) via five items, and *supportive supervision* via three items (e.g., whether their supervisor understands their family demands). The flexibility scales, particularly the operational flexibility scale, clearly resemble the concept of job control widely regarded as an important job characteristic in occupational health psychology, for example, in the job demand-control model by Karasek (1979; Karasek & Theorell, 1990; Karasek, Brisson, Kawakami, Houtman, Bongers, & Amick, 1998). Only the supportive items include the word "family."

The *third* scale by Tammy Allen (2001) measures work–family culture via Family Supportive Organization Perceptions (FSOP) with 14 items. Although uni-dimensional, the measure clearly includes items that capture somewhat different aspects of work–family culture. On the basis of our content analysis, the scale of Family Supportive Organization Perceptions seems to contain items related to psychological commitment (e.g., "Employees who are highly committed to their personal lives cannot be highly committed to their work," reverse scored) and to time-related commitment (e.g., "The ideal employee is the one who is available 24 hours a day," reverse scored). These items resemble the time demands scale of Thompson et al. (1999). There are also items that assess to what extent family life is allowed to be visible in the organization (e.g., "Employees should keep their personal problems at home," reverse scored), and items related to flexibility (e.g., "Offering employees flexibility in completing their work is viewed as a strategic way of doing business). This latter category of items ultimately strives for capturing whether employees consider flexibility as "a strategic way of doing business," that is, whether employees perceive their company as granting these policies out of business concerns.

According to Allen (2001), the Family Supportive Organization Perceptions scale concentrates specifically on employees' global perceptions with the respect to the family supportiveness of the organization. She does not include managerial or supervisor support in the scale, but instead measures this aspect via a separate scale. In fact, she is critical of those studies that have connected the global supportiveness of organizations with managerial or supervisor supportiveness (e.g., Thompson et al., 1999). Allen considers that these are two different concepts, and that they should be kept separate. This critique was also partly behind the development of the Family Supportive Organization Perceptions scale.

Recently, Haas et al. (2002) published a study that introduces a *fourth* measure of work–family culture. They used a procedure that measured culture both at the company (5 scales) and at the work group level (3 scales). However, we shall only mention here three of the scales concerned with culture on the company level, as the other scales are either closely bound up with the specific sample and topic examined in the study (i.e., working fathers and their use of parental leave) or they do not measure new aspects (e.g., supervisor and work group support). In their study, Haas et al. (2002) do not use the concept of work–family culture; instead they speak about organizational culture. The three cultural aspects we considered especially relevant are as follows: (1) *Masculine ethic* (5 items, e.g., to what extent your organization "has high demands for achievement," "is competitive"), which may hinder employees from successfully combining work and family demands, and which is often deeply embedded in organizations. If masculine ethic exists (or predominates) in an organization, it values, for example, competitiveness, aggressiveness, high goal-orientation, and material success. (2) *Caring ethic* in contrast (8 items, e.g., to what extent your organization "encourages collaboration within the company," "shows respect for individual rights") provides employees with better options to combine their work and family life. If caring ethic prevails, an organization emphasizes, for example, empathy, helpfulness, nurturing, and long-term orientation. In other words, the culture is employee centered. (3) *Equal employment opportunity ethic* (4 items, e.g., "To what extent is raising women's pay an important priority just now?") refers to an organization's commitment to improve the position of women (e.g., pay levels, opportunities for management positions) and shows that an organization values women's work. All three scales reflect the extent to which the organizational culture is still male dominated and based on the notion that family and work are separate spheres.

Evaluation of Work–Family Culture Measures

It appears that work–family culture has been operationalized primarily at the level of the behavioral norms and expectations prevailing in organizations. Generally, these norms and expectations can be seen as indicative of the extent to which male norms (e.g., full-time job, preferring work to family, working overtime) continue to function as the criteria of the ideal worker. However, only a few multidimensional definitions and measures of work–family culture were found.

Family supportiveness (i.e., an organization's supportiveness toward the demands of its employees' families) is the single dimension, which was most often referred to in measures of the family supportiveness of the organization (Allen, 2001), managers and supervisors (Campbell Clark, 2001; Thompson et al., 1999), or colleagues (Haas et al., 2002). Supportiveness belonged to every measure in one form or another. It seems, however, that for the supportiveness dimension, an additional conceptual and empirical distinction is needed, for example, among the concepts of the family-supportive organization (FSOP), general perceived supportiveness of the organization (POS), and social support.

The level of involvement—in terms of either psychological identification or time committed to the domains of work or family—an organization expects from employees was present in three measures (Allen, 2001; Haas et al., 2002; Thompson et al., 1999). Job control, or flexibility, in one form or another was, in turn, contained in two scales (Allen, 2001; Campbell Clark, 2001). However, in our view flexibility definitions and measures do not reflect either organizational or work–family culture as such; instead job control is an important job characteristic (see van der Doef & Maes, 1999, for a review) and flexibility is a significant feature related to work–family policies. The career consequences associated with benefit utilization was rather surprisingly assessed only in one measure, that is, in the scale of Thompson et al. (1999). Nonetheless, because of the rapid changes taking place in working life, which is increasingly characterized, for example, by various forms of atypical work, we consider career consequences to be an important aspect of work–family culture.

The variations found in the content of the various work–family culture measures used indicate a need to properly reconsider these measures both conceptually and empirically. First, we do not know to what extent the measures currently available empirically capture the same aspects of work–family culture. Only Behson (2002) measured work–family culture by two different measures: the correlation between the family-supportive organization perceptions (FSOP) scale and a supportive work–family culture (measured by the scales of Thompson et al., 1999) turned out to be 0.69 in her study. Second, it would be reasonable to carefully examine the general multidimensional organizational culture scales, e.g., Organizational Culture Assessment

Instrument (OCAI; Cameron & Quinn, 1999), Organizational Culture Inventory (OCI; Cooke & Lafferty, 1987), Value Survey Module (VSM; Hofstede, 1994), and Denison Organizational Culture Survey (DOCS; Denison, 1990, 2001), in order to shed further light onto the relationship between organizational culture and work–family culture. The existing scales of organizational culture could be more extensively used in studying the role of culture in the work–family interface (e.g., Haas et al., 2002).

Our review also revealed that the psychometric evaluation—construct validity, in particular—of the existing work–family culture scales has been either relatively simple (e.g., exploratory factor analysis) or insufficiently reported (e.g., when confirmatory factor analysis was conducted). Therefore, more sophisticated analytical methods should be applied in examining the psychometric properties of work–family culture scales in the future. This also applies to general organizational culture measures, of which psychometric evaluations have also been rarely performed (see Ashkanasy, Wilderom, & Peterson, 2000).

Three out of the four measures reviewed were developed in the United States, where there is little expectation of a role for the state. The only exception was the measure by Haas et al. (2002), which was developed in Sweden, a Nordic country where work–family policies go well beyond the minimum standards set by the European Directives. However, similar value typologies or profiles—such as the masculine and caring ethics used by Haas and her colleagues—can be found in many general organizational culture surveys, which originate from the United States. For example, in the Organizational Culture Assessment Inventory (OCAI; Cameron & Quinn, 1999), marketing (masculine ethic) and clan (caring ethic) cultures are hypothesized to be opposite cultural profiles (see also Denison, 2001; Hofstede, 2001).

Bearing in mind that the objective of all these scales is to evaluate organizational culture within the work–family context, this raises an important question: how appropriate and psychometrically sound would these scales turn out to be in some other context, i.e., across different samples (organizations or subunits) within the same country or among different countries (cross-national comparison)? Only the measure of Thompson et al. (1999) was utilized in modified versions by European researchers recently (see Table 4.1; Dikkers et al., 2004; Mauno, Kinnunen, & Piitulainen, 2004). In these studies, the measure has at least turned out to be reliable in terms of internal consistency. In future, we need to develop, test, and compare different scales, both nationally and cross-nationally.

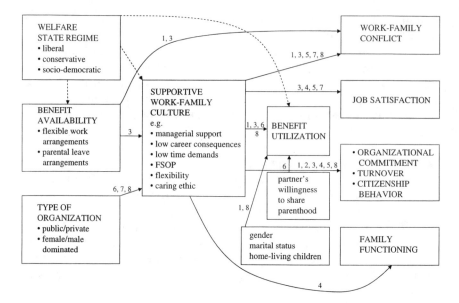

FIG. 4.1.   A summary of the main relationships found between variables in the
empirical studies of work–family culture.
Note. Figures refer to the study identification numbers presented in Table 4.1.

Outcomes of Work–Family Culture

The main findings of the studies presented in Table 4.1 are summarized in Figure 4.1. In the figure, the relationships among various
phenomena found in the studies are marked using the study identification numbers presented in Table 4.1. The findings can be roughly
divided into two main categories, which are the links between work–
family culture and the use of work–family policies and the outcomes
for well-being. We shall discus these two groups of findings separately.

Outcomes for the Utilization of Work–Family Policies.   The findings concerning
the relationship between work–family culture and the use of work–
family policies are in line with our expectations: a supportive family–
work culture seems to increase the use of work–family policies. More
specifically: (a) Benefit utilization (together 16 specific benefits, e.g.,
absence autonomy, flextime, family care leave) was greater by employees who perceived more supportive work–family cultures (high managerial support, low career consequences and low organizational time
demands) than by those with less supportive cultures (Thompson
et al., 1999). (b) Individuals who reported favorable Family Supportive Organization Perception responses also reported a greater use of

flexible work–family arrangements (e.g., flextime, compressed working week, part-time work; Allen, 2001). (c) Fathers' participation in parental leave was greater in organizational cultures showing high caring and low masculine ethic (Haas et al., 2002). (d) A supportive culture was positively related to the use of flextime and working from home; however, users of childcare arrangements and parental leave perceived more barriers (i.e., high career consequences and time demands) in the culture (Dikkers et al., 2004).

In addition, the use of work–family policies is dependent on employees' background factors: Employees who are female, married, or have children living at home are more likely to use work–family arrangements (together 16 specific benefits, e.g., absence autonomy, flextime, parental leaves) than others (Thompson et al., 1999; see also Dikkers et al., 2004). Also, a partner's attitudes matter: a mother's reported willingness to share parenting was a significant contributor to a father's decision whether or not to take parental leave (Haas et al., 2002).

However, from another American study (not referred to in either the Table 4.1 or Fig. 4.1) concerning the use of work–family benefits (Secret, 2000), it emerged that in fact parents of dependent children were no more likely than other employees to use benefits but specific family problems (e.g., family-related crisis, child-care problems) contributed to female employee use of paid leave and mental health benefits (e.g., parenting or work stress workshops). Further, size of workplace (large), sector (nonprofit and public), and culture (supportive managers and staff) were linked to employee benefit use. On the other hand, a study among Canadian managers (Barham, Gottlieb, & Kelloway, 2002) showed that managers were more willing to grant alternative working arrangements (e.g., reduced working hours) to subordinates than to managerial employees, to women than to men, and to employees with responsibilities for children rather than for older relatives.

The work–family cultures prevailing in organizations turned out to be linked to the type of organization in question. This emerged from all three studies, in which the employee samples were organization-based. In the Finnish study (Mauno et al., 2004) work–family culture (high managerial support, low career consequences, and low organizational time demands) was perceived as more supportive within the female-dominated public sector (e.g., municipal education department) than in the male-dominated private sector (e.g., paper mill). The Swedish study (Haas et al., 2002) also showed that among companies where male workers formed the majority, there were differences in the perceived cultures. For example, three companies (motor, finance, and transport) were committed to masculine ethic (or male culture), although the scores were relatively low. In addition, caring ethic (or female culture) varied according to the organization, being highest in the motor company and lowest in the metal company. However, all six companies were above the median value and could be categorized as employee-centered. Also, in the Dutch study (Dikkers et al., 2004), the culture differed between the two male-dominated private firms studied: it seemed to be perceived as more supportive but simultaneously as more constraining in the consultancy firm than in the manufacturing company.

Finally, as cross-cultural studies have shown (den Dulk et al., 1999; Lewis & Smithson, 2001), we have to take into account the welfare regime existing in each country: The type of welfare state is linked to benefit availability and utilization as well as to work–family culture, that is, to the sense of entitlement to support in work and family life (these links are marked by broken lines in Fig. 4.1).

Outcomes for Well-Being. In examining the well-being outcomes of work–family culture, the theoretical assumption is, on the one hand, that a supportive work–family culture should make an organization a more pleasant place to work. This, in turn, should affect an employee's work experiences positively (see Allen, 2001; Behson, 2002). A supportive culture may signal to employees that the organization is willing to look after the well-being of its personnel (e.g., Cameron & Quinn, 1999; Goodman, Zammuto, & Gifford, 2001; Peterson & Wilson, 2002; Sparrow, 2001). On the other hand, on the basis of the value congruence perspective, it is hypothesized that similarity between values of an organization and those of an individual employee fosters well-being (e.g., Kristoff, 1996; Meglino, Ravlin, & Adkins, 1989; O'Reilly et al., 1991; Peterson & Wilson, 2002; Sparrow, 2001). In the work–family context, this perspective implies that when a person perceives work–family issues as personally important, his or her organization should also value these issues, e.g., by fostering a supportive work–family culture.

As can be seen in Figure 4.1 (see also Table 4.1), previous empirical studies show, in line with the theory, that a supportive work–family culture is associated with several positive outcomes. More specifically, family supportive organization perceptions are linked to a better balance between the demands of work and family and between job satisfaction and organizational commitment (Allen, 2001; Behson, 2002). Similarly, a supportive work–family culture in terms of high managerial support, low career consequences, and low organizational time demands contributes to a better work–family balance (Dikkers et al.,

2004; Mauno et al., 2004; Thompson et al., 1999), job satisfaction (Mauno et al., 2004), and organizational commitment (Dikkers et al., 2004; Lyness, Thompson, Francesco, & Judiesch, 1999; Thompson et al., 1999). Only one study has looked at the outcomes for family well-being: operational flexibility (i.e., flexibility of the work itself) was associated with better family functioning (Campbell Clark, 2001).

In addition, benefit availability has also been reported as directly linked to the well-being outcomes (Allen, 2001; Thompson et al., 1999). However, this relationship may be mediated by a supportive work–family culture as Allen (2001) showed in her study. Family supportive organization perceptions (FSOP) fully mediated the relationship between the availability of family benefits (especially flexible work arrangements) and the outcome variables of work–family conflict, job satisfaction, and organizational commitment. Thus, family-supportive benefit availability was indirectly related to work–family conflict and job attitudes through family-supportive organization perceptions.

Evaluation of Previous Work–Family Culture Studies

As our review indicates, work–family culture has not yet been extensively studied. Thus far, most studies have been conducted in the United States among rather small samples consisting of individuals employed in a variety of organizations. However, because work–family culture is specific to an organization (or a unit inside the organization) organization-based samples should be utilized. The three studies mentioned earlier in which the samples were organization-based (Dikkers et al., 2004; Haas et al., 2002; Mauno et al., 2004), showed that work–family cultures varied between organizations and were linked to the type of organization.

It seems that studies have tended to focus on the direct relationships between work–family culture and different outcomes. The findings have shown that an unsupportive work–family culture has its strongest links with work–family conflict, job dissatisfaction, and low organizational commitment. The correlations between work–family culture and each well-being outcome seem to vary according to the work–family culture measure used. In general, they range from .25 (family supportive organization perceptions and job satisfaction; Behson, 2002) to .55 (work–family culture and work–family conflict; Thompson et al., 1999). Although, on the basis of these findings, we may easily conclude that a supportive work–family culture is beneficial for the well-being of the employees and of the organization, we have to remember that all the studies produced so far have been cross-sectional. Therefore, it is difficult to make causal conclusions about the direction of these links. It is equally possible that the level of employees' well-being affects their work–family culture perceptions or that this link is reciprocal rather than one-sided. In addition, the close links between work–family culture and work–family conflict may challenge their conceptual distinction.

In the future, more attention should be given to the indirect relationships between work–family culture and its expected outcomes; we do not know how the positive effects of a supportive work–family culture are translated into an individual's well-being. For example, it is possible that benefit utilization or perceived work–family conflict function as mediators in the relationship between a supportive work–family culture and individual or organizational well-being. This is indicated by the preliminary findings of a Dutch study, which showed that work–family conflict partially mediated the associations between a supportive culture and job satisfaction (Peeters, Montgomery, & Schaufeli, 2003). In addition, the well-being outcomes for the family domain have not received much attention (see Campbell Clark, 2001, for an exception). It is quite reasonable to expect that these effects in particular might be indirect, that is, mediated by other factors (e.g., work–family conflict). However, most urgently we are in need of longitudinal studies to obtain more reliable evidence about the link between cultural variables and well-being.

DISCUSSION

Summary of Empirical Findings and Ideas of Theories

The studies reviewed show that in organizations a supportive work–family culture or family-friendliness contributes to the use of work–family arrangements and to having beneficial effects on the well-being of employees and organizations. In fact, it seems that a supportive work–family culture contributes more to achieving a work–life balance and to well-being (job satisfaction, organizational commitment) than to the actual use of work–family arrangements. Owing to the fact that all the studies done thus far have been cross-sectional, we have to wary of overly simple interpretations of the findings. Nevertheless, they suggest that by improving work–family culture in a more supportive direction, the well-being of employees and organizations might also be improved.

Although some organizational culture researchers are very skeptical regarding cultural interventions, arguing that organizational culture is very hard to change by such means (see e.g., Martin, 2002; Schein, 1999), there are also those who believe in this possibility. For example, the functional approach (e.g., Cameron & Quinn, 1999; Denison, 2001) to work–family culture research implies that work–family culture can be consciously manipulated; i.e., interventions targeted at changing work–family culture in a more supportive direction are possible. In the future, this assumption should be tested by conducting quasi-experimental studies, in which work–family culture and its potential outcomes are evaluated at least at two points in time while a specific work–family program (the realization of measures to change the prevailing work–family culture in a more supportive direction) operates as an intervention between these two measurement points.

At first, however, the field of work–family culture would benefit from further theoretical advances. For example, it would be useful to analyze thoroughly the relationship between the concepts of work–family culture and organizational culture, as general organizational culture theories (e.g., Cameron & Quinn, 1999; Hofstede, 2001; Schein, 1985, 1990, 1999) have not been extensively used in either defining or operationalizing the concept of work–family culture. In addition, integrating general work–family theories (e.g., work–family conflict theory or role enhancement theory; see Geurts & Demerouti, 2003) into the framework of work–family culture would also provide a new starting point for theoretical discourse at the work–family interface. For example, the conceptual relationship between individual perceptions of work–family culture and the work-to-family or family-to-work conflict needs further clarification. As previous studies have clearly shown (e.g., see Geurts & Demerouti, 2003, for a review), the family-to-work conflict is rather seldom reported. The reason for this may lie more in the prevailing culture than in reality; the ideal worker does not let family matters interfere with work.

Relevance for Practice

The observation by Thomas and Ganster (1995) provides a possible starting point to the building of family-friendly organizations; a family-supportive work environment is composed of family-supportive policies and family-supportive supervisors, because both components exemplify organizational efforts to support employee needs to balance work and family responsibilities. Because organizations are always operating as a part of larger sociopolitical cultures or regimes, where the role of the state varies in offering work–family policies, the national context plays an important role. For example, Susan Lewis

(1997, p. 18) has clearly stated that more fundamental change will require state intervention and support, "Some companies do implement family-friendly policies without government intervention, but these are limited and therefore cannot create a family-friendly society. The broader social culture within which organizations operate will thus remain the same without state action." Therefore, the Nordic countries—where governments do legislate for family-friendly provisions—may operate as models for other countries in campaigns for more state support for work and family in countries with fewer state supports (see Lewis & Smithson, 2001).

The involvement of managers is crucial in building family-friendly organizations, as previous studies have also revealed (e.g., Campbell Clark, 2001; Haas et al., 2002; Thompson et al., 1999). If the work–family balance is not considered a valuable issue by top managers, neither family-friendly strategies nor family-friendly practices are probable. First, the importance of the work–family balance should be made an espoused value in written documents (e.g., HR strategy) characterizing an organization's goals, investments and future perspectives (see e.g., Schein, 1999). Secondly, this should be done at each level and in each department of the organization including headquarters and subsidiaries. Naturally, this does not yet guarantee that personnel will actually perceive the prevailing culture—in particular, its everyday practices—as family-friendly or supportive. According to Schein (1990, 1999), it is this kind of contradiction between public values and prevailing practices (or basic assumptions) that most visibly reveals the culture within a particular organization. Third, to achieve a more fundamental shift the strategic changes or new values have to be put into practice, which is the most difficult step.

Consider, for example, a situation in which the aim is to change top managers' basic assumptions concerning the responsibilities of an organization. If the top managers profoundly believe that the organization by no means is responsible for employees' personal lives it is very difficult to create a family-friendly organizational culture. The process of change in this type of situation usually starts only when the organization is faced with internal or external threats that jeopardize its business ideas or other central operations, e.g., when a labor shortage threatens the organization, top managers may start to reassess issues concerning the work–life balance. However, there are also doubts about whether the business rationale can bring about fundamental change if it is not combined with a sense of corporate social responsibility (Lewis, 1997).

Equal opportunities arguments for family-friendly policies have played a significant role in emphasizing the need to challenge traditional models of work (Lewis, 1997). In practice, however, the focus has often been on policies, which enable women to enter and remain in a workforce constructed by men for men without family involvement. As Lewis (1997, p. 19) puts it "Family-friendly policies which involve different ways of working will not be indicative of real culture change unless they are taken up by men as well as women, and diverse and pluralistic patterns of work and careers are equally valued." This raises also the question of how far radical workplace cultural change can be achieved without comparable change within the division of labor on a societal level.

ACKNOWLEDGMENTS

The publication took place within the research project "The Interaction between Demands of Work and Family from the Viewpoints of Women, Men and Marital Couples," which was financially supported by the Academy of Finland (grant no. 49215).

REFERENCES

Ashkanasy, N., Wilderom, C. P., & Peterson, M. F. (2000). *Handbook of organizational culture & climate.* Thousand Oaks, CA: Sage.

*Allen, T. D. (2001). Family-supportive work environments: The role of organizational perceptions. *Journal of Vocational Behavior, 58,* 414–435.

Bailyn, L. (1993). *Breaking the mold: Women, men and time in the new corporate world.* New York: The Free Press.

Bailyn, L. (1997). The impact of corporate culture on work–family integration. In S. Parasuraman & J. H. Greenhaus (Eds.), *Integrating work and family: Challenges and choices for a changing world* (pp. 209–219). Westport, CT: Quorum Books.

Barham, L., Gottlieb, B., & Kelloway, E. (2002). Variables affecting managers' willingness to grant alternative work arrangements. *The Journal of Social Psychology, 138,* 291–302.

*Behson, S. J. (2002). Which dominates? The relative importance of work–family organizational support and general organizational context on employee outcomes. *Journal of Vocational Behavior, 61,* 53–72.

Blair-Loy, M., & Wharton, A. S. (2002). Employees' use of work–family policies and the workplace social context. *Social Forces, 80,* 813–845.

Cameron, K. S., & Quinn, R. (1999). *Diagnosing and changing organizational culture.* Reading, MA: Addison-Wesley.

Campbell Clark, S. (2000). Work/family border theory: A new theory of work/family balance. *Human Relations, 53,* 747–762.

*Campbell Clark, S. (2001). Work cultures and work/family balance. *Journal of Vocational Behavior, 58*, 348–365.

Cooke, R. A., & Lafferty, J. C. (1987). *Organizational culture inventory*. Plymouth, MI: Human Synergistics.

Czarniawska-Joerges, B. (1992). *Exploring complex organizations: A cultural perspective*. Newbury Park: Sage.

Davey, K. M., & Symon, G. (2001). Recent approaches to the qualitative analysis of organizational culture. In C. L. Cooper et al. (Eds.), *The international handbook of organizational culture and climate* (pp. 123–143). UK: Wiley.

Denison, D. R. (1990). *Corporate culture and organizational effectiveness*. New York: Wiley.

Denison, D. R. (1996). What IS the difference between organizational culture and organizational climate? A native's point of view. *Academy of Management Review, 21*, 619–654.

Denison, D. R. (2001). Organizational culture: Can it be key lever for driving organizational change? In C. L. Cooper et al. (Eds.), *The international handbook of organizational culture and climate* (pp. 346–372). UK: Wiley.

den Dulk, L., van Doorne-Huiskes, A., & Schippers, J. (1999). *Work–family arrangements in Europe*. Amsterdam: Thela Thesis.

*Dikkers, J., den Dulk, L., Geurts, S., & Peper, B. (2004). *Work–life culture in two organizations in the Netherlands*. Mahwah, NJ: Lawrence Erlbaum Associates.

Eisenberger, R., Huntington, R., Hutchison, S., & Sowa, D. (1986). Perceived organizational support. *Journal of Applied Psychology, 71*, 500–507.

Geurts, S. A. E., & Demerouti, E. (2003). Work/non-work interface: a review of theories and findings. In M. J. Schabracq, J. A. M. Winnubst, & C. L. Cooper (Eds.), *The handbook of work and health psychology* (pp. 279–312). Chichester, UK: Wiley.

Goodman, E. A., Zammuto, R. F., & Gifford, B. D. (2001). The competing values framework: understanding the impact of organizational culture on the quality of working life. *Organization Development Journal, 19*, 58–68.

*Haas, L., Allard, K., & Hwang, P. (2002). The impact of organizational culture on men's use of parental leave in Sweden. *Community, Work & Family, 5*, 319–341.

Hofstede, G. (1994). *Values survey module 1994 manual*. Maastricht, The Netherlands: University of Limburg.

Hofstede, G. (2001). *Culture's consequences: Comparing values, behaviors, institutions, and organizations across nations*. London: Sage.

Isaac, R. G., & Pitt, D. C. (2001). Organizational culture. It's alive! It's alive! But there's no fixed address. In R. T. Golembiewski (Ed.), *Handbook of organizational behavior* (2nd ed., pp. 113–144). New York: Marcel Dekker.

Judiesch, M. K., & Lyness, K. S. (1999). Left behind? The impact of leaves of absence on manager's career success. *Academy of Management Journal, 42*, 641–651.

Karasek, R. (1979). Job demands. Job latitude and mental strain: Implications for job redesign. *Administrative Science Quarterly, 24*, 285–308.

Karasek, R., & Theorell, T. (1990). *Healthy work*. New York: Basic Books.

Karasek, R., Brisson, C., Kawakami, N., Houtman, I., Bongers, P., & Amick, B. (1998). The Job Content Questionnaire (JCQ): An instrument for internationally comparative assessments of psychosocial job characteristics. *Journal of Occupational Health Psychology, 3*, 322–355.

Kotter, P., & Heskett, J. (1992). *Corporate culture and performance*. New York: The Free Press.

Kristoff, A. L. (1996). Person-organization fit. An integrative review of its conceptualizations, measurement, and implications. *Personnel Psychology, 49*, 1–49.

Lewis, S. (1997). Family friendly employment policies. A route to changing organizational culture or playing about at the margins. *Gender, Work and Organization, 4*, 13–23.

Lewis, S. (1999). How to voice the needs to reconcile work and family in the workplace? *European diversities. Combining work and family in different settings of working life, family life and culture*. Seminar report (pp. 43–51). Finland, Helsinki: Stakes.

Lewis, S. (2001). Restructuring workplace cultures: the ultimate work–family challenge? *Women in Management Review, 16*, 21–29.

Lewis, S., & Smithson, J. (2001). Sense of entitlement to support for the reconciliation of employment and family life. *Human Relations, 54*, 1145–1481.

Lundberg, C. C. (2001). Working with cultures: Social rules perspective. In C. L. Cooper, S. Cartwright, & P. C. Earley (Eds.), *The international handbook of organizational culture and climate* (pp. 325–347). Chichester, England. John Wiley & Sons Ltd.

*Lyness, K. S., Thompson, C., Francesco, A–M., & Judiesch, M. K. (1999). Work and pregnancy: Individual and organizational factors influencing organizational commitment, time of maternity leave and return to work. *Sex Roles, 41*, 485–508.

Martin, J. (2002). *Organizational culture. Mapping the terrain*. Thousand Oaks: Sage.

*Mauno, S., Kinnunen, U., & Piitulainen, S. (in press). Work–family culture in four organizations in Finland: Examining antecedents and outcomes. *Community, Work and Family*.

Meglino, B. M., Ravlin, E. C., & Adkins, C. L. (1989). Work values approach to corporate culture: A field test of the value congruence process and its relationships to individual outcomes. *Journal of Applied Psychology, 74*, 424–432.

O'Reilly, C. A., Chatman, J., & Caldwell, D. E. (1991). People and organizational culture. A profile comparison approach to assessing person-organization fit. *The Academy of Management Journal, 34*, 487–516.

Peeters, M., Montgomery, A., & Schaufeli, W. (2003, May). *The role of family supportive organization perceptions in three Dutch organizations*. Paper presented at the 11th European Congress of Work and Organizational Psychology, Lisbon, Portugal.

Peterson, M., & Wilson, J. (2002). A culture-work-health model and work stress. *American Journal of Health Behavior, 26*, 16–24.

Sackmann, S. (2001). Cultural complexity in organizations: the value and limitations of qualitative methodology and approaches. In C. L. Cooper et al. (Eds.), *The international handbook of organizational culture and climate* (pp. 143–163). UK: Wiley.

Schein, E. (1985). *Organizational culture and leadership*. San Francisco: Jossey-Bass.

Schein, E. (1990). Organizational culture. *American Psychologist, 45*, 109–119.

Schein, E. (1999). *The corporate culture survival guide—Sense and nonsense about culture change*. San Francisco: Jossey-Bass.

Secret, M. (2000). Identifying the family, job, and workplace characteristics of employees who use work–family benefits. *Family Relations, 49*, 217–226.

Sparrow, P. (2001). Developing diagnostics for high performance organization cultures. In C. L. Cooper et al. (Eds.), *The international handbook of organizational culture and climate* (pp. 84–106). UK: Wiley.

Thomas, L. T., & Ganster, D. C. (1995). Impact of family-supportive work variables on work–family conflict and strain: A control perspective. *Journal of Applied Psychology, 80*, 6–15.

*Thompson, C., Beauvais, L., & Lyness, K. (1999). When work–family benefits are not enough: The influence of work–family culture on benefit utilization, organizational attachment, and work–family conflict. *Journal of Vocational Behavior, 54*, 329–415.

Treas, J., & Widmer, E. D. (2000). Married women's employment over the life-course: Attitudes in cross-national perspective. *Social Forces, 78*, 1409–1143.

van der Doef, M., & Maes, S. (1999). The Job Demand-Control(-Support) Model and psychological well-being. A review of 20 years of empirical research. *Work & Stress, 13*, 87–114.

Note: References included in the review analysis (Table 4.1) are marked with an asterisk (*).

5

Work–Life Balance and the Effective Management of Global Assignees

Paula Caligiuri
Rutgers University, USA, and Università Bocconi, Italy

Mila Lazarova
Simon Fraser University, Canada

BACKGROUND FOR THIS CHAPTER

In today's highly competitive global business environment, multinational companies recognize that effective management of human resources is critical for gaining a competitive advantage. This competitive necessity has increased attention to human resources issues, such as fostering a global corporate culture, developing global leaders, sourcing and staffing talent around the world, and the like. Consistent with these strategic human resources issues, many organizations relocate their key employees to other countries on global assignments to enhance their leaders' cross-cultural competences, fill staffing needs in subsidiaries, manage projects, transfer knowledge and corporate culture, or work on multinational teams. Global assignments are considered highly developmental for managers and are frequently used as a part of a leadership development strategy within international firms.

Global assignments provide individuals and, in turn, organizations the opportunity to gain first-hand knowledge about the complexities of international operations, the characteristics of a given national market, the business climate within a given country, the structure of that market system, specific knowledge about individual customers and suppliers located within a country or region, and much more country-specific information. If managed correctly, the knowledge global assignees transfer from the company's headquarters to its subsidiaries (and vice versa) can strengthen the competitive basis of the international firm. Such knowledge, creation, and transfer are at the heart of building and sustaining a competitive advantage in multinational companies.

Recent reports on global relocation trends suggest that even during times of economic downturns, when downsizing and outsourcing are much more common than workforce expansion, most companies do not predict reductions of their global assignees. The 2002 Global Relocation Report surveyed 181 companies with over 35,000 global assignees in 130 countries. This study reported that 82% of the international assignments were over 1 year in length (GMAC et al., 2003). Similarly, Harris, Petrovic, and Brewster (2001) reported that 53% of respondents surveyed in European and U.S.-based companies had more than 50 employees on long-term assignments (more than 1 year), as opposed to only 18% for short-term assignments. Comparable results have been reported from Australian organizations as well (Fenwick, 2001).

Although such evidence suggests that global assignment trends are enduring and pervasive around the world, a large majority of global organizations report that finding employees willing to accept these important global positions is becoming increasingly more difficult (Windham International & National Foreign Trade Council, 1994; Windham International, National Foreign Trade Council & Society for Human Resource Management, 1999; GMAC et al., 2002, 2003). The top reasons that employees are reluctant to accept global assignments include the accompanying partner's resistance to the relocation, concerns about family adjustment, the disruption of the accompanying partner's career, concern for elderly parents, and the disruption of the children's education (Borstoff, Harris, Field, & Giles, 1997; Brett & Stroh, 1995; Handler, Lane, & Maher, 1997; Harvey, 1996; Pellico & Stroh, 1997; Scullion, 1994; Swaak, 1995; Suutari & Riusala, 2000).

Research has also suggested that for those employees who accept global assignments, success in the foreign location is not only a function of their own skills, abilities, knowledge, and experience. On the contrary, the success of global assignees is often dependent on nonwork factors such as their cross-cultural adjustment and the adjustment and satisfaction of their accompanying partner and/or children.

Studies of global assignment success found that accompanying partners' inability to adjust to the global assignment was one of the most frequently cited reasons for the assignment failure (Tung, 1981). As such, an accompanying partners' adjustment may be a key antecedent related to how well a global assignee performs on his or her global assignment (Black & Gregersen, 1991; Black & Stephens, 1989).In fact, the global assignees' entire family (accompanying partner and/or children) has been shown to affect the work-related outcomes of global assignments (Caligiuri, Hyland, & Joshi, 1997; Caligiuri, Hyland, Joshi, & Bross, 1998; Fukuda & Chu, 1994).

Clearly, the success of global assignees is of strategic importance to organizations operating around the world. However, from a human resource perspective, global assignments are especially challenging to manage effectively. Given that work-related global relocation permeates every aspect of an employee's life, it is important to better understand the ways in which organizations can help encourage work–life balance among their global assignees. The objective of this chapter is to develop deeper awareness of work–life balance issues in the global assignment context.

Given the changing demographic characteristics of the expatriates (see Text Box 1), we choose to broaden the discussion of balance

---

TEXT BOX 1

GLOBAL ASSIGNEE DEMOGRAPHICS

The Global Relocation Report from 2002 offers a basic demographic sketch of global assignees.

More than 80% of global assignees are men between 30 and 49 years old. Most global assignees are married (about 65%), accompanied by a spouse (in about 87% of the cases) and have children (in about 59% of the cases). About half of global assignees' spouses have worked before the assignment, but only a fraction of them work during the assignment (see also Suutari & Riusala, 2000).

Certain characteristics of the "typical" global assignee have been changing steadily over the past 50 years. Today's global assignees are younger, with younger (school-age) children, and more likely to be female. Although this new generation is less likely to be married, those who are married are more likely to have a spouse or partner with a career of his or her own. As a result, it is much more challenging for these families to manage the dual-career reality of the assignment.

beyond work–*family* balance. Recent data suggest that the traditional definition of family (accompanying partner and children) only applies to a portion of global assignees. Many others are single, are in committed relationships, have a domestic life partner, are single parents, or provide care for elder parents or other extended family members. The unique context created by global assignments demands the use of a more inclusive term, work–*life* balance. This term recognizes personal life challenges faced by expatriates that extend beyond balancing work and family life. We define work–life balance as maintaining a happy and healthy personal life while being successful at work and as attaining a broadly defined sense of personal fulfillment (Hemingway, 2000).

The chapter is organized into three sections. The first section explores the work–life balance challenges and opportunities created by global assignments—for individuals and their accompanying partners and children. The second section offers ways in which organizations can improve the nonwork aspects of global assignees' lives in an attempt to improve their work–life balance. The last section of this chapter discusses some important areas for future research.

WORK–LIFE BALANCE DURING GLOBAL ASSIGNMENTS: POSITIVE AND NEGATIVE COUNTERWEIGHTS

The Assignee

There are many ways in which the demands of a global assignment will affect work–life balance of the global assignee. Countervailing influences on an individual's sense of work–life balance can be either positive, improving an individual's sense of work–life balance, or negative, decreasing an individual's sense of work–life balance. These influences, positive and negative, are described in the next section.

The Negative. Perhaps the greatest impediment to a global assignee's sense of work–life balance is the *culture shock* that he or she may feel as a result of living in the host country. Culture shock relates to the psychological disorientation experienced by individuals when they find themselves living and working in a culture different than their own. It may result in anxiety caused by the loss of familiar signs, symbols, and cues for interpreting daily life. When new environmental cues are not recognized, customary frames of reference are challenged, calling into question an individual's sense of self (Oberg, 1960). Research suggests that culture shock involves feelings, such as confusion over expected role behaviors, helplessness at having little, if any, control over the environment, sense of doubt when old values (which had been held as absolute) are brought into question, feelings of being rejected (or at least not accepted) by members of the new culture, and lowered self-esteem because of personal ineffectiveness (Ferraro, 2002). Given that the organization was the reason for the move to the host country, culture shock can be detrimental to an individual's sense of work–life balance, as he or she may blame the organization for any negative feelings during the adjustment process.

Thankfully, culture shock does not last throughout the entire duration of the assignment. Most global assignees will make a gradual adjustment to the host country and most of the negative aspects of culture shock will abate. Some individuals, however, may experience more severe cases of culture shock, which could be accompanied by symptoms such as homesickness, psychological withdrawal or isolation, need for excessive amounts of sleep, compulsive eating, alcoholism, substance abuse, and other stress-related physical ailments (Ferraro, 2002). Even in cases of "normal" adjustment, however, individual concerns are still present. Jet lag, physical exhaustion, overwork, and burnout are common complaints among global assignees, especially if their work requires frequent travel especially at early stages of their assignments. Thus, even in the best of cases in which culture shock is minimal, some negative factors on the global assignee's sense of work–life balance may exist.

The Positive. On the positive side, global assignments may actually enhance work–life balance of individuals. For internationally minded individuals, global assignments can be fascinating learning experiences; they can enhance one's personal development and can frame one's sense of work–life balance positively. This suggests that individuals' predispositions toward global work will moderate the relationship between the global assignment and work–life balance. For example, some people who enjoy travel, enjoy learning languages, are intellectually curious, and the like, could view a global assignment as highly consistent with their self-identity. As such, an opportunity to experience another culture (while gainfully employed) would be viewed very positively and may even improve one's sense of work–life balance. This self-identity and predisposition toward global activities are important moderators for the extent to which a global assignment will affect work–life balance. Given that a global assignment suggests that "work" has permeated every aspect of one's life, these moderators become extremely important (Caligiuri, 2000).

In addition to providing multiple opportunities for enhancing one's personal experiences, global assignments can often be associated with improvements on the "work" side of the work–life balance scale. Those assignees who value growth opportunities see professional development as a clear positive outcome of their global assignment. They report that the uniqueness of their international experience has enabled them to develop valuable knowledge, skills, and abilities that greatly enhance their professional expertise and improve their job performance (Adler, 1981, 1997; Caligiuri & DiSanto, 2001; Inkson et al., 1997; Pickard & Brewster, 1995; Tung, 1998). As a result, the enhanced set of professional skills and development opportunities could increase one's work satisfaction and thus one's sense of work–life balance. Of course, this relationship could be weakened if the sending organization does not value global experience—and unfortunately, this is a challenge for some multinational firms.

The Family: Direct Influence on the Assignee's Work–Life Balance

Whereas the previous section describes positive and negative ways in which individuals can experience work–life balance on global assignments, many additional factors affect the individual's sense of work–life balance. In most cases, global assignees lives are embedded into those of their partners, children, friends, and other loved ones. Partners and children, who often accompany them to the host country, have their lives disrupted for the sake of the assignees' job. Their experiences can often have a profound influence on the assignee's sense of work–life balance and, subsequently, on the outcome of global assignments.

Many researchers have found a positive relationship between family members' adjustment and the global assignee's adjustment and a negative relationship between family adjustment and global assignee withdrawal cognitions (Black, Gregerson, & Mendenhall, 1992; Black, Mendenhall, & Oddou, 1991; Caligiuri et al., 1998; Harvey, 1985, 1995; Shaffer, Harrison, & Gilley, 1999; Shaffer & Harrison 2001; Tung, 1981). For example, a recent study suggested that although adjustment with nonwork-life was not an important predictor of withdrawal cognitions of global assignees without families, it became increasingly important for people with more family obligations. Thus, global assignees with greater family responsibilities paid increasingly more attention to nonwork factors in making withdrawal decisions, eventually considering those family obligations the most important factor in determining whether to withdraw (Shaffer & Harrison, 1998). Exploring similar questions in a sample of married expatriates, Takeuchi, Yun, and Tesluk (2002) found support for significant (and reciprocal) links between the spouse's general adjustment and assignee's general and work adjustment. Further, the adjustment variables were positively related to assignees' general satisfaction, job satisfaction, and intention to return early from assignment (Takeuchi, Yun, & Tesluk, 2003). Shaffer and Joplin (2001) further suggested that whereas expatriates appear to be able to maintain their work concerns at work and not transfer them in their private lives, their family concerns are more likely to interfere with their work. This suggests that nonwork factors are more likely to influence work than vice-versa (Shaffer & Joplin, 2001; Takeuchi et al., 2002).

Family members are an enduring source of identity for global assignees during the transition to the new environment. If partners and children adjust, the global assignee has the benefit of strong family ties that will buffer him or her against the challenges of the assignment, thus increasing one's sense of balance. For this reason, families are a critical foundation of cross-cultural adjustment. As DeLeon and McPartlin (1995) suggested "providing social and psychological support, family life is the main source of security to counteract a profound experience of instability during a long term foreign assignment" (p. 203).

Depending on the family members, the experience of living internationally can be either negative or positive. Based on family systems theory, Caligiuri, Hyland, Joshi, and Bross (1998) found that family-level characteristics such as communication, adaptability, and support are positively related to family adjustment, and that family adjustment, in turn, is related to global assignee adjustment. Copeland and Norell (2002) suggested that shared perceptions of international relocation, family cohesion, and communication are of critical importance for achieving work–life balance on global assignments. Harvey (1996) also suggested that a noncompetitive and reciprocal family unit is important for success on global assignments. In short, the health of the family unit (expressed by cohesion, support, and communication) can be an important determinant of how a given family experiences a move and whether the influence of the family on work–life balance will be negative or positive.

The Negative. In cases where the accompanying partner and children cannot adjust to the host national environment, the relationships within the family may suffer. At the extreme, Reynolds and Bennett (1991) compared a global assignment to "psychological assault on the family" and argue that the strains placed on the relationships can ultimately break the unity of the family and result in divorce (Linehan & Scullion, 2001b; Harvey, 1985). The anxiety and irritability resulting from culture shock can become a major source of marital conflict and relationship dissatisfaction (Pellico & Stroh, 1997; Harvey 1985; Brett & Stroh, 1995). When spillover is this negative, stress and tension can be generated in the couple resulting from demands of both the work and the personal life sphere (Harris, 2002). The resulting stress negatively affects the global assignees sense of work–life balance.

The Positive. On the positive side, global assignments present all family members with opportunities to experience new surroundings and new cultures together, to make friends from different nationalities, to learn a new language, or pursue new educational opportunities (Elron & Kark, 2000; De Leon & McPartlin, 1995). The transition to another country may, in fact, be beneficial to the couple and family as a unit (Caligiuri, Hyland, Joshi, & Bross, 1998). Considering that most families or couples will move to another country knowing only each other, there will be a period of time (before new friendships are made) when they are the sole source of support, friendship, and socialization for each other. For cohesive and adaptive families and couples, global assignments can actually strengthen and deepen their relational bonds as they experience their new environment together (Caligiuri et al., 1998). These positive outcomes of living internationally for couples and families should not be overlooked.

POSITIVE AND NEGATIVE COUNTERWEIGHTS OF THE GLOBAL ASSIGNMENT FOR THE WORK–LIFE BALANCE OF ACCOMPANYING PARTNERS AND CHILDREN

The previous section demonstrated the various ways accompanying partners and children could affect the global assignee sense of work–life balance. In the following section, we explore the challenges and benefits to accompanying partners and children while living in a host country.

Challenges and Benefits for Accompanying Partners

The Negative. Research has shown that even though all members of a global assignee's family may undergo the negative effects of culture shock, accompanying partners are likely to undergo a more difficult adjustment period than global assignees. While dealing with a sense of separation and loss, global assignees still have their jobs and professional commitments as integral parts of their identity. The accompanying partner's contacts are limited primarily, at least initially, to the global assignee community—in contrast to the global assignee who interacts with the local community through his or her work and is placed in circumstances allowing faster familiarization with the host culture. In fact, the partner's daily activities and contacts with the local culture are generally not assisted by host national colleagues, further exacerbating the sense of psychological disorientation and lengthening the adjustment period (Briody & Chrisman, 1991; Punnett, 1997; Harvey, 1985, 1996; Pellico & Stroh, 1997; Shaffer & Harrison, 2001).

Lack of interaction with the host national community may lead to a heightened perception of social isolation causing the accompanying partners to feel much more isolated compared to the assignees. Traditional community supports and family ties are not readily available, and there are not enough enduring sources of the partners' self-identity remaining (especially for working professionals) to compensate for these losses (Gaylord, 1979; Brett, 1980). Given these compounded effects of culture and loss of self-identity, accompanying partners can be even more adversely affected by the global relocation (Copeland & Norell, 2002; Harvey, 1985; Pellico & Stroh, 1997; Tung, 1986; Shaffer & Harrison, 2001). As with culture shock, the negative effects generally subside over time as the accompanying partner makes friends or finds meaningful work in the host country. Accompanying partners with professional careers may find global assignments particularly challenging because, as recent evidence suggests, very few are able to find employment at the host location, even if they were employed full time prior to expatriation (GMAC et al., 2003; Suutari & Ruisala, 2000). The most common reasons for this inability to find work include various host country regulations related to work permits, language barriers, and a simple lack of available positions. This "dual career problem" has been cited as the main reason some married global assignees do not relocate with their spouse, and, as one can imagine, cited as one of the most likely causes of assignment dissatisfaction with the assignment (Handler, Lane, & Maher, 1997; Pellico & Stroh, 1997; Suutari & Riusala, 2000; GMAC et al., 2003; Swaak, 1995; Harvey, 1996).

The implication is that many accompanying partners' careers are put on hold, normally for a period of a few years. In today's dynamic environment of professional careers, such loss of career continuity may be quite damaging. Moreover, for many of those employed prior to the assignment, inability to get engaged in productive activities outside the home can contribute to increased stress (Punnett, 1997). Even though accompanying partners voluntarily choose to place their careers on the backburner, losing one's job is still a stressful experience. Accompanying partners not only lose their income, but also lose another source of social and professional identity; this loss compounds

---

TEXT BOX 2

MALE ACCOMPANYING PARTNERS

In the past, accompanying partners were more likely to be women. With the increase of the number of women undertaking global assignee assignments (see Text Box 1), this is beginning to change. Although the trend is natural, it should be noted that the experiences of male accompanying partners could be somewhat more frustrating than those of female accompanying partners. Within the traditional "expatriate enclaves," male partners are sometimes perceived as unusual and out of place, even among their compatriots.

Within the expatriate communities (a frequently cited source of support), male accompanying partners have reported experiencing difficulties participating in activities organized by female accompanying partners within the expatriate enclaves—either because they do not feel well accepted, do not feel comfortable being the only man in a group of women, or because the activities are not of interest to them (Harris, 2002).

This reluctance sometimes extends to socializing with other global assignees and their families. Research suggests that whereas 70% of female accompanying partners feel included in socializing that takes place with other global assignees, less than 40% of male accompanying partners do. Male accompanying partners may need a different type of support, compared to nonworking female accompanying partners, and such support may be difficult to find (Punnett, 1997; Moore, 2002; Elron & Kark, 2000).

---

the feelings of low self-esteem, social isolation, and anxiety normally experienced during international transitions (Elron & Lark, 2000; Pellico & Stroh, 1997; Hardill & MacDonald, 1998; Harvey, 1995; Swaak, 1995; Reynolds & Bennett, 1991).

The Positive. On the other hand, global assignments can be extremely positive for accompanying partners, as they provide many opportunities for personal enrichment. Once the initial challenges have subsided, many experiences that can only be brought about by a global assignment are, in fact, viewed as very positive. For example, accompanying partners may become fluent in the host national language, develop profound understanding of the host culture, pursue hobbies, or professional interests. Often the friendships developed during this unique period are also very deep.

In addition to personal benefits, global assignments present many opportunities for professional development for career-oriented accompanying partners, even if not formally employed. Many career-oriented accompanying partners will pursue various entrepreneurial options, explore possible career changes by updating skills in an area in which they are not experts, or keep up their professional skills through becoming active members of professional organizations. They can get involved in volunteer activities or unpaid internships, or if their profession allows it they can undertake consulting projects (Reynolds & Bennett, 1991).

Challenges and Benefits for Children

The Negative. In addition to the accompanying partners, the children of expatriates may also experience problems in adjustment. Uprooting a child from a place that is an important identity source can be a stressful experience (Harvey, 1985). In addition to concerns over availability of high quality education, one also needs to consider the emotional stress children undergo during periods of transition. Children can face obstacles such as saying goodbye to friends, making new friends, starting a new school, communicating through language barriers, having inadequate peer relations, lacking in peer acceptance (especially problematic for teenagers), and overall disruption to personal life. If not adequately supported by the parents, children may feel lonely and isolated, uncertain about their identity, and experience diminished self-esteem. The transition poses extraordinary demands on children of all ages, and it is critical that parents acknowledge this and do their best to help children through this adjustment phase (Borstoff et al., 1997; Brett, 1980, De Leon & McPartlin, 1995; Harvey, 1985). As one can imagine, this child–parent spillover effect can have a powerful effect on the work–life balance of the global assignee.

The Positive. Living in another country can also be very positive for children. Crossing cultural boundaries successfully can engender self-confidence and self-control and perceptions of control over the environment, especially in the case of children. De Leon and McPartlin (1995) argued that if expatriation occurs during the critical development stages, children's maturity could be enhanced as the children develop an international perspective. Domestic relocation literature has also suggested that mobile children are higher achievers (for example, do better academically) than stable children because of the role of the geographic relocation as a stimulating growth experience. Further, it has been proposed that mobile children have greater tolerance for new or uncertain situations and exhibit less anxiety in both acute and chronic stressful situations. Some evidence also exists that mobile children place greater value on autonomy and independence than children who are stables (Brett, 1980).

It has recently been suggested that many expatriate children become "third culture kids" (TCKs), children who have lived in more than one country and have been exposed to more than one different culture for a period of time (Selmer & Lam, 2002). Their unique experiences make them establish a frame of reference different from, but influenced by all cultures they have been exposed to. Research by Selmer and Lan (2002) provided some preliminary evidence that adolescent expatriate children exhibit characteristics that differentiate them from their "single culture" peers. Comparing samples of British expatriate adolescents living in Hong Kong, local Hong Kong adolescents living in Hong Kong, and local British adolescents living in Britain, Selmer and Lan (2002) found that TCKs, to a larger extent than their host and home peers, had perceptions of international experience, open mindedness toward other cultures, respect and tolerance of others, flexibility, and their own cultural identity. TCKs also reported a higher preference for international careers, travel and future orientation, foreign language orientation, and lower settling-down preferences. Clearly, the global assignment has a far-reaching impact on the development of expatriate children.

GLOBAL ASSIGNEES' WORK–LIFE BALANCE: ORGANIZATIONS CAN STEADY THE SCALE

An interesting paradox operates when considering the relationship between global assignees' work-life balance and the organizations that send them on assignment. Consider the following questions:

Global assignments permeate every aspect of an individual's life. In this context, how should organizations intervene to ensure that global assignees achieve work–life balance?

Global assignment success may be better predicted by nonwork factors, than work factors. To what extent should organizations be involved in the lives of their employees' partners, children, or other extended family members, to maximize the likelihood of success?

Depending on the organizational culture of the multinational corporation, a company may approach these issues differently. Most organizations pragmatically understand that in order to manage the risk of a potential unsuccessful assignment, they must manage the effect of nonwork factors. They recognize the powerful influence that accompanying partners and children can have on the work–life balance of the global assignees, and in turn, their job performance. As such, these organizations opt to become more involved in the nonwork aspects of their assignees and families. Treading carefully to preserve individual privacy, organizations (to varying degrees) have developed programs, policies, and practices designed for global assignees and their family members to utilize. This next section highlights some examples of these practices that organizations have developed to encourage global assignees' work–life balance. The practices fall into six general categories: predeparture decision making, cross-cultural training, in country support, career assistance, accompanying partner support, and general work–life assistance.

Predeparture Decision Making

The first, and perhaps the most critical, step in helping employees maintain work–life balance while on a global assignment happens before the global assignment even begins. As discussed in a previous section, individuals and their partners, if positively predisposed to global experience, will likely accept and enjoy global assignments (Brett & Stroh, 1995; Caligiuri et al., 1998). As such, many organizations have developed methods that will enable future global assignees and their accompanying partners to make a thoroughly realistic and informed decision. There are three common elements in all of these predeparture decision-making programs. The first element is that organizations start early by engaging employees to consider a global assignment (in the context of their career and personal life circumstances), even before a specific position becomes available. The second element is to involve the family as early as possible in the decision-making process (Caligiuri et al., 1998; Harvey, 1985). The third element is to maintain enough flexibility in the system to allow for de-selection at every phase. The best selection decision will be mutual among the employee, his or her organization, and his or her family.

In this predeparture decision-making phase, future global assignees should understand both the advantages and disadvantages the international move may have on them and their family members (Elron & Kark, 2000). To this end, some multinational corporations offer a visit to the host country prior to accepting the assignment (i.e., a look–see visit); they may offer formal and informal opportunities to discuss their move with former global assignees (i.e., repatriates).

Organizations should consider the facts that all the information they offer an expatriate prior to the assignment will influence his or her expectations and that the goal for managing those expectations should be *accuracy*.

Cross-Cultural Training

Cross-cultural training is defined as any planned intervention designed to increase the knowledge and skills of global assignees to live and work effectively and to achieve general life satisfaction in an unfamiliar host culture (Kealey & Protheroe, 1996). For more than 20 years, cross-cultural training has been advocated as a means of facilitating effective cross-cultural interactions and cross-cultural adjustment (Brewster, 1995; Caligiuri, Phillips, Lazarova, Tarique, & Burgi, 2001; Katz & Seifer, 1996; Kealey & Protheroe, 1996). There has been a positive trajectory of growth with respect to multinational corporations who are offering cross-cultural training. For instance, in the early 1980s, Tung (1981, 1982) found that only 32% of multinational corporations offered cross-cultural training, whereas almost 20 years later, the 1998 Global Relocation Trends Survey Report indicates that 70% of the 177 multinational corporations surveyed provide at least one day of cross-cultural training (Windham International & National Foreign Trade Council, 1998). Research has shown that a well-designed cross-cultural training program can enhance the learning process of the global assignee and thus facilitate effective cross-cultural interactions, cross-cultural adjustment, and work–life balance (Black & Gregersen, 1991; Caligiuri, Phillips, Lazarova, Tarique, & Burgi, 2001).

In addition to cross-cultural training, multinational corporations are offering other types of formal training to global assignees and their partners and children to help them achieve greater work–life balance. One type of formal training is language-skills training—often offered both predeparture and within the host country. Another type of training, albeit less common, is stress management training offered to help individuals manage their expectations prior to and their stressors during a global assignment.

In-Country Support

Although much of the cross-cultural training described in the previous section happens prior to departure, many additional programs offered in-country are beginning to become increasingly more popular. Support programs, such as culture coaches, destination services, and online support networks are becoming more popular. In some cases, companies are sponsoring these programs in-house, whereas others are seeking outside vendors. The most formal type of support program that companies offer is the International Employee Assistance Programs. These programs are available to handle extreme (and even not so extreme) personal concerns and mental and emotional challenges (e.g., depression, anxiety, and alcoholism).

In structuring global assignments, there are some additional best practices that companies have used to help global assignees maintain their work–life balance. For one, organizations can limit additional work-related travel of the global assignee, especially in the beginning of the global assignment, or they can reduce the number of working hours required at the onset of the assignment. Another policy is to offer frequent home visits for global assignees managing certain nonwork situations (e.g., caring for an elderly parent or maintain a long distance relationship). In many respects, these are the most sensitive of all practices in helping employees maintain their work–life balance while on assignments. In many cases, organizations have offered them in a cafeteria-style benefits package, where individuals can select the programs that they need and want, without any questions asked to preserve individuals' privacy.

Career Assistance

Organizations offering career-related assistance to their global assignees often do so to prevent the global assignees from leaving their organization upon repatriation. The added benefit is that career counseling may also reduce work-related anxiety and man enable the global assignee to achieve greater balance. There are many variations of formal career management and succession planning systems organizations use to achieve these goals. In addition to those formal organizational systems, some organizations provide a mentor to help global assignees with some of the more subtle aspects of career management. In combination, these practices have a positive effect of the global assignee and the organization hoping to maintain their human talent.

Accompanying Partner Support

As Suutari and Riusala (2000) suggested, there are many discrepancies between dual-career needs of the accompanying partner and extent to which they are available in organizations. In 2002, the Global Relocations Trends survey found that 56% of the companies made provisions for accompanying partners' careers: 36% offered education or training assistance, 31% of offered career enhancement reimbursement, 28% offered career planning assistance, and 21% offered assistance finding employment. These percentages are a large increase from even 5 years ago, reflecting the increased corporate involvement in the nonwork aspect of their employees' lives.

There are other tangible services that companies offer accompanying partners on global assignments. These include: monetary policies such as paying fees required by employment agencies in the host countries, offering seed money to start a new business, paying fees to join professional associations, compensation of accompanying partner lost wages and benefits, or offering financial support to engage in volunteer service (Pellico & Stroh, 1997; Punnett, 1997). Other tangible services companies offer are nonmonetary but are also considered extremely useful for accompanying partners. These include: organization-sponsored support groups for partners (Punnett, 1997), employment networks coordinated with other global firms (Punnett, 1997), and office space in the host location for the purpose of job hunting (Elron & Kark, 2000). It is interesting to note that Pellico and Stroh (1997) found a surprising lack of awareness among accompanying partners about the types of programs available to them through their partners' organization. In part, this could be due to the fact that firms respect employee privacy and do not contact the accompanying partners directly. The information, therefore, is second-hand through the employees who may, in some cases, have personal reasons for not relaying the information or may not view the information as necessary.

General Work–Life Assistance

Every individual, couple, and family has unique needs that may affect their success and happiness living in another country. As such, most international HR professionals encourage the maximum flexibility and privacy in all global assignment support programs. For example, a global assignee with a special needs child may require a certain type of educational or medical assistance before the assignment can become viable. Some organizations offer support for global assignees engaging in a commuter marriage as a result of the global position (Harris, 1993). Other organizations, in an effort to solve problems such as the dual-career concern, may encourage a greater use of short-term assignments, generally not involving the relocation of the assignee's partner and children (Harris, 1993).

DIRECTIONS FOR FUTURE RESEARCH

Although much of the research literature to date has focused on many important issues concerning global assignees' work–life balance, several important unanswered questions remain. The three areas we believe to be most important are highlighted below: (a) the applicability of domestic work–life balance models to global assignees' work–life balance; (b) the focus on the long-term effects of global assignments on assignees and their families, both positive and negative; and (c) value-added research on whether organizational interventions improve work–life balance among global assignees. Each of these three will be described in greater detail below.

Global and "Domestic" Work–Life Models

With respect to the first, researchers should focus on whether "domestic" work–life balance models apply to the global assignment context. It is true that the global assignment context is unique because, by definition, work (i.e., the assignment) permeates every aspect of the global assignee's life. That said, future research should determine whether global assignees differ from domestic employees in terms of the way they experience of work interference with personal life. Do some global assignees perceive the assignment differently and view assignments as less intrusive?

One of the most interesting issues to be examined in a global context involves the relative influence of "work interference with life" and "life interference with work" on various outcomes. Domestic literature (in most instances, U.S.-based) has placed more emphasis on "work interference with life" as a predictor of important individual and organizational variables. On the other hand, most research on global assignments has focused on "personal life interference with work," exploring the broad and complex effects of the assignees' private lives on various aspects of their work. What often remains unacknowledged is that during global assignments, work becomes much more pervasive and fully permeates assignees' personal lives. Assignments are often associated with higher work responsibilities and a need to operate efficiently in an unfamiliar environment. This is likely to lead to more time and energy being put into work.

Given this context, future research will be well advised to broaden its focus and investigate both directions of interference (personal life to work and work to personal life) in a more systematic manner. The past two decades have provided a large body of literature on the dimensionality of work–life balance in the domestic context (for example, Dixbury, & Higgins, 1991; Edwards & Rothbard, 2000; Frone, Yardley, & Markel, 1997; Greenhaus, 1988; Greenhaus & Beutell, 1985). Building on Shaffer, Harrison, Luk, and Gilley's work (2001), future research on global assignees should examine these existing domestic work–life balance models for applicability to the context of international work.

Finally, recent work on the construct of work–life balance has suggested that "balance" implies more than just the absence of interference, but rather also includes possible synergies from the interaction between work and personal life (Fisher, 2001). A focus on work–life *enhancement* in the context of global assignments (i.e., the extent to which one's personal life is enhanced by work and vice versa while on assignment) is another promising direction for future research.

Longitudinal Effects of Global Assignments on Work–Life Balance

In this chapter, we tried to present a balanced approach to the topic of work–life balance in global assignments—presenting both the negative and the positive ways in which global assignments affect individuals and their sense of balance. Future research should follow global assignees and their families' longer term to determine whether there are any lasting and predictable outcomes, such as marital strength, open mindedness, or health effects. In particular, it would be especially interesting for research to focus on whether accompanying partners and children experience any long-term positive outcomes after global assignments? Anecdotally, this would seem to be the case.

Organizational Interventions to Improve Work–Life Balance

Although this chapter offered many possible ways in which organizations can help to improve the perception of balance among global assignees, very few of them have been evaluated for effectiveness. Unfortunately, in times when budgets are tight and organizations are looking for ways to contain costs, certain programs (such as many of those mentioned in this chapter) are at risk of being cut. Academics should partner with practitioners to conduct action-oriented research on the effectiveness of these various programs. Although field research such as this is challenging, it would be a tremendous contribution to guide practitioners how to best manage their decreasing global assignment budgets.

Given the growing expense of traditional global assignments, the increased concern for security, and familial preferences, multinational corporations have been trying various alternatives to long-term assignments. Some of these alternatives include one-way or permanent moves, short-term assignments (less than one year), commuter assignments, and extended business travel without relocation. One of the rationales of introducing such alternative assignments has been that they would be associated with fewer disruptions in the personal and family life of employees who undertake them.

A recent study suggested, however, that these arrangements are not the "panacea" they promise to be. Harris and her colleagues (Harris & Brewster, in press; Harris, Petrovic, & Brewster, 2001) surveyed respondents from 65 European and American MNEs. Their results strongly indicated that alternatives to long-term global assignments bring about some serious work–life balance issues, such as long hours working on a project, burnout, travel fatigue, and "resentment at time spent away from family." It is critical that future research expands research on the topic of alternative assignments and the influence they have on work–life balance of the individual employees and their family members. Such research is especially important in view of the few existing organizational policies that regulate these types of global assignments.

We believe that this chapter provided sufficient evidence for the way in which global assignments affect assignees' work–life balance and areas that warrant future investigation. Every year international work activity increases, and the benefits to global firms are discussed and often touted. Researchers should expand our field of focus to determine the effects of the international work activity on individuals and their families and on organizations. Human resource practitioners, alike, should seek out international practices to optimize both the needs of their global organization and the needs of their globally active employees. Technology, transportation, and ease of communication have certainly lowered barriers to globalization in today's ever-shrinking world. It should be our role now, as academics and practitioners, to lower the barriers for the people and help them achieve happy, fulfilled, and more global lives.

REFERENCES

Adler, N. J. (1997). Global leadership: Women leaders. *Management International Review, 1*(Special Issue), 171–196.

Adler, N. J. (1981). Re-entry: Managing cross-cultural transitions. *Group and Organizational Studies, 6*, 341–356.

Black, J. S., & Gregersen, H. B. (1991). The other half of the picture: Antecedents of spouse cross cultural adjustment. *Journal of International Business Studies, 22*, 461–477.

Black, J. S., Gregersen, H. B., & Mendenhall, M. E. (1992). Toward a theoretical framework of repatriation adjustment. *Journal of International Business, 24*, 737–760.

Black, J. S., Mendenhall, M., & Oddou, G. (1991). Toward a comprehensive model of international adjustment: An integration of multiple theoretical perspectives. *Academy of Management Review, 16*, 291–317.

Black, J. S., & Stephens, G. K. (1989). The influence of the spouse on American expatriate adjustment and intent to stay in Pacific Rim overseas assignments. *Journal of Management, 15*, 529–544.

Borstorff, P. C., Harris, S. G., Field, H. S., & Giles, W. F. (1997). Who'll go? A review of factors associated with employee willingness to work overseas. *Human Resource Planning, 20*, 29–40.

Brett, J. M. (1980). The effect of job transfer on employees and their families. In C. L. Cooper & R. Payne (Eds.). Current concerns in occupational stress. John Wiley & Sons, Ltd.

Brett, J. M., & Stroh, L. K. (1995). Willingness to relocate internationally. *Human Resource Management, 34*, 405–424.

Brewster, C. 1995. The paradox of expatriate adjustment. In J. Selmer (Ed.), *Expatriate management: New ideas for international business:* xii, 325. Westport, Conn.: Quorum Books.

Brewster, C., & Pickard, J. (1994). Evaluating Expatriate Training. *International Studies of Management & Organization, 18*(3), 18–35.

Briody, E. K., & Chrisman, J. B. (1991). Cultural adaptation on overseas assignments. *Human Organizations, 50*, 264–282.

Caligiuri, P. M. (1998). *Evaluating the success of global assignments: Performance measurement in a cross-national context.* Paper presented at the 1998 Academy of Management Meeting, San Diego, CA.

Caligiuri, P. M. (2000). The big five personality characteristics as predictors of expatriate's desire to terminate the assignment and supervisor-rated performance. *Personnel Psychology, 53*, 67–88.

Caligiuri, P. M., & Di Santo, V. (2001). Global competence: What is it, and can it be developed through global assignments? *Human Resource Planning, 24*(3), 27–35.

Caligiuri, P. M., Hyland, M. M., & Joshi, A. (1998). Families on global assignments: Applying work/family theories abroad. In M. A. Rahim & R. T. Golembiewski (Eds.). *Current topics in management*, Vol. 3. (pp. 313–328). Greenwich, CT: JAI Press.

Caligiuri, P. M., Hyland, M. M., Joshi, A., & Bross, A. S. (1998). Testing a theoretical model for examining the relationship between family adjustment and expatriates' work adjustment. *Journal of Applied Psychology, 83*(4), 598–614.

Caligiuri, P. M., Joshi, A., & Lazarova, M. (1999). Factors influencing the adjustment of women on Global assignments. *International Journal of Human Resource Management, 10*, 163–179.

Caligiuri, P. M., & Lazarova, M. (2001). *Strategic repatriation policies to enhance global leadership development.* Invited book chapter for M. Mendenhall, T. Kuehlmann, & G. Stahl (Eds), *Developing Global Business Leaders: Policies, Processes and Innovations.* Quorum Books.

Caligiuri, P. M., Phillips, J., Lazarova, M., Tarique, I., & Burgi, P. (2001). The theory of met expectations applied to expatriate adjustment: The role of cross-cultural training. *International Journal of Human Resource Management, 12*(3), 357–372.

Copeland, A. P., & Norell, S. K. (2002). Spousal adjustment on international assignments: The role of social support. *International Journal of Intercultural Relations, 26,* 255–272.

De Leon, C. T., & McPartlin, D. (1995). *Adjustment of expatriate children.* In J. Selmer (Ed.), *Expatriate management: New ideas for international business.* Westport, CT: Quorum Books.

Dixbury, L. E., & Higgins, C. A. (1991). Gender differences in work-family conflict. *Journal of Applied Psychology, 76,* 60–74.

Dowling, P., Welch, D., & Schuler, R. (1998). *International Human Resource Management* (3rd ed). Cincinnati, OH: South-Western College Publishing.

Edwards, J. R., & Rothbard, N. P. (2000). Mechanisms linking work and family: Clarifying the relationship between work and family constructs. *Academy of Management Review, 25,* 178–199.

Elron, E., & Kark, R. (2000). *Women managers and international assignments: Some recommendations for bridging the gap.* In M. Mendenhall & G. Oddou (Eds.), *Readings in international human resource management.* Cincinnati, OH: South-Western College Publishing.

Ensher, E. A., Murphy, S. E., & Sullivan, S. E. (2002). Reel women: Lessons from female TV executives on managing work and real life. *Academy of Management Executive, 16,* 106–120.

Evans, P., Pucik, V., & Barsoux, J. L. (2001). *The global challenge: Frameworks for international human resource management.* New York: McGraw-Hill Irwin.

Fenwick, M. (2001). *New forms of international working: Evidence from Australia.* In H. DeCieri (Chair) *International Human Resource Strategies: New perspectives, new work.* Symposium presented at the 61st Annual AOM Meeting, Washington, DC.

Ferraro, G. P. (2002). *The cultural dimension of international business* (4th ed). Upper Saddle River, NJ: Pearson Education, Inc.

Fisher, G. G. (2001). *Work/personal life balance: A construct development study.* Unpublished Doctoral dissertation, Bowling Green State University, Bowling Green, OH.

Frone, M. R., Yardley, J. K., & Markel, K. S. (1997). Developing and testing an integrative model of the work-family interface. *Journal of Organizational Behavior, 50,* 145–167.

Fukuda, J., & Chu, P. (1994). Wrestling with expatriate family problems: Japanese experience in East Asia. *International Studies of Management & Organization, 24*(3), 36–47.

Garonzik, R., Brockner, J., & Siegel, P. A. (2000). Identifying international assignees at risk of premature departure: The interactive effect of outcome favorability and procedural fairness. *Journal of Applied Psychology, 85*, 13–20.

Gaylord, M. (1979). Relocation and the corporate family: Unexplored issues. *Social Work, 24*, 186–191.

Glanz, L., & van der Sluis, E. C. (2001). Employing organisations and expatriate spouses: Balancing self-knowledge and knowledge about options. *Career Development International, 6*(3), 169–175.

GMAC Global Relocation Services, National Foreign Trade Council, & Society for Human Resource Management Global Forum (2002). Global Relocation Trends 2001 Survey Report. GMAC Warren, NJ: Relocation Services.

GMAC Global Relocation Services, National Foreign Trade Council, & Society for Human Resource Management Global Forum (2003). Global Relocation Trends 2002 Survey Report. Warren, NJ: GMAC Relocation Services.

Grant-Vallone, E. J., & Ensher, E. A. (2001). An examination of work and personal life conflict, organizational support, and employee health among international expatriates. *International Journal of Intercultural Relations, 25*, 261–278.

Greenhaus, J. H. (1988). The intersection of family and work roles: Individual, interpersonal and organizational issues. *Journal of Social Behavior and Personality, 3*(4), 23–44.

Greenhaus, J. H., & Beutell, N. J. (1985). Sources of conflict between work and family roles. *Academy of Management Review, 10*, 76–88.

Guzzo, R. A., Noonan, K. A., & Elron, E. (1994). Expatriate managers and the psychological contract. *Journal of Applied Psychology, 79*, 617–626.

Haines III, V. Y., & Saba, T. (1999). International mobility policies and practices: Are there gender differences in importance ratings? *Career Development International, 4*, 206.

Handler, C. A., Lane, I. M., & Maher, M. (1997). Career planning and expatriate couples. *Human Resource Management Journal, 7*, 67–79.

Hardill, I., & MacDonald, S. (1998). Choosing to relocate: AN examination of the impact of expatriate work on dual career households. *Women's Studies International Forum, 21*, 21–29.

Harris, H. (1993). Women in international management: Opportunity or threat? *Women in Management Review, 8*, 9–14.

Harris, H. (1995). Organizational influences on women's career opportunities in international management. *Women in Management Review, 10*, 26–31.

Harris, H. (2002). Think international manager, think male: Why are women not selected for international management assignments. *Thunderbird International Business Review, 44*, 175–203.

Harris, H., & Brewster, C. (in press). "*Alternatives to traditional international assignments*" in Mayrhofer, W., Stahl, G. and Kuhlmann, T. *Innovative Ansaetz im internationalen Personalmanagement* (Innovating HRM), Hampp, Mering.

Harris, H., & Brewster, C. (2003) (in press). *Alternatives to traditional international assignments* in Mayrhofer, W., Stahl, G. and Kuhlmann, T. *Innovative Ansaetze im internationalen Personalmanagement* (Innovating HRM), Hampp, Mering.

Harris, H., & Kumra S. (1999). *Sex-Role Stereotypes in Management: Of Square Pegs and Round Holes.* Paper presented at the British Academy of Management Annual Conference, Manchester 1–3 September 1999.

Harris, H., Petrovic, J., & Brewster, C. (2001). "New Forms of International Working: The Panacea to Expatriation Ills?", Paper presented at the Global HRM Conference, ESADE Barcelona, 20–22 June 2001.

Harvey, M. (1985). The executive family: An overlooked variable in international assignments. *Columbia Journal of World Business, 20,* 84–92.

Harvey, M. (1995). The impact of dual career families on international relocations. *Human Resource Management Review, 5,* 223–244.

Harvey, M. (1996). Addressing the dual-career expatriation dilemma. *Human Resource Planning, 19*(4), 18–39.

Harvey, M. (1997). Dual-career expatriates: Expectations, adjustment and satisfaction with international relocation. *Journal of International Business Studies, 28,* 627–658.

Harvey, M., & Weise, D. (1998). Global dual-career couple mentoring: A phase model approach. *Human Resource Planning, 21*(2), 33–48.

Hays, R. D. (1972). Ascribed behavioral determinants among US expatriate managers. *Journal of International Business Studies, 2,* 40–46.

Hemingway, M. (2000). *Roles outside of work: What is the "life" in work-life balance?* Paper presented at the Society of Industrial and Organizational Psychology Annual Meeting, New Orleans, LA.

Inkson, K., Pringle, J., Arthur, M. B., & Barry, S. (1997). Expatriate assignment versus overseas experience: Contrasting models of international human resource development. *Journal of World Business, 32*(4), 351–368.

Izraeli, D., Banai, M., & Zeira, Y. (1980). Women executives in MNC subsidiaries. *California Management Review, 23,* 53–63.

Kealey, D. L., & Protheroe, D. R. (1996). The effectiveness of cross-cultural training for expatriates: An assessment of the literature on the issue. *International Journal of Intercultural Relations, 20*(2), 141–165.

Lazarova, M. B., & Caligiuri, P. (2001). Retaining repatriates: The role of organization support practices. *Journal of World Business, 36,* 389–401.

Linehan, M., & H. Scullion. (2001a). An Empirical Study of Work–Family Conflicts in International Assignments: The Experiences of Female Expatriates in Europe, *Management Development Journal of Singapore, 10,* 1–9.

Linehan, M., & Scullion, H. (2001b). Work–Family Conflict: The Female Expatriate Perspective, *International Journal of Applied Human Resource Management, 2*(2), 5–13.

Linehan, M., & Scullion, H. (2001c). European female expatriate careers: Critical success factors. *Journal of European Industrial Training, 25,* 392–418.

Linehan, M., Scullion, H., & Walsh, J. S. (2001). Barriers to women's participation in international management. *European Business Review, 13*, 10–18.

Linehan, M., Scullion, H., & Walsh, J. S. (2000). The Growth of Female Expatriation and Male Spouses in Europe: The Challenges for International Human Resource Management. *The International Journal of Applied Management Human Resource Management, 1*, 37–48.

Linehan, M., & Walsh, J. S. (2000). Work–Family Conflict and the Senior Female International Manager, *British Journal of Management, 11*, Special Issue, 49–58.

Moore, M. J. (2002). Same ticket, different trip: Supporting dual-career couples on global assignments. *Women in Management Review, 17*(2), 61–67.

Oberg, K. (1960). Cultural shock: Adjustment to new cultural environments. *Practical Anthropology, 7:* 177–182.

Pellico, M. T., & Stroh, L. (1997). *Spousal assistance programs: An integral component of the international assignment. New approaches to employee management, 4*, 227–243.

Punnett, B. J. (1997). Towards effective management of expatriate spouses. *Journal of World Business, 32*, 243–257.

Reynolds, C., & Bennett, R. (1991). The career couple challenge. *Personnel Journal*, March 1991, 46–49.

Scullion, H. (1994). Staffing policies and strategic control in British multinationals. *International Studies of Management and Organization, 24*, 86–104.

Selmer, I., & Lam, H. (2002). Using Former "Third-Culture Kids" as a Recruitment Source for Business Expatriates with Successful Potential. *BRC Papers of Cross-Cultural Management* (CCMP #200205). Hong Kong Baptist University.

Shaffer, M., & Harrison, D. A. (1998). Expatriates' psychological withdrawal from international assignments: Work, non-work, and family influences. *Personnel Psychology, 51*, 87–118.

Shaffer, M. A., & Harrison, D. A. (2001). Forgotten partners of international assignments development and test of a model of spouse adjustment. *Journal of Applied Psychology, 86*, 238–254.

Shaffer, M. A., & Harrison, D. (1998). Expatriates' psychological withdrawal from international assignments: Work, non-work, and family influences. *Personnel Psychology, 51*, 87–118.

Shaffer, M., Harrison, D., & Gilley, D. M. (1999). Dimensions, determinants, and differences in the expatriate adjustment process. *Journal of International Business Studies, 30*, 557–581.

Shaffer, M., Harrison, D., Luk, D. M., & Gilley, D. M. (2000). Spouse adjustment to international assignments: Direct determinants and the moderating effects of coping strategies. *Management Research News, 23* (2-4), 29–31.

Shaffer, M. A., Harrison, D. A., Gilley, K. M., & Luk, D. M. (2001). Struggling for balance amid turbulence on international assignments: work–family conflict, support and commitment. *Journal of Management, 27,* 99–121.

Shaffer, M. A., & Joplin, J. R. W. (2001). Work family conflict on international assignments: Time and based determinants and performance effort consequences. *AOM Proceedings 2001 IM,* I1–I6.

Stephens, G. K., & Black, S. (1991). The impact of spouse's career orientation on managers during international transfers. *Journal of Management Studies, 28,* 417–428.

Stroh, L. K., Varma, A., & Valy-Durbin, S. J. (2000). Why are women left at home: Are they unwilling to go on international assignments? *Journal of World Business, 35*(3), 1–15.

Stryker, S., & Serpe, R. T. (1982). Commitment, identity salience and role behavior: theory and research examples. In W. Ickes & E. Knowles (Eds.), *Personality Roles and Social Behavior* (pp. 199–218). York: Springer.

Stryker, S., & Serpe, R. T. (1994). Identity salience and psychological centrality: Equivalent, overlapping, or complementary concepts? *Social Psychology Quarterly, 57,* 16–35.

Suutari, V., & Riusala, K. (2000). Expatriation and careers: Perspectives of expatriates and spouses. *Career Development International, 5*(2), 81–90.

Swaak, R. A. (1995). Today's expatriate family: Dual career and other obstacles. *Compensation and Benefits Review, 27*(6), 21–26.

Takeuchi, R., Yun, S., & Tesluk, P. E. (2002). An examination of cross-over and spill-over effects of spousal and expatriate cross-cultural adjustment on expatriate outcomes. *Journal of Applied Psychology, 87,* 655–666.

Taylor, S., & Napier, N. (1996). Working in Japan: Lessons from women expatriates. *Sloan Management Review, 37,* 76–84.

Tung, R. L. (1981). Selection and training of personnel for overseas assignments. *Columbia Journal of World Business, 16,* 68–78.

Tung, R. L. (1982). Selection and training procedures of U.S., European, and Japanese multinationals. *California Management Review, 25,* 57–71.

Tung, R. L. (1986). Corporate executives and their families in China: The need for cross-cultural understanding in business. *Columbia Journal of World Business, Spring 1986,* 21–25.

Tung, R. L. (1998). American expatriates abroad: From neophytes to cosmopolitans. *Journal of World Business, 32*(2), 125–144.

Westwood, R. I., & Leung, S. M. (1994). The female expatriate manager experience: Coping with gender and culture. *International Studies of Management and Organization, 24,* 64–85.

Windham International & National Foreign Trade Council. (1994). *Global Relocation Trends 1994 Survey Report.* New York: Windham International.

Windham International & National Foreign Trade Council. (1998). *Global Relocation Trends 1998 Survey Report.* New York: Windham International.

Windham International & National Foreign Trade Council, & Institute for International Human Resource Management. (1999 May). *Global Relocation Trends 1999 Survey Report.* New York: Windham International.

6

Work–Nonwork Culture, Utilization of Work–Nonwork Arrangements, and Employee-Related Outcomes in Two Dutch Organizations

J. S. E. Dikkers
*Radboud University
Nijmegen*

S. A. E. Geurts
*Radboud University
Nijmegen*

L. den Dulk
Utrecht University

B. Peper
*Utrecht University and
Erasmus University
Rotterdam*

ABSTRACT

The main aim of the current study was to examine work–nonwork culture (WNC) in association with the actual utilization of six work–nonwork arrangements (WNAs; part-time work, working from home occasionally, telework, flexible work schedules, child-care arrangements, and parental leave), and three employee-related outcomes (i.e., work–nonwork interference, fatigue, and organizational commitment). Two samples were used consisting of 638 employees from a Dutch financial consultancy firm (Fincom) and 269 employees from a Dutch manufacturing company (Mancom). WNC was measured with a newly developed instrument tapping two dimensions, that is, support and barriers. The results in one organization (Fincom) showed that the more supportive employees perceived the WNC, the more they utilized WNAs. In neither company was a higher utilization of WNAs associated with a lower level of work–nonwork interference (WNI). Employees from both organizations experienced less WNI the more they perceived the WNC as favorable (i.e., high support and low barriers). Within Fincom, WNI seemed to mediate the relationship between a favorable WNC and fatigue. Implications for future research and practice are discussed.

INTRODUCTION

Background and Aim of Study

Changes in work and family life are visible in all Western countries, although the pace and nature of developments may differ across countries. The traditional family pattern in Europe of breadwinner father and homemaker mother is being challenged by the growing number of dual-income families, and more generally, by the rise of women's employment. Consequently, a growing number of people have substantial responsibilities at work in addition to their responsibilities at home. A survey among a representative sample of the U.S. workforce showed that 30% experienced major conflict between work demands and family responsibilities, often referred to as work–family, or work–nonwork interference (Bond, Galinsky, & Swanberg, 1998). As a response to this development, national governments and a growing number of organizations in Western Europe have adopted work–nonwork arrangements (WNAs) to create a supportive environment for employees with care responsibilities (e.g., Den Dulk, 2001; Evans, 2001).

In the Netherlands, the focus of this study, the government started to develop provisions for working parents in the 1990s. Today, Dutch working parents are entitled to 16 weeks maternity leave and 2 days paternity leave; 6 months half-time, unpaid parental leave; and 10 days emergency leave in case of a sick relative. Working part-time is also a common strategy to combine work and family life in the Netherlands, in particular among women (Den Dulk, Van Doorne-Huiskes, & Peper, 2003). If fact, 73% of Dutch women and 21% of Dutch men are employed part-time; these are the highest percentages in Europe (Commission DG Employment and Social Affairs, 2003). Although public childcare is still limited in the Netherlands (Porte-gijs, Boelens, & Keuzenkamp, 2002), an increasing number of companies offer their employees child-care support or other WNAs, such as working from home occasionally and flexible start and finishing times (Den Dulk, 2001; Remery, Van Doorne-Huiskes, & Schippers, 2002).

A distinction can be made between flexible and care-related arrangements; the first type of WNAs is aimed at improving the (spatial or temporal) flexibility of employees' jobs, whereas the second type of WNAs assists employees (particularly parents) in their care-giving activities. Although research on utilization of this kind of arrangements is limited, findings indicate that the presence of facilities does not guarantee the actual use of facilities (cf. Grootscholte, Bouwmeester, & de Klaver, 2000; Den Dulk, 2001). Organizational culture in particular is considered relevant regarding the utilization of WNAs offered.

Thompson, Beauvais, and Lyness (1999) defined work–nonwork culture (WNC) as "the shared assumptions, beliefs, and values regarding the extent to which an organization supports and values the integration of employees' work and family lives" (p. 394). They distinguished among three main WNC components, that is: (a) managerial support for the work–nonwork balance, (b) negative career consequences associated with utilizing WNAs, and (c) organizational time expectations that may interfere with nonwork (family) responsibilities. Allen (2001) extended this conceptualization of WNC by distinguishing between perceived support for the nonwork domain from the supervisor and from the organization as a whole (i.e., Family-Supportive Organization Perceptions; FSOP).

Considering these two WNC conceptualizations of WNC, support for the utilization of WNAs is clearly a central dimension. However, next to the support workers get from their supervisors and from the organization as a whole, one can also imagine that support from colleagues matters when people consider using WNAs. Therefore, support is defined here as the extent to which employees feel themselves supported in using WNAs by the organization they work for, by their supervisors, and by their colleagues. Apart from support, barriers can be considered a second central dimension of WNC because workers are less inclined to use WNAs the more they believe it might negatively affect their career (Thompson et al., 1999). In the current study, barriers are defined as the extent to which employees feel hampered in using WNAs by negative career consequences associated with their use and by organizational time demands prioritizing work above nonwork.

The main aim of the current study is to examine WNC in association with the utilization of WNAs, and three employee-related outcomes (i.e., work–nonwork interference, fatigue, and organizational commitment). Five research questions will be answered: (1) What is the utilization of available work–nonwork arrangements? (2) Is work–nonwork culture related to work–nonwork arrangement utilization? (3) Are culture and/or utilization of arrangements related to work–nonwork interference? (4) Is work–nonwork interference associated with fatigue and/or organizational commitment? and (5) Does work–nonwork interference play a mediating role in the association between culture and/or utilization of arrangements on the one hand and fatigue and/or commitment on the other hand?

Theoretical Framework

The theoretical framework of the current study is provided by two theories. The first one is the theory of reasoned action (Ajzen & Fishbein, 1974, 1980). According to this theory, social norms form important determinants of behavior. From this perspective, we can expect that utilization of WNAs (i.e., behavior) is, among other things, determined by employees' perceptions of the social norms within the organization, considering the utilization of WNAs. Some organizations do not support their employees in finding ways to balance their work with their private lives (Allen, 2001; Thompson et al., 1999). In this kind of organization, employees will not feel supported by their supervisors or by their organization in making use of the WNAs available. Also, in some organizations the amount of time spent at work is often interpreted as an indication of employees' contributions and career dedication. (Lewis & Taylor, 1996; Perlow, 1995; Starrels, 1992). In summary, these social norms may make employees reluctant to take time off or to reduce their work hours to attend to family responsibilities.

In the current study, social norms concerning the utilization of WNAs are examined by measuring the two proposed dimensions of WNC (i.e., support and barriers). In a favorable WNC, employees perceive high support (from the organization, supervisors, and colleagues) and low barriers (i.e., negative career consequences, and time demands) in using WNAs. In an unfavorable WNC, employees perceive low support and high barriers in using WNAs. Following the theory of reasoned action (Ajzen & Fishbein, 1974, 1980), we expect that the more favorably employees perceive the WNC (i.e., low barriers and high support), the more they will use WNAs (Hypothesis 1).

The second theoretical model this study is based on is the Effort–Recovery Model (E–R Model; Meijman, 1989; Meijman & Mulder, 1998). The central assumption of this model is that employees build up negative load effects during the work day. This does not necessarily lead to negative consequences for employees' health and well-being as long as employees are given ample time to recover from these effects. However, there are three types of situations in which an employee cannot recover sufficiently from these negative load effects: (1) the amount of private time can be insufficient to recover from load effects built up at work resulting from long work hours (caused by organizational time demands and negative career consequences associated with working less hours); (2) demands do not cease to exist after work because new demands are made upon the individual in the private situation (e.g., domestic and care-giving tasks); and (3) employees can suffer from a slow process of unwinding (sustained activation; see Ursin, 1980), which can hamper relaxation after work. These three situations may cause employees to experience work–nonwork interference (WNI). Hereby, a distinction can be made between time- and strain-based work–nonwork interference (Greenhaus & Beutell, 1985). Time-based WNI develops when time devoted to work obligations makes it physically impossible to meet obligations in the private domain. Strain-based WNI refers to the extent to which strain developed in the work domain hampers functioning in the private domain.

It is reasonable to assume that using WNAs may help employees to balance their work and private lives more effectively. Based upon the E–R Model (Meijman, 1989; Meijman & Mulder, 1998), we expect that the more favorable employees perceive the WNC (i.e., low barriers and high support), the less WNI they will experience (Hypothesis 2a). Also, we expect that the more employees use WNAs, the less WNI they will experience (Hypothesis 2b).

In the three situations in which sufficient recovery is at stake, a downward spiral may be activated. That is, the employees who are still not fully recovered must invest additional effort to perform adequately during the next work day, resulting in higher load effects that make an even higher appeal on the recovery process. If this negative spiral of incomplete recovery and additional effort continues, the employee will suffer an even greater decrease in well being (e.g., prolonged fatigue, chronic stress, and sleep deprivation) and in motivation in the long run (see Geurts & Demerouti, 2003, for a review). Therefore, we expect that the more (time- or strain-based) WNI employees experience, the more fatigue and the less organizational commitment they will report (Hypothesis 3). We further expect that WNI is likely to play a mediating role in the relationship between WNC and the utilization of WNAs, on the one hand, and fatigue and organizational commitment, on the other (Hypothesis 4).

As a framework to test these hypotheses, our research model is introduced in Figure 6.1.

In this model, the central research variables (i.e., WNC, WNA utilization, WNI, fatigue, and commitment) are presented together with their supposed associations (i.e., Hypotheses 1 to 4) reflected by the respective numbers. For exploratory aims, we will start with examining the utilization the respondents made of available WNAs.

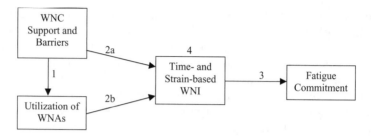

FIG. 6.1. Research model with central research variables and hypotheses 1 to 4.

METHOD

Sample

Data were collected through a survey held in two Dutch multinationals. The first organization is a financial consulting firm with headquarters in the United States, further referred to as Fincom. This organization is a typical example of a postindustrial knowledge company. Of all 5,200 employees working in this company, a select sample of 1,604 people was drawn. In total, 638 questionnaires were returned (40% response rate). Only recently, Fincom has paid attention to the work–nonwork balance of her employees. Several arrangements were implemented: flexible start and finish times, the possibility to work part-time, and a teleworking scheme (i.e. home-based telework for at least one full working day a week). Parental leave was already implemented in Fincom because employees in the Netherlands are legally entitled to take leave when they have a child younger then 8 years of age. Informally, there is also the possibility to work from home occasionally. Additionally, Fincom offers partial financial compensation for the use of child-care arrangements by employees.

The second organization is a male-dominated manufacturing company in the electronic industrial sector, which has its headquarters in the Netherlands, further referred to as Mancom. This organization is a typical industrial manufacturing company. In this company, questionnaires were sent to all 1,381 employees, of which 533 questionnaires were returned (39% response rate). Because employees who worked in shifts were not able to use all WNAs selected in the present study, we decided to select only employees who worked during the day ($N = 269$). Mancom has a long history and image of taking care of employees and their families. This organization offers employees all of the WNAs that Fincom offers. Mancom does not help their employees search for child-care institutions, but, like Fincom, offers them financial compensation.

At Fincom, 44% of all employees are female, and workers are 34 years of age on average. A large majority of the employees (70%) are highly educated, 25% are educated at the average level, and 5% have had an education at lower levels. A considerable proportion of all employees (37%) live together or are married without children. Exactly one third of Fincom employees live together with children, and 18% of all employees are single without children living in the household. On average, Fincom employees work 40 hours per week, while being contracted for 36 hours. Also, 37% of all employees are employed in supervisory positions.

Most employees working at Mancom are male (87%) and are 43 years old on average. Of all employees, 9% have a low education, 32% have been educated at the average level, and 52% have studied at a high level. Of all Mancom employees, 9% are single without children, and 29% live together or are married without children, and a large proportion of employees (56%) have a partner and children. Mancom employees work 45 hours per week, on average, although they are contracted for 39 hours per week. In addition, 33% of all employees are employed as supervisors.

When comparing the demographics of employees working at both organizations, we can conclude that Fincom employees are more often women $(\chi^2_{(1,907)} = 84.44, p < .001)$, younger $(t_{(1,907)} = -12.85, p < .001)$, and higher educated $(t_{(1,907)} = 7.35, p < .001)$ compared to Mancom employees. Employees working at Mancom, on the other hand, more often have a partner $(\chi^2_{(1,907)} = 25.29, p < .001)$ and children $(\chi^2_{(1,907)} = 43.53, p < .001)$ living in the household. In addition, employees working at Mancom work slightly more hours per week according to contract $(t_{(1,907)} = -10.13, p < .001)$ than those employed at Fincom. In summary, the two organizations selected for the current study belong to different branches of industry and, therefore, differ in their employees' demographics, which enables cross-validation of findings.

Measures

Utilization of Work–Nonwork Arrangements. Employees were given a short introduction into the subject of WNAs, both within the general Dutch legal context and within the organization in which they work. They were asked to indicate whether they (had) used the six WNAs available in both organizations (0 = no; 1 = yes), that is: (a) working part-time, (b) teleworking (i.e., structurally working from home for at least one day per week to avoid commuter traffic), (c) flexible work times (i.e., variability in starting and finishing times), (d) working from home occasionally, (e) financial support for child-care costs, and (f) parental leave. Also, a sum score was calculated reflecting total WNA utilization by adding employees' utilization of the six separate WNAs varying from score 0 (no WNA used) to score 6 (all six WNAs used).

Work–Nonwork Culture. WNC was measured by a self-developed 18-item questionnaire inspired by questionnaires constructed by Thompson et al. (1999) and Allen (2001). In this newly constructed measure, five subscales could be distinguished: (1) Organizational support (4 items; e.g., "In this organization, it is considered important that beyond their work, employees have sufficient time left for their private life," "In this organization, people are sympathetic towards employees' care responsibilities"); (2) supervisor support (3 items; e.g., "My superior supports employees who want to switch to less demanding jobs for private reasons," "My superior supports employees who (temporarily) want to reduce their working hours for private reasons"); (3) colleague support (4 items; e.g., "My colleagues support employees who (temporarily) want to reduce their working hours for private reasons," "My colleagues help me out when I am (temporarily) preoccupied with my care responsibilities"); (4) negative career consequences (4 items; e.g., "Employees who (temporarily) reduce their working hours for private reasons are considered less ambitious in this organization," "To turn down a promotion for private reasons will harm one's career progress in this organization"); and (5) organizational time demands (3 items; e.g., "In order to be taken seriously in this organization, employees should work long days and be available all the time," "In this organization employees are expected to put their job before their private life when necessary"). Answer alternatives ranged from totally disagree (= 1) to totally agree (= 5).

To determine whether the two WNC dimensions proposed in the introduction (i.e., support and barriers) underlay the five subscales, a second-order Principal Components Analysis (PCA) was performed in each organization. The three support subscales loaded high on factor one representing support (factor loadings ranged from .58 to .85; e.v. $= 2.55$; $R^2 = .51$ in Fincom, and from .68 to .77; e.v. $= 2.04$; $R^2 = .41$ in Mancom), whereas career consequences and time demands loaded high on a second factor representing barriers (from .79 to .87; e.v. $= 1.00$; $R^2 = .20$ in Fincom, and from .78 to .82; e.v. $= 1.06$; $R^2 = .21$ in Mancom). These findings support our assumption that WNC is characterized by two different (albeit related $r = -.42$,

$p < .001$ in Fincom, and $r = -.33$, $p < .001$ in Mancom) dimensions, that is, support and barriers. Support scores were then calculated by averaging the three support subscales (organizational, colleague, and supervisor) with high scores reflecting high support ($\alpha = .73$ in Fincom and $\alpha = .62$ in Mancom). Scores on barriers were calculated by averaging the subscales career consequences and time demands, with high scores reflecting high barriers ($r = .47$, $p < .001$ in Fincom, and $r = .37$, $p < .001$ in Mancom).

Work–Nonwork Interference. We used the SWING (Survey Work–Nonwork Interference NijmeGen; Geurts, Taris, Kompier, Dikkers, Van Hooff, & Kinnunen, 2004; Van der Hulst & Geurts, 2001; Wagena & Geurts, 2000) to measure time- and strain-based WNI. Example items of the 4-item subscale measuring time-based WNI are: "How often does it happen that...you have to cancel appointments with your spouse/family/friends due to work-related commitments?...Your work schedule makes it difficult for you to fulfill your domestic obligations?" Strain-based WNI was also measured with four items; example items are: "How often does it happen that...you are irritable at home because your work is demanding?...You find it difficult to fulfill your domestic obligations because you are constantly thinking about your work?" Answer alternatives were: 1 = never, 2 = sometimes, 3 = often, and 4 = always for both scales, with high scores reflecting high levels of WNI. Scores were calculated by averaging employees' scores on the four items measuring either time-based WNI ($\alpha = .79$ in Fincom and $\alpha = .72$ in Mancom) or strain-based WNI ($\alpha = .82$ in Fincom, $\alpha = .82$ in Mancom). For each WNI-scale, higher scores reflect a higher level of WNI.

Fatigue. This second employee-related outcome measure consisting of four items was deduced from an adapted version of the Checklist Individual Effort (Checklist Individuele Spankracht/CIS; Vercoulen et al., 1994), named the Fatigue Assessment Scale (FAS; Michielsen, 2002). Employees indicated whether the following statements reflected how they usually felt: (1) "I get tired very quickly" (in both samples), (2) "Physically, I feel exhausted" (in both samples), (3) "I feel tired" (in the Fincom sample) and "I am bothered by fatigue" (in Mancom), and (4) "I feel well rested" (recoded in the Fincom sample) and "I have got enough energy for everyday life" (recoded in the Mancom sample). Answer alternatives were: 1 = never, 2 = sometimes, 3 = regularly, 4 = often, and 5 = always, with higher scores reflecting higher levels of fatigue. Scores were calculated by averaging employees' scores on these four items ($\alpha = .84$ in Fincom and $\alpha = .85$ in Mancom).

Organizational Commitment. The third employee-related outcome was measured with five items that were derived from Allen and Meyer (1990). Employees indicated to what extent they agreed with five statements concerning organizational commitment. Example items: "I would like to stay in this organization for the rest of my life," and "I have got the feeling that I belong to this organization." Answer alternatives ranged from totally disagree (=1) to totally agree (=5), with higher scores reflecting a higher level of commitment ($\alpha = .78$ in Fincom and $\alpha = .84$ in Mancom).

Covariates. In some analyses, we wanted to control for the influence of third variables possibly disturbing the associations between the variables under study. The four covariates we selected were: (1) gender (1 = women, 2 = men); (2) age; (3) education (1 = basic school to 8 = academic); and (4) children living in the household (0 = no children living in the household, 1 = children living in the household).

Analysis

To get a first impression of employees' scores on the central research variables and their associations, descriptive statistics were calculated (i.e., means, standard deviations, and intercorrelations). For exploratory purposes, we also examined the use employees made of the six available WNAs. In addition, we compared the WNA utilization of men and women with the help of Chi-square tests.

In order to test Hypothesis 1 (i.e., the more favorably employees perceive the WNC, the more WNAs they will use), hierarchical linear regression analyses were performed. Total WNA utilization (0–6) was entered into the equation as the dependent variable and the four covariates (i.e., gender, age, education, and children living in the household) were entered as the independents in a first step. In a second step, WNC support and barriers were added to the covariates.

To determine whether the use of the six separate WNAs differed for employees perceiving the WNC as either favorably or unfavorably, Chi-square tests were performed in which the use of each of the six WNAs (with score 0 = WNA not used, and score 1 = WNA used) was compared for employees scoring either high ($\geq$ score 3) or low (< score 3) on WNC support and barriers.

To test Hypothesis 2a (i.e., the more favorably employees perceive the WNC, the less WNI they will experience) and Hypothesis 2b (i.e., the more WNAs employees use, the less WNI they will experience), we again performed hierarchical linear regression analyses. This time, time- or strain-based WNI were the dependent variable. The covariates were entered as independents in a first step. In a second step, the two WNC dimensions support and barriers were added to the covariates, and in a third and final step total WNA utilization (0–6) was added.

To determine whether the more WNI employees experience, the more fatigue and the less organizational commitment they report (Hypothesis 3), identical hierarchical regression analyses were performed. Fatigue and commitment were now entered as the dependent variables, however, and time- and strain-based WNI were added to the independents in a fourth and final step.

Finally, we explored the possible mediating role of WNI in the association between WNA utilization and WNC on the one hand (independents), and fatigue and commitment (dependents) on the other hand (Hypothesis 4) by first performing a regression analysis with fatigue as a function of the four covariates, WNC support and barriers, and total WNA utilization (Step 1). In a second step, time- and strain-based WNI were added to the independents (Step 2). A similar regression analysis was performed with commitment as the dependent variable. Consequently, we could test the three conditions for mediation as proposed by Baron & Kenny (1986), that is: (1) the independent variable must be significantly associated with the mediator, (2) the mediator must be associated with the dependent variable, and (3) the previously significant association between the independent and dependent variable must disappear totally (full mediation) or decrease significantly (partial mediation) when the mediator is controlled for.

RESULTS

Descriptive Statistics

Means, standard deviations, and intercorrelations for all research variables are given in Table 6.1 for both organizations. Because the correlation between time- and strain-based WNI was strong in both organizations ($r = .56$, $p < .001$ in Fincom, and $r = .43$, $p < .001$ in Mancom), we conducted a principal components analysis (PCA) with Varimax rotation to determine whether the two scales formed distinct types of WNI. The four strain-based items loaded high on factor one representing strain-based WNI (factor loadings ranged from .72 to .84; e.v. $= 3.93$; $R^2 = .49$ in Fincom, and loadings ranged from .74 to .85; e.v. $= 3.47$; $R^2 = .43$ in Mancom), whereas the four time-based items

TABLE 6.1
Means, Standard Deviations, and Intercorrelations of Research Variables in Fincom and Mancom

Variables	Fincom M	Fincom SD	Mancom M	Mancom SD	1	2	3	4	5	6	7	8	9	10
1. Gender	1.55	0.50	1.87	0.33	—	.09	.31**	.08	-.13*	.10*	.24**	.08	-.08	.14**
2. Age	34.31	9.70	43.19	9.08	.20**	—	-.10	.35**	.01	.01	-.03	.00	-.14**	.21**
3. Education	6.81	1.47	5.86	1.91	.09	-.23**	—	.03	-.24**	.31**	.33**	.21**	.08	-.02
4. Children	0.34	0.47	0.57	0.50	.19*	.06	-.00	—	-.03	.06	.04	.03	-.07	.17**
5. WNC support	3.30	0.60	3.19	0.54	-.01	-.13	.05	.07	—	-.42**	-.31**	-.29**	-.15**	.28**
6. WNC barriers	3.61	0.70	3.52	0.70	.06	.19*	.09	-.00	-.33**	—	.39**	.26**	.18**	-.11*
7. WNI time-based	1.98	0.53	1.96	0.51	-.02	.02	.10	-.04	-.21**	.22**	—	.56**	.37**	.06
8. WNI strain-based	1.86	0.49	1.99	0.53	.08	.18*	.03	.00	-.25**	.24**	.43**	—	.40**	-.10*
9. Fatigue	2.50	1.22	2.20	0.77	-.10	.15	-.16*	-.14	-.15	.10	.29**	.45**	—	-.07
10. Commitment	3.51	0.66	3.70	0.83	.04	.27*	-.07	.19*	.17*	.02	.02	.00	-.07	—

Note. Correlations above the diagonal reflect those of Fincom employees (*N* = 638), and correlations below the diagonal represent those of Mancom employees (*N* = 269).

* = *p* < .01, ** = *p* < .001.

Gender: 1 = woman, 2 = man; Education: 1 = primary school, 2 = lower vocational, 3 = average level grammar school, 4 = short average vocational, 5 = average vocational, 6 = higher level grammar school, 7 = higher vocational, 8 = academic; Children: 0 = no children, 1 = children living in the household.

TABLE 6.2
WNA Utilization by (Subgroups of) Employees Within Fincom and Mancom

	Fincom				Mancom			
WNA	Total N	%	Men %	Women %	Total N	%	Men %	Women %
Flexible working times	316	51	53	48	215	80	80	81
Working from home	245	40	47	30	41	16	16	9
Working part-time	179	29	14	49	1	1	0	3
Telework	79	13	16	9	22	9	9	6
Child-care arrangements	70	12	9	16	9	4	3	7
Parental leave	30	5	2	8	1	1	1	0

loaded high on a second factor representing time-based WNI (from .65 to .80 e.v. = 1.19; R^2 = .15 in Fincom, and loadings ranged from .64 to .73; e.v. = 1.38; R^2 = .17 in Mancom). Thus, we can conclude that time- and strain-based WNI are two related but not identical types of WNI.

What Is the Utilization of Available WNAs? (Question 1)

Table 6.2 presents the proportion of (female and male) employees in each organization that utilize each of the six available WNAs. Of all available WNAs, employees working at Fincom used flexible working times most frequently (51% of all employees used this WNA). Working from home occasionally (40%) and working part-time (29%) were also used by substantial groups of Fincom employees. Arrangements that were used to a lesser extent were telework (13%), child-care support (12%), and parental leave (5%), respectively.

Additionally, women used working part-time ($\chi^2_{(1,616)}$ = 92.77, $p < .001$), child-care arrangements ($\chi^2_{(1,606)}$ = 7.25, $p < .01$), and parental leave ($\chi^2_{(1,604)}$ = 11.67, $p < .001$) more often than men, whereas men, on the other hand, used telework ($\chi^2_{(1,609)}$ = 6.22, $p < .05$) and working from home ($\chi^2_{(1,614)}$ = 18.03, $p < .001$) more frequently than women.

Within Mancom, the WNA that was used most frequently was flexible working times (80%), followed by working from home (16%). For the remaining four WNAs, utilization was very low (i.e., between 1–9%). Women worked part-time more often than men ($\chi^2_{(1,260)}$ = 7.42, $p < .01$), although in general women did not use this WNA frequently.

TABLE 6.3
Hierarchical Linear Regression Analysis with Total Work–Nonwork Arrangement
Utilization as a Function of the Four Covariates, and WNC Support and Barriers

	Total WNA Utilization	
	Fincom	Mancom
Variables	β	β
Gender	−.15***	—
Age	—	—
Education	.19***	.31***
Children	.43***	—
WNC support	.11**	.10
WNC barriers	.12**	—
	ΔR^2	ΔR^2
Covariates	.23***	.11***
WNC	.02**	.01
Total	.25***	.12***

Note. Only beta-coefficients of $\beta \geq .10$ are mentioned (Cohen, 1977).
$^* = p \leq .05$, $^{**} = p \leq .01$, $^{***} = p \leq .001$.

Is WNC Related to Utilization of WNAs? (Question 2)

The results of hierarchical regression analyses with total WNA utilization as a function of the four covariates, and WNC support and barriers are given in Table 6.3 for both organizations. Within Fincom, three covariates explained a substantial proportion ($R^2 = 23\%$, $p < .001$) of the total variance explained in total WNA utilization ($R^2 = 25\%$, $p < .001$); women used more WNAs than men, the higher employees were educated the more WNAs they used, and employees with children living in the household used more WNAs than those without children (living in the household). WNC support and barriers added 2% ($p < .01$) to the variance explained by the covariates; employees used slightly more WNAs, the more they perceived support and barriers.

Concerning the use of specific WNAs, Fincom employees who perceived the WNC as supportive worked part-time slightly more often (32% of all employees perceiving high support) than those perceiving the WNC as less supportive (22% of those perceiving low support; $\chi^2_{(1,609)} = 6.37$, $p < .05$). Also, employees experiencing high barriers worked at home occasionally more often (42%) than those perceiving the barriers as low (30%; $\chi^2_{(1,606)} = 5.94$, $p < .05$). To determine whether the associations found between utilization of these two WNAs and WNC differed for men and women, the Chi-square tests were performed for men and women separately. The association between WNC barriers and use of working from home occasionally appeared to be significant for female employees only ($\chi^2_{(1,264)} = 9.65$, $p < .01$). Thus, female employees perceiving the barriers as high worked at home occasionally more often than those perceiving the barriers as low.

Within Mancom, education explained most of the variance ($R^2 = 11\%$, $p < .001$) in total WNA utilization; the higher employees were educated, the more they used WNAs. WNC support and barriers added an insignificant part (1%) to the variance explained, and also WNC support and barriers were not significantly associated with WNA utilization.

In summary, Hypothesis 1 (the more favorably employees perceive the WNC, the more they will use WNAs) is supported for only the Fincom workers, and only for the support dimension of WNC. Thus, Fincom employees used slightly more WNAs, the more they perceived support.

Are WNC and/or Utilization of WNAs Related to WNI? (Question 3)

The results of the hierarchical regression analyses with time- and strain-based WNI as a function of the four covariates, WNC support and barriers, and total WNA utilization are given in Table 6.4. The covariates explained some variance in time-based WNI within Fincom only ($R^2 = 12\%$, $p < .001$); men experienced more time-based WNI than women, and employees experienced more time-based WNI the higher their education. WNC support and barriers explained additional variance in the first type of WNI in both organizations ($R^2 = 11\%$, $p < .001$ in Fincom, and $R^2 = 6\%$, $p < .001$ in Mancom); employees experienced less time-based WNI, the higher the support and the lower the barriers they perceived. Utilization of WNAs did not explain a significant proportion of variance in time-based WNI ($R^2 = 1\%$, ns in Fincom, and $R^2 = 0\%$, ns in Mancom).

Concerning strain-based WNI, the covariates explained 4% ($p < .001$ in Fincom, and $p < .05$ in Mancom) of the total variance in both companies. Additionally, WNC support and barriers explained 8% ($p < .001$) of variance in both companies; employees reported less strain-based WNI, the higher the support and the lower the barriers they perceived. Utilization of WNAs did not explain any additional variance.

In addition, we performed post-hoc regression analyses to determine whether the utilization of the six separate WNAs was related to time- and strain-based WNI. Within Fincom, the use of part-time work and working from home occasionally was associated with time-based

TABLE 6.4
Hierarchical Linear Regression Analysis with Time- and Strain-based WNI
as a Function of the Four Covariates, WNC Support and Barriers, and Total
WNA Utilization

Variables	Time-based (Fincom) β	Strain-based (Fincom) β	Time-based (Mancom) β	Strain-based (Mancom) β
Gender	.15***	—	—	—
Age	—	—	—	.14*
Education	.15***	.11**	—	—
Children	—	—	—	—
Support	−.15***	−.21***	−.16**	−.18**
Barriers	.26***	.13**	.15*	.16*
Total WNA utilization	—	—	—	—
	ΔR^2	ΔR^2	ΔR^2	ΔR^2
Covariates	.12***	.04***	.02	.04*
WNC	.11***	.08***	.06***	.08***
Total WNA utilization	.01	.00	.00	.00
Total	.24***	.12***	.08**	.12***

Note. Only beta-coefficients of $\beta \geq .10$ are mentioned (Cohen, 1977).
* $= p \leq .05$, ** $= p \leq .01$, *** $= p \leq .001$.

WNI ($\beta = -.10$, $p < .05$, and $\beta = .18$, $p < .001$, respectively); part-time work employees experienced slightly less time-based WNI than full-time employees; employees working from home every now and then experienced more time-based WNI than those not working from home occasionally. The use of working from home and child-care arrangements were related to strain-based WNI ($\beta = .14$, $p < .001$, and $\beta = -.15$, $p < .001$, respectively); employees working from home occasionally experienced slightly more strain-based WNI than those not using this facility; and employees using child-care arrangements experienced slightly less WNI than those not using child-care arrangements. Within Mancom, the use of child-care arrangements was related to time-based WNI ($\beta = -.15$, $p < .05$); employees using child-care arrangements experienced less time-based WNI than those not using any child-care arrangements.

In summary, Hypothesis 2a (the more favorably employees perceive the WNC, the less WNI they will experience) is supported by these findings. Employees in both organizations experienced less time- and strain-based WNI, the more they perceived the WNC in their organization as favorable (high support and low barriers). Hypothesis 2b (the more employees use WNAs, the less WNI they will experience) is not

TABLE 6.5
Hierarchical Regression Analysis with Fatigue and Commitment as a Function of the Four Covariates, WNC Support and Barriers, Total WNA Utilization, and Time-based and Strain-based

Variables	Fatigue (Fincom) β	Commitment (Fincom) β	Fatigue (Mancom) β	Commitment (Mancom) β
Gender	−.16***	.12**	−.11	—
Age	−.11**	.17***	—	.28***
Education	—	—	−.17**	—
Children	—	.12**	−.14*	.18**
Support	—	.30***	—	.21***
Barriers	—	—	—	—
Total WNA utilization	—	—	—	—
Time-based WNI	.24***	.21***	.13*	—
Strain-based WNI	.27***	−.14**	.40***	—
	ΔR^2	ΔR^2	ΔR^2	ΔR^2
Covariates	.04***	.07***	.07***	.11***
WNC	.03***	.09***	.02	.03**
Total WNA utilization	.00	.00	.00	.01
WNI	.16***	.03***	.19***	.00
Total	.23***	.19***	.28***	.15***

Note. Only beta-coefficients of $\beta \geq .10$ are mentioned (Cohen, 1977).
* = $p \leq .05$, ** = $p \leq .01$, *** = $p \leq .001$.

supported generally. More specifically, employees working part-time (Fincom) and those using child-care arrangements (both companies), experienced less WNI than employees working full-time (Fincom) and those not using child-care arrangements (both organizations). Thus, Hypothesis 2b is supported partially for two specific WNAs.

Is WNI Associated with Fatigue and/or Organizational Commitment? (Question 4)

The results of hierarchical regression analyses with fatigue and commitment as a function of the four covariates, WNC support and barriers, total WNA utilization, and time- and strain-based WNI are given in Table 6.5. Concerning fatigue, the covariates explained some variance in both companies ($R^2 = 4\%$; $p < .001$ in Fincom, and $R^2 = 7\%$; $p < .001$ in Mancom). WNC explained some additional variance in fatigue in Fincom ($R^2 = 3\%$; $p < .001$). Support and barriers, however, were not associated with fatigue in either company nor was utilization of WHAs. WNI did explain a significant amount of variance in fatigue ($R^2 = 16\%$; $p < .001$ in Fincom, and $R^2 = 19\%$; $p < .001$ in Mancom); employees reported more fatigue the more they experienced time- and strain-based WNI.

Concerning organizational commitment, the covariates explained some variance in both companies ($R^2 = 7\%$; $p < .001$ in Fincom, and $R^2 = 11\%$; $p < .001$ in Mancom). WNC explained some additional variance in commitment ($R^2 = 9\%$; $p < .001$ in Fincom, and $R^2 = 3\%$; $p < .01$ in Mancom); employees were more committed to the organization, the more they perceived the WNC as supportive. Utilization did not explain any additional variance in commitment. WNI explained 3% ($p < .001$) of the variance within Fincom only; employees felt more committed, the more time-based and the less strain-based WNI they experienced.

In summary, Hypothesis 3 (the more WNI employees experience, the more fatigue and the less organizational commitment they will report) is partially supported. Employees reported more fatigue, the more they experienced time- and strain-based WNI. The associations with organizational commitment were in the expected direction for strain-based WNI, but in the opposite direction for time-based WNI.

Does WNI Mediate the Association Between WNC and/or Utilization of WNAs on the One Hand, and Fatigue and/or Commitment on the Other Hand? (Question 5)

In Table 6.6, the results of a regression analysis with fatigue as a function of the four covariates, WNC support and barriers, total WNA utilization (Step 1), and time- and strain-based WNI (Step 2) are given.

First, the three mediation conditions proposed by Baron and Kenny (1986) were tested within Fincom: (1) the associations between WNC support and barriers on the one hand, and time- and strain-based WNI on the other, were significant ($\beta = -.15$, $p < .001$, and $\beta = .26$ $p < .001$, respectively, for time-based WNI, and $\beta = -.21$, $p < .001$, and $\beta = .13$, $p < .01$ for strain-based WNI), (2) both time- and strain-based WNI were associated with fatigue ($\beta = .24$, $p < .001$, and $\beta = .27$, $p < .001$, respectively), and (3) the previously significant associations between WNC support and barriers on the one hand, and fatigue on the other hand ($\beta = -.11$, $p < .05$, and $\beta = .13$, $p < .01$, respectively), reduced and were no longer significant (see Table 6.6) when the two types of WNI were entered into the equation in the second step ($\beta = -.01$, n.s., and $\beta = .03$, n.s.); this implies a full mediation of the association between WNC and fatigue by WNI.

TABLE 6.6
Hierarchical Regression Analysis with Fatigue as a Function of the Four
Covariates, WNC Support and Barriers, Total WNA Utilization (Step 1), and
Time-based and Strain-based WNI (Step 2)

Variables	Step 1 (Fincom) β	Step 2 (Fincom) β	Step 1 (Mancom) β	Step 2 (Mancom) β
Gender	−.12**	−.16***	—	−.11
Age	−.11**	−.11**	.13*	—
Education	—	—	−.13*	−.17**
Children	—	—	−.14*	−.14*
Support	−.11*	—	—	—
Barriers	.13**	—	—	—
Total WNA utilization	—	—	—	—
Time-based WNI	—	.24***	—	.13*
Strain-based WNI	—	.27***	—	.40***

	ΔR^2			ΔR^2
Covariates		.04***		.07***
WNC		.03***		.02
Total WNA utilization		.00		.00
WNI		.16***		.19***
Total		.23***		.28***

Note. Only beta-coefficients of $\beta \geq .10$ are mentioned (Cohen, 1977).
* = $p \leq .05$, ** = $p \leq .01$, *** = $p \leq .001$.

Within Mancom, WNI could not mediate the relationship between WNC and fatigue as the relationship between WNC and fatigue was not significant (see Table 6.5). In addition, WNI did not mediate the association between WNC and commitment in either company, because the third mediation condition (Baron & Kenny, 1986) was not met within Fincom (i.e., the association between WNC support and commitment did not decrease or disappear when WNI was entered into the equation), and the second and third condition were not met within Mancom (i.e., WNI and commitment were not significantly associated, and the association between WNC and commitment was not significant).

In summary, Hypothesis 4 (WNI mediates the association between WNA utilization and WNC on the one hand, and fatigue and commitment on the other hand) is partially supported in Fincom. The more unfavorably Fincom employees perceived WNC (low support and high barriers), the more they experienced time- and strain-based WNI, which in turn is associated with feelings of fatigue.

DISCUSSION

The aim of the current study was to examine work–nonwork culture (WNC) in association with the utilization of six work–nonwork arrangements (WNAs) and three employee-related outcomes (i.e., work–nonwork interference (WNI), fatigue, and organizational commitment). To determine whether these variables were related, we used a self-developed measure of WNC tapping two dimensions of WNC: support and barriers. In addition, we studied the actual utilization of six specific WNAs, and we selected two types of WNI often distinguished in the literature (i.e., time- and strain-based WNI). Finally, we examined the associations between these central research variables in two Dutch organizations from different branches of industry.

Like the few studies examining the utilization of WNAs (see Allen, 2001 and Thompson et al., 1999), we found that employees from both companies used flexible WNAs more often than child-related WNAs. This is not surprising because the first type of arrangements can be used by all workers, whereas only parents are eligible to use the second type of arrangement. Additionally, working part-time was used more frequently by women than by men in both companies. As mentioned in the introduction, working part-time is a common strategy to combine work and family life in the Netherlands, in particular among women (Den Dulk et al., 2003). A post-hoc Chi-square test within Fincom revealed that women did indeed work part-time mostly in order to take care of their children, whereas men used this WNA mostly to study ($\chi^2_{(6,295)} = 44.24$, $p < .001$).

Although in some studies conducted in the United States, WNC was found to be related to utilization of WNAs (e.g., Thompson et al., 1999), the findings from the current study were less straightforward. We can only conclude for one of our cases (Fincom) that a more supportive WNC was related to a slightly higher utilization of WNAs, but that the perception of barriers was also related to a higher utilization of WNAs. These findings are reflected at a more specific level in a positive association between WNC support and part-time work (employees who perceived the WNC as more supportive more often worked part time than full time), and a positive association among women between WNC barriers and working from home occasionally (female workers perceiving high barriers worked from home more frequently than those perceiving the barriers as low). One explanation for these findings might be that particularly employees who actually use WNAs are at risk of being confronted with such barriers. Those not using any WNAs have not been confronted with such resistance and may, therefore, have very favorable perceptions of the WNC.

Another important finding is that employees did not experience less WNI the more WNAs they used. WNI was associated with the use of some specific WNAs; however, the use of part-time work (Fincom) and the use of child-care arrangements (both companies) were related to lower levels of WNI, whereas working from home was associated with higher levels of WNI (both organizations). Possibly, particularly employees who experience problems in combining work and family are the ones using WNAs. Maybe we did not find a lower level of WNI among employees working from home because these employees still experienced a higher level of WNI than those without any work–family problems.

Furthermore, the more favorably employees from both organizations perceived the WNC (i.e., high support and low barriers), the less time- and strain-based WNI they experienced. Although this association is in congruence with our expectations, it is difficult to explain through which mechanism culture can impact WNI, if not through the utilization of WNAs as we concluded earlier. It is, therefore, perhaps more plausible that employees experiencing low levels of WNI have (possibly too) favorable perceptions of the WNC (reversed causation).

Also, employees from both companies were more fatigued, the more they experienced time- and strain-based WNI. Within Fincom, WNI played a mediating role in the association between WNC and fatigue. However, WNI was not associated consistently with commitment. That is, only within Fincom, a higher level of strain-based WNI was related to a lower level of commitment. However, within Fincom, we found a positive association between time-based WNI and organizational commitment. This finding can possibly be explained by changing the path of causation ("reversed" causation); employees who are very committed to their organization are probably also the ones to spend long hours at work and to experience high levels of time-based interference with their nonwork domain.

Limitations and Suggestions for Future Research

First, the present study examined the associations between WNC support and barriers, the actual utilization of six WNAs, time- and strain-based WNI, fatigue, and commitment. However, the cross-sectional design of the study made it impossible to draw any causal inferences.

One can, for example, only conclude from our findings that WNC and WNI are associated in both organizations under study, but whether a favorable culture (low support and high barriers) causes lower levels of WNI (i.e., "normal" causation), or whether those employees experiencing lower levels of WNI hold a more positive view toward the organization than those with higher levels of WNI (i.e., "reversed" causation), remains unclear. To make such causal inferences, future research should use longitudinal designs to measure the central research variables at multiple points in time. Consequently, one can determine in which direction variables are related to each other (i.e., normal or reversed causation). In addition, one can only examine possible beneficial impacts of WNAs when measuring the development of WNI over time among employees who started to utilize one or more WNAs (natural experiments)

Second, it is important to note that the companies selected in this study are characterized by comparable levels of WNC support and barriers (i.e., moderate levels of support and moderate to high levels of barriers). Future research should also include cases with different types of WNC in order to find out how support and barriers are related to WNA utilization and other employee-related outcomes. In addition, cross-national research could examine how WNC is affected by national culture and the level of public policies and legislation issued in different countries (e.g., Peters & Den Dulk, 2003). If these studies show WNC to vary according to type of company or nation, this might have some implications for our theoretical framework, which currently does not consider these possible influences. Consequently, a broader framework including both the national and organizational context should be used to study WNC.

Third, we considered the six WNAs that were already implemented in the two companies under study. The rather low utilization found in the current study might be caused by a divergence between the WNAs implemented and employees' needs. For example, the two companies included did not implement a compressed work week. It is plausible, however, that many full-time working employees would desire working longer hours during the day but less days a week. By neglecting such alternative but possibly strongly desired WNAs, any result relating to WNA utilization could be influenced. Future research should take into account both desired and frequently used WNAs in order to examine WNA utilization as completely as possible.

Practical Implications

Although the current study has its weaknesses, we believe that it contributes to the work–nonwork practice and literature. First, organizations have to take into account both dimensions of work–nonwork culture included in the present study. That is, some employees may feel supported by the organization, their supervisor, and their colleagues in the utilization of WNAs, whereas others may feel hampered by time demands and career consequences. Consequently, support alone is a necessary but insufficient condition for an organization to be considered as favorable.

Second, flexible WNAs were used most frequently in both organizations, and child-related arrangements were used least. Interestingly, women used child-related arrangements more often than men, and men (Fincom) used flexible WNAs (i.e., telework and working from home) more often than women. In addition, some WNAs were associated with WNC differently within Fincom (i.e., part-time work was associated with high support, whereas working from home was related to high barriers). As shown earlier, women worked part-time in order to perform care-giving tasks in their nonwork domain, but men used this specific WNA for other purposes (study). Perhaps organizations can explore which arrangements are most helpful in balancing work and family life and which arrangements are beneficial in other respects. In this manner, (a) employers are aware which WNAs are most desired by (which subgroups of) employees, and (b) a division can be made between WNAs used for work-related purposes and those used for balancing work and family life.

Third, the introduction of WNAs in organizations is most often considered a good practice toward the needs of employees. However, as we pointed out, in practice not all WNAs are always beneficial for all employees. Therefore, implementation of WNAs can lead to difficult discussions on the question of who benefits most from WNAs, employees or employers. Rapoport, Bailyn, Fletcher, and Pruitt (2002) introduced the concept of the Dual Agenda to overcome this kind of discussions. The idea of the Dual Agenda is to change workplace practices in such a way that they simultaneously enhance organizations' efficiency and employees' well-being. For instance, Perlow (1997) describes an experiment within a large organization in the United States in which several departments started to let employees work for several hours without being disturbed (i.e., no meetings, no phone calls, and no colleagues asking questions). In this experiment, people could work more efficiently and they could leave earlier, benefiting both the organization and her employees. In terms of the Dual Agenda, WNAs are not considered to be trade-offs between the interests of employee and employer, but beneficial for both (cf. Kolb & Merrill-Sands, 1999; Rayman et al., 1999).

Fourth, WNC support and barriers appeared to be related to employees' time- and strain-based WNI, fatigue, and (although somewhat inconsistently) to organizational commitment in the hypothesized directions. In both organizations, employees experienced less WNI and less feelings of fatigue the more they perceived the WNC as favorable (high support and low barriers). In addition, WNC support was positively related to organizational commitment. Organizations, should, therefore—even apart from taking into account the utilization of the WNAs available—build a culture that is concerned with supporting and not hampering employees' attempts to better integrate their work with their nonwork lives. One way to start such a culture change is to conduct a survey among all employees in which they are asked to indicate how they feel about their company's culture. If a proportion of employees feels their culture hampers the use of WNAs, brainstorming or groupthink sessions could be held with all key parties involved (i.e., HR managers, supervisors, and employees). In this manner, employers are alerted to the way their employees perceive them to be either supportive or hampering toward the use of WNAs, and all relevant parties are involved in the process of problem solving.

REFERENCES

Ajzen, I., & Fishbein, M. (1974). Factors influencing intentions and the intention-behavior relation. *Human Relations, 27,* 1–15.

Ajzen, I., & Fishbein, M. (1980). *Understanding attitudes and predicting social behavior.* Englewood Cliffs, NJ: Prentice Hall.

Allen, T. D. (2001). Family-supportive work environments: The role of organizational perceptions. *Journal of Vocational Behavior, 58,* 414–435.

Allen, N. J., & Meyer, J. P. (1990). The measurement and antecedents of affective, continuance, and normative commitment to the organization. *Journal of Occupational Pscyhology, 63,* 1–18.

Baron, R. M., & Kenny, D. A. (1986). The moderator–mediator variable distinction in social psychological research: Conceptual, strategic, and statistical considerations. *Journal of Personality and Social Psychology, 51,* 1173–1182.

Bond, J. T., Galinsky, E., & Swanberg, J. E. (1998). *The 1997 national study of the changing workplace.* New York: Families and Work Institute.

Cohen, J. (1977). *Statistical power analysis for the behavioral sciences.* London: Academic Press.

Commission DG Employment and Social Affairs. (2003). *Employment in Europe 2003. Recent Trends and Prospects.* Commission DG Employment and Social Affairs Unit A.1 Employment Analysis. Brussels.

den Dulk, L. (2001). *Work–family arrangements in organizations. A cross-national study in the Netherlands, Italy, the United Kingdom and Sweden.* Amsterdam: Rozenberg Publishers.

den Dulk, L., Doorne-Huiskes, A., van, & Peper, B. (2003). Arbeid en zorg in Europees perspectief. Arbeidspatronen van werkende ouders. [Work and caregiving in a European perspective. Work patterns of working parents]. *Tijdschrift voor Arbeidsvraagstukken, 19*, 69–82.

Evans, J. (2001). *Firms' contributions to the reconciliation between work and family life.* (Occasional paper). OECD. Paris

Geurts, S. A. E., & Demerouti, E. (2003). Work–non-work interface: A review of theories and findings. In M. Schabracq, J. Winnubst, & C. L. Cooper (Eds.), *Handbook of work and health psychology* (pp. 279–312). Chichester, UK: Wiley.

Geurts, S. A. E., Rutte, C., & Peeters, M. (1999). Antecedents and consequences of work–home interference among medical residents. *Social Science and Medicine, 48*, 1135–48.

Geurts, S. A. E., Taris, T., Kompier, M. A. J., Dikkers, J. S. E., Van Hooff, M., & Kinnunen, U. (2004). *Measuring positive and negative work-home interaction: Development and validation of a new questionnaire.* Manuscript submitted for publication.

Greenhaus, J. H., & Beutell, N. J. (1985). Sources of conflict between work and family roles. *Academy of Management Review, 10*, 76–88.

Grootscholte, M., Bouwmeester, J. A., & de Klaver, P. (2000). *Evaluatie Wet op het ouderschapverlof. Onderzoek onder rechthebbenden en werkgevers.* [Evaluation of the Law on parental leave. Research among rightful claimants and employers]. Den Haag: SZW.

Kolb, D. M., & Merrill-Sands, D. (1999). Waiting for outcomes: Anchoring a dual agenda for change to cultural assumptions. *Women in Management Review, 14*, 194–202.

Lewis, S., & Taylor, K. (1996). Evaluating the impact of family-friendly employer policies: A case study. In S. Lewis & J. Lewis (Eds.), *The work family challenge: Rethinking employment* (pp. 112–127). London: Sage.

Meijman, T. F. (1989). *Mentale belasting en werkstress: een arbeidspsychologische benadering* (Mental pressure and work stress: a work psychological approach). Assen, the Netherlands: Van Gorcum.

Meijman, T. F., & Mulder, G. (1998). Psychological aspects of workload. In P. J. D. Drenth, H. Thierry, & C. J. de Wolff (Eds.), *Handbook of work and organizational psychology* (pp. 5–33). Hove, UK: Psychology Press.

Michielsen, H. J. (2002). Working our fatigue: Conceptualization, assessment, and theory. Wageningen: Ponsen & Looijen.

Perlow, L. A. (1995). Putting the work back into work/family. *Group and Organization Management, 20*, 227–239.

Perlow, L. A. (1997). *Finding time: How corporations, individuals, and families can benefit from new work practices.* Ithaca, NY: Cornell University Press.

Peters, P., & den Dulk, L. (2003). Cross cultural differences in managers' support for home-based telework. A theoretical elaboration. *International Journal of Cross Cultural Management, 3*, 329–346.

Portegijs, W., Boelens, A., & Keuzenkamp, S. (2002) *Emancipatiemonitor 2002*. Den Haag: Sociaal en Cultureel Planbureau.

Rapoport, R., Bailyn, L., Fletcher, J. K., & Pruitt, B. H. (2002). *Beyond work–family balance: Advancing gender equity and workplace performance*. San Francisco: Jossey-Bass.

Rayman, P., Bailyn, L., Dickert, J., Carré, F., Harvey, M., Krim, R., & Read, R. (1999). Designing organizational solutions to integrate work and life. *Women in Management Review, 14*, 164–176.

Remery, C., Van Doorne-Huiskes, A., & Schippers, J. (2002). *Zorg als arbeidsmarktgegeven: werkgevers aan zet* [Caregiving as a fact of the labour-market: Employers' next move]. Tilburg: OSA-publicatie.

Starrels, M. E. (1992). The evolution of workplace family policy research. *Journal of Family Issues, 13*, 259–278.

Thompson, C. A., Beauvais, L. L., & Lyness, K. S. (1999). When work–family benefits are not enough: the influence of work–family culture on benefit utilization, organizational attachment, and work–family conflict. *Journal of Vocational Behavior, 54*, 392–415

Ursin, H. (1980). Personality, activation and somatic health: A new psycho-somatic theory. In S. Levine & H. Ursin (Eds.), *Coping and health* (pp. 259–279). New York: Plenum Press.

Van der Hulst, M., & Geurts, S. A. E. (2001). Associations between overtime and psychological health in high and low reward jobs. *Work and Stress, 15*, 227–240.

Vercoulen, J. H. M. M., Swanink, C. M. A., Fennis, J. F. M., Galama, J. M. D., van der Meer, J. W. M., & Bleijenberg, G. (1994). Dimensional assessment of chronic fatigue syndrome. *Journal of Psychosomatic Research, 38*, 383–392.

Wagena, E., & Geurts, S. A. E. (2000). SWING: Ontwikkeling en validering van de 'Survey Werk-thuis Interactie-Nijmegen' [Development and validation of the Survey Work-home Interaction-Nijmegen]. *Gedrag & Organisatie, 28*, 138–158.

7

Organizational Change, Globalization, and Work–Family Programs: Case Studies from India and the United States

Winifred R. Poster
University of Illinois, Urbana-Champaign

Organizational change has been an overlooked dimension of international work–family research. Although this field has carefully examined origins and patterns of work–family policy across different national contexts, the frame is often limited to single moments in time. In response, this paper emphasizes the importance of change to the dynamics of work–family policies. First, rather than treating organizations (and households) as static phenomena, I argue they are better conceptualized in terms of ongoing transformations resulting from broader structural changes, both global and local. Second, although many studies investigate the sources of work–family programs in organizations, I ask about their long-term implications and specifically the extent to which they can be sustained in the face of global changes (Glass and Estes, 1997). Finally, I examine the role that global inequality plays in these processes. I will show how firms have varying abilities to develop and maintain work–family policies as a consequence of the global hierarchies in which they are embedded.

This analysis is based on case studies of three high-tech firms from India and the United States. Their work–family policies range from alternative work arrangements, such as flextime and flexplace, to material benefits of paid parental leave and on-site childcare. I recount how, during the period of 1989 to 1995, these firms experienced four types of organizational changes: employment insecurity, occupational restructuring, organizational restructuring, and corporate re-ownership. Because of varying positions in the global hierarchy, they respond in different ways and have different outcomes for their work–family policies. One model is *endurance*, as a U.S. firm (AmCo) survives through crises with minimal disturbance to policies. The second model is *disruption*, as an Indian firm (IndCo) undergoes major restructuring and a dismantling of its policies. The third model is *flexibility*, as a U.S. transplant firm in India (TransCo) expands the range of policies but reduces accessibility to lower level employees.

I use this range of outcomes to argue that: (a) Southern firms face greater pressure from globalization, and moreover, are less equipped to manage similar types of organizational changes than those in the North; and (b) the transnational corporation experiences flexibility both horizontally and vertically, which allows it to absorb and magnify strains relative to its parent company in the North.[1] The implications for future study of work–family policies include more longitudinal studies of organizational change, more studies of Southern organizations and transnational corporations, and more studies of the potential benefits of organizational change.

LITERATURE ON WORK–FAMILY POLICY

Traditional Accounts: Snapshots in Time

Thanks to a blossoming interdisciplinary field of work–family research, increasing attention has focused on international variations in work–family policy. Two factors in particular are typically emphasized as sources of this variation: state structures and cultural ideologies. For instance, national governments play a role in the design and implementation of supportive work–family arrangements (Bailyn, 1993; Ferber and O'Farrell, 1991; Haas et al., 2000; Kalleberg and

---

[1] I use the terms "Northern" versus "Southern" nations to draw attention to economic inequalities between countries that are roughly drawn on geo-political lines. Like many academic terms though, these concepts are flawed. I urge readers to consider the complexities, such as the presence of marginalized nations in the Northern hemisphere, and powerful nations in the South.

Rosenfeld, 1995; Kamerman, 1979; Lewis and Lewis, 1996). Northern European states such as Sweden and Denmark offer a wide range of benefits including subsidized, guaranteed childcare and parental leave, and options for part-time work, whereas governments such as the United States, the U.K., and Australia provide fewer benefits such as short and/or unpaid parental leave and little support for childcare (O'Connor et al., 1999). These patterns are often theoretically linked to different types of welfare state regimes (Esping-Andersen, 1990). The first example above, for instance, represents a social democratic welfare state, which takes broad responsibility for the funding and regulation of work-family programs, whereas the latter example reflects a liberal welfare state, which takes limited responsibility and instead passes it off to the corporate sector (see den Dulk, Chapter 8, this volume).

Cultural arguments focus on the way ideologies of family, work, and gender shape organizational policies. One popular approach is that of "individualism" versus "collectivism" (Hofstede, 1991; Triandis, 1995). Several chapters in this volume also touch on cultural themes, although not explicitly in relation to organizational policies (Gelfand and Knight, Chapter 14; Westman, Chapter 9; Yang, Chapter 11). Societies with "collectivist" cultural norms are more likely to prioritize social responsibility for the group (and family) and therefore offer more work-family programs, whereas those with "individualist" cultures are more likely to emphasize personal responsibility for managing work-family relations and therefore offer weaker benefits. In some cases, these cultural notions are linked to particular national ideologies; in China and Taiwan, for instance, collectivism is said to be rooted in Confucianism and its values of avoiding conflict and respecting hierarchies (Ling and Powell, 2001; Wharton and Blair-Loy, 2002). In other accounts, cultural notions are linked to gender (Gornick et al., 1998; Kalleberg and Rosenfeld, 1995; Kamerman, 1979). Countries with more ideological support for gender equality are associated with stronger work-family policies, in that they promote women's right to equal or continuous employment and men's responsibility for housework and childrearing (Chow and Berheide, 1994). Although there are many additional arguments explaining international variation in work policies (such as labor markets, GDP, and the social activism of leftist and religious groups, etc.; Ferber and O'Farrell, 1991; Misra, 2003), those regarding state structures and cultural ideologies seem to have the most frequent and vocal presence in the literature.

Such research has been crucial in directing scholarly attention to international dynamics of work-family policies and in developing

theoretical models for their origins and development. This is especially important given the lack of an international focus in the work–
family field. With regard to India and the United States in particular, these factors of state and culture also account for much of the
variation in their work–family policies (Komarraju, 1997; Poster and
Prasad, 2005; Sekaran, 1992), as I will describe more below. However, this literature is hampered by an assumption of atemporal-
ity, which in turn, characterizes work–family policies as timeless or
stable.

There are some practical reasons for this. One is methodological,
given that most international studies (both the quantitative and qualitative) tend to be cross-sectional or time-specific, in which change can
be hard to see unless you are looking for it (Gornick et al., 1998). It
also may be related to geographic scope, given that most of the studies
focus on Europe (especially the West), or else more recently industrialized Asia, where change has been less radical than other regions of
the world.

In addition, some of the assumed stability of work policies is theoretically embedded in this research. This is especially true with the
examples above of "culture" and "state." This is more explicit in some
cases, such as with Hofstede (1991) who argues that cultural diversity is permanent (or at least "will remain with us," p. 238); whereas
in other cases, this is implied because the variables themselves have
a presumed timeless quality, because they are so historic (as with
ideologies like Confucianism) or because of their size or institutional
embeddedness (such as the state). Another theoretical limitation is
the level of analysis. Even though these studies are "international,"
their explanatory variables are still "national" and because of this,
they often overlook relations between countries as a source of work–
family policy.

Identifying Forms of Organizational Change

As an alternative, I would like to propose the value of focusing on
change in international work–family policy. "Change" in the U.S. work–
family literature has been conceptualized largely in terms of organizational transformations. Here are some examples.

One form of change is *employment insecurity*. This refers to periods of economic strain and crisis such as recession. During these
times, jobs become more fragile, and organizations are pressured
to reduce work–family programs (Cubbins, 1998). A second form
change is *occupational restructuring*. This refers to transformations
in the conception and structure of jobs—from notions of full-time,

permanent employment, to those of "contingent work" which is part-time, temporary, or outsourced (Gonyea and Googins, 1996). The notable feature of these jobs is that they often carry little or no work–family benefits (Wallace, 1998).

A third type of organizational change is that of *corporate ownership*. This refers to increasing mergers, alliances, and partnerships among organizations in the past few decades (Aguilera et al., 2004; Fligstein, 1990). Although careful managerial strategies can overcome the challenges of integrating two sets of employee programs (Schweiger et al., 1992), mergers can also create a high level of anxiety and insecurity for employees when they lead to obligatory relocation to new sites, layoffs, or attrition as employees find that their old ways of doing things are rejected by the new management.

Finally, a fourth important type of change is *organizational restructuring*. This reflects the transformation from postwar ("Ford-ist") organizational forms emphasizing hierarchy, standardization, and routinization, to those of newer ("Toyota-ist") organizational forms, involving looser decision-making structures and physical dispersals of work sites across locations (Smith, 1997). Some workers find new decentralized arrangements favorable, as they free women workers from a "'male model' of continuous employment 'for life'" and provide greater flexibility in managing work and family (Brannen et al., 2001). However, such changes can also subvert previous social contracts between workers and employers, by shifting from an emphasis on "service, solidarity, and continuity," and toward "an erosion of employment rights," reduced work–family benefits, and heightened insecurity and layoffs.

These accounts illustrate how organizations have regular cycles of change and how these cycles have important consequences for work–family policy. To elaborate on these accounts, I illustrate how global dynamics intervene with these dynamics of change. I focus on India and the United States as countries that represent two sides of this globalization experience. Thus, I show that although all the firms in my study undergo many of the same organizational changes described above, the Indian-based firms experience them with much more strain and with more radical consequences than the U.S. firm. Next, I describe how and why globalization reshapes these dynamics for workers in the South.

The Impact of Globalization

Several important global transformations have magnified inequality across Northern and Southern nations since the 1990s. At the core was a major restructuring of political and economic authority across Northern nations—what is called the "globalization project"—and its consolidation of power in transnational banks and corporations (McMichael, 2000). Here are some of the key features of the globalization project, with special attention to India and the United States.

First, there has been a shift in the holders of global economic power, particularly regarding international finance. The late 1980s to early 1990s marked a period when development planning was transferred from previous Cold War superpowers to new global finance managers and institutions. This is when the seven most wealthy nations consolidated their efforts into a single entity to form the "Group of 7" (G-7, now the G-8), which manages global markets and institutes their plans through new governance bodies: the International Monetary Fund, the World Bank, and the World Trade Organization. At the same time, the Indian state was in financial trouble. British colonialism had destabilized the local economy, for instance through its East India Company which undermined a formerly thriving industry in cotton manufacturing. This is why the Indian government turned to the Soviet Union for aid after its independence in 1947, and subsequently turned to the IMF for debt relief in 1991 when the Soviet state fell.

The consequence of this action—and the second factor of the globalization project for India—is a restructuring of state governments. A requirement for IMF loans is a "structural adjustment program," which includes set of measures to ensure economic growth and debt repayment. To do this, states must radically transform their functions and operations, which includes liberalizing and globalizing their economies. In India, for example (Kapur and Cossman, 1996): "These new economic policies, which have taken the form of liberalization of trade, deregulation of investment, privatization of industry, and devaluation of the currency have begun to fundamentally transform the Indian economy, with a view to increasing export production, and decreasing state spending" (p. 148). This reflects the mandate of the globalization project, which says that the path to development is not in state governments, but in the markets of the private sector, especially at the global level.

The impact of structural adjustment policies on workers in the formal labor market and benefits such as work–family programs is manifold (Deshpande and Deshpande, 1992; Ghosh, 1994; Ranadive, 1994). For instance, although the Indian state has relatively strong parental leave benefits, proposals have been submitted to restrict the guarantee of three months paid leave to the first two children (Kapur and Cossman, 1996). There has also been a dismantling of the former social contract of job security and protection. Under debate in parliament at present is a plan to curtail job security benefits by limiting its application to organizations with fewer workers. In addition, there has also been a disempowerment of unions, as managers have responded to labor disputes since liberalization with lockouts and closures (Sundaramurthy, 1994). Thus, in a variety of ways, global pressure has reduced the strength of Southern firms, which in turn is transferred to their employees and work–family policies.

The third feature of the globalization project that has impacted India and the companies of the study is a consolidation of market power by transnational corporations (TNCs) (McMichael, 2000): "TNCs account for two thirds of world trade. From 1970 to 1998, the number of TNCs rose from 7,000 to 60,000, with more than 500,000 foreign affiliates. The combined sales of the largest 350 TNCs in the world exceed the GNPs of all Third World countries" (quotation reduced for brevity, pp. 95–96). The growth of these firms in the last decade is partly related to changes in the technology of production (Hoogvelt, 1997):

> First, the start-up costs of . . . automation technologies . . . are enormous, and in fact represent a shift from labour to capital intensity of awesome dimension. Second, these generic technologies are subject to rapid technological obsolescence; this has led to very short product life cycles placing an ever greater premium on access to financial resources, multiplant production and extensive marketing networks (pp. 109–110).

Because these technologies have become so expensive and short-lived, there is a growing need to enter multiple national markets at once to cover costs.

A particularly important feature of these TNCs is their flexibility. Rather than previous systems of mass production, which tended to be "rigid" (i.e., one product is made in one way and in one place), TNCs increasingly use a "flexible" system of production in which their geography is dispersed, their functions are diversified, their pace is unstable and fast and their plans are short-term and changeable. Furthermore, although the meaning of flexibility is partly structural, describing changes from a unified to a diverse organizational form, it is also relational, referring to global political maneuverability and the ability to exploit Southern sites, markets, and populations in new ways. Two types of flexibility describe the dynamics of TNCs in my case study.

Horizontal flexibility describes the increasing global interconnectedness of TNCs with other local firms. Indeed, rather than unitary, monolithic organizations, TNCs take the form of a "global web": "The transnational enterprise has evolved from company organization to a loosely confederated network structure (global web) in which many discrete fabrication activities and services are brought in for the short term" (Hoogvelt, p. 127). One of the implications of this horizontal flexibility is an increasing number of mergers across borders: "Few companies [even transnational corporations] are large enough to go it alone" (Hoogvelt, p. 110). Indeed, between 1992 and 2000, the number of acquisitions between the United States and foreign companies rose from 500+ to 2,500+ (Aguilera, Dencker, & Escandell, 2004). At the same time, such partnerships are more difficult to sustain than domestic ones. Especially across Northern and Southern contexts, these mergers are often aggravated by tensions between organizational cultures. In the process, work–family policy can be one of the major conflicts.

Vertical flexibility describes the intra-organizational changes within global firms, specifically regarding the treatment of labor. It refers to the way TNCs attenuate their connection and/or responsibility to employees through a variety of strategies. For professionals, it means weaker attachment to the firm, but magnified international demand and competition for their services (Hoogvelt, 1997): "Many high-value added activities that are contributed by 'disembodied knowledge workers', are not only 'externalized', they are also extremely *mobile*. Marketing experts, computer consultants, legal affairs specialists, financial accountants and top managers can go to wherever they can obtain the highest price for their services" (Hoogvelt, pp. 145–146). At the bottom end of job hierarchy, unskilled labor is made flexible in another way. Although these workers remain tied to the production site to a greater degree than high-skilled workers, their job conditions (security, rewards, etc.) are decreased. Indeed, TNCs increasingly employ Southern workforces in a variety of tenuous capacities: "[global] decentralization of operational activity fundamentally changes the capital-labor relation—through part-time employment, if-and-when contracts, and through self-employment and piecemeal work and so on" (Hoogvelt, p. 145).

This process of labor flexibilization is facilitated even further by the actions of local governments. In the face of the severe economic tensions brought on by the dynamics described above (global finance, state reconstruction, etc.), Southern states often turn to TNCs as a source of jobs and capital. One strategy is to set up "export processing zones" (EPZs), which offer a number of infrastructure, tax, and financial incentives. The Indian state, in an act that symbolizes this process, was the first nation in the world to do so (Kumar, 1989). What is especially noteworthy about EPZs for our purpose is how they exempt TNCs from local labor laws. In this way, Southern states collude with international capital to undermine organizations' responsibility for work–family policies.

My Argument

I will show how organizational change is fundamental to the firms in my study, in that each displays at least one of the four types described earlier. However, dynamics of the globalization project aggravate the impact of those changes at the Indian firms, relative to the U.S. firm. First, I show how *IndCo* displays the same changes of "organizational restructuring" and "employment insecurity" as AmCo. However, because of global pressures of economic marginalization and state reconstruction, IndCo has weaker resources to respond to them and weaker ability to preserve its work–family policies. Second, I show how *TransCo* displays changes of "corporate ownership" and "occupational restructuring" similarly to AmCo. However, the dynamics of transnational corporations exacerbate the effects at two levels. Horizontal flexibility makes TransCo more vulnerable to transnational clashes of corporate culture, especially regarding work–family policies. Vertical flexibility leads to privileges for globally mobile, elite workers, and marginalization for the low-skilled workers, which ultimately stratifies work–family policies.

AMCO, TRANSCO, AND INDCO: THE RESEARCH SITES AND METHODOLOGY

This analysis is based on case studies of three computer companies with similar industry and market characteristics, but different locations and positions in the global economy. The first is *AmCo*,[2] an American company located in Silicon Valley, California. It is a founding company for the high-tech industry and has subsidiaries all around the world. The second company, *TransCo*, is one of these subsidiaries situated in New Delhi, with its factory in Bangalore. Thus, it has American ownership, management, and policies, but it is entirely staffed by Indians (with few American expatriates). The third company, *IndCo*, is the Indian counterpart to AmCo. It is owned by Indians and located in New Delhi. Like AmCo, it has been a leading high-tech company in its country (at the time of the study at least) and has subsidiaries worldwide, including California. All three companies have software

---

[2]Company names in this study have been changed to preserve employee anonymity. This also includes names of companies with which these firms have had partnerships or mergers.

development and hardware production operations and all have similar gender ratios in their workforces, roughly 25–30% female.

Data collection occurred in 1995 and 1996. Therefore, the analysis considers recent changes in the companies for the previous five years or so, through retrospective accounts of managers and workers. TransCo was selected and approached first, given that it was one of the leading computer firms in both India and the United States. Contacts made during fieldwork at this site enabled access to both of the other firms: to AmCo, by a visit from the vice president of the U.S. head office; and to IndCo, by suggestion from the TransCo president of a comparable firm. Given that all three firms were the first approached and agreeable to participate, I perceived a lack of a bias because of organizational attrition from the sample.

Qualitative methodology was selected for this project in order to collect rich, detailed descriptions of the organizational settings, which cannot be garnered through surveys alone. Therefore, fieldwork was conducted at each location and involved three activities. Work relations were observed for informal types of relations, such as hierarchical versus participatory interactions, and so forth. Company documents such as organizational charts and corporate philosophies were examined for support of work–family issues. At each site, ethnographic analysis was conducted at two units: the corporate office and a factory. In the corporate offices, jobs typically involve management, marketing, engineering, accounting, administration, and so on. In the factories, jobs involve circuit board manufacturing and computer assembly.

Finally, semi-structured interviews were conducted with both workers and managers. Formal (closed-ended) questions were used to assess demographic and educational backgrounds, work histories, and household characteristics, and so forth. Informal (open-ended) questions were used to elicit unconstrained responses regarding experiences of work–family interface and organizational change. The sample selection was based on employee lists provided by the human resource department. Respondents were chosen randomly, although the samples were balanced according to gender and occupational level. The total number of interviews at AmCo was 34, at TransCo 60, and at IndCo 51. Interviewees were told that this was a study about employment in transnational firms, rather than work–family issues in particular, so as to not bias the responses. Interviews were conducted onsite, either in English or in Hindi with the assistance of an interpreter, and lasted about an hour. Features of the samples are presented in Table 7.1.

The work–family policies in these firms are listed in Table 7.2. The range of what is included as a "work–family policy" is broader

TABLE 7.1
Background Characteristics of Employees

	AmCo			TransCo			IndCo		
	Total n = 34	Women n = 17	Men n = 17	Total n = 60	Women n = 29	Men n = 31	Total n = 51	Women n = 26	Men n = 25
Average Age (Years)	40	42	38	32	31	34	34	33	35
Education									
Highest Degree (%):									
High School/ Technical Certificate	35	35	35	28	24	32	41	42	40
Graduate	50	53	49	50	66	36	37	38	36
Post-Graduate	15	12	18	22	10	32	22	20	24
Family									
Currently Married (%)	58	50	65	67	62	71	80	73	88
Spouse Works (%)	82	100	67	74	100	59	63	100	32
Average # of Children	2	2	2	1	1	1	1.5	1	2
Household Structure (%):									
Single Family	66	56	81	58	59	58	49	50	48
Joint Family	34	44	19	42	41	42	51	50	52

TABLE 7.2
Work–Family Policies

	AmCo	IndCo	TransCo
Job Restructuring Programs	Flex-time (2.5 hr range) Flex-place Part-time Work Job Sharing	None	Flex-time (1.5 hr range) Flex-place Alternative Work Options (Combines Flex-place and Flex-time)
Material Family Benefits	Unpaid Parental Leave, for Both Biological and Adopted Children (2 Months)	Paid Maternity Leave (3 Months, Up to Two Times), Plus Miscarriage or Abortion Leave (6 Weeks Paid)	Paid Maternity Leave (for Biological Children: 3 Months, Plus Birthing Costs) (for Adopted Children: 6 Weeks, Plus 6 Weeks Unpaid, Plus Legal and Medical Expenses)
Leave	Unpaid Personal Leave (6 Months–1 Year)		
Childcare Benefits	Tax Exemptions for Childcare Costs (Dependent Care Assistance Plans)	On-site Childcare Center at the Factory	Tuition Subsidies for Primary and Secondary Level Schooling, for up to 2 Children (For Executive Employees Only)
Homecare Benefits	Data Not Available	*For Executives:* Home Rental, Lunch, Books and Periodicals, Clothing, Hard Furnishings (Furniture), Soft Furnishing (Linens), Driver *For Clerical Staff:* Rent *For Production Staff:* Transportation Shuttles, Subsidized Lunches, On-Site Doctor	*For Executives:* Driver, Servants, Soft Furnishings (Linens, Crockery, and Cutlery), Periodicals, Athletic Club Membership, and 70 Other Benefits *For Production Staff:* Transportation Shuttles

than in many conventional accounts. The idea for this conceptualization is to capture policies offered by organizations that may be informal or nontraditional (at least from an academic perspective), but nonetheless beneficial to workers and their families. In Table 7.2, we see that AmCo is strong on "alternative work arrangements," or in other words, programs that modify schedules or places work to accommodate family demands. These include flex-time, telecommuting, job sharing, and part-time work. However, AmCo is much weaker on material benefits, especially compared to IndCo. This firm offers extensive and well-subsidized parental leave, along with a full package of home care benefits: coverage for rent, clothing, books, furniture, personal drivers for corporate staff; and transportation shuttles, cafeteria meals, onsite day-care centers, and doctors for production staff. TransCo combines elements of both programs, in a manner that is uncommon for other firms. This is described in detail in another paper (Poster, 2000), but will be addressed here in the upcoming section on TransCo.

RESULTS: THREE MODELS OF GLOBAL ORGANIZATIONAL CHANGE

These cases represent three models of organizational change in the global economy. Table 7.3 summarizes the features of these models, in terms of each firm's: (1) position in the global economy; (2) experience of organizational change; and (3) outcome for employment relations. Implications for work–family policies in particular are discussed in the following section.

Endurance

AmCo illustrates a model of endurance. As a Northern firm—and moreover, the parent of a multinational corporation—it represents a privileged position in the global hierarchy. Among the three firms, it is best able to insulate itself from external pressures. Therefore, it survives through this period of change with the least impact on employees.

Organizational Changes. Ironically, AmCo experienced the greatest range of organizational changes at this time relative to both IndCo or TransCo. First, there was a merger with a local telecommunications company. This generated a number of structural changes for employees of the target company, but not for long. A male technician

TABLE 7.3
Models of Global Positioning and Organizational Change

	Endurance	Disruption	Flexibility
Position in Global System	Southern Organization (AmCo)	Northern Organization (IndCo)	Transnational Organization (TransCo)
Type of Organizational Change	Employment Insecurity (Job Shuffling) Organizational Restructuring (Authority Decentralization) Occupational Restructuring (Contingent Work) Corporate Ownership (Mergers)	Employment Insecurity (Layoffs) Organizational Restructuring (Spacial Decentralization)	Occupational Restructuring (Contingent Work) Corporate Ownership (Mergers)
Global Forces		State Reconstruction Economic Marginalization	Flexible Global Production
Impact on Employment: Job Structures	Jobs Maintained but Moved	Layoffs, Speedup, and Disempowerment of Workers	Upgrading of Corporate Jobs, Downgrading of Factory Jobs
Work–Family Policy	*Suspension* of Policies (Flextime)	*Termination* of Policies (Onsite Daycare Centers, Doctors)	Intensified *Stratification* in Access to Policies

explains: "I started with a company called OtherCo[3] that AmCo acquired five years ago. So I have been working with AmCo for the last five years. [A lot] has changed with operators, technicians, and managers since AmCo bought the company. But right now, it's like one big company. You wouldn't even know it was OtherCo." There are many reasons why this merger was so smooth, including the fact that the acquiring firm was much larger than the target firm. In addition, a contributing factor was the fit between employee expectations from the old firm and the policies of the new firm. In other words, OtherCo workers appreciated AmCo's work–family policies in a way that we will not see later in the cross-border mergers by TransCo.

AmCo was also undergoing a transformation of the organizational structure—specifically, a decentralization of work relations and a shift away from hierarchy toward teams. A female supervisor on the production floor explains: "We're moving from directly supervising people, to just coaching the team, so that the operators work within their team to try and solve things and come up with solutions. [The view is that] a large population of people should make all those decisions." However, there are two reasons why this policy has not significantly altered jobs at AmCo. One is that the teams have not been fully implemented here, especially compared to other firms in the region. The supervisor continues: "It's actually going on in this whole valley, and there are not too many supervisors anymore. Everybody we've talked to is basically doing this—*but they are a lot further ahead than we are.*" The second reason is that the team model has been less successfully implemented in the corporate areas relative to the factory:

> I understand that some people have actually tried it in the office areas. It seems like it could work because many times you need the support of another person if you're going to be gone, on leave, or if you are not available. Also, you could go help somebody else if you run out of work. But it has been difficult in the offices because people usually are in a cubicle all to their own, and they're focused on what they're doing. So, it probably could work, or maybe it just needs more fine-tuning. Whereas in production, it's a little easier.

Thus, decentralization has been slow to catch on here.

The third change at AmCo is occupational restructuring, through an increasing reliance on contingent workers. A female operator

---

[3]See note 2.

explains, "We've had new people coming into our area, and they are hiring a lot of temps. It's kind of hard. When you've been working with someone for years and years, it's a little bit different having people come in fairly new." The most extensive uses of temporary workers seem to be in other departments however, or else in previous periods of speedup. A male technician describes: "In the past when we were going 24 hours a day, 7 days a week, we had a lot of temporary workers: out of a work group of 60, we had about 45 temporary workers." Indeed, at the time of these interviews, there were few temporary workers in the factory and none in the sample.

Impact on Employees. Relative to these three types of organizational change, the only one that had a very significant impact on workers at AmCo is employment insecurity. Given the recessions of the early 1990s, the firm experienced pressures to reduce staff. One corporate office employee in facilities explains: "We're in a 'redeployment mode' in our department. *Redeployment mode?* [Laugh] These new words. [It means] a downsizing. As we go through the downsizing stuff, there are jobs that will be outsourced." Thus, some workers were laid off as the company cut back on staff and outsourced some of the tasks. However, for the majority of employees, the more common procedure was shuffling workers around various departments of the company. A female operator in the factory explains what the experience meant: "I was doing one job for a while and then they "accessed" everybody. *What does that mean – "access"?* They are cutting down on people, and then we get to look around for another job in the company."

These experiences of job insecurity generate many strains for AmCo workers. One is increased tension *among* employees, as they now have to compete with their colleagues for scarce "core" positions. The facilities executive above recounts: "The job I have now is a core position, and so it has security. Management identified three more core positions, and there are six people in our group out of fourteen who will be eligible for those positions. So when the opportunity arises, we will be competitive for those three positions." Second, the repeated "redeployment" of employees means that many workers submit to a career of intra-office movement, as this female engineer in the corporate office describes: "I've actually got friends who are on their fifth access, which means that five times they have been rolled over. It comes to the point where their only job is to find a job." Still others describe an insecurity of being in a constant state of unknowing about the fate of their jobs, as a corporate employee in applications support explains:

> It's almost as though with all the changes in management, all of the changes in—not policy, but it's the change in structure that's ongoing—you just have to be more careful of what you are saying, because people are nervous. They're nervous because all of a sudden, their new managers are in Atlanta, their department is being shifted, and it is all going to be housed in Boise, and they think: "What's going to happen to me?" Everybody is very cautious, and you have to be more careful.

Thus, clearly, these changes in jobs created a degree of hardship and anxiety for AmCo employees.

Yet, the unique feature of AmCo (especially compared to IndCo) is its general ability to maintain a "no fire" policy through this crisis. Many employees in the corporate office praise the firm for this commitment to job security, such as this male engineer: "It's not like other companies. I haven't seen anybody get laid off from this company in seven years. You might have seen companies hiring like crazy, and at the same time firing people. But we have job security, and if you are accessed in a group, they give you lots of options." Furthermore, even with the downsizing, some departments in the firm were expanding. A female supervisor in the factory confirmed: "We've interviewed quite a few people in the last year and a half, because we've had such a big hiring." Thus, in many ways, employment security is better here than at other firms.

Disruption

IndCo illustrates the model of disruption. As a Southern-based company, it faces more severe external pressures than AmCo—in particular, global pressures of state reconstruction and economic marginalization. Given that IndCo has fewer resources with which to manage these strains, it requires more drastic organizational strategies. Thus, although IndCo experiences fewer of the "organizational changes" in Table 7.3, it experiences more substantial consequences on employment and work–family policy, including layoffs, labor speedup, and a termination of many material benefits.

Global Pressures. Prior to 1991, IndCo was a relatively successful company in India. It was top ten in its market and invented a crucial piece of hardware for PCs that spread worldwide in the 1980s. Plus, as the demand for computers rose, IndCo increased production by 300%. However, several shifts in global production derailed their upward progress by the 1990s. The first was a change in the high-tech industry, reflecting the rapid obsolescence of technology, as discussed earlier. The factory manager explains:

> A reason for the changing scene is that the computer industry has a very short life span for any product. The time it takes to come from United States, Japan, or any other country to India is about 6 months. The demand for those items starts here, and in a year or so, it goes down. So any product which comes here, within 6 months or 1 year, it has become obsolete. There is a change.

At the same time, there was an escalating need for volume of production: "The expectations of the division, of the management have increased. The reason is that we had very little volumes. If we don't have volume, we cannot stand in the market. The poor volumes of U.S. companies may be a very high target for us. And if you are talking big volumes, you have to have automation." Thus, global economic marginalization—especially relative to the United States—puts these firms at a disadvantage. Another pressure was change in the technology of the production process. Along with speed and volume, IndCo needed to improve automation:

> When we set up this factory, we had a big plan on having a lot of automation here. We thought that we will have automatic packing machines, lifting machines, trolleys here and there. We don't have much except that we have glow soldering machines and some electrical screwdrivers. It's because we are not in that good of a financial position to do the investment.

A pivotal turning point for IndCo was when the state liberalized its economy and changed regulations on trade. By opening local markets to imports, it greatly intensified competition for computer parts. This had a profound effect on IndCo's strategy for production:

> Because of the government policies, we had to take a decision not to invest too much money here—it was not viable to have the big production plan. Earlier we used to do the assembly of cables and cards ourselves. We used to get components like resistors, capacitors, and circuit boards separately, then assemble, do the testing, and make the machines. But then the import duty on assembled machines was reduced, and the profit for manufacturing was too small. So we decided to do basically machine integration.

Thus, this combination of factors ultimately influenced IndCo's leaders to change the core process of the factory from manufacturing to assembly. Moreover, the new state laws had the counter-productive effect of *discouraging* investment in the factory.

Organizational Changes. As a response to these strains, IndCo managers felt that organizational restructuring was necessary. One form of this was decentralization. More radical than the decentralization at AmCo (which involved decision-making structures and teams), the decentralization at IndCo involved its physical space. IndCo undertook a "trifurcation" of its factory, in which a large production facility in New Delhi was divided into three smaller facilities. This trifurcation was largely motivated by the new state policies. To promote the high-tech business in particular, the state set up industrial parks called "Electronics Cities," which provided infrastructural support and tax incentives. The factory manager continues: "We were getting a sales tax advantage here, so we decided to open this new factory. Initially, we had plans to have our R&D and purchase department and some other functions, so that is why you see big land here." This new factory was now located many miles away from the head office in New Delhi, in a city called Gurgaon. Although these state initiatives were designed to promote and expand private industries in India, they had the opposite effect in this case—redistributing and downsizing the scale of production at IndCo.

Simultaneous to this, IndCo underwent a second major change involving employment insecurity—layoffs. The IndCo president explains what this meant for the occupational structure and size of the labor force: "We reduced or eliminated layers. From nine or—in some cases—eleven layers, we came down to three or five layers. We had 928 persons, and we came down to 460. [And later] closed one full factory." Even for those who remained, there was a fresh feeling of anxiety. For many of these workers, the possibility of being fired was a new concept, as previous socialist labor policies had protected workers in many organizations. The female factory supervisor recounts:

> In government organizations, job security is there. But in a private organization, they can always chuck you out if they are not satisfied. That is in the appointment letter, there is a clause. If you are not satisfying their job requirements, they can ask you to leave. So, I do feel that a private organization is comparatively harder.

Thus, with state liberalization, these workers experience the precariousness of the capitalist employment contract more immediately.

New Tensions for Employees. There were many reverberations from these changes for workers. The first is a speedup of the work process. At the corporate office, executives felt this speedup in terms of long hours, and informal pressure to work harder and perform more. This female quality manager explains: "There is a different organization culture right now. People are staying back [late], coming on Sundays, coming on holidays, and all that. A culture is drumming up. It has become an 'in' thing. And people who are doing that are being benefitted. What the organization requires right now, maybe we are unable to deliver that." Production workers experience this speedup of work in a more concrete and visible way. The factory manager explains this by contrasting work pressure at the older factory in New Delhi: "Though we are producing many more machines than Delhi, we have less employees. In Delhi, we were dealing with around 70, 80, or maybe 100 machines in a month. *Today we are producing about 500 machines in a month—with just 1/10th of the staff.*" A shopfloor employee describes the change from her view: "When the [old] factory was there, the manpower was high so the work expected from one person was less compared to what it is now. So people never used to feel that loaded." Likewise, another says: "This is a change. Over there, the staff was good quantity-wise. So, one person was not responsible for so much. There was sufficient responsibility. But nowadays, everybody is loaded with work."

A second newfound tension was commuting, for the factory workers in particular. The President explains, "Most of the workers are from Delhi, and previously more than 50% of the workers were staying next to the [old] factory. So normally, they would have taken about 5, 10, 15 minutes to reach the factory. Now they have to spend about 2 hours more—one hour for coming, one hour for going." A female factory worker describes the tension it creates for their households: "Two hours is basically needed for commuting. Even if we leave at 7 or 7:30 a.m., we reach home by 6:30 or 7 p.m. So there is hardly any time for your family."

An especially significant consequence of the shift was a demobilization of the union. IndCo was the only one of three companies to ever have a union. However, through the decentralization of the factory, the union lost its base and its momentum. A woman on the factory shopfloor explains: "Here the union is not as effective as it was in Delhi. It is not effective. First, the number of people is less, and second, everyone is loaded with work." Some of the workers believe that demobilizing the union was a motivating factor for the trifurcation in the first place. Whatever the source, the loss of the power of the union was significant because it had been the driving force behind a number of family benefits for the workers, as described below.

There were a few positive outcomes for workers that accompanied the strains from this transition. For instance, during the layoffs, most workers who left the firm received a cash compensation. The factory manager claims that about 95% of the workers took a "golden handshake," which ranged from about $5,000 for managers to $2,500 for operators (equal to about 6 months salary for the former, and 2 years for the latter). Another positive outcome was a new provision for transportation. The factory manager says: "When the shift took place, then we came with an agreement because of the distance problem. We decided we will compensate some part in the form of money, and we will also provide transport. Because probably that was the best we could have done for them." These vans are a big help because public transportation is very difficult in New Delhi. Even with the added convenience of company vans, however, these workers still have to take buses after the vans drop them off downtown rather than at their homes.

Flexibility

TransCo illustrates a third model of flexibilization. With its global resources as a transnational corporation, it evades many of the tensions that IndCo experiences, such as employment insecurity and organizational restructuring. Instead, it experiences other types of change—corporate ownership (i.e., mergers) and occupational restructuring (i.e., contingent work). Many of these processes are similar to those at AmCo, but more extensive and/or conflictual at TransCo given the intervening factor of globalization. First, the mergers are complicated by clashing corporate policies (including work–family) given that the firms come from different national institutional contexts. Second, contingent work is exacerbated by the firm's use of global space to privilege upper level employees and marginalize lower level workers. These dynamics reflect the dynamic of global flexibility at TransCo.

Organizational Changes. Because of TransCo's horizontal flexibility, mergers are more integral to the ongoing dynamics of the firm than at AmCo. Local partnerships and alliances were necessary from the very beginning as a means of gaining an edge on regional markets and incorporating functions into the firm (i.e., suppliers, vendors, labor, etc.). In fact, the original establishment of TransCo in India was dependent upon a joint venture with a local distributor. This was a pre-1991 requirement by the state. However, "with the liberalization and government policy, etc.," as the Vice President explains, "now the joint venture arrangement had come to an end and AmCo had the feasibility to go in for a 100% subsidiary operation."

Such mergers were also fraught with tension. One alliance with MergerCo[4] illustrates how the clash of corporate cultures and policies from multiple international sources can aggravate a merger. On one hand, the target firm had elements of the "local" Indian system: "Employee management in local companies is completely different— whether you go to the MergerCo's, or the Birla's, the Tata's, the Modi's, [each of these being Indian firms] or whoever. Very, very different. They basically tow the line of the boss. And if it happens to be a family-owned company, it's even worse. They have an approach of: 'If it's not broken, why fix it?'" Added to this, the target company also had holdover elements of the former British imperial administration: "If you walked into their office, they still have this British system of standing up, and saying, 'Yes sir,' and 'Good morning, sir,' and all that nonsense. We don't have it. It's all first-name basis—that's part of the AmCo corporate philosophy." Ultimately, the flatter hierarchy of AmCo clashed with the vertical style of Indian and British firms. Because these corporate cultures are trinational—U.S., British, *and* Indian—the merger is further complicated.

A second type of organizational change that TransCo experiences more acutely than AmCo is occupational restructuring. This reflects the vertical flexibility of TransCo as a TNC, in the form of a greater share of contingent workers relative to both other firms. TransCo had recently increased its temporary workforce to a proportion far exceeding that of AmCo. About two thirds of the factory staff at TransCo was temporary—80 workers, split in two shifts.

It is not a coincidence that TransCo has such a large share of contingent work relative to AmCo. Indeed, this trend represents another type of flexibility among TNCs—the ability to transfer organizational strain between parent and subsidiary. The TransCo factory manager explains how the growing flexibilization of offshore labor is part of AmCo strategy: "In Singapore, the AmCo unit has a large flex force. And in Spain, we have a strength of 150 factory workers, out of which 145 of them are flex." Even workers at AmCo see this trend. One factory worker (who described being moved to different jobs around the firm) explains the fate of her department: "There were quite a few people that were accessed—hundreds. They [AmCo managers] were doing away with the division—moving it. That one went overseas to

---

[4]See note 2.

Singapore." As we know from the factory manager, the jobs in Singapore (like those at TransCo in India) are far inferior to those at AmCo. In this sense, AmCo is shielding its own workers from occupational downgrading by transferring the marginal jobs abroad. (This is perhaps one of the ways that AmCo survived the downsizing pressures common in Silicon Valley at that time.) Thus, global flexibility means greater marginalization of Southern workers through the TNC.

Impact on Employees. The conditions of temporary work at TransCo are precarious in a number of ways. The least severe perhaps is alienation from routine organizational activities and practices. Temporary workers are left out of many daily events that otherwise reflect a fairly inclusive and dominant corporate culture. For instance, these workers do not receive evaluations or feedback on their work. A female production supervisor at TransCo explains:

> We have a performance evaluation for every employee on a regular basis, six months to yearly. When they are permanent, I meet them at least once in a year, and really discuss what their strengths and weaknesses are, what they could do to improve, and how to convert their weaknesses into strength. But with the flex, we don't have this for them. That is something which is missing at the moment.

Unlike permanent workers, therefore, these temps are unable to improve their skills, perhaps one of the only potentially transferable human capital benefits of the job. Similarly, these workers are excluded from access to certain kinds of information. Another production manager explains:

> They are not part of a lot of things. We include them in communication events, like every month where everyone comes together to celebrate birthdays. But some of the company information is not given out to them, specifically not any company related information – things like earnings statements or organizational changes. Because it's valuable information for the company. And given that workers go off to another industry, the competitors can use it against you.

Regardless of how useful such information would be for individual workers, the exclusion indicates how TransCo treats temporary workers with suspicion.

There are other more tangible effects of temporary work. Short duration is the obvious one—production workers are there merely

6 months. According to a factory manger, this is partially due to local laws about contingent work: "The temporary people—they are here for a short time. The government requires certain rules—that they are not here for more than 6 months. So you have to keep shifting them out. The turnover is quite high." At the time of my study, this type of employment was unusual for the industrial park in Bangalore where TransCo is located. Comparing his firm to another nearby high-tech TNC, the factory supervisor estimated that his wages are "...probably less. Just a little less. But remember that they [i.e., the other TNC's workers] are permanent, and these are flex. The job is not secure." Thus, although TransCo's wages are slightly higher than similar permanent jobs, they come at the high cost of short duration.

Furthermore, another downside of temporary work relative to other local production jobs is exclusion from unionizing. A factory supervisor comments: "I don't know if it is possible to have a union for a flex force. The fact is that we don't have any union." It is unclear whether or not this is a formal global policy for AmCo, but it is certainly a pattern in many of AmCo's other factories around the world. The factory manager confirmed that AmCo subsidiaries in Spain and Singapore are also without unions.

DISCUSSION: DIVERGENT OUTCOMES FOR WORK–FAMILY POLICY

These models of organizational change have significant implications for the success or failure of work–family policy. Here, I link each model to varying outcomes of suspension, termination, or stratification of work–family programs (summarized in Table 7.3).

AmCo and the Endurance Scenario

AmCo emerged from its experience of change with the least disturbance to its work–family policies. As listed in Table 7.2, AmCo has a large range of programs, and they were maintained throughout this period, even for the low-skilled workers. This also applies to the "redeployed" workers, as the female engineer quoted earlier continues: "Even the accessed workers are continuing to be paid, and they continue to get their benefits. Nobody said 'goodbye.' We have a very unique, different company."

The most serious consequence of these organizational changes on work–family programs was a temporary *suspension* of its flextime program. There were varying accounts of how widespread this suspension was throughout the firm. Some employees described it as departmentally specific. "I know that AmCo has flexible time," a male production assistant says, "but this flexible time does not apply to all departments. It depends upon the department." Other employees described it as temporally sporadic. A female production worker echoes, "We have flexible timings. We *could* come in at 2:30–3:00pm. But not right now. It depends on the work, how it is set up. It is up to the manager, and the management level." Still other employees predicted that the suspension would be wide-scale and permanent, such as this female production technician: "They want to change it. There will not be any flexibility anymore. They have changed the time: everybody comes in 6:30 a.m. to 3:00 p.m. And when the second shift takes over, we just leave." Whatever the future scenario for flextime, the majority of the other policies (including parental leave) remain intact through the transition. In this sense, AmCo illustrates an "endurance" of its policies through dynamics of organizational change.

IndCo and the Disruption Scenario

IndCo's more dramatic experience of factory decentralization and layoffs lead to a *termination* of several work–family programs. One of these was cash bonuses. The factory manager explains: "We used to give cash awards or some amount two or three times a year. We would find out two or three people, and give them awards every 2–3 months or something like that. That scheme initially went up very well, but those types of practices have been stopped—it collapsed."

Another casualty of the transition was an onsite daycare center. A female personnel administrator explained how this originated at the old factory in New Delhi, where she used to be a shopfloor manager: "We made this creche for the women in the factory. I started it from scratch. It started in 1986 and wound off in 1992, so it was functional for six years. But now that factory is closed." She explained that there is no plan to reinstate childcare centers at any of the sites, even though it is at the top of women's policy needs. A female software engineer explains:

> Now we have a lot of women who have got small kids and they are facing problems in terms of managing their babies. Earlier there were not so many women in the company, so they had never thought about having a day care. But now definitely. We have been pushing it, but managers are not so positive about it. It is not being considered a very important issue.

Furthermore, a number of other material benefits from the old factory disappeared—including an onsite doctor, adequate food in the cafeteria, and higher wages. A male personnel administrator recounts:

> When I joined here some labor trouble was going on. All the female workers were fighting against the management. They were fighting for their demands—wage increases and better facilities. Like for married females, we were having a creche for their children. They were also asking for better food and milk, and that a full-time doctor should be provided. I said this is all reasonable. There is no question of discussion. They were asking for a 1500 Rupee raise in their salary. That is unreasonable, so 500 Rupees was the raise.

The crucial factor in this scenario is the presence of the union. Previous work–family benefits were achieved through the union's collective action and would be hard to recover without its continued support.

In these ways, IndCo represents the most "disruption" in the organizational change process in comparison to the two other firms in this study. First, it experienced the greatest loss in terms of the content of work–family policies. IndCo's policies had been material in form, which are more beneficial to workers in some ways than alternative work arrangements such as flextime and flexplace (Poster, 2000; Poster and Prasad, 2005). Second, it experienced the greatest extent of loss. IndCo is the only firm of three in which work–family policies were terminated, rather than suspended or reduced in access. Finally, whereas TransCo's experience of change accompanied an expansion of policies for workers at the top of the firm, this was not the case at IndCo.

TransCo and the Flexible Scenario

TransCo's global flexibility means that work–family policy outcomes are more complicated and multifaceted. Here I outline the outcomes for external versus internal employee programs.

Horizontal flexibility resulted in transnational conflicts among the work–family policies of the partnering firms. Consider the contrasts between policies at MergerCo and TransCo. MergerCo offered generous material compensation, but at the cost of high job insecurity and fear. As the TransCo President describes it:

> MergerCo corporation has a specific type of culture which I don't agree with. It's because the way they treat their people: "I can give you a little higher salary, and a few stock options, and you won't go and work anywhere else. And if you don't perform, I'll fire you. Instantly. Without

second thought. Without a word of training, coaching, or whatever." It's by fear that they make things work. You don't have to motivate.

In contrast, TransCo offered weaker material benefits, but greater job autonomy and alternative work options: "We are in an environment where we are very flexible. We have flexi-time. For the first time in this country, we introduced it. We are now looking at umpteen ways of work-life balance, which is unheard of in other companies so far."

Eventually, there was a clash in these orientations toward work–family policy, with one emphasizing material benefits and the other alternative work arrangements. Such tensions were difficult to resolve, as the President continues:

> Culture has a lot to do with alliances, joint ventures, strategic relationships, partnerships, and companies that you buy—and a lot to do with business results. When there's a misfit—a *cultural* misfit—you really screw up the organization. Today, five years later, we're still trying to work on what's best in both the cases. Integrating a culture that's completely different—to get a mix of both. We're still struggling with it.

A few years after my fieldwork, the merger failed. Thus, this case shows how *work–family policies* are significant enough to get in the way of mergers. It also explains why TransCo experiences greater difficulty in its mergers than does AmCo. TransCo's mergers are more complicated because of the multiple national origins of the policies that have to be reconciled, and especially because of their global scale across Northern and Southern nations. So, whereas TransCo's horizontal flexibility means that it engages in more external alliances than does AmCo, it also means that these alliances are more difficult to complete.

Vertical flexibility in work–family programs results from differential global pressures at different levels of the firm's job structure. At the top, TransCo faces a crisis of retention for its "high-value" employees (i.e., the engineers and technical experts, but also the sales, marketing, and finance personnel). With the increasing global mobility of this professional and technical staff, TransCo experienced an immediate threat of losing them to other firms—not only in India, but also in the United States and other countries. The TransCo President explains:

> There's a 35% turnover in the computer companies—because of intense competition from outside. In the past, employees were in a situation where they were lucky if they got jobs in India. Today, it's the other way around. There's a demand on people all of a sudden. Competitors are

coming from around the world so they can steal your people. And more than half of [our employee departures] are leaving to go *outside* the country for jobs.

Although IndCo certainly faces this labor market pressure as well, TransCo is uniquely positioned to respond to it. As a TNC, it has access to global resources in the form of both capital and policy design from its parent company. In turn, TransCo uses work–family benefits as a means to retain their professional staff. They offer a vast array of programs that are, moreover, unusually innovative (Poster, 2000): they combine IndCo's style of material benefits (such as paid maternity leave) with AmCo's style of alternative work arrangements (such as flextime). Some of these policies—such as children's school subsidies and the "alternative work options" program—are not even offered at AmCo's global units in other countries.

However, TransCo's temporary employees are eligible for neither the employee benefits nor work–family programs. This reflects their global strategy of labor flexibilization, in which the parent company utilizes temporary workers in Southern nations precisely for the purpose of avoiding corporate responsibilities such as employee benefits. It also reflects localized complicity, in that the Indian state provides exemptions from a wide array of labor regulations for transnational corporations in export processing zones. An example is one of the hallmarks of the state's labor policy—the Maternity Benefit Act—which is not mandatory for TNCs hiring temporary workers (Gothoskar, 1992). Ultimately then, this dual strategy of flexible employment—select treatment of high-skilled workers and marginalization of low-skilled workers—results in bifurcated access to work–family policy at TransCo.

In the end, this stratification of work–family policy far exceeds that of IndCo or AmCo. We can see this in their structures of wages (Table 7.4). For instance, TransCo managers earn 12 times more than the monthly salaries of their operators, whereas IndCo managers earn 8 times more, and AmCo managers earn only 2 times more. So, although AmCo wages are generally higher than those of the other firms, TransCo displays the most egregious vertical differentiation in rewards.

This said, there are also some benefits of organizational change at TransCo. For the permanent workers at TransCo (mostly at higher occupational levels), work–family benefits exceed those of many local firms. For the temporary workers, TransCo has also provided some advantages in terms of job opportunities in a context where unemployment rates are very high. Finally, regardless of occupational level,

TABLE 7.4
Average Monthly Salary by Job Level and Gender

Job Level	AmCo			TransCo[a]			IndCo[a]		
	Total $n = 31$	Women $n = 15$	Men $n = 16$	Total $n = 56$	Women $n = 29$	Men $n = 27$	Total $n = 48$	Women $n = 24$	Men $n = 24$
All Levels	$3,766	$3,500	$4,017	$ 547	$372	$ 729	$352	$253	$455
Management	$4,720	$3,867	$6,000	$1,076	$625	$1,230	$731	$557	$811
Executive, Sales, Engineer	$5,449	$5,338	$5,523	$ 513	$431	$ 612	$316	$333	$296
Administrator, Secretary[b]	$4,583	$4,583	—	$ 349	$349	—	$164	$199	$136
Operator, Technician	$2,273	$2,137	$2,391	$ 90	$ 60	$ 107	$ 90	$ 90	$ 91

[a]Wages at IndCo and TransCo have been converted from rupees, at a rate 34.5 rupees per dollar (applicable to the year of the interview).
[b]Blank entries indicate a lack of respondents in the sample for this category.

working in a transnational corporation has status in India, as it provides potential access to international contacts. Still, what is unique
about TransCo, relative to IndCo and AmCo, is its flexibility. On one
hand, it uses its flexibility of global capital and positioning to avoid
many of the tensions faced by IndCo in organizational change; on the
other hand, it uses its flexibility to absorb and magnify the global tensions faced by AmCo, particularly by implementing cost-cutting labor
strategies abroad.

CONCLUSION

This analysis has illustrated how three similar high-tech companies
operating in the same period of the early 1990s experienced three different outcomes in their work–family programs. AmCo, representing
a model of "endurance," was able to retain most of its programs, aside
from a suspension of flextime; whereas IndCo, representing "disruption," was forced to terminate many of its programs including onsite
day-care centers, medical staff, and cash bonuses. TransCo, as the
model of "flexibility," fashioned an inverted pyramid out of its policies by expanding those at the top of the occupational hierarchy and
narrowing those at the bottom.

My argument is that these outcomes are related to the positions
of these firms in the global economy. AmCo, as a Northern firm,
is better able to insulate its work–family policies from cyclical patterns of global economic strain. In contrast, IndCo, as a Southern
firm, is forced to sacrifice many of its work–family policies because
of formidable pressures of global economic marginalization and state
reconstruction. Finally, TransCo represents the global privileges and
tensions of a transnational corporation, which has the horizontal flexibility to absorb organizational strains from its parent company, and
the vertical flexibility to marginalize its low-skilled workforce and ultimately stratify its policies.

Given that this is a case study analysis, it is important to note
the specificity of these particular firms and the ways they may differ from others in their contexts. AmCo, for instance, is especially
committed to work–family issues (often listed in publications of the
"best places to work"). Although AmCo is definitely representative of
other large Fortune 500 firms, it may not be representative of other
U.S. firms. Some argue these larger firms have more resources to
offer work–family benefits, and are furthermore not "typical" workplaces because most people work for small firms. AmCo may also
be somewhat unique in its "endurance" relative to other U.S. firms.

During the time period of this study, many other Silicon Valley firms folded. Moreover, shortly after the study was conducted—in the early 2000s—the high-tech industry went through an historic recession. Tens of thousands of jobs were lost in Silicon Valley, along with 41% of the computer jobs in New York, making it the worst hiring slump in 20 years (Mahler, 2003). Thus, not all firms survive as well as AmCo.

IndCo is also somewhat unique in its context. Again, it represents a high-end workplace, as only a small percentage of the total population works in the formal labor market. Still, among middle class employers, IndCo represents a relatively average firm. On one hand, it offers a wider package of work–family benefits relative to firms in other industries and relative to government organizations. On the other hand, it offers fewer benefits than many leading Indian firms (especially given the growth and changes in Indian firms subsequent to this period). Finally, it is important to note that not all Indian companies experience disruption to the same degree that IndCo did. Indeed, many survived this period with much more ease, an example of which is the highly successful global Indian firm, Infosys. My point, however, is that although all these firms are single cases, they represent broad trends in the positions of dominant and subordinate firms in the global economy.

This study contributes to the literature on international work–family policies in several ways. First, it challenges the assumptions of stability in work–family policy and suggests that policies should instead be conceived in terms of change. Second, this study suggests that in international contexts, dynamics of change are often globally interactive rather than merely internal to national contexts. In this study, the "globalization project" drives many of these patterns, through the consolidation of global finance, IMF loans, state restructuring, and the growth of transnational corporations with their new forms of flexible global production. These factors intensify organizational change for Southern nations, so that the *same* basic organizational changes taking place in AmCo have far greater consequences for work–family programs than in IndCo and TransCo.

For instance, although AmCo workers faced *employment insecurity* in terms of job shuffling, IndCo workers faced labor speedups and massive layoffs. Similarly, whereas AmCo workers faced *organizational restructuring* in the form of authority decentralization and use of teams, IndCo faced a more invasive form of decentralization involving the physical displacement of workers and new tensions of commuting. Third, whereas AmCo's changes in *corporate ownership* were relatively smooth, those at TransCo were intensified by conflicting organizational cultures and orientations toward work–family policy. Finally, whereas AmCo workers faced minimal or localized *occupational restructuring* in terms of contingent work, TransCo organized its production force almost entirely around it. Even if AmCo is heading in this direction as well, many indicators suggest that the casualization of labor is greater in Southern countries, and is likely to increase (International Labour Office, 2001).

This said, there are some theoretical limitations to the comparison of cases in this study. One is the differential costs of these work–family policies, which may affect their outcomes during organizational change. In other words, AmCo's policies (e.g., flextime) are cheaper to implement than IndCo's (e.g., childcare). This begs the question of how these firms would have responded if their policies had been more similar to begin with: Would AmCo have been more likely to disrupt its policies if they had been more expensive? Would IndCo have been more likely to retain its policies if they had been cheaper? Thus, future research should address the connections between the longevity of policies and their costs during similar types of change.

In addition, the emphasis on *global* factors in this study may compromise due attention to the *local* ones. Many work–family scholars point to the importance of local pressure from institutional environments (Goodstein, 1994; Kelly, 1999; Osterman, 1995) and managerial rationality (Milliken, Martines, and Morgan, 1998) as determinants of organizational policy. Likewise, further research is needed to address the impact of external labor markets (Poelmans, Chinchilla, and Cardona, 2003). For instance, while I have maintained that the labor market for high-tech professionals is tight on a global level (to which TransCo was in a unique position to respond in its work–family benefits), it is possible that the local labor markets of these firms were more varied.

Still, these findings recast traditional explanations of international work–family policies. Arguments regarding states and cultures described in the introduction are put under question in these firms, as organizational changes brought on by global dynamics are undermining or complicating them. For instance, although the Indian state may have been responsible in establishing strong supports for workers and their families (through legislation such as the Factories Act, the Minimum Wage Act, the Maternity Leave Act, etc.), few of these laws continue to have much force in practice given the societal transformations of the early 1990s. IndCo shows decreasing ability to offer provisions such as day-care centers, despite state policies that uphold them. TransCo has even less obligation to offer benefits such as maternity leave, given its exemptions from most labor legislation as a TNC in an export processing zone.

The same is true for cultural influences, which also are attenuated in this period. Whereas "collectivist" ideologies may have originally contributed to strong benefits for the family in India (Komarraju, 1997), such factors lack the economic or political fortitude to withstand recent forces of the global economy. A prime example is IndCo's policy of job security. IndCo had been implementing this policy for decades (even though as a private organization, it was not legally required to so in the eyes of the state). However, this changed when the firm faced the pressures of economic liberalization and ultimately had to abandon it in order to implement layoffs. The effects of national culture are dissipating in the face of organizational change in TransCo as well. Under the globalizing dynamics of cross-border mergers (Aguilera and Dencker, 2004 forthcoming), "culture" is being fragmented and reshaped as organizational policies from different nations come into contact. Furthermore, TransCo's outcome as an United States/British/Indian hybrid in its alliance with MergerCo shows how "culture"—as a unitary entity—no longer exists in isolation. Rather, organizational forms and polices are increasingly under negotiation, integration, and reformation in the face of globalization. In all these ways, organizational change—as prompted by global factors—is recasting traditional accounts of work–family policy.

For the future, this study suggests many potentially useful ways to study organizational change and globalization of work–family policy. One such direction would be longitudinal research on work–family policies—both at the organizational and state level. This study has shown how policies can be much more tenuous and loosely embedded in organizations than commonly assumed. Therefore, it would be helpful to track them more regularly over the long term to make sure they are protected (and of course improved). It would also be interesting to know more about the contexts where policies are likely to survive the longest, and what kinds of social factors have made it possible.

A second area of study is research on work–family policies in the South. The analysis of IndCo in particular reveals how work–family policies in Southern nations can be more vulnerable to forces of change than those in the North. Therefore, research on how to sustain work–family policies in these contexts would be helpful. Given that the international work–family literature is currently focused on Western Europe, the United States, and other advanced industrial nations such as Japan, the field would benefit from research on Africa, Latin America, the Middle East, and Southeast Asia.

A third area of study is the transnational movement of work–family policies. For instance, the case of TransCo is somewhat unique in displaying both innovations and misuses of work–family policy, and it would be interesting to know if this is confirmed in other case studies of TNCs. Moreover, TransCo illustrates a case in which the *flaws* of U.S. policies are exacerbated overseas. Many studies have pointed out how there is a stratification of work–family policies in the United States along lines of race, class, gender, and marital status (Bergmann, 1998; Glass and Estes, 1997; Wexler, 1997). Although this is also true of AmCo, this study has shown how global forces have magnified such dynamics in TransCo. Finally, given the difficulties of negotiating work–family programs in TransCo's mergers, it would be interesting to know more about successes and failures of integrating such policies in other transnational corporate alliances.

Finally, research should address the relative benefits and costs of organizational change for work–family policy. An optimistic finding of this study is that organizational change can create positive outcomes for work–family policies (alongside the negative ones). In fact, this happened in all three firms: In AmCo, managers demonstrated an unusual commitment to job security; in IndCo, managers offered new policies for transportation in TransCo, managers developed a wide array of work–family benefits for employees at the top of the firm and, at the very least, new employment opportunities for those at bottom. Thus, more investigation is needed to disentangle the processes by which change turns good versus bad, and to help determine what types of organizational changes are conducive to better work–family policies.

ACKNOWLEDGMENTS

Data collection was conducted with support from the National Science Foundation, the University of California at Berkeley Professional Studies Abroad in India Program, and a Stanford University McCoy Fellowship. Analysis was supported by the Center for International Business Education and Research, and the Vice Chancellor's Research Board at the University of Illinois at Urbana-Champaign. I am grateful to the participants of the study for their generous offerings of time and knowledge and to Steven Poelmans and two anonymous reviewers for their excellent comments. The opinions expressed herein are those of the author alone.

REFERENCES

Aguilera, R., & Dencker, J. (2004, forthcoming). "The role of human resource management in cross-border mergers and acquisitions." *International*

Journal of Human Resource Management. Urbana-Champaign: University of Illinois.

Aguilera, R. V., Dencker, J. C., & Escandell, X. (2004). "Disentangling Embeddedness: An Empirical Analysis of Global Acquisitions in the 1990s." In *03-0110 College of Business Working Papers.* Urbana, IL: University of Illinois, Urbana-Champaign.

Bailyn, L. (1993). *Breaking the mold: Women, men, and time in the new corporate world.* New York: The Free Press.

Bergmann, B. (1998). Watch out for 'family friendly' policies. *Dollars and Sense, 215,* 10–11.

Brannen, J., Lewis, S., Moss, P., Smithson, J., & McCarraher, L. (2001). "Workplace change and family life: Report on [two cases] for the Tedworth Foundation." Manchester, UK: Manchester Metropolitan University.

Chow, E. N., & Berheide, C. W. (1994). *Women, the family, and policy: A global perspective.* Albany, NY: State University of New York Press.

Cubbins, L. A. (1998). Employer-based health insurance in a changing economy. In D. Vannoy & P. J. Dubeck (Eds.), *Challenges for work and family in the twenty-first century* (pp. 183–199). New York: Aldine de Gruyter.

Deshpande, S., & Deshpande, L. K. (1992). New economic policy and female employment. *Economic and Political Weekly, 27,* 2248–2252.

Esping-Andersen, G. (1990). *Three worlds of welfare capitalism.* Princeton, NJ: Princeton University Press.

Ferber, M. A., & O'Farrell, B. (1991). *Work and family: Policies for a changing work force.* Washington, DC: National Academy Press.

Fligstein, N. (1990). *The transformation of corporate control.* Cambridge, MA: Harvard University Press.

Ghosh, J. (1994). Gender concerns in macro-economic policy. *Economic and Political Weekly, (April 30),* 2–4.

Glass, J. L., & Estes, S. B. (1997). The family responsive workplace. *Annual Review of Sociology, 23,* 289–313.

Gonyea, J. G., & Googins, B. K. (1996). The restructuring of work and family in the United States: A new challenge for American corporations. In S. Lewis & J. Lewis (Eds.), *The work–family challenge: Rethinking employment* (pp. 63–78). London: Sage.

Goodstein, J. D. (1994). Institutional pressures and strategic responsiveness: Employer involvement in work–family issues. *Academy of Management Journal, 37,* 350–382.

Gornick, J. C., Meyers, M. K., & Ross, K. E. (1998). "Public policies and the employment of mothers: A Cross-National Study." *Social Science Quarterly, 79,* 35–54.

Gothoskar, S. (1992). Struggles of women workers in the pharmaceutical industry in Bombay. In S. Gothoskar (Ed.), *Struggles of women at work* (pp. 132–143). New Delhi: Vikas Publishing House.

Haas, L., Hwang, P., & Russell, G. (Eds.). (2000). *Organizational change & gender equity: International perspectives on fathers and mothers at the workplace.* Thousand Oaks: Sage.

Hofstede, G. (1991). *Cultures and organizations: Software of the mind.* London: McGraw-Hill.

Hoogvelt, A. (1997). *Globalization and the postcolonial world.* Baltimore, MD: Johns Hopkins University Press.

International Labour Office. (2001). *World employment report 2001: Life at work in the information economy.* Geneva: International Labour Office.

Kalleberg, A. L., & Rosenfeld, R. A. (1995). Work in the family and in the labor market: A cross-national, reciprocal analysis. In G. L. Bowen and J. F. Pittman (Eds.), *The work and family interface: Toward a contextual effects perspective* (pp. 409–421). Minneapolis: National Council on Family Relations.

Kamerman, S. B. (1979). Work and family in industrialized societies. *Signs, 4,* 632–650.

Kapur, R., & Cossman, B. (1996). *Subversive sites: Feminist engagements with law in India.* New Delhi: Sage.

Kelly, E. (1999). Theorizing corporate family policies: How advocates built "the business case" for "family-friendly" programs. *Research in the Sociology of Work, 7,* 169–202.

Komarraju, M. (1997). The work–family interface in India. In S. Parasuraman, J. H. Greenhaus, (Eds.), *Integrating work and family: Challenges and choices for a changing world* (pp. 104–114). Westport, CT: Praeger.

Kumar, R. (1989). *India's export processing zones.* Delhi: Oxford University Press.

Lewis, S., & Lewis, J., (Eds.), 1996. *The work–family challenge: Rethinking employment.* London: Sage.

Ling, Y., & Powell, G. N. (2001). Work–family conflict in contemporary China: Beyond an American-based model. *International Journal of Cross-Cultural Management, 1,* 357–373.

Mahler, J. (2003). Commute to nowhere. *New York Times Magazine, (April 13),* 44–75.

McMichael, P. (2000). *Development and social change: A global perspective* (2nd ed.). Thousand Oaks, CA: Pine Forge Press.

Milliken, F. J., Martines, L. L., & Morgan, H. (1998). "Explaining organizational responsiveness to work–family issues." *Academy of Management Journal, 41,* 580–592.

Misra, J. (2003). Women as agents in welfare state development: A cross-national analysis of family allowance adoption. *Socio-Economic Review, 1,* 185–214.

O'Connor, J. S., Orloff, A. S., & Shaver, S. (1999). *States, markets, families.* Cambridge, UK: Cambridge University Press.

Osterman, P. (1995). Work–family programs and the employment relationship. *Administrative Science Quarterly, 40,* 681–700.

Poelmans, S. A. Y., Chinchilla, N., & Cardona, P. (2003). "The adoption of family-friendly HRM policies." *International Journal of Manpower, 24,* 128–147.

Poster, W. R. (2000). "Challenges for work–family policy in global corporations: Lessons from high-tech companies in India and the United States." In *Work and Family: Expanding the Horizons*. San Francisco, CA: UC Berkeley Center for Working Families, Business and Professional Women, Sloan Foundation.

Poster, W. R., & Prasad, S. (2005, forthcoming). "Work–family relations in transnational perspective: Case studies from India and the United States." *Social Problems 52*. Chicago, IL: American Sociological Association.

Ranadive, J. R. (1994). Gender implications of adjustment policy programme in India. *Economic and Political Weekly, (April 30)*, 12–18.

Schweiger, D. M., Ridley, R. R., Jr., & Marini, D. M. (1992). "Creating one from two: The merger between Harris Semiconductor and General Electric Solid State." In S. E. Jackson (Ed.), *Diversity in the workplace: Human resources initiatives* (pp. 167–202). New York: Guilford Press.

Sekaran, U. (1992). "Middle-class dual-earner families and their support systems in India." In S. Lewis, D. N. Izraeli, & H. Hootsmans, (Eds.), *Dual-earner families: International perspectives* (pp. 46–61), London: Sage Publications.

Smith, V. (1997). New forms of work organization. *Annual Review of Sociology, 23*, 315–39.

Sundaramurthy, N. (1994). NEP and trade union response. *Economic and Political Weekly, (June 18)*, 1551–1552.

Triandis, H. C. (1995). *Individualism and collectivism*. Boulder, CO: Westview Press.

Wallace, M. (1998). Downsizing the American dream: Work and family at century's end. In D. Vannoy and P. J. Dubeck (Eds.), *Challenges for work and family in the twenty-first century* (pp. 23–47). New York: Aldine de Gruyter.

Wexler, S. (1997). Work–family policy stratification: The examples of family support and family leave. *Qualitative Sociology, 20*, 311–323.

Wharton, A. S., Blair-Loy, M. (2002). The "overtime culture" in a global corporation: A cross-national study of finance professionals' interest in working part-time. *Work and Occupations, 29*, 32–63.

8

Workplace Work–Family Arrangements: A Study and Explanatory Framework of Differences Between Organizational Provisions in Different Welfare States

Laura den Dulk
Utrecht University

INTRODUCTION

This paper focuses on workplace work–family arrangements, i.e., measures supporting working parents developed by employers, such as flexible working hours, child-care support, and leave arrangements. A cross-national comparison is made between employers in the Netherlands, Italy, the United Kingdom, and Sweden. So far, most research on work–family arrangements in organizations has been done in Anglo-Saxon countries such as the United States, Australia, and the United Kingdom (e.g., den Dulk, 2001; OECD, 2001). These are countries in which working parents are encouraged to rely on their own resources for combining work and family life, and government intervention is minimal. Europe, however, is characterized by countries with different welfare state regimes, and the question can be raised how these different institutional contexts influence the adoption of work–family arrangements by employers.

A cross-national comparison, in fact, raises the question how employers' provisions are linked toward their national context. Lewis (1997) stated that there are basically two arguments concerning this relationship. The first argument says that the presence of public facilities makes it less likely that employers will create their own additional provisions. It is the absence of public policy that stimulates a tradition of corporate welfare. The alternative argument, however, is that public provision of work–family policies has the potential to create a climate in which employers are stimulated to supplement basic entitlements (Lewis, 1997, p. 98). Another possibility is that, instead of influencing each other, both public policy and organizational practices are affected in their own way by developments in society, such as the aging and feminization of the workforce, the growing number of dual-earner families, and changing norms and values related to work and family life.

Research so far shows that work–family arrangements are most common in public sector organizations and large organizations (e.g., Evans, 2001; OECD, 2001). Employer's surveys in Anglo-Saxon countries suggest that organizations mainly offer flexible work arrangements, such as flexible working hours and part-time work. Leave arrangements and child-care support are less common (OECD, 2001). Data from employee surveys suggest that employers in member states of the European Union, such as Germany, Austria, and South European countries, more frequently offer extra-statutory leave and child-care arrangements than do employers in the United States or Canada (OECD, 2001). However, data based on self-reported data from employees has to be interpreted with caution. Employees are not always aware whether their workplace is indeed offering additional facilities or are merely following statutory entitlements.

In this chapter, findings from a telephone survey among a sample of Dutch, Italian, British, and Swedish service employers with more than 100 employees are presented. However, first a theoretical framework is discussed, which tries to explain the adoption of work–family arrangements in organizations across different countries. The third section discusses the research design and the social policy context in the four countries in more detail. In the fourth section, the findings of the cross-national study are presented. In the final section, findings are discussed and concluding remarks are formulated.

THEORETICAL FRAMEWORK

To explain employers' involvement in the development of work–family arrangements across countries, insights of the institutional theory and rational-choice theory are used.

Institutional Theory

Research aimed at explaining the adoption of work–family arrangements by organizations often use a theoretical framework based on institutional theory (e.g., Goodstein, 1994; Ingram and Simons, 1995; Osterman, 1995). The institutional perspective posits that organizations will adopt innovations in order to increase their legitimacy. Institutional theorists argue that organizations either adopt new practices because these are seen as the proper way to organize or adopt new practices in response to coercion by powerful institutional forces that control critical resources (e.g., DiMaggio & Powell, 1983; Tolbert & Zucker, 1996). The existing studies all start with the basic assumption that there is a growing institutional pressure on employers to develop work–family arrangements because of changes in the workforce, i.e., more working women, more dual-earner families, more public attention, and, in varying degrees in different welfare states, more state regulations and legal obligations. Within the institutional perspective, the influence of the legal and normative environment on organizational structures and practices is emphasized (DiMaggio & Powell, 1983; Scott, 1995). Employers not only have to meet economic considerations, but also need to respond to regulations, norms, laws, and social expectations (Goodstein, 1994). Early institutional theorists have been criticized for considering organizations as passive actors that merely conform to institutional pressures. Moreover, research has shown that organizations differ in the way and extent they respond to the increasing need for supportive work–family arrangements. To explain differences in employers' behavior, Oliver (1991) developed a typology of organizations' responses to institutional pressures. Employers may fully conform to institutional pressures, make symbolic gestures, or resist or even manipulate the institutional environment. Institutional factors and organizational interests both determine which strategy is chosen.

Two studies done in the United States on the development of work–family arrangements in organizations applied the typology of Oliver (1991). Both Goodstein (1994) and Ingram and Simons (1995) assumed that some employers are more sensitive to institutional pressure than other employers. They expected, for instance, that large organizations, because of their visibility in society, are more likely to conform to institutional pressure than are small organizations. Moreover, they assumed that when responsiveness to institutional pressures is perceived as having a positive effect on technical outcomes, such as absenteeism and turnover rates, organizations are even more likely to conform. A compromise and an avoidance strategy are both likely in a situation of strong institutional pressures and perceived negative effects on technical outcomes. Whether the avoidance or compromise strategy is chosen depends primarily on the dependence of the organization on critical institutional actors. For instance, for an organization that is highly dependent on government orders or on its public image, an avoidance strategy can be risky. Finally, the manipulation strategy is more likely, according to Goodstein (1994), when there are weak institutional pressures and a positive view on the effects or technical outcomes.

In the studies by Goodstein (1994) and Ingram and Simons (1995), the strength of institutional pressures is connected with organizational characteristics, such as the size of the organization, proportion of women employees and women managers, and whether an organization is part of the public or private sector. Empirically, these factors have been quite successful in predicting the degree of institutional compliance, but the results on the role of technical considerations were more mixed. Goodstein (1994) found that perceived benefits from child care increases responsiveness, whereas Ingram and Simons could not confirm this finding.[1] In both studies, technical considerations were based on the perception of respondents rather than direct measurements of the costs and benefits of work–family arrangements. Because the institutional context also affects the perception of organizational actors, it is difficult to distinguish the separate role of organizational interest and institutional views. In addition, it remains unclear how technical and institutional pressures are weighed against each other.

The theoretical framework of Tolbert and Zucker (1996) provides some additional insights on this issue. They argue that in the first

---

[1]The fact that technical determinants were measured differently in the two studies could play a role. Ingram and Simons (1995) measured benefits from work–family arrangements with a question about the degree to which an organization had problems when employees with young children missed work because child-care services were not available. Goodstein (1994) asked about the perceived effects of child-care services on recruitment, retention, absenteeism, employee morale, etc. and whether the costs and liability were considered to be an obstacle.

instance, organizations act on the basis of their own interests; later, "when practices become more widespread the more likely are organizations to view it as an optimal choice, and the less influential will be individuals' independent judgments of the value of the choice" (Tolbert & Zucker, 1996, p. 181). The level of institutionalization and thereby the power to determine organizational behavior varies across countries. As a result, rationality may be more or less bounded in the different stages of institutionalization. In the preinstitutionalization stage, the creation of work–family arrangements, such as leaves and child-care facilities, is largely an independent activity. Work–family arrangements are adopted as a solution to a particular organizational problem. Objectification may result in more widespread adoption and less critical evaluation by individual organizations. However, Tolbert and Zucker (1996) devote less attention to the perspective that organizations can influence the environment and try to change it according to their needs. Scott (1995) argues that organizations not only make individual choices, but also can respond collectively to institutional pressure. Moreover, responses made by groups of employers have the potential to shape the nature of environmental demands.

Rational Choice Approach

The rational choice perspective provides an interesting framework to explain why organizations make various decisions about the adoption of work–family arrangements. In fact, whereas the decision-making mechanism remains theoretically implicit in the institutional approach, the choice of actors is central to the rational choice approach. The rational choice approach assumes that actors generally strive for the maximum realization of their goals given the constraints they face (e.g., Coleman, 1990). Within this perspective, employers are considered as active actors who make choices whether or not to adopt work–family arrangements. Generally, actors will choose the alternative or combination of alternatives with the highest net benefit. Resources and constraints, i.e., the specific circumstances of the actors, influence the costs and benefits of available options. In the classic economy, time and money are seen as (the only relevant) resources and constraints in relation to decisions people make. In sociological analysis, the notion of relevant resources and constraints is extended by institutional conditions such as laws, regulations, norms, and expectations (e.g., van der Lippe, 1993).

In choosing their responses or behavior, employers are not just surrounded by laws, norms and social expectations, but also by labor market conditions, economic perspectives, and the availability of personnel. Within this context, employers may choose to adopt work–family arrangements in order to attract and retain valuable or scarce personnel. In other words, employers will adopt arrangements if the benefits exceed the implementation costs. This does not mean that institutional pressure from legislators or other important institutional agencies are not important; on the contrary, institutional conditions, such as the level and nature of government involvement influence decisions made by employers. However, employers may respond differently to these institutional pressures because they face different organizational circumstances, which they take into account when considering the costs and benefits of available options.

Integration of Theoretical Perspectives

By integrating the institutional and rational choice approach, it becomes possible to explain why organizations respond differently to institutional pressures and why some organizations even initiate the development of work–family arrangements when institutional pressures are low. Both perspectives are considered as complementary, and when integrated into a theoretical framework, they offer a more complete explanation of variation in employers' response. In our framework, the choice to introduce a certain type of work–family arrangement depends on the costs and benefits of the arrangements for the organization, which in their turn are related to the organizational and institutional context. By specifying relevant conditions, the variation in employers' responses is explained.

Focusing on the employer as a general actor, who is, by assumption, acting intentionally, it is important to identify the possible goals employers aim to realize. The maximum realization of profit is considered the ultimate goal of employers. However, modern employers need to strive for other goals as well, for instance, reputation or status in society, harmonious relations with their employees, and a secure market position. How do work–family arrangements contribute to the profit or status of an organization? Despite the fact that work–family arrangements do involve costs, they may nevertheless contribute to the profit or budget of the organization by reducing absenteeism and turnover rates. For example, work–family arrangements make it easier for women to combine paid work with caring tasks. Hence, by offering, for instance, a child-care arrangement when public provision is low more women may return from maternity leave (Glass & Fujimoto, 1995). Secondly, in an environment where support for working parents is considered important, the provision of work–family arrangements can contribute to the status and societal reputation of an organization. A good reputation attracts not only customers, but also sufficient supply of labor. Thirdly, employers try to avoid conflict within the organization. If employees or trade unions make a strong request for the implementation of certain work–family arrangements, the employer may conform in order to reduce the risk of a conflict and to maintain harmonious relations. Finally, employers strive toward a secure market position. The position of a private company is related to its market-share or productivity. For public organizations, a secure position is related to its (political) legitimacy. If the introduction of work–family arrangements increases the productivity and legitimacy of the organization, the provision of these arrangements contributes to a secure position. However, if an organization is in an insecure position, the employer is less likely to introduce and implement work–family arrangements because of the costs involved.

Organizational Characteristics and Institutional Context

Research shows that the size of an organization is positively related to the presence of work–family arrangements (e.g., Evans, 2001; Forth, Lissenburgh, Callender, & Millward, 1997; Ingram & Simons, 1995; Osterman, 1995). Visibility, economics of scale, and the presence of a specialized HR department can explain this finding. Because of their visibility, large organizations are more sensitive to institutional pressure to develop facilities than smaller ones. Resistance could result in public disapproval, whereas responsiveness could benefit the image and social status of the employer. In addition, there are economies of scale for large organizations in benefit provisions (Osterman, 1995). Moreover, large organizations often have specialized human resource staff, which is more likely to be aware of increasing demands for work–family arrangements and will have more expertise to react to these developments (Morgan & Milliken, 1992). Thus for smaller organizations work–family arrangements are more costly to adopt.

> H1   The greater the size of an organization, the more likely that employers will adopt work–family arrangements

The costs and benefits of work–family arrangements are influenced by the fact that an employer is a public or a private sector organization. For instance, public organizations are more likely to be evaluated according to government standards and norms, whereas for private companies, profit-related arguments are more important. In particular when government policy stimulates organizations to support working parents, the costs of not responding to public pressure to develop work–family arrangements are higher for public organizations than for private ones.

> H2   Public sector organizations are more likely to adopt work–family arrangements than are private sector organizations

The characteristics of the workforce are another important feature, which influences the balance of costs and benefits of work–family arrangements. The number of female employees is important in this respect. Because women are more likely to be responsible for caring tasks than are men, the effects of work–family arrangements on productivity, absenteeism, and turnover can be significant in organizations with a large proportion of women in the workforce. However, a large proportion of female employees can also result in a strong request for facilities such as child care. A high demand for facilities increases the costs and may be a reason to decide against the introduction of work–family arrangements. An alternative choice open to employers is to employ women with caring responsibilities in occupations and positions in which productivity losses and turnover costs are low (Glass & Fujimoto, 1995), thereby avoiding the necessity of work–family arrangements. Hence, if the proportion of women employees is very large, the net benefits of work–family arrangements are lower for organizations because of the relatively high costs involved related to (potential) high utilization of facilities. Both the proportion and the position of female employees are relevant. Generally, retention of personnel becomes more important in terms of costs and benefits, when an employer invests more in its personnel. For instance, loss of women in managerial positions means a loss of human capital and is costly. Besides the organizational benefits of keeping valuable personnel, female managers can serve as "agents of change." Female managers are in a position to stimulate the development of work–family arrangements in the organization (e.g., Ingram & Simons, 1995).

> H3   The greater the proportion of female employees within an organization, the more likely that employers will adopt work–family arrangements.
> H4   The greater the proportion of female managers within an organization, the more likely that employers will adopt work–family arrangements.

Eligibility requirements to use work–family policies frequently include a regular contract. As a result, people with affixed-term contracts are often not entitled to facilities provided by the employer. Moreover, flexible workers often work in jobs with low replacement cost. Therefore, a large proportion of employees with a fixed-term contract will decrease the likelihood of employer's involvement in work–family arrangements, because the net benefits will be lower.

> H5   The greater the proportion of employees with a fixed-term contracts, the less likely that employers will adopt work–family arrangements.

The economic position of an organization or company is also linked to the development of facilities. A good or stable economic position creates room for risk taking and investments. There are also more resources to adopt new practices, although this is less the case when a company has an unstable or bad economic position. Unfortunally, this study does not contain sufficient data to include this variable in the analysis.

Institutional Context.   The effect of organizational conditions is also influenced by the institutional context in which an organization operates. In countries with a high level of public child-care services, it is not necessary for employers to duplicate this provision. On the other hand, child care is more likely to become an employer's issue in countries where statutory provisions are low (Harker, 1996).

In general, government policy can influence employers' provisions in various ways. Legislation and government regulations intervene directly in organizational practices; i.e., organizations are obliged to implement statutory provisions. However, it can also be argued that compulsory policies have a further indirect effect: Legislation helps to create a normative climate, which gives rise to new social expectations regarding organizational practices. "When a new law provides the public with new expectations or new bases for criticizing organizations, or when the law enjoys considerable societal support conditions, apparent noncompliance is likely to endanger loss of public approval" (Edelman, 1990, p. 1406). The introduction of more and better public provisions has the potential to create a public awareness of the problem of balancing work and family life. Thus, besides legal sanctions, legislation can create normative pressure on organizations to adopt certain facilities (Edelman, 1990). Rostgaard (1999) refers to this as a "spill over effect" between public provisions and policies at the organizational level. "Instead of a zero-sum game, it may therefore be held that occupational welfare is more complementary than substitutional here, furthering the notion of a more pluralistic welfare mix where statutory and occupational benefits complement each other" (Rostgaard, 1999, pp. 53–54).

Policies to stimulate and support employer's provisions, such as subsidies and recommendations, are another way to influence the behavior of employers, i.e., by reducing the costs involved. Government involvement can contribute to the institutionalization of work–family arrangement in a country. When public provisions are absent, it is likely that social expectations regarding the involvement of employers are less salient. In this context, the introduction of facilities depends mainly on organizational characteristics, such as the proportion of female employees in the workforce. Besides the level of public provisions, labor market conditions and the economic climate in a country are also of importance. In a situation of economic growth and competition for trained and skilled staff, work–family arrangements can be used to attract personnel. This is less needed when it is easy to get new employees.

To summarize, both a positive and a negative relationship between the degree of public provisions in a country and the development of work–family arrangements in organizations can be expected. First, it can be hypothesized that the net benefits of work–family arrangements increase with the presence of public provisions. Legislation helps to create a normative climate that gives rise to new social expectations regarding organizational practices. To avoid public disapproval and improve the image of the organization or to maintain a good relationship with employees, employers may decide to comply with institutional pressure. In addition, government policy may reduce the costs of work–family arrangements by offering, for instance, subsidies or tax deduction for part of the cost involved. Based on this hypothesis, a positive relation between government provisions and employer's provisions is expected. Although, employers may offer additional provisions, it does not make sense for employers to offer facilities for which the government takes full responsibility. As a result, the range of work–family arrangements offered by employers may be more limited than in a country with limited public provisions.

In the absence of statutory provisions, there is, in fact, more scope for employers to introduce work–family arrangements, especially when there is a growing need among employees for supportive measures. In the (almost) absence of legislation, the introduction of arrangements offers a competitive advantage over other employers. Work–family arrangements can serve as a recruitment tool or as a means to reduce turnover of personnel. If public provisions are (virtually) absent, however, social expectations regarding employers' involvement are likely to be less strong, and introduction of work–family arrangements will depend mainly on organizational circumstances, such as a shortage of personnel or large proportion of female staff.

Legislation may contribute to the institutionalization of work–family arrangements. On the basis of the theoretical framework of Tolbert and Zucker (1996), it can be expected that in a situation where work–family arrangements are relatively new and not yet institutionalized, employers are more likely to consider the costs and benefits of arrangements and choose arrangements that best fit the needs of the organization at a particular time. Hence, employers will show variation in extent and types of work–family arrangements they realize. When work–family arrangements are more or less taken for granted, employers are less likely to evaluate arrangements on the specific needs of the organization; instead they will assume that it is beneficial for the organization to implement arrangements.

H6   Social policy hypothesis:
a. Countries with high statutory provisions are not less likely to have a high share of employers that have adopted work–family arrangements than employers in countries with low statutory provisions.
b. In countries with low statutory provisions, employers will show larger differences between employers in number and types of work–family arrangements adopted than employers in countries with high statutory provisions.

RESEARCH DESIGN AND THE CHOICE OF COUNTRIES

Cross-national research on employer's provisions is limited, despite the fact that the institutional context is considered to be a relevant factor for the introduction of work–family arrangements in organizations. To examine the implications of the institutional context for the implementation of work–family arrangements in organizations, a cross-national comparison is needed. The choice of countries in this study is based on Esping-Andersen's (1990, 1999) typology of welfare state regimes. The Netherlands, Italy, the United Kingdom, and Sweden represent different welfare state regimes in which the state, the market, and the family shape different backgrounds in which the combination of work and family life is addressed (see Table 8.1).

Choice of Countries

Sweden was included in the research as an example of a social–democratic welfare state regime in which both the labor market participation of women and men is advocated. The Swedish government takes responsibility for a broad range of social issues including public work–family arrangements such as public day care and

TABLE 8.1
Classification of Countries in Different Welfare State Regimes

Social-Democratic Regime	Conservative Regime	Liberal Regime
Norway	Austria	The United States
Denmark	Belgium	Canada
Finland	France	Australia
	Germany	Ireland
	Spain	New Zealand
	Japan	
Sweden	Italy	The United Kingdom
	The Netherlands	

Source: Esping-Andersen, 1999.

advanced statutory leaves. Compared to the other three countries, there is a longer tradition of support for dual-earner families in Sweden. Already in the 1960s, Sweden developed supportive policies for working parents. As a result, the fact that a majority of people combine work with caring responsibilities is taken for granted in the Swedish context. Other countries that resemble the social democratic welfare state regime are Norway, Denmark and Finland.

Within Europe, the United Kingdom most closely represents the liberal welfare state. In a liberal welfare state regime, government involvement and regulation for employers are limited and the development of work–family arrangements is left to market forces. Men and women are treated as equal despite differences in caring responsibilities (Plantenga & van Doorne-Huiskes, 1993). The adoption of work–family arrangements is framed as a business case, in which costs and benefits for the organization are central. Because of the near absence of public provisions, there is a lot of scope for employers to develop work–family arrangements.

The Netherlands and Italy were chosen as different examples of the conservative/corporatistic welfare state regime. In both countries, the role of the family is more important than in the social–democratic regime, and externalization of care is limited. Especially, in Italy, the traditional family is expected to take care of the welfare of relatives. Within Europe, the division of paid and unpaid work between men and women is most traditional in Italy, and informal help regarding the care for young children is very important (SCP, 2000). Labor market participation of Italian women is low compared to other EU countries (Trifiletti, 1999). Another reason for including Italy in this study is that Italy is considered to be a classic example of the corporatistic welfare state regime (Esping-Andersen, 1990, 1999), whereas the Netherlands is a more ambiguous case.

The Dutch welfare state is characterized by a mix of social–democratic and corporatistic features (Wildeboer Schut, Vrooman, & de Beer, 2000). However, regarding the division of paid and unpaid labor between women and men, the Netherlands can be considered an example of the corporatistic welfare state regime. For a long time, Dutch government policy was based on the traditional division of paid and unpaid labor between men and women. Furthermore, even though the Dutch government improved public provisions for working parents during the 1990s, the level of facilities and the labor market participation of women still lag behind the level found in social–democratic countries such as Denmark and Sweden (SCP, 2000). In the Netherlands, the social norm that a child should be cared for by the parents (i.e., the mother) themselves is still prevalent. The ideal model for a family with children is two parents working part-time; however, in practice it is the woman who uses part-time work as a strategy to combine work and family life, whereas the man remains full-time employed when he becomes a father (SCP, 2000). In Sweden, full employment of both partners is stimulated. Only in the first year of a child's life is full-time care by parents facilitated, after that parents are supposed to return to paid employment. Hence, in a corporatistic welfare state regime, statutory provisions that support the combination of work and caring responsibilities are minimal compared to those in the social–democratic welfare state; i.e., there is a larger role for the family but less so for the market as is the case in the liberal regime. Table 8.2 gives a brief overview of the legislation on child care and leave arrangements in the Netherlands, Italy, the United Kingdom, and Sweden. Public policies supporting working parents were implemented at a much earlier date and at a more substantial level in Sweden than in the other three countries.

As is shown in Table 8.2, the statutory leaves in Sweden are longer, and loss of income is compensated at a higher level than in the other three countries. In addition, the statutory leave system is complemented by the universal availability of public child-care services.

In the Dutch context, the state is not viewed as the sole provider of support for working parents. Instead, employers' organizations, trade unions, and individual organizations are viewed as active participants who should contribute to the development of work–family arrangements. The Parental Leave Act, for example, is considered as a minimum, which can be supplemented by collective agreements or policies of individual firms. The Dutch government also actively encourages employers to participate in the provision of child care. In the Netherlands, child care is organized as a public–private partnership

TABLE 8.2

Statutory Leave Arrangements and Public Child Care in the Netherlands, Italy, the United Kingdom, and Sweden.

	The Netherlands	Italy	United Kingdom	Sweden
Maternity leave	16 weeks, fully paid leave	5 months, paid at 80% of earnings	52 weeks, 6 weeks fully paid, 20 at a flat rate[a]	50 days pregnancy allowance paid at 80% of earnings; leave taken after childbirth is taken out the parental leave period.
Paternity leave	Two days, paid leave[b]	None	Two weeks[b]	10 days, paid at 80% of earnings
Parental leave	6 months, part-time leave per parent, unpaid	10 months, paid at 30% of earnings for a child under 3. Parents get one month extra when the father takes at least 3 months leave[c]	3 months unpaid leave per parent[b]	16 months per child: 13 months paid at 80% of earnings; 3 months at a flat-rate payment
Short-term care leave	10 days emergency leave, partly paid[b]	Unpaid leave until the child is 3 years old	None	60 days a year per parent when a child or the normal caregiver is ill.
Long-term care leave	None	None	None	60 days cash benefits to care for closely related persons, paid at 80% of earnings
Child care	Stimulation policy, limited number of public child-care places	Limited public childcare for children under 3; pre-primary school for children aged 3–6	Public childcare is very limited and targeted at children in need	All working and studying parents have the right to a place in public childcare for a child between 1–12 years
Reduction of working hours	Right to reduce or extend working hours unless it conflicts with business needs[b]	None	None	All working parents with a child under 8 years of age have the right to shorten their working week by 25% or 12.5% (i.e., to work a six- or seven-hour work day).

[a]At the time of research, statutory maternity leave in the United Kingdom was 14 weeks for all working women and women were entitled to 40 weeks leave if they were in employment with the same employer longer than 2 years.

[b]Not yet available at the time of the research (1998).

[c]At the time of the research, statutory parental leave in Italy was 6 months, paid at 30% of earnings.

between government and employers. In 1989, employers contracted 13% of child-care places. In 1998, this was already 44% (Niphuis-Nell, 1997).

In the Italian context, work–family issues have only recently appeared on the public and political agenda, and the social partners have not yet given much attention to the combination of work and family life (Bergamaschi, 1999; Del Boca, 1998). However, this might change in the near future. An increasing focus on work–family issues in the political debate may have spillover effects on the negotiations between employers and trade unions. At the time of the research, Italy was still characterized by low state involvement and relatively low expectations of employers' involvement in work–family arrangements. The family is considered to be the main provider of care services. It is the state's duty to support rather than substitute the family's caring burden (Trifiletti, 1999). In the United Kingdom, care for children is likewise seen as a private matter. However, the reasons for minimal state provisions are different from those in a conservative welfare state regime. Both in Italy and the Netherlands, the role of the family is emphasized, and less so the role of the market as a provider of care services (Esping-Andersen, 1999).

By comparing countries that differ in their so-called welfare mix, the question is raised how employer provisions are related to their national context. The social policy hypothesis formulated in the previous section specified for the four countries included in this study are as follows:

a. Swedish employers are not less likely to be involved in work–family arrangements than British, Italian or Dutch employers.
b. British employers will show largest differences between employers in number and types of work–family arrangements adopted while Swedish employers will show the smallest differences between employers in number and types of work–family arrangements adopted.

Research Design

This chapter reports on a study conducted among medium- and large-sized service sector organizations in the four different countries. Although this is a relatively small-scale study, the use of identical surveys provides comparative data on employers' provisions of work–family arrangements in the four countries. National studies are difficult to compare because of different samples, unit of analysis, and measurement.

In the period 1998–1999, a telephone survey was conducted among service sector employers with 100 or more employees. The sample includes government and health care organizations, retail companies, financial and business services, hotels and restaurants, and transport and communications companies. In total, 375 organizations participated in the research: 113 Dutch organizations (a response rate of 38%), 95 Italian (a response rate of 46%), 67 British (a response rate of 18%), and 100 Swedish organizations (a response rate of 39%[2]). Directors of personnel were approached for an interview and asked about the availability of work–family arrangements and relevant organizational characteristics.

To select the samples in the different countries, national databases were used. In the Netherlands and Italy, the sample of private sector companies was drawn from the register of the Chamber of Commerce. The sample of government and health care organization was selected at random from publications that list these kinds of organizations (the Staatsalmanak, 1997 and Pyttersen's Nederlandse Almanak, 1998; Guida Monaci, 1998). In Italy, the research was restricted to the northern and central regions of Italy.[3] In the United Kingdom, there was no register available that includes all British private and public sector organizations. Therefore, a private database of large private and public sector organizations was used for the sample of British employers. In Sweden, Statistics Sweden (SCB) selected a sample of both public and private sector organizations.

When comparing the samples of the four countries regarding size and the profit/nonprofit distinction, significant differences become visible. However, multiple comparison (post-hoc tests, Bonferroni, $p < .05$) shows that these differences are solely caused by the British sample. The British sample is less comparable to those in the other three countries: Large organizations and public sector organizations are overrepresented compared to the Dutch, Italian, and Swedish samples (see Table 8.3). When comparing among countries, this

---

[2] In total, 74 Swedish organizations refused to participate. Eighty-four organizations were never reached; they did receive a letter and were contacted for an interview, but the interviewer never spoke to the respondent. In the end, these respondents were not contacted again because of sufficient response. If these latter organizations would not be calculated as nonresponse, the response rate would be 58%.

[3] The case of Italy shows that differences within countries can be larger than those among countries. Taking into account the limited size of the sample in each country, it was decided to exclude southern regions of Italy. The central focus of the research is on the relation between government policy and organizational policies. Therefore, those regions most similar to the other three countries, i.e., north and central Italy, were included.

TABLE 8.3
Number and Percentage of Employers According to Sector and Company Size, in
the Dutch, Italian, British and Swedish Sample

	NL	IT	UK	SW
Profit	68 (60%)	45 (47%)	28 (42%)	51 (51%)
Nonprofit[a]	45 (40%)	50 (53%)	39 (58%)	49 (49%)
Industry				
Public adm./health care	44 (39%)	39 (41%)	38 (57%)	42 (42%)
Financial/business services	24 (21%)	26 (27%)	6 (9%)	27 (27%)
Trade, transport & comm.				
hotels & restaurants	35 (31%)	20 (21%)	17 (25%)	16 (16%)
Otherwise	10 (9%)	10 (11%)	6 (9%)	15 (15%)
Number of Employees				
100–200[b]	37 (33%)	20 (21%)	8 (12%)	37 (37%)
200–500	28 (25%)	29 (31%)	13 (19%)	21 (21%)
500 or more	48 (43%)	46 (48%)	44 (66%)	42 (42%)
Total	113 (100%)	95 (100%)	67 (100%)	100 (100%)

[a]Including semi-profit organizations (charities or cooperatives).
[b]There are a few organizations that, at the time of research, had less than a hundred
employees.

has to be taken into account. Differences found among the British
organizations and the Dutch, Italian, and Swedish organizations
might be caused by sample differences instead of different institutional contexts.

When comparing our samples with national statistics, it becomes
clear that large organizations are overrepresented in this study. This
is true for all countries. In addition, financial and business services
companies are underrepresented in the British sample.[4] In Sweden,
not only large organizations are overrepresented, but also government
and health care organizations (Statistics Sweden, 1998, p. 281).

Because this research is restricted to medium-sized and large-sized
organizations in the service sector, outcomes cannot automatically be
generalized to all organizations and sectors of industries in the four
countries. On the basis of other research (e.g., Forth et al., 1997;
SZW, 1997; Bernasco, 1998), it is likely to assume that among small

[4]In our British sample only 15% of private sector companies are financial or business services, whereas national statistics show that 43% of service sector companies
with 100 or more employees are financial or business services enterprises (National
Statistics, 2000).

employers and manufacturing companies the adoption of work–family arrangements will be less widespread.

Measurement of Work–Family Arrangements

When measuring employer's involvement in work–family arrangements in four different countries, one must take into account the fact that levels and nature of public provisions vary across the countries. Because of this, a distinction was made between work–family arrangements that supplement or those that substitute statutory provisions. In case of statutory provisions being available, personnel directors were asked whether their organization supplemented these. In case of absence of statutory provisions, respondents were asked whether their organization had any provisions itself. For instance, in the United Kingdom, employers were asked whether their organization had introduced parental leave. In the United Kingdom, no parental leave legislation existed at the time of the research, in contrast to the other three countries, where statutory parental leave was available. Hence, Swedish, Dutch, and Italian employers were asked whether their organization *supplemented* statutory parental leave regulations.

In the survey, the director of personnel was asked whether the following work–family arrangements were present in his/her organization (arrangements that either supplement or substitute legislation): child-care arrangements, the possibility to work part-time, flexible start and finishing times, a compressed working week, telework, working occasionally a day from home, maternity leave, parental leave, paternity leave, short-term emergency leave for family reasons, long-term leave to care for ill relatives, and career breaks. Both formal policies and informal arrangements were taken into account.

Measurement of Organizational Characteristics

The distinction between public and private sector organizations is based on the profit/nonprofit distinction. Size is measured as the natural logarithm of the total number of employees on the payroll. The proportion of women employees is measured as the percentage of women employees present in the organization; the percentage of women managers in the highest three levels in the organization is taken as an indication of the proportion of women managers. Finally, the percentage of employees with a fixed-term contract is taken into account.

RESULTS

What kind of work–family arrangements have been implemented within organizations in the four countries under study? The findings in Table 8.4 show that a majority of Dutch organizations have adopted child-care arrangements (70%), compared to a minority of Italian (11%) and British organizations (27%). Only two of the hundred Swedish organizations offer child-care provisions. One of the two Swedish companies with child-care arrangements has a contract with a local child-care facility (close to the workplace); the other supports a parents' cooperative and family service. Dutch employers most often hire child-care places for their employees or offer financial support. Workplace nurseries, on the other hand, are more common among British employers, although there are also other child-care arrangements available, such as holiday play schemes, contracted places, financial support, and information and referral services that employees can use to find suitable child-care services.

Whereas the Dutch employers focus on child care, Swedish employers often adopt flexible work arrangements. Almost all Swedish employers offer flexible hours (92%), as do the majority of Italian, Dutch and British employers. Other flexible work arrangements,

TABLE 8.4
Work–Family Arrangements in Organizations, Percentage of Employers

W/F Arrangement	NL $N = 113$	IT $N = 95$	UK $N = 67$	SW $N = 100$	χ^2
Child care	70	11	27	2	142,962**
Maternity leave	13	51	70	5	113,804**
Parental leave	42	32	13	17	24,247**
Paternity leave	11	58	79	4	154,519**
Short-term leave	63	31	93	1	162,762**
Long-term leave	50	94	60	11	134,786**
Career break	44	68	51	72	23,195**
Part-time work	96	94	100	67[a]	—
Flexitime	70	64	64	92	25,338**
Telework	20	5	25	39	33.068**
Compressed work week	30	5	40	47	43,969**
Working from home occasionally	10	0	12	16	15,591*

$*p < .01. **p < .001.$
[a]67% of Swedish employers supplement the right of parents with young children to reduce their working hours.

i.e., the possibility to telework, a compressed work week, and working occasionally from home, are also most common among Swedish employers. In contrast, very few Italian employers offer such schemes. Dutch and British employers more closely resemble Swedish employers, being actively involved in the development of flexible work arrangements.

In addition, the majority of Swedish employers (67%) supplement the right of working parents with young children to work shorter hours; they do so either by offering this arrangement to parents with children over 8 years old or by offering the possibility to reduce the number of hours worked with more than 25%, or by allowing a combination of both arrangements. Furthermore, 93% of the Swedish employers also offer the possibility of part-time work to employees without young children. In general, the option of part-time work exists in almost all organizations in all four countries, although the number of people who actually work part-time varies greatly. Again, in Italian organizations, the number of part-timers is much lower than in the other three countries, which reflects the fact that working part-time is less common in Italy (den Dulk, 2001).

Both Italian and British employers are most active in the field of leave arrangements. Swedish employers do not often supplement the statutory leave system, but if they do, they usually offer a policy on career breaks. Dutch employers also pay relatively little attention to leave arrangements; a relatively large proportion of Dutch employers does not offer any form of leave arrangement (20%). In contrast, all Italian and almost all British organizations have introduced at least one form of leave arrangements, and in many cases they offer more than that. The British employers participating in this study focus on short-term leave, such as paternity leave for fathers and short-term emergency leave for family reasons, and enhanced maternity leave. Italian employers more frequently offer long-term leave to care for seriously ill relatives.

To summarize, there is extensive variation among the employers in the four countries regarding the type of work–family arrangements adopted. In general, Swedish service employers with a hundred or more employees offer additional provisions in the form of flexible work arrangements. Dutch employers pay more attention to child care, but relatively little to the development of leave arrangements. In contrast, British and Italian employers mainly focus on leave arrangements.

When looking at the total number of work–family arrangements in organizations (excluding part-time work), we see that, on average, British employers have adopted the largest number of work–family arrangements. British employers provide on average a total number of six work–family arrangements, whereas Swedish employers have adopted on average three, and Dutch and Italian employers four arrangements. British employers not only provide more work–family arrangements, but also the differences among organizations are larger in the United Kingdom than in the other three countries, especially where profit-sector organizations are concerned (the standard deviation is 2.8 for the total British sample). For instance, 25% of the British organizations implemented more than seven arrangements; on the other hand, 27% have three or less work–family arrangements. In the Swedish sample, smaller differences are found, and there are relatively few extreme cases (standard deviation is 1.5). With respect to the average total number of work–family arrangements, the Dutch and Italian sample appears to be relatively similar, but larger differences are found among Dutch employers (standard deviation is 2.4 compared to 1.9 in the Italian sample). There are a few organizations that have adopted none of the work–family arrangements: five Dutch private sector companies, three Swedish, and two British companies do not provide any arrangements at all.[5] A British governmental organization has adopted the maximum number of arrangements: it provides 13 different types of provisions.

Linear regression can show the effects of different organizational characteristics while controlling for other variables. Five independent variables are included: the profit/nonprofit distinction, size of the organization, percentage of women employees, percentage of women managers, and proportion of employees with a fixed-term contract.

Table 8.5 shows that the fit of the regression model for the total number of work–family arrangements adopted by organizations varies among countries. For Sweden, none of the organizational characteristics have a significant effect.[6] The highest explained variance is found in the British sample: 64%. For the Dutch and Italian sample the amount of explained variance is 44 and 38%, respectively. In the United Kingdom and the Netherlands, the profit/nonprofit distinction is the most important variable. In Italy, the size of the organization seems to be the most important factor, when other variables are controlled.

---

[5]The companies without work–family arrangements do not show a certain profile with respect to size or sector, except for the fact that they are all private sector companies.

[6]The distinction profit/nonprofit is the most relevant variable ($t = -1.4$; $p = .17$).

TABLE 8.5
Linear Regression of the Total Number of Work–Family Arrangements in
The Netherlands, Italy, United Kingdom, Sweden

	NL	IT	UK	SW
	Beta	Beta	Beta	Beta
Profit/nonprofit (profit = 1)	−.56***	−.30***	−.76***	−.21
Size	.28***	.44***	.22*	.18
% women	.06	.01	.03	.08
% women managers	.03	.05	−.20	−.07
% fixed-term	−.02	.10	.04	−.16
Adjusted R^2	.44	.38	.64	.06
N	91	92	47	86

*$p < .1$.   **$p < .05$.   ***$p < .01$.

DISCUSSION

Looking back on the findings, we have seen that in three of the four countries public sector organizations and large organizations tend to have more work–family arrangements than do private sector organizations and smaller organizations. This finding confirms the hypothesis that public sector organizations and large organizations are more likely to adopt work–family arrangements than are companies and smaller organizations. The results do not confirm the hypothesis that the greater the proportion of female employees and female managers the more likely employers will adopt work–family arrangements. The same applies to the hypotheses on the proportion of employees with a fixed-term contract. No significant effect is found regarding this variable in the regression analysis.

In Sweden, differences between organizations are small, and organizational characteristics have no explanatory power. In the other three countries, differences among employers are larger regarding the number and types of work–family arrangements adopted. This finding confirms the hypotheses that in countries with low statutory provisions, employers show smaller differences in number and types of work–family arrangements adopted than employers in countries with high statutory provisions. The largest variance is found among British employers, followed by Dutch employers and Italian employers. The results also indicate that organizational characteristics have the most predictive power in the British sample. British employers in this study have adopted, in fact, the largest number of work–family arrangements and Swedish employers the smallest number. These findings contradict our hypotheses that countries with high statutory provisions are not less likely to have a high share of employers that have adopted work–family arrangements than countries with low statutory provisions. Hence, our findings suggest that it is the (near) absence of public provisions that lead to larger employers' involvement rather than the presence of advanced public provisions. However, it must be taken into account that the large average number of work–family arrangements in the British organizations is related to the fact that large and public sector organizations are overrepresented in the British sample compared to the other three countries. These sample differences, and the low response rates in this country, could also explain the high average number of work–family arrangements.

Theoretical and Practical Implications

Dutch employers were the most active regarding childcare provisions. This finding is confirmed by other research (e.g., Evans, 2001; OECD, 2001; Peters et al., 2000). The large involvement in child care is related to the way child care is organized in the Netherlands. Of the three countries, the Dutch government most actively encourages employers to participate in the provision of child care. British employers often find child care expensive and difficult to arrange (den Dulk, 2001). This suggests that stimulation measures aimed at reducing the costs for employers or offering an infrastructure that makes it easier to arrange child care might result in more involvement of employers. Only two of the Swedish employers had a child-care arrangement for their employees; this is against the background of a substantial public child-care system. The other three countries are characterized by a shortage of child-care facilities for working parents. Like the British employers, few Italian employers had adopted a child-care facility. In Italy, child care is not considered as a responsibility of employers but is seen as a task of the (local) government. Do our findings on the introduction of child-care arrangements suggest that minimal public provisions, rather than no or many public provisions stimulate employers to develop child care? Not necessarily, it could also be the case that other institutional conditions other than government policy may explain the relatively large involvement of Dutch employers providing child care. The preference for child care instead of leave arrangements among Dutch employers compared to Italian and British employers may also be caused by the economic climate in the Netherlands. At the time of the research, the Netherlands was characterized by economic growth and shortage of personnel. In Italy, in contrast, economic recovery was slow and long-term unemployment and unemployment among young people was still high (SCP, 2000). Economic growth and shortage of personnel makes it more attractive for Dutch employers to invest in child-care facilities rather than leave arrangements. If leave is taken, an employee is temporarily absent from work, whereas child-care facilities may increase the availability of personnel. However, also in Britain there was a situation of economic growth (SCP, 2000). Nevertheless, British employers tend to introduce (short-term) leave arrangements rather than child-care provisions. An explanation for this finding might be that in a liberal welfare state regime, such as Britain, no specific type of facility is stimulated among employers. Organizations choose those arrangements that best fit the needs of the organization, and low costs options are preferred. Child-care arrangements are relatively expensive whereas short-term leave can be classified as a relatively cheap and relatively easy to implement.

In this study, both the Netherlands and Italy are classified as examples of corporatistic–conservative welfare state regimes. A specific characteristic of the corporatistic welfare state regime is the intensive debate between government, employers' organizations and trade unions on employment conditions. Collective agreements are relatively more important and consequently; there is more similarity among organizations than in a liberal regime. A difference found between Dutch and Italian employers was that the Dutch employers more often offer child care and flexible work arrangements, whereas Italian employers focus mainly on leave arrangements. Specific institutional conditions can explain these differences. In Italy, the trade union opposition toward flexible work arrangements and the dominant view that child care is a responsibility of the (local) government leads to more attention to leave arrangements. In the Netherlands, attention to child care and flexible work and a favorable economic climate have lead to less attention for leave arrangements.

Few Swedish employers did supplement public leave and child-care provisions. However, when taking both statutory and employers' provisions into account, Sweden still has the highest level of provisions. In the other three countries, employers are on average more active, but never fully substitute statutory provisions. Active government involvement does not necessarily mean that the incentive for employers to develop facilities themselves disappears. Within a social–democratic regime, too, it can be profitable to supplement statutory provisions to a higher degree than one's competitors.

Work–family arrangements are increasingly becoming part of the fringe benefits offered by employers. A main characteristic of employers' provisions is however, that they are not evenly distributed:

as arrangements are more often found in some types of organizations than in others. As a result, employers' provisions lead toward inequality of access. To offer equality of life chances or equal access to facilities, public provisions are also needed. A positive relation between government and employers' involvement can ensure equal access and, at the same time, can stimulate organizations to develop facilities that suit the specific needs of both the organization and the employees.

Future Research

To elaborate on the findings of this study, future research should, on the one hand enhance the scope of research, i.e., extend the research to other countries and to samples of organizations including all industries and sizes. When extending the scope of the research to organizations of all sizes and sectors of industries and to other countries, more detailed information about the relative role of organizational characteristics, institutional conditions at the level of industry, and at the national level will be available. If more countries were included in the analysis, it would be possible to statistically analyze the effect of national conditions on the relation between organizational factors and the adoption of work–family arrangements in a multilevel model. Interesting countries to include in future research would be, for instance, France and Belgium, which both deviate from the conservative regime because of their relatively highly developed family policies; Asian countries such as Japan, where both the market and the family are important providers of welfare (Esping-Andersen, 1999); and Eastern European countries because of the changing role of the state toward work–family policies in these countries. When more countries are included it would be interesting to examine whether interaction effects between institutional conditions organizational characteristics are of importance.

The influence of institutional conditions at the level of industries has not been taken into account in this study. This would have implied the selection of a larger sample, which was not possible in the scope of this study. It can be assumed, however, that collective agreements at the level of industries influence the adoption of certain types of facilities (e.g., SZW, 1997).

Like most other research done in this field, the focus of the research has been on large- and medium-sized organizations. There has been in fact little research done on small employers and the development of work–family arrangements, despite the fact that 99% of enterprises in the EU are small- or medium-sized (250 employees or less; Eurostat, 1996) and that the situation in smaller organizations differs in many respects from larger organizations. For many small organizations, the introduction of work–family arrangements are often too costly. However, on the other hand, they tend to be less formalized and departmentalized, but more centralized than large organizations (e.g., Kalleberg, Knokke, Marsden, & Spaeth, 1996), which may stimulate creative solutions regarding the work–life balance of employees. Future research should also focus on small employers and the self-employed and the costs and benefits of different types of work–family arrangements for these organizations. For national governments, it would be valuable to find out how one can effectively stimulate the development and implementation of work–family arrangements in organizations of all sizes.

This research has focused on the presence of facilities rather than on the actual use. A case study approach could further investigate how and when employees use available provisions and how this is affected by the organizational culture; i.e., the norms and values at the workplace about what is and is not done and how this, in turn, is affected by the national culture prevalent in a particular country. In-depth research may also increase our knowledge about informal work–family arrangements in the context of small organizations. Moreover, future research could elaborate on how various flexible work arrangements, including new developments, such as self-managing teams and portable human capital, affect to the balance of work and family life and by which intentions they are implemented.

ACKNOWLEDGMENT

The Netherlands Organization of Scientific Research (NWO) financially supported this study (number 510-02-0009).

REFERENCES

Bergamachi, M. (1999). Equal opportunities and collective bargaining in Italy. The role of women. *The European Journal of Women's Studies, 6,* 133–148.

Bernasco, W., de Voogd-Hamelink, A. M., Vosse, J. P. M., & Wetzels, C. M. M. P. (1998). Trendrapport Vraag naar arbeid 1998. OSA publicatie A-163. Servicecentrum Uitgevers: The Hague.

Coleman J. S. (1990). *Foundations of social theory.* Cambridge: Harvard University Press.

Del Boca, D. (1998). Labour Policies, Economic Flexibility and Women's Work: The Italian Experience. In E. Drew, R. Emerek, & E. Mahon (Eds.), *Women, work and the family in Europe.* London/New York: Routledge.

DiMaggio, P. J., & Powel, W. W. (1983). The Iron Cage Revisited: Institutional Isomorphism and Collective Rationality in Organizational Fields. *American Sociological Review, 48*, 147–160.

Dulk, L. den (2001). Work–family arrangements in organisations, a cross-national study in the Netherlands, Italy, the United Kingdom and Sweden. Amsterdam: Rozenberg Publishers.

Edelman L. B. (1990). Legal environments and organizational governance: The expansion of due process in the American workplace. *American Journal of Sociology, 95*, 1401–1440.

Esping-Andersen, G. (1990). *The three worlds of welfare capitalism.* Cambridge: Polity Press.

Esping-Andersen, G. (1999). *Social Foundations of Postindustrial Economies.* New York: Oxford University Press.

Evans, J. M. (2001). *Firms' contribution to the reconciliation between work and family life.* Occasional papers No. 48. Paris: OECD.

Eurostat (1996). *Enterprises in Europe, Fourth Report.* Office for Official Publications of the European Communities: Luxembourg.

Forth, J., Lissenburgh, S., Callender, C., & Millward, N. (1997). *Family friendly working arrangements in Britain, 1996.* Research Report No. 16. Policy Studies Institute, Department for Education and Employment.

Glass, J. L., & Fujimoto, T. (1995). Employers characteristics and the provision of family responsive policies. *Work and Occupation, 22*, 380–411.

Goodstein, J. D. (1994). Institutional pressures and strategic responsiveness: Employer involvement in work–family issues. *Academy of Management Journal, 37*, 350–382.

Guida Monaci (1998). *Annuario Generale Italiano.* Rome: Author.

Harker, L. (1996). The Family-Friendly Employer in Europe. In: S. Lewis & J. Lewis (eds.), *The Work-Family Challenge, Rethinking Employment.* London: Sage.

Ingram, P., & Simons, T. (1995). Institutional and resource dependence determinants of responsiveness to work–family issues. *Academy of Management Journal, 38*, 1466–1482.

Kalleberg, A. L., Knokke, D., Marsden, P. V., & Spaeth, J. L. (Eds.). (1996). *Organizations in America. Analyzing their Structures and Human Resource Practices.* New York: Sage.

Lewis, S. (1997). An international perspective on work–family issues. In S. Parasurama & J. H. Greenhaus (Eds.), *Integrating work and family choices for a changing world.* Westport: Quorum.

Lippe, T. van der (1993). *Arbeidsverdeling tussen mannen en vrouwen.* Amsterdam: Thesis Publishers.

Morgan, H., & Milliken, F. J. (1992). Keys to action: Understanding differences in organizations' responsiveness to work and family issues. *Human Resource Management, 31*, 227–248.

National Statistics (2000). *Small and Medium Enterprise (SME), Statistics for the United Kingdom, 1999.* Statistical Bulletin. Sheffield: Research and Evaluation Unit Small Business Service.

Niphuis-Nell, M. (1997). Beleid inzake herverdeling van onbetaalde arbeid. In: *Sociale atlas van de vrouw, deel 4: veranderingen in de primaire leefsfeer.* SCP: Rijswijk.

OECD (2001). *Employment Outlook 2001.* Paris: Organisation for Economic Co-operation and Development.

Oliver, C. (1991). Strategic responses to institutional processes. *Academy of Management Review, 16,* 145–179.

Osterman, P. (1995), Work–family programs and the employment relationship. *Administrative Science Quarterly, 40,* 681–700.

Peters, A., F de Yong and Sardjce, U. H. I. (2000). Arbeid en zorg in CAO's 1998. The Hague: Elsevier bedrijfsinformatie.

Plantenga, J., & van Doorne-Huiskes, J. (1993). Verschillen in arbeidsparticipatie van vrouwen in Europa, de rol van verzorgingsstaten. *Tijdschrift voor Arbeidsvraagstukken, 9,* 51–65.

Pyttersen's Nederlandse Almanak. (1998). *Pyttersen's Nederlandse Almanak.* Houten: Bohn Staflen van Loghum.

Rostgaard, T. (1999). *The Configuration of Corporate Social Responsibility— The Role of the Enterprise in a New Welfare Model.* Research Program No. 6: The Open Labour Market. Copenhagen: The Danish National Institute of Social Research.

Scott W. R. (1995). *Institutions and organizations.* Thousand Oaks, CA: Sage.

SCP (2000). *Sociaal en Cultureel Rapport 2000. Nederland in Europa.* Sociaal en Cultureel Planbureau: The Hague.

Staatsalmanak (1997). *Staatsalmanak voor het Koninkrijk der Nederlanden 1998.* The Hague: Sdu Uitgevers.

Statistics Sweden (1998). Statistical Yearbook of Sweden 1999. Stockholm: Author.

SZW (1997). *Emancipatie in arbeidsorganisaties.* Arbeidsinspectie, Ministerie van Sociale Zaken en Werkgelegenheid: The Hague.

Tolbert P. S., & Zucker, L. G. (1996). The Institutionalization of Institutional Theory. In S. R. Clegg, C. Hardy, & W. R. Nord (Eds.), *Handbook of organization studies.* London: Sage.

Trifiletti, R. (1999). Work–family arrangements in Italy. In L. den Dulk, J. van Doorne-Huiskes, & J. Schippers (Eds.), *Work–family arrangements in Europe.* Amsterdam: Thela-Thesis.

Wildeboer Schut, J. M., Vrooman, J. C., & de Beer, P. T. (2000). *De maat van de verzorgingsstaat. Inrichting en werking van het sociaal-economisch bestel in elf westerse landen.* The Hague: Sociaal en Cultureel Planburau.

III

Cross-Cultural Perspective

9

Cross-Cultural Differences in Crossover Research

Mina Westman
Tel Aviv University, Israel

ABSTRACT

Studies investigating the crossover of stress and strain between partners have shown that job demands are transmitted from job incumbents to their partners, affecting their psychological and physical health. Three main mechanisms have been suggested to account for the apparent effects of a crossover process, involving, respectively, common stressors, empathic reactions, and an indirect mediating process. Most findings have demonstrated a unidirectional crossover from husbands to wives but not from wives to husbands. However, a few studies have detected symmetrical bidirectional crossover effects from one spouse to another. One of the possible explanations suggested for the inconsistency in findings is a moderating effect of gender interacting with culture. In cultures characterized by a traditional gender ideology, the crossover process is mostly unidirectional, from husbands to wives. However, in cultures characterized by a nontraditional gender ideology the crossover process is mostly symmetrical and bidirectional. Recommendations for future research are proposed and the implications for organizational theory are discussed.

This chapter deals with research on the impact of culture in the crossover of stress and strain from one spouse to another. The first section defines the crossover concept and presents its possible mechanisms. Next, gender is introduced as a possible moderating variable in the stress–strain process, extrapolating to its role in the crossover process. The last section deals with the impact of culture on the role of gender in the crossover process.

THEORETICAL FRAMEWORK

The Crossover Process Between Spouses

There is ample evidence that job stress has an impact on workers' mental and physical well-being. However, less attention has been paid to crossover: the reaction of individuals to the job stress experienced by those with whom they interact regularly. Bolger, DeLongis, Kessler, and Wethington (1989) differentiated between two situations: *spillover*—stress experienced in one domain of life results in stress in the other domain for the same individual; and *crossover*—stress experienced in the workplace by the individual leads to stress or strain being experienced by his or her spouse at home. Whereas spillover is an *intra-individual* transmission of stress, crossover is a dyadic, *interpersonal* transmission of stress or strain. Thus, crossover research focuses on the phenomenon of stress experienced in the workplace by the individual leading to stress and strain being experienced by the individual's spouse at home.

Empirical evidence demonstrates that job stress and psychological strain, such as depression and burnout of one spouse, affects the physiological and psychological health of the other spouse. Studies on crossover of stress and strain from one spouse to the other have been conducted in Australia (e.g., Morrison & Clements, 1997); England (e.g., Jones & Fletcher, 1993); Finland (e.g., Mauno & Kinnunen, 2002); Israel (e.g., Westman & Etzion, 1995); the Netherlands (e.g., Bakker & Schaufeli, 2000); Russia (e.g., Westman, Vinokur, Hamilton, & Roziner, 2004); and the United States (e.g., Barnett, Raudenbush, Brennan, Pleck, & Marshall, 1995).

This chapter is based on empirical studies that investigated the crossover process from different angles. Some focused on the crossover of job *stress* from the individual to the spouse (e.g., Burke, Weir, & DuWors, 1980), some examined the process whereby *job stress* of the individual affects the *strain* of the spouse (e.g., Jones & Fletcher, 1993; Long & Voges, 1987), and others studied how psychological *strain* of one partner affects the *strain* of the other (e.g., Mitchell, Cronkite, & Moos, 1983; Westman & Vinokur, 1998).

Five major outcomes have been frequently investigated: burnout (e.g., Bakker & Schaufeli, 2001; Westman, Etzion, & Danon, 2001), depression (e.g., Katz, Beach, & Joiner, 1999; Vinokur, Price, & Caplan, 1996), work–family conflict (e.g., Hammer, Allen, & Grigsby, 1997; Hammer, Bauer, & Grandey, 2003; Westman & Etzion, in press) cross-cultural adjustment (Takeouchi, Seokhwa, & Tesluk, 2002), and marital dissatisfaction (e.g., Westman et al., 2004). Although most researchers investigated the crossover effects of one partner's psychological well-being on the other, a few (e.g., Fletcher, 1983, 1988) studied the crossover of physical health between marital partners.

Previous studies (Westman, 2001, 2002), based on the crossover literature and on models of job stress and the work–family interface, have proposed a comprehensive framework to integrate the literature conceptually, and in particular have delineated the mechanisms that underlie the crossover process.

Westman and Vinokur (1998) specify three main crossover mechanisms, which result respectively from common stressors, empathetic reactions, and an indirect mediating interaction process. The *common stressors* mechanism refers to common stressors in a shared environment that increase both partners' strain. What appears to be a crossover effect is the result of common stressors in a shared environment increasing the strain in both partners. This suggests that people in close relationships may experience shared stressors (e.g., economic hardship) creating psychological strain in both of them. Hobfoll and London (1986) suggested that many stressors make simultaneous demands on both individuals in a dyad. The common stressors affecting both partners will impact the strain of both partners and the positive correlation detected between the strains of the spouses will *appear as resulting from* a crossover effect. Thus, Westman and Vinokur (1998) suggested that the contribution of common stressors in a shared environment to the increase in stress that affects both partners' strain needs to be considered as a spurious case of crossover. *Direct empathetic crossover* implies that stress and strain are transmitted from one partner to another directly as a result of empathetic reactions. The basis for this view is the finding that crossover effects appear between closely related partners who care for each other and share the greater part of their lives together. Literally, the root meaning of the word empathy is "feeling into." Starcevic and Piontek (1997) define empathy as interpersonal communication that is predominantly emotional in nature. It involves the ability to be affected by the other's affective state and to be able to read in oneself what that affect has been. Similarly, Lazarus (1991, p. 287) defines empathy as "sharing another's feelings by placing oneself psychologically in that person's circumstances"; that is, the core relational theme for empathy involves a sharing of another person's emotional state, distressed or otherwise. Accordingly, strain in one partner produces an empathetic reaction in the other that increases his or her own strain. This view is supported by social learning theorists (e.g., Bandura, 1969; Stotland, 1969) who have explained the transmission of emotions as a conscious processing of information. They suggest that individuals imagine how they would feel in the position of another and thus come to experience and share their feelings.

Finally, *indirect crossover of strain* is a transmission mediated by interpersonal exchange. Thus, indirect crossover occurs when an increase in the strain of one partner triggers a provocative behavior or exacerbates a negative interaction sequence with the other partner, often expressed as social undermining behavior toward the other person and perceived as such by the partner (Duffy, Ganster, & Pagan, 2002; Vinokur & van Ryn, 1993). The strain of one person that leads to his or her social undermining behavior toward the other acts as a stressor for the recipient of this behavior, and this stressor causes the recipient's strain level to increase. Here, one's strain results in an increase in the strain of the other, but the crossover does not occur unless it is bridged or mediated by another intermediate process of negative interactions.

The explanation that the crossover process is mediated by negative social interactions is supported by empirical findings from two lines of research. First, research documents that frustration is often an outcome of stressful conditions that trigger aggression (Berkowitz, 1989). Second, the literature on family processes also reports that stressed couples exhibit high levels of negative conflictual interactions (Schaefer, Coyne, & Lazarus, 1981).

It should be noted that the three distinct mechanisms of crossover can operate independently of one another. Moreover, because they are independent and are not mutually exclusive, it is of course quite possible that more than one mechanism contributes to the crossover process and that some of the proposed mechanisms operate in conjunction with one another. There are also certain other possible mechanisms that have not yet been explored, such as similarity between spouses, modeling, quality of relationship between spouses, and personality factors such as negative and positive affectivity. For this reason, investigating and explaining crossover processes and their effects in any specific context or relationship requires an analytic model that takes into account all the relevant potential contributors to crossover effects.

Direction of Crossover: Unidirectional vs. Bidirectional

The literature shows that crossover may be unidirectional (from one spouse to another) or bi-directional (from one spouse to another and vice versa). Most stress crossover studies have been unidirectional, examining and finding effects of husbands' job stress on the well-being of their wives (e.g., Jackson & Maslach, 1982; Long & Voges, 1987; Pavett, 1986; Rook, Dooley, & Catalano, 1991), and have related to the wives as the passive recipients of stress and strain from their husbands, neither assessing nor controlling wives' job and life stress.

Later crossover studies focus on both spouses and examine bi-directional crossover of stress or strain. Jones and Fletcher (1993), the first to also measure wives' job stress, found transmission of husbands' job demands on wives' anxiety and depression after controlling wives' job stress. However, they did not find transmission of anxiety and depression from wives to husbands, perhaps because the women in their sample did not experience high levels of stress. Similarly, Westman et al. (2001), investigating a sample of Israeli couples working in the same downsizing organization, found crossover of burnout from husbands to wives but not from wives to husbands. A recent longitudinal study of officers in the Russian army and their wives (Westman et al., 2004) also detected strong crossover effects of marital dissatisfaction from husbands to wives but no significant crossover from wives to husbands.

Though these studies did not detect crossover of stress and strain from wives to husbands, evidence concerning gender differences in the crossover process is not consistent. Recent studies of dual-career families found bi-directional crossover effects of stress or strain (e.g., burnout, work-family conflict, depression, anxiety, and distress) for both spouses (e.g., Barnett et al., 1995; Hammer et al., 1997; Hammer et al., 2003; Mauno & Kinnunen, 2002; Westman & Etzion, 1995; Westman et al., 2002). Thus, Westman and Etzion (1995) demonstrated a crossover of burnout from career officers to their spouses and vice versa, after controlling husbands' and wives' own job stress and resistance resources (control and social support). Takeouchi, Seokhwa and Tesluk (2002) also found bi-directional crossover of cross-cultural adjustment from Japanese expatriates to their spouses and vice versa, while Hammer et al. (1997; 2003) found a bi-directional crossover of work-family conflict from husbands to wives and vice versa. Similarly, Westman et al. (2002) found crossover of work-family conflict from women in the Air Force to their spouses and vice versa. Adding to this cross-sectional literature, the bi-directional nature of the crossover effect has been demonstrated in longitudinal designs. Thus, Barnett et al. (1995) and Westman and Vinokur (1998) found bi-directional crossover of distress from husbands to wives and from wives to husbands over time. Also, Westman, Etzion and Horovitz (2004), focusing on the crossover of state anxiety between spouses in *working couples* when one of them faces unemployment, found a significant bi-directional crossover effect of state anxiety from the unemployed to the spouse and from the spouse to the unemployed at both waves of their longitudinal study after controlling for all relevant variables.

One possible explanation for the inconsistency in the direction of the crossover process may be the role of gender. As already noted, some of the findings indicate that the crossover process is unidirectional, or at least stronger from husbands to wives, who are more frequently the recipients of the husbands' stress and strain. There are at least three groups of findings that support this contention. (a) Women experience higher levels of distress and therefore are less resilient when facing the stress and strain of their husbands. Tousignant, Brosseau, and Tremblay (1987) indicated that one of the most consistent results in mental health research is that women report significantly more symptoms than men do. Furthermore, recent studies suggest that the level of depressive symptoms in women continues to be higher than in men despite substantial gains in education and career opportunity (Mirowski & Ross, 1995). (b) Women are more empathetic to the stress of their husbands and therefore more vulnerable to crossover effects. Larson and Almeida (1999) maintain that the finding that wives are more frequently the receivers in the crossover process may reflect their deliberate efforts to be empathetic toward their husbands and a general tendency to have more permeable boundaries than men. (c) Women are more vulnerable to crossover effects because of their role as providers of social support. Riley and Ekenrode (1986) noted that significant others are influenced by each other's distress indirectly, via the other's reduced social support, noting that demand for social support caused a drain in others in the dyad or in the social group.

Thus, there is some indication that women are more susceptible than men to the impact of stressors affecting their partners (Kessler, 1979). Kessler and McLeod (1984) suggested that because of their greater involvement in family affairs, women become more sensitive not only to the stressful events that they experience themselves, but also to those that affect their spouses. The evidence that gender has an impact on perceived stress and strain is also relevant to the second suggested mechanism of the crossover process—direct crossover between spouses. Gender is a potential moderator of the impact of one's stress on the spouse's strain because of differences in the traditional role demands and expectations for men and women (Lambert, 1990).

The Impact of Culture

The inconsistencies in the evidence concerning gender differences in the crossover process lead us to assume a possible impact of culture on the role of gender in general and on the crossover process in particular. According to Shafiro, Himelein, and Best (2003), the differences in gender attitudes among diverse cultures have been of enduring interest to cross-cultural researchers investigating the extent to which women from different cultures differ in their beliefs concerning gender roles and male–female interactions.

Bearing in mind that work and family systems operate within, influence, and are influenced by the wider social, economic, and political context, which includes cultural norms and values, and gender-role ideology, it is important to investigate whether culture has an impact on the crossover process and its consequences. This issue is particularly important and timely in view of the ever-growing need for multinational organizations to be aware of the impact of cultural influences on their operations and to develop culturally appropriate strategies to prevent stress and strain crossover and its consequences.

As job and family stress and the importance of family and work may differ from culture to culture, several questions arise. Do societies differ in the importance they attach to work and family? Do employees from different cultures perceive stress and strain differently? Does culture have an influence on the mechanisms through which the crossover process occurs? Are there cultural differences in gender role ideologies? Does the "breadwinner" role differ across cultures? And, are the perspectives concerning crossover of stress and strain from one spouse to another generalizable? In order to answer these and additional questions, it is proposed to investigate the impact of culture on the crossover process of stress and strain.

The following sections aim to show how cultural and organizational contexts and value differences among cultures (e.g., the importance of work and family, the impact of gender, gender ideology) influence the experience, levels, direction, antecedents, and outcomes of the crossover process in the different cultures.

A handful of studies have investigated cross-nation differences in employee well-being, but not enough data exist to paint a complete picture. However, cultural differences were found concerning the perception of stress and strain and in the relationship between stress and strain (Perrewe et al., 2003; Spector et al., 2001). Perrewe et al.'s

(2003) findings clearly indicate that the actual levels of role conflict, role ambiguity, and burnout differed significantly across the nine cultures of this study. In addition, the level of perceived self-efficacy also varied significantly. Furthermore, self-efficacy was relevant as a mediating effect on the role stressor–outcome relationship, but it was not universal for all stressors, nor totally consistent across all countries. Spector et al. (2001) found that the relationship between locus of control and psychological well-being was consistent across all 24 nations in their study. However, relations between locus of control and physical well-being failed to show consistent findings across nations. They concluded that manifestation of control can differ across societies.

Based on these findings, it is suggested to introduce culture to the crossover research as one of the possible predictors of stress that interacts with gender, the focus being on the issue of whether the impact of gender on the crossover process differs from culture to culture according to the role of gender in that culture. Among the main issues in this context are the role of men as breadwinners and gender differences in coping strategies. This line of research will further our knowledge of the relationship among gender, stress, and the partner's stress and cultural differences in gender roles that impact the stress–strain relationship.

As Ellsworth (1994) maintains, it makes sense that there are differences across cultures and that they differ in their definitions of novelty, hazard, opportunity, attack, gratification, loss, and appropriate responses. Cultural belief systems also define events as the result of circumstances or to a person's own efforts, as good or as bad, as controllable or uncontrollable; differences in such cultural appraisals affect people's emotional responses to events. There is, moreover, empirical evidence of different strain levels in various countries (Perrewe et al., 2003), and many emotions observed in everyday life seem to depend on the dominant prevailing social frame and therefore cannot be separated from culture-specific patterns of thinking, acting, and interacting.

Cultural Dimensions

During the past decades, several cultural frameworks have been developed to classify cultures in terms of varius dimensions and values (Hofstede, 1980; Schwartz, 1992; Triandis, 1995). We found the dimensions suggested by Hofstede to be most suitable in analyzing crossover research from the cultural perspective. Hofstede (1984, 1994) concluded from his studies of culture that values of different societies differ substantially along four basic dimensions. His four-value framework (Hofstede, 1984) focuses on power distance, individualism–collectivism, masculinity–femininity, and uncertainty avoidance. *Power distance* reflects the extent to which members of a given culture accept unequal power distribution within institutions and organizations in a society, from relatively equal to extremely unequal. *Uncertainty avoidance* represents the extent to which people in a society feel threatened by ambiguous or unstructured situations. *Individualism–collectivism* refers to whether individualistic or collective action is the preferred way to deal with the issue. *Individualism* reflects a culture's emphasis on the goals and needs of the individual rather than as members of the group. *Collectivism* indicates interdependence among the employees and the organization bearing responsibility for the employees. *Masculinity* relates to the extent to which members of a culture prefer stereotypical masculine values such as extrinsic reward, with a focus on assertiveness and material success rather than stereotypical feminine values such as caring for others and solidarity. *Femininity* is the extent to which members of a culture prefer values such as concern for people, importance of social goals, empathy, relations, and help. Highly masculine cultures have more rigid gender roles than highly feminine cultures.

All these dimensions may be relevant in one way or another to crossover research, but the most relevant ones seem to be masculinity–femininity and to a certain extent, individualism–collectivism. In collectivistic cultures couples may be more inclined to perceive a common mission than in individualistic cultures. According to Triandis (1995), in collectivistic cultures, people define themselves according to group membership (e.g., family) and emphasize group norms, goals, and needs over personal norms, goals, and needs. In individualistic cultures, people tend to be less interconnected and more independent, focusing on personal goals and preferences.

A *masculine* culture tends to value assertiveness, roughness, material success, acquisition of money and material possessions, pursuit of advancement, and the like. Achievement is defined in terms of recognition and wealth; work is a more central feature of life, people prefer more salary to shorter working hours, and company interference in private life is accepted. There are greater value differences between men and women in the same jobs, and women are expected to be soft and focus on quality of life.

A *feminine* culture is characterized by cooperation, more importance is attached to a congenial atmosphere, and achievement is defined in terms of human contacts and the living environment. Work is less central in people's lives, and the value differences between men and women in the same jobs are smaller if they exist at all.

Boss (2001) emphasized the need to take into account the community and cultural contexts in which the family resides to understand why and how families are stressed and how they respond to stress. Thus, in interpreting the pattern of results from crossover research, we need to consider the roles of women within the context of the culture. The characteristics of individualism and collectivism and of masculinity and femininity lead us to the following propositions presented in Table 9.1:

1. There is a difference in the direction and main mechanisms of crossover in different cultures depending on the sociocultural and contextual variables operating in various cultures.
   (a) There is a bidirectional direct crossover of stress and strain between spouses in cultures characterized by individualism and to some degree in culture characterized by femininity. There is a unidirectional crossover (from husbands to wives) in cultures characterized by collectivism and in culture characterized by masculinity.
   (b) There is a direct crossover of stress and strain via empathy in cultures characterized by collectivism and in culture characterized by femininity more than in cultures characterized by individualism and in cultures characterized by masculinity.
   (c) Common stressors increase the stress and strain of both spouses in cultures characterized by collectivism and in culture characterized by femininity more than in cultures characterized by individualism and in cultures characterized by masculinity.
   (d) In cultures characterized by individualism and in cultures characterized by masculinity the indirect crossover process via undermining (especially from husbands to wives) will be more prevalent, than in cultures characterized by collectivism and in cultures characterized by femininity.

Gender Role Ideology

Although the masculinity–femininity and individualism collectivism factors have the greatest impact on the prevalence, direction, and symmetry of crossover processes, the conclusions regarding the moderating effects of gender in crossover research must be drawn with

TABLE 9.1
Crossover Mechanisms and Cultural Dimensions

Cultural Dimensions	Crossover Mechanisms			Crossover Direction	
	Empathy	Undermining*	Common Stressors	Bidirectional	Unidirectional*
Individualism	Low to moderate	High	Low to moderate	High	
Collectivism	High	Low to moderate	High		High
Masculinity	Low	High	Low to moderate		High
Femininity	High	Low	High		High

*from husbands to wives.

251

great caution because in many studies, gender is confounded with the primary breadwinner role in the family and its association with power relationships. It may be the case that the findings of moderating effects of gender are actually the moderating effects of the primary breadwinner role in these relationships. Gender role ideology seems to vary by culture. To illustrate, the dimension of individualism and collectivism relates to gender role ideology. In collectivistic countries, gender role ideologies are more traditional whereas in countries high in individualism gender role ideologies are more egalitarian. Gender role ideologies play a significant role in determining the direction and intensity of the crossover process (Westman et al., 2004). Williams and Best (1990) found more liberal gender role attitudes in countries that emphasized individualism and de-emphasized authoritarian power structure. The desire for independence and self-sufficiency that characterizes individualism led Shafiro et al. (2003) to hypothesize and find that such qualities in women tend to be associated with more liberal attitudes toward gender roles.

The importance of gender ideologies can be illustrated by three crossover studies conducted in Finland (Mauno and Kinnunen, 2002), in the United States (Barnett et al., 1995), and in Russia (Westman, et al., 2004). Whereas Mauno and Kinnunen (2002) and Barnett et al. (1995) found bidirectional symmetrical crossover from one spouse to another in dual earner couples, Westman et al. (2004) found a strong crossover of marital dissatisfaction from husbands to wives and no crossover of marital dissatisfaction from wives to husbands in a Russian sample. The inconsistency in findings seems to stem from the differences in characteristics of the samples. Whereas the Finish and U.S. samples consisted of nontraditional dual-career/earner couples, the Russian sample consisted of mostly dual-earner couples who held a traditional gender ideology. An elaboration of the Russian sample will explain the differences.

According to a Russian dictionary, a breadwinner is "the person who feeds and provides sustenance to someone." Though the key factor in acquiring "breadwinner" status is the ability to secure the means on which the family lives, it may be influenced by traditional perceptions instilled in the process of socialization concerning the proper function, role, and duties of men and women in the family. The reasons for some household members being called breadwinner may be traditional sociocultural norms concerning the perception of female and male duties and may also be gender values that are deeply rooted in the consciousness of both men and women. Thus, the gap between the traditional, ideal division of labor between men and women and the actual practice may be greater in Russian society than it is in other cultures.

Various studies of the Russian family suggest that even in a family with husband and wife sharing the breadwinning role in a more or less egalitarian manner, they still hold traditional gender role attitudes. Kiblitskaya (2000) argues that even when women take on the responsibility for providing for the family and even when they are highly successful, this does not necessarily result in the transformation of power in relations in the family: "While women may appear to be in control, they generally still accept the idea that the men should be in control" (p. 68). The women still long for men to fulfill the role of the traditional breadwinner as much as the men desire to resume their place as head of the family. Women usually want only a modified version of tradition.

Most of the couples in Westman et al. (2004) study were dual-career or dual-earner couples. However, in terms of gender ideology, these couples could be described as traditional. When asked about their agreement with the statement "A husband should be head of the family," 64% of the women and 80% of the men agreed with it. Furthermore, when asked about who is doing the housework, 34% of the husbands reported they engage in housework in comparison to 73.4% of the wives.

In contrast, the breadwinner role is not as rigid in Finland and in the United States. Roehling and Moen (2003) maintain that beginning in the 1960s, the traditional breadwinner–homemaker lifestyle, which was the norm for middle-class married couples, gave way to the dual-earner couple, dyads in which both members work for pay. Today, dual-earner couples are the norm, representing 54% of married couples in the United States in 2001.

The studies that demonstrated symmetrical bidirectional crossover effects included what can be described as nontraditional dual-career couples who also hold nontraditional attitudes toward gender family roles (e.g., Barnett et al., 1995; Mauno and Kinnunen, 2002). The available data regarding the couples in the Westman et al. (2004) study suggest that although they too share the role of breadwinning and may be described as dual-career or dual-earner couples, they still hold traditional gender attitudes. These attitudes express themselves in viewing the husband as the head of the family and the wife as the one in charge of housework. We argue that these traditional attitudes toward gender roles in the family account for the unique unidirectional crossover effects found in this study because these traditional attitudes shape the expectations of the husband and wife from each other, their interactions, and their emotional responses to these interactions.

An additional illustration of the differences between traditional and nontraditional gender ideologies is evident from findings concerning the third crossover mechanism, the indirect crossover of strain mediated by interpersonal exchange. Whereas findings concerning the role of undermining as a mediating variable were consistent for both husbands and wives in American and Israeli samples (e.g., Westman & Vinokur, 1998; Westman et al., 2001), the findings in the Russian sample (Westman et al., 2004) were different. For the husbands, the increased undermining behavior from the wives resulted in a strong significant increase in their marital dissatisfaction. However, this effect was negligible and statistically not significant for the wives. That is, increased undermining from the husbands did not have an effect on the wives' marital dissatisfaction. This finding may result from traditional gender ideology regarding husbands' undermining behavior toward their wives as normative whereas wives undermining behavior toward their husband causes husbands' marital dissatisfaction because this is an unacceptable behavior.

DISCUSSION

The reviewed literature leads to the conclusions that in order to detect and understand the role of gender in crossover research, we have to look at the impact of culture on this process. Yanmg, Chen, Choi, and Zou (2000) maintain that work and family issues are *intricately* related to the cultural beliefs, values, and norms. As crossover research focuses on stress and strain crossing over from these domains, they are influenced by culture.

Culture has an important role in crossover research as it impacts the stress and strain transmitted between spouses. However, the main impact of culture is its interaction with gender. This interaction impacts the symmetry and direction of the crossover process and the impact of the communication style (e.g., social undermining) of the couple. Thus, culture and gender affect both the direct and indirect mechanisms of the crossover process.

The introduction of cultural diferences may add an additional important dimension to crossover research, especially the focus on gender and gender role ideology differences in various cultures. There are several aspects of the relationship between gender and crossover that merit further research because of their societal implications. One is the impact of stress on gender roles and the impact of the crossover

process on the entire family. As the number of women affected physically and psychologically by stress, strain, and the crossover process increases, the need for a thorough study of its effects becomes
urgent. Furthermore, because of the increasing number of studies
finding unidirectional crossover from husbands to wives, crossover
should be recognized as an addition to the list of stressors that are
more prevalent among women than among men. Knowledge about the
contribution of gender and culture will enrich our understanding of
the crossover process and will facilitate preventive measures for the
individual and for the family.

All the reviewed studies investigated negative crossover, such as
when job stress of one spouse affects the stress or strain of the other
spouse. However, just as stressful demands or a bad day at work
have a negative impact on the partner's well-being, positive job or
family events may also cross over to the partner and have a positive
effect on his or her well-being. Whereas crossover is usually defined
as a transmission of stress, we can broaden the definition into transmission of positive events or feelings as well. One can think of many
instances of positive crossover, such as enjoyable experiences at one's
job leading to job satisfaction crossover and eliciting a good mood
in the partner at home. Conversely, family life can support, facilitate,
or enhance work life. Supportive family relationships and attitudes
can create positive crossover to the work set. Investigating positive
crossover can enhance theoretical thinking and make practical contributions to crossover literature. The increased amount of attention being paid in the work–family domain indicates a potential of crossover
of positive events and feelings such as work–family facilitation (Wayne,
Musisca, & Fleeson, 2004), positive spillover between work and family (Grzywacz & Marks, 2000), and work–family balance (Clark, 2000;
Greenhaus, Collins, & Shaw, 2003). This is also a promising domain
for cross-cultural research.

Future research on crossover in general and on the impact of culture on the process of crossover in particular should provide additional possible mechanisms of the crossover process focus on positive crossover between spouses and include personality variables as
moderators of this process. Furthermore, methodology should improve by designing more longitudinal designs and by using experimental designs to support the suggested mechanisms. Cross-cultural
studies on the issue of crossover should be encouraged. To date,
we have findings from crossover studies in several countries and
cultures but none of them compared different cultures. There is a
need for an international group who will study the phenomenon of
crossover cross-culturally. Such studies would supply the theoretical

background for interventions focusing on the dyad and not only on the individual.

Greenhaus and Parasurmann (1999) are to be applauded for their recommendation that investigations of cross-cultural and cross-national influences play a prominent role in the future research agenda on the work–family interface. It is to be hoped that this line of research on the factors influencing the role of gender in different cultures will continue.

To date, most crossover studies have employed English-speaking samples or have been conducted in industrialized western countries. All the crossover studies consist of data collected only in one country. Because of the impact of culture, it is impossible to isolate effects or rule out alternative explanations for the findings. Of utmost importance to the study of crossover is the observation that within different cultural frameworks, coping, mental health, and well-being can take different forms and are likely to be associated with different ways of feeling. Furthermore, building a crossover framework needs this cultural aspect because any theory claiming universality must be demonstrated to hold cross culturally. The more a theory receives cross-cultural confirmation, the more closely it approximates universal generality (Kagitcibasi, 1994).

REFERENCES

Bakker, A. B., & Schaufeli, W. B. (2000). Burnout contagion process among teachers. *Journal of Applied Social Psychology, 30*, 2289–2308.

Bandura, A. (1969). *Principles of behavior modification*. New York: Holt, Rinehart, & Winston.

Barnett, R. C., Raudenbush, S. W., Brennan, R. T., Pleck, J. H., & Marshall, N. L. (1995). Changes in job and marital experience and change in psychological distress: A longitudinal study of dual-earner couples. *Journal of Personality and Social Psychology, 69*, 839–850.

Berkowitz, L. (1989). Frustration-aggression hypothesis: Examination and reformulation. *Psychological Bulletin, 106*, 59–73.

Bolger, N., DeLongis, A., Kessler, R., & Wethington, E. (1989). The contagion of stress across multiple roles. *Journal of Marriage and the Family, 51*, 175–183.

Boss, P. (2000). *Family stress management*. Newbury Park, CA: Sage.

Burke, R. J., Weir, T., & DuWors, R. E. (1980). Work demands on administrators and spouse well-being. *Human Relations, 33*, 253–278.

Clark, S. C. (2000). Work/family border theory: A new theory of work/family balance. *Human Relations, 53*, 747–770.

Duffy, M., Ganster, D., & Pagon, M. (2002). Social undermining in the workplace. *Academy of Management Journal, 45*, 331–351.

Ellsworth, P. C. (1994). *Sense, culture, and sensibility.* In S. Kitayama & H. R. Markus (Eds.), *Emotions and culture: Empirical studies of mutual influence* (pp. 23–50). Washington, DC: American Psychological Association.

Fletcher, B. (1983). Marital relationships as a cause of death: An analysis of occupational mortality and the hidden consequences of marriage—some U.K. data. *Human Relations, 36,* 123–134.

Fletcher, B. (1988). Occupation, marriage, and disease specific mortality concordance. *Social Science and Medicine, 27,* 615–622.

Greenhaus, J., Collins, K., & Shaw, J. (2003). The relations between work–family balance and quality of life. *Journal of Vocational Behavior, 63,* 510–531.

Greenhaus, J., & Parasuraman, S. (1999). *Research on work, family and gender: Current status and future directions.* In G. N. Powell (Ed.), *Handbook of gender and work.* London: Sage.

Grzywack, J., & Marks, N. (2000). Reconceptualizing the work–family interface: An ecological perspective on the correlates of positive and negative spillover between work and family. *Journal of Occupational Health Psychology, 5,* 111–126.

Hammer, L. B., Allen, E., & Grigsby, T. D. (1997). Work–family conflict in dual-earner couples: Within individual and crossover effects of work and family. *Journal of Vocational Behavior, 50,* 185–203.

Hammer, L. B., Bauer, T., & Grandey, A. (2003). Work–family conflict and work-related withdrawal behaviors. *Journal of Business and Psychology, 17,* 419–436.

Hobfoll, S. E., & London, P. (1986). The relationship of self concept and social support to emotional distress among women during war. *Journal of Social Clinical Psychology, 12,* 87–100.

Hofstede, G. (1984). The cultural relativity of the quality of life concept. *Academy of Management Review, 9,* 389–398.

Hofstede, G. (1994). Images of Europe. *Netherland Journal of Social Sciences, 30,* 63–82.

Jackson, S. E., & Maslach, C. (1982). After-effects of job-related stress: Families as victims. *Journal of Occupational Behavior, 3,* 63–77.

Jones, F., & Fletcher, B. (1993). An empirical study of occupational stress transmission in working couples. *Human Relations, 46,* 881–902.

Kagitcibasi, C. (1994). A critical appraisal of individualism and collectivism: Toward a new formulation. In U. Kim & H. Triandis (Eds.), *Individualism and collectivism: Theory, method, and applications.* Cross-cultural research and methodology series (Vol. 18, pp. 52–65). Thousand Oaks, CA: Sage.

Katz, J., Beach, S., & Joiner, T. (1999). Contagious depression in dating couples. *Journal of Social and Clinical Psychology, 18,* 1–13.

Kessler, R. C. (1979). A strategy for studying differential vulnerability to the psychological consequences of stress. *Journal of Health and Social Behavior, 20,* 100–108.

Kessler, R. C., & McLeod, J. D. (1984). Sex differences in vulnerability to undesirable life events. *American Sociological Review, 49*, 620–631.

Kiblitskaya, M. (2000). Russian females breadwinners: The changing subjective experience. In S. Ashwin (Ed.), *Gender, state and society in Soviet and Post-Soviet Russia* (pp. 55–70). London: Rutledge.

Lambert, S. J. (1990). Processes linking work and family: A critical review and research agenda. *Human Relations, 43*, 239–257.

Larson, R., & Almeida, D. (1999). Emotional transmission in the daily lives of families: A new paradigm for studying family process. *Journal of Marriage and the Family, 61*, 5–20.

Lazarus, R. S. (1991). *Emotion & adaptation.* New York: Oxford.

Long, N. R., & Voges, K. E. (1987). Can wives perceive the source of their husbands' occupational stress? *Journal of Occupational Psychology, 60*, 235–242.

Mauno, S., & Kinnunen, U. (2002). Perceived job insecurity among dual-earner couples: Do its antecedents vary according to gender, economic sector and measure used? *Journal of Occupational and Organizational Psychology, 75*, 295–314.

Mirowski, J., & Ross, C. E. (1995). Sex differences in distress. Real or artifact? *American Sociological Review, 60*, 449–468.

Mitchell, R., Cronkite, R., & Moos, R. (1983). Stress, coping and depression among married couples. *Journal of Abnormal Psychology, 92*, 433–448.

Morrison, D., & Clements, R. (1997). The effects of one partner's job characteristics on the other partner's distress: A serendipitous, but naturalistic, experiment. *Journal of Occupational and Organizational Psychology, 70*, 307–324.

Pavett, C. M. (1986). High-stress professions: Satisfaction, stress, and well-being of spouses of professionals. *Human Relations, 39*, 1141–1154.

Perrewe, P., Ralston, D., Hochwarter, W., Westman, M., Rossi, A. M., Vollmer, G., Wallace, A., Tang, M., Wan, P., Maignan, I., Van Deusen, C. A., & Castro, S. (2002). Are work stress relationships universal? A nine-region examination of the culture study of the relationships of role stressors, general self-efficacy and burnout. *Journal of International Management, 8*, 163–187.

Riley, D., & Eckenrode, J. (1986). Social ties: Costs and benefits within different subgroups. *Journal of Personality and Social Psychology, 51*, 770–778.

Roehling, P., & Moen, P. (2003). Dual-earner couples. In *A Sloan Work and Family Electronic Encyclopedia Entry*.

Rook, S. K., Dooley, D., & Catalano, R. (1991). Stress transmission: The effects of husbands' job stressors on emotional health of their wives. *Journal of Marriage and the Family, 53*, 165–177.

Schaefer, C., Coyne, J. C., & Lazarus, R. S. (1981). The health-related functions of social support. *Journal of Behavioral Medicine, 4*, 381–406.

Schwartz, S. (1992). Universals in the content and structure of values: Theoretical advances and empirical tests in 20 countries. *Advances in Experimental Social Psychology, 25*, 1–65.

Shafiro, M., Himelein, M., & Best, D. (2003). Ukrainian and US American Female: Differences in individualism/collectivism and gender attitudes. *Journal of Cross-Cultural Psychology, 34*, 297–303.

Spector, P., Cooper, C. L., Sanchez, J. I., O'Driscoll, M., Sparks, K., Bernin, P., Büssing, A., Dewe, P., Hart, P., Lu, L., Miller, K., Renault de Moreas, Ostrognay, G. M., Pagon, M., Pitariu, H., Poelmans, S., Radhakrishnan, P., Russinova, V., Salamatov, V., Salgado, J., Shima, S., Ling Siu, O., Stora, J. B., Teichmann, M., Theorell, T., Vlerick, P., Westman, M., Widerszal-Bazyl, M., Wong, P., & Yu, S. (2002). A twenty-four-nation study of work locus of control, well-being and individualism: How generalizable are western work findings? *Academy of Management Journal, 45*, 453–466.

Starcevic, V., & Piontek, C. M. (1997). Empathic understanding revisited: Conceptualization, controversies, and limitations. *American Journal of Psychotherapy, 51*, 317–328.

Stotland, E. (1969). *Exploratory investigations of empathy.* In L. Berkowitz (Ed.), *Advances in experimental social psychology* (Vol. 4, pp. 271–314), New York: Academic Press.

Takeouchi, R., Seokhwa, Y., & Tesluk, P. (2002). An examination of crossover and spillover effects of spousal and expatriate cross-cultural adjustment on expatriate outcomes. *Journal of Applied Psychology, 87*, 655–666.

Tousignant, M., Brosseau, R., & Tremblay, L. (1987). Sex biases in mental health scales: Do women tend to report less serious symptoms and confide more than men? *Psychological Medicine, 17*, 203–215.

Triandis, H. C. (1995). *Individualism and collectivism.* Boulder, CO: Westview.

Vinokur, A., Price, R. H., & Caplan, R. D. (1996). Hard times and hurtful partners: How financial strain affects depression and relationship satisfaction of unemployed persons and their spouses. *Journal of Personality and Social Psychology, 71*, 166–179.

Vinokur, A., & van Ryn, M. (1993). Social support and undermining in close relationships: Their independent effects on mental health of unemployed persons. *Journal of Personality and Social Psychology, 65*, 350–359.

Wayne, J. H., Musisca, N., & Fleeson, W. (2004). Considering the role of personality in the work–family experience: Relationships of the big five to work–family conflict and facilitation. *Journal of Vocational Behavior, 64*, 108–130.

Westman, M. (2001). Stress and strain crossover. *Human Relations, 54*, 557–591.

Westman, M. (2002). *Crossover of strain in the family and in the workplace.* In P. Perrewe & D. Ganster (Eds.), *Research in occupational stress and well-being* (Vol. 2). Greenwich, CT: JAI Press/Elsevier Science.

Westman, M., & Etzion, D. (1995). Crossover of stress, strain and resources from one spouse to another. *Journal of Organizational Behavior, 16*, 169–181.

Westman, M., Etzion, D., & Danon, E. (2001). Job insecurity and crossover of burnout in married couples. *Journal of Organizational Behavior, 22*, 467–481.

Westman, M., & Etzion, D. (in press). *The crossover process of work–family conflict from one spouse to another*. Journal of Applied Social Psychology.

Westman, M., & Vinokur, A. (1998). Unraveling the relationship of distress levels within couples: Common stressors, emphatic reactions, or crossover via social interactions? *Human Relations, 51*, 137–156.

Westman, M., Vinokur, A., Hamilton, L., & Roziner, I. (2004). Crossover of marital dissatisfaction during downsizing: A study of Russian army officers and their spouses. *Journal of Applied Psychology, 89*, 769–779.

Williams, J. E., & Best, D. L. (1990). *Sex and psyche: Gender and self viewed cross-culturally*. Newsbury Park, CA: Sage.

Yang, N., Chen, C. C., Choi, J., & Zou, Y. (2000). Sources of work–family conflict: A sino-U.S. comparison of the effects of work and family demands. *Academy of Management Journal, 43*, 113–123.

10

The Work–Family Interface in Urban Sub-Saharan Africa: A Theoretical Analysis

Samuel Aryee
Hong Kong Baptist University

Women in sub-Saharan Africa have a long history of participation in income-generating activities, albeit in the informal sector of the economy. However, better educational and economic opportunities coupled with urbanization and industrialization have led to their growing participation in formal wage employment. A significant number of these women are mothers involved in dual-earner families whereas a minority are heads of single parent families. The constraints of formal wage employment, such as lack of flexibility and changing gender roles, suggest that employed parents in sub-Saharan Africa face the challenge of balancing work and family just like their counterparts in the developed economies of the West and increasingly in Asia. However, unlike their counterparts elsewhere, there is a paucity of research on the dynamics of the work–family interface in sub-Saharan Africa. Lewis and Cooper (1999, 389) noted that:

> In the context of globalization of markets, the growth of multinational organizations and technological advances, not only work and family but also national and cultural boundaries are disappearing. It will be increasingly important for the work–family agenda to recognize the

261

different ways in which work and family issues are constructed cross-nationally.

Although as previously noted, women in sub-Saharan Africa have always participated in income-generating activities, the rising cost of living has made it necessary for women to assume a co-provider role. Further, the cultural endorsement of marriage and procreation (which suggests that most individuals will at some point in their adult life participate in work and family roles) and the general absence of government and organizational family-friendly initiatives, underline the susceptibility of employed parents to difficulties in combining work and family roles. Research on the work–family interface in sub-Saharan Africa will contribute to an understanding of the contextual influences that shape the operation of the work–family interface in this continental region and thereby help ascertain the generalization of findings in the predominantly Western literature. Additionally, an understanding of the dynamics of the work–family interface will provide the knowledge base for global firms to design culturally appropriate organizational family-friendly initiatives to assist employed parents in sub-Saharan Africa balance their work and family roles. Given that formal wage employment is urban-skewed, the discussion in this chapter focuses on employed parents in urban sub-Saharan Africa.

Sub-Saharan Africa describes the region that stretches from south of the Sahara Desert to the southern tip of the continent and includes western, eastern, central, and southern Africa. Although the 46 countries that constitute this continental region are heterogeneous in terms of their colonial past, ethnic groups, and languages, they share a number of similarities, which include low levels of industrialization (with the exception of South Africa), massive rural–urban migration patterns, low rates of participation in formal wage employment, and a culturally collectivistic ethos. Because their similarities outweigh their differences, it is appropriate to treat sub-Saharan Africa as a homogenous entity in terms of the challenge of combining work and family roles.

THEORETICAL FRAMEWORK

Underpinned by role theory and informed by the scarcity hypothesis, the extant Western literature on the work–family interface has focused predominantly on the conflict that individuals with significant work and family responsibilities experience when they attempt to combine these responsibilities. The scarcity hypothesis is predicated on the assumption that individuals have a fixed amount of psychological and physiological resources to expend on their role obligations. Consequently, involvement in multiple roles will exhaust or drain these resources and ultimately impair one's psychological and physiological functioning (Edwards & Rothbard, 2000; Marks, 1977; Sieber, 1974; Zedeck & Mosier, 1990). Greenhaus and Beutell (1985, p. 77) define work–family conflict "as a form of inter role conflict in which role pressures from the work and family domains are mutually incompatible in some respect." Researchers have since embraced a bidirectional conceptualization of work–family conflict—family–work conflict describes the experience of family interfering with performance of the work-role while work–family conflict describes the experience of work interfering with the performance of the family role (Gutek, Searle, & Klepa, 1991). Figure 10.1 presents a conceptual model of the predominantly Western research on the work–family interface. Informed by Cohen and Wills' (1985) causal chain linking stress and well-being, this research examined the antecedents of family–work and work–family conflict and their moderators as the first point in the causal chain linking stress and well-being. The second point is represented by research that examined the outcomes of family–work and work–family conflict and moderators of these relationships. The rest of this section is devoted to a review of the research summarized in Figure 10.1.

Following from Greenhaus and Beutell's (1985) definition of work–family conflict, the extant research focused on strain- and time-based antecedents of family–work and work–family conflict. Although there is recognition that work and family domains are permeable (Eagle, Miles, & Icenogle, 1997; Pleck, 1977), much of this research focused on within domain stressors as antecedents of conflict originating within that domain. Performance of work and family roles require considerable amounts of time and energy, both of which are scarce resources. Consequently, instances that require simultaneous performance of work and family roles tend to precipitate time-based stressors or deplete one's energic resources which leads to family–work and work–family conflict.

Strain-based antecedents in the work domain include role conflict, role ambiguity, role overload, lack of autonomy, and job insecurity (Frone, Russell, & Cooper, 1992; Greenhaus & Beutell, 1985; Grandey & Cropanzano, 1999; Parasuraman, Purohit, Godshalk, & Beutell, 1996). These antecedents trigger tension and frustration culminating in work–family conflict. Time-based antecedents in the work domain are number of hours devoted to work per week and schedule inflexibility (Greenhaus & Beutell, 1985; Parasuraman et al., 1996; Thomas

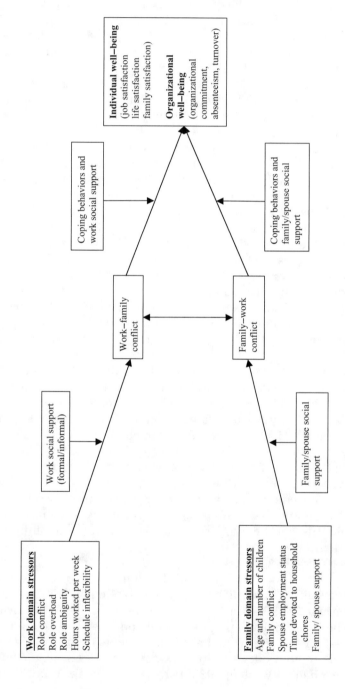

FIG. 10.1.   A western–model of the work–family interface.

& Ganster, 1995). Pertaining to the family domain, strain-based antecedents include family conflict, financial strain, and family expectations (Carlson, Kacmar, & Williams, 2000; Cooke & Rousseau, 1984; Frone, Yardley, & Markel, 1997; Kinnunen & Mauno, 1998), whereas time–based antecedents include number and age of children, spouse's work role salience, and spouse employment status (Bedeian, Burke, & Moffett, 1988; Carlson & Kacmar, 2000; Frone et al., 1997; Higgins, Duxbury, & Irving, 1992; Parasuraman et al., 1996).

Based on the stress model that underpins much of the research on the work–family interface, research has examined the moderators of the preceding antecedents and the stress reaction of family–work and work–family conflict. Typically, domain social support has been examined as moderator. Social support describes an interpersonal transaction that involves emotional concern, instrumental aid, information, or appraisal (House, 1981) and is generally conceived of as a coping mechanism in the stress literature (Gore, 1987). Sources of social support in the work domain include supervisor and co-worker support (Carlson & Perrewé, 1999; Etzion, 1984; Parasuraman, Greenhaus, & Granrose, 1992; Thomas & Ganster, 1995) and may be described as informal support. Formal sources of social support describe organizational family-friendly initiatives designed to assist employed parents reduce work–family conflict. These initiatives may help reduce work–family conflict by providing greater flexibility, reducing work hours, and providing child-care assistance (Glass & Estes, 1997). Family domain support has been conceptualized primarily in terms of spousal and/or family support (Adams, King, & King, 1996) and has been shown to ameliorate the negative consequences of family stressors on the experience of family–work conflict (Frone et al., 1997; Parasuraman et al., 1992). Essentially, interpersonal relationships within both the work and family domains constitute critical resources in attenuating the influence of domain stressors on work–family and family–work conflict.

As shown in Figure 10.1, work–family and family–work conflict have been linked to myriad individual and organizational outcomes such as job and life satisfaction, depression, organizational commitment, absenteeism, turnover, and role performance (Allen, Herst, Bluck, & Sutton, 2000; Bedeian et al., 1988; Frone et al., 1997; Parasuraman et al., 1996). As earlier noted, the second point in the causal chain linking stress and well–being (Cohen & Wills, 1985) suggests that adequate support intervenes between stress and well–being by reducing the stress reaction. Accordingly, much research has examined social support and coping behaviors as moderators of the relationship between work–family and family–work conflict on their demonstrated outcomes (Aryee, Luk, Leung, & Lo, 1999; Kossek, Noe, & DeMarr, 1999; Matsui, Oshawa, & Onglatco, 1995). Social support at this point in the causal chain linking stress and well-being performs a buffering role (Greenhaus & Parasuraman, 1994). This is because it enhances one's cognitive and behavioral coping abilities thereby enabling one to manage the stressful situation more effectively.

In summary, this section provided a brief review of the predominantly Western literature on the work–family interface and noted that the literature is underpinned by a stress perspective. The review suggests that the influence of role-related stressors (time- and strain–based) on work–family and family–work conflict is moderated by social support. Further, work–family and family–work conflict have negative consequences on individual and organizational well–being, which may be moderated by social support and coping behaviors. In the next section, we provide a discussion of the sociocultural and economic context of the work–family interface in urban sub-Saharan Africa and highlight salient contextual influences that shape the operation of the work–family interface.

The Family Context in Urban Sub-Saharan Africa

As in many parts of the world, the family constitutes the backbone of life in sub-Saharan Africa. The nuclear family into which individuals are born is an integral part of an extended family system that comprises a group of kinsfolk who share a common origin or descent. The collectivistic nature of African society is demonstrated through participation in social relationships in the context of the extended family. Family ties are particularly evident during significant periods in the life of a member, such as birth, marriage, and death. Given the emphasis on family, considerable cultural premium is attached to marriage and procreation. Although social life continues to take place in the context of the extended family, there is a discernible emphasis on the nuclear family particularly in the urban areas. In this section, we focus on the implications of family demands for the challenge of combining work and family roles. The high cost of raising children particularly in urban areas has led to a relative reduction in family size and the previously prevalent practice of polygamous marriage is experiencing a decline. However, family size in urban sub-Saharan Africa remains large requiring considerable investment of time and energic resources compared to the average family in the industrialized world.

In addition to the heavy parental demands, performance of household chores is aggravated by the absence of modern household conveniences. In much of sub-Saharan Africa, the rapid pace of urbanization has put considerable strain on the provision of utilities, such as electricity and water, resulting in frequent power outages and irregular water supply. Low reliability in the supply of utilities influences not only the timing of the performance of household chores but also the amount of effort that goes into such chores. Regardless of a household's ability to afford modern electrical household appliances, the frequent power outages creates uncertainty about when certain domestic chores can be performed, whereas some, such as family meals, will have to be prepared on a daily basis necessitating frequent trips to the markets. Consequently, time devoted to household chores and the demands performance of these chores make on energic resources of employed parents in urban sub-Saharan Africa are much greater than in the West.

Another feature of the family context in urban sub-Saharan Africa is elder care. In a context where nursing homes or homes for the aged remain foreign concepts, adult children (particularly daughters) are culturally expected to assume responsibility for the care and maintenance of their elderly parents. This is a particularly important responsibility because governments in sub-Saharan Africa do not provide social assistance for the elderly. Although the housing situation in urban sub-Saharan Africa makes this a short–term arrangement, it is not unusual for elderly parents to live with their adult children. Even when elderly parents live apart from their adult children, these children still have to visit frequently and generally assume responsibility for parenting their parents. Intergenerational parenting or caregiving contributes to the challenge of combining work and family roles in urban sub-Saharan Africa relative to the West.

Mikell (1997) identified retention of the ideology and language of familism in spite of changes in actual kinship behavior, as a trend that characterizes the contemporary family in sub-Saharan Africa. Although a nascent sense of individualism consequent upon urbanization and modernization has weakened extended family ties, it has yet to foster the demise of the extended family. As noted earlier, social life continues to take place in the context of the extended family. Obligations to the extended family albeit to a shrinking field of relatives, require considerable amount of time and energic resources. For example, funerals are rather elaborate for non-Muslims, and mourning periods may range from a couple of days to about 2 months depending on the closeness of the relationship. Further, extended family members who travel from rural areas to urban areas in search of employment or on a social visit may stay with a relative for short periods. Unlike the West, extended family obligations make demands on the time and energic resources of employed parents in urban sub-Saharan Africa contributing to the challenge they face in combining work and family roles.

Although elder care and obligations to the extended family make demands on the time and energic resources of employed parents in urban sub-Saharan Africa, it is worth noting, however, that relations with elderly parents and the extended family constitute sources of support. It is not unusual for elderly parents (usually grandmothers) to move in with an adult child to provide care for an infant beyond the period of the paid maternity leave. As a statutory benefit, the period of the paid maternity leave ranges from 30 to 105 days in sub-Saharan Africa (Neft & Levine, 1997, 74). Further, children of poor relatives are also often sent from rural areas to perform domestic responsibilities such as cooking and washing. In exchange for their services, they receive vocational training (Fapohunda, 1982). Even when social and spatial mobility make it difficult to obtain social support from elderly parents and/or mothers-in-law or kinsfolk, employed parents hire a "houseboy" and/or "housegirl." The "housegirl" usually assumes such domestic responsibilities as cooking and washing, whereas the "houseboy" performs such tasks as gardening, ironing, and yard maintenance. Domestic helpers are generally recruited from rural areas. In addition to providing for their board and lodging, they are paid a monthly stipend. Employment of domestic helpers constitutes the preserve of middle-class families because of the expense involved. For the vast majority of working class families, trusted neighbors (who become fictional kinsfolk in an urban setting) keep an eye on the children while older children help with domestic chores. In general, employed parents in urban sub-Saharan Africa have better access to social support (instrumental and emotional) than their Western counterparts, which attenuates the challenge of combining family and work roles.

The preceding discussion has highlighted distinctive features of the family context in urban sub-Saharan Africa relative to the West and the challenges and opportunities they present in terms of combining family and work roles. These challenges and opportunities can be distilled into propositions that suggest differences in the antecedents of family–work conflict in urban sub-Saharan Africa relative to the West.

Proposition 1: Family size (age and number of children) will be more strongly related to family–work conflict in urban sub-Saharan Africa than in the West.

Proposition 2: Absence of modern household appliances and irregular supply of utilities will be related to family–work conflict in urban sub-Saharan Africa but not in the West.

Proposition 3: Care of elderly parents as live-ins and/or dependents will be more strongly related to family–work conflict in urban sub-Saharan Africa than in the West.

Proposition 4: Obligations stemming from extended family ties will be related to family–work conflict in urban sub-Saharan Africa but not in the West.

The Work Context in Sub-Saharan Africa

The structure of the economies of sub-Saharan African countries comprises agriculture, industry, manufacturing, and service sectors. For many of these countries, agriculture has traditionally made a disproportionate contribution to gross domestic product (GDP). As shown in Table 10.1, the value-added contribution of agriculture as percent of GDP has been declining, although it remains relatively high compared to high income countries such as Britain and the United States. Further, the contribution of industry and manufacturing to GDP over the two time periods is rather modest. However, the service sector has emerged as a major contributor to GDP in countries such as Botswana, Ghana, Kenya, Mali, and South Africa, although its contribution in Cameroon, Nigeria, and Togo has experienced relative decline.

Much of the nonagricultural labor force in sub-Saharan Africa participates in the formal and informal sectors of the economy. The formal or modern sector is characterized by wage employment with defined terms of employment. This sector employs a small proportion of the labor force relative to the economically active population. As will be discussed later, wage employment in urban sub-Saharan African countries is declining sharply. The informal sector comprises "a range of economic units in urban areas which are largely owned and operated by single individuals with little capital and labor" (ILO World Labor Report, 1997/98).

The economies of sub-Saharan African countries have experienced low growth rates over the past three decades or so. The poor economic performance of the vast majority of countries in the region has been attributed to myriad factors including deteriorating terms of trade for its primary products, low capital investment, less investment in people, political instability, and the debt burden. To arrest the deteriorating trend in economic performance, a number of countries in sub-Saharan Africa implemented International Monetary Fund (IMF) and World Bank initiated structural adjustment programs. Although economic revitalization in Uganda and Ghana is credited to the structural adjustment program, it is argued that overall, these programs

TABLE 10.1
Structure of Output (Economy)

Economy	Gross Domestic Product Millions of Dollars		Value Added as a % of GDP Agriculture		Industry		Manufacturing		Services	
	1980	1998	1980	1998	1980	1998	1980	1998	1980	1998
Angola	—	6,648	—	14	—	54	—	5	—	32
Benin	1,405	22,322	35	39	12	14	8	8	52	47
Botswana	1,105	5,690	11	4	45	46	5	5	44	51
Cameroon	6,741	8,736	31	42	26	22	10	11	43	36
Cote d' Ivoire	10,175	11,041	26	25	20	23	13	19	54	52
Ghana	4,445	7,501	58	37	12	25	8	8	30	38
Kenya	7,265	11,083	33	29	21	16	13	10	47	55
Malawi	1,238	1,643	44	39	23	19	14	15	34	41
Mali	1,787	2,695	48	45	13	21	7	6	38	34
Nigeria	64,202	41,353	21	32	46	41	8	5	34	27
Senegal	2,986	4,836	19	17	15	23	11	15	66	59
South Africa	78,744	116,730	7	4	50	38	23	24	43	57
Tanzania[a]	—	7,917	—	46	—	14	—	7	—	40
Togo	1,136	1,510	27	42	25	21	8	9	48	37
Uganda	1,244	6,653	72	43	4	18	4	9	23	39
Zambia	3,884	3,352	14	16	41	30	18	12	44	55
Zimbabwe	6,679	5,908	16	18	29	24	22	17	55	58
World	10,939,459t	28,854,043t	7w	5w	38w	-w	25w	20w	56w	61w
Sub–Saharan Africa	270,391	316,517	18	17	39	34	16	19	43	50
United Kingdom	537,389	1,357,429	2	2	43	31	27	21	55	67
United States	2,709,000	8,210,600	3	2	33	27	22	18	64	71

Note. [a]Data cover mainland Tanzania only.
Source. World Bank (2000). Entering the 21st century: World Bank development report 1999/2000.

have had a negative social impact. Retrenchments in the civil service and the inability of the private sector to absorb the retrenched workers has led to a growing informalization of the economies of sub-Saharan African countries (ILO World Labor Report, 1997/98). It should, however, be noted that the economic performance of African countries as a whole has improved moderately in the past 3 years. For example, real GDP growth in 2001 was estimated at 3.4% compared to 3.2% in 2000 and the number of countries that experienced negative growth declined from 9 to 5 (African Development Bank Report, 2002).

The preceding discussion of the economic performance of sub-Saharan African countries and organizational responses to a dismal economic environment provide a necessary backdrop for a discussion of features of the work context that constitute challenges for combining work and family roles in urban sub-Saharan Africa. A source of challenge or stress is job insecurity. In the past decade or so, much has been written about the changing nature of the employment relationship in the developed economies and the job insecurity that this has precipitated (Kissler, 1994; Lewis & Cooper, 1999; Parks & Kidder, 1990; Rousseau & Wade-Benzoni, 1995). The nature of the employment relationship is shaped in part by the cultural context (Thomas, Au, & Ravlin, 2003). The collectivistic orientation of sub-Saharan African countries as embodied in the extended family system finds expression in the organizational context as organizational familism. The extended family is characterized by the exchange of socioemotional and economic resources among its members. Aryee (2004) noted that much like the extended family, organizational familism leads to an expectation on the part of employees that the organization will take care of their socioemotional and material needs in exchange for promoting the interests of the organization. The implementation of structural adjustment and, more recently, economic liberalization programs has changed the traditional employment relationship. Under pressure to respond to market forces, many public and private sector organizations have retrenched employees, signaling the dawn of an emergent transactional employment relationship. Consequently, job insecurity has emerged as a major source of stress in urban sub-Saharan Africa. Although job insecurity is also prevalent in the developed economies, the absence of public social assistance programs makes the threat of job insecurity much more stressful and constitutes a salient source of stress in the work domain. Lewis and Cooper (1999, 385) noted that "With the fundamental shift away from long–term careers in one or two organizations, work–family research can no longer afford to neglect the impact of the erosion of job security."

Job insecurity in a context of high unemployment has revolution-
ized work habits in urban sub-Saharan Africa. For example, it has
minimized tardiness and increased the amount of time employees
spend in the workplace. There is evidence in the predominantly Western literature that employees are working longer hours leading to increased levels of work–family conflict (Major, Klein, & Ehrhart, 2002;
Wallace, 1999). In the context of sub-Saharan Africa, the concept of
working hours needs to be broadened to include not only hours spent
in formal employment but also time devoted to income generating activities. A growing number of employees in urban sub-Saharan Africa
moonlight as petty traders. A major determinant of the increased
hours devoted to income generating activities is inadequate or low
pay. In tandem with the decline in employment opportunities in the
formal sector is a fall in wages as inflation eroded the real value of
wages. Real wages reportedly declined by about 30% between 1980
and 1986, and the real minimum wage fell by 20% (ILO World Labor
Report, 1993). Indeed, Ghadially and Kumar (1989), using a sample of Indian teachers, reported inadequate pay as a major stressor
but not role overload, which has been shown to constitute a stressor in the Western literature. Inadequate pay is not only a potential
source of stress in urban sub-Saharan Africa but also motivates an
increased investment of time and energic resources into income generating activities, another potential source of stress. However, in the
collectivistic societies of sub-Saharan Africa, time devoted to income-
generating activities is not considered as a sacrifice of the family but
rather, as a sacrifice for the family (Aryee, Fields, & Luk, 1999; Yang,
Chen, Choi, & Zou, 2000). This is in contrast to an individualistic
society where, because of the emphasis on personal accomplishment
and achievement, time devoted to work is considered as fulfilling personal ambition and, therefore, a sacrifice of the family. Based on the
preceding arguments, we expect inadequate pay to be more strongly
related to work–family conflict in urban sub-Saharan Africa relative
to the West. However, we expect time devoted to income-generating activities not to be as strongly related to work–family conflict in urban
sub-Saharan Africa as in the West.

The implementation of structural adjustment and economic liberalization programs has put considerable emphasis on performance
as a primary determinant of continued employment. The previous
life–time employment particularly in the public sector meant that
employees experienced little or no pressure to perform to their potential. Consequently, stress from work-related demands, a major
source of stress in the predominantly Western literature, was rather
inconsequential in urban sub-Saharan Africa. Although the increased

emphasis on performance in response to competitive pressures has precipitated performance anxiety, it is doubtful whether work-related demands would constitute a major source of stress as in the West. This is because performance is not as closely linked to rewards in urban sub-Saharan Africa as in the West. Human resource practices in sub-Saharan Africa have been noted to have a particularistic tone (Kamoche, 1993). Although many organizations have adopted the bureaucratic means of formalism and hierarchy, the cultural premium placed on interpersonal relations has led to a situation in which these bureaucratic means have been harnessed to particularistic ends. The high power distance that characterizes sub-Saharan African countries has found structural expression in centralized decision making in organizations. In a context of resource scarcity and limited opportunities for improving one's economic circumstances, employees are acutely aware of their dependence on supervisors. In the absence of objective criteria on which reward decisions are based, personal favors play an important role in decisional outcomes. Anxiety about resource allocation decisional outcomes has led to proactive behaviors on the part of employees to influence these outcomes leading to a high degree of organizational politics. Although perceptions of organizational politics have been noted to constitute a source of stress (Ferris, Frink, Galang, Zhou, Kacmar, & Howard, 1996), its influence on work–family conflict has not been examined. In view of the preceding arguments, we expect anxiety about resource allocation decisional outcomes to be more strongly related to work–family conflict in urban sub-Saharan Africa than in the West.

Social support has long been recognized as a critical resource in ameliorating the negative consequences of stress on well-being (Cohen & Wills, 1985; House, 1981). Research on the work–family interface has identified supervisor and co-worker support as informal sources of support in reducing work–family conflict (Anderson, Coffey, & Byerly, 2002; Greenhaus & Parasuraman, 1999; Thomas & Ganster, 1995). The emphasis on interpersonal relations suggests that supervisor and co-worker support will also constitute a critical resource in reducing work–family conflict in urban sub-Saharan Africa, as shown in the Western literature. Currently, the emphasis in workplace social support is on formal rather than informal support. Formal workplace social support is defined by organizational family-friendly initiatives or policies. Glass and Finley (2002, 321) classified these policies into three categories: parental leave (policies and benefits that reduce work hours to provide time for family caregiving), flexible work arrangements (policies designed to give workers greater flexibility in scheduling hours, while not decreasing average hours worked per week), and employer-supported child care (policies designed to provide work-place social support for parents). The reinforcement of such policies by an organizational family-friendly culture may reduce work–family conflict (Clark, 2001; Thomas & Ganster, 1995; Thompson, Beau-vais, & Lyness, 1999). In urban sub-Saharan Africa, the challenge of managing the work–family interface has yet to emerge as a legitimate business concern. With the exception of paid maternity leave (a statu-tory benefit) and days off to take care of sick children and to attend funerals, employed parents depend on their resourcefulness to man-age the work–family interface. Lacking the formal workplace social support available to their counterparts in the developed economies of the West, we expect workplace social support (formal) not to play a sig-nificant role in reducing work–family conflict in urban sub-Saharan Africa as in the West.

Our propositions linking stressors in the work context to work–family conflict in urban sub-Saharan Africa are:

Proposition 6: Job insecurity will be more strongly related to work–family conflict in urban sub-Saharan Africa than in the West.

Proposition 7: Inadequate pay will be more strongly related to work–family conflict in urban sub-Saharan Africa than in the West.

Proposition 8: Time devoted to income-generating activities will not be related to work–family conflict in urban sub-Saharan Africa but will be related to work–family con-flict in the West.

Proposition 9: Anxiety over resource allocation decisions (organiza-tional politics) will be more strongly related to work–family conflict in urban sub-Saharan Africa than in the West.

Proposition 10: Workplace social support (formal) will more strongly reduce work–family conflict in the West relative to ur-ban sub-Saharan Africa.

TOWARDS A MODEL OF THE WORK–FAMILY INTERFACE IN URBAN SUB-SAHARAN AFRICA

The gist of the preceding section is that the Western-inspired model of the work–family interface (specifically, work–family and family–work conflict) does not fully reflect the dynamics of the work–family in-terface in urban sub-Saharan Africa. Figure 10.2 presents a model of the work–family interface that incorporates contextual influences

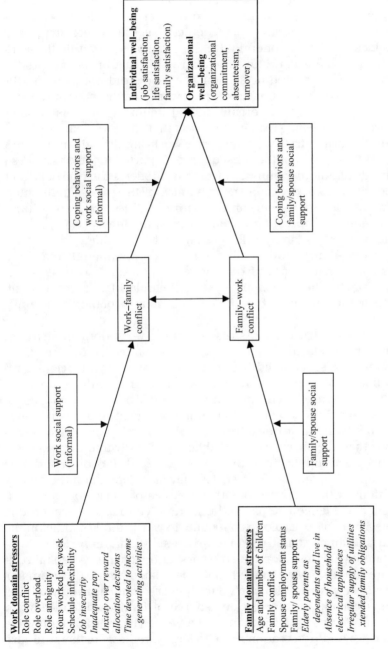

Work domain stressors
Role conflict
Role overload
Role ambiguity
Hours worked per week
Schedule inflexibility
Job insecurity
Inadequate pay
Anxiety over reward
allocation decisions
Time devoted to income
generating activities

Work social support
(informal)

Coping behaviors and
work social support
(informal)

Work–family
conflict

Family–work
conflict

Coping behaviors and
family/spouse social
support

Family/spouse social
support

Family domain stressors
Age and number of children
Family conflict
Spouse employment status
Family/ spouse support
Elderly parents as
dependents and live in
Absence of household
electrical appliances
Irregular supply of utilities
xtended family obligations

Individual well-being
(job satisfaction,
life satisfaction,
family satisfaction)

Organizational
well–being
(organizational
commitment,
absenteeism,
turnover)

FIG. 10.2. A model of the work–family interface in urban sub-
Saharan Africa.

*Italicize stressors are context-specific.

(sociocultural and economic) and purports to extend the Western-inspired model of the work–family interface. Essentially, the model posits that there are similarities and differences in the antecedents of work–family and family–work conflict. The differences stem from the sociocultural and economic stressors that operate within the work and family domains in urban sub-Saharan Africa. Consistent with the discussion in the preceding section, the model did not focus on the demonstrated negative consequences of work–family and family–work conflict on individual and organizational well-being. This is because there are no compelling reasons to expect that employed parents in urban sub-Saharan Africa will experience work–family and family–work conflict differently from the consequences reported in the extant Western literature. Another omission from our model is the role of gender in moderating experience of the dynamics of the work–family interface. Watanabe, Takahashi, and Minami (1997) noted two cultural universals in the operation of the work–family interface: (a) gender inequality whereby family roles are allowed to intrude into women's work, whereas men's work roles can intrude upon family and (b) a gender-role transition away from role separation and toward a gender-neutral society. These phenomena suggest similarities rather than differences in the influence of gender on the dynamics of the work–family interface.

As shown in Figure 10.2, stressors in the work domain stem not only from role–related demands but also from interpersonal relations with supervisors. As noted previously, unclear performance and reward allocation criteria generate considerable anxiety that employees proactively manage by engaging in ingratiatory behaviors such as favor rendering. In a context of high unemployment, job security may depend not so much on objective criteria but on relations with supervisors. Further, the absence of formal family-friendly initiatives suggest that workplace support in terms of work schedule flexibility and time off to respond to family emergencies may also depend on the quality of relations with supervisors. Other sources of work domain stressors, such as inadequate pay and time devoted to income-generating activities, are not expected to contribute to work–family conflict in the West to the same extent they do in urban sub-Saharan Africa.

Pertaining to family domain stressors, although interpersonal relations are important, we argued that role related demands are major sources of stress and ultimately, family–work conflict. Family-related demands constitute a far greater source of family–work conflict in urban sub-Saharan Africa than in the West. The cultural emphases on marriage and procreation leads to large families. Further, the care of elderly parents, and in some cases as dependents, increases the parental demands on adult children. This is further aggravated by intergenerational differences in values and the ensuing conflict. Family-related demands may also stem from social and financial obligations to the extended family. It must, however, be emphasized that elderly parents and the extended family constitute potential sources of support in terms of child care and performance of household chores. Thus, although family–related demands constitute stressors, they may also serve as a support network to a degree that is unknown in the West. Lastly, the absence of modern household appliances, especially in working class homes, coupled with the irregular supply of water and frequent power outages add to the time devoted to performing household chores and demands on energic resources leading to family–work conflict.

DISCUSSION

This chapter sought to extend the Western model of the work–family interface by theoretically examining contextual influences on the dynamics of the work–family interface in urban sub-Saharan Africa. It was argued that the processes through which stressors in the work and family domains culminate in work–family and family–work conflict and their resulting outcomes in terms of individual and organizational well-being may generalize across cultural contexts. However, differences in sociocultural and economic contexts suggest that sources of stress in the work and family domains may differ not only across sociocultural contexts but also across levels of economic development. For example, pertaining to the level of economic development, it was noted that power outages and frequent interruptions in water supply in urban sub-Saharan Africa increase the time devoted to performing household chores and the demands on energic resources. Further and because of the stress model that informs research on the dynamics of the work–family interface, social support is considered a critical resource in mitigating the experience of and the negative consequences of work–family and family–work conflict. It was argued that although the role of social support in the dynamics of the work–family interface may generalize across sociocultural contexts, the sources of support may differ across contexts. Social support may be obtained from work and family domains. However, the conspicuous absence of formal workplace social support suggests that in urban sub-Saharan Africa, social support is obtained primarily from the family domain. In spite of the relative weakening of the extended family system, elderly parents and female relatives constitute a social support system. As previously noted, the relationship between adult children and their elderly parents is a symbiotic arrangement that on one hand is a source of stress and on the other, a source of social support. Given the pace of urbanization and modernization, it remains to be seen how long employed parents in urban sub-Saharan Africa can continue to depend on female relatives as a support system. Oppong (1997) pointed to a possible future scenario when she noted that "Increasing social and spatial mobility is having insidious effects upon kin solidarity, which in a former era ensured survival in time of crisis and disaster."

As Watanabe et al. (1997) observed, gender inequality constitutes a universal feature of the work–family interface. As elsewhere, employed mothers in urban sub-Saharan Africa are primarily responsible for household and child-care responsibilities and therefore, "suffer from the double day that afflicts most working women in the West" (Parpart, 1990, 173–174). In a study of urban Yoruba mothers, Di Domenico, de Cola, and Leishman (1987) reported women's suggestions for change and improvement centered on child-care arrangements and flexibility. Specifically, they indicated shorter working hours, part-time jobs, some form of financial assistance for improved care, and provision of nursery schools. The findings of Di Domenico et al.'s (1987) study suggest an organizational and even societal role in assisting employed parents to combine their work and family roles. The rationale for the adoption of such policies has been based on the negative implications of work and family imbalance for work attitudes and behaviors such as low levels of commitment, lateness, absenteeism, turnover, and low productivity (Glass & Finley, 2002; Thomas & Ganster, 1995). Given the expense involved in implementing employer-supported child care, organizations in urban sub-Saharan Africa should experiment with formal family-responsive policies such as parental leave (e.g., leave for emergency child care, illness) and flexible work arrangements (e.g., flextime) in addition to informal policies such as supervisor support. In a study of employed parents in Ghana, Aryee, Tan, & Debrah (2004) reported that informal policies such as supervisory support and work schedule flexibility influenced the work outcomes of job satisfaction and psychological withdrawal behavior through perceived organizational support. In effect, the increasingly tenuous nature of the family-based social support system suggests an organizational role in assisting employed parents in urban sub-Saharan Africa integrate their work and family responsibilities.

A major limitation of research on the work–family interface is the focus on conflict or stress. Greenhaus (1989, 30) noted "Much of the research on the relationship between work and family has been somewhat negative in that, it tends to emphasize the dysfunctional consequences of work–family interactions." Although conflict and stress are inherent in the operation of the work–family interface, there is recognition of the social psychological benefits that stem from participating in the work and family domains (Barnett, 1998; Thoits, 1983). Based on the expansion/enhancement hypothesis, and in order to redress the conflict paradigm in research on the work–family interface, there is a growing interest in understanding how work and family experiences enrich the lives of individuals (Barnett, 1998; Frone, 2003; Greenhaus & Parasuraman, 1999). The enhancement hypothesis posits that rather than lead to the depletion of an individual's psychological and physiological resources, involvement in multiple roles provides a number of benefits that may outweigh the costs leading to net gratification rather than strain. Because conflict and enhancement are inherent in participation in work and family roles, a better understanding of the work–family interface requires an integration of the scarcity and enhancement hypotheses or as Frone (2003) noted, should include both conflict and facilitation. He defined work–family facilitation as "the extent to which participation at work (home) is made easier by virtue of the experiences, skills and opportunities gained or developed at home (work)." Frone (2003) suggested a four-fold taxonomy of work–family balance along the primary dimensions of (i) direction of influence between work and family roles (work to family versus family to work) and (ii) type of effect (conflict versus facilitation). Empirical research in both Western and non-Western contexts has since provided empirical support for Frone's four-fold taxonomy of work–family balance (Aryee, Srinivas, & Tan, in press; Grzyuracz & Marks, 2000; Wayne, Musisca, & Fleeson, 2004).

SUGGESTIONS FOR FUTURE RESEARCH

In addition to a rigorous empirical examination of the propositions, several issues that stem from the discussions in this chapter suggest directions for research on the dynamics of the work–family interface in urban sub-Saharan Africa. First, research should examine how employed parents socially construct the work–family interface. Specifically, research using qualitative techniques such as in-depth interviews should examine the subjective experience of conflict and facilitation and the ways in which work and family roles are socially constructed that contribute meaning to the lives of employed parents in urban sub-Saharan Africa. This form of grounded research will help conceptualize and develop indigenous measures of conflict and facilitation components of work–family balance.

Second, the adaptive strategies used by employed parents in urban sub-Saharan Africa deserve research attention. In a recent study based on a U.S. sample, Becker and Moen (1999) identified three such strategies—placing limits, having a one-job, one-career marriage, and trading off. It has been noted that in collectivistic societies, time devoted to work is considered a sacrifice for the family and not of the family (Yang et al., 2000). In view of this, research should examine the extent to which Becker and Moen's (1999) findings in the individualistic context of the United States generalize to the collectivistic societies of sub-Saharan Africa.

Third, research should examine a comprehensive model of the work–family interface in urban sub-Saharan Africa. This model should not only focus on the antecedents and outcomes of work–family balance (conflict and facilitation) but on the moderators and mediators of these relationships. Some moderators that could be examined in the context of urban sub-Saharan Africa include socioeconomic status, gender, ethnicity, and sector of employment (formal or informal). Globalization and the implementation of economic liberalization policies in sub-Saharan Africa have exposed indigenous organizations to competitive pressures from global firms. These competitive pressures are forcing indigenous organizations to rethink the role of human resources in organizational performance (Kamoche, Debrah, Horowitz, & Muuka, 2004). Given the demonstrated negative consequences of work–family imbalance in the Western literature, indigenous organizations should consider implementing family-responsive initiatives to assist employed parents reduce work–family conflict or enhance work–family facilitation. Accordingly, a final direction for future research is to examine employed parents' preferences for family-responsive initiatives.

In conclusion, this chapter has provided a theoretical analysis of the contextual influences on the dynamics of the work–family interface in urban sub-Saharan Africa. As balancing work and family roles becomes a challenge in almost all contemporary societies, work–family research should embrace an international or cross-cultural focus if it is to provide a more complete and culturally-informed understanding of the dynamics of the work–family interface. It is hoped that the discussions in this chapter and the suggested directions for future research will contribute to this enterprise and thereby provide insights into "... ... the different ways in which work and family issues are constructed cross–nationally" (Lewis & Cooper, 1999, 389).

REFERENCES

Adams, G. A., King, L. A., & King, D. W. (1996). Relationships of job and family involvement, family social support, and work–family conflict with job and life satisfaction. *Journal of Applied Psychology, 81*, 411–420.

African Development Bank (2002). *Africa Development Report. Rural development for poverty reduction in Africa.* London: Oxford University Press.

Allen, T. D., Herst, D. E. L., Bluck, C. S., & Sutton, M. (2000). Consequences associated with work-to-family conflict: A review and agenda for future research. *Journal of Occupational Health Psychology, 5*, 278–308.

Anderson, S. E., Coffey, B. S., & Byerly, R. T. (2002). Formal organizational initiatives and informal workplace practices: Links to work–family and job-related outcomes. *Journal of Management, 28*, 787–810.

Aryee, S. (2004). *Human resources management in Ghana.* In K. Kamoche, Y. A. Debrah, F. Horowitz, & G. N. Muuka (Eds.), *Managing human resources in Africa* (pp. 121–133). London: Routledge.

Aryee, S., Fields, D., & Luk, V. (1999). A cross-cultural test of a model of the work–family interface. *Journal of Management, 25*, 491–511.

Aryee, S., Luk, V., Leung, A., & Lo, S. (1999). Role stressors, interrole conflict, and well-being. *Journal of Vocational Behavior, 54*, 259–278.

Aryee, S., Srinivas, E. S., & Tan, H. H. (in press). Rhythms of life: Antecedents and outcomes of work–family balance in employed parents. *Journal of Applied Psychology.*

Aryee, S., Tan, H. H., & Debrah, Y. A. (2004). *Family-supportive work environment and perceived organizational support: Mechanism and outcomes.* Manuscript submitted for publication.

Barnett, R. C. (1998). Toward a review and reconceptualization of the work/family literature. *Genetic, Social, and General Psychology Monographs, 124*, 125–182.

Becker, P. E., & Moen, P. (1999). Scaling back: Dual-earner couples' work–family strategies. *Journal of Marriage and the Family, 61*, 995–1007.

Bedeian, A. G., Burke, B. G., & Moffett, R. G. (1988). Outcomes of work–family conflict among married male and female professionals. *Journal of Management, 14*, 475–491.

Carlson, D. S., Kacmar, K. M., & Williams, L. J. (2000). Construction and initial validation of a multidimensional measure of work–family conflict. *Journal of Vocational Behavior, 56*, 249–276.

Carlson, D. S., & Perrewé, P. L. (1999). The role of social support in the stressor–strain relationship: An examination of work–family conflict. *Journal of Management, 25*, 513–540.

Clark, S. C. (2001). Work cultures and work/family balance. *Journal of Vocational Behavior, 58*, 348–365.

Cohen, S., & Wills, T. A. (1985). Stress, social support, and the buffering hypothesis. *Psychological Bulletin, 98*, 310–357.

Cooke, R., & Rousseau, D. (1984). Stress and strain from family roles and work–role expectations. *Journal of Applied Psychology, 69*, 252–260.

Di Domenico, C., de. Cola, L., & Leishman, J. (1987). *Urban Yoruba mothers at home and at work*. In C. Oppong (Ed.), *Sex roles, population and development in West Africa* (pp. 118–132). Portsmouth, NH: Heineman.

Eagle, B. W., Miles, E. W., & Icenogle, M. L. (1997). Interrole conflicts and permeability of work and family domains: Are there gender differences? *Journal of Vocational Behavior, 50,* 168–184.

Edwards, J. R., & Rothbard, N. P. (2000). Mechanisms linking work and family: Specifying the relationships between work and family constructs. *Academy of Management Review, 25,* 178–199.

Etzion, D. (1984). Moderation effect of social support on the stress–burnout relationship. *Journal of Applied Psychology, 69,* 615–622.

Fapohunda, E. R. (1982). *The child-care dilemma of working mothers in African cities. The case of Lagos, Nigeria.* In E. G. Bay (Ed.), *Women and work in Africa* (pp. 277–288). Boulder, CO: Westview Press.

Ferris, G. R., Frink, D. D., Galang, M. C., Zhou, J., Kacmar, K. M., & Howard, J. E. (1996). Perceptions of organizational politics: Predictions, stress-related implications and outcomes. *Human Relations, 49,* 233–266.

Frone, M. R. (2003). *Work–family balance.* In J. C. Quick & L. E. Tetrick (Eds.), *Handbook of occupational health psychology* (pp. 143–162). Washington, DC: American Psychological Association.

Frone, M. R., Russell, M., & Cooper, M. L. (1992). Antecedents and outcomes of work–family conflict: Testing a model of the work–family interface. *Journal of Applied Psychology, 77,* 65–75.

Frone, M. R., Yardley, J. K., & Markel, K. (1997). Developing and testing an integrative model of the work–family interface. *Journal of Vocational Behavior, 50,* 145–167.

Ghadially, R., & Kumar, P. (1989). Stress, strain and coping styles of female professionals. *Indian Journal of Applied Psychology, 26,* 1–8.

Glass, J. L., & Estes, S. B. (1997). The family responsive workplace. *Annual Review of Sociology, 23,* 289–313.

Glass, J. L., & Finley, A. (2002). Coverage and effectiveness of family-responsive workplace policies. *Human Resources Management Review, 12,* 313–337.

Gore, S. (1987). Perspectives on social support and research on stress moderating processes. *Journal of Organizational Behavior Management, 8,* 85–101.

Grandey, A. A., & Cropanzano, R. (1999). The conservation of resources model applied to work–family conflict and strain. *Journal of Vocational Behavior, 54,* 350–370.

Greenhaus, J. (1989). The intersection of work and family roles: Individual, interpersonal and organizational issues. In E. B. Goldsmith (Ed.), *Work and family: Theory research and applications.* Newbury Park: Sage.

Greenhaus, J. H., & Beutell, N. J. (1985). Sources of conflict between work and family roles. *Academy of Management Review, 10,* 76–88.

Greenhaus, J. H., & Parasuraman, S. (1994). Work–family conflict, social support, and well–being. In M. J. Davidson & R. J. Burke (Eds.), *Women in management: Current research issues* (pp. 213–229). London: Paul Chapman.

Greenhaus, J. H., & Parasuraman, S. (1999). Research on work, family, and gender: Current status and future directions. In G. N. Powell (Ed.), *Handbook of gender and work* (pp. 391–412). Thousand Oaks, CA: Sage.

Grzywacz, J. G., & Marks, N. F. (2000). Reconceptualizing the work–family interface: An ecological perspective on the correlates of positive and negative spillover between work and family. *Journal of Occupational Health Psychology, 5,* 111–126.

Gutek, B. A., Searle, S., & Klepa, L. (1991). Rational versus gender role expectations for work–family conflict. *Journal of Applied Psychology, 76,* 560–568.

Higgins, C. A., Duxbury, L. E., & Irving, R. H. (1992). Work–family conflict in the dual-career family. *Organizational Behavior and Human Decision Processes, 51,* 51–75.

House, G. S. (1981). *Work stress and social support.* Reading, MA: Addison-Wesley.

ILO (1993). *World Labor Report.* Geneva: International Labor Office.

ILO World Labor Report (1997–1998). *Industrial relations, democracy and social stability.* Geneva: International Labor Office.

Kamoche, K. (1993). *Toward a model of HRM in Africa.* In J. B. Shaw, P. S. Kirkbride, & K. M. Rowland (Eds.), *Research in personnel and human resources* (Supplement 3; pp. 259–278). Greenwich, CT: JAI.

Kinnunen, U., & Mauno, S. (1998). Antecedents and outcomes of work–family conflict among employed women and men in Finland. *Human Relations, 51,* 157–177.

Kissler, G. D. (1994). The new psychological contract. *Human Resource Management, 33,* 335–352.

Kossek, E. E., Noe, R. A., & DeMarr, B. J. (1999). Work–family role synthesis: Individual and organizational determinants. *International Journal of Conflict Resolution, 10,* 102–129.

Lewis, S., & Cooper, C. L. (1999). The work–family research agenda in changing contexts. *Journal of Occupational Health Psychology, 4,* 382–392.

Major, V. S., Klein, K. J., & Ehrhart, M. G. (2002). Work time, work interference with family and psychological distress. *Journal of Applied Psychology, 87,* 427–436.

Marks, S. R. (1977). Multiple roles and role strain. *American Sociological Review, 42,* 921–936.

Matsui, T., Oshawa, T., & Onglatco, M. L. (1995). Work–family conflict and the stress-buffering effects of husband support and coping behavior among Japanese married, working women. *Journal of Vocational Behavior, 47,* 178–192.

Mikell, G. (1997). Modern crisis and the renegotiation of African familial relations. In G. L. Anderson (Ed.), *The family in global transition* (pp. 141–178). St. Paul, MN: PWPA Book.

Neft, N., & Levine, A. D. (1997). *Where women stand: An international report on the status of women in 140 countries.* New York: Random House.

Oppong, C. (1997). African family systems and socio–economic crisis. In A. Adepoju (Ed.), *Family, population and development in Africa* (pp. 158–182). London: Zed Books Ltd.

Parks, J. M., & Kidder, D. L. (1990). Till death do us part... ...changing work relationships in the 1990s. In C. L. Cooper & D. M. Rousseau (Eds.), *Trends in organizational behavior* (Vol. 1, pp. 111–136). New York: Wiley.

Parpart, J. L. (1990). Wage earning women and the double day: The Nigerian case. In S. Sticher & J. L. Parpart (Eds.), *Women, employment and the family in the international division of labor* (pp. 161–182). London: MacMillan.

Parasuraman, S., Greenhaus, J. H., & Granrose, C. S. (1992). Role stressors, social support and well–being among two–career couples. *Journal of Organizational Behavior, 13*, 339–356.

Parasuraman, S., Purohit, Y. S., Godshalk, V. M., & Beutell, N. J. (1996). Work and family variables, entrepreneurial career success, and psychological well–being. *Journal of Vocational Behavior, 48*, 275–300.

Pleck, J. H. (1977). The work–family role system. *Social Problems, 24*, 417–427.

Rousseau, D. M., & Wade-Benzoni, K. A. (1995). Changing individual–organization attachments: A two–way street. In A. Howard (Ed.), *The changing nature of work* (pp. 290–322). San Francisco: Jossey-Bass.

Sieber, S. D. (1974). Toward a theory of role accumulation. *American Sociological Review, 39*, 567–578.

Thoits, P. A. (1983). Multiple identities and psychological well-being: A reformulation and test of the social isolation hypothesis. *American Sociological Review, 48*, 174–187.

Thomas, D. C., Au, K., & Ravlin, E. C. (2003). Cultural variation and the psychological contract. *Journal of Organizational Behavior, 24*, 451–471.

Thomas, L. T., & Ganster, D. C. (1995). Impact of family-supportive work variables on work–family conflict and strain: A control perspective. *Journal of Applied Psychology, 80*, 6–15.

Thompson, C. A., Beauvais, L. L., & Lyness, K. S. (1999). When work–family benefits are not enough: The influence of work–family culture on benefit utilization, organizational attachment, and work–family conflict. *Journal of Vocational Behavior, 54*, 392–415.

Wallace, J. E. (1999). Work to non-work conflict among married male and female lawyers. *Journal of Organizational Behavior, 20*, 797–816.

Watanabe, S., Takahashi, K., & Minami, T. (1997). The emerging role of diversity and work–family values in a global context. In P. C. Earley & M. Erez (Eds.), *New perspectives on international industrial/organizational psychology* (pp. 319–332). San Francisco: New Lexington Press.

Wayne, J. H., Musisca, N., & Fleeson, W. (2004). Considering the role of personality in the work–family experience: Relationships of the big five to work–family conflict and facilitation. *Journal of Vocational Behavior, 64*, 108–130.

Yang, N., Chen, C. C., Choi, J., & Zou, Y. (2000). Sources of work–family conflict: A Sino-US comparison of the effects of work and family demands. *Academy of Management Journal, 41*, 113–123.

Zedeck, S., & Mosier, K. L. (1990). Work in the family and employing organization. *American Psychologist, 45*, 240–251.

ANNEX

Case Study: It's Tough Being a Dual-Earner Couple in Timbuktu

Veronique and her husband, Henri, are members of the growing number of dual-earner couples in the ancient city of Timbuktu, in the West African country of Mali. They have two children, Henri Junior, aged 5 and Louise, aged 7. They attend an international school in downtown Timbuktu. Veronique is employed by a subsidiary of a French cosmetics manufacturing company as an executive assistant to the managing director. Her job requires her to work long hours and the occasional overnight work-related trips. Although she considers her role as mother and spouse important to her identity, she derives considerable satisfaction from her job. Indeed, she claims that her work-related experiences have helped her at home in terms of delegating, communication, and organizing. Her husband, Henri, attests to his wife's effectiveness in the performance of her domestic responsibilities. He also thinks Veronique is not utilizing her potential to the fullest and has been encouraging her to pursue a Master's degree in business administration to prepare for a career change.

Henri works as an assistant financial controller with an American mining operation headquartered in Timbuktu. His work requires frequent business-related travels to the company's operations in the West African sub-region. Although he is among the top 2% of salaried professionals in that country, the family needs Veronique to be a co-provider. This is because of the financial demands that Henri's family makes on him. Indeed, he is helping to put two of his younger siblings through school. Veronique considers Henri an unusual husband because of his pro-liberal views in a society where gender roles are firmly etched on the consciousness of individuals. Henri shares household and child-care responsibilities with Veronique when he is not away on business trips, which is more the norm than the exception. However, Henri's mother, who lives with them, frowns on this and complains about her son being a hen-pecked husband. This is a source of tension between Veronique and her mother-in-law. The mother-in-law helps out with domestic responsibilities when her rheumatic pains are bearable, which is not very often. Because she does not speak

French and her grandchildren do not speak her dialect, there is little interaction between her and the grandchildren.

As an indication of their middle class status, Veronique and her family have a range of modern electrical household appliances. However, frequent power outages make it impossible for them to use these appliances so household chores are performed manually. In addition, the tap runs only between 3 and 5 am so she has to be up early to store water. The demands of her household responsibilities make her perennially tired. To manage her work and family responsibilities, she has occasionally expressed an interest in working part-time. However, this form of flexible work arrangement is not available to Malians in formal wage employment. Recently, her boss complained about her tardiness and reminded her of the company's expectation that employees keep their work and family roles separate. With her pride hurt, Veronique thought about quitting her job or even withdrawing from paid employment but she knew that was not an option. Henri also complains about his limited family time and even turned down a promotion to the position of financial controller. Although it has been evident to them that they needed to take a fresh look at their lives, they have always resisted the thought. That was before Veronique met a childhood friend who complained about her baggy eyes and haggard looks.

QUESTIONS

1. List the work and family demands that Henri and Veronique face as a dual-earner couple. Would you attribute these demands to the sociocultural context of Mali?
2. Do you think the work and family domains are differentially permeable for Henri and Veronique? Explain your answer.
3. Explain negative and positive spillover as used in the work–family literature. Discuss instances of each in the case.
4. How would you describe Veronique's company's work–family culture? Could such a culture constitute a source of competitive advantage? Why or why not?
5. As an HR consultant, how would your understanding of the sociocultural context of Mali and its level of economic development influence the family-friendly initiatives you would recommend to a global firm intending to set up an operation in that country?

11

Individualism–Collectivism and Work–Family Interfaces: A Sino–U.S. Comparison

Nini Yang
San Francisco State University

INTRODUCTION

For most men and women today, work and family are central institutions in life, and the work–family relationship has been the object of much research. Perhaps because of the increased percentage of women, of dual-earner couples, and of single-parents in the workplace, many recent studies have focused on work–family conflict (e.g., Doby & Caplan, 1995; Frone, Russel, & Cooper, 1992, 1997; Higgins & Duxbury, 1992; Kossek & Oseki, 1998). Data have shown that role conflicts caused by simultaneous demands from work and nonwork life domains are both stressful and costly to individual employees and to organizations. Lost workdays, unproductive work time, and high health insurance claims contribute to the significant economic costs associated with work–family tensions (e.g., Frone, Russel, & Cooper, 1997; Vanderkolk & Young, 1991; Yang, 1993). Effects of work–family conflict have created a new emphasis on balancing life across the two domains. Where, by tradition, families have always been dependent on the product of work (e.g., earning income through employment), the contemporary socioeconomic paradigm has presented a new reality: Organizational productivity and competition have become increasingly dependent on the strengths families give to workers. Meanwhile, economic globalization and business expansions across national borders have made work–family issues increasingly important to organizational performance and competition worldwide. International businesses and domestic organizations with diverse employees need to be aware of cultural influences on differing patterns of work–family interfaces in order to develop appropriate human resource strategies and programs to deal with work–family matters.

Researchers have called for a more expansive conceptualization of work–family adjustment patterns in order to understand the mechanisms that result in different personal and organizational outcomes. Various factors that may influence the magnitude of work–family conflict and employee behavioral reactions to it have been proposed. They range from work and family related social support and gender role explanations (e.g., Greenhaus & Parasuraman, 1994; Gutek, Searle, & Klepa, 1991; Yang, 1993) to cultural differences such as normative emphasis on segmentation versus integration of work and family role obligations and relative role priorities (e.g., Lobel, 1991; Schein, 1984; Yang, Chen, Choi, & Zou, 2000). However, difficulty with the literature on the work–family relationship is that the existing work–family concepts are primarily developed in western industrial societies, most notably in the United States. There has been little direct test assessing how people in culturally distinct societies may view and experience the work–family relationship differently, and how variations of cultural values may have differential effects on patterns of work–family interfaces and their outcomes. It remains to be shown how work–family relationships are structured in different cultures and whether the nature and magnitude of work and family pressures are culturally linked.

The present study extended prior work in the work–family area in three ways. First, it expanded existing work–family frameworks to include a cross-cultural comparison. Participants included working people in the United Sates and in the People's Republic of China. This approach allowed one group or category of people to be distinguished from another, so that potential errors in confounding cultural differences with organizational or personal factors were reduced. Second, this study examined antecedents and outcomes of work–family conflict with special attention to possible buffering effects of two opposite cultural orientations commonly called individualism and collectivism. Schein (1984) and Triandis (1989) posit that there are variations in the ways separate roles are integrated by individuals in different cultures. Compartmentalization between work and family roles may be most typical of individualistic cultures, whereas in collectivistic cultures, there is more integration of multiple roles played by an individual (Redding & Martyn-Johns, 1979; Schein, 1984; Triandis, 1989; Yang, 2000; Yang et al., 2000). Cultures also differ in allocating time and assigning priority between work and family (Hofstede, 1980; Schein, 1984; Yang et al., 2000). Following this line of argument, work and family role expectations, as embodied in cultural categories and social norms, are important factors moderating patterns of work–family adjustment and outcomes. Third, this study explored the bidirectional construct of work–family conflict in a cross-cultural context. The distinction between global work–family conflict (GWFC) and two direction-specific measures of work–family interferences (W→F vs. F→W) made it possible to compare how culture may influence the magnitude of work–family role pressures and employees' perceptions of conflict origins and consequences.

As more women, ethnic minorities, and immigrants enter the U.S. labor pool, concerns of work versus family expectations may vary tremendously among individual employees. Workforce diversity, including the family structural diversity, has led to an increased emphasis on quality of life and family-friendly policies at the workplace. As well, more than two decades of promoting economic reform and the family planning policy have seen some shift toward more competition at the workplace and family structural changes in China (Chen, 1995; Child, 1994; Triandis, 1995; Yang et al., 2000). The marked differences between the two nations' cultural traditions and the significant socioeconomic shifts within each should provide sufficient variation for testing both between-cultures variance in work–family conflict and outcomes and within-culture differences as a function of family situation, work situation, work–family interfaces, and the prevailing cultural norms of individualism versus collectivism.

A COMPARATIVE MODEL OF WORK–FAMILY INTERFACES

Taking the ideas discussed above about the work–family relationship and the potential effects of cultural differences on it, a comparative model can be described to specify interrelationships among work and family situations, individual beliefs, prevailing cultural norms, role conflict, and outcomes (Figure 11.1). The model suggests that an employee's multiple role requirements (i.e., family and work demands) would exert direct impacts on the experience of work–family conflict, which in turn would influence personal and organizational outcomes

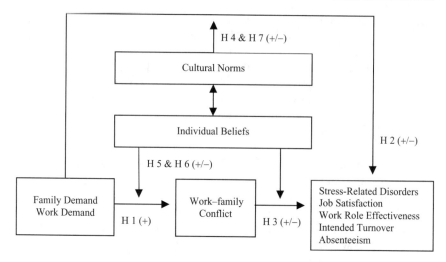

FIG. 11.1. A comparative model of work–family interfaces in culturally distinct societies.

such as stress-related disorders, job satisfaction, work role effectiveness, absenteeism, and intended turnover. The strength of these relationships, however, would be moderated by the traditional values of a culture (the American or the Chinese in the present context) either independently or through their interactions with individual beliefs characterized as individualistic or collectivistic.

Work–Family Conflict

To the extent that people in culturally distinct societies may view the work–family relationship differently, this study proposes that perceptions of work–family interfaces and their consequences are culturally linked. To investigate this proposal, I used a widely held view of work–family conflict conceptualized by Kahn, Wolfe, Quinn, Snoek, and Rosenthal (1964). Kahn et al. (1964) defined work–family conflict as a form of interrole conflict in which pressures from work and family domains tend to be mutually incompatible. This definition is consistent with those of other authors (e.g., Greenhaus & Beutell, 1985; Kanter, 1977) and implies that satisfaction or success in one life domain entails sacrifices in the other, because work and family environments have distinct norms and role expectations. To further conceptualize work–family interfaces, global work–family conflict (GWFC) was broken down into two specific dimensions: work interference with family (W→F) and family interference with work (F→W). This approach is consistent with those employed by several authors (e.g., Frone et al.,

1992; Greenhaus & Parasuranman, 1994; Gutek et al., 1991; Yang, 1993), which have noted the importance of the bidirectional conceptualization of work–family conflict. On the work side, for example, the number of hours worked per week, the amount and frequency of overtime, inflexible work schedules, excessive work load, and conflicting or ambiguous job requirements are sources of W→F conflict. On the other hand, the amount of time spent in carrying out family responsibilities, the amount of housekeeping and child-care tasks, household compositions, and family size are typical demographic variables associated with F→W conflict. The bidirectional nature of work–family conflict suggests that unfulfilled family obligations may interfere with one's day-to-day functioning at work; and conversely, a stressful work situation may interfere with one's family-related obligations.

To investigate the relationship of work–family conflict to employees' well-being and work behaviors within the context of a multivariate model, I drew a conceptual distinction between work interference with family (W→F) and family interference with work (F→W). At the same time, global work–family conflict (GWFC), without decomposing its directionalities, still merits cross-cultural research attention. First, culture influences the concept of work–family relationship itself (e.g., as two separate life domains or more as a unitary whole), which may moderate the magnitude of role incompatibility and hence perceptions of work–family conflict. Second, whereas previous research in the United States may argue that global work–family conflict measures mainly work interference with family (e.g., Frone et al., 1992; Gutek et al., 1991), it is unclear how people in different cultures, such as the Chinese, would perceive what work–family conflict means. To explore these questions, this study included both direction-specific measures and a global measure of work–family conflict.

Neither work nor family is a closed system. Structural conditions in one life domain may influence individual behavioral reactions in the other. A particular role requirement may not be in itself stressful, but it may still significantly increase the level of stress when added to other role requirements placed on a person. Work–family conflict may result in poor health and disturbed role performance. Most often, researchers assess work–family conflict through self-report questionnaires, under the assumption that these self-reports reflect objective circumstances. This assumption exemplifies what has been called a rational view of the work–family relationship (Near, Rice, & Hunt, 1980). Under the rational view, the relationship between one's work and family demands and perceptions of work–family conflict is quite straightforward: There is a direct correspondence between objective conditions and self-reports of work–family conflict. The amount of work–family conflict one perceives rises in proportion to the amount of time and energy one expends in meeting work and family demands. Consequently, employees who are exposed to higher levels of work and family demands will be more likely to report experiences of negative effects of work–family conflict on quality of life and behavioral outcomes. Previous research has identified three major types of work–family conflict: time-based, strain-based, and behavior-based (Greenhaus & Beutell, 1985). Consistent with the rational view, work and family must compete for an individual's scarce time and energy. Time-based conflict arises when time spent on role performance in one life domain precludes time spent on the other lifer domain. Time spent on role performance may also deplete energy or generate strain. Strain-based conflict arises when strain in one role affects one's performance in another role. Behavior-based conflict refers to the incompatibility of behavior patterns that are desirable in work versus family domains. This study was focused on time-based conflict while recognizing that the concept also includes time-induced strain and subsequently stress-related symptoms and impaired behavioral outcomes.

From the concept of work–family conflict and based on the rational view of its antecedents and consequences, I drew the following hypotheses:

Hypothesis 1: As work and/or family demands increase, employees in both individualistic and collectivistic societies will experience higher degrees of work–family conflict.

Hypothesis 2a: As work and/or family demands increase, employees in both individualistic and collectivistic societies will experience higher degrees of negative personal and organizational outcomes (e.g., stress-related disorders, absenteeism, and job turnover).

Hypothesis 2b: As work and/or family demands increase, employees in both individualistic and collectivistic societies will experience lower degrees of positive personal and organizational outcomes (e.g., job satisfaction and work role effectiveness).

Hypothesis 3a: In both individualistic and collectivistic societies, work–family conflict will be positively related to negative personal and organizational outcomes (e.g., stress-related disorders, absenteeism, and job turnover).

Hypothesis 3b: In both individualistic and collectivistic societies, work–family conflict will be negatively related to positive personal and organizational outcomes (e.g., job satisfaction and work role effectiveness).

Individualism–Collectivism and Work–Family Relationships

The key to the distinction between individualism and collectivism is the degree to which people in a country prefer to act as individuals as opposed to preference to act as members of groups (Hofstede, 1993; Triandis, 1995). This distinction is at the root of some basic differences in social behavior. In regard to the work and family relationship, it is argued that individualists would prefer a clear separation between the two life domains, presumably because they believe that individuals can function successfully in one without any influence from the other (Schein, 1984). Individualists value independence, and for them, group and personal goals are unrelated (Triandis, 1989). In contrast, collectivists prefer more integration of work and family life domains, presumably because they are concerned with interdependence and group harmony (Schein, 1984; Shenkar & Ronen, 1987; Yang, 2000). For collectivists, the group (whatever it may be) is the basic unit of survival, and privacy is reduced because of the heightened interaction between the individual and the collective (Hui, 1988).

The traditional values of a culture generally are taken for granted by people and operate unconsciously. The self (the internal features of an individual rather than the norms of a collective), however, is more dynamic. It varies in different situations (e.g., at school versus at home; see McGuire, McGuire, & Cheever, 1986), or when group structures are different (e.g., nuclear versus extended families; see Hofstede, 1991). Furthermore, there are cultural variations in the way separate roles are integrated into the self (Redding & Martyn-Johns, 1979; Schein, 1984; Triandis, 1989). In a collectivistic society, the self is more likely considered as a unitary whole. In an individualistic society, separations of different selves (e.g., private self versus collective or public self of a person) are more likely. Schein (1984) posits that an individual's commitment to family does not necessarily conflict with commitment to work and career in societies that make less of a separation between work and family and where family norms support a strong work ethic. Such conflict is much more likely to arise in the United States where self and family developments are posed as counter to the demands of work and where dual-career families are becoming increasingly legitimized. In the United States, an individual's career connotes personal ambition and achievement. If the main purpose of work is to further one's own career, a good family person should not allow work to interfere with family, as symbolized by a saying "leaving one's work at the office" (Schein, 1984, p. 74). Combining them is viewed as nonroutine or creative.

Consistently, Yang et al. (2000) noted that in collectivism-oriented cultures, such as China, sacrificing family time for work is viewed as self-sacrifice and a short-term cost incurred to gain long-term benefits of the family; whereas in individualism-oriented cultures, such as the United States, such behavior is often perceived as sacrificing family for one's own career or personal achievement, which is likely to cause dissatisfaction in other family members. There has been some empirical evidence in the United States that as work interfered with family, family members, instead of providing support to the distressed workers, withdrew such support (Adam, King, & King, 1996). Combined, these ideas and research findings indicate more value congruence across work and family commitments in China but more incompatibility in the United States. Previous research also suggests that at the cultural level, individuals in a collectivistic society are more likely to receive social support, which acts to buffer life stress. Hofstede (1980) contrasted individualistic with collectivistic societies where people are born into extended families or kinship systems that protect them in exchange for loyalty. There is also an emphasis on membership in the corporate family where employees seek life-long employment and have emotional dependence on organizational support in their personal lives (Trompennaars, 1994). In China, even after decades of economic reform, employees still have strong organizational or work group identity, and Chinese corporations continue to be the primary provider of social welfare benefits to individual employees and their families (Child, 1994).

Extending these implications of cross-cultural differences in work–family interfaces, it seems plausible to expect that culture will moderate role coordination across different life domains, which is to say that work and family adjustment may be achieved differently in individualistic and collectivistic cultures. Value congruence across roles may be more common in a collectivistic culture than in an individualistic one; and incompatibility between work and nonwork role requirements may be more typical of an individualistic culture than of a collectivistic culture. Thus cultural differences in individualism-collectivism values will moderate the impact of stress produced by work and family stressors and hence the probability of impaired health and behavioral outcomes. Simply put, employees in collectivistic cultures may experience lower levels of work–family conflict than their counterparts in individualistic ones. Consequently, they may also experience fewer symptoms of time-, strain-, and behavior-based role conflicts. From this line of conceptualization, I drew the following hypotheses:

Hypothesis 4: Perceptions of work–family conflict will be stronger in the United States than in China.

Hypothesis 5: Perceptions of work–family conflict will be more strongly related to impaired personal well-being and organizational outcomes in the United States than in China.

Hypothesis 6: Work and family demands will be more strongly related to impaired personal well-being and organizational outcomes in the United States than in China.

Cultural Patterns and Relative Role Priorities

Cultures differ in the extent to which they conceive of the self as distinct from the group. Although many individual cultures cluster in the middle range of the individualism–collectivism dimension, according to Hofstede (1993), the United States is highest on individualism among the 53 countries and regions he studied, and China is strongly collectivistic. For this study, therefore, it is assumed that samples of individuals from the United States and P.R. China will be clearly distinguishable on the individualism–collectivism cultural dimension.

Previous cross-cultural research suggests that employees differ in their relative commitments to work and family and that variation within a culture may be greater in those societies that have norms supporting freedom of choice (Schein, 1984). In the United States, for examples, two sets of norms pertain to the work–family relationship. One set of norms may clearly specify that occupational demands must be treated with higher priority than family demands, yet the other set of norms may support decisions of any given individual to decline occupational requirements for personal or family reasons. On the one hand, if a career is accepted, the individual is expected to give full commitment (Schein, 1984). On the other hand, when work and family conflict, Americans are expected to side with family (Yang et al., 2000). In this aspect, cultural norms are self-instructed by members of a culture to do what is perceived as correct and appropriate in certain situations. One can expect a wide range of work involvement and personal priorities within the U.S. society.

Cultures differ tremendously in how important it is that work leave enough time for personal and family life (Hofstede, 1980), and demand from the domain on which the society at large sets higher priority exerts greater role pressure through social expectations and norms (Yang et al., 2000). Researchers tend to agree that Western individualistic societies value family and personal time more strongly than Eastern collectivistic societies (e.g., Hofstede, 1980; Lai, 1995; Shenkar &

Ronen, 1987). Comparing sources of work–family conflict, Yang et al. (2000) found that family demand had greater impact on work–family conflict in the United States than it did in China, whereas work demand had greater impact on work–family conflict in China than it did in the United States. These differences highlight potential effects of culture on assigning relative role priorities to work versus family. The cultural norm of collectivism in China legitimizes giving higher priority to work by emphasizing reciprocity between family and other larger collectives such as the workplace. When there is a conflict of interests, employees are expected to side with work, inducing work interference with family. The cultural norm of individualism in the United States tends to go opposite; in dealing with other nonfamily collectives, individualists by definition place priority on self and family interests (Hofstede, 1980, 1991). Furthermore, the family value has been enhanced in the U.S. society by a more general emphasis on quality of life and family-friendly policies at the workplace. More Americans seek self-fulfillment through expressive individualism, such as quality time and relationship with family, than through utilitarian individualism, such as advancement in organizations and fast-track careers.

The above contrasts and research findings lead to a cultural perspective on the bidirectional nature of work–family conflict. That is, demand is greater from the life domain on which cultural norms set higher priority, the life domain with higher priority exerts greater role pressure and hence greater impact on role conflict. From the cultural relativity of role priority between work and family and extending the cultural differences in sources of work–family conflict, I drew the following hypotheses:

Hypothesis 7: Perceptions of work interference with family will be stronger in China than in the United States.

Hypothesis 8: Perceptions of family interference with work will be stronger in the United States than in China.

METHODS

Data Collection

Data were collected by surveying four organizations in the United Sates and four organizations in the People's Republic of China. Survey questionnaires were distributed through internal organizational systems. The general purpose of the survey was explained in a cover letter. Questionnaires were anonymous and participation voluntary. The sampled populations were employees in varied job categories,

TABLE 11.1
Sample Compositions by Job Categories (In Percentage)

Occupation[a]	U.S.[b]	China[c]
Operative	25.8	32.5
Staff	43.9	35.0
Professional	15.4	15.9
Managerial	14.9	16.6

[a]Operative includes shop-floor workers and operators.
Staff includes administrative clerks and service employees.
Professional includes employees holding professional job titles, e.g., engineering, accounting, etc.
Managerial includes managers/supervisors across organizational functions and levels.
[b]U.S. subjects, $N = 254$.
[c]Chinese subjects, $N = 192$.

both male and female, who worked at least 20 hours per week. Table 11.1 presents sample compositions by job categories.

Participating organizations in China included two manufacturing companies, a municipal administration office, and an educational institution of which participants were evening students holding full- or part-time jobs in medium-sized companies of a light industry. A total of 192 people filled out the survey questionnaires. Participating organizations in the United States included a multidivisional manufacturing company, a major airline company, a state government department, and a public educational institution of which participants were nontraditional students pursuing a business degree while holding full- or part-time jobs. A total of 254 questionnaires were completed. The cross-organizational response rate was about 41%.

Sample Characteristics

In both the United States and China, there was considerable family diversity in the surveyed workforces. In the United States, about 48% of the respondents were in dual-employee families and about 11% in single-parent families. About 43% of the respondents claimed child-care responsibilities for children in the household, and about 18% claimed child-care responsibilities for children not in the household. Some 32% of the respondents had elder-care responsibilities for people aged 60 through 95, and 22.5% provided care for other persons in their lives, not identified as either children or elderly people. In China, respondents in dual-employee and single-parent families were about 52% and 4%, respectively. About 39% of the respondents claimed child-care responsibilities for children in the household, and about 4% claimed child-care responsibilities for children not in the household. Some 37% of the respondents had elder-care responsibilities for people aged 60 through 93, and 18% provided care for other persons in their lives, not identified as either children or elderly people. No significant difference was found in gender compositions and job categories between the two independent samples. American respondents, on average, were about 4 years older than were their Chinese counterparts.

Measurements

Measures of family demand, work demand, work–family conflict (GWFC, W→F, and F→W), and personal and organizational outcomes were administered to the two independent samples. All the measures were translated from English to Chinese using a back-translation method (Brislin, 1970).

Family demand (FD) was measured by seven items of Yang's (1993) scale querying family role pressures on a person's time and energy (e.g., "How much time do you spend on home/family related activities such as taking care of children or others?" "How often do family responsibilities make you feel tired out?"). The response scale ranged from 1 (almost none/never) to 5 (very much/always). The coefficient alphas in the present study were .83 and .86 for Chinese and American samples, respectively. Work demand (WD) was measured by six items from Spector's (1975) Organizational Frustration scale, which taps work role pressures for a person's time and energy (e.g., "I often feel that I am being run ragged."). The response scale ranged from 1 (completely disagree) to 5 (completely agree). The coefficient alphas were .64 and .75 for the Chinese and American samples, respectively.

Six items of Yang's (1993) Global Work–Family Conflict (GWFC) scale were used to indicate the extent to which work and family compete for a person's time and energy (e.g., "How much conflict do you feel there is between the demands of your job and your family life?" "How often do you feel that you don't have the time and energy to meet the demands of being both an employee and a family member?"). Respondents rated each question from 1 (not at all/never) to 5 (a lot/very often). The coefficient alphas were .73 and .84 for the Chinese and American samples, respectively. Two specific dimensions of work interference with family (W→F) and family interference with work (F→W) were measured by Yang's (1993) scales. The W→F conflict measure consisted of nine items concerning how often demands from the work domain interfere with one's family-related activities such as child care, elder care, household tasks, and relationships with specific family members (e.g., "How often does your job interfere with your effort to perform child-care tasks you think you should do as a mother or father?"). The F→W conflict measure contained six items concerning how often demands from the home/family domain interfere with one's effort to cope with work-related issues such as job performance, job commitment, absenteeism, and relationship with people at work (e.g., "How often do you family responsibilities interfere with how well you do your job?"). Each item used a five-point rating from 1 (never) to 5 (very often). The coefficient alphas were .91 (W→F) and .79 (F→W) for the Chinese sample, and .91 (W→F) and .88 (F→W) for the American sample.

Outcome variables fell into two categories: employees' well-being (i.e., stress-related disorders and overall job satisfaction), and work behaviors (i.e., work role effectiveness, intended turnover, and absenteeism). Stress-related disorders were assessed using both physical and psychological items adapted from the Quality of Employment Survey (Quinn & Staines, 1979), which had 13 items measuring symptoms such as "trouble getting to sleep," "heart pounding or racing," and "feeling nervous or fidgety and tense." The response scale ranged from 1 (never) to 4 (often). The coefficient alphas were .85 and .78 for the Chinese and American samples, respectively. Five items of the Facet-Free Job Satisfaction scale (Quinn & Staines, 1979) were used to measure overall job satisfaction (e.g., "All in all, how satisfied would you say you are with your job?"). The response scale ranged from 1 (not at all satisfied) to 5 (very satisfied). The coefficient alphas were .78 and .80 for the Chinese and American samples, respectively. Six items of Yang's (1993) Work Role Effectiveness were used to tap an employee's job performance and interpersonal skills (e.g., "In the last three months, how often have you done more than is minimally required of you by your job?"). The response scale ranged from 1 (never) to 4 (often). The coefficient alphas were .66 and .71 for the Chinese and American samples, respectively. Three items from Yang's (1993) Propensity for Job Turnover were used to tap an employee's disposition toward work role withdrawal because of unsolved environmental demands (e.g., "How likely is that you will actively look for a new job in the next year?"). The response scale ranged from 1 (not at all likely) to 5 (extremely likely). The coefficient alphas were .60 and .87 for the Chinese and American samples, respectively. Absenteeism was measured in two categories: complete work days and partial work days missed. Respondents were instructed to count all kinds of absenteeism in 3 months preceding the survey: excused and unexcused, planned and unplanned, and paid and unpaid. No distinction was made between voluntary and involuntary absence (e.g., because of illness or child care) because the concern in the present study was the degree of absenteeism rather than its justification or controllability.

The internal coefficients of the measurements varied between samples, with three alphas relatively low for the Chinese sample (below .70). The difference could be attributed to two potential factors: language and survey experience. All questions were originated in English and translated to Chinese. Although the back-translation method was used to ensure the content equivalence (Brislin, 1970), the source version of the instrument might still contain some culture connection (not completely culture free). It should also be recognized that surveys are far less common in China than in the United States. Most of the Chinese participants in this study had no prior experience answering survey questionnaires. Given the complexity of cross-cultural research and the multifaceted nature of the comparative model developed by the present study, these reliability coefficients were considered satisfactory.

RESULTS

By and large, data revealed four major findings. First, in both China and the United States, as work and/or family demands increased, employees experienced higher degrees of work–family conflict, and impaired personal well-being and organizational outcomes. Regardless of culture, work–family conflict was positively related to negative personal and organizational outcomes (e.g., stress-related disorders, intended turnover, and absenteeism) and negatively related to positive outcomes (e.g., overall job satisfaction and work role effectiveness). These results are in keeping with Hypotheses 1, 2a, 2b, 3a, and 3b, indicating that work–family conflict is a cross-cultural phenomenon in both individualistic and collectivistic societies. Second, American respondents reported greater global work–family conflict than did Chinese respondents, indicating there are higher levels of incompatibility between work and family life domains in an individualistic culture than in a collectivistic culture. Third, regardless of culture, work–family conflict was found to be bidirectional in nature (W→F and F→W), depending on from which life domain (work or family) the conflict originates. Chinese respondents reported greater work-interference with family than did their American counterparts, indicating there is more work intrusion into family in a collectivistic culture than in an individualistic one. No significant difference was found in levels of family interference with work (F→W) between the two groups. These results are in support of Hypotheses 4 and 7, but not in support of Hypothesis 8. Fourth, global work–family conflict (GWFC) showed similar patterns of impacts on personal and organizational outcomes in the predicted directions across cultures, whereas direction-specific measures of role conflict (W→F and F→W) showed different patterns of outcome results. Specifically, the magnitudes of work and family role pressures and subsequent interrole disruptions on personal and organizational outcomes were stronger and broader in the U.S. sample than in the Chinese sample. These results are clearly consistent with Hypotheses 5 and 6. Combined, results indicate that culture (American vs. Chinese) has an important role in predicting degrees of work–family conflict by moderating the magnitude of multiple role pressures (i.e., work and family demands) on a person's time and energy and also by influencing cognitions of the conflict origins (i.e., W→F vs. F→W). More detailed statistics follow.

Work and Family Situations by Culture

In addition to perceptions of family demand, the survey obtained three other quantitative variables reflecting family/home circumstances (i.e., total number of dependents based on the sum of children, elderly persons, and others taken care of by the respondent; total number of hours spent on various household tasks per week such as house cleaning and laundry, cooking, household shopping, maintenance, and yard work, etc.; and percentage of those household tasks generally performed by the respondent). Correlations between perceived family demand on the one hand, and on the other hand, number of care responsibilities, number of weekly hours spent on household tasks, and percentage of household tasks performed by the respondents were .33, .61, and .31 ($p < .001$), respectively, for the Chinese sample, and .32, .45, and .36 ($p < .001$) for the American sample. There were, however, some significant differences in the home–family structural conditions between American and Chinese respondents. Descriptive statistics and comparisons of mean ratings by culture (Tables 11.2 and 11.3) indicated that American respondents reported greater care responsibilities ($t = 2.77$, $p < .01$), whereas Chinese respondents reported more time spent on household tasks ($t = -2.27$, $p < .01$). Within-sample, gender was positively related to perceptions of family demand for both American ($r = .16$, $p < .05$) and Chinese respondents ($r = .24$, $p < .01$), indicating that regardless of culture, women employees experienced higher degrees of family–home-related role pressures than did their male counterparts. Gender was negatively related to perceptions of work demand for American

TABLE 11.2
Descriptive Statistics and Comparisons of Mean Ratings by Culture

	U.S.		China		
Sample Background Descriptions	Mean	S.D.	Mean	S.D.	t
Hours spent on household tasks per week	34.07	31.73	45.14	33.66	−2.27**
Percentage of household tasks performed	2.41	2.49	1.77	.95	2.08
Number of family/home care responsibilities	2.58	2.81	1.69	1.65	2.77**
Primary paid work hours per week	43.90	5.05	42.14	4.03	2.53**
Primary unpaid overtime per week	1.89	5.35	1.71	4.70	.18

$^{**}p < .01.$

respondents ($r = -.21$, $p < .01$), indicating that male employees experienced higher degrees of work-related role pressures than did female employees, but gender made no significant difference for Chinese respondents. Overall, American respondents perceived higher degrees of family demand than did Chinese respondents ($t = 4.96$, $p < .0001$).

T-values also indicated that American respondents reported more weekly time commitment to their primary paid work than did

TABLE 11.3
Comparisons of Mean Ratings of Family Demand, Work Demand, Work–Family
Conflict, and Personal and Organizational Outcomes by Culture

	U.S.		China		
Effects	Mean	S.D.	Mean	S.D.	t
Subjective family demand	3.64	.75	3.15	.65	4.96****
Subjective work demand	2.93	.80	2.88	.76	.48
Family interference with work (F→W)	1.77	.68	1.91	.68	−1.51
Work interference with family (W→F)	2.48	.93	2.84	1.15	−2.44**
Global work–family conflict (GWFC)	2.68	.95	2.33	.73	2.96**
Stress-related disorders	1.94	.60	1.97	.59	−.32
Overall job satisfaction	3.28	1.08	3.01	1.09	1.80*
Work role effectiveness	3.14	.58	3.37	.54	−2.31**
Intended turnover	2.58	1.12	2.89	.90	−2.24**
Complete work days missed	2.49	3.16	1.80	1.74	1.15
Partial work days missed	1.50	1.92	1.81	2.89	−.69

$^{*}p < .05.$ $^{**}p < .01.$ $^{****}p < .0001.$

Chinese respondents ($t = 2.53$, $p < .01$). Primary paid work hours per week, however, were not significantly related to perceptions of work demand for either of the two groups. It was the unpaid overtime that contributed to degrees of perceived work demand for both American ($r = .30$, $p < .001$) and Chinese respondents ($r = .29$, $p < .01$), but there was no significant difference in weekly unpaid overtime between the two groups. Consistent with these results, no significant difference was found in perceptions of work demand between the two groups.

In general, these primary assessments are consistent with the rational view of the work–family relationship, and suggest comparability of the two cultural samples with respect to their work and family situations.

Multiple Role Pressures and Work–Family Conflict

Both family and work demands were found significantly related to perceptions of global work–family conflict (GWFC) in each of the two cultural contexts (Tables 11.4 and 11.5). Direction-specific measures of work–family conflict indicated that perceptions of family demand were significantly related to degrees of family interference with work (F→W) for both American ($r = .46$, $p < .001$) and Chinese respondents ($r = .24$, $p < .01$). Perceptions of work demand, on the other hand, were significantly related to degrees of work interference with family (W → F) for both American ($r = .31$, $p < .001$) and Chinese

TABLE 11.4
Correlation Matrix of Family Demand, Work Demand, Work–Family Conflict,
Personal and Organizational Outcomes, and Individualism–Collectivism
Index (China)

Measures	FD	WD	F → W	W → F	GWFC
Family interference with work (F→W)	.24**	.34***	—	—	—
Work interference with family (W→F)	−.14	.32***	.02	—	—
Global work–family conflict (GWFC)	.41***	.35***	.53***	.16*	—
Stress-related disorders	.28**	.47***	.37***	.28**	.39***
Overall job satisfaction	−.38***	−.11	−.18*	−.16*	−.34***
Work role effectiveness	.06	−.23*	−.11	−.07	−.32**
Intended turnover	.04	−.02	.14	−.08	.16*
Complete work days missed	.10	−.10	−.002	.13	.38**
Partial work days missed	.05	−.18	−.09	−.04	.06
Gender	.24**	−.02	.13	.08	.05

$^*p < .05.$ $^{**}p < .01.$ $^{***}p < .001.$

TABLE 11.5
Correlation Matrix of Family Demand, Work Demand, Work–Family Conflict,
Personal and Organizational Outcomes, and Individualism–Collectivism
Index (U.S.)

Measures	FD	WD	F → W	W → F	GWFC
Family interference with work (F→W)	.46***	.21**	—	—	—
Work interference with family (W→F)	.51***	.31***	.45***	—	—
Global work–family conflict (GWFC)	.75***	.25**	.74***	.63***	—
Stress-related disorders	.41***	.18*	.48***	.43***	.44***
Overall job satisfaction	−.26**	−.31***	−.21**	−.23**	−.29***
Work role effectiveness	−.15*	−.43***	−.44***	−.29***	−.23**
Intended turnover	.22**	.28**	.16*	.16*	.20*
Complete work days missed	.02	.01	.03	−.02	.07
Partial work days missed	.24**	.04	.32***	−.05	.21**
Gender	.16*	−.21**	−.15	−.03	.12

$^*p < .05.$ $^{**}p < .01.$ $^{***}p < .001.$

respondents $(r = .32,\ p < .001)$. These results clearly support Hypothesis 1.

Personal and Organizational Outcomes

As shown in Tables 11.4 and 11.5, family demand was found significantly related to stress-related disorders and overall job satisfaction in the predicted directions for both American and Chinese respondents. Family demand was also significantly related to work behavior-oriented outcomes in the predicted directions (i.e., work role effectiveness, intended turnover, and absenteeism in terms of partial workdays missed) for American respondents, but not for their Chinese counterparts. As well, work demand was significantly related to stress-related disorders and work role effectiveness in the predicted directions for both American and Chinese respondents. Work demand was also significantly related to lower job satisfaction and higher propensity for job turnover for American respondents, but not for Chinese respondents. No significant correlations were found between work demand and absenteeism for either of the two groups.

These findings provide support for Hypotheses 2a and 2b. The relationships between work and family role pressures and those personal and organizational outcomes, however, were stronger and broader in the U.S. sample than in the Chinese sample. Of 10 predicted correlations (two demand variables vs. five outcome variables), 9 were

significant for American respondents, whereas only 4 were significant for Chinese respondents, results that were consistent with Hypothesis 6.

Work–Family Conflict

For both American and Chinese respondents, global work–family conflict (GWFC) was negatively related to employees' overall job satisfaction and work role effectiveness, but positively related to their
stress-related disorders and intended job turnover. As for absenteeism, GWFC contributed to the loss of complete workdays in China
($r = .38$, $p < .01$), but to the loss of partial workdays in the United
States ($r = .21$, $p < .01$). Correlation results also showed that both
direction-specific measures of work–family conflict (W→F and F→W)
were significantly related to employees' well-being (i.e., stress-related
disorders and overall job satisfaction) in the predicted directions,
regardless of culture. There were, however, clear between-groups
differences in the correlations involving other outcomes reflecting
employees' work behaviors. Although both W→F and F→W conflict
dimensions showed significant correlations with work role effectiveness and intended turnover in the predicted directions for American respondents, neither of the two conflict measures was related to
those work behavior-oriented outcomes for Chinese respondents. Furthermore, family interference with work (F→W) was found positively
related to absenteeism in terms of partial workdays missed for American respondents ($r = .32$, $p < .001$), whereas it showed no similar
relationship with either type of absenteeism for Chinese respondents.

These results are consistent with Hypothesis 3a and 3b. In general, regardless of culture, work–family conflict was found positively
related to negative personal and organizational outcomes (increasing stress-related disorders, intended turnover, and absenteeism) and
negatively related to positive outcomes (reducing both overall job satisfaction and work role effectiveness). In comparison, global work–
family conflict (GWFC) revealed similar patterns of personal and organizational outcomes between the two cultural groups. All of the
five predicted correlations were significant across cultures. Direction-
specific measures of W→F and F→W interferences, on the other hand,
showed different patterns of outcome results between the two cultural
groups. Overall, both W→F and F→W conflict measures revealed
stronger and broader relationships with the outcome variables for
American respondents than for Chinese respondents. Of 10 predicted
correlations (two dimensions of work–family conflict vs. five outcome
variables), 9 were significant for American respondents, while only

4 were significant for Chinese respondents, results that were consistent with Hypothesis 5, which proposed between-cultures differences in work–family conflict and outcomes.

Between-Cultures Differences

In order to detect cultural effects on work–family conflict and outcome variables, a series of factorial analysis of variance were conducted. All variables were entered simultaneously with country as the between-subject factor, and work and family demand measures as the within-subject factors. Results (Table 11.6) showed country-culture as a significant factor affecting each of the three work–family conflict measures in addition to main effects of work and family demands. In comparison, work demand showed a much stronger main effect on W→F conflict ($ss = 29.19$, $p < .0001$) than did family demand ($ss = 9.55$, $p < .05$). Family demand showed a much stronger main effect on F→W conflict ($ss = 10.37$, $p < .0001$) than did work demand ($ss = 3.89$, $p < .05$). These results provided empirical evidence for the bidirectional construct of work–family conflict in a cross-cultural context.

With respect to personal and organizational outcomes, country-culture appeared as a significant factor affecting employees' overall job

TABLE 11.6
Factorial Analysis of Variance on Work–Family Conflict (Unique Sums of Squares, All Effects Entered Simultaneously)

Dependent Variables	Sources of Variance	Sum of Squares	F
Global work–family	Within-subject	63.92	18.27****
conflict (GWFC)	Family demand	48.32	27.62****
	Work demand	15.60	8.92****
	Between-subject	6.33	14.48****
	Country	6.33	14.48****
Family interference	Within-subject	17.00	5.43****
with work (F→W)	Family demand	10.37	6.62****
	Work demand	3.89	2.48*
	Between-subject	1.99	5.09*
	Country	1.99	5.09*
Work interference	Within-subject	41.63	5.76****
with family (W→F)	Family demand	9.55	2.64*
	Work demand	29.19	8.08****
	Between-subject	6.29	6.96**
	Country	6.29	6.96**

$*p < .05.$ $**p < .01.$ $****p < .0001.$

TABLE 11.7
Factorial Analysis of Variance on Personal and Organizational Outcomes (Unique
Sums of Squares, All Effects Entered Simultaneously)

Dependent Variables	Sources of Variance	Sum of Squares	F
Stress-related disorders	Within-subject	17.93	7.01****
	Family demand	9.82	8.64****
	Work demand	5.89	5.18***
	Between-subject	.24	.86
	Country	.24	.86
Job satisfaction	Within-subject	32.00	3.36***
	Family demand	17.21	4.06**
	Work demand	6.07	1.41
	Between-subject	9.23	8.70**
	Country	9.23	8.70**
Work role effectiveness	Within-subject	8.79	3.34***
	Family demand	2.03	1.77
	Work demand	4.84	4.02**
	Between-subject	2.36	8.19**
	Country	2.36	8.19**
Intended turnover	Within-subject	27.58	3.20***
	Family demand	10.36	2.71*
	Work demand	9.76	2.55*
	Between-subject	7.06	7.38**
	Country	7.06	7.38**
Complete work days missed	Within-subject	57.95	.74
	Family demand	11.88	.34
	Work demand	36.23	1.04
	Between-subject	13.67	1.58
	Country	13.67	1.58
Partial work days missed	Within-subject	119.08	3.33***
	Family demand	29.11	1.83
	Work demand	95.20	5.99****
	Between-subject	.71	.18
	Country	.71	.18

$^*p < .05.$ $^{**}p < .01.$ $^{***}p < .001.$ $^{****}p < .0001.$

satisfaction ($ss = 9.23$, $p < .01$), work role effectiveness ($ss = 2.35$, $p < .01$), and intended turnover ($ss = 7.06$, $p < .01$), in addition to main effects of work and family demands, but not on absenteeism and stress-related disorders (Table 11.7). These results, along with correlations and t-values discussed below, provided empirical support for the cultural perspective on work–family relationship.

A series of T-tests were conducted to compare mean ratings of three types of work–family conflict and five types of personal and organizational outcomes by culture. *T*-values (Table 11.3) indicated that whereas American respondents perceived higher degrees of global work–family conflict (GWFC: $t = 2.96$, $p < .001$), Chinese respondents perceived higher degrees of work-interference with family (W→F: $t = -2.44$, $p < .01$). No significant difference was found in levels of family interference with work (F→W) between the two groups. Hypotheses 4 and 7 were therefore supported, but Hypothesis 8 was not.

With respect to positive personal and organizational outcomes, American respondents showed higher levels of overall job satisfaction than did Chinese respondents ($t = 1.80$, $p < .05$), whereas Chinese respondents showed higher degrees of work role effectiveness ($t = -2.31$, $p < .01$). As for negative personal and organizational outcomes, Chinese respondents had a stronger tendency for job turnover ($t = -2.24$, $p < .01$) than did American respondents, but no significant differences were found in either stress-related disorders or absenteeism between the two groups.

These findings along with correlation results discussed earlier provide support for Hypotheses 5 and 6. First, W→F, F→W, and GWFC consistently revealed stronger and broader relationships with impaired personal well-being and organizational outcome variables in the United States than in China. Second, demands of work and family consistently showed stronger and broader relationships with outcome variables in the United States than in China. Third, family demand appeared more strongly linked to W→F, F→W, and GWFC for American respondents than for their Chinese counterparts (Tables 11.4 & 11.5). These results also add empirical evidence that work–family conflict is not a unitary construct, but rather a bidirectional one. Although, as predicted, the American respondents reported higher degrees of global work–family conflict than did their Chinese counterparts, we cannot come to a simple conclusion that role integration reduces all kinds of role conflict without looking into the two specific conflict dimensions (W→F and F→W). Furthermore, as shown in Tables 11.4 and 11.5, global work–family conflict (GWFC) was strongly related to both W→F ($r = .74$, $p < .001$) and F→W ($r = .63$, $p < .001$) measures of role interference for American respondents, whereas for Chinese respondents, it showed a stronger relationship with family interference with work (F→ W: $r = .53$, $p < .001$) than with work interference with family (W→F: $r = .16$, $p < .05$). These results suggest that people of different cultures (e.g., Americans vs. Chinese) may not share a similar understanding of what work–family conflict means to them even if the instruments are composed of equivalent questions.

DISCUSSION AND CONCLUSIONS

Major Findings and Theoretical Implications

This study produced empirical evidence for the relevance and utility of a cross-cultural approach to understanding potential factors that influence work–family interfaces. It has several important implications for future research. First, in theorizing the potential cultural effects of individualism–collectivism, the study incorporated specific cultural constructs such as cultural preference for work–family segregation versus integration, incompatibility versus value congruence between work and family role expectations, and cultural relativity of assigning role priority between work and family. In addition to main effects of work and family stressors, factorial analyses of variance showed significant impacts of country on all three measures of work–family conflict (i.e., GWFC, W→F, and F→W). Higher levels of global work–family conflict found in the U.S. sample confirmed the conceptualization that role incompatibility between work and family life domains is more typical of an individualistic society than of a collectivistic society such as China. The difference can be partially because of cultural relativity of role segregation versus integration. Role integration, however, does not automatically reduce all types of conflict.

The differentiation of W→F versus F→W interferences provided an opportunity to examine how relative role commitments, as embodied in cultural norms, may influence the conflict origin and consequences. The positive relationship found between collectivism and work interference with family (W→F) challenged some traditional assumptions that collectivism leads to role integration, which in turn reduces role conflict. It suggests instead that, in China, collectivists are exposed to more intrusion of work into the home/family life domain. The reverse relationship (F→W), however, may not obtain. In a sense, this is not surprising; collectivism as a value system entails some personal sacrifice for the benefit of the group. Collectivism expects an individual not only to be more aware of group needs but also to be more willing to subjugate personal life to group interests. Chinese traditional values of collectivism emphasize reciprocity between an individual and a collective or between a smaller collective (*xiao-jia* or small family, e.g., an individual's family) and a larger collective (*da-jia* or bigger family, e.g., a corporate family). Home/family is part of a person's private life or a smaller collective, whereas a workplace or an organization to which an individual belongs is a larger public collective. In regard to the work–family interface, one's identification with a larger collective, such as a workgroup or an organization, may require one to sacrifice some personal or family commitment, but not the other way around. In other words, the cultural norms of collectivism in China legitimize giving priority to work.

The difference found in levels of W→F interference between American and Chinese respondents can be attributed partially to the relative role priorities set by different social norms and partially to their differing value congruence between work and family. Individualism, by definition, emphasizes privacy and personal responsibility for one's immediate family. The cultural norms of individualism in the United States illustrate legitimacy and primacy of family over other collectives; a good family person should not allow work to interfere with family. Collectivism, in contrast, emphasizes group interests over personal interests, and privacy is reduced because of heightened interdependence among group members. The cardinal value of reciprocity entails that assuming extra work responsibilities and assignments is for the long-term benefit of the family even if that may disrupt family life temporarily. These speculations of course call for further empirical testing.

Second, findings of this study should inspire more cross-cultural research addressing the bidirectional construct of work–family interface and related outcomes. Factorial analysis of variance showed that work demand had a much stronger main effect on W→F conflict than did family demand, whereas family demand had a much stronger main effect on F→W conflict than did work demand across countries (U.S. and China). These results provide empirical evidence of the bidirectional construct of work–family conflict in a cross-culture context. However, there still are questions to be explained and global work–family conflict still merits research attention.

Previous research in the United States posits that mixed measures of work–family conflict assess primarily the experience of W→F conflict (e.g., Frone et al., 1992; Gutek et al., 1991). For Chinese respondents, however, this study indicated that the mixed measure of work–family conflict (GWFC) assessed primarily the experience of F→W conflict, suggesting that people of different cultures (e.g., American vs. Chinese) may not share a common understanding of what work–family conflict means even if the instruments are composed of equivalent questions. This matter clearly calls for further research.

Third, the distinction between two direction-specific measures of work–family conflict (W→F vs. F→W) in this study made it possible to compare antecedents and outcomes of different types of work–family conflict. Overall, both W→F and F→W conflict measures revealed much stronger and broader relationships with personal and organizational outcomes in the American sample than in the Chinese sample. There may be two reasons for the remarkable difference in the effects of direction-specific measures of work–family conflict (W→F vs. F→W) between the two cultural groups. One potential reason is that, in China, collectivists' willingness to subjugate personal life (e.g., one's family responsibility) to the interests of a collective (e.g., loyalty and commitment at work) may reduce strains of unaccomplished role requirements at home. In a culture, where family norms support a strong work ethic or work role priority, one's family commitment does not necessarily conflict with one's work commitment. Similarly, if work norms honor family relations, an employee's work commitment may be compatible with his or her family needs (e.g., one's high commitment at work may bring honor, security, and social welfare benefits to one's family). Another potential reason is that, in the United States, family structural changes (e.g., increased dual-earner families, married-like couples, and single-parent families) and workplace changes (e.g., increased unpaid overtime, commuting, and flexible workplace) have made it increasingly difficult to compartmentalize different life domains as a traditional way of life. One's equal identification with separate referent groups (work vs. family) or viewing work and family as competitors for one's limited time and forcing negotiations over work–family boundaries may entail more difficulty in balancing multiple role requirements, especially when some sacrifice has to be made for one over another. These lines of argument, of course, call for further conceptualization and empirical research.

Fourth, within-sample comparisons raised some key issues that merit further attention. One issue has to do with gender, which was found positively related to levels of family demand for both American and Chinese respondents, indicating that regardless of culture, women employees are exposed to higher degrees of family/home-related role pressures than are their male counterparts. Gender was negatively related to perceptions of work demand for American respondents, indicating that male employees experienced higher degrees of work-related role pressures than did female employees, but gender made no significant difference for Chinese respondents. The difference can be attributed to increased dual-earner families and women's participation in the U.S. workforce where nuclear families are traditionally preferred and men are still considered primary bread-earners. Other family structures are often called "nontraditional" or "uncharted."

Another issue is that work and family role pressures predicted intended job turnover in the U.S. sample, but had little effect in the Chinese sample. Nevertheless, Chinese respondents, on average, scored higher on intended job turnover than did American respondents.

These findings suggest that other factors, such as social and economic changes in a society, may outweigh effects of multiple role stressors and work–family conflict on job turnover. By tradition, job mobility is higher in the United States than in China where lifetime employment is more common, as in other collectivistic societies such as Japan. Collectivism is characterized by a tight social framework in which people expect in-groups (such as an organization to which they belong) to look after them and protect them. In exchange for this security, in-group members feel they owe absolute loyalty to the group. In China, such loyalty (as a normative contract or a psychological condition between individual employees and their working organizations) has become more uncertain in the context of the nationwide economic reform, which has been promoted for more than 2 decades. Job security is no longer taken for granted because many state-owned organizations have been forced to downsize or to privatize. Meanwhile, private enterprises and foreign investments have been growing rapidly, creating new job opportunities. Not only have these changes made job mobility possible, but also they have made it attractive to people who see their jobs as less secure or not paid comparably well. Cultural traditions may then encourage individual adaptations to collective changes. In such a dynamic environment, adaptations are so essential for survival and prosperity of both individual employees and their working organizations that individual employees' loyalty to a particular organization or vice versa may become less relevant at the cultural level. In the United States, on the other hand, the job market hard hit by the economic recession and large waves of corporate downsizing and outsourcing have constrained people's job mobility, and job security has become a salient issue for both workers and managers. In order to remain competitive, an increased emphasis on group-oriented teamwork, along with organizational reengineering, has gradually brought value changes to the U.S. workplace. Despite the enhanced value of family in the U.S. society, giving higher priority to family over work or allowing family to interfere with work may weaken an individual's career or job security, which could be part of the reason that this study did not find significant difference in levels of family interference with work between the United State and China. Taking into consideration the socioeconomic changes occurring in the two countries, our mixed findings can be attributed partially to individual employees' learning and adaptations to changes in each of the cultural contexts (American and Chinese). On this premise, a general theoretical model can be proposed to account for effects of cultural change on work–family interfaces.

Research Design and Limitations

Cross-cultural research often confronts questions such as whether the subjects selected are representative of the culture. Berry (1980) stressed that sample representativeness is relative to research purposes. If one's research goal is to achieve universal generalization, cultures should be sampled in consideration not only of the range, but also of representativeness. If the goal is to explore systematic co-variations between cultural and behavioral variables, then cultures are selected, not for their representativeness, but for their differences along the chosen variables. The same reasoning applies to sampling strategy at the individual level. If individuals are being selected because they represent some variables of interest, then whether they are representative of some population is not important. The present study was focused on the cultural dimension of individualism–collectivism. Although many countries cluster in the middle range of the this dimension, according to Hofstede (1993), the United States is highest on individualism among the 53 countries and regions he studied, whereas China is strongly collectivistic. The striking cultural difference in individualism–collectivism values between China and the United States is widely recognized by many other cross-cultural researchers (e.g., Chen, 1995; Child, 1994; Triandis, 1995). This study, therefore, assumed that samples of individuals from the United States and P.R. China would be clearly distinguishable on the individualism–collectivism cultural dimension. The present study did not attempt to discover universal generalizations that explain cultural variations. Rather, its purpose was to explore how the work–family interface is influenced independently and/or jointly by prevailing cultural norms and individual employees' work and family situations. Different cultures, American and Chinese, were selected as a way to maximize variations in the work–family relationship and not for their representativeness. Cultural representativeness would be better served by maximizing homogeneity within the respective cultures, but that would defeat the purpose of within-culture analysis. For our research purposes, subjects were selected, not because they represented particular cultures, but because they represented differences on the variables of interest.

Despite major findings and theoretical implications discussed above, this study has some limitations. First, compared with U.S.-based work–family research, this study appeared simplistic in terms of the variable refinements and statistical analyses. Second, although the results by and large are consistent with hypothesized cultural expectations, the study did not test the moderating effects of culture directly. Survey data collected at the one point of time cannot determine the causal effects. Factorial analysis, t-values, and correlations cannot determine direct or interaction effects of culture and other variables. Third, the study did not find empirical evidence for greater family interference with work (F→W) in the United States, although perceptions of family demand were significantly higher in the U.S. sample than in the Chinese sample, which was consistent with the family role priority argument. One possible reason for the lack of evidence is the limitation of time-based role conflict that this study was focused on. Another reason might be the dynamic socioeconomic changes taking place in both surveyed countries, which may affect some basic assumptions about work and family in each cultural environment.

Practical Implications

We are living in times of increased labor force diversity and economic globalization. Although there are dramatic social and economic changes taking place in each of the surveyed countries, these changes do not involve rejecting cultural traditions; rather, they flourish in the general framework of cultural traditions. Both individuals and organizations have to learn about and adapt to these changes. A better understanding of cultural differences in work–family interfaces can be useful for organizational effectiveness and individual prosperity.

This study provided important implications for work–family-related organizational learning and interventions. First, as described earlier, in both the United States and China, there was considerable family diversity in the surveyed organizations. Although objective home/family conditions predicted employees' perceptions of family demand in each of the samples, the magnitude of family role pressures varied between the two cultural groups. American respondents reported more home/family care responsibilities than did Chinese respondents; Chinese respondents reported more time spent on household tasks. There may be two major reasons for these differences. One is that, in China, the long-standing family planning policy has reduced the number of children to one per couple in many households, thereby decreasing family care responsibilities. In the United States, an increased divorce rate, delayed marriages, and transformation of work have increased the number of married-like couples, single-parent families, and dual-earner families, thus increasing family/home care responsibilities. Another explanation is that the national wealth and overall quality of life in the United States make it possible for people to spend less time performing household tasks than do people in China, where household appliances such as dishwashers and vacuum cleaners are not common, and where most home/family responsibilities remain time consuming. These findings suggest that, in the United States, organization-sponsored child-care and elder-care programs may be more effective in supporting employees' efforts to balance role pressures between home and work. In China, on the other hand, flexible work hours or longer weekends may be more helpful in facilitating employees' time allocations between work and family.

Second, in both China and the United States, unpaid overtime predicted perceptions of work demand, whereas primary paid work hours showed little impact. To help employees cope with work role pressures effectively, more attention should be focused on effective management of unpaid overtime, regardless of culture. Recognition of employees' unpaid overtime, making work itself more meaningful and reducing unnecessary unpaid overtime may be helpful. To be effective, these efforts clearly need organizational commitment.

Third, in both China and the United States, work–family conflict induced absenteeism but in different categories: causing organizational losses of complete workdays in China and of partial workdays in the United States. These results are consistent with previous research (Yang, 1993), which has stressed the differential effects of work–family conflict on absenteeism. At a family-supportive work setting, managerial accommodations for employees in order to cope with work–family conflict may entail increased losses of partial workdays, but this type of absenteeism can be balanced off by reduced losses of complete workdays. From an organizational perspective, effective management of work–family matters requires a basic understanding of what kind of absenteeism is involved and to which specific culture context an organization is attached.

Finally, cultural training is particularly important for managing expatriate performance. As managers go abroad, it is important that they understand differences in both value systems and social structures, including family structures. As individuals in collectivistic societies are expected to subordinate personal interests to group interests, U.S. organizations should prepare their expatriates for these cultural expectations in order to work more effectively with local co-workers. When personal sacrifice is expected, effective communication with one's spouse and children can be critical for expatriates' family stability, which is an important factor predicting overseas performance and adaptation. When organizations carry over individualistic values into a collectivistic society, or vice versa, managers should be aware of potential impacts that may have on employees' work–family adjustments.

REFERENCES

Adams, G. A., King, L. A., & King, W. D. (1996). Relationship of job and family involvement, family social support, and work–family conflict with job and life satisfaction. *Journal of Applied Psychology, 81*, 411–420.

Berry, J. W. (1980). *Acculturation as varieties of adaptation*. In A. Padilla (Ed.), *Acculturation: Theory, models and some new findings* (pp. 9–25). Boulder, CO: Westview Press.

Brislin, R. (1970). Back translation for cross-culture research. *Journal of Cross-cultural Psychology, 1*, 185–216.

Chen, C. C. (1995). New trends in rewards allocation preferences: A Sino-U.S. comparison. *Academy of Management Journal, 38*, 408–428.

Child, J. (1994). *Management in China during the age of reform*. New York: Cambridge University Press.

Doby, V. J., & Caplan, R. D. (1995). Organizational stress as threat to reputation: Effects on anxiety at work and at home. *Academy of Management Journal, 38*, 1105–1123.

Frone, M. R., Russel, M., & Cooper, M. L. (1992). Antecedents and outcomes of work–family conflict: Testing a model of the work–family interface. *Journal of Applied Psychology, 77*, 65–78.

Frone, M. R., Russel, M., & Cooper, M. L. (1997). Relation of work–family conflict to health outcomes: A four year longitudinal study of employed parents. *Journal of Occupational Health Psychology, 1*, 57–69.

Greenhaus, J. H., & Beutell, N. J. (1985). Sources of conflict between work and family roles. *Academy of Management Review, 10*, 76–88.

Greenhaus, J. H., & Parasuraman, S. (1994). *Work–family conflict, social support, and well-being*. In M. J. Davison & R. J. Burke (Eds.), *Women in management: Current research issues* (pp. 213–229). London: Chapman.

Gutek, B. A., Searle, S., & Klepa, L. (1991). Rational versus gender role explanations for work–family conflict. *Journal of Applied Psychology, 76*, 560–568.

Higgins, C. N., & Duxbury, L. E. (1992). Work–family conflict in the dual-career family. *Organizational Behavior and Human Decision Processes, 51*, 51–75.

Hofstede, G. (1980). *Culture's consequences: International differences in work related values*. Beverly Hills, CA: Sage.

Hofstede, G. (1991). *Cultures and Organizations: Software of the mind*. UK: McGraw-Hill.

Hofstede, G. (1993). Cultural constraints in management theories. *Executive: An Academy of Management Publication, 8*, 81–94.

Hui, C. H. (1988). Measurement of individualism–collectivism. *Journal of Research in Personality, 22*, 17–36.

Kahn, R. L., Wolfe, D., Quinn, R., Snoek, J. D., & Rosenthal, R. A. (1964). *Organizational stress: Studies in role conflict and ambiguity*. New York: Wiley.

Kanter, R. (1977). *Men and women of the corporation.* New York: Basic Books.

Kossek, E. E., & Oscki, C. (1988). Work–family conflict policies, and the job–life satisfaction relationship: A review and directions for organizational behavior—Human resources research. *Journal of Applied Psychology, 83,* 139–149.

Lai, G. (1995). Work–family roles and psychological wellbeing in urban China. *Journal of Health and Social Behavior, 36,* 11–37.

Lobel, S. A. (1991). Allocation of investment in work and family roles: Alternative theories and implications for research. *Academy of Management Review, 16,* 507–521.

McGuire, W. J., McGuire, C. V., & Cheever, J. (1986). The self in society: Effects of social contexts on the sense of self. *British Journal of Social Psychology, 25,* 250–270.

Near, J. P., Rice, R. W., & Hunt, R. G. (1980). The relationship between work and non-work domains: A review of empirical research. *Academy of Management Review, 5,* 415–429.

Quinn, R. P., & Staines, G. L. (1979). *The 1977 quality of employment survey.* Ann Arbor: University of Michigan.

Redding, S. G., & Martyn-Johns, T. A. (1979). *Paradigm differences and their relation to management, with reference to South-East Asia.* In G. W. England, A. R. Neghandhi, & B. Wilpert (Eds.), *Organizational functioning in a cross-cultural perspective* (pp. 103–125). Kent, OH: Kent State University Press.

Schein, E. H. (1984). Cultural as an environmental context for careers. *Journal of Occupational Behavior, 5,* 71–81.

Shenkar, O. R., & Ronen, S. (1987). Structure and importance of work goals among managers in the People's Republic of China. *Academy of Management Journal, 30,* 564–576.

Spector, P. E. (1975). Relationships of organizational frustration with reported behavioral reactions of employees. *Journal of Applied Psychology, 60,* 635–637.

Triandis, H. C. (1989). Cross-cultural studies of individualism and collectivism. In J. Berman (Ed.), *The Nebraska symposium on motivation* (pp. 41–133). Lincoln: University of Nebraska Press.

Triandis, H. C. (1995). *Individualism and collectivism.* Boulder, CO: Westview.

Trompennaars, F. (1994). *Riding the waves of culture: Understanding diversity in global business.* New York: Irvin.

Vanderkolk, B. S., & Young, A. A. (1991). *The work and family revolution: How companies can keep employees happy and business profitability.* New York: Facts on File, Inc.

Yang, N. (1993). *Work-family conflict and supervisor support.* Eastern Academy of Management Best Paper Proceedings, pp. 174–177. Providence, Rhode Island: ZAM.

Yang, N. (2000). *Cultural relativity of employee motivation: When West meets East.* In C. M. Lau, K. S. Law, D. K. Tse, & C. S. Wong (Eds.), *Asian management matters: Regional relevance and global impact* (pp. 7–57). London: Imperial College Press.

Yang, N., Chen, C.C., Choi, J., & Zou, Y. (2000) Sources of work–family conflict: A Sino-U.S. comparison of the effects of work and family demands. *Academy of Management Journal, 43,* 113–123.

12

Easing the Pain: A Cross-Cultural Study of Support Resources and Their Influence on Work–Family Conflict

Margaret A. Shaffer
Hong Kong Baptist University

Anne Marie Francesco
Hong Kong Baptist University

Janice R. W. Joplin
University of Texas at El Paso

Theresa Lau
Hong Kong Polytechnic University

ABSTRACT

The purpose of this chapter is to present the results of a cross-cultural study examining various resources that help individuals cope with competing demands from the work and family domains. To enhance our understanding of work–family conflict in different countries, we conducted focus groups in China, Hong Kong, Mexico, Singapore, and the United States. Integrating findings from the focus groups with those from the literature, we developed a classification system for organizing support resources. Domain-specific support resources include social and instrumental forms of support within the family and work/organizational domains. Domain-spanning resources include personal resources such as individual values and differences (i.e., self-reliance) and national resources such as laws that affect work and family systems. Cross-cultural comparisons are made and implications for researchers and organizations are discussed.

INTRODUCTION

Globalization, war, terrorism, SARS, and financial crises are just some of the major events affecting the quality of life for individuals around the world. Concurrent with these events, and perhaps as a result of them, even traditionally stable institutions such as work and family are experiencing revolutionary changes. Shifts in work and family characteristics and structures—such as increased participation of women in the work force, longer working hours, more dual-career/income families, and expanded responsibilities for child-care as well as eldercare—affect how individuals enact their work and family roles and how they cope with competing demands emanating from these two domains (Bond, Galinsky, & Swanberg, 1998). In this chapter, we focus on resources that help people in different countries handle conflicts that erupt as a result of competing demands between work and family.

Work–family conflict (WFC) is defined as a form of interrole conflict that occurs when responsibilities from the work and family domains are incompatible (Greenhaus & Beutell, 1985). Although WFC was originally viewed as a unidirectional construct, recent studies have supported two directions: work interference with family (WIF) and family interference with work (FIW) conflict (e.g., Adams, King, & King, 1996). Inputs to these two forms of WFC are generally domain-specific (i.e., work and family) variables that either make greater *demands* on an employee's limited time and energy, or that provide supplemental or support *resources*, freeing up some of that limited time and energy (see Frone, 2003, for a review).

Despite the predominant Western initiative in work–family research, the universality of WFC is recognized (e.g., Aryee, 1992) and several recent studies in nonwestern countries support this notion (e.g., Aryee, Fields, & Luk, 1999; Lee & Choo, 2001; Ng, Fosh, & Naylor, 2002; Skitmore & Ahmad, 2003; Yang, Chen, Choi, & Zou, 2000). In reviewing the literature from different cultures,[1] we noted some common themes across studies, regardless of the culture sampled. One commonality is the underlying assumption that human energy is limited and that those who take on multiple roles (i.e., work and family) will experience role conflict. That is, work–family conflict occurs when participation in one domain (e.g., work) diminishes the energy available for the other domain (e.g., family).

---

[1]Empirical studies cited in this paper were conducted in the United States unless otherwise specified.

Notwithstanding some evidence that participating in multiple roles may be beneficial for physical and mental health of individuals (Barnett & Hyde, 2001), the majority of the literature continues to focus on the scarcity theory rather than the expansion of roles theory. The scarcity theory contends that the resulting tension between the two domains is especially stressful because they are of similar salience and because they are dependent on each other for resources (Greenhaus & Beutell, 1985). Another commonality is that domain-specific demands, especially work and family time pressures, are major sources of work–family conflict (e.g., Aryee et al., 1999; Lee & Choo, 2001).

Findings regarding the influence of support resources are, however, inconclusive. Regardless of cultural origin, research involving support resources has been haphazard and piecemeal, with researchers generally focusing on just one or two forms of support. As with demands, these resources have been mainly confined to the work and family domains (Frone, 2003). Only a few studies have looked at personal sources of support such as personality characteristics (e.g., Bernas & Major, 2000; Grandy & Cropanzano, 1999; Grzywacz & Marks, 2000). As far as we know, no researchers have considered the effects of national level forms of support (i.e., legal protections and policies) on work–family conflict. This may be because cross-cultural WFC research has generally been limited to samples within one cultural context (see Yang et al., 2000, for an exception).

The purpose of this chapter is to identify resources that may help employees in various countries effectively cope with the stresses of competing work and family demands. Our objectives are to (1) develop a comprehensive classification scheme that includes both domain-specific (i.e., work and family) and domain-spanning resources (i.e., personal and national); (2) compare resources across cultures, noting cultural differences; and (3) consider the complex role that various forms of resources might play in the process of coping with work–family conflict. The research reported here is part of a larger study of life balance and work–family interface across five cultural locations: China, Hong Kong, Mexico, Singapore, and the United States. In the next section, we review resources that have been associated with work–family conflict. Then we describe our research approach, present our classification of support resources, and describe patterns of similarities and differences in resources used across the five countries in our study. To conclude, we discuss why and how these resources help employees cope with work–family conflict.

LITERATURE REVIEW

Resources for Coping with WFC

Traditional approaches to work and/or family stress and to work–family conflict are based on the notion that (dis)stress occurs when someone perceives environmental demands to outstrip personal resources (e.g., McGrath, 1976). Integrating this argument with stress theory, Hobfoll (1989) developed the Conservation of Resources model, which was used by Grandey and Cropanzano (1999) to explain work–family conflict. According to this model (Hobfoll, 1989), individuals seek to obtain and retain resources. When there is an actual or potential loss of resources, individuals may experience stress. In the case of work–family conflict, distress occurs when resources are lost in the process of juggling activities within the work and family domains. Although most work–family researchers have focused on domain-specific resources, the Conservation of Resources model (Hobfoll, 1989) is a more general framework that recognizes a wider range of resources, including those that may span domains such as personal characteristics and contextual conditions. We will now review previous research that has considered the influence of work and family domain-specific resources and domain-spanning personal resources.

Work Resources.   Organizational resources include both social and instrumental forms of support. Social support refers to positive affective experiences; within the work domain these may involve either supervisors or coworkers. Social support from both supervisors and coworkers is believed to be an important coping mechanism in dealing with the strain of WFC (Schwartz, D., 1994). An unsympathetic supervisor in the workplace has been one of the most important sources of work–family problems (Galinsky & Stein, 1990), yet social support in the workplace may reduce role stressors and time demands and decrease WFC (Carlson & Perrewé, 1999). For example, stress is often alleviated when understanding supervisors accommodate employees' needs for flexible schedules, are tolerant of employees' personal calls, and offer kind words when family problems arise (e.g., Batt & Valcour, 2003).

Instrumental resources refer to concrete organizational benefits or practices that are intended to reduce or prevent stress. These include telecommuting; flex-time; part-time; job sharing; employer supported childcare and care of the elderly; career break; enhanced maternity, paternity, and family leave; and making the workplace more appealing to men and women with family responsibilities (Hochschild, 1997). Of these, flex-time is one of the most popular work–family benefits that can help to reduce work and family conflict (Fredriksen-Goldsen & Scharlach, 2001). Flexible work arrangements allow employees to manage their personal lives and work more effectively; thus it is regarded as a good buffer against the encroachment of work on the family domain (Skitmore & Ahmad, 2003). Insofar as child-care arrangements are a major source of strain for parents with infants or toddlers, they are especially likely to endorse child-care centers as a means of reducing conflict between work and family (Fredriksen-Goldsen & Scharlach, 2001).

Family Resources. Researchers have also conceptualized family resources in terms of social and instrumental forms of support. Social (or emotional) support refers to positive affective experiences with family members (and friends), such as caring, listening sympathetically, and providing empathy. It has long been espoused to have positive effects on individual well-being (Joplin, Nelson, & Quick, 1999). This type of support can come from several sources, including spouse, children, other family members, and friends. Emotional support from the family has been directly associated with lower levels of work–family conflict (Adams et al., 1996; Frone, Yardley, & Markel, 1997) and indirectly, through its effects on family stress (Bernas & Major, 2000). A lack of support is especially problematic. Carlson and Perrewé (1999) found that not having family social support was predictive of higher levels of family role conflict, family time demands, and family role ambiguity.

Instrumental support refers to more tangible expressions such as actually lending a hand to complete a task. The family environment may be enhanced with instrumental forms of support such as domestic help, child- or elder-care provisions, and help provided by family members. Outside assistance with family, especially for women in dual career marriages, is critical for many families (Duxbury & Higgins, 1991). Hiring caretakers for family members is often a resource for families, especially when family members are satisfied with the quality of the care (Bedian, Burke, & Moffett, 1988). However, as much as reliable help can be supportive, lack of confidence in hired help, such as domestic helpers in Hong Kong (Fu & Shaffer, 2001), can be another source of stress. Similarly, evidence regarding the effects of instrumental support in the form of familial assistance with household chores is inconclusive (Baruch & Barnett, 1986; Swanberg, 1997).

Personal Resources.   This set of resources includes personal values and characteristics or traits of the individual that enable one to cope with stress. Values attributed to the work and family life roles have implications for the experience of work–family conflict; however, their effects are complex. The limited studies that have examined relationships between life role values indicate that these values influence the levels of work–family conflict (Cinamon & Rich, 2002) and the process whereby individuals experience work–family conflict (Carlson & Kacmar, 2000). In particular, work and family values, measured in terms of importance, centrality, and priority, were involved in several significant interactions involving antecedents and consequences of both work-to-family and family-to-work conflict (Carlson & Kacmar, 2000).

From a stress resource perspective, individual differences are important means for combating stress and its adverse consequences (Cohen & Wills, 1985; Hobfoll, 1989). Of the Big 5 personality traits, emotional stability (i.e., neuroticism) and extraversion have been associated with lower levels of both dimensions of work–family conflict (Grzywacz & Marks, 2000). Various other personal traits have also been related to work–family conflict. These include perceptions of control over work and family demands (Duxbury, Higgins, & Lee, 1994), hardiness, which is defined in terms of a sense of personal control over events (Bernas & Major, 2000), self-efficacy (Erdwins, 2001), and locus of control (Noor, 2002).

Research Questions About Resources

As we noted earlier, the research on coping resources has been haphazard and inconclusive. It has also been limited to single country samples, thus precluding a consideration of national level resources that may help individuals cope with competing work and family demands. Such national resources include government legislation regarding terms of employment that employers are legally required to follow (e.g., hours, holidays), and other work and family related legislation (e.g., income tax policies). For example, one of the most basic is legislation that limits allowable work hours or days. This creates a legal ceiling in terms of what an organization can demand and should limit time pressures in the work domain that lead to work–family conflict. Similarly, the provision of vacation and public holidays also can help to reduce time pressure from the work domain. Limited vacation time, however, may create relatively more time pressure from the work domain, which may lead to greater WFC. Income tax law is an example of other forms of legislation not directly related to terms of employment that may affect WFC. Various policies may encourage or discourage individuals from marrying or having children. Economic incentives or disincentives influence family domain instrumental support in terms of financial resources and may also have an indirect influence in terms of societal expectations of marriage and family that could lead to more or less WFC.

Applying the framework proposed in the Conservation of Resources model (Hobfoll, 1989), we would like to consider both domain-specific (work, family) and domain-spanning resources (personal, national):

Research Question 1: What are the various resources available to individuals for coping with competing demands from work and family?

Another issue has to do with cross-cultural similarities and differences in resources for coping with WFC. During the past few decades, several cultural frameworks have been developed to classify cultures in terms of various dimensions and values (e.g., Hofstede, 1980; Kluckhohn & Strodtbeck, 1961; Ronen & Shenkar, 1985; Schwartz, S. H., 1992, 1994). Often defined in terms of shared values and meanings, culture develops through the socialization processes of institutions, such as work and family, and it influences how individuals perceive, feel, and behave. Although WFC is a universal phenomenon, culture may account for some observed differences in how the interface between work and family is experienced. For example, in a comparison of American and Chinese employees, Yang et al. (2000) found several differences. Americans experienced greater family demands, and these demands had a greater impact on their WFC. In contrast, work demands led to more WFC for Chinese employees. In the United States, overwork was generally perceived as sacrificing family for one's own career; in China, it was perceived as sacrificing self for the family. Moreover, American cultural norms put family before work, and Chinese norms put work before family (Yang et al., 2000).

Although individuals within cultures will vary in terms of their cultural values and orientations, the different cultural frameworks provide norms that are useful in describing and understanding cultures in general. In comparing the five countries in our study, Hong Kong, China, and Singapore tend to group together in a far eastern cluster (Ronen & Shenkar, 1985). With respect to Hofstede's (1980) value dimensions, these same three locations have comparable ratings on the dimensions of power distance, individualism, and masculinity. They are also quite similar across Trompenaars' (1993) dimensions, except China is rated as more emotional, and Hong Kong and Singapore are considered more neutral in expressing emotions. In contrast, across cultural frameworks, the United States and Mexico are both distinct from each other and from the far eastern locations. These differences across cultures lead us to our next research question:

Research Question 2: In comparing resources for coping with WFC across cultures, what are the major similarities and differences?

METHOD

To answer these research questions, we conducted focus groups in five geographic regions: China, Hong Kong, Mexico, Singapore, and the United States. We chose these locations because of their diversity in terms of macro-level systems and practices. Of these regions, Hong Kong and Singapore are unique in that they combine both Asian and western cultural influences. The inclusion of Mexico adds a Latin dimension that is often ignored in cross-cultural research. Subjects were professionals from a major city in each of the five countries of interest. In this way, we controlled for possible confounding effects of rural versus city experiences.

Participants were invited by one of the researchers or their contacts to participate in a focus group discussion on the subject of work–family balance. We chose to collect data from focus groups as this method is particularly appropriate to generate and stimulate ideas (Cooper & Schindler, 1998) and to provide participants a chance to react to somewhat vague concepts (Johnson, 1988). It is especially useful in the exploratory and developmental phases of research so that ideas can be generated to submit to further testing using other approaches (Carson, Gilmore, Perry, & Gronhaug, 2001). As the purpose of the larger study that this is a part of is to clarify the interface between work and family and to gain an in-depth understanding of this phenomenon, focus groups provided us with the scope and flexibility needed to explore the opinions and attitudes of respondents more fully across our five locations.

The average size of our focus groups was 10 participants. The largest group, which was in Mexico, consisted of 25 participants. To conform to the recommended size of 6 to 12 participants (Carson et al., 2001; Greenbaum, 2000), we divided this group into two for the purpose of discussion (Langer, 2001), but responses were combined for analyses. Because our focus was on (relatively) young professionals, participants were graduate students, holders of a master's or other advanced degree, or the spouse of someone in either of the previous two categories. Subjects were selected to represent

TABLE 12.1
Demographic Characteristics of Focus Group Participants

	China	Hong Kong	Mexico	Singapore	United States
Gender					
Male	56%	40%	56%	67.7%	42%
Female	44%	60%	44%	33.3%	58%
Age (average years)	34.22	37.5	31.67	44	30.68
Education					
Associate's degree	33.3%	10%			
Bachelor's degree	33.3%	50%	44%	14%	63%
Master's degree	33.3%	40%	56%	86%	37%
Marital status					
Married	66.7%	80%	44%	71%	37%
Single	33.3%	20%	56%	29%	63%
Children					
Number (median)	1	2	1	2	2
Age (average years)	4.71	12.3	7.29	12.2	16.18
Family structure					
Nuclear family	66.7%	80%	89%	66.7%	89%
Extended family	33.3%	20%	11%	33.3%	11%

diverse work–family structures such as dual-income couple, traditional couple, and single working person. Among these categories, we further tried to vary number and age of children and whether or not the participants' parents needed or provided help. At the same time, we tried to control demographic characteristics across samples to facilitate comparability of data (see Table 12.1).

The first author and one other researcher were present at each of the five focus groups. A consistent approach was maintained in conducting the focus groups: (a) introduction of researchers and participants, (b) presentation of the background and rationale of the study, and (c) discussion based on a set of semistructured questions on the following aspects of work–family conflict and balance: definition, causes, outcomes, examples of those who are good or poor at balancing, and coping mechanisms. Our intention was to encourage participants to share their experiences in juggling work and family activities. All discussions were tape recorded with the permission of the participants.

The data were analyzed according to procedures suggested by King (1994). First, a research assistant prepared a transcript of the tape (and for the Mexico City group, simultaneously translated it into English). The accuracy was then verified by one of the researchers. Based on a preliminary reading of the transcripts and a consideration of the questions that were asked during the focus groups, another research assistant and all the authors developed initial categories representing the work–family interface and its antecedents and consequences (i.e., work–family conflict; work, family, and personal demands and resources; and work, family, and personal outcomes). At the same time, the research assistant reviewed the transcripts and divided the comments into interpretable single-thought "segments" so that the data could be coded. One researcher then reviewed these transcripts.

In the next step, each segment was tagged with a unique alphanumeric code for identification. The code indicated the city where the remark was made and a number that was assigned in numerical order within each city. The research assistant and all four authors then independently coded the segments into the established categories. Although there was a high degree of initial agreement on categorization, we followed an iterative process, discussing and recoding items until complete agreement was reached for all items. In the next step, the categories were divided up among the researchers, and each of us was responsible for an overall interpretation and to identify similarities and differences across cultures. A second researcher independently repeated this process, and the results from the two were integrated.

RESULTS

Our first research question was concerned with identifying the various resources available to individuals for coping with competing demands from work and family. Based on the coding process described above and our literature review, we developed the resource categories shown in Table 12.2. These include the domain-specific resources of work and family/friends and the domain-spanning resources, personal and national. In this section, we will describe the major findings for each of these categories, including those related to our second research question on cultural similarities and differences.

The two major sources of work support were social and instrumental. Social support was primarily from the supervisor with some "nice" co-workers mentioned. Overall, our respondents felt that an understanding boss could help them to balance work and family:

> The company where I work is local, very local, but a lot of ladies choose to stay, because they find that the bosses are more understanding. It's like a big family.
>
> —A Singapore Focus Group Participant

TABLE 12.2
Resources for Coping with WFC

Domain-Specific Resources			Domain-Spanning Resources	
Work	Family/Friends		Personal	National
Social support	Social support		Individual differences	Legally required terms of
Supervisors	Spouse		Big 5 personality traits	employment
Co-workers	Children		Self-reliance	Hours of work
Instrumental support	Other family members		Locus of control	Days off
Family friendly practices	Friends		Hardiness	Maternity/paternity leave
	Instrumental support		Self-efficacy	Other work and family-related
	Domestic helpers		Personal values	government legislation
	Child care		Work	Income tax policy
			Family	Education policy

Often a supportive boss was described as female, married, and/or family-oriented. The value of a supportive supervisor as a work resource and the types of behaviors that constituted supportive seemed similar across countries. For example, the supportive boss valued education and made it easier for subordinates to pursue further education.

The other type of work support resource was instrumental support in the form of family-friendly practices that helped employees balance work and family. The majority of these were benefits that helped parents to take care of their children, and they were usually used by female employees. Examples of organizational practices that were helpful included flextime, part-time work, and telecommuting:

> My company offered flexible working hours to one of the colleagues because she was struggling most of the time because of family problems. We need to be fair, so we suggested her to take shorter lunch breaks, coming half an hour earlier but leaving earlier.
> —A Hong Kong Focus Group Participant

Benefits such as child-care services, recreation clubs, sports, and vacations were also mentioned. However, it seemed that these types of practices were prevalent only in the United States. Our respondents in other countries mentioned these as uncommon, unusual, or only found in large multinationals.

The second type of domain-specific support was from family and friends, which was further subdivided into social support and instrumental support. Clearly, the greatest amount of social support was provided by immediate family members, usually the spouse or parents of the employee. In Mexico City and Shanghai, our participants mentioned that it was common for unmarried adults to live with their parents. Because the parents took care of most household responsibilities such as cleaning and cooking, it left the singles with little to take care of at home. In Hong Kong and Mexico City, it was common for grandparents, usually grandmothers, to look after the children while their parents worked:

> When I come back she and he [the children] are sleeping . . . . Thanks to my mother I have the balance because my mother takes care of them . . .
> —A Mexico Focus Group Participant

The participants from China, the United States, and Hong Kong also talked about delegating or sharing of work at home among family members.

Few participants mentioned friends as sources of support. In fact, although the few comments received about friends indicated they were positive sources of support, because work and family concerns dominated, the participants often did not have time to contact friends.

There was also instrumental support from the family domain in the form of domestic helpers and childcare. Comments about paid help as a source of support were mainly from Asian participants. In Singapore and Hong Kong, it was common to have full-time maids. However, although they were considered as a support resource, there were often conflicts with the maids that created additional stress:

> They usually give all the housework for the maids and then they just keep ringing up from work [to check on what the maid is doing].
>
> —A Hong Kong Focus Group Participant

In Mexico City and Shanghai, part-time maids were more common, whereas in the United States having household help was less common and generally only on a once-per-week basis. In Hong Kong and Shanghai, families often employed tutors to help with the children's schoolwork, and in all locations, teachers were hired for instruction such as piano lessons.

One of the domain-spanning types of support resources was personal. These included individual differences such as personality traits and personal values relating to work and family. From our focus groups there were some comments relating to self-reliance as a support resource:

> For me, I just have to decide and say, "I can control that; I cannot control that." And once I define that, I focus on what I can control and that usually helps me solve my problems or helps me deal with my problems. But once I've decided that I can't control something, I don't worry about it. I actually leave it up to the other person to fix it because I can't do it.
>
> —A United States Focus Group Participant

In the United States, religion and extracurricular activities were seen as positive, and in Mexico, improving time and self management was seen as a source of support.

Comments from focus group participants in all five countries suggest that life role values are an important resource for individuals as they struggle to balance both work and family responsibilities:

TABLE 12.3
National Resources

Legally Required Terms of Employment

	China	Hong Kong	Mexico	Singapore	United States
Workweek	40 hours	Limits for women and young people	42 to 48 hours	Not specified	40 hours
Overtime	Paid 150% of daily wages; 200% paid on rest days	No limit (but one day of rest for each 7 days worked)	Limited to 3 hours per day	Limited to 72 hours per month; paid 1.5 times hourly pay	Paid at 1.5 times regular rate of pay
Rest days	1 day per week	1 day/7 days, no extra pay for work on rest day	1 day/6 days, double pay plus salary for work on rest day	1 day /week, 1/2 day at 1 day's pay, 1/2 to full day, paid for 2 days	Varies by state from 1 day to more, no pay provisions
Vacation	Not specified	7 to 14 days depending on the length of service	6 days or more. Compulsory to give and take vacation	7 to 14 days entitlement	Not specified
Public holidays	Three week long holidays.	12 days	7 days + Christmas bonus of 15 days' pay	11 days	10 federal holidays, varies by state

Maternity, paternity leave	Minimum of 90 days for maternity; up to 15 days for paternity. Full pay and no dismissal allowed	Minimum of 10 weeks for maternity; no dismissal of pregnant employee allowed	Pregnant women cannot work after 10 pm, overtime, or in risky areas; post-birth government services & 1% dowry	8 weeks maternity if employed over 180 days or >1 children; pregnant worker cannot work between 11 pm and 6 am	12 weeks unpaid parent leave for new born, adopted, foster child; unlawful to discriminate against pregnant applicants or employees

Other Work- & Family-Related Legislation & Services Provided

Income tax policy	Fined if more than one child			Tax relief for married $9000 (1st) to $18000 (3rd) baby bonus	Until 2003, income tax "marriage penalty"
Other Legislation			College grants & scholarships		Tax deductible child care

Note. Data for this table were complied from U.S. Census Bureau, 2000 (2003) and CIA (2003); International Labour Organization (2003); Mancomext (2003); Mexico Connect (2003); Singapore Government (2003).

Spending time with family and being at work are both important, but it's difficult to do both. Basically I need to be working all the time if I want to have a promotion. You know, if you leave early from your job usually the boss says things like "What, you don't want to be promoted?"

—A Mexico Focus Group Participant

Finally, the last category of support resources was domain-spanning national resources. In all countries, the participants mentioned that government provided basic supports, but more seemed to be provided by the Singaporeans and Chinese. Because some of our participants raised the issue of government support resources yet little research had been conducted in this area, we undertook to compare legally required terms of employment and other work- and family-related government legislation in the five countries. Our results are presented in Table 12.3.

DISCUSSION

In this chapter, we have identified a spectrum of resources that are specific to either the work or family domains and that span these domains (i.e., personal and national resources). According to the Conservation of Resources model (Hobfoll, 1989), these resources may help employees effectively cope with the stresses of competing work and family demands. Having noted some similarities and differences across cultures, we now turn our attention to a discussion of how these resources may influence WFC. To understand why support resources help employees cope with WFC in different countries, we consider some cross-cultural factors that may influence this process. Based on this discussion, we then suggest directions for future research and implications for organizations.

In contrast with demands associated with WFC, support resources seem to play a more complex role in the WFC process. Although some researchers have examined the direct effects of social support on WFC (e.g., Adams et al., 1996), others have considered more indirect effects such as antecedents to demands (e.g., Cohen & Wills, 1985), mediating relationships (e.g., Gore, 1987), and moderating relationships (e.g., Frone, Russell, & Cooper, 1995). Although there is some evidence that social support has the strongest influence on WFC through its influence on antecedent stressors or demands (Carlson & Perrewé, 1999), the role of other forms of support resources has not been clarified. Given the mixed support for both direct and indirect models, it seems likely that coping resources may impact WFC in different ways and at different times.

Our investigation of the WFC experiences of employees in five countries suggests that several cultural factors may influence this process. Research on the meaning of work indicates that there is substantial variation in work centrality, the degree of general importance and value attributed to the role of working in one's life (England, 1986; MOW International Research Team, 1987). In an eight-country study, the United States had the fourth highest average work centrality score, Japan had the highest, and Britain the lowest (MOW International Research Team, 1987). In cultures where work is viewed as more important, family members may be more accepting of work being conducted in the home environment than employers are of family issues being attended to in the work setting. In other words, the family is more elastic than is the work domain (Gutek, Searle, & Klepa, 1991), and such elasticity could serve as a resource for employees. However, in cultures where work is regarded as less important, the family may not be so tolerant of work interference in the family domain, and the elasticity of the family domain may not serve as a resource.

Social and instrumental support in either domain may vary as a result of cultural differences. In more collectivistic societies that are group oriented, individuals may provide social support as a matter of duty or obligation (Triandis, 1995). Because of the importance of each individual to the collective, there may be more opportunities for people to receive social support. Similarly, collectivists may give more instrumental support to members of their own group. For instance, it is quite common in collectivist societies for grandparents or other relatives to help look after children. Support may also be influenced by gender role expectations. Where traditional gender roles are the norm, females will be expected to take on a heavier burden at home, even if they have a job outside, and males may be reluctant to provide any instrumental support to reduce the load. Moreover, cultural norms that put family before work, such as in the United States (Yang et al., 2000), seem to be associated with a higher incidence of company-provided family-friendly benefits.

Because personal resources are by definition individually based and culture is an important influence on the individual, cultural differences also account for variations in these resources. For example, life role values may be related to individualism and collectivism. Because collectivists are more group-oriented, they might on average put higher value on the family role. With respect to self-reliance, a personal resource that emerged from our focus groups, collectivists may have a greater tendency to be overdependents (i.e., rely on too many people and too much information), whereas individualists may tend more toward counterdependency (i.e., tendency to withdraw from social activity and work alone). In other words, it is possible that group-oriented collectivists may become even more dependent on others and that self-oriented individualists even more dependent on themselves.

Finally, with respect to national resources it seems that these are similar in nature to instrumental resources offered in the work and family domains and thus can have a direct influence on the WFC process. Most of these national resources relate to time and money; i.e., they restrict the amount of time that someone should work and legally mandate the provision of financial resources either from the employer or directly from the government under certain circumstances. Thus, for example, the legally mandated overtime pay can be used to obtain childcare, and thus directly reduce potential WFC. Because such legislation varies considerably from country to country, we would expect these differences to be reflected in national differences in WFC. However, because one consistent theme from our focus group participants was that actual time worked far exceeded legal limits on work hours, this phenomenon may obscure some of the variation in country to country data.

Implications

Except for national resources, each type of resource that we have discussed has been researched to some extent in the past. However, most of these studies were done only in one country, the United States. Thus, the major question of how support resources influence work–family conflict across cultures has not really been tested. The focus group research that we present in this chapter has been helpful in giving us an in-depth look at a small group of professionals' opinions about work–family conflict and relevant resources in five countries. However, the limited scope of this study, in terms of both number of participants and number of countries, demands that further research be carried out using larger samples, more countries, and other methodologies. Although focus groups allowed us to obtain rich descriptive data, this method does not lend itself to testing causal relationships. Studies, such as the one done by Carlson and Perrewé (1999), that compare models with support variables as antecedent, intervening, moderating, and independent variables would also help to discern how these different resources influence WFC in different countries.

The results of past research and our own focus group study have indicated cross-cultural differences that have organizational implications. For example, when a society expects and approves of family domain instrumental support such as childcare provided by a family member, employer-sponsored day care may be viewed as an unnecessary or even useless benefit by employees. Thus, multinationals must be attuned to different societal needs and expectations when it comes to providing such types of benefits. Another example relates to possible gender effects on levels of WFC as a result of societal gender role expectations. Ambivalence about the role of women as professionals versus their traditional role at home combined with an expectation that women should be responsible for taking care of children and the home may lead to higher levels of WFC for women and consequent negative effects on job performance, satisfaction, and other outcomes. As mentioned earlier, much more comprehensive cross-cultural research is needed to ascertain the precise influence of support resources on the work–family conflict process within and across cultures.

To conclude, this chapter has identified and organized the various resources that help individuals cope with competing demands from the work and family domains across countries. We have integrated findings from the literature with the results of our five-country focus group study in China, Hong Kong, Mexico, Singapore, and the United States. The classification system that we have developed encompasses domain-specific support resources including social and instrumental forms of support within the work and family domains and domain-spanning resources including personal and national resources. We have found that these resources vary considerably across countries, and we propose how and why they may influence work–family conflict. It is clear that large-scale cross-cultural research is needed to gain further understanding of this phenomenon.

REFERENCES

Adams, G. A., King, L. A., & King, D. W. (1996). Relationships of job and family involvement, family social support, and work–family conflict with job and life satisfaction. *Journal of Applied Psychology, 18,* 411–420.

Aryee, S. (1992). Antecedents and outcomes of work–family conflict among married professional women: Evidence from Singapore. *Human Relations, 45,* 813–837.

Aryee, S., Fields, D., & Luk, V. (1999). A cross-cultural test of a model of the work–family interface. *Journal of Management, 25,* 491–511.

Barnett, R. C., & Hyde, J. S. (2001). Women, men, work, and family. *American Psychologist, 56,* 781–796.

Baruch, G. K., & Barnett, R. (1986). Role quality, multiple role involvement, and psychological well-being in midlife women. *Journal of Personality and Social Psychology, 51,* 578–585.

Batt, R., & Valcour, P. M. (2003). Human resource practices as predictors of work–family outcomes and employee turnover. *Industrial Relations, 42,* 189–220.

Bedian, A. G., Burke, B. G., & Moffett, R. G. (1988). Outcomes of work–family conflict among married male and female professionals. *Journal of Management, 14,* 475–491.

Bernas, K. H., & Major, D. A. (2000). Contributors to stress resistance: Testing a model of women's work–family conflict. *Psychology of Women Quarterly, 24,* 170–178.

Bond, J. T., Galinsky, E., & Swanberg, J. E. (1998). *The 1997 national study of the changing workforce.* New York: Families and Work Institute.

CIA, "The World Factbook 2003," http://www.cia.gov/cia/publications/factbook/index.html, Accessed March 15, 2003.

Carlson, D. S., & Kacmar, K. M. (2000). Work–family conflict in the organization: Do life role values make a difference? *Journal of Management, 26,* 1031–1054.

Carlson, D. S., & Perrewé, P. L. (1999). The role of social support in the stressor–strain relationship: An examination of work–family conflict. *Journal of Management, 25,* 513–540.

Carson, D., Gilmore, A., Perry, C., & Gronhaug, K. (2001). *Qualitative marketing research.* London: Sage.

Cinamon, R. G., & Rich, Y. (2002). Profiles of attribution of importance to life roles and their implications for the work–family conflict. *Journal of Counseling Psychology, 49,* 212–220.

Cohen, S., & Wills, T. A. (1985). Stress, social support, and the buffering hypothesis. *Psychological Bulletin, 98,* 310–357.

Cooper, D. R., & Schindler, P. S. (1998). *Business research methods.* Boston: McGraw-Hill Irwin.

Duxbury, L. E., & Higgins, C. A. (1991). Gender differences in work–family conflict. *Journal of Applied Psychology, 76,* 60–74.

Duxbury, L. E., Higgins, C., & Lee, C. (1994). Work–family conflict: A comparison by gender, family type, and perceived control. *Journal of Family Issues, 15,* 449–466.

England, G. W. (1986). National work meanings and patterns—Constraints on management action. *European Management Journal, 4,* 176–184.

Erdwins, C. J. (2001). The relationship of woman's role strain to social support, role satisfaction, and self-efficacy. *Family Relations, 50,* 230–238.

Fredriksen-Goldsen, K. I., & Scharlach, A. E. (2001). *Families and work: New directions in twenty-first century.* New York: Oxford University Press.

Frone, M. R. (2003). Work–family balance. In J. C. Quick & L. E. Tetrick (Eds.), *Handbook of occupational health psychology* (pp. 143–162). Washington, DC: American Psychological Association.

Frone, M. R., Russell, M., & Cooper, M. L. (1995). Relationship of work and family stressors to psychological distress: The independent moderating influence of social support, mastery, active coping, and self-focused attention. In R. Crandall & P. L. Perrewé (Eds.), *Occupational stress: A handbook.* Washington, DC: Taylor & Francis.

Frone, M. R., Yardley, J. K., & Markel, K. S. (1997). Developing and testing an integrative model of the work–family interface. *Journal of Vocational Behavior, 50,* 145–167.

Fu, C., & Shaffer, M. (2001). The tug of work and family: Direct and indirect domain-specific determinants of family interference with work and work interference with family. *Personnel Review, 30,* 502–522.

Galinsky, E., & Stein, P. (1990). The impact of human resource policies on employers. *Journal of Family Issues, 11,* 368–383.

Gore, S. (1987). Perspectives on social support and research on stress moderating processes. In J. M. Ivancevich & D. C. Ganster (Eds.), *Job stress: From theory to suggestion.* New York: Haworth Press.

Grandey, A. A., & Cropanzano, R. (1999). The conservation of resources model applied to work–family conflict and strain. *Journal of Vocational Behavior, 54,* 350–370.

Greenbaum, T. (2000). *Moderating focus groups.* Thousand Oaks, CA: Sage.

Greenhaus, J. H., & Beutell, N. J. (1985). Sources of conflict between work and family roles. *Journal of Management Review, 10,* 76–88.

Grzywacz, J. G., & Marks, N. F. (2000). Reconceptualizing the work–family interface: An ecological perspective on the correlates of positive and negative spillover between work and family. *Journal of Occupational Health Psychology, 5,* 111–126.

Gutek, B. A., Searle, S., & Klepa, L. (1991). Rational versus gender role explanations for work–family conflict. *Journal of Applied Psychology, 76,* 560–568.

Hobfoll, S. E. (1989). Conservation of resources: A new attempt at conceptualizing stress. *American Psychologist, 44,* 513–524.

Hochschild, A. (1997). *The time bind: When work becomes home and home becomes work.* New York: Henry Holt.

Hofstede, G. (1980). *Culture's consequences: International differences in work related values.* Beverly Hills, CA: Sage.

International Labour Organization. NATLEX, Accessed March 17, 2003, http://natlex.ilo.org/scripts/natlexcgi.exe?lang=E

Johnson, R. R. (1988). *Marketing News, 22,* October 24, 21.

Joplin, J. R. W., Nelson, D. L., & Quick, J. C. (1999). Attachment behavior and health: Relationships at work and home. *Journal of Organizational Behavior, 20,* 783–796.

King, N. (1994). The qualitative research interview. In C. Cassell & G. Symon (Eds.), *Qualitative methods in organizational research: A practical guide.* London: Sage.

Kluckhohn, F., & Strodtbeck, F. L. (1961). *Variations in values orientations.* Evanston, IL: Peterson.

Langer, J. (2001). *The mirrored window: Focus groups from a moderator's point of view.* Ithaca, NY: Paramount Market Publishing.

Lee, S. K. F., & Choo, S. L. (2001). Work–family conflict of women entrepreneurs in Singapore. *Women in Management Review, 16,* 204–221.

Mancomext, "Mexico Business Opportunities and Legal Framework" XV. Labor, http://www.mexico-trade.com/exchange.html#1f, Accessed March 19, 2003.

McGrath, J. E. (1976). Stress and behavior in organizations. In M. D. Dunnette (Ed.), *Handbook of industrial and organizational psychology*. New York: Wiley.

Mexico Connect, American Chamber Mexico, "Mexico Labor Market and Laws," http://www.mexconnect.com/mex_/laborlaw.html, Accessed March 19, 2003.

MOW International Research Team. (1987). *The meaning of work: An international perspective*. London: Academic Press.

Ng, W. C., Fosh, P., & Naylor, D. (2002). Work–family conflict for employees in an east Asian airline: Impact on career and relationship to gender. *Economic and Industrial Democracy, 23*, 67–105.

Noor, N. M. (2002). Work–family conflict, locus of control, and women's well-being: Tests of alternative pathways. *Journal of Social Psychology, 142*, 645–662.

Ronen, S., & Shenkar, O. (1985). Clustering countries on attitudinal dimensions: A review of and synthesis. *Academy of Management Review, 10*, 435–454.

Schwartz, D. (1994). *An examination of the impact of family-friendly policies on the glass ceiling*. New York: Families and Work Institute.

Schwartz, S. H. (1992). Universals in the content and structure of values: Theoretical advances and empirical tests in 20 countries. *Advances in Experimental Social Psychology, 25*, 1–65.

Schwartz, S. H. (1994). Beyond individualism/collectivism: New cultural dimensions of values. In U. Kim, H. C. Triandis, C. Kagitcibasi, S. C. Choi, & G. Yoon (Eds.), *Individualism and collectivism: Theory, Method and Applications*. Thousand Oaks, CA: Sage.

Singapore Government, Welcome 2 Employment Town, http://www.employmenttown.gov.sg/ecareer/solutions/1,1260,3-6,00.html, Accessed March 18, 2003.

Skitmore, M., & Ahmad, S. (2003). Work–family conflict: A survey of Singaporean workers. *Singapore Management Review, 25*, 35–52.

Swanberg, J. E. (1997). Job family role strain: Understanding the experience of lower wage service employees. *Dissertation Abstracts International, 58*, 5-A.

Triandis, H. C. (1995). *Individualism and collectivism*. Boulder, CO: Westview.

Trompenaars, F. (1993). *Riding the waves of culture: Understanding diversity in global business*, London: The Economist Books.

U.S. Census Bureau, "2000 Census Data," http://blue.census.gov/cgi-bin/ipc, Accessed March 11, 2003.

Yang, N., Chen, C. C., Choi, J., & Zou, Y. (2000). Sources of work–family conflict: A Sino-US comparison of the effects of work and family demands. *Academy of Management Journal, 43*, 113–123.

IV

Case Studies

Case Study 1

Emigration to Mexico: Promotion and the Dual-Career Couple

Nuria Chinchilla and Steven Poelmans
IESE Business School/University of Navarra

EMIGRATION TO MEXICO: PROMOTION AND THE DUAL-CAREER COUPLE (A)

We had another fight today. This time Ana seemed a lot angrier than on other occasions. She said this was the worst Christmas she'd had for a long time. She's very tense, and I know it's my fault.

It all started almost as a bit of excitement, an adventure. My boss asked me if I'd like to go to Mexico DF for a month to look into the possibility of establishing a subsidiary there. It was only going to be for a month and then I'd come back to Spain. I'd learn all about the Latin American market. It would be fun and professionally enriching... It all sounded very appealing. But everything has happened so fast. After a month in Mexico, the outlook was highly promising, and then came the serious offer. I can't say whether I was expecting it, whether it's what I wanted to happen, or whether I just did my best to make a good job of researching the opportunities in Mexico. But the fact is they came to me with this offer... and I can't pretend I'm not extremely excited about it. Three years in DF, setting up the subsidiary, with general management responsibilities, and with what looks to be a very much brighter career prospect when I get back to Spain. And with a salary—during those three years—three times what I'm getting now, plus a car and a big house, all paid for. When I get back to Spain, the salary will drop back in line with my new position, but I imagine it will be a very good position. In a word, a big promotion.

At first, I was flattered. Of all my colleagues (a lot of whom would give anything for this opportunity) they chose me. I liked that, but I couldn't really believe it. Later, when I thought about the responsibility it involved, how much I'd learn, the money... then I started to take it seriously. Very seriously. Some friends told me I should go for it. Even my parents seemed to be in favor.

But, obviously, there was always Ana to be thought about.

Ana, my wife, is the person I love and respect more than anyone. We were together for more than 7 years before we got married, though we lived in different cities: Ana in La Coruña, I in Madrid. But we persevered. We met whenever we could, when we didn't have exams, putting up with the long coach rides to and fro, spending what little money we had as students. And almost every day we spent apart we would wait till 10 at night to speak to each other on the phone (at the off-peak rate), just for a few minutes, a few coins' worth, from public phone boxes because our parents were fed up with having to pay our bills, and so they forced us to use our initiative. But we persevered. And our love for one another grew. Until, in the end, we gave all those who had been betting on when we would split up a big disappointment by getting married. Ana came to Madrid with me. She set up a practice as a tax accountant, on her own, without any help. And she was very successful. She won a lot of clients and carved out a niche for herself. She started to bring in a very good income and gained confidence in her own abilities. She made friends. She was happy.

It is now more than 4 years since we got married. We were getting closer and communicating more. I felt very lucky: she was the best, and she still is. But now, along comes this.

I know that, for me, this is a unique opportunity. She knows it too. But if we go to Mexico, she'll have to close down her practice, which is a very important part of her life. She's very good at what she does and she'll lose everything she has fought so hard for, everything that gives her so much satisfaction and fulfillment. She won't be able to set up a practice like that in Mexico. The legislation is different. The culture is different. It would take years! And when we get back to Spain, her old clients will have found another accountant to look after their affairs. She'll have been away for 3 years, after all! She'll lose everything, there's no escaping that fact.

The other night I really understood the dilemma she's in. We were having dinner with another couple who have spent several years in

DF and have just recently come back to Spain. The husband said to us:

> My wife was in a similar position as you: a graduate, with a good job in Spain. But when we got to Mexico, she was out of work. I was earning a fortune, but she was relegated to the position of the bored housewife, stuck at home all day (in DF it can be dangerous to go out at certain times of day). In the end, though, she found work as a secretary in DF, and at least it meant she had some pleasure in life. If you want, I could recommend Ana for the secretarial post my wife just left.

Poor fellow, he wasn't joking. He was deadly serious. He really wanted to help us! It was awful!

I glanced at Ana but her forced smile made me freeze. To think of Ana, a real career woman, a fighter, highly respected in her field, adviser to some very important companies, speaker at numerous conferences and seminars... to think of Ana going around begging for a clerical job just so she didn't feel bored, so she didn't turn into a bored housewife!

My employer won't allow her to work with me (company rules), and they can't find her a job elsewhere. Nor would she want to do just any old job they offered her: she's too clever for that and she needs a challenge.

I know that she would sacrifice herself for me, but what I am asking of her is very tough. In fact, it's devastating; there's no other word for it. But there's no question of me going without her. No way. She came to Madrid to be with me. She has backed me to the hilt. She comes first.

If, instead of me, it was Ana who had the big opportunity, would I go and live abroad for her sake, find whatever job I could and give up everything I've worked so hard for here? Would I make the sacrifice for my wife as I'm asking her to do for me? That is the question I hardly dare ask myself out loud when she is around.

I thought of telling her *she* should decide: whatever she decided, I'd go along with it. But she's too good. She said to me:

> You're really excited about it, aren't you? It's a once-in-a-lifetime opportunity, isn't it? And we don't have any children yet. So this is the right time to do it. Do you think I could be happy, thinking I'd spoiled your career? You are my life. If it's up to me to decide, I can tell you it's already settled: we're going.

That same evening, Ana started burning her bridges. She phoned her father and told him she was going to live in Mexico. Ever since then my father-in-law has hated me. I'm the one who's stolen away his favourite daughter (all the family knows that my father-in-law has a particular fondness for Ana). First I carry her off to Madrid, and now I'm planning to whisk her off even further away: Come on! Mexico here we come!

After she'd spoken to her father, Ana cried for a bit. She couldn't help it. I promised her we wouldn't go, but at the same time I couldn't help putting pressure on her: I did my best to make her see all kinds of advantages in the move. To be honest, I think I just couldn't let this opportunity go so easily. I don't know if I did the right thing, but I do know that it broke my heart to see her like that. I was being pulled in two different directions at once: my love for my wife was commanding me to stay, while my excitement at the prospect of going abroad was yelling at me to try to persuade her and get her to agree to go there with me for 3 years, even if it did mean giving up her practice.

She cried a lot, but she never said we must stay, not once. She's far too good, and far too tough, for that. All she asked was that I let her cry a little, she would soon get over it. But she hasn't got over it. Now, instead of crying, whenever we broach the subject we end up fighting. We try not to argue, but we end up losing our patience and flying off the handle.

I don't want to force her, but one of us is going to have to make a sacrifice, that's for sure. It would be easier for me if I could accuse her of being selfish, but she isn't. If anyone here is being selfish, it's me.

I don't know what to do. I don't know what's best. At this stage I can't expect her to believe me if I say I'll stay and it doesn't really matter to me: she knows me too well for that. I started all this trouble. How will we feel later, a year or two from now, if I make the sacrifice and we stay here? And how will we feel if she makes the sacrifice and we go?

Mexico can be a dangerous place for families. I've heard there are quite a few broken marriages. It's much easier for Spaniards to get involved in extramarital affairs, even without looking for it, even trying to avoid it. Spaniards from the mother country are highly respected and well treated in Mexico. They're looked up to. A person can easily start to get an exaggerated opinion of himself, start thinking he's something special, lose his head. A lot of people say it changes your character, people get arrogant or vain. If Ana and I were to separate, I would be the most wretched person on earth. We love each other dearly, and we deserve to be together. In fact, we battled to stay together—for 7 long years.

All the same, this is a great opportunity for me, and 3 years goes in no time. And when we come back, we can be a happy, wealthy family. I'll have an excellent job. And if then we have children, we'll be able to offer them the very best. And she'll be able to start up her practice again...or at least, I hope she will.

Sometimes I think it would be better if Ana thought of herself more, if she was more selfish. That way I would feel better about insisting on what I want. But although right now she's earning more than me, even so I know she wants to go for my sake—for my sake and for no other reason. She says she really believes in me, even at the worst times when we start to lose our temper and quarrel.

Don't be angry, Ana. It'll be all right. We'll make the decision that's best for the both of us, just you wait and see. So please don't be angry any more. You mean everything to me, too.

EMIGRATION TO MEXICO: PROMOTION AND THE DUAL-CAREER COUPLE (B)

Ever since my husband was offered the job in Mexico, I've been in a state of panic. The pressure has been tremendous. Pressure and panic—that just about sums up how I've been feeling. Let me try to explain.

Until not so long ago, I was perfectly settled in my adopted city, despite the fact that my parents live far away in another town. Life revolved around my husband and my work as a liberal professional. We have a lot of friends. Although they are friends of both of us, I have to admit that most of them come from my husband's side, as all of my friends are people I met at school or university who have stayed in the city where my parents are living now (and where I used to live until I got married).

My life was more or less anxiety-free. I had a job that I enjoyed, I had a very good income, and so did my husband.

Then, more or less out of the blue (to be honest, I suppose it wasn't quite like that, but it certainly seemed like it to me), my husband was offered the chance to go to Mexico for a month to sound out the market and investigate the opportunities for opening a subsidiary of his company there. He's naturally hard-working and ambitious, so the assignment really appealed to him (in fact, it was the sort of challenge he needed, as he'd been telling me for some time that his immediate boss was stifling his initiative). So, without giving it another thought, he told them he'd love to go.

We talked about it at home, and he assured me it would only be for a month, and of course I was foolish enough to believe it. I didn't think it would be too difficult, being apart for a month, seeing as we'd already lived apart for so many years (more than 7) before we got married, living in different cities, seeing each other only in the holidays and occasionally on weekends.

So my husband went to Mexico and came back, as planned, after one month. That was just before Christmas. As soon as he got back, he was summoned to various meetings with his bosses and, to cut a long story short, everything had gone so well that the obvious happened: they suggested that he go and live in Mexico for 2 to 3 years, at least.

I'll never forget the day he came home with that bombshell! We've always been in the habit of talking things over with one another very openly, so he more or less came straight out with it: "They've offered me the chance to go and live in Mexico, and I have to give them an answer straightaway." (My husband is a very impatient man, and although in fact they hadn't demanded an immediate reply, he'd decided that he had to give them a definite yes or no more or less the next day.) That was on a Thursday or Friday, and he more or less said he had to tell them one way or the other the following Monday or Tuesday.

You can imagine how I felt. Initially, I just gaped at him and said, "How can we possibly be expected to make such an important decision in such a short time?"

The upshot of it all is that, after talking it over and clarifying the fact that we didn't have to give an answer immediately, this last Christmas has been the worst I've ever had.

My husband and I have been talking about it nonstop. We try to weigh the pros and cons, but there doesn't seem to be much point. It's already tacitly understood that we're going to say yes, and that turning the offer down isn't really an option.

The basic problem, I suppose, is very simple: one of us is going to have to sacrifice his career to some extent. For him this is the chance of a lifetime (he'll be general manager of the Mexican subsidiary, and he's very young to hold such an important position, commanding such a big salary). If we don't go, we'll always have the knowledge that his career could have turned out very differently. There doesn't seem to be any alternative.

At the moment, I have my own practice, based in a room in our house, and I'm on a good income (in fact, right now I'm earning more than my husband). And yet, perhaps because it's just my little room, my practice doesn't seem as important as the opportunity he has been offered. There may be a bit of male chauvinism in it, of course (the woman is the one who has to sacrifice herself first), and also—there's no point in denying it—a good deal of resignation on my part.

We've been over it again and again with one another (although I sometimes wonder if we aren't merely going around in circles) and also with my parents. I'm not very sure what his parents think, although I know they're not very keen on the idea of his going to live so far away. What I do know, though, is how badly my parents have reacted, particularly—it's only fair to say—my father.

My practice is a continuation of my father's practice. I started working alongside him in his practice, and when I got married I opened a branch office. That is enough on its own to make my father balk at the idea of my throwing overboard all that I've accomplished with such effort, building on his achievements. To make things worse, I'm the apple of his eye. The implication being that he doesn't just disapprove of my giving it all up and going to live in Mexico, with no job to go to, just like that; no, he absolutely detests the idea. But instead of trying to persuade me or argue his case, he just flatly opposes the plan and refuses to understand what I'm going through.

> The reasons he has given why I shouldn't go to Mexico run more or less along these lines: You're talking about going to live in an underdeveloped, male chauvinist country where you're going to find social life hell and where you're not going to find a job to match your qualifications. You've been told it'll be for two or three years, but it'll end up being for the rest of your life. And above all, as you know full well, even if you do come back, you can kiss your practice goodbye. If you tell your clients you're going, you'll never get them back. And don't go thinking I'll help you out, because I won't. If you come back, you'll have to get yourself a job in some company or other, but you can forget about being a liberal professional again.

I don't suppose it's quite the reaction he expected, but this has brought out the rebellious streak in me. I'm not going to be bullied. So I said to him, "I refuse to let anyone blackmail me like this. My husband comes first. I definitely will go now, you can be sure of that, because there's no point in staying here if my own father can't be bothered to make the effort to understand me in a situation as important as this."

This is not something that has happened all in one day, but over several days, and sometimes over the phone, though there was one day recently when, for some reason to do with his work, my father and I had a face-to-face confrontation. And that was even worse, because he refused to budge and what really upset me was that I could see the expression on his face: hard and inflexible.

On top of all this, whenever we've told our friends about the job offer, they've all said what a marvelous opportunity it is, an offer we can't refuse (it's so easy to have opinions about things that affect other people and not yourself!). One very close friend of mine laughingly said to me, "I'd be on the plane already." But I wonder if, when it came to the crunch, he'd be prepared to move, even if it was just to another part of Spain.

We really need to think things through more carefully, but I feel as if we're being swept along by events. The only thing I know for sure is that either we go to Mexico or my husband's career will be nipped in the bud.

So in a way I'm resigned to the fact that I'm going to Mexico. I've started to lose all interest and enthusiasm for my work and feel depressed most of the time, even though deep inside I'm still hoping for some magic solution that will solve all my problems. It will have to be a solution that doesn't involve going to Mexico but that will save me from having to spend the rest of my life feeling I've ruined my husband's career.

The way things are right now, all I can do is pray, and that's exactly what I do constantly, asking God to help me find the solution that I'm incapable of finding for myself.

Instructor's Manual for Case Study 1

Barbara Beham and Steven Poelmans
IESE Business School/University of Navarra

CASE OVERVIEW

The case deals with the decision of a dual-career couple on whether to accept an offer provided by the company for the husband to go abroad. The events surrounding the decision are separately told from the perspective of Ana and her husband.

Ana and her husband live together in Madrid, Spain. Upon getting married, Ana moved from La Coruña to Madrid. She started a small practice as a tax accountant in a branch of her father's practice. Ana is very successful in her job, currently earning more than her husband. A few weeks ago, her husband's company offered him a job in Mexico. He has been there for a month, checking the possibility of establishing a subsidiary. As the outlook was highly promising, they offered him a job for 3 years in Mexico DF, setting up the subsidiary with general management responsibilities and with very good career prospects when returning to Spain. Her husband claims he has to make his decision within a few days.

Accepting the offer would mean that Ana has to give up her practice. As legislation is different in Mexico she would not be able to set up a new practice there. Company policies do not allow her to work at her husband's company, and there is no other support for spouses available. For her husband it is an once-in-a-lifetime opportunity. If they do not go, they may have to come to the realization that his career could have turned out very different. It seems that someone has to make a sacrifice.

KEY ISSUES

The case is designed to allow the development of a discussion on the following issues:

- Work–family conflict
- Dual-career couples
- Crossover effects of stress and strain
- Work–life policies in organizations
- Expatriation/global assignments
- Cultural influences on work–family conflict

TEACHING

This case can be used in courses dealing with organizational behavior, career management, or human resource management. Although MBA students (especially international students with a partner) might be able to relate best to this case it could also be used in an undergraduate course.

The case can be discussed in one class session of one to two hours duration. The class could begin with the simple question to the students on what the couple should do in that situation: go or not go. The different positive and negative arguments can be discussed and summarized on the black board. As part of this exercise, the students could also make an estimate of purely monetary arguments. This can then be followed by one of the following questions.

QUESTIONS FOR DISCUSSION

Work–family conflict and dual-career couples:

1. In your opinion, should the couple take or reject the career opportunity in Mexico? Why?
2. What suggestions would you make to the couple or to people facing a similar situation?

3. What are some major factors that are causing the conflict and stress between the Spanish couple in the case?
4. According to the case and based on your knowledge, what are some work–family matters that are unique for dual-career couples?
5. How would the storyline play out if it was the female partner within the couple who received the job offer in Mexico? Would the decision be different?

Crossover effects of stress and strain:

1. Can you detect some crossover processes in the current situation? Direct? Indirect? Unidirectional? Bidirectional? What aspects of culture will affect the crossover of stress and strain between them?
2. Imagine the future if Ana does decide to move to Mexico with her husband? What are some of the repercussions of Ana's move to Mexico that could negatively affect her husband's job performance?
3. What role do extended family members and friends play? Are they a source of support or an additional source of strain? Would their reactions be different if this case occurred in the United States? What about China?

Cultural influences on work–family conflict:

1. What cultural factors are influencing the work–family conflict that Ana and her husband are experiencing?
2. What do you think women in other countries would do if they were in Ana's position?
3. How might the concept of acculturative stress relate to this case?

Work–life policies in organizations and expatriation:

1. What role does the company play in this situation? What could the company do to help the couple make the important decision of whether to accept a global assignment?
2. From Ana's perspective, what could her husband's organization do to help her, personally and professionally, if she decides to relocate with her husband?
3. The case emphasizes the negative implications on Ana's career if relocation is chosen. What might be some positive aspects, in terms of Ana's personal and professional development, if

relocation is chosen? Can the company do something to create or enhance opportunities for positive experiences?

4. A commuter relationship is not mentioned in the case. Why not? What organizational interventions would make a commuter relationship possible and relieve some of the unnecessary stress being placed on Ana?

THEORETICAL LINKS

One theoretical approach in analyzing this case would be *identity theory* (Burke, 1991). Much of the stress that Ana is experiencing (and that is playing out in the form of work–family conflict) is the result of incongruence between her identity as a professional woman and her identity as a wife.

Burke, P. J. (1991). Identity processes and social stress. *American Sociological Review, 56,* 836–849.

Another theoretical approach is the *conservation of resources theory.* According to this theory (Hobfoll, 1989), individuals seek to obtain and retain resources. When there is an actual or potential loss of resources, individuals may experience stress. In the case of work–family conflict, distress occurs when resources are lost in the process of juggling activities within the work and family domains. Although most work–family researchers have focused on domain-specific resources, the Conservation of Resources model (Hobfoll, 1989) is a more general framework that recognizes a wider range of resources, including those that may span domains such as personal characteristics and contextual conditions.

Hobfoll, S. E. (1989). Conservation of resources: A new attempt at conceptualizing stress. *American Psychologist, 44,* 513–524

Social identity theory says that individuals classify themselves as members of social groups. Individuals have multiple identities that derive from their interaction with others. The extent of identification with each role varies with the person and goals shared with others (Tajfel & Turner, 1985). Applied to the work–family context, a person may achieve work–family balance by (a) ensuring that conflicting identities are separated or (b) by applying consistent personal values across identities. Social identity theory proposes that people can invest in several roles and feel satisfied, as long as one of the two aforementioned conditions is met (Lobel 1991a).

Lobel, S. A. (1991a). Allocation of investment in work and family roles: Alternative theories and implications for research. *Academy of Management Review, 16,* 507–521.

Tajfel, H., & Turner, H. (1985). The social identity theory of intergroup behaviour. In S. Worchel & W. Austin (Eds.), *Psychology of intergroup relations* (2nd ed., pp. 7–24). Chicago: Nelson-Hall.

The case can also be analyzed in the light of *decision process theory of work and family*, which concentrates on decisions actors make. Within this framework, work–family conflict can still be seen as an external or internal stressor, as is the case of role theory, spillover theory, and self-discrepancy theory, but the decision process theory fundamentally conceives work–family conflict as the intermediate result of decisions made in the course of time. It centers on decisions proceeding and following conflict rather than on the consequences of work–family conflict. The decision of Ana and her husband is a difficult one, and there is no absolute right or wrong choice. The couple should learn more about the Mexican culture and work environment, particularly for Ana, who seems to have no direct personal experience about the country. The couple also needs to communicate more openly about how they feel about the career dilemma and each other. The decision is not just for one person's career or sacrifice, but should be a joint decision with mutual understanding and mutual support between the couple.

Poelmans, S. (2004). The decision process theory of work and family. In E. E. Kossek and S. Lambert (Eds.), *Managing work–life integration in organizations: Future directions for research and practice.* Mahwah, NJ: Lawrence Erlbaum Associates.

Hofstede (1997) compared *cultural differences* among 53 countries and regions. Relevant to the current case, the following table contrasts the value variations between Spain and Mexico.

Country	Power Distance	Individualism-Collectivism	Masculinity-Femininity	Uncertainty Avoidance
Spain	Medium	Individualist	Feminine	High
Mexico	High	Collectivist	Masculine	High

Yang, Chen, Choi, and Zou (2000) contend that cultures differ in the extent to which they separate self, work, and family. In a collectivistic society such as China, work is viewed as self-sacrifice for the benefit of the family, whereas in an individualistic society such as the United States, sacrificing family for work is often perceived as for one's own career and a failure to care for significant others in one's family. In the current case, the husband and wife consistently see persistence for his or her own career as forcing the other to "make a sacrifice" or "being selfish." Such perception of career relative to family and separation of self, career, and family are consistent with Spain's individualistic cultural orientation. They also help explain why the couple seems to make every effort to avoid someday thinking, "I'd spoiled your career."

According to Schein (1984), culture influences the concept of career itself, the importance of career relative to personal and family issues, and the legitimacy of managerial career. In an individualistic society, one's career connotes personal ambition and achievement and should not interfere with family, otherwise it is likely to cause dissatisfaction in other family members. In the current case, the career opportunity for the husband is likely to interfere with the family (e.g., family relationship and the wife's career), which clearly has caused pressure and depression for the wife. On the other hand, both have the legitimacy to choose between personal career and family.

Hofstede, G. (1997). *Culture and organizations*: Software of the mind. New York: McGraw Hill.

Schien, E. H. (1984). Culture as an environment context for careers. *Journal of Occupational Behavior, 5,* 71–81.

Yang, N., Chen, C. C., Choi, J., & Zou, Y. (2000). Sources of work–family conflict: A Sino-U.S. comparison of the effects of work and family demands. *Academy of Management, 43,* 113–123.

The *concept of acculturative stress* (Chapter 2, this volume) states that immigrants have to develop acculturation coping strategies. One of these strategies is marginalization as Berry and Sam (1997) note as one of the coping strategies migrants follow. Ana may risk being marginalized to some extent during the move in Mexico by possibly being underemployed. Despite her high skill level, she too has to manage legal challenges arising from employment and immigration laws. She and her spouse will need to make decisions regarding the degree to which she will adapt to Mexico's traditional mores or carry their family cultural system followed in Spain abroad.

Berry, J. W., & Sam, D. L. (1997). Acculturation and adaptation. In J. W. Berry, M. H. Segall *et al.* (Eds.), *Handbook of cross-cultural psychology* (pp. 291–326). Boston: Allyn and Bacon.

The case is also a good example of *crossover effects*. Crossover effects occur when the stress and strain of one partner are transmitted to the other partner. In this case the anxiety of one partner is clearly affecting the anxiety experienced by the other partner. For more information on crossover effects involving work and family:

Hammer, L. B., Bauer, T. N., & Grandey, A. A. (2003). Work–family conflict and work-related withdrawal behaviors. *Journal of Business and Psychology, 17,* 419–436.

Westman, M., & Etzion, D. (1995). Crossover of stress, strain and resources from one spouse to another. *Journal of Organizational Behavior, 16*, 169–181.

Some research examined the impact of relocating for a spouse on the career of the trailing partner. For example, the new jobs for spouses tend to be poorer in terms of pay and benefits and promotion opportunities (Eby, 2001).

Eby, L. T. (2001). The boundaryless career experiences of mobile spouses in dual-earner marriages. *Group & Organization Management, 26*, 343–368.

Further information on supporting dual-career families on *global assignments*, can be found in the following articles:

Handler, C. A., Lane, I. M., & Maher, M. 1997. Career planning and expatriate couples. *Human Resource Management Journal, 7*, 67–79.

Harvey, M. (1995). The impact of dual career families on international relocations. *Human Resource Management Review, 5*, 223–244.

Harvey, M. (1996). Addressing the dual-career expatriation dilemma. *Human Resource Planning, 19*(4), 18–39.

Moore, M. J. (2002). Same ticket, different trip: Supporting dual-career couples on global assignments. *Women in Management Review, 17*(2), 61–67.

Pellico, M. T., & Stroh, L. (1997). Spousal assistance programs: An integral component of the international assignment. *New approaches to employee management, 4*, 227–243.

Suutari, V., & Riusala, K. (2000). Expatriation and careers: Perspectives of expatriates and spouses. *Career Development International, 5*(2), 81–90.

EPILOGUE

Ana and her husband did not go to Mexico. At the time of their decision, the economic and political situation in Mexico changed and became risky: The peso was devaluated and the government changed. In the end, the company decided not to expose the couple to this risk. Her husband spent one year traveling back and forth. He set up the subsidiary and later received an opportunity to move to another location in Spain.

Case Study 2

Launching Flexible Work Arrangements within Procter & Gamble EMEA

Steven Poelmans
IESE Business School / University of Navarra

Wendy de Waal-Andrews
London Business School

LAUNCHING FLEXIBLE WORK ARRANGEMENTS WITHIN PROCTER & GAMBLE EMEA (A)[1]

Launching the new flexible work arrangements was a big step forward for Procter & Gamble's diversity program in EMEA. It made it possible for employees to work part-time, to work at a more convenient time or location, and to take several types of leave of absence. Not only did it allow young mothers to combine child care and work, it also offered a solution for many other conflicts between work and private life. P&G would be able to retain more women, and women would be able to reach higher positions in the organization.

The launch had been prepared meticulously by the team of diversity managers. The president had been involved from the beginning and sponsored the project. The general manager of each country was involved prior to the communication phase. Each of them was to lead the communication and be the face of the new policy in his or her

---

[1] EMEA is the regional area covering Europe, the Middle-East and Africa. Procter & Gamble is present in over 30 countries in this area. Appendix A gives more information on the operations in EMEA.

country. The HR managers and the diversity managers were there to support the general managers. Also, there was merchandising material for the employees: a brochure with all the details in it, a flexible work arrangement site, a video and even a discussion area on the intranet site where people could post their comments.

Getting Ready for Diversity

In the United States a study of employee turnover in 1991 uncovered an alarming trend: Two out of every three good performers who quit P&G were women. A survey of women P&G wanted to retain revealed that only a very few dropped out of the labor force. The rest moved on to high-profile, high-stress jobs. Almost half were surprised to learn that P&G regretted losing them.

In EMEA there were signs of a similar trend. P&G improved the HR data systems and learned that although around 50% women were recruited, the director level was predominantly male. In exit interviews, women were increasingly saying there was a lack of balance between their personal life and work. In the 1980s, long working hours had become widespread; but people entering the company in the 1990s were much more worried about retaining a balance. It was obvious that something had to be done, and gender became the priority in the new diversity initiative.

Diversity and the Organization

In the early 1990s, Procter & Gamble didn't have a clear diversity program in EMEA. Some business units were taking actions, but there wasn't a consistent strategy. The company wanted to give diversity a place in the organization. Early in 1998 a number of new positions were created. Each western European country was assigned a diversity manager. Both western Europe and CE-MEA[2], the two regions forming EMEA, were assigned a regional diversity manager.

The new positions were not full-time tasks. A diversity manager at national level spent about 10 to 15% of his/her time on diversity, and one at regional level about 40 to 50%. Most national diversity managers worked in HR the rest of the time and reported to the HR

[2]Central Eastern Europe, Middle East, and Africa.

manager of the country. They were usually employees in their late 20s who had been with the company for around 5 years.

The regional diversity managers reported to the regional HR manager. They were responsible for keeping track of employee needs in the region—using tools such as surveys, focus groups, and external contacts and publications—and for leading policy improvements and initiatives to promote diversity (an organization chart is included in Appendix B.)

In some countries, groups of P&G women had been getting together informally for some time. As part of the diversity initiative, these local initiatives were given a more official status. The so-called women's business networks acted as a sounding board for the diversity managers. The networks came together on a regular basis to discuss issues and ideas, and then provided the diversity managers with important insight in the concerns of P&G women.

Flexible Working Arrangements

Identifying the Need. To find out why women were not progressing to the same level in the company as men, the diversity managers held a survey. Interviews took place across Europe in the form of focus groups. One or more focus groups were organized per country, depending on the size of the local workforce, and a total of around 400 people were interviewed.

The focus groups each consisted of six to eight randomly selected employees, male and female, and were led by the country's diversity manager. The participants sat in a room and were provoked in a positive way to have a discussion about flexibility. The discussions started with questioning why people didn't progress and why women left the company. The discussion leader gave data on the positions of women within the company to stimulate people to think and come up with questions and solutions.

Flexibility came out of the survey as one of the major issues. Women felt they had to make a choice between their work life and their family life and were asking for more flexibility.

Specifying the Policies. Once the survey had identified flexibility as an important employee need, it was the task of the diversity managers to propose in what way the company should meet the demand. To compare their ideas with the external situation they used two benchmarks.

The law	Some countries decreed a high level of flexibility for employees by law, whereas others didn't give any. The diversity managers studied the level of flexibility required by law in their country.
Other companies	Diversity was an area in which P&G wanted to be at the leading edge.
	Through their inter-company HR networks, the diversity managers found out what other organizations were doing in terms of flexibility. Different publications appeared in the press that gave further insight into the progress other companies were making.

The diversity managers started to understand what flexibility would mean for P&G in practical terms. They decided which types of arrangements were the most realistic and most crucial for the company. There were four arrangements: reduced work schedules, family care leave, personal leave of absence, and flexible work schedule. Three others were considered to need a trial period to determine if implementing them was really viable: job sharing, working from home, and compressed work week.

Developing Policies. Once the diversity managers had identified the requirements, it was the task of the policy manager to put the actual policies on paper, in line with the company's purpose, values, and principles (cf. Appendix C). In P&G, a policy manager is a specialist in policy design. He or she advises on P&G standards and formulation and if necessary does further research. In line with the collaborative work style in P&G, drawing up the policies was a joint effort. The policy manager went through the design with the diversity managers, questioning each detail and its argumentation: "Why three months leave of absence? Why after 5 years? Why not after three years?" and so on. In a back and forth discussion lasting several weeks, they fine-tuned all the details and developed a set of policies to be nominated for approval.

The policies were the same for the entire region and reflected the minimum flexibility the company was offering. In cases in which the law prescribed a higher level of flexibility or better conditions, the law was to be followed.

Approval. The regional diversity manager for western Europe handed in the recommendation to Wolfgang Berndt, the president of

EMEA, for approval. Wolfgang Berndt was one of the biggest sponsors of the flexibility program. He commented on a couple of details, but basically he agreed with the recommendation. After making sure the policies were in line with what other companies were doing, he approved them. (See Appendix D for the final result.)

Once the approval had been obtained, the diversity managers directly started with the preparations for the deployment of the policies. The deployment of the policies was split in two phases:

1. The communication phase—to provide information and create awareness.
2. The actual implementation phase—to initiate use.

Prior experience with large implementations had taught P&G that the different issues that arise in the different phases could be dealt with better this way.

Communication

The national general managers had been appointed as the "faces" of the flexibility program. They were the ones to communicate the policies to the employees. The diversity managers realized that it would not have the same impact if they did the communication themselves or if HR did it. To maximize the credibility of the program, the general managers needed to sponsor it, and the employees had to be aware of that.

The program was launched in 1998. The general managers were given 3 months to complete the communication. They had a video to show and folders to give to each employee describing all the details of the policies and specifics on how to obtain more information. The video was shown in sessions with up to 300 employees. It pictured P&G employees from all levels of the organization, including the president, giving their opinion on work–family balance and flexibility and talking about the importance of the program. The general manager was present at each video session to answer questions. In large countries, such as Germany and the UK, several sessions were needed to show the video to all the employees. The time frame of 3 months was necessary to accommodate this.

It was in the communication stage that the general managers were really involved for the first time. Prior to the actual launch, they were presented with the key numbers of the survey, and they were informed of the flexibility initiative that was planned as a result. To most managers, it was clear that there was a problem and that something had to be done. However, the reactions were not all the same. Although some general managers wanted to start moving directly and wondered why nothing had been done sooner, others refused to accept that there was a problem in their own country and questioned the numbers and conclusions of the survey.

Although in the end all general managers communicated the policies, some did so more wholeheartedly than others. Some deployed the policies just because they had to. They felt that if all the countries were doing so and their people would know that, they could not stay behind. They communicated the policies, but they didn't encourage people to use them.

The diversity managers dealt with less supportive countries in three different ways:

1. *Talk with them:* The diversity managers explained and re-explained the importance of the flexibility program. They emphasized the fact that the president was sponsoring it and the need that had been expressed by employees. Even so, there were countries that did not buy in.
2. *Coach the local diversity/HR manager:* The national diversity managers and HR managers in countries that were unsupportive received extra coaching from the other diversity managers. Together they tried to find better ways of approaching and convincing the general managers in question.
3. *Reward the others:* It was impossible to make all countries embrace the policies immediately. The diversity managers focused on the countries that cooperated and hoped the others would follow. They published successes on the first page of the intranet, visible for everyone. The free positive publicity functioned as a reward for the cooperative countries and an incentive for the others to do better.

Implementation

Having the policies and communicating them was not enough. People needed to know a number of practical things. They would have to know the procedure to follow: how to use the policies, what steps to take, and with whom to talk. They also needed to know which criteria they would have to meet to be granted a request for flexibility. To ensure the policies were used in the same way over all EMEA, the procedure and criteria were defined regionally.

Procedure	An employee had always first to speak to his/her manager. The manager made the final decision because it was basically a business decision. The diversity managers and HR managers were available for support. If a manager said no, the diversity and HR managers could try to help change the manager's mind and build the new culture.
Criteria	The criteria were generic criteria. For instance, "the business cannot suffer from your decision of going to a reduced schedule." No numeric or more specific criteria were available.

Helena Josue

When the flexible work arrangements were introduced, Helena was working as HR manager for Portugal and was diversity manager for Iberia (the area covering Portugal and Spain). By January 2000, she had moved on to the position of regional diversity manager and HR manager for Western Europe, which she combined with a number of marketing and communication responsibilities, all from a HR perspective. From her new position, she kept track of the progress of the flexibility program.

At first, things seemed to go well. There were managers that took to the policies more than others, but there were no real problems. Problems arose when people started to ask for the policies. There were a lot of questions. Managers wondered what to do with the work if they'd have someone working part-time or wanting to take 3 months off.

She noticed things didn't all work out as planned. Some countries didn't sponsor the arrangements as much as they could. Employees in these countries could only make use of the arrangement in highly exceptional circumstances. However, even in the countries that were cooperating, there were some managers (department managers reporting to the general manager) that didn't accept the policies at all. Or down one level more, an employee's immediate manager could be a person that actually said, "Your job cannot be done with a flexible arrangement. We won't even consider it."

Then there were clashes with culture. In departments with a lot of women, the policies had gone down very well. However, it had not gone so well in some predominantly male dominated environments, where they believed it to be part of their workload to plan meetings or see customers at 7 or 8 in the evening. These men were suddenly confronted with women saying things like, "Well actually I can't go, because I've got reduced work and I need to be home to see my children at 4 in the afternoon."

People thought it would never work in marketing, for instance, that you could not have a brand manager working a reduced work schedule. It was unheard of and would never happen.

There were certain levels in the organization that assumed they could not use the policies. Directors assumed they couldn't use them. Also, if you were really low in the organization, you didn't dare ask. Some younger people that had been working with the company for 3 or 4 years were scared, because they thought it would be seen as lack of commitment.

There was the perception among some people that if you didn't have a family you couldn't use these policies. If you didn't have a child, why would you ask for a reduced work schedule? If you didn't have to look after a sick parent, you couldn't have 3 months leave of absence.

And people kept questioning things: "What happens if suddenly the whole workforce decides to work 80% of the time? That means we've lost 20% productivity from the whole company." Helena knew it would be a huge problem and could only hope that it would never get to that stage.

Some managers simply didn't accept that there are differences between men and women in the workplace. For them there wasn't a problem, and therefore the flexibility arrangements were not necessary. Some men thought that if women couldn't work then it was obviously because of their abilities. If there were no women directors, that didn't mean there was another reason, it just meant they were incapable of working.

In early 2001, people in some business units wondered if the flexible work arrangements still existed. Helena knew they weren't there yet, and wondered what she should do.

BIBLIOGRAPHY

Larkin, P. (2000). P&G making gains in hiring, keeping more women leaders, *Cincinnati Post*, 29/02/2000.

Appendix A

LAUNCHING FLEXIBLE WORK ARRANGEMENTS WITHIN PROCTER & GAMBLE EMEA (A)

Fact sheet Procter & Gamble EMEA

Fact sheet Procter & Gamble EMEA

FINANCIAL INFORMATION   Years ended June 30

Worldwide (millions of dollars)

	1995–1995	1996–1997	1997–1998
Net sales	$35,284	$35,764	$37,154
Net earnings	$3,046	$3,415	$3,780
Basic net earnings per common share ($/share)			
	$2.14	$2.43	$2.74

Europe* (millions of dollars)

	1995–1995	1996–1997	1997–1998
Net sales	$11,458	$11,587	$11,835
Net earnings	$793	$956	$1,092

* Includes Middle East and Africa.

EUROPEAN OPERATIONS

P&G sells its products in more than 140 countries and has worldwide operations in more than 70 countries including in the following European countries:

Austria	1967	Netherlands	1964
Belarus	1995	Norway	1993
Belgium	1955	Poland	1991
Bulgaria	1994	Portugal	1989
Croatia	1996	Romania	1994
Czech Republic	1991	Russia	1991
Denmark	1992	Slovak Republic	1993
Estonia	1996	Slovenia	1996
Finland	1971	Spain	1968
France	1954	Sweden	1969
Germany	1960	Switzerland	1953
Greece	1960	Turkey	1987
Hungary	1991	Ukraine	1995
Ireland	1980	United Kingdom	1930
Italy	1956	Uzbekistan	1996
Kazakhstan	1996	Yugoslavia	1996
Lithuania	1997		
Latvia	1995		

Note. Year listed indicates when business was first established.

Source: European supplement to 1998 annual report.

EMPLOYEES

Europe	31,469
Middle East & Africa	4,801
North America	43,385
Latin America	12,849
Asia	17,583
Worldwide	110,087

MANUFACTURING FACILITIES

P&G Europe has manufacturing facilities in the following countries:

Belgium	Ireland	Russia
Czech Republic	Italy	Spain
France	Poland	Sweden
Germany	Portugal	Turkey
Hungary	Romania	United Kingdom

RESEARCH & DEVELOPMENT

P&G has worldwide 17 major research centers of which 5 are located in Europe:

Strombeek-Bever (Brussels), Belgium:
Applied research and product development for laundry and cleaning products

Schwalbach (Frankfurt), Germany:
Applied research and product development for paper products and beverages

Rusham Park (Egham), United Kingdom:
Applied research and product development for health and beauty care products

Newcastle, United Kingdom:
Applied research and product development for laundry and cleaning products

Italian Research Center (Rome, Pescara), Italy:
Applied research and product development for laundry, cleaning and paper products

R&D in figures (1997–1998)

Budget (millions of dollars)	Worldwide	$1,546
	Europe	$318

R&D employees	Worldwide	$8,240
	Europe	2,110

Appendix B

LAUNCHING FLEXIBLE WORK ARRANGEMENTS
WITHIN PROCTER & GAMBLE EMEA (A)

Organization structure of diversity team

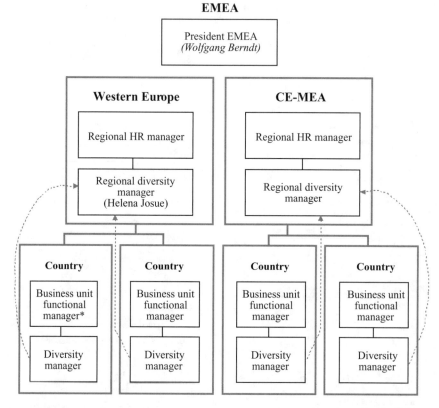

*Diversity managers spend on average 10–15% of their time on diversity. They report to the functional manager they do the rest of their work for. Usually this is HR work and their manager is the HR manager.

Appendix C

LAUNCHING FLEXIBLE WORK-ARRANGEMENTS
WITHIN PROCTER & GAMBLE EMEA (A)
Purpose, values, principles

Core Values

Procter&Gamble
Purpose, values, principles

P&G IS ITS PEOPLE AND THE CORE VALUES BY WHICH THEY LIVE

P&G People. We attract and recruit the finest people in the world. We build our organization from within, promoting and rewarding people without regard to any difference unrelated to performance. We act on the conviction that the men and women of Procter & Gamble will always be our most important asset.

Leadership. We are all leaders in our area of responsibility, with a deep commitment to deliver leadership results. We have a clear vision of where we are going. We focus our resources to achieve leadership objectives and strategies. We develop the capability to deliver our strategies and eliminate organizational barriers.

Ownership. We accept personal accountability to meet the business needs, improve our systems and help others improve their effectiveness. We all act like owners, treating the Company's assets as our own and behaving with the Company's long-term success in mind.

Integrity. We always try to do the right thing. We are honest and straightforward with each other. We operate within the letter and spirit of the law. We uphold the values and principles of P&G in every action and decision. We are data-based and intellectually honest in advocating proposals, including recognizing risks.

Passion for Winning. We are determined to be the best at doing what matters most. We have a healthy dissatisfaction with the status quo. We have a compelling desire to improve and to win in the marketplace.

Trust. We respect our P&G colleagues, customers, consumers and treat them as we want to be treated. We have confidence in each other's capabilities and intentions. We believe that people work best when there is a foundation of trust.

Principles

These are the principles and supporting behaviors which flow from our Purpose and Core Values.

We Show Respect for All Individuals
– We believe that all individuals can and want to contribute to their fullest potential. – We value differences.

– We inspire and enable people to achieve high expectations, standards and challenging goals. – We are honest with people about their performance.

The Interests of the Company and the Individual Are Inseparable
– We believe that doing what's right for the business with integrity will lead to mutual success for both the company and the individual. Our quest for mutual success ties us together. – We encourage stock ownership and ownership behavior.

We Are Strategically Focused in Our Work
– We operate against clearly articulated and aligned goals and strategies. – We only do work and only ask for work that adds value to the business. – We simplify, standardize, and streamline our current work whenever possible.

Innovation Is the Cornerstone of Our Success
– We place great value on big, new consumer innovations. – We challenge convention and reinvent the way we do business to better win in the marketplace.

We Are Externally Focused
– We develop superior understanding of consumers and their needs. – We create and deliver products, packaging and concepts which build winning brand equities. – We develop close, mutually productive relationships with our customers and our suppliers. – We are good corporate citizens.

We Value Personal Mastery
– We believe it is the responsibility of all individuals to continually develop themselves and others. – We encourage and expect outstanding technical mastery and executional excellence.

We Seek to Be the Best
– We strive to be the best in all areas of strategic importance to the Company. – We benchmark our performance rigorously versus the very best internally and externally. – We learn from both our successes and our failures.

Mutual Interdependency Is a Way of Life
– We work together with confidence and trust across functions, sectors, categories, and geographies. – We take pride in results from reapplying others' ideas. – We build superior relationships with all the parties who contribute to fulfilling our Corporate purpose, including our customers, suppliers, universities, and governments.

Appendix C (continued)

Appendix C (continued)

Purpose

P&G people are committed to serving consumers and achieving leadership results through principle-based decisions and actions.

We will provide products and services of superior quality and value that improve the lives of the world's consumers.

As a result, consumers will reward us with leadership sales, profit and value creation, allowing our people, our shareholders, and the communities in which we live and work to prosper.

CORE VALUES

Sustainability

Sustainable Development, or sustainability, integrates economic progress, social development and environmental concerns with the objective of ensuring a quality of life for future generations at least as good as today's.

P&G directly contributes to sustainable development by providing products and services that improve the lives of consumers, whether in terms of health, hygiene or convenience. Through our activities, we also contribute to the economic and social well-being of a range of other stakeholders, including employees, shareholders, local communities in which we operate, and more widely to regional, national and international development. So, P&G contributes to sustainable development both through "what we do" and "how we do it", including ensuring we address any environmental and social issues associated with our products and services.

Source: P&G internet site www.pg.com (About P&G > Overview & Facts > Purpose and Values).

Appendix D

LAUNCHING FLEXIBLE WORK-ARRANGEMENTS WITHIN PROCTER & GAMBLE EMEA (A)

Embracing Flexibility brochure

With our corporate Values and Principles, P&G inextricably links the needs of the business to the needs of the employees, generating a synergy where everybody comes out ahead.

Now I want us to make a leap forward. It's time for us to embrace diversity, to accelerate the development of a workforce that is diverse in terms of background, culture and gender. I am personally committed to Embracing Diversity not because it's the fair thing to do but because I believe that a diverse workforce leads to diverse thinking, which in turn leads to more innovative ideas and thus to a more competitive company.

To reach that destination, we have developed a variety of flexible work arrangements –a diversity of routes, mapped out in this brochure– designed to meet the needs of a diverse workforce.

We're calling them Flexibility Guidelines and they are a big opportunity for all of us. An opportunity to work better and live better and for P&G to compete better. This will also bring us closer to our 2005 stretch, innovation and speed goals. I see these guidelines as just the start of a long journey whose destination is a company in which diverse management styles are encouraged and nurtured so all employees can harness their strengths better and perform better.

Yours sincerely,
Wolfgang C. Berndt

P&G committed to diversity

Reviewing the results

Our new Flexibility Guidelines are not just noble words. They are being taken very seriously by the Company and will be implemented with full organizational commitment and the progress we make will be measured and kept under constant review.

> The results will be stracked in employee surveys together with focus groups to assess changes in the culture and in job satisfaction.

> We will continuously track the diversity of the workforce.

> Behaviour that encourages diversity will be rewarded

Networking

> We will appoint a person in each country or region who will be your HR "Diversity" contact.

> We are currently supporting "Diversity" groups to monitor progress. These teams will propose to their HR contact action plans aimed at improving diversity in their region.

We also invite you to view the "Diversity" video and check out the complete version of the guideliness on the P&G intranet.

Embracing diversity

Appendix D (continued)

FLEXIBILITY

General principles

> The new flexible work arrangements detailed in this brochure are open to you whatever your level in the company.

> When considering a flexible work arrangement, first have a talk with your manager to review whether it fits in with both your personal needs and the nees of the business. The next step then is for your locations's "HR" contacts to get involved to work out a personalised plan for you.

> Having embarked on one of the new flexible work arrangements, you will continue to be evaluated and rated according to your business achievements.

> Where the opinion involves working fewer hours your salary will be reduced pro-rata.

> The new flexible work arrangements are not enticements or benefits. Implementation will depend on whether the option meets a combination of both your needs and the company's needs at the time you make the request.

Please note: This brochure is intended only to give you a general overview of the Flexibility Guidelines. The complete guidelines can be found on the P&G intranet or obtained through your HR contact.

Can I reduce my working week
*without reducing
my work prospects?*

> **Reduced Work Schedules**

At some periods in your life you may need more flexibility. The underlying principle is that what's good for you is good for the company. And vice versa.

The idea is to enable you– whether you're a man or a woman– to continue on your career path while working either fewer days per week or fewer hours per day. This solution will be possible if your work lends itself to this kind of arrangement.

> Fewer days per week or fewer hours per day.

> Available if it fits in with the demands of your work.

> You'll be treated as a full time employee for training and assignment planning.

Your work expectations will be scaled back accordingly and you will be evaluated against these reduced expectations.

> Promotion will be based on your contribution to the business. It will require that there is an open position, that you are the most qualified candidate for it and that this new position can be managed within a reduced work schedule.

> Your salary and benefits will be reduced on a pro-rata basis.

Embracing diversity

Appendix D (continued)

Maternity leave, paternity leave.

Taking more time.

> **Family Care Leave**

The aim is to enable you to take unpaid leave of absence over and above the legally mandated maternity/paternity leave to care for each new child born or adopted in case your local country law doesn't provide this. This option is available to both men and women.

> Whether you are a new mother or a new father, you can take a year's unpaid leave beyond the statutory maternity/paternity (if not provided by local law) leave to enable you to spend more quality time with your family at this special time in your life.

> During your leave of absence, a "keep in touch" plan set up by your last manager will operate.

> Some of your benefits (such as stock purchase plans) will continue to be valid during your absence for a period not extending beyond five years.

Got a 7-year itch?

Scratch it.

> **Personal Leave of Absence**

A diverse workforce necessarily has diverse interests and needs.
The personal leave of absence allows you as a full time employee to take a sabbatical of up to three months every seven years.

> You can request a leave of absence of up to three months' unpaid leave after five years with the company and subsequently every seven years.

> This leave will preferably be taken between assignments and therefore you should give at least six months' notice to your manager to facilitate assignment planning.

> Providing it does not generate a conflict of interest, you are free to use the time you take off in any way you wish.

> The timing will be subject to the needs of the business and what stage of an assignment you are at.

Embracing diversity

Appendix D (continued)

Unexpected overnight trip?

We'll help with the child care.

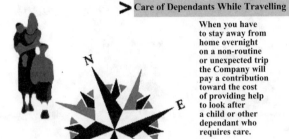

> **Care of Dependants While Travelling**

When you have to stay away from home overnight on a non-routine or unexpected trip the Company will pay a contribution toward the cost of providing help to look after a child or other dependant who requires care.

**Want to start your day early
and leave early?**

We're with you.

> **Flexible Work Schedule**

For a whole host of personal reasons it may be more convenient for you to start your workday earlier-or later-than most people. Our point of view is that if this kind of flexibility is compatible with your work, we'll support you.

> Business units or individuals who are full time employees can establish their own schedules provided an adequate number of hours fall within the regular working hours of that site.

> The nature of your work is the key factor to be taken into account in determining if an alternate schedule is workable.

Embracing diversity

Appendix D (continued)

> **JOB SHARING, WORKING FROM HOME, COMPRESSED WEEK.**

Experience a new flexible work arrangement.

Flexible working at P&G

Flexible working at P&G will continue to evolve. Potential new flexible work arrangements under consideration are job sharing, working from home, and a compressed work week. If you believe one of these arrangements would suit you we can explore these options together.

Job sharing

> You work part time with another part time employee sharing between you the work load of a full time job.

Working from home

> Enabling up to 50% of your work time to be spent at home.
> The decision to enable this will depend on the demands of your job and the needs of the business, as well as your country's legislation.
> If you have children, you must continue to use normal child care just as though you were continuing to work full time in the office.
> The Company will support you technologically.

Compressed week

> Here you could choose to work longer hours some days so as to be able to take off a half or full day during the week.
> In total you would still work a full number of hours and remain a full time employee.
> Feasibility will depend on local legal regulations.

Embracing diversity

FLEXIBILITY GUIDELINES

Want to know more...

... Just click on the P&G Flexible Work Arrangements intranet site.

It will contain:

> the new policies outlined in detail
> contact names for help/advice
> the name of the HR contact in your business unit.

Embracing diversity

LAUNCHING FLEXIBLE WORK ARRANGEMENTS WITHIN PROCTER & GAMBLE EMEA (B)

On June 8, 2000, an executive change took place within Procter & Gamble. Durk I. Jager, the CEO, stepped down and was succeeded by Alan G. Lafley. It was a positive change for the diversity program. Although Durk Jager had always been an enthusiastic sponsor of the initiative, his role had been a passive one. Alan Lafley went a step further and actively pushed the program. He didn't only sponsor it, he set targets and led the program. His involvement gave the diversity initiative more energy, visibility, and importance.

As part of a restructuring program, Lafley enlarged the network of diversity managers in western Europe. Where previously there had been only one diversity manager per country, now there was one for each business unit. This meant nearly doubling the number of diversity managers in the region.

Lafley decided to make the diversity program part of the regional action plan. This meant that for the first time the general managers of the countries were responsible for taking measures concerning diversity. If the diversity managers proposed an action to be taken in the region and the idea was approved, the general managers were responsible for making it happen.

Flexible Work Arrangements

The flexible work arrangements had developed since their launch in 1998. Working from home and job sharing had become part of the official set of policies available to all employees. Compressed work week, however, had not lost its trial status. In P&G people let their work schedule depend on the amount of work that needed to be done and didn't keep to a strict 8 hours a day. In this culture, a compressed week proved difficult to implement.

Despite the positive developments, Helena Josue was not happy with the situation. In the summer of 2001, she was faced with a decreasing awareness among employees of the flexible work arrangements. She thought she might be able to halt the trend with a new communication preface, but she knew the problem was not simple. Employees needed to know that the arrangements still existed and that they could use them. At the same time, managers had to accept that the arrangements were available to all employees in the company. Without the support of the managers, the arrangements would not give employees more flexibility.

Helena thought two independent approaches were needed to really bring the flexible work arrangement back to life; one aimed at employees and the other at managers. The communication had to be separate from that of the diversity program. This would underline that flexible work arrangements were not only for women, but for both genders.

Helena agreed with the diversity managers to take a number of actions to reach the employees. The site would be brought back to life, including a new discussion area, and there were going to be new merchandising materials available all over the region. An agency had been hired to find more creative ways of increasing employee awareness. One idea was to make use of the paper placemats used in the cafeterias. They would be printed with success stories of people using the arrangements for years and then being promoted. Employees would be able to read these while having lunch.

Helena thought she needed facts to convince the managers to support the arrangement. She agreed with the diversity managers that they would collect two sets of data. The first would be used to develop a "fact book." This was to be an overview of what was happening externally and would contain information on what other companies were doing. The goal was to make the general managers realize that it was not just "those crazy people from P&G" trying to make them do this, but that it was part of a general trend.

The second set of data would be obtained from people inside the company. They would hold surveys to collect data on the type of arrangements people wanted. Managers would not just be able to see that flexible work arrangements were being introduced outside P&G but also that people, their people, wanted them.

When handing the data to the managers, all the communication was going to start at the top, with the general managers. They were the ones who had to pass on the message to their leadership team.

Hopefully in one year, two years, three years maximum, this will change the culture and flexwork arrangements will be something that we don't even talk about any more.

The re-launch was planned for December 2001.

Instructor's Manual for Case Study 2

Barbara Beham and Steven Poelmans
IESE Business School / University of Navarra

CASE OVERVIEW (PART A)

The case describes the launch of new flexible work arrangements at Procter & Gamble EMEA (regional area covering Europe, the Middle East, and Africa). P&G had realized that two out of three good performers who quit were women. The process to counteract turnover in female employees started in 1998 with the introduction of diversity managers in the region. A survey to identify the needs of P&G's female employees was held, and the issue was discussed in focus groups.

After having identified flexibility as an important employee need, policy managers at P&G developed policies valid for the entire region. It was decided to implement four types of flexible work arrangements: reduced work schedules, family care leave, personal leave of absence, and flexible work schedules. Three others were to be tested during a trial period: job sharing, working from home, and compressed work week.

The deployment of the policies was split in two phases: the communication phase, to provide information and create awareness and the actual implementation phase, to initiate the use of those policies. General management was first involved in the communication stage and not all managers supported the implementation. By talking to them, coaching the local diversity manager/HR manager and rewarding highly cooperative countries the diversity managers tried to deal with less supportive countries.

Several problems arose when employees started to ask for the policies. Not all countries sponsored the arrangements as they could. Employees working at certain organizational levels assumed that they could not use the policies. There was the perception among some people that if you don't have a family, you couldn't use these policies. In early 2001, people in some business units wondered if the flexible work arrangements still existed.

KEY ISSUES

The case is designed to allow the development of a discussion on the following issues:

- Managing diversity in organizations
- Managing the work–family interface in companies
- The adoption, design, implementation, and utilization of (flexible work arrangements or family-friendly) human resource policies.
- Change management

TEACHING

This case can be used in courses dealing with human resource management, organizational behavior, or change management. Although master students studying (human resource) management might be able to relate best to this case, it could also be used in an undergraduate course. The case can be discussed in one class session of one to two hours duration.

As an introduction to the class, the instructor can ask students to define diversity and ask them whether they think diversity is necessary for organizations, and if so, why and under what circumstances? What are the dangers of too little or too much diversity? Students are then invited to take the role of an outside consultant. They have to analyze the secondary and root causes creating the difficulties in implementing the flexible work arrangements. Before jumping to conclusions and solutions, the students are asked to identify who is responsible for preventing or eliminating these different barriers and sources of resistance. At this point, the instructor can insert a short intervention explaining the basics in change management. Last but not least, the instructor can ask the students to make recommendations of how to ensure the use of the flexible work arrangements on the basis of their analysis.

QUESTIONS FOR DISCUSSION

Diversity in organizations:

1. Why do companies strive for diversity among their employees? What are the pros and cons of a diverse workforce? What criteria should be kept in mind when creating an efficient, diverse workforce?
2. What are the challenges when creating diversity, at the interindividual, group, and organizational level?

Adoption of flexible work arrangements:

1. Why are companies starting to adopt flexible work arrangements? What is the link with diversity?

2. Identify possible flexible work arrangements and discuss their advantages and disadvantages, first from the point of view of the employee and then of the organization.
3. Can flexible work arrangements be applied to all organizational levels? Why (not)?

Change management/implementation of flexible work arrangements:

1. Identify and discuss the different steps of the organizational change process? What went wrong at P&G?
2. Make an analysis of the costs and benefits of flexible work arrangements for the company. Take into account recruiting and replacement costs and effects on the image of the organization.
3. Who are crucial actors in the change process? How have they been involved in the process?
4. What role does company culture play in the implementation process?
5. What incentives are needed, and how can they be introduced in an organization to make their managers become more responsive toward their employees needs?
6. Can one conclude that support from managers would have guaranteed the success of flexible work practices in P&G?

Utilization of flexible work arrangements:

1. Does national culture shape organizational culture? Which of the two types is more important?
2. To what extent does national culture influence the allowance (by managers) and utilization (by employees) of flexible work arrangements in organizations?
3. What other factors influence the allowance and utilization of flexible work arrangements in a firm?
4. What difficulties do managers have to cope with when allowing flexible work arrangements such as parental leaves and reduced work hours to employees?

THEORETICAL LINKS

With the incorporation of women in the labor force dual-earner families have become the norm in the United States and the majority of European countries. In order to align business needs and the needs of these collective, companies have started to implement family-supportive human resource policies (Lobel & Kossek, 1996). Most studies until now have focused on explaining the adoption of these policies in terms of institutional pressures (Goodstein, 1994; Ingram & Simons, 1995; Osterman, 1995; Poelmans, Chinchilla, & Cardona, 2003) or rational choices of human resource managers as interpreters of institutional pressures (Kossek, Dass, & DeMarr, 1994; Milliken, Martins, & Morgan, 1998; Poelmans et al., 2003). These studies concluded that larger companies operating in tight labor markets with low unemployment (Goodstein, 1994; Ingram & Simons, 1995) are especially inclined to adopt these policies. Work–life policies may also be a rational attempt to create high commitment in employees (Osterman, 1995; Poelmans et al., 2003), something that will be increasingly important in a knowledge and service society.

Goodstein, J. D. (1994). Institutional pressures and strategic responsiveness: Employer involvement in work–family issues. *Academy of Management Journal, 37*, 350–382.

Ingram, P., & Simons, T. (1995). Institutional and resource dependence determinants of responsiveness to work–family issues. *Academy of Management Journal, 38*, 1466–1482.

Kossek, E. E., Dass, P., & DeMarr, B. (1994). The dominant logic of employer-sponsored work and family initiatives: Human resource managers' institutional role. *Human Relations, 47*, 1121–1149.

Lobel, S., & Kossek, E. (1996). Human resource strategies to support diversity in work and personal lifestyles: Beyond the "family-friendly" organization. In E. Kossek & S. Lobel (Eds.), *Managing diversity: Human resource strategies for transforming the workplace* (pp. 221–244). Cambridge, MA: Blackwell.

Milliken, F. J., Martins, L. L., & Morgan, H. (1998). Explaining organisational responsiveness to work–family issues: The role of human resource executives as issue interpreters. *Academy of Management Journal, 41*, 580–592.

Osterman, P. (1995). Work/family programs and the employment relationship. *Administrative Science Quarterly, 40*, 681–700.

Poelmans, S., Chinchilla, N., & Cardona, P. (2003). Family-friendly HRM policies and the employment relationship. *International Journal of Manpower, 24*, 128–147.

The *implementation of work–family initiatives* like flexible work arrangements is a complex problem that involves many stages, variables, and implied organizational actors. Poelmans (2005, Chapter 16 this volume) distinguishes four steps in the implementation process: adoption, design, implementation, and allowance. The first step is to decide whether or not to take any initiative at all, which in the literature has been referred to as "the adoption" of work–family policies (den Dulk, 2005, Chapter 8 this volume). Once managers in a company have decided to adopt work–family policies the focus shifts to the question which specific policies should be adopted, and how to compose them in a coherent HR bundle. The case illustrates that companies invest a lot of resources (human, financial) in designing policies. Proctor & Gamble conducted a survey in all the subsidiaries in Europe to identify the needs of the employees, and a policy manager was assigned to develop the policies and check them off with diversity managers in different countries in an iterative process of fine-tuning the policies. In addition, the company decided to immediately implement four policies and try three other policies out on a trial period.

In the implementation step (perceived) organizational and managerial support is absolutely necessary. If formal policies are not backed up by sufficient support, they may be of very little use (Thompson, Lyness, & Beauvais, 1999; Poelmans, Chapter 16, this volume). In the case of Procter & Gamble, the fundamental problem experienced by the diversity manager was neither an adoption nor a design issue. It was an implementation problem.

In the last step of the implementation process, the allowance decision has to be made: When and how can an individual employee actually be allowed to take up a work–family arrangement as requested? (Poelmans, Chapter 16, this volume.) Powell and Mainiero 1999 have demonstrated that the more managers see flexible work arrangements as potentially disruptive for business, the more they will resist them.

The logic driving managers and employees to negotiate access to work–life benefits can be explained using social exchange theory (Blau, 1964; Homans, 1958). Lambert (2000) used this theory to explain the relationship between the presence of work–life policies and organizational citizenship behavior in the firm. Poelmans integrated social exchange theory in his decision process theory, distinguishing between pure contractual relationships between employer and employee, where equity theory applies, and social exchange relationships in these dyads, where social exchange theory would apply. According to Poelmans (2004), if employees experience a favorable (input/benefits—costs) ratio in comparison with other jobs in the same company or alternative companies in the sector, with work–life policies representing a higher employer input or employee benefit and lower costs for the employee, they will be inclined to stay with the same firm. In the case of the contrary, they may be inclined to break the contract, unless the cost of breaking the contract offsets the balance (in case of a contractual relationship) or if ties of loyalty impede them to discontinue the social exchange relationship.

Blau, P. (1964). *Exchange and power in social life*. New York: Wiley.

Den Dulk, L. (2005). Workplace work–family arrangements: A study and explanatory framework of differences between organizational provisions in different welfare states. In S. Poelmans (Ed.),

Work and Family: An International Research Perspective. Mahwah, NJ: Lawrence Erlbaum Associates.

Homans, G. C. (1958). Social behavior and exchange. *American Journal of Sociology, 63,* 597–606.

Lambert, S. J. (2000). Added benefits: The link between work–life benefits and organizational citizenship behavior. *Academy of Management Journal, 43,* 801–815.

Poelmans, S. (2004). The decision process theory of work and family. In E. E. Kossek & S. Lambert (Eds.), *Managing work–life integration in organizations: Future directions for research and practice.* Mahwah, NJ: Lawrence Erlbaum Associates.

Poelmans, S. (2005). Organizational research on work and family: Recommendations for future research. In S. Poelmans (Ed.), *Work and family: An international research perspective.* Mahwah NJ: Lawrence Erlbaum Associates.

Powell, G. N., & Mainiero, L. A. (1999). Managerial decision making regarding alternative work arrangements. *Journal of Occupational and Organizational Psychology, 72,* 41–56.

Thompson, C. A., Lyness, K. S., Beauvais, L. L. (1999). When work-family benefits are not enough: The influence of work-family culture on benefit utilization, organizational attachment, and work-family conflict. *Journal of Vocational Behavior, 54,* 392–415.

There is a growing body of research that assesses the positive impact of work–life programs. A study conducted by AT&T found that the average cost of leave for new mothers was 32% of the annual salary: 39% for management and 28% for nonmanagement. By comparison, the cost of turnover was 150% of the annual salary for management and 75% for nonmanagement. Thus, it is far less expensive to support a parental leave than to replace the employee permanently (Galinsky & Johnson, 1998).

Flexible time policies reduce absences and positively affect worker satisfaction and retention. A study at Johnson & Johnson (J&J), for example, found that the average number of days of absenteeism among all J&J workers declined over the 2-year period following the introduction of more generous and flexible time and leave policies. And an integrated array of work–life programs and policies also positively affects performance and commitment (Galinsky & Johnson, 1998).

Galinsky, E., & Johnson, A. A. (1998). *Reframing the business case for work–life initiatives.* New York: Families and Work Institute.

Several studies have revealed that the implementation of policies does not guarantee their actual utilization, because the company culture and more specifically managers and colleagues may not be supportive at all. A supportive *family–work culture* seems to increase the use of work–family policies. More specifically: (1) Benefit utilization (together 16 specific benefits, e.g., absence autonomy, flextime, family care leave) was greater by employees who perceived more supportive work–family cultures (high managerial support, low career consequences, and low organizational time demands) than by those with less supportive cultures. (2) Individuals who reported favorable Family Supportive Organization Perception responses also reported a greater use of flexible work–family arrangements (e.g., flextime, compressed working week, part-time work; Kinnunen, 2005, Chapter 4 this volume).

Peters & den Dulk (2003) assume that managers' attitudes toward telework are affected by the national culture and the organizational context they work in, and also the characteristics of the employee requesting telework and the content of the request. Managers working in an organizational context that is more supportive for telework will be more willing to grant a telework request.

Kinnunen, U., Mauno, S., Geurts, S., & Dikkers, J. (2005). Work–family culture in organizations: Theoretical and empirical approaches. In S. Poelmans (Ed.), *Work and family: An international research perspective.* Mahwah NJ: Lawrence Erlbaum Associates.

Peters, P., & den Dulk, L., den (2003). Cross cultural differences in managers' support for home-based telework. A theoretical elaboration. *International Journal of Cross Cultural Management, 3,* 329–346.

EPILOGUE (CASE PART B)

In 2000, CEO Durk I. Jager stepped down. He was succeeded by Alan Lafley. Because Durk's role in the whole implementation process was supportive but passive, this change in top management had a positive impact on the diversity program. The network of diversity managers was enlarged and the program became part of the regional action plan with the general managers being responsible for measuring diversity. Despite those positive developments, awareness among employees of flexible work arrangements was decreasing in 2001. Helena Josue, the regional diversity manager and HR manager for Western Europe, planned a re-launch of the work arrangements based on two different approaches: one aimed at employees and the other at managers. A new discussion area, new merchandising material and the development of a "fact-book" was planned.

The re-launch was planned for December 2001.

V

Conclusions and Recommendations for Future Research

13

Methodological Issues in Work–Family Research in an Era of Globalization[1]

Rabi S. Bhagat and Balaji C. Krishnan
University of Memphis

ABSTRACT

Methodological issues for improving the robustness of work–family
research are reviewed. Special attention is given to the complexities
of understanding relative demarcation of work and nonwork (family)
boundaries, as globalization spreads rapidly in different parts of the
world. Four issues are examined in depth, and a framework is proposed for understanding the contrasting perspectives of various research methods. These methods are to be undertaken at different stages
of research to understand the interactions between work and family. It
is argued that the methods are equally important, and their employment
should be carefully monitored at different stages of the research project.
Recent trends in demographic shifts in the West are reviewed, and their
research implications for work–family research are discussed.

[1]Karen South Moustafa provided insightful suggestions in the preparation of this
chapter. Work on this project was facilitated by a sabbatical granted to the first author
by the Fogelman College of Business and Economics at the University of Memphis,
Memphis, TN, USA.

Methodological issues in work–family research will become increasingly complex as we deal with the dilemmas of globalization. Many joys and difficulties that people face are a function of the rapid changes in the interconnected economy that exists in many parts of the world. Even though globalization directly affects less than 10% of the world's population, the discontent unleashed by forces of globalization affects more than half (Stiglitz, 2002).

One of the major underlying reasons for much of the early work focusing on work–family interaction was to ensure that the "long arm of the job" did not significantly affect the structure and functioning of workers' families (Kornhauser, 1965). Much of this research was conducted in the United States, starting after World War II, when the U.S. economy was beginning to expand rapidly. There was intense interest in making sure that the mental health of the industrial worker and his family was not significantly affected by intrusion of work pressures and conflicts. Industrial psychologists, occupational sociologists, and government officials concerned with occupational hazards were the primary researchers in this area. Some of the findings resulted in the establishment of government programs directed at appropriate interventions in maintaining a balance between work and family, as deemed fit during that time.

Research in other parts of the world, particularly in western Europe, East Asia, Africa, and Latin America, was conducted by cultural anthropologists and sociologists. Many findings were based on anecdotal evidence and gave us interesting stories about how the progress of industrialization, as reflected in the increased emphasis on work values, might have changed the patterns and rhythms of family life. Remember that the research investigating the interaction between work and family was carried out in an era in which globalization was not, by any means, the dominant force that it has become in the last two decades.

In this chapter, we address some of the fundamental methodological issues that we must wrestle with in order to gain knowledge that will (a) maintain the unstoppable progress of global and the internet economy and (b) provide appropriate, timely and contextually relevant solutions to the problem of work and family interaction. The following issues are paramount:

Issue 1: What aspects of work–family research need to be studied in this era of globalization?
Issue 2: Why are we studying work–family interaction in the context of the present study?
Issue 3: How do we choose an appropriate research method?
Issue 4: How do we analyze the data and arrive at valid conclusions?

We first look at the aspects of work–family research that need further illumination in the era of globalization.

ISSUE 1: WHAT ASPECTS OF WORK–FAMILY RESEARCH NEED TO BE STUDIED IN THIS ERA OF GLOBALIZATION?

We understand some of the historical reasons why those in the fields of applied psychology, occupational sociology, and industrial economics are interested in the topic. However, the current reasons for studying work–family interactions in the era of globalization are not as clear. With the movement of global capital, workers' families are being affected in countries such as Indonesia, Malaysia, Nigeria, Mexico, China, India, and, more recently, in western countries. Global capital does not have a caring heart. Its primary loyalty lies in sustaining the return of the stakeholders in worldwide capital markets. Global corporations are there to produce a product or service at the least possible price, which is made available to a global marketplace. If workers' families experience significant dislocations, stressful lives, or various dysfunctional consequences from job loss or overwork and increased role conflict, it may not be a major concern of global corporations.

Consider the situation in the United States: Corporations that cared about the well-being of their workers and families in the 1950s and 1960s, such as IBM, 3M, General Motors, and Ford, are moving many of their less profitable functions overseas. Outsourcing of services and production is the dominant norm in the global economy. Companies that once employed a large American workforce are now employing workers in other countries that are characterized by lower labor costs. Although it may cost less to employ a Mexican or Chinese worker to produce a television, the fact remains that the assembly workers in the United States lose jobs when production is outsourced to other locations. There is nothing in international trade regulations to prevent the flow of global capital or the establishment of subsidiaries in different parts of the world. In fact, the jobs that fled the United States for Mexico are now fleeing Mexico as the labor cost increases—and will go to countries such as Guatemala and El Salvador.

Business process outsourcing has become the norm (*Business-Week*, December 8, 2003). As mentioned earlier, a number of industries are moving their manufacturing to other countries because of the availability of cheap labor. This trend has continued with service components, including customer support, billing, and medical transcription, to name a few. Jobs considered entry level in the U.S. are attractive to the citizens of Asia in general, and India in particular. However, these employees are required to work during U.S. working hours, i.e., between 7 p.m. and 6 a.m. at their local time. Manufacturing industries have used this work timing around the world, but the requirement to work nights is becoming widespread as these countries compete for western service jobs. Moreover, in the "information economy," knowledge is the key input from labor. This leads to workers carrying their work-related problems home with them, which certainly has implications for researchers in the work–family domain.

ISSUE 2: WHY ARE WE STUDYING WORK–FAMILY INTERACTION IN THE CONTEXT OF THE PRESENT STUDY?

Presumably, one of the fundamental reasons for studying work–family interaction is to maintain the sanctity and temporal boundaries of both work and family domains. If research is conducted to develop family-friendly work organizations, then the focus is necessarily managerial in nature. On the other hand, if research is conducted to understand some of the clear and subtle effects of work pressures and conflicts on the maintenance of family in the idiosyncratic social and cultural milieu in which the family functions, then the focus should be more humanistic and less concerned with managerial issues.

As early as 1976, Argyris (1976) noted that much of the logic behind the inquiries of industrial psychologists was Aristotelian in character, in which the explanation lay in the properties of the phenomenon under study and not in its relationships among other phenomenon, which would be the Galilean mode of thought (characterized by much of the work–family research). The cultural variation of the meanings that humans put on the significance of work and nonwork (family) activities in different parts of the worlds has not been fully explored. Such explorations are driven by more Aristotelian logic. We urge that the early stages of research investigations of work–family relationships be guided by this line of thinking.

About 30 years ago, Triandis (1973) noted that work has social and culturally specific meanings, and these meanings often transcend economic compensation. Work allows people to form social groups, creates a feeling of self respect and identity, and offers an individual status in the pecking order of his or her society. This pattern has remained invariant for much of human history. The work of emperors, priests, artisans, judges, carpenters, and others has distinctive significance for each occupational group.

The United States, the world's most dominant economy, has over 40,000 different occupational groups (*Dictionary of Occupational Titles*, US), although many have similar properties in terms of how work in the occupations might characterize the psychological and physiological well-being of individual workers and therefore are often clustered into occupational categories. The point remains that each occupation has distinguishing features that must be considered before undertaking investigations into work–family relationships. For future research to have important consequences for our rapidly globalizing world, it is of crucial importance that we first examine the psychological boundaries of work and nonwork as distinct categories before we engage in studying the type of relationships that are likely to be found across various occupational groups.

ISSUE 3: HOW DO WE CHOOSE AN APPROPRIATE RESEARCH METHOD?

The answer to this question might seem obvious to western researchers who focus largely on quantitative methods involving research instruments with appropriate psychometric properties. This trend has characterized much research on work–family balance, conflict, and related issues for the past 3 decades. Although such methods are appropriate for research in Western societies, use of ethnographic, anthropological, focus group, and participant observation research methods are much more appropriate for exploring work–family issues in societies in which the demarcation of work and nonwork boundaries are not only unclear, but also tend to vary according to the seasons of the year (i.e., religious festivals and rituals). Research in various areas of cross-cultural psychology and management has also shown that patterned rituals separate work from nonwork (Triandis, 1973, 1994). Before embarking on examinations of work and nonwork interactions, it is useful to develop appropriate methodologies for understanding the cultural and contextual variations in these rituals. For example, Bhawuk (2003) argued that spirituality, which is an enshrined value in Indian culture, is responsible for sustaining creative activities in the domain of both work and nonwork, and such work is impossible to quantify without initial qualitative work.

Following Runkel and McGrath (1972) and Pedhazur and Schmelkin (1991), we suggest the use of a framework for facilitating research in this area, as shown in Figure 13.1. Work–family research that maximizes the generalizability of findings is typically conducted by sample surveys and formal theories using archival data. Such research is typically conducted by cross-cultural sociologists interested in the patterning of work–family as a function of industrialization and globalization and also by economists who use census data to draw broad conclusions. A good example of this research is found in the

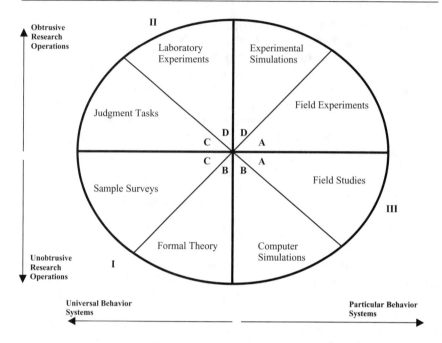

A. Settings in natural settings
B. No observation of behavior required
C. Behavior not setting dependent
D. Contrived and created settings

I.   Research strategies with maximum concern for generalizability of results.
II. Research strategies with maximum concern for precise measurement of variables.
III. Research strategies with maximum concern for incorporating contextual characteristics of the settings.

FIG. 13.1. Research strategies for work–family interactions. Adapted from Runkel, P. J., & McGrath, J. E. (1972). *Research on Human Behavior: A Systematic Guide to Method* (p. 85). New York: Holt, Rinehard, & Winston.

work of economists who report that television viewing among children in Singapore and Hong Kong, where dual-career parents are the norm, is about the same as in the U.S. Singapore and Hong Kong are vertical collectivistic societies (Triandis, 1994, 1995; Bhagat, Kedia, Harveston, & Triandis, 2002), and familism has traditionally been more important in these societal contexts.

Precision of measurement is the focus of studies that use field experiments and experimental simulations. The interest of the researchers using these methodologies is typically on the nature of causality between sets of antecedents and outcomes. If researchers were interested in understanding the satisfaction of wives of Japanese executives with their marital bond, one interesting way of testing a hypothesis would be to compare the wives of two Japanese executive groups, with one having an increased work load compared to another. Laboratory experiments and computer simulations are rare in this area, but creative uses with simulations might reveal some intricate patterns of interactions that would not otherwise be discovered.

Field experiments and field studies are typically more suited for research examining interaction, such as spillover, compensation, and reciprocal and instrumentality models (Burke & Greenglass, 1987; Frone, 2003). Field studies are easy to conduct using construct valid measures of various components of demand conflict experiences in the domain of work and family. There have been a plethora of cross-sectional studies involving significant correlations among important constructs such as job satisfaction in the domain of work and life satisfaction in the domain of nonwork and family. Causal correlational designs, which also reveal patterns of causality among variables such as work load in the domain of work and its subsequent effect on different outcome variables (e.g., quality of child care, quality of family interactions, use of time) have also been examined, but are not as frequent (Burke & Greenglass, 1987; Quick, Cooper, Nelson, Quick, & Gavin, 2003).

We suggest that research in culturally dissimilar settings should involve methodologies that develop appropriate theoretical frameworks, particularly in the early stages. For example, there is little to be gained in studying work–family balance in tribal communities in the rain forest areas of Brazil, unless one has also gained understanding of the significance of cultural values, customs, and rituals that have been studied in depth using anthropological field surveys. As the world globalizes and as global corporations expand their operations in culturally dissimilar parts of the world, this area of research involving the use of formal theory and anthropological field surveys will become increasingly important.

In the second stage of the research, researchers should use sample surveys and various types of judgment-task designs to get a broader feel for an array of variables involved in work–family interactions. Broad sample surveys using questionnaires and interviews can yield massive amounts of data, and patterns of intercorrelations among these variables can provide interesting insights that might otherwise not have been found.

In the next stage, the importance of knowing causality arises. This can only be resolved by taking a limited set of variables and conducting laboratory experiments in the actual settings of work and family or, alternatively, by inviting the participants to university research settings. This line of research is almost totally absent in the work–family domain, perhaps because of the inherent difficulties. However, diary studies in which husbands and wives keep notes pertaining to the quality of their marital interactions as a function of periodic changes in pressures from work and family have been conducted (e.g., Kasl & Jones, 2003). In our opinion, such studies are most interesting, especially in the parts of the world where the use of electronic technology can aid these studies. It would also be an interesting idea to study the impact of issues such as "social desirability bias" and the "importance of norms" on the diary entries. Culture could impact the responses and statements that the respondents could admit to.

In other words, all of these research strategies (depicted in Figure 13.1), are important, but at different stages of the process. It is not important that all of the researchers interested in studying work–family interactions use *all* of these techniques. Mastery of all techniques would be impossible. Researchers should use those particular techniques that are appropriate for the type of research questions that they are asking. However, all of these methods should be examined for their comparative strengths and weaknesses before a strategy is developed.

The technique of triangulation (Jick, 1979), in which a number of methods are employed to test convergent validity of the constructs employed, is laudable, but it has not been the dominant norm in this area of research. We recommend that future researchers be concerned with triangulating distinct methods and then with examining the validity of the findings arrived at through different methods. Though time consuming, it is vital to the formalization of theories in this field of research.

ISSUE 4: HOW DO WE ANALYZE THE DATA AND ARRIVE AT VALID CONCLUSIONS?

Different types of data are analyzed by using different statistical and analytical techniques. Data obtained through participant observation and qualitative techniques are analyzed differently than a massive amount of numerical data concerning such measures as growth rates of a given region and family life satisfaction obtained from surveys. The first type of studies are analyzed by techniques found in such volumes as Denzin and Lincoln (1998), whereas the second type is best tested by using techniques discussed in Edwards (2003) and later validated by methodologies discussed in Edwards (2003) and Althauser and Heberlein (1970).

A number of researchers have conducted meta-analytical studies that aggregate data across multiple industries and multiple job descriptions. Similarly some researchers have focused on vertical data, including different job descriptions, in a single company. Other researchers have focused on a single job description across multiple companies, i.e., work–family research among salespeople. For examples, see the work of Baltes and Briggs (1999); Brown and Booth (2002); Griffeth, Hem, and Gaertner (2000); Hechanova, Beehr, and Christiansen (2003); Lau, Wing, and Ho (2003); and Reynolds (2003). Given the multiple levels of data aggregation and the vast variation in the type of research done, it is essential that additional meta-analyses be undertaken. This will help us understand how relationships among variables related to this area of research, i.e., job satisfaction and turnover, vary across job descriptions and industries. Moreover, meta-analysis will help us to resolve the problem arising from differing results for relationships among the same constructs reported in different studies.

In addition, researchers have studied the relationship between antecedents and consequences, modeled as path analysis, using Structural Equation Modeling (SEM). In SEM, interest usually focuses on latent constructs—abstract psychological variables such as stress or job satisfaction—and measurement is recognized as difficult and error-prone. By explicitly modeling measurement error, SEM allows to derive unbiased estimates for the relations among the latent constructs being studied and is being widely used in many areas of social science research.

In cross-cultural and cross-national research, it is important to examine the robustness of the relationships among constructs across cultures. Therefore, researchers should use various invariance techniques to rigorously test for differences in the strength of the relationships among constructs at different levels. Steekemp and Baumgartner (1998) provide a good list of invariance tests that needs to be conducted in cross-national research. Conceptual equivalence can be examined in proper empirical terms only after testing the invariance of constructs across dissimilar national and cultural contexts.

In reviewing the literature on the methodological robustness of the studies in this area, we have the distinct impression that the quality of quantitative data has improved in terms of psychometric reliabilities and validities, and the results are appropriate. However, the lack of relevance of much of the data in generalizing the findings to dissimilar contexts is problematic. Once again, it is important for us to remind ourselves of the purpose of the study and how the findings of the study will be useful. Although it might be beneficial for sustaining a research career, a series of investigations with limited scope is likely to be of little use in developing sharper insights into the functioning of work–family interactions. The issues of work–family interactions are important, as the editor and other authors in this volume have noted. They will become even more important as globalization un- leashes some of its unintended consequences, as noted by Greider (1997), Stiglitz (2002), and as discussed in terms of its implications by Bhagat, Baliga, Moustafa, and Krishnan (2003); Gareis and Barnett (2002); Hofstede (2003); Smith (2003); and others.

Florida (2002) argued that only the "creative class," those who pro- duce knowledge and use the knowledge in innovative ways, will be relatively unaffected by the flow of global capital from their regional areas. In other words, individuals performing more routine and eas- ily replicable jobs are vulnerable to dislocation caused by globaliza- tion. Even among the creative classes who function in a nonvertical la- bor market, time pressures on work–family interaction are increasing (Florida, 2002). In fact, in the United States, since the 1960s, marriage rates have declined whereas births out of wedlock, cohabitation, and divorce have increased, along with strong criticisms of marriage as a flawed societal institution. The 2002 U.S. Census shows a postmari- tal society, with single households comprising 26% of all households (which is larger than married households with children). Marriage is often characterized as an oppressive relationship, and more is being written on alternative forms of marriage (Carol Sanger, Columbia Law School Professor, quoted by Lewin, 2003). Whatever the case may be, in many western societies, ideas emphasizing two people in a com- mitted, permanent, caring relationship with children are noticeably declining. Conlin (2003) noted that the new U.S. demographics (in which half of the households are headed by unmarried people) will have a significant impact on the nature of functions of business, poli- tics, and society.

Researchers interested in developing new insights into the effects of work on family and family on work should concern themselves with this new trend in the data in the United States and elsewhere and should examine the relevance in the construction of hypotheses. Gone are the days when occupational self-identity was the sole concern of the male head of the household. Many women in both western and nonwestern societies sacrifice their families for their careers.

A related note in enhancing the significance of research findings is to incorporate culture-specific, i.e., emic (Peterson & Quintanilla, 2003), perspectives. Such perspectives will highlight both culture- and region-specific responses to pressures of globalization and its effects on work–family interactions.

CONCLUSION

We have argued in this chapter that research in the work–family domain will increase as the world globalizes rapidly. A recent investigation by Spector et al. (2004) illustrates a good trend of theory driven cross-national work with important conclusions. Similar research will enhance the robustness of our findings in this area. Florida's work (2002) on the rise of the creative class should provide some of the theoretical foundations for deriving propositions in the area. Time crunch, a concept discussed by Florida and others, is not only affecting work–family relationships in the G7 countries, but is also spreading to countries such as India, Ireland, Singapore, Hong Kong, and Egypt, where global companies are locating their call center operations and other low cost service activities. In an interesting discussion on this topic, *BusinessWeek* (March 3, 2004) noted that Indian women who work in call center operations experience significant bouts of depression because they are not able to fulfill some of the normal requirements of their familial duties in the collectivist context of Indian society.

To conduct methodologically sophisticated research, it is important to be sensitive to the reasons for conducting this research. Research conducted to enhance managerial strategies in managing work–family interactions is likely to be characterized by a different tone than that conducted to enhance human welfare in general and maintenance of the family unit, which has served humankind for centuries. Different types of methodologies are appropriate, and in fact there is no dearth of appropriate methodologies for conducting even the most complex research questions in this domain. Cultural variations should be adequately addressed by incorporating various culture-specific research methods, as discussed in Triandis (1994), Hui and Luk (1997), and van de Vijver and Leung (1997). Work–family research is of great importance in guiding some of the multinational and global corporations in the design of appropriate organizational and human resource policies. We believe that methodologically sophisticated, theory-driven research addressing all aspects of work–family interaction can begin to yield the kind of information and knowledge that we need to overcome some of the dysfunctional consequences of rapid globalization. Scholars such as Stiglitz (2002) will be pleased if some of the discontents associated with globalization can be checked by use of meaningful research outcomes in this important area of human functioning.

We strongly suggest that, with appropriate answers to the four questions raised in this chapter, research in work–family interaction in an era of globalization will be not only promising, but rewarding for years to come. "Dreams come true for those who persist despite adversities" should become the motto of researchers concerned with topics as vital as this.

REFERENCES

Althauser, R. P., & Heberlein, T. A. (1970). Validity and the multitrait-multimethod matrix. In E. F. Borgatta & G. W. Bohrnstedt (Eds.), *Sociological methodology* (pp. 106–127). San Francisco: Jossey-Bass.

Argyris, C. (1976). Problems and new directions for industrial psychology. In M. D. Dunnette (Ed.), *Handbook of Industrial and Organizational Psychology* (pp. 151–184). Chicago: Rand McNally College Publishing.

Baker, S., Kriplani, M., Hof, R. D., & Kersletter, J. (2004). Software, Business Week, March 1, 2004.

Baltes, B. B., & Briggs, T. E. (1999). Flexible and compressed workweek schedules: A meta-analysis of their effects on work-related criteria. *Journal of Applied Psychology, 84*, 496–513.

Bhagat, R. S., Baliga, B. R., Moustafa, K. S., & Krishnan, B. (2003). Knowledge in cross-cultural management in the era of globalization: Where do we go from here? In D. Tjosvold & K. Leung (Eds.), *Cross-cultural management: Foundations and future* (pp. 155–176). Aldershot, UK: Ashgate Press.

Bhagat, R. S., Kedia, B. L., Harveston, P., & Triandis, H. C. (2002). Cultural variations in the cross-border transfer of organizational knowledge: An integrative framework. *Academy of Management Review, 27*, 204–221.

Bhawuk, D. P. S. (2003). Culture's influence on creativity: The case of Indian spirituality. *International Journal of Intercultural Relations, 27*, 1–22.

Brown, S. L., & Booth, A. (2002). Stress at home, peace at work: A test of the time bind hypothesis. *Social Science Quarterly, 83*, 905–920.

Burke, R. J., & Greenglass, E. R. (1987). Work and family. In C. L. Cooper & I. T. Robertson (Eds.), *International review of industrial and organizational psychology, 1987* (pp. 273–320). New York: Wiley.

Conlin, M. (2003). Unmarried America. *BusinessWeek, October 20*, 106–116.

Denzin, N. K., & Lincoln, Y. S. (Eds.) (1998). *Collecting and interpreting qualitative materials*. Thousand Oaks, CA: Sage.

Edwards, J. R. (2003). Construct validation in organizational behavior research. In J. Greenberg (Ed.), *Organizational behavior: The state of the science* (2nd ed., pp. 327–372). Mahwah, NJ: Lawrence Erlbaum Associates.

Florida, R. (2002). *The rose of the creative class: And how it's transforming work, leisure, community, and everyday life.* New York: Basic Books.

Frone, M. R. (2003). Work–family balance. In J. C. Quick & L. E. Tetrick (Eds.), *Handbook of occupational health psychology* (pp. 143–162). Washington, DC: American Psychological Association.

Gareis, K. C., & Barnett, R. C. (2002). Under what conditions do long work hours affect psychological distress? *Work & Occupations, 29,* 483–497.

Greider, W. (1997). *One world: Ready or not.* New York: Crown Business.

Griffeth, R. W., Hem, P. W., & Gaertner, S. (2000). A meta-analysis of antecedents and correlates of employee turnover: Update, moderator tests, and research implications for the next millennium. *Journal of Management, 26,* 463–488.

Hechanova, R., Beehr, T. A., & Christiansen, N. D. (2003). Antecedents and consequences of employees' adjustment to overseas assignment: A meta-analytic review. *Applied Psychology, 52,* 213–236.

Hofstede, G. (2003). The universal and the specific in the 21st century management. In D. Tjosvold & K. Leung (Eds.), *Cross-cultural management: Foundations and future* (pp. 29–42). Aldershot, UK: Ashgate Press.

Hui, H., & Luk, C. L. (1997). Industrial/organizational psychology. In J. W. Berry, M. H. Segal, & C. Kagitcibasi (Eds.), *Handbook of cross-cultural psychology* (Vol. 3, pp. 371–412). Boston: Allyn & Bacon.

Jick, T. D. (1979). The triangulation method. *Administrative Science Quarterly, Dec.*

Kasl, S. V., & Jones, B. A. (2003). An epidemiological perspective on research design, measurement, and surveillance strategies. In J. C. Quick & L. E. Tetrick (Eds.), *Handbook of occupational health psychology* (pp. 379–398). Washington, DC: American Psychological Association.

Kriplani, M., Ergardio, P., & Hamon, S., *The Rise of India,* BusinessWeek Dec. 8, 2003.

Kornhauser, A. L. (1965). *Mental health of the industrial worker.* New York: Wiley.

Lau, V. C. S., Wing, T. A., & Ho, J. M. C. (2003). A qualitative and quantitative review of antecedents of counterproductive behavior in organizations. *Journal of Business & Psychology, 18,* 73–99.

Lewin, T. (2003). For better or worse: Marriage's stormy future. *The New York Times, November 23, Section 4,* 1, 4.

Pedhazur, E. J., & Schmelkin, L. P. (1991). *Measurement, design, and analysis: An integrated approach.* Mahwah, NJ: Lawrence Erlbaum Associates.

Peterson, M. F., & Quintanilla, S. A. R. (2003). Using emics and etics in cross-cultural organizational studies: Universal and local, tacit and explicit. In D. Tjosvold & K. Leung (Eds.), *Cross-cultural management: Foundations and future* (pp. 73–102). Aldershot, UK: Ashgate Press.

Quick, J. C., Cooper, C. L., Nelson, D. L., Quick, J. D., & Gavin, J. H. (2003). Stress, health, and well-being at work. In J. Greenberg (Ed.),

Organizational behavior: The state of the science (2nd ed., pp. 53–90). Mahwah, NJ: Lawrence Erlbaum Associates.

Reynolds, J. (2003). You can't always get the hours you want: Mismatches between actual and preferred work hours in the U.S. *Social Forces, 81,* 1171–1199.

Runkel, P. J., & McGrath, J. E. (1972). *Research on human behavior: A systematic guide to method.* New York: Holt, Rinehard, & Winston.

Steekemp, J. E. M., & Baumgartner, H. (1998). Assessing measurement invariance in cross national consumer research, *Journal of Consumer Research 25* (June), 78–90.

Smith, P. (2003). Meeting the challenge of cultural difference. In D. Tjosvold & K. Leung (Eds.), *Cross-cultural management: Foundations and future* (pp. 59–72). Aldershot, UK: Ashgate Press.

Spector, P. E., Cooper, C. L., Poelmans, S., Allen, T. D., O'Driscoll, M., Sanchez, J. I., Siu, O. L., Dewe, P., Hart, P., & Lu, Luo. (2004). A cross-national comparative study of work–family stressors, working hours, and well-being: China and Latin America versus the Anglo world. *Personnel Psychology, 57,* 119–142.

Stiglitz, J. E. (2002). *Globalization and its discontents.* New York: Norton.

Triandis, H. C. (1973). Work and nonwork: Intercultural perspectives. In M. D. Dunnette (Ed.), *Work and nonwork in the year 2001* (pp. 29–52). Monterey, CA: Brooks/Cole.

Triandis, H. C. (1994). *Culture and social behavior.* New York: McGraw-Hill.

Triandis, H. C. (1995). *Individualism and collectivism.* Boulder, CO: Westview Press.

Van de Vijver, F. J. R., & Leung, K. (1997). Methods and data analysis of comparative research. In J. W. Berry, Y. H. Poortinga, & J. Pandey (Eds.), *Handbook of cross-cultural psychology* (2nd ed., Vol. 1, pp. 257–300). Needham Heights, MA: Allyn & Bacon.

14

Cross-Cultural Perspectives on Work–Family Conflict

Michele J. Gelfand and Andrew P. Knight
University of Maryland

Research on the interface between work and family has exploded over the past 2 decades. Grounded in diverse theoretical foundations ranging from crossover theory (e.g., Westman & Etzion, 1995) to institutional perspectives (e.g., Arthur, 2003), scholars have recently made great strides in exploring how the relationship between work and family impacts various outcomes. The breadth of outcomes investigated at the individual level is staggering. Researchers have considered attitudinal outcomes, including attitudes such as job satisfaction (e.g., Kossek & Ozeki, 1998) and organizational commitment (e.g., Lyness & Thompson, 1997); behavioral outcomes, such as organizational citizenship behaviors (e.g., Lambert, 2000), substance abuse (e.g., Allen, Herst, Bruck, & Sutton, 2000), and absenteeism (e.g., Thomas & Ganster, 1995); and, health outcomes, including both psychological (e.g., Frone, Russell, & Cooper, 1997) and physical ailments (e.g., Adams & Jex, 1999). At the organizational level, scholars have focused their attention primarily on organizational culture (e.g., Thompson, Beauvais, & Lyness, 1999) and family-friendly practices (e.g., Lambert, 2000). Taken as a whole, these findings reinforce the notion that work–family research has the potential to practically benefit individuals and organizations in a diverse number of areas.

Yet as this volume attests, the contemporary global economy requires an understanding of how the work–family relationship operates within and across cultures. It is in this regard that this volume, with its special focus on international issues, makes important theoretical and empirical contributions. Below, we highlight some key contributions that the chapters collectively make to the study of work–family issues. As we will discuss, the chapters make significant progress in moving the field toward an open-systems perspective, in explicating what is universal (etic) versus culture-specific (emic) regarding work–family phenomena, and in illustrating how work–family cultures develop at the organizational level of analysis. We then discuss some critical challenges and opportunities for the future study of culture and work–family conflict.

ORGANIZATIONS AS EMBEDDED OPEN SYSTEMS

The chapters of this volume advance work–family theory through their explicit consideration of organizations as open systems, that is, as influenced by the overarching contexts in which they operate (Katz & Kahn, 1978). Since Katz and Kahn's landmark publication, decades of research in organizational behavior have illustrated that environmental inputs can have a marked impact upon the types of behaviors, processes, and structures that are enacted within organizations. In keeping with this spirit, scholars in this volume make clear that the environmental context has a significant impact on work–family practices within organizations. The focus on context throughout the volume is wide in its scope—from differences in sociopolitical contexts (e.g., welfare state regimes) to differences in sociocultural contexts (e.g., cultural values). As good systems theorists, scholars in this volume have also considered how changes in the environment can have wide-ranging implications for work–family issues.

For example, with regard to the sociopolitical context of work–family issues, den Dulk (Chapter 8) provides an insightful analysis of how welfare state regimes shape the number and types of work–family provisions offered by organizations. Kinnunen and Mauno (Chapter 4) show how legislation impacts work–family culture, which in turn influences various outcomes such as personal well-being. Shaffer, Francesco, Joplin, and Lau (Chapter 12) explicate how cultural values, such as individualism–collectivism and gender role ideologies, can impact work–family conflict and the support resources available to cope with this conflict. Their study is an important first step in developing a cross-cultural conceptualization of work–family support resources. Likewise, Westman (Chapter 9) cogently makes a case for the organization as an open system in her incorporation of cultural values into crossover theory. Westman argues that values, such as individualism–collectivism and masculinity–femininity, interact with gender to affect the symmetry and direction of the crossover processes.

Finally, by focusing on environmental changes, two chapters provide compelling evidence for an open-systems approach. In his chapter on work–family issues in sub-Saharan Africa, Aryee (Chapter 10) emphasizes the dynamic nature of the work–family relationship under fluctuating environmental conditions. His portrayal of sub-Saharan Africa's changing sociocultural context, in which people must negotiate novel barriers to work–family balance, stresses the importance of considering temporal trends in work–family issues. Interestingly, Aryee argues that national policies lag behind the cultural changes of sub-Saharan Africa, exaggerating the effects of work–family conflict. Poster (Chapter 7) also explicitly treats the work–family relationship as a dynamic phenomenon, determined, in part, by continuously transforming global and local sociopolitical and economic structures. Her longitudinal study examines how organizations differentially respond to change, with respect to work–family policies. Poster's attention to how global changes affect work–family policies in a number of contexts fills a conceptual void in the work–family literature.

THE IMPORTANCE OF TESTING UNIVERSALS

A second theoretical contribution made by this volume is its emphasis on testing for universal work–family relationships. The work–family literature is dominated by Western research using Western samples (Poelmans, et al., 2003). Thus, an exploration of work–family relationships cross-culturally is necessary to determine which relationships are etic (or universal) and which are emic (or culture-specific). The chapters in this volume show some surprising results regarding universality. For example, Spector, Allen, Poelmans, and Cooper (Chapter 3) provide quantitative support for the idea that work–family relationships, as explicated by western research, vary across cultures. Spector et al.'s data not only show mean differences across

18 countries on all of the variables studied (work–family pressure, job satisfaction, mental well-being and physical well-being), but furthermore, show that many relationships found to hold in western countries were weak or nonexistent in eastern countries. For example, they found a significant relationship between work–family pressure and work hours in western countries, but in eastern countries such a relationship was not significant. Likewise, Yang (Chapter 11) provides significant quantitative support for the moderating role of culture in work–family research. Although she found support for similarities between the United States and China with respect to the relationship between work–family conflict and negative outcomes (both at the individual and organizational levels), her results also suggested that individualism–collectivism moderates the relationship among various role pressures (i.e., work and family demands) and work–family conflict, such that the effects of work and family demands on work–family conflict are diminished by collectivism, as opposed to individualism. Yang's findings clearly demonstrate the importance of including cultural moderators in conceptualizations of work–family relationships.

CULTURE AT OTHER LEVELS OF ANALYSIS

Finally, this volume makes considerable theoretical contributions by considering culture with respect to work–family issues beyond the societal level but also at the organizational level as well. Kinnunen and Mauno (Chapter 4) provide an insightful review of the literature on work–family culture and the various scales that have been developed to assess culture at the organizational level. Although they found little consistency across studies with regard to the measure used to assess work–family culture—thereby making comparisons of results difficult—their review does support the notion that work–family culture is related to individual outcomes, such as job satisfaction and organizational commitment. By synthesizing previous research on organizational culture, Kinnunen and Mauno provide the foundation upon which sound theory and measurement can be developed. Along the same lines, Geurts et al. (Chapter 6) provide interesting data, which show that a positive work–family culture at the organizational level is critical for predicting the likelihood that employees will actually use available work–family provisions, such as flextime and child care. Their findings clearly indicate that without a supportive organizational culture, work–family provisions are less likely to be effective, resulting in increased work–family conflict among employees.

Taken as a whole, this volume makes significant contributions by showing that the cultural context of organizations is critical for an understanding of work–family issues. In continuing to develop our global understanding of the work–family relationship, however, a number of theoretical challenges still face international work–family researchers. In this final section, we highlight a number of critical areas for future research on work–family issues, including the need for the development of multilevel theories, the need to develop global constructs with culture-specific sensitivity, the need to move beyond examining dichotomies of individualism and collectivism, and the need to examine the global context of organizations as it affects work–family dynamics. Each is discussed in turn.

MULTILEVEL CONTEXT OF WORK–FAMILY RESEARCH

Work–family conflict is inherently a multilevel phenomenon, requiring an understanding of factors at the societal, organizational, team, and individual levels of analysis (Poelmans, 2003). Much of the research on work–family conflict, however, is limited in its multilevel scope (Korabik, Lero, & Ayman, 2003) and has a rather individualistic bias—focusing largely on individual level attributes, perceptions, attitudes, and outcomes. It is critical, therefore, that the next wave of work–family research move beyond this individual level focus to start tackling the multilevel terrain in which work–family issues exist.

In adopting a multilevel focus, there are a number of avenues of work–family research that are ripe for investigation, including single-level models that move beyond the individual level, cross-level models that link higher order levels with lower levels, and cross-level models that link lower levels with higher levels. With respect to single-level models, although we are beginning to develop more sophisticated models at the individual level—those that link work–family conflict with individual outcomes such as satisfaction, commitment, psychological strain, and depression—there is a dearth of research on the antecedents and consequences of work–family issues at higher levels of analysis. For example, at the organizational level, future research would benefit from examining what organizational characteristics (e.g., industry, size, technology) predict work–family phenomena at the organizational level (e.g., work–family friendly organizational cultures and climates). Further, it is critical to begin examining the *organizational outcomes* that are associated with work–family cultures at this level. Are individual level models isomorphic at the organizational level? Are positive work–family cultures associated with higher organizational satisfaction, lower organizational turnover rates, and/or enhanced organizational reputations and performance? Given that employees tend to treat customers consistently with how they are treated (Schneider, White, & Paul, 1998), it stands to reason that work–family cultures can indeed spill over to aggregate customer experiences, which can ultimately affect organizational performance. Further, moving beyond outcomes directly related to organizations, do work–family cultures affect outcomes (beyond the individual level) that are more relevant for society at large? For example, are work–family cultures related to divorce rates of employees? Do work–family cultures affect the development of children? At present, there is little data that can address these issues. From a practical point of view, illustrating that work–family issues have consequences that matter beyond the individual level could be imperative for gaining management commitment to these issues.

In addition to developing single-level models, it is critical to begin to develop cross-level models of work–family issues. In one respect, models that illustrate top-down processes—in other words, how higher level contextual factors affect phenomena at lower levels of the system (Kozlowski & Klein, 2000)—are ripe for development. For example, there is emerging evidence that documents the linkage between societal and organizational culture in the areas of leadership (Gelfand, Bhawuk, Nishii, & Bechtold, 2004), and it seems reasonable to assume that societal culture and state ideology affect the development of organizational cultures that are beneficial or detrimental to work–family issues. As mentioned previously, some of the chapters in this volume address the embeddedness of organizations in their overarching social and national contexts, but there remains much room for theoretical and empirical assessment of linkages across levels.

Going down one level of analysis, it is also important to continue to examine cross-level relationships between work–family organizational cultures and individual attitudes and behaviors. For example, research could explore the relationship between work–family culture and destructive job behaviors. We might also begin to examine moderated cross-level relationships, asking questions such as: Does work–family organizational culture affect individual outcomes only for certain types of people or people in certain types of jobs? Or, more specifically, what types of people stand to benefit the most from positive work–family cultures? Research addressing such issues could demonstrate the importance of focused managerial attention on work–family concerns.

Finally, although we have discussed top-down processes, it is equally important for research to examine bottom-up processes in organizations that elucidate work–family dynamics. Here we refer to the types of individual and group characteristics that emerge to predict higher level phenomena such as work–family organizational cultures and the adoption of work–family practices. Research is needed to examine what personalities and/or individual attributes are associated with the development of work–family initiatives and supportive work–family cultures. What types of people, in aggregate, lead to supportive work–family cultures, and what types of people, in aggregate, lead to unsupportive work–family cultures? In societies in which being seen as a family-friendly organization can lead to improved financial performance (see Arthur, 2003), how can organizations market themselves to attract employees that will help create a positive work–family culture? Further, how might organizations select individuals (and/or train them) to support and enact such a culture (cf. Schneider, Smith, & Sipe, 2000)? Jumping levels of analysis, how might the aggregate work–family cultures of a nation's organizations impact national policies, legislation, and sociopolitical culture? In addition to studying organizational culture as a consequent of societal characteristics, we could investigate its role as an antecedent to such attributes. By examining such bottom-up processes, we might gain a new perspective on the relationship between work, family, and culture.

THINKING GLOBALLY, DEFINING LOCALLY

Inherent to all cross-cultural research is the tension between *etics* (what is universal) and *emics* (what is culture-specific). As noted above, much progress has been made in work–family research in trying to empirically assess whether research in the west is in fact generalizable to other cultures. Yet a lurking problem in research in the field (and in cross-cultural studies in general) is the use of *imposed etic constructs* (Berry, 1980), wherein researchers simply import constructs and measurements that have been developed in the United States (or another country) for use in work–family research in other cultures. This is a risky strategy because such measures may miss important cultural elements (e.g., may have *construct deficiency*) and may include completely irrelevant elements (e.g., may have *construct contamination*). Thus, by starting (and ending) with western constructs, we may be missing important aspects of work–family that are relevant in other cultures. As Azuma (1984) cogently remarked "when a psychologist looks at a non-Western culture through Western glasses, he may fail to notice important aspects of the non-Western culture since the schema for recognizing them are not provided by his science." (p. 49)

Future research on work–family issues needs to develop global (etic) constructs while also being mindful that such constructs may be operationalized in culture-specific ways. As an analogy, in the area of leadership, cross-cultural research has revealed that classic dimensions of leadership, namely, *initiating structure* and *consideration* are found in other cultures, yet the specific behaviors that are associated with these dimensions vary considerably across cultures. The same behavior—talking about one's subordinate behind his or her back for instance—is seen as an indicator of considerate behavior in Japan, yet is seen as an indicator of inconsiderate behavior in the United States (Smith, Misumi, Tayeb, Peterson, & Bond, 1989). Likewise, in the domain of work–family issues, at the organizational level, the construct of "work–family culture," or that which supports and value the integration of work and family lives (Kinnunen & Mauno, chapter 4; Thompson, Beauvais, & Lyness, 1999) is likely to be universal; yet the types of values, assumptions, and practices that constitute work–family cultures will invariably differ across societal cultures. For example, the manifestations of perceived organizational support may vary across cultures. Kashima and Callan (1994) argue that managers in Japan adopt metaphors of the Japanese family when managing (Kashima & Callan, 1994), and engage in "family" like practices such as assisting employees in finding spouses. Aycan (2004) also notes that in cultures that emphasize paternalism, such as Turkey, managers assume the role of a "father" who is highly involved in the lives of employees. Managers not only advise employees in professional matters (e.g., career planning, job training), but also provide counsel on personal and family matters as well (e.g., providing marriage counseling, resolving disputes between husbands and wife). Indeed, supervisor support is expected to extend beyond the immediate employee relationships to include family members and to include attending congratulatory events (e.g., weddings, graduations), condolences (funerals). In addition, supervisors even provide financial support of family members when needed.

To be sure, these practices may not be entirely unfamiliar to managers in the west. Practices that are recommended for U.S. managers dealing with expatriate employees who must adjust to life away from their domestic organizations (e.g., providing partner support; see Caligirui & Lazarova, chapter 5) have some resemblance to paternalistic practices that are typical in nonexpatriate contexts in other cultures. Yet even in expatriate contexts, paternalistic practices are likely to be viewed as an invasion of privacy and *not* supportive in western cultures. More generally, this discussion suggests that what constitutes the dimension of managerial support may vary across cultures. Accordingly, existing work–family culture measures, which have largely been developed in the United States (e.g., see Chapter 4 by Kinnunen & Mauno, for a review), are likely in need of expansion to be relevant in other cultural contexts.

TOWARD A MULTIFACETED VIEW OF SOCIETAL CULTURE

A perusal of this volume and the literature more generally illustrates that individualism and collectivism (IC) is the most researched dimension among scholars studying work–family issues. This is perhaps not surprising given that IC is also the favorite heuristic in cross-cultural psychology (Segall & Kagitçibasi, 1997). Nevertheless, future research needs to move beyond simple dichotomies of individualism and collectivism in order to capture the complexity of the constructs. For example, Triandis and colleagues (Singelis, Triandis, Bhawuk, & Gelfand, 1995; Triandis, 1995; Triandis & Gelfand, 1998) have shown that there are important distinctions among individualistic and among collectivistic cultures—termed horizontal and vertical individualism and collectivism. Although the United States is generally an individualistic culture, it also emphasizes achieved status and competition (termed "vertical individualism"; Triandis and Gelfand, 1998). By contrast, according to Triandis and Gelfand (1998), other individualistic cultures, such as Australia and Sweden, emphasize equality and eschew status differences (termed "horizontal individualism"). Likewise, not all collectivistic cultures are alike; some emphasize ascribed status (e.g., Japan) whereas others emphasize equal status (e.g., an Israeli Kibbutz). There are many further distinctions among individualism and collectivism (Triandis, 1995), and work–family research needs to capture this complexity so as to avoid oversimplifying this dimension.

Future research should also continue to incorporate other dimensions of culture into theory and research on work and family issues, as an exclusive focus on IC and work–family issues is highly limiting in its scope. Lytle, Brett, Barsness, Tinsley, and Janssens (1995) identified many value dimensions on which national cultures vary (see their Table 1) that may be relevant to work–family issues. More recent research on cultural values by the GLOBE research project (House, Hanges, Javidan, Dorfman, & Gupta, 2004) is also very relevant to work–family issues. For example, dimensions such as *societal performance orientation* may be related to increased work–family conflict, whereas *societal humane-orientation* may be related to increased social and institutional support for work–family issues.

Dimensions such as gender egalitarianism may also moderate gender differences in work–family conflict that are well-documented in the literature (see Westman, Chapter 9). Moving beyond values, Leung, Bond, and colleagues (2002) advanced a taxonomy of beliefs that vary across cultures, which may also be relevant to phenomena discussed in this volume. For example, an emphasis on *spirituality* may have relevance to how people cope with stress derived from work–family issues. Likewise, Peng and Nisbett's (1999) notion of cultural differences in cognition or *dialectic thinking*, the tolerance for contradiction that is derived from ancient Chinese philosophy, may have relevance for the types of metaphors that underlie work–family issues (e.g., work–family "conflict" vs. balance) across cultures. Time orientation (Kluckhohn & Strodtbeck, 1961) is also a key societal dimension that needs to be explored in work–family research. For example, work–family conflict is likely to be more acute in cultures that emphasize a monochronic view of time (in which people tend to experience time as a linear, limited, and valuable commodity, and there is an emphasis on doing only one thing at a time and adhering to plans), as compared to cultures that emphasize a polychronic view of time (in which people are involved with many things simultaneously, and plans often change to accommodate demands arising from the interpersonal dynamics). Cultural differences in *time urgency* (Waller, Conte, Gibson, & Carpenter, 2001), entrainment processes (Ancona & Chong, 1996), and metaphors for time (Gelfand & McCusker, 2002) are also likely to be highly relevant for experiences of work–family conflict across cultures. More generally, by broadening the cultural dimensions considered, we will ultimately be better able to understand and explain more phenomena related to work–family issues across societies.

THE DYNAMICS OF CHANGE: WORK–FAMILY RESEARCH IN A GLOBAL CONTEXT

With few exceptions (Aryee, Chapter 10; Poster, Chapter 7) much of the research in this area offers a static view of culture and work–family issues. A key challenge for future research will be to understand how culture is challenged, and changed and to move away from culture as a static "essence." For example, one key driver of change that needs to be incorporated into work–family research is *globalization*. Today, many companies operate globally and are characterized by complex arrangements that cross national borders in the form of multinational companies, international mergers and acquisitions, joint ventures, and international alliances. Moving beyond domestic boundaries presents a number of fascinating questions for work–family research. For example, how do global organizations operating across national boundaries build hybrid cultures (Earley & Malikowsi, 2000) that incorporate values related to work–family issues from multiple societal contexts? How can such organizations contend with satisfying the work–family needs of a heterogeneous workforce? How must national policies and/or legislation adapt to ensure that the work–family expectations of a global workforce are met? In terms of multinational mergers and acquisitions, how can disparate work–family values be reconciled during the restructuring of an organization to embrace a multinational workforce? How can organizations avoid ethnocentricity in designing work–family benefit programs? Such issues bring sensitive issues to the bargaining and negotiation tables of multinational corporations.

Another critical issue for future research is the impact that globalization has on work–family practices in developing nations. As Poster (Chapter 7) has shown, the impact of globalization is clearly unequal across societies. Work–family policies in rich nations are more likely to be insulated from massive organizational and societal changes. However, in developing nations, whereas the global context of organizations can be an economic stimulant for the society at large, it can also disrupt and reduce the emphasis on work–family practices. Being sensitive to the differential impact of globalization on developing nations presents a significant challenge to cross-cultural work–family researchers. Indeed, societal changes in developing nations may be particularly detrimental to women. For example, in Aryee's (Chapter 10) insightful analysis, despite larger changes in the sub-Saharan African cultural practices (e.g., family child-care arrangements), deep assumptions regarding the role of women remain unchanged, making the integration of work and family even more difficult than in years past. Along the same lines, research is needed to give voice to segments of societies that are left behind or marginalized, as Kossek and her colleagues' analysis clearly shows. Incorporating multiple socioeconomic groups will help move the work–family literature away from being relevant only to middle-class, privileged members of society.

CONCLUDING REMARKS

In conclusion, this volume, which puts work–family theory and research within a global framework, adds significantly to the existing work–family literature. Most importantly are its recognition of environmental forces that influence how organizations operate, an emphasis on the continued testing of universal versus locally identified work–family relationships, and an appreciation of how culture can operate at many different levels, such as the organizational level. All of this is to say "Well done!" The search for broader and deeper theory on work–family issues is off and running with the publication of this book. There is still much to explore, and the future of research on the intersection of work and family is exciting. It promises scholars the opportunity to impact the global community by contributing to an understanding of how two of the most important aspects of many people's lives interrelate.

ACKNOWLEDGMENT

The authors express their gratitude to Steven Poelmans for his feedback on the current chapter.

REFERENCES

Adams, G. A., & Jex, S. M. (1999). Relationships between time management, control, work–family conflict, and strain. *Journal of Occupational Health Psychology, 4,* 72–77.

Allen, T. D., Herst, D. E., Bruck, C. S., & Sutton, M. (2000). Consequences associated with work-to-family conflict: A review and agenda for future research. *Journal of Occupational Health Psychology, 5,* 278–308.

Ancona, D., & Chong, C-L. (1996). Entrainment: Pace, cycle, and rhythm in organizational behavior. *Research in Organizational Behavior, 18,* 251–284.

Arthur, M. M. (2003). Share price reactions to work–family initiatives: An institutional perspective. *Academy of Management Journal, 46,* 497–505.

Aycan, Z. (2004). Managing inequalities: Leadership and teamwork in developing country context. In H. Lane, H. Mendenhall, & M. Maznevski (Eds.), *International handbook of management* (pp. 406–423). New York: Blackwell.

Azuma, H. (1984). Psychology in a non-western country. *International Journal of Psychology, 19,* 45–56.

Berry, J. W. (1980). Introduction to methodology. In H. C. Triandis & J. W. Berry (Eds.), *Handbook of cross-cultural psychology* (Vol. 2, pp. 1–28). Boston: Allyn and Bacon.

Earley, P. C., & Mosakowski, E. (2000). Creating hybrid team cultures: An empirical test of transnational team functioning. *Academy of Management Journal, 43,* 26–49.

Frone, M. R., Russell, M., & Cooper, M. L. (1997). Relation of work–family conflict to health outcomes: A four-year longitudinal study of employed parents. *Journal of Occupational and Organizational Psychology*, *70*, 325–335.

Gelfand, M. J., Bhawuk, D. P., Nishii, L., & Bechtold, D. (2004). Individualism and collectivism: Multilevel perspectives and implications for leadership. In R. J. House, P. J. Hanges, M. Javidan, P. W. Dorfman, & V. Gupta (Eds.), *Culture, leadership, and organizations: The GLOBE study of 62 cultures.* Thousand Oaks, CA: Sage.

Gelfand, M. J., & McCusker, C. (2002). Metaphor and the cultural construction of negotiation: A paradigm for theory and research. In M. Gannon & K. L. Newman (Eds.), *Handbook of cross-cultural management* (pp. 292–314). New York: Blackwell.

House, R. J., Hanges, P. J., Javidan, M., Dorfman, P. W., & Gupta, V. (2004). *Culture, leadership, and organizations: The GLOBE study of 62 cultures.* Thousand Oaks, CA: Sage.

Kashima, Y., & Callan, V. J. (1994). The Japanese workgroup. In H. C. Triandis, M. D. Dunnette, & L. M. Hough (Eds.), *Handbook of industrial and organizational psychology* (2nd ed., Vol. 4, pp. 606–649). Palo Alto, CA: Consulting Psychologists.

Katz, D., & Kahn, R. L. (1978). *The social psychology of organizations* (2nd ed.). New York: Wiley.

Kluckhohn, F., & Strodtbeck, F. (1961). *Variations in value orientation.* Evanston, IL: Row, Peterson.

Korabik, K., Lero, D. S., & Ayman, R. (2003). A multi-level approach to cross cultural work–family research. *International Journal of Cross Cultural Management*, *3*, 289–303.

Kossek, E. E., & Ozeki, C. (1998). Work–family conflict, policies, and the job–life satisfaction relationship: A review and directions for organizational behavior-human resources research. *Journal of Applied Psychology*, *83*, 139–149.

Kozlowski, S. W. J., & Klein, K. J. (2000). A multilevel approach to theory and research in organizations: Contextual, temporal, and emergent processes. In K. J. Klein & S. W. J. Kozlowski (Eds.), *Multilevel theory, research, and methods in organizations: Foundations, extensions, and new directions* (pp. 3–90). San Francisco, CA: Jossey-Bass.

Lambert, S. J. (2000). Added benefits: The link between work–life benefits and organizational citizenship behavior. *Academy of Management Journal*, *43*, 801–815.

Leung, K., Bond, M. H., de Carrasquel, S. H., Munoz, C., Hernandez, M., Murakami, F., Yamaguchi, S., Bierbrauer, G., & Singelis, T. (2002). Social axioms: The search for universal dimensions of general beliefs about how the world functions. *Journal of Cross-Cultural Psychology*, *33*, 286–302.

Lyness, K. S., & Thompson, D. E. (1997). Above the glass ceiling? A comparison of matched samples of female and male executives. *Journal of Applied Psychology*, *82*, 359–375.

Lytle, A. L., Brett, J. M., Barsness, Z. I., Tinsley, C. H., & Janssens, M. (1995). A paradigm for confirmatory cross-cultural research in organizational behavior. *Research in Organizational Behavior*, *17*, 167–214.

Peng, K., & Nisbett, R. E. (1999). Culture, dialectics, and reasoning about contradiction, *American Psychologist, 54,* 741–754.

Poelmans, S. (2003). Editorial: The multi-level 'fit' model of work and family. *International Journal of Cross Cultural Management, 3,* 267–274.

Poelmans, S., Spector, P. E., Cooper, C. L., Allen, T. D., O'Driscoll, M., & Sanchez, J. I. (2003). A cross-national comparative study of work/family demands and resources. *International Journal of Cross Cultural Management, 3,* 275–288.

Schneider, B., Smith, D. B., & Sipe, W. P. (2000). Personnel selection psychology: Multi-level considerations. In K. J. Klein & S. W. Kozlowski (Eds.), *Multi-level theory, research, and methods in organizations* (pp. 91–120). San Francisco, CA: Jossey-Bass.

Schneider, B., White, S., & Paul, M. C. (1998). Linking service climate and customer perceptions of service quality: Test of a causal model. *Journal of Applied Psychology, 83,* 150–163.

Segall, M. H., & Kagitcibasi, C. (1997). Introduction. In J. W. Berry, M. H. Segall, & K. Kagitcibasi (Eds.), *Handbook of cross-cultural psychology.* Needham, MA: Allyn & Bacon.

Singelis, T. M., Triandis, H. C., Bhawuk, D. P. S., & Gelfand, M. (1995). Horizontal and vertical dimensions of individualism and collectivism: A theoretical measurement refinement. *Cross-Cultural Research, 29,* 240–275.

Smith, P. B., Misumi, J., Tayeb, M., Peterson, M., & Bond, M. H. (1989). On the generality of leadership style measures across cultures. *Journal of Occupational Psychology, 62,* 97–109.

Thomas, L. T., & Ganster, D. C. (1995). Impact of family-supportive work variables on work–family conflict and strain: A control perspective. *Journal of Applied Psychology, 80,* 6–15.

Thompson, C., Beauvais, L., & Lyness, K. (1999). When work–family benefits are not enough: The influence of work–family culture on benefit utilization, organizational attachment, and work–family conflict. *Journal of Vocational Behavior, 54,* 329–415.

Triandis, H. C. (1995). *Individualism & collectivism.* Boulder, CO: Westview Press.

Triandis, H. C., & Gelfand, M. (1998). Converging measurement of horizontal and vertical individualism and collectivism. *Journal of Personality and Social Psychology, 74,* 118–128.

Waller, M. J., Conte, J. M., Gibson, C. B., & Carpenter, M. A. (2001). The effect of individual perceptions of deadlines on team performance. *Academy of Management Review, 26,* 586–600.

Westman, M., & Etzion, D. (1995). Crossover of stress, strain, and resources from one spouse to another. *Journal of Organizational Behavior, 22,* 467–481.

15

Emphasizing the Family in Work– Family Research: A Review of Current Research and Recommendations for Future Directions

Jennifer M. Bowes
Macquarie University–Sydney

This chapter presents a family researcher's perspective of the links between work and family by reviewing the literature on the effects of work on families, using the ecological framework of Bronfenbrenner (1986, 1979, 1997) and by suggesting new areas for research, particularly areas that involve an international perspective in a research area dominated by U.S.-based insights into work and family.

Considerable literature has built on the impact of the demands and characteristics of paid work on the family life of workers. This research has investigated the impact of paid work on the relationships with partners and children within workers' families. Family functioning and parenting have also been the focus of research. Other research again has focused on the workers themselves and their strategies to balance work and family responsibilities. More recently, there has been increasing interest in the impact of the working conditions of parents on the development of their children, seldom the focus of work–family research from an organizational perspective (Rothausen, 1999). In addition, some concern has been voiced about effects not just on families but on communities of trends in the workplace, particularly the trend in several developed countries toward the working of longer and nonstandard hours, such as evenings and weekends.

The aim of this chapter is to review this literature, to highlight some major findings and research approaches, and to identify the topics that have as yet received little research attention, together with research approaches that appear particularly useful in this area of investigation. Much of the research on work and family derives from the United States and other developed countries, such as Australia and the United Kingdom. The review takes these studies as a starting point, then discusses how a wider international perspective can open up this area of research to new ideas and different findings. The chapter presents three research questions that could be valuable for future research in work and family, particularly if the issues are investigated in an international or cross-cultural context.

FRAMEWORK FOR LITERATURE REVIEW AND CHAPTER

The concern in this chapter with the impact of work characteristics and patterns on communities, societies, and families stems from two sources. The first is a shift in child development and family research toward consideration of children and their parents in community context rather than as individuals in isolation (see Bowes, 2004). This shift has been strongly influenced by the work of Bronfenbrenner (1986, 1979, 1997), who has urged that an ecological approach be taken in research on child development. In Bronfenbrenner's systems-based approach, children and families are considered in the context of settings such as school, workplace, and community, which have direct impact on them, and in the context of less direct yet considerable influences such as the cultural and legislative characteristics of their society. Recently, Bronfenbrenner's framework has been applied to the work and family area, and this approach shows considerable promise for the broadening of work–family theory (Barnett, 1998; Barnett & Hyde, 2001) and research (Grzywacz & Marks, 2000).

A second reason for looking beyond the family to wider contexts in considering work and family in this chapter is its relevance for social policy. Work–family issues have implications for multiple areas of policy from industrial relations and workforce planning to the consideration of societal resources to assist families to achieve a work–family balance that is productive and healthy for them and for their society. Community as a context has only recently been included in theory and research on the work–family interface (see Voydanoff, 2003 for a summary).

The chapter begins with a review of research on the impact of paid work on individual workers, their families, and their communities. Following the review of selected research on work and family in the United States and similar countries, several other international studies are considered. Although not as numerous, these international studies clearly expand research perspectives on the impact of parental employment on families by bringing different groups of workers to the fore and by considering cultural values as an integral mediating factor in the impact of work on family in different countries. The chapter concludes with suggested directions for further research in this area. Suggestions are made about research topics, research methods, and international perspectives for a work–family research agenda for the future.

REVIEW OF LITERATURE

Over the past decade, research has increased markedly in this area, appearing in journals from a range of discipline areas including applied psychology, family studies, industrial relations and labor, management, sociology, women's studies, business, demography, and developmental psychology articles (Drago & Kashian, 2003). In response, there have been several excellent bibliographies and reviews published in this area (Barnett, 1998; Gottfried, Gottfried, & Bathurst, 2002; Lilly, Pitt-Catsouphes, & Googins, 1997; Perry-Jenkins, Repetti, & Crouter, 2000), electronic data bases and newsgroups established (for example, the Work–Family Research Database at Boston College and The Penn State-based Workfam Newsgroup in the United States, and the Work and Family Internet Discussion List in Australia), and a paper identifying key journals for work–family articles (Drago & Kashian, 2003). Because of the availability of these resources, this review does not attempt to be comprehensive. Rather, the aim is to develop a framework to review selected current research, to identify gaps and to pose new questions about the work–family interface, particularly questions that extend internationally.

The review is mainly of research conducted in the United States, Australia, and the United Kingdom and discussion of studies is presented in relation to three broad research questions:

- What are the effects of parental employment on family life?
- What are the strategies used by employed parents to reconcile work and family responsibilities?
- What are the effects of parental employment on communities?

The first two questions are common ones in the current research base, although the research on these questions tends to focus on some aspects of the issue and neglect others as the review shows. The third question is relatively unexplored yet is included to indicate an impact of work conditions that extends beyond the families of workers, which needs to be considered within an ecological framework.

What Are the Effects of Parental Employment on Family Life?

The first and most obvious effect of parental employment on family life is its financial benefit. The negative impacts on child development and family functioning of economic hardship are well documented (Duncan, Brooks-Gunn, Young, & Smith, 1998; Galinsky & Swanberg, 2000; Heyman, Boynton-Jarrett, Carter, Bond, & Galinsky, 2003; Lerner, 2003). Adequate income reduces family stress and allows families to purchase necessities and other benefits for their children (McLoyd, 1993; Yeung, Linver, & Brooks-Gunn, 2002). Research has found that other benefits for families from parental employment include higher career aspirations of girls with mothers in paid work (Hoffman & Youngblade, 1999; Wright & Young, 1998) and the development in children of knowledge about work (Bowes & Goodnow, 1996).

Most recent research in the work and family field focused on workers and how they manage the demands of their job and their family, particularly when these demands compete with (Hammer & Thompson, 2003) or spillover (Crouter, 1984; Repetti & Wood, 1997) into the other domain. A particular concern has been how women manage to reconcile the demands of work and family. This concern reflects a general expectation in many cultures that women are responsible for the bulk of the emotional and household work within the family (Barnett & Hyde, 2001; Hochschild, 1999; Pocock, 2003; Rothausen, 2003).

When women entered the workforce in large numbers from about the 1960s in the United States and internationally (OECD, 2002), the issue of work–family balance became prominent in research. Women in these countries, particularly middle-class women, have in the past few generations particularly "kept the home fires burning" for the male worker, taking care of the unpaid work in the home involved in household work, care of children, relationships with extended family and community ties through friendships and volunteer work (Barnett & Hyde, 2001; Hochschild, 1999; Pocock, 2003; Rothausen, 2003). The societal change in the United States and other countries with women's movement into the workplace has raised the issue of how these unpaid activities, essential to family and community life, can be sustained even when many women are working a "second shift" of housework after their paid work each day (Hochschild, 1989).

The work–family spillover for male workers has only recently been of interest to family researchers, mainly in the context of research on fathering (Amato, 1998; Furstenberg, 1998; Gottfried et al., 2002; Lamb, 1997; O'Brien & Shemilt, 2003; Petre, 1998; Weston, Qu, & Soriano, 2002). Expectations that fathers will take a greater role in child care and household work in the United States and other developed countries have led to this change in research focus. There is little research on fathering in relation to work roles in developing countries, and the impact of work on men's caring roles in relation to extended family or community service are unexplored.

In response to the broad research question of the effects on family life of parental employment, studies are reviewed below that relate to two major elements of family life that might be affected by spillover from paid work: care of family members and household work.

Care of Family Members. Employment, particularly if work conditions are inflexible, with long hours or shift work at the times when families are usually together, has the potential to interfere with the physical and emotional care that takes place within families. Research in this area has focused on the care of children but families are also involved in the care of partners, parents, and family members with disabilities and chronic illness, all of which can be affected by spillover from the workplace and can impact on level of participation in employment.

In relation to partners, demanding work conditions that reduce the time and attention available for partners have been shown in Australian research to have a negative impact on marital relationships (Pocock, van Wanrooy, Strazzari, & Bridge, 2001; Pocock, 2003). The degree of control that partners feel they have over work schedules is another important factor, with one study reporting an initially surprising finding of higher marital satisfaction for American female physicians in full-time than in part-time work. This was due to the "low schedule control" part-time female physicians felt they had over household work compared to their control over schedules in their paid work (Barnett & Gareis, 2002). The greater relative control over work schedules in paid work is perhaps one of the reasons for the greater psychological and physical health reported by women in paid work compared to women working only at home (Barnett & Hyde, 2001).

The impetus for a great deal of work–family research has been a concern that relationships with children may be affected if parents, particularly mothers, are unable to attend to their children's needs because of their absence during work hours or if work pressures spill over to alter their behavior at home. Such concern is in the context of families often having little available support for parenting from extended family and community members so that all caring for family members occurs within the nuclear family (Pocock, 1993). In countries or cultural groups in which support from extended family and local community members still operates, different research assumptions need to be made about care responsibilities.

The concern about reduced time for mothers to spend with their children has been allayed by time-use studies that indicate that the time mothers spend in care of children does not differ by employment status of the mother (full-time, part-time, or no paid work). This result has been found in studies in Australia (Bittman, 1991; Craig, 2002a), Germany (Ahnert, Rickert, & Lamb, 2000) and in the United States (Bianchi, 2000). To achieve this time for child care, employed mothers reduce the time they spend in household work and time for sleep and recreation (Bianchi, 2000; Craig, 2002b; Galinsky & Swanberg, 2000). In Canada, however, Cook and Willms (2002) looked beyond time spent with children to the activities parents engaged in with their children. They found that mothers who worked outside the home reported, on average, fewer incidents than mothers at home of activities that are linked to positive child development such as laughing, playing, talking to, and reading with their children. This finding suggests that more research attention is needed on the activities parents engage in with their children rather than simply the time spent.

Fathers in the United States from dual-earner families have been found to spend more time caring for their children as their partner's work hours increase, "buying" this time by reducing their free-time activities. In contrast to mothers, fathers' time with their children was found to leave unaffected their time spent in sleep and household work (Bittman, 1991; Craig, 2002a; Galinsky & Swanberg, 2000). For fathers, increases in their own hours of paid work have been associated with less time spent caring for their children (Gottfried et al., 2002). From this research, it appears that mothers and fathers show different patterns of time use in relation to work and family, reflecting traditional gender roles. In other research from the United States, however, there is evidence that traditional gender roles may be changing—if not in parenting, then in other work and family issues. In their review of work and family research, Barnett & Hyde (2001) reported, for example, that negative feelings within couples about females earning more than males were less common now than in the 1970s and 1980s.

In terms of the effect of maternal employment on children, Gottfried et al. (2002) identified two waves of research: the first compared the children of mothers who were in the workforce with the children of mothers who were not, and the second wave investigated the processes that mediate the relationship between employed mothers and the development of their children. They concluded from their review of research that parenting was a key mediating variable linking parental work and child outcomes. The impact of work on parenting can be seen in several studies. In a study of rural fathers in the United States, for example, type of work was found to influence approaches to parenting (Whitbeck, Simons, Conger, Wickrama, Ackley, & Elder, 1997). Fathers who experienced autonomy and were self-directed at work were less likely to use harsh parenting and more likely to use reasoning in disciplining their children than fathers who had less autonomy at work. In another example, parental work affected children through its impact on parenting. Crouter, Bumpus, Maguire, & McHale (1999) found that high levels of pressure at work for dual-earner mothers and fathers in the United States spilled over into the home to produce more parental conflict with adolescents and lower levels of psychological well-being in those children.

Work demands have been found to affect parents' monitoring of their children's activities (Crouter, McGuire, Helms-Erikson, & McHale, 1999) and their knowledge about their children's lives in middle childhood (Bumpus, Crouter, & McHale, 1999). Other key variables found to mediate effects of maternal employment on parenting include socioeconomic status and maternal depression (Hoffman & Youngblade, 1999) and mother's satisfaction with their work role (Gottfried et al., 2002).

Gottfried et al. (2002) concluded from their review of the literature on maternal and dual-earner employment and parenting that exposure and response to stress and parental self-efficacy explained more about parenting than did employment status. The authors suggested that because maternal employment appeared to have no specific effects on parenting, employed mothers needed to be included in the mainstream of research on parenting and no longer treated as a separate category.

Although it is rare that this issue gains any prominence in the work–family literature, family researchers have also been concerned about indirect effects on children from parental work. These effects may derive from the care settings children experience while parents are at work. Research into the effects of child care in day-care centers in the early years of children's development has found that quality of care is a key variable mediating positive child outcomes, particularly in the cognitive domain (Brooks-Gunn, Han, & Waldfogel, 2002; NICHD Early Child Care Research Network, 2003). More research is needed into the multiple forms of nonparental care that children attend beyond the formal child care that forms the basis of most of this research.

A few studies have asked children themselves about their views on their parents' work (Commonwealth Department of Family and Community Services, 2002; Galinsky, 1999). In these studies, children in the United States and Australia have indicated a positive response to their parents' employment, although they also gave reports of mood spillover from work; spillover that quickly dissipated in most cases. It would be interesting to compare these findings to children's perceptions of parents' moods when one or both parents were not in employment. The voices of children are rarely heard in research on work and family, and there is a need to explore further how children's life at home and in various forms of child care is affected by their parents' work, through talking directly to the children.

Caring for elderly parents is also part of the responsibilities of workers in the "sandwiched generation" who care for children at home and whose parents are becoming elderly and in need of care (Hammer & Neal, 2003). With demographers forecasting a larger proportion of elderly people living longer in developed countries and workers retiring later from the workforce (OECD, 2002), new research is needed to determine successful strategies for workers to cope with the care of two or more generations in addition to their employment.

Parents of workers can also be affected by the workplace participation of their adult children as they are often involved in the care of preschool-aged children, sometimes maintaining participation in the workforce themselves at the same time (Bengston, 2001; Goodfellow & Laverty, 2003; Millward, 1998). In caring for grandchildren on a regular basis, grandparents often share the care and upbringing of young children with parents and other carers in formal and informal child care (Bowes, Wise, Harrison, Sanson, Ungerer, Watson, & Simpson, 2003), leading to a sharing of parenting roles (Ahnert, Rickert, & Lamb, 2000; Bianchi, 2000). The role of extended family members in supporting parents to balance work and family needs more research both in the United States and in other countries, where the role of grandparents may differ considerably.

Family members with disabilities or chronic illness add an additional demand to the caring responsibilities of employed family members. Caring for children with disabilities has been shown to constrain the employment participation of mothers (Porterfield, 2002). There has been little research, however, on employed mothers of children with disabilities or with a chronic illness to investigate how they fulfill their responsibilities at work and home. This is an important topic for family researchers as this group of workers is often a hidden group in western societies.

A final concern in reviewing the effects of parental employment on family life is with the well-being of employed family members themselves in their efforts to meet the demands of both work and family. Negative effects have been found deriving from the management of multiple roles (Voydanoff & Donnelly, 1999) and role conflict in general (Greenhaus & Singh, 2003). Qualitative research in Australia, for example, has shown a widespread varying degree of personal distress in workers. Some individuals, rather than "balancing" or "reconciling" work and family, have reported in interviews and focus groups feeling "torn apart" by competing demands of work and family (Pocock, 2003). Employed parents say they are "pushed for time" (OECD, 2002) and are reported as suffering from guilt and exhaustion from long hours of work, reduced sleep, and multiple jobs (Pocock, 2001; Pocock, 2003; Pocock et al., 2001). Reports of such psychological distress have urgent implications for workplaces and for research into how workplaces can assist workers to find a level of balance that allows them to operate productively at work and at home.

Other research, however, suggests that workers can experience benefits from multiple roles (Barnett, 1998; Barnett & Hyde, 2001). In addition to the kind of negative spillover from work to home and home to work suggested above, positive spillover was reported in both directions in a recent representative sample of American workers (Grzywacz & Marks, 2000). In this study, family support led to positive spillover to work and decision latitude at work was associated with positive spillover to home. The authors argue that work and family research needs to move away from the assumption that spillover between work and family will always be negative.

Household Work. Involvement in the workforce has implications for the division of labor at home. Analysis has shown that women undertake the bulk of unpaid work in households, including housework and child care. This is the case for women who are not in the workforce and for those who are, whether they work part-time or full-time. It also appears in research from the United States and Australia that women working full-time cut down on time spent on housework in order to spend as much time with their children as other mothers do (Bianchi, 2000; Commonwealth Department of Family and Community Services, 2002; Pocock, 2003).

There is little evidence for fathers filling in the resulting gap in housework but some evidence of fathers' increasing involvement in child care. A recent UK analysis reported an eightfold increase in UK fathers' daily time spent with children, claiming that fathers are now doing a third of child care (O'Brien & Shemilt, 2003). In addition, children are also involved in household work, with their views on participation and payment for that participation varying according to whether they come from an individualistic or collectivist country (Bowes, Flanagan, & Taylor, 2001). This kind of research is useful in its indication of who is doing what to sustain and maintain daily functioning of families according to their degree of involvement in the workforce.

The observation is often made that the domestic division of labor is a major trigger for marital separation and divorce. An insight into the link between division of labor in the home and the quality of the relationship with a partner was provided by Goodnow and Bowes (1994) who asked 50 couples who said that they shared housework equally, about their feelings and interpretations surrounding the division of household labor. Most couples explained that the impetus for their sharing was to preserve an equal, fair, and caring relationship. Often they had seen previous relationships or their parents' relationships as unbalanced in power ("master–servant" relationships), lacking in consideration and unjust in the distribution of labor. Similar results have been found in research on American "peer marriages" (Schwartz, 1994). This kind of research is important to supplement time-use data by investigating the meanings placed on the tasks of household work and care of children and on the strategies used to negotiate satisfactory and workable arrangements at home, particularly in relation to paid work responsibilities.

In summary, in family and developmental psychology, a great deal of research has investigated the effects of parental employment on family life. In contrast to organizational research that tends to focus on the worker, this body of research shows that other family members, notably children, can be subject to the positive and negative spillover from their parents' workplaces. Extended family members are also affected by the employment of their adult children, particularly when they take on roles of regular care for grandchildren. Employment has also been shown to have an impact on division of labor in the home with implications for the relationship between partners.

What Are the Strategies Used by Employed Parents to Reconcile Work and Family Responsibilities?

A particularly interesting direction in the work–family research has been an inquiry into the strategies used by parents in their attempts to manage work and family. Becker and Moen (1999) referred to "scaling back" at work to allow time to meet family commitments. Many women workers in the United States, Australia, and The Netherlands, for example, scale back from full-time to part-time work, reduce their work hours to fit family schedules such as school hours or leave the workforce altogether when their children are young (Barnett & Gareis, 2002; OECD, 2002; Pocock et al., 2001; Watson, Buchanan, Campbell, & Briggs, 2003). In doing so, women join the "mommy track," effectively sidelining their chances for career advancement for the sake of their families. Men also scale back their work or leave the workforce for family reasons (Hand & Lewis, 2002), with fathers in the UK reported to be willing to work less if the lost income can be replaced by an increase in their partner's income (O'Brien & Shemilt, 2003).

Strategies also include workers taking advantage of leave entitlements, flexible hours, job sharing arrangements, and other "family-friendly" provisions that may be available in their workplaces. Research, however, has indicated reluctance among workers to take advantage of these provisions because of the feared perception by their colleagues and bosses that they are not sufficiently committed to their work (Hochshild, 1997; Pocock, 2001; Watson et al., 2003).

Bittman (2003), for example, analyzed the effects on families of parents working on Sundays in Australia. Families in Australia traditionally spend time together on Sundays. Time with children and sharing meals with the family were found to be affected by Sunday work as most workers were working full days rather than short shifts. A study of employed parents who worked nonstandard hours in the UK also indicated that time and activities with families and children were the main areas in which workers made adjustments (Millward, 2002). It appears that "scaling back" is also happening at home to accommodate the demands of work schedules; this has implications for children, family functioning, and the social capital available for local communities (Pocock, 2001). There is some evidence that when parents are working nonstandard hours and are not present at mealtimes or on weekends on a regular basis, children are more likely to exhibit behavior problems (Millward, 2002; Strazdins, Lim, Korda, & Broom, 2003).

In summary, research needs to investigate scaling back and other strategies that workers are using in contexts other than work. Research suggests that workers may be adjusting their behavior in terms of some aspects of parenting, their relationships with their partner, and their responsibilities to extended family members, and, as suggested in the next section, their contributions to the community.

What Are the Effects of Parental Employment on Communities?

The impact of participation in paid work extends beyond individual families to local communities. As yet research has been limited on this topic but several researchers have made important observations on the community impact of changing working patterns, again in developed countries. Hochschild (1997) has argued, on the basis of her sociological research on workers in a large American company, that work is the new site for the friendships and connections that in the past characterised local community life. Her observation was that for many workers, the workplace has become the haven that the home used to be and that the increasing amounts of time workers are spending at work in the United States was having an impact not only on their families but also on their communities.

A similar observation was made by Pocock (2003) about the impact of widespread workforce participation in Australia. She noted a decrease in levels of volunteer work and community service, reflecting the absence of the women who would have taken on these roles in the past. Time-use research has shown that employed mothers reduce their social life to enable more time for child care (Bianchi, 2000; Bittman, 1991; Craig, 2002b; Galinsky & Swanberg, 2000). In doing so, however, mothers have fewer connections with neighbors and smaller networks of friends outside the workplace to call on for support, especially in emergencies such as when children are ill. In the absence of such resources, more research is needed on the sources of assistance available to parents from the workplace and the community when family emergencies arise and work and family commitments compete directly (Bond, Galinsky, & Swanberg, 1998).

INTERNATIONAL PERSPECTIVES ON WORK AND FAMILY

As can be seen from the review above, most of the research on the work–family interface that appears in the literature derives from the United States and, to a lesser extent, from other developed countries. It is important to remember that characteristics of the workplace, family life, and cultural values vary throughout the world and that the findings of much current published work–family research may not be able to be generalized to other countries. Indeed, investigation of work–family issues in a range of different countries is likely to throw up new issues that are currently not on the research agenda in mainstream work–family research. The need to adopt an international perspective is essential to broaden our understanding of issues and processes in the work–family interface and also to understand the position of workers in an increasingly global economy.

The focus of this book on international perspectives on work and family provides a wider perspective than is usual in considering both issues and research approaches in this area. As has been seen in previous chapters of this book, an international perspective can bring to our attention new kinds of workers such as "global" workers whose travel or relocation to other countries brings different challenges and opportunities for the workers and their families. Research from other countries can also highlight how cultural differences in gender, for example, can affect the degree of spillover of work stress between partners. Cross-cultural comparison studies, such as the focus group study reported in Chapter 12 of work–family issues in China, Hong Kong, Mexico, Singapore, and the United States, are also extremely valuable research approaches. Comparisons among countries allow new issues and perspectives to emerge, contributing to a fuller understanding of work and family interrelationships in their wider societal context.

An example of how the global economy affects workers who are sent to other countries to work for an extended period was presented in Chapter 5. Executives, however, are not the only workers travelling internationally for their employment. Ehrenreich and Hochshield (2003) have documented the implications for women from third world countries who move to richer countries to work as nannies, maids, or sex workers. These women leave behind their families, arrange for relatives to raise their own children and work long hours over many years in an alien country. As Hochschild (2003) points out, implications of their work extend beyond individual women and their families to their countries of origin. These countries experience a "care drain" as a consequence of the emigration of these impoverished women workers. It is clear that more research is needed into global workers at all levels of the workforce hierarchy.

The issue of different cultural values influencing the work–family interface in different countries and in different cultural groups within countries has been raised in several chapters in the current volume. The relative importance of work and family affects the salience of work–family issues in different groups. Hochschild (1997, 2003) suggests that in the United States, work is regarded as more important than family, with workers preferring time spent at work to time spent at home. However, Barnett & Hyde (2001) present research that shows both women and men in the United States report placing family before work in their priorities. Family comes first for other groups such as the Chinese (see Chapter 12 of this book) and for Asian immigrant women in the United States (Grahame, 2003), with adaptations made in the face of work–family conflict taking place in different ways. From the interviews conducted by Grahame (2003) with Asian textile workers in New York, it appears that work and family are not looked on as separate domains. Workers perceived their work as something that they were doing for their family, not as an activity taking them away from their family.

In summary, this review has highlighted areas of research from a family researcher's perspective that are relatively well established, such as the effect of parental work on families, and others that are in need of more research attention, such as work pattern effects on the wider community. The research effort, however, is largely concentrated in the United States and, as such, restricted to a particular range of work conditions, and cultural values. As research reported in other chapters of these book shows, different questions and different perspectives reflecting cultural values enter the research once an international perspective is taken. The following suggestions take up some of the unanswered questions raised in the review of literature and raise new questions from an international perspective on work and family.

SUGGESTIONS FOR A RESEARCH AGENDA

Future research needs both to extend our understanding of how work impacts family and community and to inform government policy on workplace and other social support for families to enable them to balance work, family, and community responsibilities. Such information is also important for other policy concerns such as workforce and population planning, and child care provision.

The following suggestions for a future research agenda are presented within a framework that has less emphasis on work and family as opposing spheres in the lives of families and more emphasis on family adaptations. The suggestions also explore the benefits and the costs of work and family participation for parents. Research is needed to extend the topics and studies reviewed earlier in the chapter; the following three research questions are offered as ways to develop a wider framework for future work–family research, mindful of international variation in work and family and of cultural values and practices.

What Is the Impact on Individuals, Fellow Workers, Families, and Communities of New Ways of Working?

The first question stems from current changes in ways of working. Nonstandard hours of work and rapid changes in technology offer new possibilities for work–family flexibility in the United States and elsewhere but also have the potential to disrupt family and community involvement of workers. Often research assumes standard hours or averages across workers so that variations are not apparent. In Australia, for example, only 28% of couple families with children under 15 are working standard hours of 35–40 hours a week (Watson et al., 2003). Developments in information and communication technology are making work possible in sites outside the workplace, including the home. As work hours and ways of working change, research is needed on how families adapt, especially when work takes place in the home either as its primary site or as an extension of the workplace. This question is relevant for working families in all countries. As technology brings work changes, particularly changes in location to the home, different family supports may be needed to reconcile work and family responsibilities. Continuing research is needed by family researchers to discover what works best for families in different work and family arrangements in this rapidly changing area.

What Kind of Support Is Available for Working Parents and Their Families at Different Stages of Family and Career, and How Do These Supports Affect Decisions About Work–Family Adaptation?

The context of cultural and institutional constraints and support can influence decisions about work–family adaptation. These can include large decisions such as who within a working couple will further their career and who will scale back at a particular point of their family and working life, and smaller decisions such as whether to attend a business meeting or a family birthday celebration scheduled for the same time on a weekend, a vignette used in research by Greenhaus & Powell (2003). Insight into decision making in this wider context of family and career stage could provide a useful extension to our understanding of the factors involved in common adaptations to address work and family demands such as scaling back.

A great deal of research on work–family supports for employed parents focuses on the needs of workers when they first become parents. This is a key transition point for families when support is clearly needed. More research would be useful, however, on the support needs of families at different points in their family life when different issues may be salient. For example, care for sick children may be a more major concern for families with young children than for families with adolescents. Parents also have different support needs at different stages in their own careers or working lives.

Moen and colleagues conducted research on family and work trajectories (Becker & Moen, 1999; Han & Moen, 1999; Moen & Wetherington, 1992) and their life-cycle approach needs to be applied to research underpinning the policies of workplaces and governments in their support for working families. Cross-cultural research is important in this area, particularly to inform the decisions of policy makers.

How Do Families Adapt to Work Demands in Relation to Cultural Values, Institutional Constraints, and the Availability of Support?

Work is often seen in current research to be part of individual identity, and work–family adaptation the result of a competition between personal and family interests (Hall & Callery, 2003). We know, however, that in many cultures, family is the primary concern, and work is a means to further the family's interests (Grahame, 2003; Hochschild, 2003). More research is needed in countries and among immigrant groups that have less individually oriented and more family-oriented perspectives and into their related beliefs and strategies in organization of work and family life.

There is a need for future research on family adaptations to consider both the constraints and the supports available to families in making arrangements that work for them. Grahame (2003), for example, presented her research on immigrant Asian women working in the United States in a framework that acknowledged the "institutional constraints" on their choices. Within the limits of their immigrant status and restricted work options, these women were working a triple day, managing work, family, and study to better their families' prospects for the future.

Support for families in their work–family arrangements can come from government policy, workplace policy, and formal and informal support within the community. A recent OECD (2002) report compared Australia, Sweden, and the Netherlands on policies that support families with employed parents. These included policies on parental leave, child care, part-time work, flexitime, leave to care for sick children, and other family-friendly policies. Policies were shown to impact on the choices made by working parents. Parents in Sweden who were well supported by leave and child care provisions tended to remain in the workforce compared to mothers in the Netherlands who were more likely to leave the workforce on the birth of their first baby as their opportunities for employment were limited by few child care options. Such cross-cultural comparisons are extremely valuable in that they can provide data from national samples to assess the impact of different work–family policy patterns on family adaptations.

The informal support that families gain from extended family and the community is another important area of research in the work–family area. Again, studies conducted in a range of countries or cultural groups within one country could indicate different forms of adaptation made by families using these informal supports or a mix of formal and informal arrangements. In Australia, for example, formal child care is generally of good quality because of a system of accreditation for care but insufficient places are available and fees are out of the reach of many families. In response, families often develop a mix of arrangements to support parents' work hours, using different combinations of formal care and regular weekday care by grandparents, neighbors, friends, and nannies (Bowes et al., 2003; OECD, 2002). However, in Australia, grandparents are often involved in direct regular care of grandchildren in order to support their adult children's employment (Goodfellow & Laverty, 2003); in Singapore and Hong Kong, grandparents are often involved in a different kind of child care support: supervising the maids who care for their grandchildren (Leung, personal communication, 2003; Namasivayam, personal communication, 2003). These different patterns underline the need for international research on work–family adaptations in response to different institutional constraints and available sources of support.

Issues of constraints and support apply to all work–family research. The current emphasis on dual-earner middle-class families in the United States has provided much relevant information about this group of families. Research is now needed into other types of family, such as single parents, immigrant families, and refugee families in a range of countries in addition to the range of family types identified in the United States as the potential focus of work–family research (Sloan Work and Family Research Network, 2002). Many families do not have the financial resources to allow them the range of strategies we have seen in research on middle-class couples.

Disciplinary and Methodological Approaches for Work–Family Research

Research methods used in the work–family area have been diverse reflecting the interdisciplinary nature of research endeavour in this field (Drago & Kashian, 2003). Such diversity enriches the field and introduces new ways of considering work–family issues. The variety of current approaches can be seen in the following examples. Crouter et al. (1999) conducted research using questionnaires and scales within a psychological framework to identify the key variables and processes linking parental work, its spillover into the home, and the psychological well-being of young adolescents in American dual-earner families. In a contrasting approach, sociologists such as Echrenreich and Hochschild (2003) and Grahame (2003) have used in-depth interviews in their research on work–family issues for Asian migrant women in the United States.

In recent articles, Duncan and Magnussen (2002) and Porterfield (2002) suggested that an economic analysis of parenting might be a useful addition to family research into work and family. This is a relatively new framework for child and family studies and it widens the conceptual tools for analysis and interpretation in work and family research.

In terms of research methods, Gottfried et al. (2002) suggested that longitudinal research can make a particularly useful contribution to the research on effects of maternal employment on children. Until recently, this approach has not been used extensively for work–family research. It has the potential to answer questions about longer-term impacts of parental work on families and children and also the impact of decisions about work–family adaptations made at different points in family and work trajectories.

When work–family research relates to children, it is also important to take account of the ages of children involved. The ages of children affect the current issues facing parents as well as their approaches to parenting, including time spent and activities engaged in with their children (Cook & Willms, 2002; Gottfried et al., 2002). The age of workers is also important to take into account as it relates to other family and community involvements that are part of workers' responsibilities and involvements outside the workforce, which vary at different stages of their life course.

It is also important that future research on work–family uses a range of informants. Most research to date has relied on reports from workers themselves about their work and home issues. This has raised the problem in work–family research that relies on self-report that associations found may be due to common-method variance (Grzywacz & Marks, 2000). Parental reports can be usefully supplemented by reports from children about their experiences with parents' employment whether at the workplace or at home and about the impact on their life at home of their parents' work. Grandparents and other carers involved in children's lives while their parents are at work should also be informing our knowledge of how work–home arrangements operate. Data from home needs also to be matched with data from work colleagues and supervisors, and reports need to be supplemented with observational data from both workplace and home settings. The emphasis on work–home issues for women has already begun to shift to include men and their roles as partners and fathers, and this shift provides a richer and more balanced view of work–home issues than is currently available.

In conclusion, despite the wealth of recent research on the impact on families and their adaptation to parental employment, there are new questions that need to be answered. This chapter has presented a review of current research and has offered three new research areas that will develop and extend the research questions asked to date and open up new knowledge in the work and family area. Both the review of literature and the suggested research areas widen the focus of current research by extending beyond family to community and societal concerns, by adopting a more extended view of family responsibilities and sources of support beyond the nuclear family, and by seeking the different viewpoints and practices that cross-cultural research can bring. An international perspective will enrich our understanding of family functioning by extending it beyond its currently U.S.-dominated research base. The cross-cultural knowledge generated in a more international approach will inform national policies and knowledge about local work and family issues and the family implications of an increasingly mobile globalized workforce.

REFERENCES

Ahnert, L., Rickert, H., & Lamb, M. E. (2000). Shared caregiving: Comparisons between home and child care settings. *Developmental Psychology, 36,* 339–351.

Amato, P. A. (1998). More than money? Men's contributions to their children's lives. In A. Booth and A. C. Crouter (Eds.), *Men in families* (pp. 241–278). Mahwah, NJ: Lawrence Erlbaum Associates.

Barnett, R. C. (1998). Towards a review and reconceptualization of the work/family literature. *Genetic, Social and General Psychology Monographs, 124,* 125–182.

Barnett, R. C., & Gareis, K. C. (2002). Full-time and reduced-hours work schedules and marital quality: A study of female physicians with young children. *Work and Occupations, 29,* 364–379.

Barnett, R. C., & Hyde, J. S. (2001). Women, men, work, and family: An expansionist theory. *American Psychologist, 56,* 781–796.

Becker, P. E., & Moen, P. (1999). Scaling back: Dual earner couples' work-family strategies. *Journal of Marriage and the Family, 61,* 995–1007.

Bengston, V. L. (2001). Beyond the nuclear family: The increasing importance of multigenerational bonds. *Journal of Marriage and the Family, 63,* 1–16.

Bianchi, S. M. (2000). Maternal employment and time with children: Dramatic change or surprising continuity? *Demography, 37,* 401–414.

Bittman, M. (1991). *Juggling time: How Australian families use time.* Report prepared for the Office for the Status of Women, Department of Prime Minister and Cabinet. Canberra: Australian Government Printing Service.

Bittman, M. (2003). Sunday working and family time. Proceedings of the Health for Life Forum on Work, Health and Families, Canberra: Australian National University. Retrieved on 10/10/03 from http://nceph.anu.edu.au/Health_For_Life/publications.

Bond, J. T., Galinsky, E., & Swanberg, J. E. (1998). *The 1997 national study of the changing workforce.* New York: Families and Work Institute.

Bowes, J. M. (2004). *Children, families and communities: Contexts and consequences.* Melbourne: Oxford University Press.

Bowes, J. M., Flanagan, C. A., & Taylor, A. J. (2001). Adolescents' ideas about individual and social responsibility in relation to children's household work: Some international comparisons. *International Journal of Behavioral Development, 25,* 60–68.

Bowes. J. M., & Goodnow, J. J. (1996). Work for home, school or labor force: The nature and sources of children's understanding, *Psychological Bulletin, 119,* 300–321.

Bowes, J., Wise, S., Harrison, L., Sanson, A., Ungerer, J., Watson, J., & Simpson, T. (2003). Continuity of care in the early years? Multiple and change-able childcare in the early years. *Family Matters, 64,* 30–35.

Bronfenbrenner, U. (1986). Ecology of the family as a context for human development: Research perspectives. *Developmental Psychology, 22,* 723–742.

Bronfenbrenner, U. (1979). The ecology of human development. Cambridge, MA: Harvard University Press.

Bronfenbrenner, U. (1997). Developmental ecology through space and time. In P. Moen, G. H. Elder, & K. Lüscher (Eds.), *Examining lives in context* (pp. 619–648). Washington, DC: American Psychological Association.

Brooks-Gunn, J., Han, W. J., & Waldfogel, J. (2002). Maternal employment and child cognitive outcomes in the first three years of life: The NICHD study of early child care. *Child Development, 73,* 1052–1072.

Bumpus, M. F., Crouter, A. C., & McHale, S. (1999). Work demands of dual earner couples: Implications of parents' knowledge about children's lives in middle childhood. *Journal of Marriage and the Family, 61,* 465–475.

Commonwealth Department of Family and Community Services (2002). *Family and work: The family perspective.* Retrieved on 8/8/03 from http://www.facs.gov.au/.

Cook, C., & Willms, J. D. (2002). Balancing work and family life. In J. D. Willms (Ed.), *Vulnerable Children* (pp. 183–198). Alberta: University of Alberta Press.

Craig, L. (2002a). *Caring differently: A time use analysis of the type and social context of child care performed by fathers and mothers.* (Social Policy Research Centre Discussion Paper No. 116). Sydney: Social Policy Research Centre, University of NSW.

Craig, L. (2002b). *The time cost of parenthood: An analysis of daily workload.* Sydney: Social Policy Research Centre, University of NSW.

Crouter, A. C. (1984). Spillover from work to family: The neglected side of the work–family interface. *Human Relations, 37,* 425–431.

Crouter, A. C., Bumpus, M. F., Maguire, M. C., & McHale, S. (1999). Linking parents' work pressure and adolescents' well-being: Insights into dynamics in dual-earner families. *Developmental Psychology, 35,* 1453–1461.

Crouter, A. C., McGuire, M., Helms-Erikson, H., & McHale, S. (1999). Parental work in middle childhood: Links between employment and the division of housework, parent–child activities and parental monitoring. *Research in the Sociology of Work, 7,* 31–54.

Drago, R., & Kashian, R. (2003). Mapping the terrain of work/family journals. *Journal of Family Issues, 24,* 488–512.

Duncan, G. J., & Magnuson, K. A. (2002). Economics and parenting. *Parenting: Science and Practice, 2,* 437–450.

Duncan, G., Brooks-Gunn, J., Young, J., & Smith, J. (1998). How much does childhood poverty affect the life chances of children? *American Sociological Review, 63,* 406–423.

Ehrenreich, B., & Hochschild, A. R. (2003). *Global woman: Nannies, maids and sex workers in the new economy.* New York: Metropolitan Books.

Furstenberg, F. F. (1998). Social capital and the role of fathers in the family. In A. Booth and A. C. Crouter (Eds.), *Men in families* (pp. 295–301). Mahwah, NJ: Lawrence Erlbaum Associates.

Galinsky, E. (1999). *Ask the children: What America's children really think about working parents.* New York: William Morrow.

Galinsky, E., & Swanberg, J. E. (2000). Employed mothers and fathers in the United states: Understanding how work and family life fit together. In J. L. Haas, P. Hwang, & G. Russell (Eds.), *Organisational change and gender equity: International perspectives on fathers and mothers in the workplace* (pp. 15–28). Thousand Oaks, CA: Sage.

Goodfellow, J., & Laverty, J. (2003). Grandcaring: Insights into grandparents' experiences as regular child care providers. Watson, ACT: Early Childhood Australia Inc.

Goodnow, J. J., & Bowes, J. M. (1994). *Men, women and household work.* Melbourne: Oxford University Press.

Gottfried, A. E., Gottfried, A. W., & Bathurst, K. (2002). Maternal and dual-earner employment status and parenting. In M. Bornstein (Ed.), *Handbook of parenting,* Vol. 2 (pp. 207–229). Mahwah, NJ: Lawrence Erlbaum Associates.

Grahame, K. M. (2003). "For the family": Asian immigrant women's triple day. *Journal of Sociology and Social Welfare, 30,* 65–90.

Greenhaus, J. H., & Powell, G. N. (2003). When work and family collide: Deciding between competing role demands. *Organizational Behavior and Human Decision Processes, 90,* 291–303.

Greenhaus, J. H., & Singh, R. (2003). Work-family linkages. *Sloan Work and Family Encyclopedia.* Retrieved on 8/21/03 from http:/www.bc.edu/bc_org/avp/wfnetwork/rft/wfpedia/wfpWFLent.html.

Grzywacz, J. G., & Marks, N. F. (2000). Reconceptualizing the work–family interface: An ecological perspective on the correlates of positive and negative spillover between work and family. *Journal of Occupational Health Psychology, 5,* 111–126.

Hall, W. A., & Callery, P. (2003). Balancing personal and family trajectories: An international study of dual-earner couples with pre-school children. *International Journal of Nursing Studies, 40,* 401–412.

Hammer, L., & Neal, M. (2003). Sandwiched generation. *Sloan Work and Family Encyclopedia.* Retrieved on 8/21/03 from http:/www.bc.edu/bc_org/avp/wfnetwork/rft/wfpedia/wfpSGent.html.

Hammer, L., & Thompson, C. (2003). Work–family role conflict. *Sloan Work and Family Encyclopedia.* Retrieved on 8/21/03 from http:/www.bc.edu/bc_org/avp/wfnetwork/rft/wfpedia/wfpWFRCent.html.

Han, S-K., & Moen, P. (1999). Work and family over time: A life-course approach. *The Annals of the American Academy of Political and Social Science, 562,* 981–1010.

Hand, K., & Lewis, V. (2002). Fathers' views on family life and paid work. *Family Matters, 61,* 26–29.

Heyman, J., Boynton-Jarrett, R., Carter, P., Bond, J. T., & Galinsky, E. (2003). *Work–family issues and low-income families.* Retrieved on 8/8/03 from http://www.lowincomeworkingfamilies.org/.

Hoffman, L. W., & Youngblade, L. M. (1999). *Mothers at work: Effects on children's well-being.* New York: Cambridge University Press.

Hochschild, A. R. (1989). *The second shift: Working parents and the revolution at home.* New York: Viking Penguin.

Hochschild, A. R. (1997). *The time bind: When work becomes home and home becomes work.* New York: Henry Holt.

Hochschild, A. R. (1999). *The managed heart: Commercialization of human feeling.* Berkeley, CA: University of California Press.

Hochschild, A. R. (2003). *The commercialization of intimate life.* Berkeley, CA: University of California Press.

Lamb, M. E. (1997). Fathers and child development: An introductory overview and guide. In M. E. Lamb (Ed.), *The role of the father in child development* (pp. 1–18). New York: Wiley.

Lerner, J. (2003). Maternal employment and child outcomes. *Sloan Work and Family Encyclopedia.* Retrieved on 8/21/03 from http:/www.bc.edu/bc_org/avp/wfnetwork/rft/wfpedia/wfpMECOent.html.

Lilly, T. A., Pitt-Catsouphes, M., & Googins, B. K. (1997). *Work–family research: An annotated bibliography.* Westport, CT: Greenwood.

McLoyd, V. C. (1993). Employment among African-American mothers in dual-earner families: Antecendents and consequences for family life and child development. In J. Frankel (Ed.), *The employed mother and the family context* (pp. 180–226). New York: Springer.

Millward (1998). *Family relationships and intergenerational exchanges in later life* (Working Paper No. 15). Melbourne: Australian Institute of Family Studies.

Millward, C. (2002). Work rich, family poor? Non-standard working hours and family life. *Family Matters, 61,* 40–47.

Moen, P., & Wetherington, E. (1992). The concept of family adaptive strategies. *Annual Review of Sociology, 18,* 233–251.

NICHD Early Child Care Research Network (2003). Does quality of child care affect child outcomes at age $4\frac{1}{2}$? *Developmental Psychology, 39,* 451–469.

O'Brien, M., & Shemilt, I. (2003). *Working fathers: Earning and caring.* London: Equal Opportunities Commission, UK. Retrieved on 9.3.03 from http://www.eoc.org.uk.

OECD (2002). *Babies and bosses: Reconciling work and family life: Vol. 1.* Paris: Organisation for Economic Co-operation and Development.

Perry-Jenkins, M., Repetti, R. L., & Crouter, A. C. (2000). Work and family in the 1990s. *Journal of Marriage and the Family, 62,* 981–998.

Petre, D. (1998). *Father time: Making time for your children.* Sydney: Pan Macmillan.

Pocock, B. (2001). *Having a life: Work, family, fairness and community in 2000.* Adelaide: Centre for Labour Research, Adelaide University.

Pocock, B. (2003). *The work/life collision.* Sydney: The Federation Press.

Pocock, B., van Wanrooy, B., Strazzari, S., & Bridge, K. (2001). *Fifty families: What unreasonable hours are doing to Australians, their families and their communities.* Melbourne: Australian Council of Trade Unions.

Porterfield, S. L. (2002). Work choices of mothers in families with children with disabilities. *Journal of Marriage and the Family, 64,* 972–981.

Repetti, R., & Wood, J. (1997). The effects of daily stress at work on mothers' interactions with preschoolers. *Journal of Family Psychology, 11,* 90–108.

Rothausen, T. J. (1999). 'Family' in organizational research: A review and comparison of definitions and measures. *Journal of Organizational Behavior, 20,* 817–836.

Rothausen, T. J. (2003). Gender: Work–family ideologies and roles. *Sloan Work and Family Encyclopedia.* Retrieved on 8/21/03 from http:/www.bc.edu/bc_org/avp/wfnetwork/rft/wfpedia/wfpGWFIRent.html

Schwartz, P. (1994). *Peer marriages: How love between equals really works.* New York: The Free Press.

Sloan Work and Family Research Network (2002). Expanding the work–family research lens. *Research Newsletter of the Sloan Work and Family Research Network, 4.*

Strazdins, L., Lim, L. L., Korda, R. J., & Broom, D. H. (2003). *Mothers' non-standard work hours and children's well-being in a 24/7 economy.* Unpublished manuscript. Canberra: Australian National University.

Voydanoff, P. (2003). Community as a context for the work-family interface. *Sloan Work and Family Encyclopedia.* Retrieved on 8/21/03 from http:/www.bc.edu/bc_org/avp/wfnetwork/rft/wfpedia/wfpCACent.html.

Voydanoff, P., & Donnelly, B. W. (1999). Multiple roles and psychological distress: The intersection of the paid worker, spouse and parent roles with the role of the adult child. *Journal of Marriage and the Family, 61,* 725–738.

Watson, I., Buchanan, J., Campbell, I., & Briggs, C. (2003). *Fragmented futures.* Sydney: The Federation Press.

Weston, R., Qu, L., & Soriano, G. (2002). Implications of men's extended work hours. *Family Matters, 61,* 18–25.

Whitbeck, L. B., Simons, R. L., Conger, R. D., Wickrama, K. A. S., Ackley, K. A., & Elder, G. H. Jr. (1997). The effects of parents' working conditions and family economic hardship on parenting behaviors and children's self-efficacy. *Social Psychology Quarterly, 60,* 291–303.

Work and Family Internet Discussion List (Australia). Retrieved on 10/10/03 at http://www.nwjc.org.au.

Work-Family Research Database (Boston College). Retrieved on 3/9/03 at http://www.bc.edu/wfnetwork.

Workfam Newsgroup (The Pennsylvania State University). Retrieved on 3/2/03 at http://www.lsir.la.psu.edu/workfam.

Wright, D. W., & Young, R. (1998). The effects of family structure and maternal employment on the development of gender-related attitudes among men and women. *Journal of Family Issues, 19,* 300–314.

Yeung, W. J., Linver, M. R., & Brooks-Gunn, J. (2002). How money matters for young children's development: Parental investment and family processes. *Child Development, 73,* 1861–1879.

16

Organizational Research on Work and Family: Recommendations for Future Research

Steven Poelmans
IESE Business School / University of Navarra

INTRODUCTION

The studies mentioned in Part 1, which reviewed the major findings of the consequences of work–family conflict at the individual level of analysis, have made clear that there is a strong argument for preventing work–family conflict in the workplace, irrespective of the country or culture in which the company is situated. There is a great deal of anecdotal evidence—mostly in the American business press—of companies that have successfully developed and implemented family-friendly policies or practices and that have reported some beneficial effects in terms of employee well-being or productivity. Surprisingly, there is very limited scientific research on the topic. Few scholars have reported rigorous studies in a peer-reviewed journal testing the effectiveness of family-friendly policies and practices in reducing work–family conflict. The focus of research concerning organizational initiatives has been on the adoption of work–family policies, mostly from a (neo)-institutional theoretical perspective (e.g., Goodstein, 1994; Ingram & Simons, 1995; Osterman, 1995; Poelmans, Cardona, &

Chinchilla, 2003), the organizational effectiveness of these policies (e.g. Arthur, 2004; Konrad & Mangel, 2000; Lambert, 2000; Meyer, Mukerjee, and Sestero, 2001; Perry-Smith & Blum, 2000), and the impact of a (perceived) supportive organizational culture on employee benefit utilization and well-being (for an overview see Kinnunen et al., 2005, Chapter 4 in this volume).

Put into a broader context of the complex process that starts with the adoption of work–family policies by an organization and ends with the actual impact of a policy on an individual employee's work–family balance and well-being, we realize that these are merely pockets of research focusing on certain aspects and that this field still has many questions to answer in order to develop a full understanding of this complex process. The objective of this chapter is to describe the different steps in this process and draw up a broad framework in order to identify the gaps in the literature, with special attention for the importance of the international context in which organizations and employees operate.

In the course of this chapter, I will briefly describe the steps one could distinguish in the long and complex process of achieving organizational effectiveness of work–family initiatives: policy adoption, design, implementation, and allowance. These steps will be used as an organizing framework of this chapter. I will make references to the scarce work–family literature pertinent to those different steps, without having the pretension to give a systematic and exhaustive overview of the literature. My intention is primarily to situate the organizational level chapters in this volume (Part 2, Chapters 4–8) in these different steps and formulate recommendations for future research. More specifically, I will combine insights of all the above studies with general observations of the field, to draw some overall conclusions and indicate directions for future research at the meso-level of analysis. A key finding is that managers as a research target have been neglected, although they have a pivotal function in the company as both victims of work–family conflict, judges in the allowance of work–family policies to specific employees, and change agents in the attempt to make companies more family-supportive. Therefore, they need to get more attention of the work–family research community. More specifically, I suggest we need to direct more attention to managerial decision making.

ORGANIZATIONAL EFFECTIVENESS OF WORK–FAMILY INITIATIVES

A researcher concerned with the question, how and under which circumstances organizations take initiatives that are successful in reducing work–family conflict in their employees, will soon realize that he or she is facing a complex problem involving many stages, variables, and implied organizational actors. To simplify this complex process, I have distinguished four steps that can guide us: adoption, design, implementation, and allowance.

Adoption of Work–Family Policies

The first obvious step is to decide whether or not to take any initiative at all, which in the literature has been referred to as the "adoption" of work–family policies. Den Dulk (2005, Chapter 8, this volume) reviews different theoretical approaches to the adoption issue, contrasting the (neo)-institutional approach (DiMaggio & Powell, 1983; Scott, 1995; Tolbert & Zucker, 1996) with the rational choice perspective. On the basis of her in-depth study of organizational initiatives in four European countries, den Dulk shows that the adoption of work–family policies is a function of a complex interaction among the country's legislative context (level of statutory provisions), the economic climate, organizational characteristics, and negotiations between employers' organizations and trade unions on employment conditions. When taking both statutory and employers' provisions into account, den Dulk found that Sweden still has the highest level of provisions. However, it is in the UK, where government involvement is minimal, that we see more organizational initiatives, as if to fill the void left by the legislator.

These findings lend support to Hambrick and Finkelstein's (1987) claim that managers make choices within institutional constraints and seem to suggest that we need to combine insights from both institutional theory (DiMaggio & Powell, 1983; Scott, 1995; Tolbert & Zucker, 1996) and the strategic choice perspective on organizational adaptation (Child, 1972; Daft & Weick, 1984). According to the latter approach, managers decide how to respond to institutional or resource pressures, and their responses can range from defiance to full acquiescence (Oliver, 1991). It is worthwhile mentioning in this context that the study of Milliken, Martins, and Morgan (1998) who found that both institutional pressures and rational choice criteria (the extent to which HR managers conduct employees surveys, consider work–family issues as salient, and have an impact on productivity) are related with the adoption of policies. Most interesting in this context is also the finding of Osterman (1995) and Poelmans et al. (2003) that firms that especially place high value on obtaining employee commitment and that have implemented high-commitment work systems, such as quality circles, also have developed and implemented family-friendly polices, probably as an extra means to ensure employee commitment. This again illustrates an interaction between given contextual constraints (high unemployment versus scarcity in certain labor markets) and organizational needs and choices (to attempt to engage and retain employees through high commitment work systems).

The insights of taking into account both contextual constraints and organizational choice in the adoption decision has important implications for scholars studying organizational responses to work–family conflict in an international context. Their models should ideally be multilevel models or include variables that cross levels or should at least control for context variables at different levels. Whereas international researchers almost always have to make explicit the unique and idiosyncratic context in which the study is set to explain the limitation of their studies, American researchers generally do not pause with the fact that the data on which their models are built are exclusively American, and collected in a certain city or state. It is less of a concern to them because of the relative homogeneity of the American legislative and cultural context and the fact that most peer-reviewed journals in this field are American. However, in the context of continuing globalization, also of the research community, it is the responsibility of both American and non-American researchers to make explicit the context in which the study is set. This will be helpful in deciding which contextual constraints can generally be considered as having an important influence on, for instance, the adoption of policies, irrespective of the national context. Taking into account this recommendation, I would like to call for more replication studies, testing American models in different cultural contexts (cf. Osterman, 1995; Poelmans et al., 2003) or testing models that take into account national (legislative, sociocultural, economic, political) differences in multiple countries. These models would theoretically be sampled on the basis of differentiating factors, as in the study of den Dulk (2005, Chapter 8, this volume), or they would be chosen to keep other context factors such as the sector or the country constant, as in the study of Poster (2005, Chapter 7, this volume).

Design of Work–Family Policies

Once managers in a firm have decided to adopt work–family policies, our concern shifts to the question of which specific policies to adopt and how to compose them in a coherent HR bundle. This is a very practical question, which is quite a concern for policy makers, human resource and diversity managers, and change agents in the firm, but that in contrast with the previous question has hardly been addressed by researchers. The case of "Flexible Work Arrangements in Procter &

Gamble EMEA" (Poelmans & Andrews, 2005, this volume) illustrates that companies invest a lot of resources (human and financial) in designing policies. In Proctor & Gamble, a survey was conducted in all the subsidiaries in Europe to identify the needs of the employees, and a policy manager was assigned to develop the policies and check them off with diversity managers in different countries in an iterative process of fine-tuning the policies. In addition, the company decided to immediately implement four policies, and try three other policies out in a trial period. The design question is not only relevant at the beginning of the process, right after the adoption phase, but also later on in the process if managers have to redesign the policies to respond to changes in the environment. This is well illustrated in the cases described by Poster (2005, Chapter 7, this volume), in which one firm under pressure of globalization and competition had to redesign (read reduce) its policies in number and scope.

Some crucial design questions are: Are there any policies that are more suited than others in certain regions and cultures, industries and sectors, or in different types of firms? Can we match different policies with different employee needs? These research questions have been generally ignored in the work–family literature. Mostly researchers ask respondents which policies are available and/or which they have used in the past and use a sum score, implicitly assuming that these policies are universally valid and that the more policies the company adopts, the better. This assumption is dubious for several reasons.

First, as managers in firms and their consultants know very well, some policies have their complications, pitfalls, or negative side-effects (e.g., Michaels, 1992). In general, researchers point at the beneficial effects of work–family policies. For example, the results of a meta-analysis by Baltes, Briggs, Huff, Wright, and Neuman (1999) showed that flexible work schedules are associated with lower absenteeism and greater job satisfaction. These "general findings" may mislead researchers, consultants, and practitioners to believe that flexibility is a useful policy in any organization. In particular instances though, the same flexibility in working hours can lead to "boundary blurring" or the destruction of the natural boundaries between work and family. As a consequence, the responsibility of "drawing the line" is shifted toward the employees, and if they do not manage these boundaries well, they may find that this "flexibility" actually causes more work–family conflict and spillover instead of less. In the professional services sector for instance, it is common practice not only to create extreme "flexibility," but also to "bill per hour" and to tie the incentive system to number of hours worked. The toxic combination of flexibility and pay per hour generally results in eternal working hours and workaholic cultures in these firms. Another example of the "dark side" of flexibility is the use of portable computers and company mobile phones. Many firms pride themselves on this type of flexibility, because it allows their employees to avoid traffic jams and leave work at their convenience and work at other times and places, as long as they meet their objectives. Olson-Buchanan and Boswell (2004) referred to this phenomenon as the "electronic leash" and found that this policy has the opposite effect of creating work–life conflict, rather than reducing it. Also, Guerts et al. (2005, Chapter 6, this volume) found that working from home was associated with more work–nonwork interference. To conclude, the utility of a single policy should not remain unquestioned, and more research is needed to evaluate the context and conditions under which policies have a positive or negative effect. More specifically, I recommend work–family researchers to study the interaction of certain policies with certain employee needs and to study different employee groups' coping skills to see which combinations have positive or rather negative effects.

Second, whereas work–family researchers generally focus on the beneficial effects of these policies for employee well-being, managers are concerned about the bottom line. As illustrated in the Procter & Gamble case study (Poelmans & Andrews, 2005, this volume), managers had questions about the impact on the overall firm productivity and customer service if all employees in a certain department take up flexible working arrangements simultaneously. This question is of even greater concern to owners of small- and medium-sized companies where, for example, several women taking up maternity leave simultaneously can literally reduce a department's capacity by half. Meyer et al. (2001) found that not all policies contribute equally to firm profitability. For some policies, such as telework, the generalized use is a necessary condition to have a positive relationship with firm profitability. If not, it can even have a negative association with firm profitability. As each policy has its costs and benefits—and the costs are generally easier to calculate than the benefits—managers may be reluctant to adopt "bundles" of policies. They take a more cautious approach of adopting separate policies gradually over time to guarantee a use that is beneficial for both the firm and the employee. To conclude, not all policies offer the guarantee of being useful and beneficial for both the firm and the employee, but research that unveils the context, facilitating factors and conditions under which policies do have a positive financial impact, is scarce. More studies are needed to show which policies have a higher leveraging effect than others, in order to allow especially small- and medium-sized companies to decide which policies to adopt first.

Scholars studying the relationship between strategy and human resource management and how to best align them distinguish two approaches: the universalistic approach and the contingency approach. The former states that there are certain "universally valid" best practices that irrespective of the firm's strategy are more effective in achieving competitive success through the way they manage people (Huselid, 1995; Huselid & Becker, 1996; Levine, 1995; Pfeffer, 1994, 1996). According to the contingency approach, most HR activities can and should be matched to the organization's business strategy in order to be effective (Milgrom & Roberts, 1995; Schuler & Jackson, 1987). In a similar vein, work–family researchers should ask themselves whether work–family policies can be simply categorized as universally valid and by definition useful in all circumstances. Possibly a more cautious road should be taken, and that according to different contexts and internal needs, some policies are more beneficial for both the firm and the employees than others, despite the "face-value" of the most popular policies. Further research is warranted to play out the universal approach against the contingency approach and to examine which one is most fit for determining the effectiveness of organizational work–family initiatives.

Third, even if it can be demonstrated that certain policies are really universally beneficial for the well-being of employees without having any negative side-effects and on top of that have a favourable cost–benefit ratio, they may not be optimally efficient because of a less than perfect match between the policies and the employee needs. Vodafone in Spain decided to include adoptive children in their child-support policy in order to match the needs of more than just the majority of employees who have biological children. Some have argued that the mere fact that companies take initiatives to support employee care responsibilities is enough to create favourable attitudes in the organization, but failure to address specific needs in a timely way may result in frustration instead of gratitude. This point can be illustrated with the study of Kossek and Nichol (1992) who observed a "frustration effect" in employees low on the waiting lists for child-care centers. These employees perceived the child-care centers as lower in attractiveness and fairness. The timeliness of access to policies is often an implementation issue (cf. next paragraph), but anticipating and meeting the needs of all individual employees is a design problem. In the multilevel fit theory of work and family, I propose that focusing on the right "fit" of policies with employee needs may be crucial (Poelmans, 2003, p. 272) and it is also crucial to focus on the fit of these policies within the broad sociocultural and legislative context. Guerts et al. (2005, Chapter 6, this volume) showed that the majority of the variance explained in the utilization of policies is due to employee characteristics such as sex, educational level, and having children, and that there are significant differences in which policies different groups use. This implies that different employees have different needs and that a fit approach may be necessary. Frone and Yardley (1996) studied the factors that can predict the importance ratings of employees of work–family policies. They found that being female, having younger children, and experiencing family-to-work conflict is associated with higher importance ratings of family-supportive programs. Women attach more importance to job sharing and child care, and parents with younger children especially appreciate flex-time, compressed working week, child care, work at home and reduced work hours. These importance ratings may function as proxies of fit, but we also have to look at the actual effect of offering "desired" policies to employees. Obviously, testing a fit model requires more detailed data and more sophisticated statistical analyses. It may well be that treating the match between specific employees' needs and specific company policies as the antecedent of employee well-being, commitment, and productivity proves to be a more fruitful approach than simply using a policy sumscore to calculate correlations with outcome variables.

In line with this "fit" philosophy, but broadening the issue to the company philosophy and values, is the need to strive in the design of policies for "value congruence." Kinnunen et al. (2005, Chapter 4, this volume) mentioned that similarity between values of an organization and those of an individual employee fosters well-being (e.g., Kristoff, 1996; Meglino, Ravlin, & Adkins, 1989; O'Reilly, Chatman, and Caldwell, 1991; Peterson & Wilson, 2002; Sparrow, 2001). More than adopting family-supportive policies congruent with employees' expectations I claim that it will be necessary in the design of these policies to be respectful with different value dimensions in the diverse employee pool. This may be evident in the case of multinational corporations that employ individuals of diverse cultural backgrounds, but may be equally important but less evident in more homogeneous firms where managers have the tendency to ignore minorities or individuals that have specific values and needs that deviate from the majority. In this context, I would suggest that beyond cafeteria-model compensation, we need individualized work–life policy responsiveness. Whereas some work–family scholars looked at the importance of values at the individual level (Carlson & Kacmar, 2000; Lobel, 1992), I'm not aware of any studies looking at value congruence between individual employees' work and family values and organizational family-supportive policies. It may well prove to be an important predictor of employees' satisfaction with these policies and overall well-being. A suggestion for practitioners is to survey not only employees' instrumental needs as an input to design policies, but also their work and family values. An obvious variable that practitioners would never overlook but that deserves more attention from researchers is the economic viability of individualizing work–family policies.

Implementation of Policies

Whereas little is known about the optimal design and composition of policies, there exists ample literature that is relevant for the next step in the process, the implementation of work–family policies in the firm. Kinnunen et al. (2005, Chapter 4, this volume) have already extensively reviewed the literature on family-supportive organizational culture, and they amended their recommendations for future research, so I will not come back to that point here. The fundamental idea behind this research is that if formal work–family policies are not backed up by (perceived) organizational and managerial support, they may be of very little use, as can be derived from the weak or nonsignificant relationships between family policy availability and work–family conflict, and strong or significant relationships between perceived organizational support and work–family conflict (e.g. Allen, 2001; O'Driscoll, Poelmans, Spector, Kalliath, Allen, Cooper, & Sanchez, 2004). The study of Guerts et al. (2005, Chapter 6, this volume) serves as yet another illustration of the importance of perceived organizational support for reducing work/nonwork interference.

In this paragraph, I would like to point out that whereas this literature is undoubtedly very relevant for the implementation question, it is insufficient, and many questions regarding implementation remain unanswered. Once again, the Procter & Gamble case (Poelmans & Andrews, 2005, this volume) illustrates my point. The fundamental problem experienced by the diversity manager in this case is neither an adoption nor a design issue. It is an implementation problem. She is well aware of the importance of gaining support of managers at all levels of the firm, and the careful process of consultation, communication, and regional role-out is exemplary, but nonetheless insufficient. It is one thing to know that managerial support is needed, but another question is how to create and consolidate this support. Academia has been remarkably silent on that front.

Whereas in the previous paragraph I could quote some existing studies, in this paragraph I have very little references to make. Only a few exceptional studies look at the impact of flexibility policies over time (e.g., Golembiewski, Hilles, & Kagno, 1974). Kinnunen et al. (2005, Chapter 4, this volume) made the suggestion we need quasi-experimental studies in which work–family culture and its potential outcomes are evaluated at least at two points of time whereas a specific work–family program operates as an intervention between these two measurement points. In addition to this quantitative approach, I suggest we also need more in-depth ethnographic studies in order to get an insight into the facilitating and inhibiting factors and actors in the implementation process of work–family policies. Probably here it would be interesting for a work–family researcher to team up with an expert in organizational development and change to study implementation of work–family programs in firms and provide deeper insights into what generally goes wrong. I suspect they will come to the conclusion that the same principles and recommendations valid for successful strategy implementation or change management in general are relevant for implementing work–family programs: involving employees and managers in early stages of the design process; ensuring the unconditional moral and financial support of top-management; preparing the change process thoroughly anticipating different scenarios of resistance and resistive collectives; communicating continuously and in a timely way before, during, and after the change; reinforcing the new policies and expected behavioral patterns through the incentive system; training of new required skills; and ensuring supervisor support at all levels.

The contribution of Poster to this volume (2005, Chapter 7, this volume) can be considered as an exceptional and laudable effort in taking a closer look at process instead of outcomes. Her study follows three organizations over time and tries to describe responses of these firms to different types of organizational change. I would invite the author to return to her data with specific attention to managers who made and influenced decisions in the firm at pivotal stages. This brings me to a point that is extremely important both for the implementation and the allowance issue; managerial decision making.

Allowance of Policies

Partly overlapping with the previous phase is the individual allowance of a certain work–family arrangement. Here I refer to the question of when and how to decide whether an individual employee can actually be allowed to take up a work–family arrangement as requested, such as reducing the number of working hours, extending maternity leave, or initiating some type of telework. This allowance decision may range from the administration of an employee "right" acquired through an official company policy, or in a context of a company without official policies, the managerial discretion to meet an employee "request" or not. In firms with clear work–family policies, the "allowance" issue partly overlaps with the design and implementation questions, because a company may specify the rules and circumstances that govern whether an employee right should be allowed or not, and it can be considered as a specific instance of supervisor support. Partly, it is a separate issue though, because whereas the implementation issue is driven by managers who strongly believe in its utility, the actors involved in the allowance decision can range from knowledgeable managers with a fundamentally favorable attitude to managers and supervisors who only vaguely recall the company policy and who are fundamentally against anything that may disrupt their goals, work processes, and workforce needs.

To my knowledge, there are only a handful of studies that have looked at the managerial allowance decision in a work–family context (Peters & den Dulk, 2003; Powell & Marineiro, 1999). Powell and Marineiro (1999) found that employee requests perceived as disruptive for work were judged less favorably. In order to advance our insight in why managers and supervisors support or do not support family-supportive policies, practices, and initiatives, we need a better insight in the decision-making units and sources of power in firms; these key managers' decision criteria and rules, assumptions and biases; what family policy is concerned; and more than anything a comprehension of the development of decision-making processes over time in these different actors and decision-making units. Whereas some authors have studied the rationality of firms and managers in the adoption issue, little or nothing is known about the rationality of managers in the implementation and allowance phases.

STATUS OF THE FIELD AND RECOMMENDATIONS FOR FUTURE RESEARCH

Considering all the above, we have to conclude that the field of organizational work and family research is still in its infancy. Many gaps still need to be filled, and some fundamental research still needs to be initiated. Here are some of the most important weaknesses of the field.

First, theory development is poor. To my knowledge, with the exception of institutional theory and rational choice theory, which shed some light on the processes of adoption of work–family policies by organizations, no theoretical framework has been proposed to integrate insights from individual, organizational, and sociocultural studies of work and family. This may be due to the complexity of such a multilevel model. An alternative explanation is the fact that the field overemphasizes quantitative, cross-sectional, same-level studies, despite the fact that this type of study is associated with methodological problems and incapable of capturing deeper and tacit phenomena, processes in time, and cross-level interactions.

Second, the implementation of work–family programs has only partially been grounded on empirical insights and systematic studies. For instance, a striking observation is that in the majority of the studies focusing on family-friendly policies, the variable that seems to be missing is paradoxically work–family conflict. Except for some exceptions (e.g., Frone & Yardley, 1996), very few researchers have thought of what seems to be to most obvious antecedent of work–family policies: the prevalence of work–family conflict. Again, with a few exceptions (e.g., Goff, Mount, & Jamison, 1990), very few studies have looked at the most important, immediate objective of family-friendly policies, i.e. reducing work–family conflict. It seems obvious that family-friendly policies reduce work–family conflict, but another well-established research finding might point at the contrary. One of the most studied consequences of work–family policies, job satisfaction (for a review, cf. Kossek & Ozeki, 1998) can be expected to relate with longer working hours. Thus, we can logically expect more time-based work–family conflict. This paradoxical effect of work–family policies deserves to be explored more. For instance, it could well be that on the one hand, flexible work arrangements reduce work–family conflicts. Take for instance a father who can leave earlier to pick up his children from school. On the other hand, they may also reduce the number of hours spent with the family. If we take the same example, once the father has brought the children home, because of the generated job satisfaction and commitment, this same father works at his home office and spends less time with his children or experiences high levels of strain and irritability when interrupted by his children. Future research should not overlook what seems to be obvious and should include work–family conflict as a variable. It should also look at subtle effects such as the hypothesized link between work–family policies, job satisfaction, commitment, longer working hours, and less family time.

Third, *studies reporting the evaluation of the impact of work–family programs* are generally lacking or have not been reported. For instance, Meyer, Mukerjee, and Sestero (2001) looked at the relationship of certain policies with company profitability, but we need to develop a deeper insight, ideally in studies that develop over time, of the process through which policies impact individual employee well-being, productivity, customer orientation, and thus indirectly, firm performance.

Fourth, an often ignored important distinction *is the distinction between time-based, strain-based, and behavior-based work–family interference of family–work interference* (Carlson, Kacmar, & Williams, 1998). Most work–family policies are directed at alleviating time-based conflict, by making work schedules more flexible and offering "extra hands" in the form of child care to compensate for (long) working hours. But it is clear that most policies overlook strain-based work–family conflict. In other words, they do not try to alleviate directly work stress to avoid a spillover of stress to the family. This is particularly odd, because one of the most widely studied and best-established antecedents of work–family conflict is work stress. Future research on family-supportive programs should include work stress as both an independent variable (are companies characterized by high levels of work stress more inclined to implement work–family policies?) and a dependent variable (do these policies alleviate work stress?). Another avenue for research is the effect of stress management policies on work–family conflict.

A fifth striking limitation of the accumulated research findings is that very few compare countries or cultures in the presence and application of family-supportive policies (for exceptions, see Bailyn, 1992; den Dulk, 2005, Chapter 8, this volume). Taking into account the heterogeneity in legislative contexts in countries outside Canada and the United States, and the argument that institutional pressures play an important role in the adoption of work–family policies (Goodstein, 1994; Ingram & Simons, 1995), we can seriously question the generalizability of the findings of mostly American studies. Another argument is that different cultures are characterized by different work and family values, practices, and habits. This calls for cross-cultural studies of work–family policies and programs. A good illustration of the impact of cultural differences on human resource policies is the study of Raghuram, London, and Larsen (2001), who found that national differences in cultural values impact the structure of work and adoption of flexible work arrangements. One way of doing cross-cultural research is to collect data in a specific country or region and test or replicate existing (Anglo-Saxon) models. Although there are several studies looking at work–family initiatives in other cultures, only a few studies explicitly compared policies in different cultures (den Dulk, 2005, Chapter 8, this volume).

This constellation of observations seems to suggest that there is a pressing need for theory that is able to include different levels of analysis and that offers a framework to both academics and practitioners. We need the basis of such an encompassing, coherent theory to systematically study organization-wide interventions aimed at both individual and organizational performance. This theory should go beyond existing theories that are basically limited to an explanation of how work–family conflict results in employee well-being. There is nothing as practical as a good theory, especially if the theory can be helpful to explain decision making and action in real-life situations for both individuals and organizations.

There is a special need for theory and empirical research focusing on managers because they have a pivotal role in firms as victims of work–family conflict, as decision-makers in the allowance of policies to individuals, and as change agents in the effort to create more family-supportive firms. Managers play a decisive role in the adoption, design, implementation, and allowance of work–family policies, but may be seriously influenced in their decisions by the fact that they themselves have been socialized and conditioned into family-hostile firms through powerful incentive and promotion systems. Therefore, they need to receive more attention from the research community. There are several reasons to expect elevated levels of work–family conflict in managers. Higher levels of responsibility and long working hours can be expected to result in more strain-based and time-based work–family conflict, in higher levels of role overload, in role ambiguity, and in role conflict. We may add additional pressures coming from intensifying competition and turbulence in the market, and company restructurations jeopardizing their career perspectives. Managers are often members of dual-career couples, which intensifies conflict even more. At the same time, these managers seem to be pivotal for the implementation of work–family programs and for the creation of a family-friendly culture (Thompson, Beauvais, & Lyness, 1999). We can anticipate that organizations offering family-friendly policies in their effort to recruit and retain talent may create sensitivity for work–family issues in employees and societal groups in general. The latter in turn will increasingly expect or demand more flexibility and respect for diversity. This can be contrasted with the fact that for many organizations balancing work and life is a nonissue. So many managers will be confronted with contradictory expectations from organizations and employees, without even mentioning their own standards or expectations, which may or may not align with these expectations.

Despite the fact that managers as a group are experiencing all these pressures relevant for the study of work–family conflict, they have been neglected as a focus of research, probably in part because they are difficult to access–ironically because of their scarce time. This calls for more research of this specific group and for attention to their multiple roles in the field of work–family conflict, as victims, generators, and moderators of work–family conflict and as implementers and beneficiaries of family-friendly policies. The implication for practice is clear. Those firms who really wish to create a family-friendly environment should not underestimate the importance of gaining their managers' support for the formal policies. Simple briefings, information sessions, or even training sessions may not suffice to counter deeply rooted beliefs, values, and working habits of their managers, especially if these values are rooted in the organizational culture itself.

Given that post-hoc rationalizations may conceal the true nature of managerial decision-making, cross-sectional studies, surveys, and one-shot interviews may not be the most adequate methods, which may explain the paucity of research on this topic. Longitudinal and (quasi-)experimental studies that allow the study of causality or control for certain factors and that systematically manipulate other factors that may influence managerial decision-making are more difficult to conduct but urgently needed. Factors that may influence managerial decision-making may include the company culture of perceived (top) manager support, the presence of an official work–family program, the perceived accountability and the presence of incentive systems to reinforce the application of these policies, the level of perceived disruption of specific work–family arrangements, and a whole number of individual characteristics of the decision-makers, such as age, sex, level in the organization, family responsibilities, and his or her work and family values and involvement, to name just a few. Decisions are seldom made by one individual, therefore studies of decision making dyads or units are needed to look at processes of negotiation among decision-makers and between decision-makers and the beneficiaries of the policies.

To conclude, research on family-supportive policies is still in its infancy. This is clear from the fact that we miss any attempt to provide a framework or a systematic exploration of antecedents and outcomes at different levels of analysis. Managers, the pivotal actors in firms, have hardly been studied. Especially decision-making in managers is a promising research object because of its pertinence to research and direct relevance for practice. More rigorous studies, considering a wider set of contexts and methods are needed. Considering the amount of cases mentioned in the business press, there is certainly no lack of empirical data.

A FRAMEWORK FOR RESEARCH ON THE WORK–FAMILY INTERFACE

I will now introduce a framework for research on the work–family interface that can help scholars working in this field to identify one's research focus and contrast it with potential underresearched areas within the field. To structure the presentation of this framework, I have determined (a) different levels of analysis, (b) different focuses of analysis, (c) different scopes of analysis, and (d) different methodologies. I will start with explaining these different levels, scopes, focuses, and methodologies. They will provide the dimensions that will allow me to differentiate types of studies.

Level of Analysis

While choosing the level of analysis, we should distinguish the individual or interpersonal level, the organizational level, and the societal level. The motivation to consider the individual level is that work–family interference and enhancement, the core variable of research in this field, is by definition a phenomenon that is situated at the individual level. At this level, we can distinguish between specific groups. A second level that holds a lot of promise for research and that is seriously underrated is the interpersonal or dyadic level. There are quite a few studies focusing on couples of dual-earners, but I also suggest we need studies of employee–supervisor dyads. Students of organizations need to address the questions when, why, and how managers or organizations deal with work–family conflict, which brings us to the organizational level or the study of human resource strategies, policies, and practices, and more specifically to family-supportive policies and culture. An important part of the work–family literature concentrates on exactly that aspect. But also the societal level plays an important role (1) to understand the sociocultural factors driving organizations to adopt, design, implement and allow policies, and (2) to formulate government policies that can address work–family conflict in many layers of the population.

Focus of Analysis

Closely related with the level of analysis, but different, is the focus of analysis. We can focus on more fundamental questions or look at day-to-day reality to study specific practices and policies that have been developed, both by individuals and organizations. This distinction generally coincides with more theoretical versus more practitioner-oriented approaches. But we should also distinguish between purely descriptive and a rather prescriptive focus. The fundamental questions are concerned with "why," and go beyond psychological or managerial concerns to touch upon philosophical matters. They try to find answers to questions such as "Why do employees, human resource managers, top managers, supervisors assign priority to family or to work?" and "What are the exact reasons why some companies create more work–family conflict in their employees than others?" We judge that answering these fundamental questions is an absolute requisite to change focus without running the risk of addressing trivial questions. The more down-to-earth focus of analysis goes straight to specific practices and policies to study what works and what does not. This analysis can generate direct output in terms of useful advice for firms. The previously mentioned types of analysis can be rather descriptive in nature, focusing on what is the real nature of the phenomenon or what practices and policies are being used. But they can also be approached from a normative perspective, which means that we enter into the ethics of what should be priority and the most appropriate type of action for individuals and firms.

Scope of Analysis

While choosing the focus of analysis, one can concentrate on the local situation, broaden the focus to include the country or region more in general, or take an international or cross-cultural perspective. On the one hand, work–family conflict is culturally bound because of the simple fact that family plays a very different role in let us say Latin or Scandinavian countries. On the other hand, several authors have argued that the incidence of work–family conflict is associated with institutional pressures, which we can expect will be different in different countries. To allow an in-depth analysis of these institutional pressures, it can be important to focus on one nation.

Methodological Considerations

To distinguish among methodologies, we can use two dimensions: time and depth. The time dimension refers to studying the phenomenon at one moment in time or to study evolution over time. Here I refer to cross-sectional versus longitudinal studies. With depth we mean the difference between (a) large-scale quantitative data that allow estimating the importance of phenomena, and statistical relationships among variables, and (b) qualitative analysis, concentrating on individual cases, to allow a more in-depth insight in the phenomenon.

TABLE 16.1
Different Possible Studies, Taking into Account Different Levels of Analysis, Scope of Analysis, and Different Methodologies: Longitudinal vs. Cross-Sectional, Quantitative vs. Qualitative

		Qualitative		Quantitative	
		Individual/couples	*Organizational*	*Individual/couples*	*Organizational*
Cross-sectional	National	(1) In-depth interviews with couples in Spain	(2) In-depth case study of one local company with WF-policies	(3) Survey research among local managers	(4) Survey research among local (companies) HR-managers
	Cross-cultural	(5) In-depth interviews with couples in several international countries	(6) In-depth case study of several international companies with WF-policies	(7) Survey research among international managers	(8) Survey research among international (companies) HR-managers
Longitudinal	National	(9) Diary research of couples mentioned in (1) over time	(10) Follow-up study of case mentioned in (2)	(11) Panel study following local couples over time	(12) Longitudinal study of local (companies) HR-managers
	Cross-cultural	(13) Diary research of couples mentioned in (5) over time	(14) Follow-up study of cases mentioned in (6)	(15) Panel study following international couples over time	(16) Longitudinal study of international (compan.) HR-managers

TABLE 16.2

Different Possible Studies, Taking into Account Different Levels of Analysis, Focus of Analysis, Quantitative and Qualitative Research

DISCIPLINES	TOPICS		Individual	Organizational	Societal
			Philosophy/antropology/ psychology	Organizational psychology/ organizational behavior/ human respurce management	Sociology/law/industrial relations
Fundamentals	Qualitative		Antropological study of motives of specific persons, like male managers with a dual-career family	Antropological study of motives of specific organizational actors or representatives, like human resource managers	Philosophical study of motives of societies to address work and family issues
	Quantitative		Large scale, cross-sectional or longitudinal studies (focusing individuals or couples) of antecedents and outcomes of work-family conflict	Large scale, cross-sectional or longitudinal studies (focusing firms) of antecedents and outcomes of work-family policies	Sociological analysis of sociodemographic factors driving the intensification of work-family conflicts
Policies and practices	Qualitative		In-depth case studies of diary research of individuals or couples	In-depth case studies of organizations with or without family-supportive programs	In-depth case studies of nations with or without family-supportive government policies
	Quantitative		Inventarisation of individual practices	Inventarisation of organizational policies	Inventarisation of government policies

The above paragraphs have provided the different dimensions. Tables 16.1 and 16.2 give an overview of different possible studies, crossing several of these dimensions:

- Individual, inter-individual, organizational, and societal
- Theoretical/fundamental, and practitioner-oriented
- Descriptive and normative
- Local, country/regional, and international or cross-cultural
- Cross-sectional and longitudinal
- Quantitative and qualitative

Any scholar of work–family conflict can choose certain combinations of dimensions to determine his or her approach. It is clear that some approaches have been dominating the field, such as individual, local/regional, cross-sectional, and quantitative studies. To balance research in this field, I call for more inter-individual, organizational, cross-cultural, longitudinal, and qualitative studies, which paradoxically offer much more depth than do the dominant ones. Probably this is related to the overall quantitative bias in the academic community, which values numbers and quantifiable models over more complex and subtle insight. It can probably also be traced back to a certain level of convenience, because more qualitative, longitudinal and cross-cultural studies demand a great deal of preparation, field work, work to note, encode and process data, interpretation, interpretative hazards, international collaboration, time and money, and insistence to get the work published. But considering the importance of balancing work and family, both for the well-being of individuals, couples, their children, organizations and society as a whole, I believe this effort is more than justified.

A VISION FOR THE FIELD

If I were to be asked what I personally consider as the most important conclusion of this chapter, it would undoubtedly be that the field needs a fundamental shift in focus. We have been overlooking some fundamental questions because our methods do not allow us to uncover these issues. I strongly believe in the importance of tacit, immanent actions and processes, such as decision making, and in the interaction among partners and among employees and their supervisor for the understanding of the phenomenon of work–family conflict. My suggestion would be to concentrate on the interactions among multiple actors in work and life and to fundamentally conceive work–family conflict as the intermediate result of a process in time. We need a framework that considers different levels of motivation (why do people act, what is their real drive, what are their priorities and why) as drivers of interaction, and relevant decision-making processes that proceed and follow interaction, based on different types of exchange (economic, social) between multiple actors. I would suggest focusing on the ongoing process of actions, rather than on the consequences of work–family conflict. We need to give much more depth to the factors that influence actions and fundamentally treat work–family conflict at the dyad level and not at the individual level. If an organizational actor is to maintain or protect its resources or resilience, this will be the result of strengthening or weakening interactions with many others he or she is tied to in multiple dyads. But I do not assume that actors always strive to maintain their resources. Sometimes they consciously or unconsciously use or even abuse their resources to obtain certain rewards. In the course of time, an actor is confronted with both small day-to-day choices and major life and career cycle choices between work and family. Because the actor is tied to multiple others through different types of relationships, the choices the actor makes (decision making) are simultaneously an output and an input of this complex set of interactions with multiple others.

In my vision, this requires a radical shift from quantitative toward qualitative studies and from cross-sectional studies toward longitudinal studies to allow detailed investigations of processes over time and interactions between people. Taking a set of multiple dyads as the unit of analysis may allow developing a unifying theory for individual and organizational work–family conflict. Once we start considering and studying deeper decision-making criteria or values that will emerge from the analysis of decision making and interaction processes, the influence of culture will become evident. More cross-cultural studies are needed, but given my recommendation of longitudinal, qualitative studies, these cross-cultural studies will require intense collaboration among local researchers who are intimately familiar with the culture. Given the difficulty of doing qualitative, longitudinal, cross-cultural research, the inertia of the field, and the power of the reigning paradigm role theory, I suspect that what the field really needs will not actually happen, or at least, not immediately. This shift requires courage and a critical mass. I hope that with this chapter, I may trigger some change.

REFERENCES

Allen, T. D. (2001). Family supportive work environments: The role of organizational perceptions. *Journal of Vocational Behavior, 58*, 414–435.

Arthur, M. M. (2003). Share price reactions to work–family initiatives: an institutional perspective. *Academy of Management Journal, 46*, 497–506.

Bailyn, L. (1992). Issues of work and family in different national contexts: How the United States, Britain, and Sweden respond. *Human Resource Management* (Special Issue on Work and Family), *31*, 201–208.

Baltes, B. B., Briggs, T. E., Huff, J. W., Wright, J. A., & Neuman, G. A. (1999). Flexible and compressed workweek schedules: A meta-analysis of their effects on work-related criteria. *Journal of Applied Psychology, 84*, 496–504.

Carlson, D. S., & Kacmar, K. M. (2000). Work–family conflict in the organization: Do life role values make a difference? *Journal of Management, 26*, 1031–1054.

Carlson, D. S., Kacmar, K. M., & Williams, L. J. (2000). Construction and initial validation of a multidimensional measure of work–family conflict. *Journal of Vocational Behavior, 56*, 249–276.

Child, J. (1972). Organizational structure, environment, and performance: The role of strategic choice. *Sociology, 6*, 1–22.

Daft, R. L., & Weick, K. G. (1984). Toward a model of organizations as interpretation systems. *Academy of Management Review, 9*, 284–195.

DiMaggio, P. J., & W. W. Powell (1983). The iron cage revisited: institutional isomorphism and collective rationality in organizational fields. *American Sociological Review, 48*, 147–160.

Frone, M. R., & Yardley, J. K. (1996). Workplace family supportive programmes: Predictors of employed parents' importance ratings. *Journal of Occupational and Organizational Psychology, 69*, 351–366.

Goff, S. J., Mount, M. K., & Jamison, R. L. (1990). Employer supported child care, work–family conflict and absenteeism: A field study. *Personnel Psychology, 43*, 793–809.

Golembiewski, P. T., Hilles, R., & Kagno, M. S. (1974). A longitudinal study of flexitime effect: Some consequences of a OD structural intervention. *Journal of Applied Behavioral Science, 4*, 503–532.

Goodstein, J. D. (1994). Institutional pressures and strategic responsiveness: employer involvement in work–family issues. *Academy of Management Journal, 37*, 350–382.

Hambrick, D. G., & Finkelstein, S. (1987). Managerial discretion: A bridge between polar views of organizations. In L. L. Cummings & B. M. Staw (Eds.), *Research in Organizational Behavior* (Vol. 9, 369–406). Greenwich CT, JAI.

Huselid, M. A. (1995). The impact of human resource management practices on turnover, productivity, and corporate financial performance. *Academy of Management Journal, 38*, 635–672.

Huselid, M. A., & Becker, B. E. (1996). Methodological issues in cross-sectional and panel estimates of the human resource-firm performance link. *Industrial Relations, 35*, 400–422.

Ingram, P., & Simons, T. (1995). Institutional and resource dependence determinants of responsiveness to work–family issues. *Academy of Management Journal, 38*, 1466–1482.

Konrad A. M., & Mangel, R. (2000). The impact of work–life programs on firm productivity. *Strategic Management Journal, 21,* 1223–1237.

Kossek, E. E., & Ozeki, C. (1998). Work–family conflict, policies, and the job-life satisfaction relationship: A review and directions for organizational behavior—human resources research. *Journal of Applied Psychology, 83,* 139–149.

Kossek, E. E., & Nichol, V. (1992). The effects of on-site child care on employee attitudes and performance. *Personnel Psychology, 45,* 485–509.

Kristoff, A. L. (1996). Person-organization fit. An integrative review of its conceptualizations, measurement, and implications. *Personnel Psychology, 49,* 1–49.

Lambert, S. J. (2000). Added benefits: The link between work–life benefits and organizational citizenship behavior. *The Academy of Management Journal, 43,* 801–815.

Levine, D. L. (1995). *Reinventing the workplace: How business and employees can both win.* Washington, DC: Brookings Institution.

Lobel, S. A. (1992). A value-laden approach to integrating work and family life. *Human Resource Management* (Special Issue on Work and Family), *31,* 249–266.

Meglino, B. M., Ravlin, E. C., & Adkins, C. L. (1989). Work values approach to corporate culture: A field test of the value congruence process and its relationships to individual outcomes. *Journal of Applied Psychology, 74,* 424–432.

Meyer, C. S., Mukerjee, S., & Sestero, A. (2001). Work–family benefits: Which ones maximize profits? *Journal of Management Issues, 8,* 28–44.

Michaels, B. (1992). Work and family pitfalls. *Executive Excellence,* January 1992.

Milgrom, P., & Roberts, J. (1995). Complementarities and fit. Strategy, structure, and organizational change in manufacturing. *Journal of Accounting and Economics, 19,* 179–208.

Milliken, F. J., Martins, L. L., & Morgan, H. (1998). Explaining organizational responsiveness to work–family issues: The role of human resource managers as issue interpreters. *Academy of Management Journal, 41,* 580–592.

O'Driscoll, M., Poelmans, S. A. Y., Spector, P. E., Cooper, C. L., Allen, T. D., & Sanchez, J. I. (2004). Family-responsive interventions, perceived organizational and supervisor support, work–family conflict, and psychological strain. *International Journal of Stress Management, 10,* 326–344.

Oliver, C. (1991). Strategic responses to institutional processes. *Academy of Management Review, 16,* 145–179.

Olson-Buchanan, J. B., & Boswell, W. R. (2004). *Correlates and consequences of being tied to an electronic leash.* Paper presented at the 2004 Society for Industrial and Organizational Psychology Conference. Chicago.

O'Reilly, C. A., Chatman, J., & Caldwell, D. E. (1991). People and organizational culture. A profile comparison approach to assessing person-organization fit. *Academy of Management Journal, 34,* 487–516.

Osterman, P. (1995). Work–family programs and the employment relationship. *Administrative Science Quarterly, 40,* 681–700.

Perry-Smith, J. E., & Blum, T. C. (2000). Work–family human resource bundles and perceived organizational performance. *The Academy of Management Journal, 43,* 1107–1117.

Peters, P., & den Dulk, L. (2003). Cross-cultural differences in managers' support for home-based telework: A theoretical elaboration. *International Journal of Cross-Cultural Management, 3,* 329–346.

Peterson, M., & Wilson, J. (2002). A culture–work–health model and work stress. *American Journal of Health Behavior, 26,* 16–24.

Pfeffer, J. (1994). *Competitive advantage through people.* Boston, MA: Harvard Business School Press.

Pfeffer, J. (1996). When it comes to "best practices"—Why do smart organizations occasionally do dumb things? *Organizational Dynamics, 25,* 33–44.

Poelmans, S. A. Y. (2003). Editorial. The multi-level "fit" model of work and family. *International Journal of Cross-Cultural Management, 3,* 267–274.

Poelmans, S., Chinchilla, N., & Cardona, P. (2003). Family-friendly HRM policies and the employment relationship. *International Journal of Manpower, 24,* 128–147.

Powell, G. N., & Marineiro, L. A. (1999). Managerial decision making regarding alternative work arrangements. *Journal of Occupational and Organizational Psychology, 72,* 41–56.

Raghuram, S., London, M., & Larsen, H. H. (2001). Flexible employment practices in Europe: Country versus culture. *International Journal of Human Resource Management, 12,* 738–753.

Scott W. R. (1995). *Institutions and organizations.* Thousand Oaks, CA: Sage.

Schuler, R., & Jackson, S. (1987). Organizational strategy and organizational level as determinants of human resource management practices. *Human Resource Planning, 10,* 125–141.

Sparrow, P. (2001). Developing diagnostics for high performance organization cultures. In C. L. Cooper (Ed.), *The international handbook of organizational culture and climate.* (pp. 84–106). England: Wiley.

Thompson, C. A., Beauvais, L. L., & Lyness, K. S. (1999). When work–family benefits are not enough: The influence of work–family culture on benefit utilization, organizational attachment, and work–family conflict. *Journal of Vocational Behavior, 54,* 392–415.

Tolbert P. S., & L. G. Zucker (1996). The institutionalization of institutional theory. In S. R. Clegg, C. Hardy, & W. R. Nord (Eds.), *Handbook of organization studies,* London: Sage.

Epilogue

Globalization and the Integration of Work with Personal Life

Rhona Rapoport
Institute of Family &
Environmental Research,
UK

Suzan Lewis
Manchester Metropolitan
University, UK

Lotte Bailyn
Massachusetts Institute
of Technology

Richenda Gambles
University of Oxford, UK

Some of the chapters in this book make clear that the existence of family policies is highly dependent on national context (e.g., Poster, Chapter 7, Den Dulk, Chapter 8), which in turn has an impact on people's sense of entitlement to integrate paid work and personal life in equitable ways (Lewis & Smithson, 2001). However, the chapters also show how global tendencies are interacting with national culture to produce patterns that may be far from optimal (Poster, Chapter 7). The dilemma—that global forces are calling for more and more effort in employment with very little consideration for the effect on people or societies—is what we wish to address in this chapter.

The problem is exacerbated by the fact that the major push for organizational change throughout the world comes from the west, particularly the United States and to a certain extent Britain, with their highly individualistic views of family responsibility (Den Dulk, Chapter 8, this volume). Hence, the more collective family orientation of other cultures is being undermined by the excessive push for market reform, growth, and global competitiveness. There is a danger, therefore, that the US/UK emphasis on employment at the expense of family and community concerns is being exported throughout the world, even as Americans and the British are themselves becoming aware of the dangers of such a one-sided emphasis. What is also clear is that these dominant countries are the ones with the greatest unequal distributions of income and opportunity within their own societies, and there is some evidence that this trend can be transferred to more egalitarian countries by transnational corporations (Den Dulk, Chapter 8, this volume).

What we see happening is that the invasiveness of paid work into people's lives is moving from the "developed" world to the "developing" world. Formal paid work is highly intrusive into other aspects of people's lives across contemporary western societies (Lewis, 2003a; Lewis, Rapoport, & Gambles, 2003; Taylor, 2002) and increasingly in nonwestern societies as globalisation gains pace (Poster, Chapter 7, this volume). Such one-sidedness has negative implications for gender and other equity issues, for life satisfaction, and, in general, for the development and sustainability of all peoples. Many women find they are unable to meet the increasing demands and expectations of time dedicated to paid work because of their nonpaid caring commitments (Smithson, Lewis, Cooper, & Dyer, 2004); and men—and growing numbers of women—find they are increasingly isolated from family and leisure activities in an ever-increasing climate of long hours and work intensity (Burchall et al., 1999). These trends make it difficult to increase equitable divisions of paid and nonpaid work. Further, as population age, caring for older people exacerbates pressures for many workers. Older workers may find that they too cannot or do not want to meet the increasing demands of paid work, thereby leaving them vulnerable to poverty or social isolation, although other older people might like more work but differently organized and managed.

As well as equity implications, issues of life satisfaction are equally important. As Bauman (2003) argues, intimate relationships or institutions such as families, friendships, or communities are increasingly squeezed out or subjected to consumer forces and market mentalities, and growing numbers of people reject, leave, or switch relationships and corresponding institutions. In this climate, men and women report increased loneliness, eroding support networks, or falling quality of life; trends that can also be linked with migration and international employment related travel that can take people away from their local or familial communities (Putnam, 2000; Voydanoff, in press). Some discussions are consequently examining the negative effects of current working patterns and expectations on people's sense of connectedness with others and on life satisfaction and happiness (Jacobs and Christie, 2000; Layard, 2003; Voydanoff, in press).

Linked to equity and satisfaction issues are concerns around human dignity for all. As work increasingly dominates people's lives, time for care and the value placed on care can suffer, with critical social consequences. For example, care is the third most important factor preventing child malnutrition, after food security and water sanitation facilities (UN, 1999). Crises of child, elder, and disability care are spreading throughout the world, threatening traditional cultures and exacerbating problems of poverty and quality of life (Heymann, Earle, & Hanchate, 2004; UN, 1999). There is also mounting concern over declining interest and participation in local communities and civic activities, which is threatening community sustainability and democratic and civic spirit (Blunkett, 2001; Putnam, 2000).

All in all, it is clear that current patterns of work create a lack of time and energy for the care of children, elders, and communities, as well as for pursuits that refresh the spirit and create the will and motivation for both employment and other activities.

THE INTEGRATION OF WORK AND PERSONAL LIFE AS A CENTRAL ISSUE

We argue that the ways in which people are able to integrate paid work with the rest of their lives is therefore of central social concern and can no longer be seen as a side or individual issue. The new economy, while bringing affluence to some, is widening the gaps between rich and poor. In addition, insufficient wages for people in low paid jobs means that many have to work longer and harder simply to meet basic economic needs (Toynbee, 2003). Stress, poverty, and persisting inequities, more "efficient" ways of production, low birth rates and aging populations, disability, or epidemics such as HIV/AIDS wiping out generations in some countries so that elderly parents have to raise grandchildren, are all apparent in our global world; and they are all connected with the ever-increasing centrality of paid work in people's lives. Thus, many social forces are coming together to push work–personal life integration issues onto the public radar.

Discussions around the negative implications of the invasive nature of work on the rest of life are increasingly framed as "work–life balance" in many countries, although much academic research and debate has focused on work–family conflict (see for example Goff, Mount, & Jamison, 1990; Huang, Hammer, Neal, & Perrin, 2004; Kossek & Oseki, 1998; Netemeyer, Boles, & McCurrin, 1996; Voydanoff, 2004). However, we prefer to understand these issues as "work-personal life integration." Work, after all, is part of life and, as already indicated, often too much of a part. The focus on integration rather than conflict is justified by evidence that multiple roles have the potential to create multiple sources of satisfaction (Barnett, 1998; Edwards & Rothbard, 2000; Frone, Yardley, & Markel, 1997; Greenhaus & Powell, in press; Marks, 1977; Rothbard, 2001; Ruderman, Ohlott, Panzer, & King, 2002; Sieber, 1974). We argue that the discourse of "work–life balance" is limited because it ignores the distinctions between paid and unpaid work and seems to undervalue unpaid care work by seeing it as just another part of the nonwork part of life. Furthermore, the very word "balance" seems to imply a trade-off—one side goes up, the other goes down—whereas we feel that work and personal life are not necessarily antithetical or mutually "exclusive," but rather feed into and affect each other. Indeed, there is some evidence that it may be possible to enhance both equity and satisfaction issues at the same time as workplace performance (Lewis & Cooper, in press; Rapoport, Bailyn, Fletcher, & Pruitt, 2002). Hence, "work–personal life integration," though not very felicitous, is the working terminology we use to capture the synergies and connections among the different spheres of life.

In light of the many negative implications that arise from current working practices and expectations, we argue that there is now a need to think creatively about how to envisage and implement new ways of integrating paid work with the rest of people's lives in ways that mitigate some of these inequities and enhance people's life satisfaction, productivity, and potential. However, if we do not keep the emphasis on *both* work and personal life, we end up with phenomena such as the current U.S. jobless recovery where productivity is so high that millions of people are unable to find employment. In other words, work–personal life integration issues need to form an integral part of discussions around the "new" global economy.

These are our basic premises. In the rest of this chapter we set out the need for change, and the basic questions that need to be raised by researchers, by people in organizations, and by societies more generally in order to effect such change. We then suggest one way that we feel might move us in the right direction.

THE NEED FOR CHANGE[1]

Whereas so much has changed in work and personal life, *conventional wisdom* in the mindsets of people has remained relatively

---

[1] Some of this material is based on an ongoing international study supported by the Ford Foundation: *Looking Backwards to Go Forwards: The Integration of Paid Work and Personal Life.*

intact. Despite changes in the composition of the workforce, the nature of work in the technological era, and the hype and policy initiatives to make paid work more compatible with contemporary realities, many workplace structures, cultures, and practices continue to be designed as if face time in the office is a marker of commitment and as though employees have wives at home (Bailyn, 1993; Kanter, 1977). In this chapter, we emphasize the need to rethink many of these assumptions inherent within working practices, and their effects on women and men. We want to emphasize that men's needs and men's lives are as central to this debate as women's, and, at this point in time, may offer a more effective leverage point of change. For if male workers were to make the kinds of accommodations that women are currently being forced to make, organizations might pay considerably more attention.

Change such as this, however, is difficult to effect. It takes time to challenge conventional wisdom, and one of the key needs is to create the time and space for collectively and creatively thinking about new work and personal life patterns—all of which reflect basic questions about the kind of society we want to live in. In the words of Bauman in his discussion of the human consequences of globalization, "questioning the ostensibly unquestionable premises of our way of life is arguably the most urgent service we owe to our fellow humans and our selves" (Bauman, 1998, p. 5).

There are currently forces that could be expected to push toward such a reconceptualization: the large influx of women into formal paid work settings; demographic shifts in the population, particularly its aging; concerns about equality, equity, and diversity; the needs of organizations to recruit and retain the workers and skills they need to compete effectively; and the gradual emergence of changes in the needs and desires of men to have more time for personal life and for greater involvement in home and family settings. Technology also plays a role. It could actually facilitate different models of work, though it is important to ensure that it does not increase the invasiveness of work, which is a real danger with globalization and the possibilities of a 24-hour workday (Heymann and Earle, 2001; Sullivan and Lewis, 2001).

BARRIERS TO CHANGE

With all these emerging levers for change, why do people still find it so hard to move forward? And why is there so much resistance to making real changes that would enable people to find better ways to integrate paid work with the rest of life? Primarily, we argue, it is because *fundamental questions have not been asked* in the context of work–personal life integration issues and research. Instead, solutions being proposed or taken up on the basis of research are often superficial quick fixes. Basic organizational structures, cultures, and practices have not been challenged by legislative and workplace policies (Lewis, 2003b). For example, assumptions about what it means to be a committed or competent employee have rarely been thought through. And when they are thought through (see for example Harrington, 1999; Rapoport et al., 2002; Williams, 2000), the message is very difficult to hear. Research needs to explore, for example, how closely time and effort are actually related to productivity, or whether individual measures of competence—as in most pay-for-performance systems—may actually undermine the true needs of complex knowledge work.

We also suffer from the *limited language and terminology* used to frame these issues. Although a shift from work–family and family-friendly to work–life and work–life balance reflects a broader and more inclusive way of framing the issues that enable men and those without children to identify with them, the term *work–life balance*, as already indicated, remains problematic. Our working terminology, as set out above, is by no means perfect, but aims to broaden the scope and captures the potential synergies among the different spheres of life.

A ***culture and language of busyness*** experienced at many levels of societies is also preventing fundamental questions about the integration of paid work and personal life from being asked. For example, why are certain skills valued over others, when all are needed for a caring and productive society? Or, why is there such emphasis on competition when it can lead to workers guarding their work and knowledge instead of enhancing it through collaboration (Lewis and Smithson, 1998)? The need for things to get done quickly and conveniently is linked to the power of money and consumerism that underpins the dominance of paid work in our lives (Schor, 1991). All of this reinforces individualism and contributes to the perception that solutions to work–personal life issues are individual issues when collective, collaborative, and systemic solutions might enhance both the experiences and the effectiveness of all workers.

There has also been an overwhelming ***tendency to avoid looking at deep identity and diversity issues*** existing among individuals throughout societies, as well as ignoring the reciprocal changes in relationships that are needed between people and among institutions. Although women's needs to adjust to combining paid work, family, and personal lives have been much commented on, there has been an inadequate focus throughout societies on men and their need to change in new gender relationships. However, this is shifting somewhat with studies of masculinities and fatherhood (e.g., Burghes, Clarke, & Cronin, 1998; Maier, 1999). Other deep identity issues must also be brought into the discussion. Too much of the debate has focused on professional people and white collar issues,[2] which means that work–personal life integration issues are often perceived as luxury, emotional issues rather than issues that contribute to inequities for many groups of diverse people. Attention also needs to be given to the changing nature of institutions within our lives such as work, family, communities, and the relations among and between them. As work becomes more central to people's lives, there is a need to focus on the implications of this for communities and civic participation and for families, friendships, and social networks.[3] We live in an increasingly connected world and need to understand and respect the diversities among different societies and the ways in which these can be valued rather than eroded through current exportations of western working practices, values, norms, and assumptions.

All these barriers feed into problems connected with a *failure to consider the dual or multiple agenda* (Bailyn & Fletcher, 2003; Rapoport et al., 1996, 2002). By this we mean an approach that considers personal needs—equity, diversity, and deep identity issues—alongside efficiency and competitive or productivity needs. Better policies and benefits, though critical under current conditions, seem to absolve businesses from looking more deeply at actual working practices and inherent assumptions that make it so hard to find satisfactory, equitable, and sustainable integrations of paid work and personal life. Government social policies addressing work–personal life issues are also too easily undermined by these workplace practices and assumptions (Brandth & Kvande, 2002). Real change will require challenging the status quo. Such an effort, however, takes time that is often not made available and requires wider thinking that may run contrary to current beliefs.

ASKING THE FUNDAMENTAL QUESTIONS AND BROADENING THE DEBATE

Probing deeply into ways people may be able to find more equitable, satisfying, and sustainable solutions for integrating paid work with the rest of life necessitates some reflection on the nature and place

---

[2]There are exceptions, for example the work of the Center for Gender and Organizations at the Simmons Graduate School of Management.

[3]An exception is Bookman (2004).

of paid work in people's lives and requires thinking about many of the barriers to further development that we have highlighted. Here we outline some of the fundamental questions that we believe are necessary for researchers to raise in order to move forward:

Why do societies need to continue to challenge existing gender roles and gender relationships?
Why do societies need to rethink working structures, cultures, and practices?
Is economic growth all that matters, beyond an optimal level?
How can diverse diversities be valued and respected?
How do these issues link with transnational solidarity in a globalising world?

By asking these questions and discussing the issues they raise, it may be possible for the issues seen as barriers to be turned into new levers for change. Indeed, as we show, this is beginning to happen. In discussing some of these questions and issues, we may build a broader consensus around the need for change by linking many issues facing societies today with work–personal life integration. This may encourage thinking about collaborative ways in which researchers, organizations, and societies more generally can work together to make satisfying, equitable, and sustainable changes.

Why Do Societies Need to Continue to Challenge Existing Gender Roles and Gender Relationships?

One of the barriers we mention is that the changing nature of families and work and changes in the lives and positions of women throughout much of the world have not been matched with reciprocal changes in the lives of men. Although some countries have witnessed a degree of change toward greater involvement of men in the sharing of care and other home-based responsibilities (see for example Brandth and Kvande, 2001; Hobson, 2002; Reeves 2002), this has remained limited or appears nonexistent in many other countries.

The struggles women currently face in "juggling" paid work with family responsibilities, particularly as working hours are increasing in many countries throughout the world, are well documented. We know, for example, that caring responsibilities of women or expectations that these will arise at some point in their lives have major consequences on opportunities for pay increases and promotions (Rake, 2000). We also know that caring and service work, though increasingly needed in workplaces, is valued less than other kinds of work (Fletcher, 2003), which contributes to women making up two thirds of the world's poorest people (UN, 1999).

We also need to investigate the inequities that men face in the current system. Indeed, what is often missing is the realization that so-called "choices" some women (at least those in better life circumstances) have are linked to the constraints placed on the men in their lives. Men are assumed to be the bread winners, and as pressures and expectations of commitment to paid work increase, they increasingly become more isolated from familial settings and other arenas in life (Burghes et al., 1998).

If it is to be possible to move forward with more equitable, satisfying, and sustainable ways of integrating paid work and the rest of life for both men and women, there is a need to examine ways in which gendered systems that continue to operate around outdated expectations can be restructured to get beyond current assumptions about gender identity and gender relationships. For example, in most workplaces, the definition of commitment remains rooted in a traditional concept of the ideal worker as someone for whom work is primary, time to spend at work is unlimited, and the demands of family, community, and personal life are secondary (Bailyn, 1993; Fletcher, 1999; Levine & Pittinsky, 1997; Lewis, 1997; Lewis, 2001; Rapoport et al., 2002; Williams, 2000). This notion of commitment penalizes both women who have caring responsibilities or other interests in life and men who may want to be more involved with these activities. However, it also penalizes organizations, because the relational skills that develop through domestic and care responsibilities and interactions with friends and other family members, which mirror many of the skills required in the new "relationship" economy, remain largely undervalued (Fletcher, 1999; Rapoport et al., 2002). By maintaining an illusion of total separation of this sphere from workplace settings and by discouraging many men in particular from developing these skills, inequities between women and men are reinforced and opportunities for enhancing workplace collaboration, performance, and productivity are lost. This point needs to be flagged clearly.

Challenging these outdated but pervasive gendered structures, and the inequities that arise from their persistence, means bringing men into the center of these debates. The needs and desires of both men and women and how their actions affect one another must be considered. Finding optimal solutions to benefit all will require men and women to communicate more deeply with each other about their identity issues and changing needs and to discuss them collectively. This is beginning to happen at the workplace level (Rapoport et al., 2002) and between men and women in the family context (Degroot & Fine, 2003). The Third Path Institute (http://www.thirdpath.org/), for example, is working at the couple and at the occupational level to create nongendered approaches to both work and care. However, as people find themselves considering new behavior that was formerly regarded as belonging to the other sex, resistance from men who may be reluctant to give up power in the workplace and resistance from women who may be reluctant to give up power in the home will have to be addressed.

None of this is easy. Nor is it likely that one can question assumptions and expectations about the roles of men and women at all levels of society at one time. It seems more likely that a strategy of small wins (Meyerson & Fletcher, 2000)—in some families, in some workplaces, and in some communities—is a more realistic goal. The point that there needs to be change in gendered assumptions and gendered relations to paid and unpaid work remains.

Why Do Societies Need to Rethink Working Structures, Cultures, and Practices?

Policies and benefits do lead to changes at the margins of organizations (Lewis, 1997), but they leave basic organizational structures and cultures largely unchallenged as indicated. Although policies may enable people to limit hours or take time off for other commitments in life, assumptions about what it means to be a "committed" or "competent" employee remain unchallenged. As such, people taking these benefits are often relegated or marginalized in their work, and most men—and indeed many career ambitious women—fail to use them, and thus forego the opportunity to change the ways in which they work (Bailyn, 1993; Lewis, 1997, 2001; Rapoport et al., 2002).

Policies in themselves have not enabled people to rethink and tackle persisting but outdated gendered assumptions and identities that run throughout current working practices. Nor have they facilitated a climate in which other diversity issues or inequities can be worked through. The changing needs of workers during their lifetimes, for example, need to be examined and considered in the context of current norms and assumptions surrounding working practices for younger, middle-aged, or older workers (cf. Moen, 2003). Once policies are in place, it is often assumed that employers have done what they can to enhance the integration between work and personal life. But without corresponding shifts in values and working practices, these policies can be undermined or even negated because of assumptions that they are antithetical to economic success. Research needs to continue to highlight and challenge this.

Policies also tend to focus on work–personal life integration as individual rather than systemic issues. Although some individuals may be able to opt out of professions or career tracks that are characterized by long hours at the expense of pay opportunities and promotions, this obscures the societal, economic, and cultural constraints under which these "choices" are made. When an individual is making such a "choice," the person is influenced by the workplace norms, expectations, and societal values that generate paid work and money as markers of status. These norms and expectations may deter requests for more time for family or for greater flexibility by people who seek advancement in the workplace and can result in impossible standards by which others are measured. It is important for research to demonstrate and encourage systemic solutions so that individuals do not have to make constant choices about how to work and how to cope with the current difficulties of integrating their lives. For example, in one financial analysis group of a large bank, where employees had long commutes and long work hours, an experiment that allowed employees to work from home 2 to 3 days a week proved so successful that it was later institutionalized (Rayman, Bailyn, Dickert, & Carre 1999). Not only did the workers now have easier acccss to family and community events—which they had sorely missed under their previous conditions—but also the manager had finally been able to implement a coordinating template critically important for the work of this group, which had previously been resisted. Systemic approaches involve deep organizational learning and innovation rather than organizations just making accommodations for individual needs while remaining fundamentally unchanged (Lee, MacDermid, & Buck, 2000).

Individual solutions also lead to ways of working that impede collaboration, despite rhetoric to the contrary. Thus, collectively rethinking work structures, cultures, and practices may increase workplace performance and productivity. Though, as Fletcher (2003) has shown, this is partly dependent on a reevaluation of gender identities and gendered relationships.

Is Economic Growth All That Matters? What is The "Optimal" Level?

What if paid work suffers when such changes are made—does that matter? To ask this question and be taken seriously is currently very difficult in a world in which economic values have such a high priority. At an individual level, employment has become central to identity, with perceptions of worth attached to consumer goods and money. At the organizational level, the primary focus on efficiency and profit underpins reluctance to confront real change. At the societal level, the conventional wisdom in western capitalist countries is that business growth and increasing GDP, at whatever cost, are society's primary goals. At the global level, this economic determinism fuels unsustainable inequalities: global capitalism has brought affluence to some and poverty to others. There is a need to make clear these connections and consequences.

Consideration of work–personal life integration issues highlights the need to consider both business and social imperatives; some of this is beginning to happen. Even though economic growth is one of the key dominant philosophies of our time and is perceived as a way in which we can better our lives, there is increasing awareness of the negative effects this can have on satisfaction, happiness, and sustainability. Some economists have begun to look more closely into sustainable development (Sen, 2000) and the importance of valuing and recognizing aspects of our lives such as unpaid care. They have also begun to question the primary focus on economic growth by looking at its negative implications for happiness and well-being. In the United Kingdom, for example, work done by Richard Layard focuses on the relationship between income and happiness. He argues that despite increasing levels of societal and personal wealth, many of us in the western world have not become any happier. He finds that overall happiness does not rise once a society reaches an average or optimal level of income per capita—at £10,000 or $15,000—and sets out a compelling case for redistribution and higher taxation to encourage a better work–life balance (Layard, 2003). This work now needs to be built on. Other influential economists, such as Stiglitz, also pose similar questions. After years of working as the chief economist at the World Bank, he wrote a critique of the unsustainable nature of neo-liberal economic policies that are heralded by this organization (Stiglitz, 2002). Taken together, these efforts reflect a potential seeding of change in thinking and attitudes and demonstrate that it is possible to question current wisdoms, values, and understandings and to make this heard.

How Can Diverse Diversities Be Valued and Respected?

We have already highlighted the importance of dealing with deep identity issues that arise from people's individual diversities. These relate not just to gender but also, among others, to age, social class, birthplace, nationality and ethnicity, faith, sexuality, and disability (see for example Holvino, 2001). Take, for example, social class: research on the experiences of the low paid has shown that many do not aspire for promotions because of the long hours and difficulties of integration that would arise, particularly for couples in low paid work who are already doing "shift" parenting (Crompton, 2003). It is possible, therefore, that the ways in which people currently integrate paid work with the rest of life and the commitment expectations of people in more senior positions, could prevent social mobility and thus may perpetuate cycles of low pay and poverty. So it is important to consider the extent to which people from all walks of life can integrate paid work and personal lives in equitable ways and to learn from these diverse experiences. A study of lesbian women with children, for example, found that they were able to integrate paid work more satisfactorily with the rest of life than many women living with men. These women found innovative ways to do this with a greater fluidity between their employment and domestic responsibilities, as they were not constrained by gendered assumptions within their work and personal lives (Dunne, 2000). How can these findings be built upon in heterosexual families or within wider society?

We have already mentioned the need to think more deeply about diversity and about changes within individuals throughout their lifetimes. As one Norwegian company argues, "diversity goes beyond race and gender. It has to do with perspective and it exists within individuals. Each of us is many different people at different times in our lives. Cultivate that diversity, and greater creativity will flow."[4] This highlights how a focus on and understanding of and learning from diversity can be good for workplace performance and for equity (Bailyn, 1993). In considering diversity, we also need to accept the centrality that individuals choose to give to their paid work at various points in their lives. However, at the same time, there is a need to be aware that those making a choice to emphasize the importance of paid work over other aspects of their lives often influence workplace cultures and norms, which may set impossible standards for others to meet. Examining the ways in which all types of diversity could be equally valued is becoming increasingly pressing.

How Do These Issues Link with Transnational Solidarity in a Globalising World?

In exploring some of the fundamental questions and probing into values and root causes of difficulties faced in the context of integrating our lives, it is no longer possible to ignore the wider global context. As technology and the processes of globalization open up the world,

---

[4]Interview with Hydro by Fast Company, see http://www.fastcompany.com/online/26/norskhydro.html.

our existing ways of life are being shaken up at an inexorable rate (Giddens, 1999). In this fast changing and fast moving world, the very nature of societal institutions—systems such as workplace organizations, families, and relationships within them—are changing rapidly. All of this creates new issues and challenges for the integration of paid work and personal life throughout the world, and research needs to continue to explore these emerging realities.

Globalization processes are contributing to increasing pressures and hours spent in workplace settings throughout the world. Combined with pressures of migration or the lure of international travel, these processes are fueling loneliness and erosion of social networks, as we discussed earlier. People in "developing" countries may lack economic, social, or political power to reject long hours, new locations, and increasing intensity of work. Also, people in "developed" countries are increasingly accepting long hours and increasingly intense work practices for fear they may otherwise lose their jobs to the growing global pool of talent as work can switch to cheaper locations and labor options. The reasons for and ways in which globalization affects work–personal life integration now needs to be examined in much more detail.

To think globally, however, does not preclude attention to local environments, as reflected through contemporary terms or processes such as "glocalisation," "devolution," and "the new localism" or "identity politics." Research and action in local environments are essential if different cultures and the needs of different people within them are to be respected. Despite living in an increasingly connected world, we need to give attention to understanding and respecting the differences among different societies and ways in which these can be valued rather than eroded through current exportations of western working practices, values, norms, and assumptions. A local focus, however, must always be placed within a wider global context and frame.

There have been many protests over the current effects of globalization with questioning and resistance from both the "developed" and "developing world" becoming increasingly apparent (see e.g., Rowbotham & Linkogle, 2001). The chairman of the Federal Reserve in the United States recently coined the phrase *infectious greed* to describe attitudes and trends in our globalizing world,[5] and the recent anti-war campaigns in many western countries over Iraq, demonstrate the sensitivities that are emerging over globalization and seeming western dominance or self interest. The rise of global labor markets and the rise of global conflict, terror, and war, partly perpetuated through

---

[5]See for example the Guardian (03/03/03) and the Financial Times (20/07/02).

increasing inequities and anger over western cultural domination, are coming together to heighten the debate over the ways in which globalization is going. These insecurities need to be linked firmly with the ways in which people are able to work, the ways in which they are able to integrate work with the rest of life, and the extent to which it may be possible for them to collaborate on real change in their own lives and the systems that affect them. There is a need to think about the ways in which inequities and conflicts are perpetuated by globalizing forces and how it may be possible to enjoy the positive aspects of these movements while mitigating the negative ones. In this context, we argue that there is a pressing need to examine ways of moving toward greater solidarity among different societies and to rethink working practices in ways that ensure greater understanding, respect, and equity within and among them.

MAKING CHANGES AND MOVING FORWARD

As well as broadening the scope for research, the consensus for change, and highlighting new emerging levers that could make new integrations of paid work and the rest of life possible, it is also important to think about the *processes of change* and how research can facilitate or encourage people, organizations, and societies to move forward constructively. There are no easy or quick fix answers; there is no "one-size-fits-all" solution. Issues of integrating our lives are highly complex and require deep, collective thinking and action. So how can the questions and new levers for change that have been raised in this chapter be used to generate collaborative thinking so as to encourage societies to move forward in constructive ways?

History shows that ideas that are potentially useful often do not get used until social forces are ready for inherent changes. We have indicated some of the forces of change already coming in the world. However, if these changes are to take equitable, satisfying, and sustainable forms and also maintain business imperatives (the dual or multiple agenda), there may be a need proactively to try to influence the ways these changes occur.

The Multiple Agenda and Action Research

Although there may be many ways to make change, and we hope this chapter prompts thinking and suggestions around this, we offer one possible way forward that has so far had some success at workplace levels: action research of an interactive, collaborative kind, involving people at all levels, such as grass roots, managers, and boards (see Rapoport et al., 2002, for a full description of this method). Such an approach leads to the small wins already mentioned. Although but one way forward, this approach has been shown capable of challenging norms about the necessary primacy of paid work and capable of redefining the implicit beliefs that commitment and competence are best measured by the amount of time and energy given to paid work.

The goal of this action research is to explore how effectiveness and equity concerns are both fueled by outdated working practices that fail to take account of changing business and people needs. It is based on creating time for workgroups to come together and think collaboratively about how they could change the ways in which they actually work and the value they place on different tasks. The goal is to improve both workplace performance and work–personal life integration. When this is done and supported sufficiently by management, positive and effective changes in workgroup practices are made possible.

In one organization, for example, problems relating to assumptions that committed workers are always present at fixed times and are never late or absent, were creating both efficiency and equity problems. When, contrary to established norms, workers were allowed to fix their own schedules—collectively, "as long as the work got done"—everyone gained. Both men and women were able better to integrate their work with their personal lives, and absenteeism declined by 30%. Moreover, groups began to work as more collaborative, self-managed teams (brought about by collective concern with work and schedules), a goal that had previously eluded the organization (see Rapoport et al., 2002 for this and other examples). Or, to take another example, a decision by one engineering software group to reallocate the timing of their daily activities, led to less strain on the engineers and a timelier and higher quality product (Perlow, 1997, 2002).

Although the focus of such change processes was on workplaces, many of the assumptions holding back change run throughout all levels of societies. Attention needs also to be given to changing mindsets at individual, family, community, and wider society levels (see Bookman, 2004, for an analysis of the role of community in this process). At best, such approaches can sow the seeds of change, and it will need broader and ongoing reflection on social and economic goals—on ways of meeting the multiple agenda and on diffusion of change processes—if these seeds are to flourish. However, whatever the method or processes adopted and developed by researchers in workplaces and other institutions such as families or communities, we believe that four basic principles, arising from the foregoing discussion, must inform thinking and research about the change process. These are ideals to be reached. They cannot be implemented wholesale or in every situation. They represent, however, the deeper levels of change one needs to be aware of in every concrete attempt at change.

Four Basic Principles Underlying Change

1. **Tackling deep identity issues.** We have noted people tend to want simplistic explanations and solutions to complex problems resulting in pragmatic solutions concentrated on government legislation and workplace policies. Although these are necessary, it is essential to move beyond current quick fixes and to consider the work practices, reward systems (both explicit and implicit) and other cultural expectations that generate the current dilemmas. However such an approach—whatever the method—will not work without tackling deep and diverse identity issues. For this to happen, researchers and other people need to be able to discuss *feelings* and intellectual perspectives so as to reflect on and examine their own assumptions and how these may be holding back change.

2. **Encouraging men and women to address gender issues.** We have highlighted the need of changing gender relationships and men and women's behavior. Changing gender relationships and including men in these issues are critical in moving forward. Many of the assumptions that hold back the evolution of work–personal life issues stem from gender assumptions about ways in which work should be done and separated from the rest of life. Open and honest discussions and insights are needed about the changing behavior and identity of women and men and about the difficulties faced in putting new values and ideals into practice.

3. **Recognizing multiple agendas and ways of integrating.** Work–personal life can be discussed from many viewpoints, such as workplace and government policies, benefits, child care, workplace practices and culture, or gender relationships. The interdependence of these different channels must be recognized. Unless we consider the various business and social imperatives collectively,optimal outcomes will not be reached in people's lives, in business or other work organisations in the medium or long run, or within societies globally. Attempts to make changes that have let either effectiveness or equity issues slip from view have been largely unsuccessful (Rapoport et al., 2002). For example, in a workplace context, when a focus on effectiveness is dropped, managers or employers can lose faith in initiatives to change. When a focus on equity is dropped, the energy and enthusiasm for developing new ways of working can evaporate as people see no improvements in their personal lives.

4. **Making time and space for multiple solutions.** Real change that enables different diversities that exist across and throughout the life course to be respected and valued takes time.The need to make the time and space to consider and explore these multiple solutions collectively and collaboratively is vital.

CONCLUDING NOTE

With profound changes going on in the lives of people throughout the world and in the nature of work and families, and the increasing centrality of paid work at the expense of other aspects of our lives, there is a need to challenge and rethink many existing assumptions operating throughout all levels of society. Work–personal life integration is not a side issue but a central issue in 21st century societies.

In questioning values in line with desires for good societies and good lives, it is important to come together and creatively explore new integrations of paid work and the rest of our lives. Key to this is a questioning of many accepted societal beliefs, including patterns of current work practices, structures, and cultural expectations and the relationships between men and women and the skills and values they are expected to portray.

We have outlined possible processes and principles for exploring and enacting these changes in concrete situations, highlighting the need to consider and question some of our seemingly unquestionable assumptions and the time and energy it will take to do this. Focusing on fundamental questions, priorities, and values, and making the time and space to challenge conventional wisdoms, whatever the chosen method of research or action, are now essential if there is to be progress toward new integrations that enable both a productive society and equitable, satisfying, and sustainable lives.

REFERENCES

Bailyn, L. (1993). *Breaking the mold: Women, men and time in the new corporate world.* New York: Free Press.

Bailyn, L., & Fletcher, J. K. (2003). *The equity imperative: Reaching effectiveness through the dual agenda* (CGO Insight #18). Boston: Center for Gender and Organization.

Barnett, R. C. (1998). Towards a review and reconceptualization of the work/family literature. *Genetic, Social and General Psychology Monographs, 24,* 125–182.

Bauman, Z. (1998). *Globalisation: The human consequences.* Cambridge, UK: Polity Press.

Bauman, Z. (2003). *Liquid love: On the frailty of human bonds.* Cambridge, UK: Polity Press.

Blunkett, D. (2001). *Politics and progress: Renewing democracy and civil society.* London: Politico's Publishing.

Bookman, A. (2004). *Starting in our own backyards: How working families can build community and survive the new economy.* New York: Routledge.

Brandth, B., & Kvande, E. (2001). Flexible work and flexible fathers. *Work, Employment and Society, 15,* 251–267.

Brandth, B., & Kvande, E. (2002). Reflexive fathers: Negotiating parental leave and working life. *Gender, Work and Organization, 9,* 186–203.

Burchall, B., Day, D., Hudson, M., Lapido, D., Nolan, J, Reed, H., Wichert, I., & Wilkinson, E. (1999). *Job insecurity and work intensification: Flexibility and the changing boundaries of work.* York: Joseph Rowntree Foundation.

Burghes, L., Clarke, L., & Cronin, N. (1998). *Fathers and fatherhood in Britain.* London: Family Policy Studies Centre.

Crompton, R. (2003). *Class, Gender and work–life balance.* London: London school of economics (LSE), ESRC Seminar Series, Work, life and time in the new economy.

DeGroot, & Fine (2003). Integrating work and wife: Young women forge new solutions. In *The American woman 2003–2004: Daughters of a revolution—Young Women Today.* New York: Palgrave Press.

Den Dulk, L. (2004). Workplace work–family arrangements: A study and explanatory framework of differences between organizational provisions in different welfare states. In S. A. Y. Poelmans (Ed.), *Work and family: An international research perspective.* Mahwah, NJ: Lawrence Erlbaum Associates.

Dunne, G. A. (2000). Opting into motherhood: Lesbians blurring the boundaries and transforming the meaning of parenthood and kinship. *Gender and Society, 14,* 11–35.

Edwards, J. R., & Rothbard, N. P. (2000). Mechanisms linking work and family: Clarifying the relationship between work and family constructs. *Academy of Management Review, 25,* 178–199.

Fletcher, J. K. (1999). *Disappearing acts: Gender, power, and relational practice at work.* Cambridge, MA: MIT Press.

Fletcher, J. K. (2003). *The paradox of post heroic leadership: Gender matters* (CGO Working Paper #17). Boston: Center for Gender and Organization.

Frone, M. R., Yardley, J. K., & Markel, K. S. (1997). Developing and testing an integrative model of the work–family interface. *Journal of Vocational Behavior, 50,* 145–167.

Giddens, A. (1999). *Runaway world: How globalisation is reshaping our lives.* London: Profile Books.

Goff, S. J., Mount, M. K., & Jamison, R. L. (1990). Employer supported child care, work/family conflict, and absenteeism: A field study. *Personnel Psychology, 43,* 793–809.

Greenhaus, J. H., & Powell, G. N. (in press). When work and family are allies: A theory of work–family enrichment. *Academy of Management Review*.

Harrington, M. (1999). *Care and equality: Inventing a new family politics*. New York: Knopf.

Heymann, J., & Earle, A. (2000). The impact of parental working conditions on school aged children: The case of evening work. *Community, Work and Family, 4*, 305–325.

Heymann, J., Earle, A., & Hanchate, A. (2004). Bringing a global perspective to community, work and family: An examination of extended work hours in families in four countries. *Community, Work and Family, 7*(2), 247–272.

Hobson, B. (2002). *Making men into fathers*. Cambridge, UK: Cambridge University Press.

Holvino, E. (2001). Complicating gender: The simultaneity of race, gender and class in organization change(ing) (Insight #14). Boston: Center for Gender in Organizations (CGO).

Huang, Y., Hammer, L., Neal, M., & Perrin, N. (2004). The relationship between work-to-family and family-to-work conflict: A longitudinal study. *Journal of Family and Economic Issues, 25*, 79–100.

Jacobs, M., & Christie, I. (2000). The personal is political (again): A new politics of quality of life. In A. Coote (Ed.), *The New Gender Agenda*. London: IPPR (Institute of Public Policy Research).

Kanter, R. M. (1977). *Men and women of the corporation*. New York: Basic Books.

Kossek, E. E., & Ozeki, C. (1999). Bridging the work–family policy and productivity gap: A literature review. *Community, Work and Family, 2*, 7–32.

Layard, R. (2003) *Happiness: Has social science a clue?* Lionel Robbins Memorial Lectures. London: LSE.

Lee, M. D., McDermid, S. M., & Buck, L. (2000). Organizational paradigms of reduced-load work: Accommodations, elaboration and transformation. *Academy of Management Journal, 43*, 121–122.

Levine, J., & Pittinsky, T. L. (1997). *Working fathers: New strategies for balancing work and family*. Reading, MA: Addison-Wesley.

Lewis, S. (1997). Family friendly policies: Organisational change or playing about at the margins? *Gender, Work and Organisations, 4*, 13–23.

Lewis, S. (2001). Restructuring workplace cultures: The ultimate work–family challenge? *Women in Management Review, 16*, 21–29.

Lewis, S. (2003a). The integration of paid work and the rest of life: Is post industrial work the new leisure? *Leisure Studies, 22*(4), 343–355.

Lewis, S. (2003b). Flexible working arrangements: Implementation, outcomes and management. In I. Roberson & C. Cooper (Eds.), *Annual review of industrial and organisational psychology* (Vol. 18). London: Wiley.

Lewis, S., & Cooper, C. L. (in press). *The integration of work and personal life: Case studies of organisational change*. London: Wiley.

Lewis, S., Rapoport, R., & Gambles, R. (2003). Reflections on the integration of paid work and the rest of life. *Journal of Managerial Psychology, 18*, 824–841.

Lewis, S., & Smithson, J. (2001). Sense of entitlement to support for the reconciliation of employment and family life. *Human Relations, 55,* 1455–1481.

Maier, M. (1999). On the gendered substructure of organization: Dimensions and dilemmas of corporate masculinity. In G. Powell (Ed.), *Handbook of gender and work.* Thousand Oaks, CA: Sage.

Marks, S. R. (1977). Multiple roles and role strain: Some notes on human energy, time and commitment. *American Sociological Review, 42,* 921–936.

Meyerson, D., & Fletcher, J. K. (2000). A modest manifesto for shattering the glass ceiling. *Harvard Business Review, (January-February),* 127–136.

Moen, P. (Ed.). (2003). *It's about time: Couples and careers.* Ithaca, NY: Cornell University Press.

Netemeyer, R. G., Boles, J. S., & McCurrin, R. (1996). Development and validation of work–family conflict and family–work conflict scales. *Journal of Applied Psychology, 81,* 400–410.

Perlow, L. (1997). *Finding time: How corporations, individuals, and families can benefit from new work practices.* Ithaca, NY: Cornell University Press.

Perlow, L. (2002). Who's helping whom: Layers of culture and workplace behavior. *Journal of Organizational Behavior, 23,* 345–351.

Putnam, R. D. (2000). *Bowling alone: The collapse and revival of American community.* New York: Simon & Schuster.

Rake, K. (2000). *Women's incomes over the lifetime.* London: Cabinet Office.

Rapoport, R., Bailyn, L., Fletcher, J., & Pruitt, B. (2002). *Beyond work–family balance: Advancing gender equity & work performance.* San Francisco, CA: Jossey-Bass, and London: Wiley.

Rayman, P. M., Bailyn, L., Dickert, J., & Carre, F. (1999). (With Maureen A. Harvey, Robert Krim, & Robert Read)—"Designing organizational solutions to integrate work and life", *Women in Management Review, 14,* 164–176.

Reeves, R. (2002). *Dad's army.* London: Work Foundation.

Rothbard, N. P. (2001). Enriching or depleting? The dynamics of engagement in work and family roles. *Administrative Science Quarterly, 46,* 655–684.

Rowbotham, S., & Linkogle, S. (2001). *Women resist globalisation: Mobilising for livelihood and rights.* London: Zed Books.

Ruderman, M. N., Ohlott, P. J., Panzer, K., & King, S. N. (2002). Benefits of multiple roles for managerial women. *Academy of Management Journal, 45,* 369–386.

Schor, J. (1991). *The overworked American: The unexpected decline of leisure.* New York: Basic Books.

Sen, A. (2000). *Development as freedom.* New York: Anchor Books.

Sieber, S. D. (1974). Toward a theory of role accumulation. *American Sociological Review, 39,* 567–578.

Stiglitz, J. (2002). *Globalisation and it's discontents.* London: Penguin Books.

Smithson, J., & Lewis, S. (2000). Is job insecurity changing the psychological contract? Young people's expectations of work. *Personnel Review, 29,* 680–698.

Smithson, J., Lewis, S., Cooper, C., & Dyer, J. (2004). Flexible working and the gender pay gap in the accountancy profession. *Work, Employment and Society, 18*(1), 115–135.

Sullivan, C., & Lewis, S. (2001). Home-based telework, gender and the synchronisation of work and family; Perspectives of teleworkers and their co-residents. *Gender, Work and Organisation, 8,* 123–145.

Taylor, R. (2002). *The future of work–life balance.* ESRC Future of Work Programme Seminar Series. ESRC, UK.

Toynbee, (2003). *Hard work: Life in low pay Britain.* London: Bloomsbury Publishing.

UN. (1999). United Nations development report: The invisible heart—care and the global economy. *Human Development Report 199.* Oxford: Oxford University Press.

Voydanoff, P. (in press). Implications of work and community resources and demands for marital quality. *Community, Work and Family.*

Voydanoff, P. (2004). Implications of work and community demands and resources for work-to-family conflict and facilitation. *Journal of Occupational Health Psychology,*

Williams, J. (2000). *Unbending gender: Why family and work conflict and what to do about it.* New York: Oxford University Press.

Author Index

Subject Index